Encyclopedia of
American Indian History

Encyclopedia of
American Indian History

VOLUME II

Bruce E. Johansen
Barry M. Pritzker
EDITORS

A B C ◉ C L I O

Santa Barbara, California • Denver, Colorado • Oxford, England

Copyright 2008 by ABC-CLIO, Inc.

All rights reserved. No part of this publication may be reproduced, stored in a retrieval system, or transmitted, in any form or by any means, electronic, mechanical, photocopying, recording, or otherwise, except for the inclusion of brief quotations in a review, without prior permission in writing from the publishers.

Cataloging-in-Publication Data is on file with the Library of Congress

ISBN: 978-1-85109-817-0   ebook: 978-1-85109-818-7

12   11   10   09   08   1   2   3   4   5   6   7   8

Production Editor: Vicki Moran
Editorial Assistant: Sara Springer
Production Manager: Don Schmidt
Media Editor: John Whithers
Media Resources Coordinator: Ellen Brenna Dougherty
Media Resources Manager: Caroline Price
File Manager: Paula Gerard

ABC-CLIO, Inc.
130 Cremona Drive, P.O. Box 1911
Santa Barbara, California 93116-1911

This book is also available on the World Wide Web as an ebook. Visit http://www.abc-clio.com for details.

This book is printed on acid-free paper. ∞

Manufactured in the United States of America

Contents

Volume II

Governments and American Indian History

Introduction

A BOOK CAN BE A TIME MACHINE, opening a window on the unquestioned judgments and assumptions of authors in other times. Many of these have been delivered with a sense of European-American self-congratulation. Consider John D. Hicks, who, in *The Federal Union: A History of the United States to 1865* (1937) opens a 700-page tome with the words "The civilization that grew up in the United States . . ." implying that nothing worth the name occurred before Columbus planted European seeds here (Hicks, 1937, 1). Paragraph two begins: "America before the time of Columbus had developed no great civilizations of its own" (Hicks, 1937, 1). This text states authoritatively that the Mayas, Aztecs, and Incas could not match "the best that Europe had to offer" (Hicks, 1937, 1), despite the fact that accounts of the Cortez invasion expressed a sense of awe at the Aztecs' capital city Tenochtitlan when they first saw it. In the same paragraph, Hicks develops reasons why he believes that Europeans surpassed America's "primitive civilization": "racial traits may account in part for this failure, but the importance of the environment cannot be overlooked" (Hicks, 1937, 1).

No time and no people speak with a single voice, however. So while Hicks' assumptions of racial superiority remind us of Richard Henry Pratt's advertising slogan for the boarding schools he built ("Kill the Indian, Save the Man") even Pratt's and Hicks' time were informed by other voices that asserted enduring value to Native American peoples and cultures. While Pratt's slogan is sometimes interpreted as an endorsement of genocide in our time, to him it was friendly advice to peoples whom he assumed would die culturally as well as genetically if they held fast to cultures that he considered out of date in a modern world. Multicultural ideas that inform public discourse (as well as census reports) in our time had precedents in Pratt's and Hicks' time. The majority society was just not listening. Consider Walt Whitman, for example, during 1883, as Pratt was fashioning his campaign to save Indians by killing their cultures:

As to our aboriginal or Indian population . . . I know it seems to be agreed that they must gradually dwindle as time rolls on, and in a few generations more leave only a reminiscence, a blank. But I am not at all clear about that. As America . . . develops, adapts, entwines, faithfully identifies its own—are we to see it cheerfully accepting using all the contributions of foreign lands from the whole outside globe—and then rejecting the only ones distinctly its own? (Moquin, 1973, 5–6).

One newspaper, the *Omaha World-Herald*, sent a native woman, Susette LaFlesche (an Omaha), to describe the aftermath of the Wounded Knee massacre. She was married to Thomas Tibbles. Together, a decade earlier, they had roused their city of Omaha in anger over the torturous treatment suffered by the Ponca Standing Bear and his band. Exiled in Indian Territory from their homeland along the Niobrara River (in northernmost Nebraska), the Poncas had escaped and walked home, stopping in the city, their feet bleeding in the snow, so hungry that they had chewed on their moccasins. General George Crook volunteered to be the defendant in a legal case that established the Poncas' right to return home.

History is full of surprises. The same year that Hicks' book was published, Matthew W. Stirling, chief and later director of the American Bureau of Ethnology for thirty years (1928–1958), stated in *National Geographic* that the Albany Plan of Union (1754) was fundamentally shaped by the Iroquois Confederacy through Benjamin Franklin (Stirling, 1937). Such an idea is hardly universally accepted, even in our time. For one, Steven Pinker, in *The Blank Slate,* asserted that the same idea was flimsy enough to dismiss without explanation in two words: "1960s granola" (Pinker, 2002, 298).

Historically, we stand with Whitman and Stirling. *The Encyclopedia of American Indian History* attempts to redress assumptions that any single culture is superior to any other. American Indian voices were available to historians in the 1930s; it was, after all, a time of major Native rights assertion under the Indian Reorganization Act, but many non-Native historians seemed not to be listening. The writings of Dr. Charles A. Eastman (or, to use his Dakota name, Ohiyesa) and Luther Standing Bear were widely published, among many others. Major nineteenth-century feminists (Elizabeth Cady Stanton and Matilda Joslyn Gage, to name two) had acknowledged their debt to Native matriarchal societies. Still, one can hardly imagine Hicks having any use for an encyclopedia entry titled "American Indian Contributions to the World."

We start with six essays, written by our co-editors and members of our editorial board, which focus on the themes that dominate particular eras in American Indian history. So, for example, if a reader wants to find out why the Trail of Tears migration happened when it did, s/he would find that context covered in the essay dealing with the period from 1800 to 1850. The late Vine Deloria, Jr. once advised non-Indian scholars to study the history of topics of contemporary importance to Native peoples, and a section of the encyclopedia addresses those issues that are prominent both in the history of Native peoples and in Native societies today. These entries range from archaeology and pre-contact Native history to topics like gaming and water rights, which are still so relevant. Subsequent sections deal with the most important events of American Indian history, aspects of Native cultures that have had ramifications in history, Native interactions with non-Indian governments, and the roles of both individuals and groups in American Indian history. One of the most important sections of the encyclopedia, the histories of particular Native nations, is absolutely vital to the stories we're seeking to have told and deserves to be highlighted. Also, primary sources from throughout American Indian history are presented so that readers can get a flavor of how different people viewed these events as they happened.

The occupancy of most of North America by Europeans on a sustained basis is less than 200 years old—four consecutive human lives then, less than three now. Thus, the importance of American Indian history to the recent history of all peoples on this continent is clear. The history is written in what we call our homeland—many of our cities, half the constituent states in the federal union that calls itself the United States, bear names that have Native roots.

If there is one thing we've learned from trying to organize and do justice to such a vast and important subject, it is that there is no way to present this material that is perfect for everyone. Different people learn best in different ways. However, we've endeavored to be as clear as possible, making the large number of materials and resources as easy to locate and use as possible. An encyclopedia is not a cast-iron product, but a collection of many contributors' work. In our case, this is a mixture of Native and non-Native voices. Selection of subject matter is subject to judgment, and interpretation, and will be reviewed—something or someone is included, someone or something else is ignored, or given short shrift. We can say only that we have done our best.

Bruce E. Johansen and Barry M. Pritzker, Editors
Steven L. Danver, Project Editor

References and Further Reading

Hicks, John D. *The Federal Union: A History of the United States to 1865.* 1937. Boston: Houghton-Mifflin.

Moquin, Wayne. *Great Documents in American Indian History.* 1973. New York: Praeger.

Pinker, Steven. *The Blank Slate: The Modern Denial of Human Nature.* 2002. New York: Viking (Penguin Putnam).

Pritzker, Barry M. *Native America Today: A Guide to Community Politics and Culture.* 1999. Santa Barbara, CA: ABC-CLIO.

Stirling, Matthew W. "America's First Settlers, the Indians." *National Geographic* 72:5 (1937), cited in Bruce E. Johansen, comp. *Native America and the Evolution of Democracy: A Supplementary Bibliography.* 1999, 140. Westport, CT: Greenwood.

Encyclopedia of
American Indian History

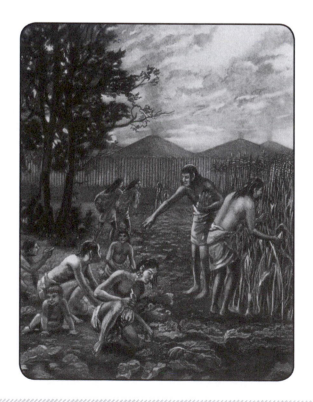

Culture and American Indian History

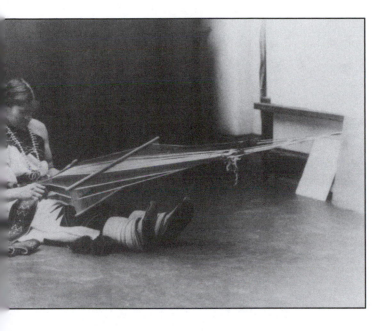

Adena Civilization

The Adena, an early eastern Woodlands civilization, existed from about 1000 BCE to 500 CE. Best known for the mounds they built, the Adenas left a substantial number of artifacts as well as evidence of early agricultural practices. The Adena homeland extended from southeastern Indiana to southwestern Pennsylvania and from central Ohio to central Kentucky and West Virginia. Adena migrants, presumably later displaced by the Hopewell, could also be found as far east as the Chesapeake Bay and as far south as Alabama.

The Adena civilization is named after the estate of Thomas Worthington, the sixth governor of Ohio. Worthington's estate, near Chillicothe, Ohio, stands near a large Adena burial mound. At the time that Worthington built his mansion in the early nineteenth century, the Adenas were not recognized as worthy of importance. For this reason, many of the Adena mounds and the artifacts within them were plowed under by farmers, destroyed to build roads, and dismantled to construct buildings. Much of the Adena legacy has thus been lost.

The Adena legacy that remains is chiefly in the form of mounds. Although the Adenas had been present in Ohio for some centuries, they apparently began constructing mounds only after about 500. These mounds, found in and around Adena villages, were conical and dome-shaped structures of earth and stone. Mounds served as territorial and perhaps diplomatic markers. Topographic prominence appears to have been an important objective in placement, although the topography has likely changed somewhat since the era of the Adenas. Mounds built by the Indians in upland locations are typically located on ridge crests, hilltops, bluff lines, and the tips of promontories so that they could be easily seen. Mounds in lowland locations are usually found on higher terraces of flood plains, sites that would allow them to be visible from the waterways or the adjacent uplands, yet secure from all but the largest floods.

Many of the surviving Adena mounds are burial mounds. These structures are normally conical in

The Great Serpent Mound in Ohio was a product of the Adena civilization. (Richard A. Cooke/Corbis)

shape and can be found in either lowland or upland locations. The burial mounds are located on the former sites of Adena wooden structures. The ground at a burial site has been ritually modified by clearing the surface vegetation or soil layer, adding sand or clay, or other sediments, and building a circular or rectangular wooden enclosure. The structures were once believed to be Adena houses but archaeologists now believe that the buildings were related to some ceremonial use, perhaps a mortuary ritual, and were never intended for habitation.

To construct a mound, the Adena began by preparing a special floor. Then, they ritually prepared the deceased for burial and interred the body in a chamber beneath or on the surface. The deceased was buried with a variety of goods. Lastly, a mound was built over and around the grave. In the early stages of the culture, low earthen hillocks were built up, basketful by basketful, over the burial pits of honored individuals. Later, high mounds were constructed of mostly earth and some stones over multiple burials, the corpses usually placed in log-lined tombs. With each new burial, another layer of dirt was added to

the mound. Often these earthen monuments were surrounded by other earthworks—rounded walls or ridges of earth, usually circular in shape. Stone mounds were built in upland locations in the Appalachian and Interior Low plateaus but the purpose of these mounds is not yet well understood.

The mounds indicate that the Adenas had a high degree of social organization. Burial mounds were repositories for the dead, but they were also monuments to the dead whose bodies they covered and enveloped. The fact that the burial mounds required special effort to construct indicates that the deceased were sufficiently respected by their group to warrant the investment of time and labor required to erect the memorial. The Adena grave goods that have been found indicate the social inequalities in the culture: engraved stone tablets, often with raptorial bird designs; polished gorgets of stone and copper; pearl beads; ornaments of sheet mica; tubular stone pipes; and bone masks.

The Adenas also constructed earthen effigy mounds—totemic animals or symbols. The best-known Adena mound is the Great Serpent Mound

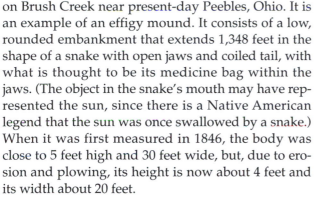

on Brush Creek near present-day Peebles, Ohio. It is an example of an effigy mound. It consists of a low, rounded embankment that extends 1,348 feet in the shape of a snake with open jaws and coiled tail, with what is thought to be its medicine bag within the jaws. (The object in the snake's mouth may have represented the sun, since there is a Native American legend that the sun was once swallowed by a snake.) When it was first measured in 1846, the body was close to 5 feet high and 30 feet wide, but, due to erosion and plowing, its height is now about 4 feet and its width about 20 feet.

Aside from their mound building, the lifestyle of the Adenas differed relatively little from that of their late Archaic period predecessors. Most Adena people apparently lived in small, widely scattered, and probably seasonally occupied sites that were ephemeral. A typical dwelling most likely was a simple and expendable wood-framed structure, perhaps formed of bent or upright saplings covered with woven branches, hides, or herb mats. Structures inhabited during the winter appear to have been more substantial, befitting the harsh winters in the area inhabited by the Adenas. The framework of Adena houses had a unique construction. Outward sloping posts, set in pairs, formed a circle. Four vertical center posts supported the high ends of the rafter poles that extended downward, beyond the wall posts, to form generous eaves. The walls were wattled and the roof was matted or thatched. There is also evidence that the Adena periodically occupied rock shelters and caves, features that are relatively numerous in the Appalachian Plateau and Interior Low Plateau.

The Adena people were primarily hunters, gatherers, and collectors. The region inhabited by the Indians was sufficiently lush enough to support a fairly sedentary lifestyle. There is some evidence of incipient agriculture in Adena culture—the cultivation of sunflowers, pumpkins, gourds, and goosefoot as food sources. It is also known that Adena Indians grew tobacco for ceremonial use.

The Adenas lived close to a number of major waterways and apparently participated extensively in trade. Adena products were apparently much sought after. They made cigar-shaped and tubular pipes of siltstone (also known as pipestone), a material that was easily drilled and easily carved and that had a nice sheen when polished. The pipes were in great demand and have been found as far away as the Chesapeake Bay area in Maryland, in New England, and in the Saint Lawrence River Valley in Canada. The pipes, as well as projectile points made of Vanport flint, were apparently exchanged for copper from the Great Lakes region and mica from the southern Appalachian Mountains. The Adena used these materials to make copper ornaments and mica crescents. They also made unique carved stone tablets. These items were small, flat rectangles, delicately carved with abstracted snake and bird designs. Since traces of pigment have been found on some, they apparently were used to stamp designs on some flat surface, perhaps bark cloth or deerskin. In addition to these objects, the Adena also crafted a wide range of stone, wood, bone, and copper tools, as well as incised or stamped pottery and clothes woven from vegetable fibers.

As is the case with so many prehistoric cultures, it is not known for certain what became of the Adena civilization. The Hopewell Indians, a subsequent mound-building people, somehow came to displace them. The Adena and Hopewell Indians shared many cultural traits, including an affinity for designing the same sort of pipes. They coexisted for five centuries but their exact relationship is not known—whether Adena peoples, or some among them, were ancestral to Hopewell, or whether Hopewell Indians invaded from elsewhere.

Caryn E. Neumann

See also Archaeology and the First Americans; Cahokia; Hopewell Culture; Mississippian Culture; Mound Cultures of North America; Ohio Valley Mound Culture; Trade.

References and Further Reading

Dragoo, Don. 1963. *Mounds for the Dead: An Analysis of the Adena Culture.* Pittsburgh, PA: Carnegie Museum.

Hamilton, Ross. 2001. *The Mystery of the Serpent Mound: In Search of the Alphabet of the Gods.* Berkeley, CA: Frog.

Hothem, Lar. 1989. *Treasures of the Mound Builders: Adena and Hopewell Artifacts of Ohio.* Lancaster, OH: Hothem House Books.

Korp, Maureen. 1990. *The Sacred Geography of the American Mound Builders.* Lewiston, NY: Edwin Mellen Press.

Shaffer, Lynda Norene. 1992. *Native Americans Before 1492: The Moundbuilding Centers of the Eastern Woodlands.* Armonk, NY: M. E. Sharpe.

Silverberg, Robert. 1986. *The Mound Builders.* Athens, OH: Ohio University Press.

Webb, William S., and Charles E. Snow. 1974. *The Adena People.* Knoxville: University of Tennessee Press.

Woodward, Susan L., and Jerry N. McDonald. 2002. *Indian Mounds of the Middle Ohio Valley.* Blacksburg, VA: McDonald and Woodward.

African Americans

Mixed genealogy between African Americans and Native Americans is not unusual. For example, Crispus Attucks, son of an African American father and a Massachuset Indian mother, was the first casualty of the Boston Massacre of March 5, 1770, the first death in the cause of the American Revolution. Attucks' father was a black slave in a Framingham, Massachusetts, household until about 1750, when he escaped and became a sailor. Attucks' mother lived in an Indian mission at Natick, Massachusetts.

Poet Langston Hughes, singer Tina Turner, actor James Earl Jones, and civil rights activist Jesse Jackson all have some black–American Indian ancestry, although their specific tribal affiliations are not known. The Pequot founders of Foxwoods, in Connecticut, the largest Indian casino in the United States, are mixed African-Indian, a fact that has provoked some critics to challenge their Indian bona fides (Benedict, 2000).

The notable abolitionist Frederick Douglass was born Frederick Augustus Washington Bailey on a farm on Lewiston Road, Tuckahoe, near Easton, in Talbot County, Maryland, in February 1818. He was the son of an unknown European-American father and Harriet Bailey, a slave who may have been partially Native American. No traces remain of the Native tribe or nation with which he may share ancestry. As a boy, Douglass's owner, Aaron Anthony, referred to him as his "little Indian boy."

In some cases, Native Americans and escaped slaves made common cause with Native Americans in sizable groups. One such example is the black Seminoles, who are sometimes called Seminole maroons by ethnologists, who live today mainly in Oklahoma, Texas, the Bahamas, and Coahuila, Mexico. Their ancestors were runaways from the plantations of South Carolina and Georgia between the late seventeenth and mideighteenth centuries who sought refuge in Spanish-controlled Florida. The name "Seminole," derived from the Spanish word *cimaroon*, meaning "fugitive" or "wild one," was incorporated into the Native language. The word "maroon," in English, stems from the same Spanish word.

Fugitive slaves from Charleston arrived in Spanish St. Augustine, Florida, as early as 1687, where many began new lives as free men and women in a multicultural community. Some of the men worked as cartwrights, jewelers, butchers, and innkeepers, while women were employed as cooks

A black Seminole named Abraham, one of many escaped black slaves absorbed into the Seminole nation. (Library of Congress)

and laundresses. Some owned small businesses. In 1838, the Spanish authorities established a settlement for escaped slaves, Gracia Real de Santa Teresa de Mose, where roughly 100 men, women, and children came into contact with various bands of Native Americans living nearby.

The Seminoles, originally one of the five Civilized Tribes (the others being the Cherokee, Choctaw, Chickasaw, and Creek) were chased into Florida in 1818 by armed forces under the command of General (and later U.S. President) Andrew Jackson. Florida was under Spanish jurisdiction (the area was ceded to the United States in 1821), and the invasion provoked a diplomatic furor. The Seminoles, many of whom were descended from Creeks, had elected to ally themselves with the Spanish rather than the United States, an act of virtual treason in General Jackson's eyes.

Jackson's pretext for invading Florida (over Spanish diplomatic objections) was the pursuit of freed slaves as well as the Seminoles. For several decades, escaped slaves made common cause with the Seminoles, sometimes mingling and at other times establishing a separate identity and preserving their own cultures and traditions. In the meantime, the Seminoles fought the U.S. Army to a stalemate. To avoid capture, the black Seminoles developed skills at guerilla warfare. They also became very adaptable, finding ways to survive in new environments, such as the Florida Everglades, that other people regarded as uninhabitable or marginal.

In addition, the Seminoles gave shelter to escaped slaves. The pretext of Jackson's raid thus was the recovery of stolen human property. After the U.S. purchased Florida from Spain, slave-hunting vigilantes invaded the area en masse, killing Seminoles as well as blacks. Later, in the 1830s, when President Jackson proposed to remove the Seminoles to Indian Territory, they refused. Moving deep into the swamps of southern Florida (an area that ironically was being used as a removal destination for other Native peoples), the Seminoles fought U.S. Army troops to a bloody stalemate during seven years of warfare. They were never defeated, and they never moved from their new homeland.

In 1823, Seminole leaders agreed to the Treaty of Moultrie Creek that ceded land and created reservations for the Seminoles. Later, as a result of U.S. removal policies, the Treaty of Payne's Landing (1832) required all Seminoles to leave Florida for Indian Territory within three years. According to the treaty, Seminoles with African American blood were to be sold into slavery.

Escaped slaves joined the Seminoles during the Second Seminole War (1835–1842), a guerilla campaign during which the blacks served prominent roles as advisors, spies, and intermediaries. At one point, General Thomas S. Jesup said it was "a Negro and not an Indian War." Jesup eventually promised the former slaves freedom if they would emigrate to the Indian Territory as part of the Seminole nation.

The war against the Seminoles was one of the most expensive Indian campaigns that the U.S. Army had waged to that time. In addition to the 1,500 soldiers killed (one for every two Seminoles eventually removed to Indian Territory), the government spent an average of $6,500 for each Native person transferred to Indian Territory. At a time when the average job paid less than $1,000 a year, this amount represented a small fortune.

Following the First and Second Seminole Wars (1817–1818 and 1835–1842), some of the black Seminoles escaped to the Bahamas. Others were separated from their Native American allies and transported to the Indian Territory (present-day Oklahoma), where they became known as Freedmen. Some moved to Mexico where their descendents, known as *Indios Mascogos*, still live. After the Civil War, some black Seminoles moved to Texas, where, during the 1870s and 1880s, they served with the U.S. Army on the Texas frontier as the Seminole Negro Indian Scouts. Today, members of the black Seminole community in Texas refer to themselves as Seminoles to set themselves apart from other blacks and to emphasize the pride that they have in their unique history of having escaped slavery.

Bruce E. Johansen

See also Black Seminoles; Slavery.
References and Further Reading
Benedict, Jeff. 2000. *Without Reservation: The Making of America's Most Powerful Indian Tribe and Foxwoods, the World's Largest Casino*. New York: HarperCollins.
Black Indians: An American Story. No date. A documentary film directed by Chip Richie, produced by Steven R. Heape, written by Daniel Blake Smith, and narrated by James Earl Jones. Available at: http://www.richheape .com/native-american-videos/Black _Indians_An_American_ Story.htm
CCNY Libraries. 1998. "The Black Seminoles' Long Road to Freedom." Available at: http://www .ccny.cuny.edu/library/News/seminoles2 .html. Accessed January 9, 2007.
Forbes, Jack D. 1993. *Africans and Native Americans: The Language of Race and the Evolution of Red-Black Peoples*. Urbana: University of Illinois Press.

Agriculture

While popular imagination sometimes stereotypes them solely as nomadic hunters, many, if not most, of North America's Native peoples practiced agriculture, or the domestication of plants for human consumption. At least half of the earth's staple vegetable foods, the most important being corn (maize) and potatoes, were first cultivated by American Indians, who often drew their sustenance from hunting, gathering, *and* agriculture. By the year 800, agriculture was an established way of life for many Native peoples in North America.

At first sight, many immigrating Europeans did not recognize Native American agriculture, because it did not resemble their own. Indians did not domesticate draft animals and only rarely plowed their fields. Sometimes crops were grown in small clearings amid forest. When Europeans first laid eyes on North America, it was much more densely

This hand-colored engraving depicts Native American farmers in Florida, circa 1562. Native American agriculture introduced many foods, including corn, squash, and chocolate to European palates. (Bettmann/Corbis)

forested than it is today. The park-like appearance of many eastern forests was a result of Native American peoples' efforts to manage plant and animal life.

Some Native peoples used fire to raze fields for farming and to drive game while hunting. These were not fires left to blaze out of control, however. For instance, Navajos who used range fires customarily detailed half of their hunting party to contain and control the fire and to keep it on the surface, where the flames would clear old brush so that new plant life could self-generate instead of destroying the forest canopy.

Agricultural Contributions to the World

Native Americans first cultivated many of the foods that today are taken for granted as everyday nourishment. The main ingredients of Crackerjacks (peanuts and popcorn), for example, are both indigenous to the Americas, as are all edible beans except horse beans and soybeans, all squashes (including pumpkins), Jerusalem artichokes, the "Irish" potato, the sweet potato, sunflowers, peppers, pineapples, watermelons, cassava, bananas, strawberries, raspberries, gooseberries, and pecans.

Native American agriculture has influenced eating habits around the world so completely that many people forget their foods' culinary origins. Before the voyages of Columbus, the Italian food of today (with its tomato-based sauces) was unknown. The Irish cooked their food without potatoes. Europeans satisfied their desire for sweets without chocolate. Corn was unknown outside the Americas. These crops were produced by experimentation by many Native American cultures over thousands of years. Knowledge of plant life was passed along from generation to generation with other social knowledge, usually by the elder women of a Native tribe or nation.

Food Production and Spiritual Life

The production of food is woven into Native American spiritual life. Among the Iroquois and many other Native peoples, for example, festivals highlight the key role of the three sisters (corn, squash, and beans). Archaeologists tell us that the food complex of corn, beans, and squash was transferred northward from Mexico as a set of rituals before it was an agricultural system. By practicing the rituals, Native Americans in the corn-growing areas of North America became farmers. Corn requires a one-160-day frost-free growing season; the northern limit of corn cultivation also often marks the limit of intensive Native agriculture.

Agriculture among Native American peoples enabled higher population densities. According to William Cronon, the Indians in Maine, who did not use widespread agriculture, sustained an average density of about forty people per 100 square miles, while Native Americans in southern New England, who raised crops (corn being their major staple), averaged 287 people (seven times as many) on the same amount of land (Cronon, 1983, 42).

Native American agriculture often seemed disorderly to European eyes, accustomed as they were to large monocultural fields of one crop. Native fields showed evidence of thought and practice, however. Samuel de Champlain described how Indians planted corn on small hills mixed with beans of several types. "When they grow up, they interlace with the corn, which reaches to the height of five to six feet; and they keep the ground free from weeds," Champlain wrote (Cronon, 1983, 43). John Winthrop, describing Indian fields in Massachusetts within a generation of the Pilgrims' arrival, said that their agriculture "load[ed] the ground with as much as it will beare" (Cronon, 1983, 44). Indian farming methods (usually the responsibility of women, except when growing tobacco) not only kept weeds at a minimum but also preserved soil moisture.

Many Native peoples offered their thanks to the plants as well as to the animals that they consumed, out of a belief that the essence of life animating human beings also is present in the entire web of animate and inanimate life and objects. Long before a science of "sustained yield" forestry evolved, Native American peoples along the Northwest Coast harvested trees in ways that would assure their continued growth, as part of a belief that trees are sentient beings. Some Native Americans charted farming cycles through complicated relationships with the sun and moon. In addition to domesticating dozens of food plants, they also harvested the wild bounty of the forests for hundreds of herbs and other plants used to restore and maintain health.

Mayan Agriculture

While the Mayas are known for their temples in such places as Tikal, Copan, and Palenque, the commoners who supported the small elite that maintained the temples, spent most of their time cultivating food, principally corn. Most of the Mayan ceremonial centers were surrounded by very large earthworks, which were used for agriculture. These artificial ramparts were not discovered by modern archaeologists until they started using satellite images of the land, because today the earthworks often are submerged in jungle and thus very difficult to see from ground level. The earthworks included complex irrigation channels and raised fields, often hewn from reclaimed swampland. The Maya dredged nutrient-rich soil from the bottoms of the irrigation ditches to fertilize fields that they raised above the flood level of the rainy season. The fields were so rich that they produced several crops a year to feed the people of the urban ceremonial centers.

The discovery of complex agricultural earthworks among the Maya caused scholars to question earlier assumptions that the Maya had practiced slash-and-burn agriculture that was said to have deforested the land, exhausted and eroded the topsoil, and played a role in the collapse of the "classic" age of the Maya. Today, the collapse of the Maya is usually ascribed not to deforestation caused by agriculture, but to ecological damage and social disorganization caused by escalating warfare between city-states. Not all of the Mayas' earthworks were constructed to aid agriculture. Some ramparts were defensive, and, as war became more common and deadly, the Mayas' complex agricultural system suffered immensely.

Pueblo Agriculture: Water Is Life

About the same time that the Mayan civilization collapsed, the ancestors of today's Pueblos were building a corn-based culture in the Chaco Canyon of present-day New Mexico. The Pueblos of the Rio Grande are cultural and economic inheritors of the Mogollon, Ancestral Puebloan, and Hohokam communities to the west and southwest of the upper Rio Grande Valley. The cultivation of corn was introduced into the area about 3000 BCE. About 2000 BCE, beans and squash were added. Cotton later became a third staple crop.

Also about 2,000 years ago, irrigation was introduced to supplement dry farming in the area. The

Pueblos used brief, heavy precipitation to advantage by constructing some of their irrigation works at the bases of steep cliffs that collected runoff. The residents of this area constructed roads that often ran for hundreds of miles to provide a way to share food surpluses; if one pueblo had a bad harvest, others would make it up. The cultivation of corn in Chaco Canyon supported a civilization that constructed the largest multifamily dwellings in North America. Such a high degree of agricultural organization supported a culture that dominated the turquoise trade in the area. Turquoise was important as a liquid asset, a medium of trade. Pueblo centers such as Pueblo Bonito became centers of trade, manufacturing, and ceremony.

The vital role of water and irrigation in Pueblo agriculture is illustrated by the fact that the great classic Pueblo civilizations were destroyed by a drought so severe that not even ingenious water management could cope with it. In the thirteenth century, residents abandoned most Pueblo settlements outside the Rio Grande Valley after fifty years of nearly rainless drought that destroyed their agricultural base.

Following the Spanish colonization of New Mexico, access to water became a crucial cause for conflict. Land without water is worthless in the arid Southwest. Paradoxically, the Pueblos in 1680 used the waters of the Rio Grande to defeat the Spanish; they staged their revolt while the river was flooding to keep Spanish reinforcements out.

The irrigation of farmland is *the* key factor in Pueblo agricultural land use. To plan, construct, and maintain elaborate land systems, cooperation between several villages was crucial. The irrigation systems needed routine maintenance that rendered clans inefficient, so nonkinship associations were created to cope with the work. This organizational framework had other community functions, and it revolved primarily around the spiritual life of the Pueblos. The basic rationale for the nonkinship associations was irrigation, however.

The Importance of Corn

Corn, the major food source for several agricultural peoples across the continent, enjoyed a special spiritual significance. Corn and beans (which grow well together because beans, a legume, fix nitrogen in their roots) were often said to maintain a spiritual union. Some peoples, such as the Omahas of the eastern Great Plains, "sang up" their corn through special rituals. Some groups cleaned their storage bins before the harvest, "so the corn would be happy when they brought it in" (Brandon, 1961, 116). The Pawnees grew ten varieties of corn, including one (called holy or wonderful corn) that was used only for religious purposes and never eaten. The Mandans had a Corn Priest who officiated at rites during the growing season. Each stage of the corn's growth was associated with particular songs and rituals, and spiritual attention was said to be as important to the corn as proper water, sun, and fertilizer. Among the Zuni, a newborn child was given an ear of corn at birth and endowed with a corn name. An ear of maize was put in the place of death as the heart of the deceased and later used as seed corn to begin the cycle of life anew. To Navajos, corn was as sacred as human life.

Corn is intertwined with the origin stories of many Native American peoples. The Pueblos say that corn was brought to them by Blue Corn Woman and White Corn Maiden, who emerged to the surface of the earth from a great underground kiva (sacred place). At birth, each infant is given the seed from an ear of corn as a fetish, to carry for life as a reminder that the Corn Mothers brought life to the Pueblos. The corn fetish has a practical side as well: Should a harvest completely fail for drought or other reasons, the fetishes may become the seed corn for the next crop.

Corn's biological name is *Zea Mays*, from which the name "maize" is derived. The first distant relatives of today's foot-long ears of corn were probably grown in central Mexico, in caves near Teotihuacán, about 7,000 years ago, from a wild grass called *teosinte*. Early corn was small, perhaps three to four inches long, with two rows of mismatched kernels. Utilization of corn spread to South America as well as to the Ancestral Puebloan country in present-day Arizona and New Mexico, first as a wild grain, then as an agricultural product, gradually gaining length and kernels along the way. Corn was firmly established as a staple in the Southwest by about 1,500 years ago. By 1,000 years ago, corn had spread over all of North and South America having the requisite warmth and growing season and had become a stable crop of many Native peoples across the hemisphere. As the use of maize spread north and south from Mexico, Native peoples domesticated hundreds of varieties and bred them selectively so that the edible kernels grew in size and numbers.

Corn was introduced in eastern North America shortly after the birth of Christ in the Old World (about 200) and had become a dominant food source across much of the region (from southern Ontario to northern Florida) by about 800. During this time, Native American farmers took part in the selective breeding of several strains of corn to increase production as well as hardiness in the face of freezes and drought. By 900, a major advance in breeding, commonly called flint or eastern eight row, secured corn's dominance of agricultural food production throughout the East because it was even hardier than earlier strains. The spread of corn as a staple crop did not reach its greatest extent until a hundred years before Columbus's first voyage.

When colonists arrived in eastern North America, many of the Native peoples they met farmed corn in large tracts. John Winthrop, governor of the Massachusetts Bay Colony, admired abandoned Native cornfields and declared that God had provided the epidemic that killed the people who had tended them as an act of divine providence, clearing the way for the Puritans. Native Americans taught the Puritans which seeds would grow in their territory. Most of the seeds that the Puritans had brought from England did not sprout when planted in the area that the colonists called "New England."

Corn also enhanced the role of agriculture in many Native American economies. The Iroquois' oral history, for example, holds that corn had a key role in establishing agriculture as a major economic enterprise. The Haudenosaunee (Iroquois) adopted corn as a staple crop and developed large-scale architecture shortly after 1000. Their ability to produce a surplus of corn played a role in the political influence of the Haudenosaunee Confederacy, which reached, through a chain of alliances, from their homelands in present-day upstate New York across much of New England and the Middle Atlantic regions.

The Iroquois' adoption of corn-based agriculture, along with cultivation of beans and squash (called the three sisters) played an important role in their adoption of a matrilineal social structure and a consensus-based political system. Before roughly the year 1000, the Iroquois were less prone to alliance and more frequently disposed to murder for revenge. An older confederacy to the north, probably the Wyandot (Huron), are said to have sent an emissary, Deganawidah, to persuade the Haudenosaunee to make peace with each other and outlaw the blood feud, which was threatening social stability.

Deganawidah and Hiawatha, the Mohawk cofounder of the Haudenosaunee Confederacy, spent most of their adult lives persuading the feuding Haudenosaunee to accept their vision of peace. According to calculations by Barbara Mann and Jerry Fields, the Confederacy was finally accepted in 1142, within living memory.

Bruce E. Johansen

See also Adena Civilization; American Indian Contributions to the World; Ancestral Puebloan Culture; Archaeology; Environment and Pollution; Haudenosaunee Confederacy, Political System; Hohokam Culture; Hopewell Culture; Mississippian Culture; Squanto; Thanksgiving Holiday, Origins; Trade; Water Rights; Women in Native Woodlands Societies; Women of All Red Nations.

References and Further Reading

Ballantine, Betty and Ian. 1994. *The Native Americans: An Illustrated History.* Atlanta, GA: Turner Publishing.

Brandon, William. 1961. *American Heritage Book of Indians.* New York: Dell.

Cronon, William. 1983. *Changes in the Land: Indians, Colonists, and the Ecology of New England.* New York: Hill and Wang.

Deloria, Vine, Jr. 1992. *God Is Red.* Golden, CO: Fulcrum.

Dozier, Edward P. 1970. *The Pueblo Indians of North America.* New York: Holt, Rinehart, and Winston.

Grinde, Donald A., Jr., and Bruce E. Johansen. 1995. *Ecocide of Native America.* Santa Fe, NM: Clear Light Publishers.

Hughes, J. Donald. 1983. *American Indian Ecology.* El Paso: Texas Western Press.

Iverson, Peter. 1992. "Taking Care of the Earth and Sky." In *America in 1492: The World of the Indian Peoples Before the Arrival of Columbus.* Edited by Alvin Josephy. New York: Alfred A. Knopf.

Sando, Joe S. 1976. *The Pueblo Indians.* San Francisco: Indian Historian Press.

American Indian Contributions to the World

For many years, immigrants to the continent they came to call North America studied history as if they had shaped its First Peoples—it was *their* westward movement, *their* religion, *their* civilization, *their* conquest. Often left unexamined until recent years are the many ways in which the more recent immigrants absorbed Native foods, sports, and social and politi-

cal ideas. Assertions also have been made that Indian contributions helped shape non-Native folksongs, the locations for railroads and highways, ways of dying cloth, and even bathing habits (Frachtenberg, 1915, 64–69; Edwards, 1934, 255–272).

The U.S. Army did more than subjugate the Plains Indians. As troops chased the Lakota, they also learned from them. Many Plains people used sign language, their smoke signals could be seen for many miles in open country, and the Sioux later devised a system of signaling by mirrors. The Army adopted some of these signaling systems (in some cases, symbol-bearing blankets became flags), and they became the basis of the techniques used in the modern U.S. Army Signal Corps.

Even after more than five centuries in America, non-Natives are still discovering the lands and inhabitants of a place their ancestors called the New World. Felix Cohen, author of the *Handbook of Federal Indian Law,* a basic reference in that field, compared Native American influence on immigrants from abroad to the ways in which the Greeks shaped Roman culture: "When the Roman legions conquered Greece, Roman historians wrote with as little imagination as did the European historians who have written of the white man's conquest of America. What the Roman historians did not see was that captive Greece would take captive conquering Rome [with] Greek science [and] Greek philosophy . . ." (Cohen, 1952, 180). Cohen wrote that American historians had too often paid attention to military victories and changing land boundaries, while failing to see that "in agriculture, in government, in sport, in education, and in our views of nature and our fellow men, it is the first Americans who have taken captive their battlefield conquerors" (Cohen, 1952, 180). American historians "have seen America only as an imitation of Europe," Cohen asserted. In his view, "[t]he real epic of America is the yet unfinished story of the Americanization of the white man" (Cohen, 1952, 180).

Cohen published his essay in 1952. His idea was not invented by a new generation of scholars, however. It was being rediscovered. Such an understanding had always existed, as evidenced by a letter that the poet Walt Whitman wrote to the Santa Fe City Council in 1883, four years after General Pratt started his Carlisle School under the slogan "Kill the Indian and save the Man" (i.e., "assimilate or die"). "As to our aboriginal or Indian population . . . ," wrote Whitman, "I know it seems to be agreed that they must gradually dwindle as time rolls on, and in

a few generations more leave only a reminiscence, a blank." He continued: "But I am not at all clear about that. As America develops, adapts, entwines, faithfully identifies its own—are we to see it cheerfully accepting . . . all the contributions of foreign lands from the whole outside globe—and then rejecting the only ones distinctly its own?" (Moquin, 1973, 5–6).

Many borrowings are indirect and so deeply engrained in present-day culture that we have forgotten, for the most part, where they came from. The word "tuxedo," for example, is anglicized from the Delaware (Leni Lenápe) word for wolf, *p'tuksit.* Neither wolves nor most American Indians wore tuxedos when this borrowing took place during the 1880s, of course. The tuxedo was first worn in a New York village by the name of Tuxedo, however. In our time a "tux" is taken to be very conventional dress, but, in the 1880s, young men wore it as an alternative to the older fashion of jackets with tails.

An Encyclopedia of Borrowings

An entire encyclopedia devoted to this idea is evidence that the idea of two-way communication has reached a degree of maturity in the academy. Such an idea has brought us a long way from the boarding school days of forced one-way acculturation. As its title suggests, Keoke and Porterfield's *Encyclopedia of American Indian Contributions to the World* is the first attempt to compile a wide array of such material under one cover. It is a wide-ranging effort, one that may surprise even the most diligent student of ways in which Native American cultures have shaped others worldwide.

The *Encyclopedia of American Indian Contributions to the World* is a groundbreaking compilation of Native American contributions to sciences, technology, foods, lifeways, government, and other aspects of history and modern life. It is also, at the same time, a monument to cultural amalgamation, a reminder that everything ultimately finds itself mixed with everything else. This was as true 500 years ago as it is in today's world of accelerated communication and transportation. Consider "Indian" (that is, Indian as in the subcontinent) curry. The spices that comprise it actually began as a chili in what is now Brazil. They were transported to India by Portuguese seafarers and then mixed with Asian spices to produce the mixture we know today. Democracy developed similarly: a piece from Greece, a dash from Rome, a sprinkle of Iroquois law, all brought together in a common porridge of English legal precedent, spoken now in English, and often served to the world as a uniquely American tradition. One wonders what the Italians ate before tomato sauce, what the Irish consumed before potatoes, and what Jewish celebrants of Hanukkah used in lieu of potatoes for their latkes.

The idea of playing a game with a bouncing ball is indigenous to the Americas, particularly to Mesoamerica, where the Aztecs and Mayas played a game that had the attributes of basketball, American football, and soccer. Europeans had no rubber before Columbus and thus no rubber balls. The Olmecs, who lived in the Yucatan Peninsula, invented a way to treat raw latex to make usable items from rubber. They used it to make balls, soles for sandals, hollow bulbs for syringes, and waterproofed ponchos. This process was similar to vulcanization, which was patented by Charles Goodyear in 1844. Many present-day ball games share both European and American Indian precedents. Baseball, for example, shares attributes of English cricket and a Choctaw game.

Many of Native America's contributions have become so familiar for so long that many of us have forgotten their origins. When we "sleep on it," for example, we forget that we are invoking an Iroquois custom, in which chiefs in council are implored to let at least one night intervene before making important decisions. The passage of time was said to allow the various members of a Haudenosaunee council to attain unanimity—"one mind"—necessary for the consensual solution of a problem. Similarly, to "bury the hatchet" refers to the Iroquois practice of sequestering weapons under the Great Tree of Peace.

Native American Sciences

Pre-Colombian American Indian astronomers (notably the Maya) used a sophisticated system to calculate celestial events such as solar eclipses. The Maya also created calendar systems that were based on detailed observations of the sun and moon. Mayan astronomers' observations were so accurate that by the fifth century they had calculated a year's length to within a few minutes of today's calendars.

Keoke and Porterfield assert that indigenous Americans employed technology that was, in some respects, more advanced than non-Native techniques. They write, for example, that American Indian metallurgists invented electroplating of met-

als hundreds of years before its discovery in Europe. The Moche, who lived on the coast of northern Peru, utilized electroplating between 200 BCE and 600 CE. Europeans did not discover the process of electroplating until Sir Humphrey Davy's experiments during the late 1700s (Keoke and Porterfield, 2002, 98).

Native Medicines in the Pharmacopoeia of the United States

Several American Indian medicines have come into use among European-Americans. By the late twentieth century, more than 200 drugs first used by American Indians were listed in the *United States Pharmacopoeia,* an official listing of all effective medicines and their uses. These include quinine, laxatives, muscle relaxants, and nasal remedies, as well as several dozen drugs and herbal medicines. To this day, scientists are discovering more beneficial drugs in plants once known only to Native Americans. One reason that many people are concerned at the demise of the Amazon rainforests is that such destruction could keep us from learning more about the Native American uses of plants there.

Native Americans in the North American Northeast used foxglove (*Digitalis purpurea*) to treat heart problems. They administered it with extreme care because high doses were needed and the plant is highly toxic. Keoke and Porterfield maintain that pre-contact American Indian healers had developed a sophisticated system of medical treatment compared to European healers of the time, who relied on bloodletting, blistering, and religious penance, as well as concoctions of lead, arsenic, and cow dung to treat disease. In addition to performing surgery, American Indians from several culture groups understood the importance of keeping wounds sterile and used botanical antiseptics. They made syringes out of bird bones and animal bladders to administer plant medicine.

Native peoples in the Americas had developed so many botanical medications by the time of contact that the Spanish King Philip II sent physician Francisco Hernando to the Americas in 1570 to record Aztec medical knowledge and bring it back to Europe. As early as 1635, after less than a generation in America, English colonists were using herbal medicines introduced to them by the Native peoples. "A Relation of Maryland," written to give prospective immigrants information on the new colony, included this passage:

This Countrey affords naturally, many excellent things for Physicke and Surgery, the perfect use of which, the English cannot yet learne from the Natives: They have a roote which is an excellent preservative against Pyson, called by the English the Snake roote. Other herbes and rootes they have wherewith they cure all manners of wounds; also Saxafras, Gummes, and Balsum. An Indian seeing one of the English, much troubled with the tooth-ake, fetched of the roote of a tree, and gave the party some of it to hold in his mouth, and it eased the pain presently (Birchfield, 1997, 5: 705–706).

By the eighteenth century, European-American observers, many of them missionaries, were compiling lists of Native herbal remedies, some of which were published in several European languages. One of these lists carried to Europe the knowledge that the bark of a particular tree that grows in North America could alleviate toothache. The Canada shrubby elder could be used to combat agues and inflammations. The Jalap root could be used as a laxative and also to relieve the pain of rheumatism; the Ipecacaunha also functioned as an enematic, as well as an antidote to snakebite. Peter Kalm, the Swedish botanist, visited the Middle Atlantic states between 1748 and 1750 to catalogue Native medicinal herbs.

Captain John Smith learned through Pocahantas that her people applied a root that she called *wighsacan* to wounds for its healing power. John Lawson, visiting the Carolinas about 1700, observed that Natives there chewed a root (which he did not name) to soothe stomach ailments. European observers also wrote of Indians who committed suicide by eating certain roots and mushrooms. William Penn wrote that a Delaware woman who had been betrayed by her husband "went out, plunk't a Root out of the Ground, and ate it, upon which she immediately died" (Birchfield, 1997, 5: 706). Native peoples often warned Europeans which plants, if eaten, could make them ill, produce skin rashes, or kill them. In some cases, Native peoples also provided antidotes. The Delaware, for example, dealt with the rash produced by contact with poison sumac by preparing a tea from the inner bark of the sour gum tree, which gave off a distinctive odor that caused Native peoples to compare it to raw fish.

Some Native plant remedies became popular among Europeans based on their biological record, while others took Europe by storm on the basis of unsupported health claims. Use of sassafras root (the "saxafras" in the "Relation of Maryland") was noted as early as Shakespeare's time. The use of sassafras tea spread throughout Europe as a general health tonic, and a trading network grew up across the Atlantic specializing in its harvest, sale, and transport. At about the same time, all sorts of extravagant claims were being made for the tonic effects of tobacco that now do not stand up to scientific scrutiny. Tobacco was said to aid digestion, cure toothaches, kill nits and lice, and even stop coughing. The advocates of tobacco seemed to draw their advice from Native peoples who often used tobacco as a ceremonial herb and who only very rarely became addicted to nicotine.

Tobacco was one of many herbal weapons in the arsenal of Native "medicine men," or shamans, across the continent. The role of the medicine man had no direct counterpart in Europe. The various Native names for the persons who performed these functions can be translated as shaman, juggler, conjurer, sorcerer, priest, and physician, as well as medicine man. Even the translation of Native words that correspond to "medicine" in English can be tricky, because Western culture has no single term that incorporates all the aspects of the shaman's work. Whereas "medicine" in English connotes the treatment of a disease with a drug or other specific remedy, a medicine man was a spiritualist, as well as a person who had learned the basics of physical medicine and herbal cures. Native shamans combined the art of mental suggestion with physical cures as well; the mental attitude of the "patient" was often considered as important as any physical cure. The casting of spells (and other kinds of sorcery) had as much to do with a person's state of mind as with physical and biological reactions.

Most Native American peoples used the byproducts of animals, as well as plants, for medicinal and cosmetic purposes. English immigrants in Virginia and Massachusetts learned early that an emollient of bear grease allowed Native people to range in the woods wearing a minimum of clothing on hot summer days without being bitten by mosquitoes and other stinging insects. Goose grease and bear fat were widely used as hair dressings, and skunk oil was sometimes applied to the chest and throat to relieve the symptoms of colds, including chest congestion. The Delawares sometimes slowed the flow of blood from a cut by inserting spider webs, which probably helped with the clotting of blood.

Witch hazel is a commonly used Native botanical remedy that has been adopted generally by non-Natives in America. Used as a first-aid treatment for insect bites and cuts, witch hazel is the distilled extract of the witch hazel bush combined with alcohol. The shrub grows commonly in the eastern United States; its leaves were boiled and applied to bites and cuts by many Native peoples in that area. The root and leaves of the wintergreen contain methyl salicylate, which is used today in creams and in other forms to treat rheumatic pain, muscular aches, and similar ailments. Salicylic acid is the main active ingredient of aspirin, probably the most widely used relief for minor pain in modern times. The inner bark of the white pine (the national symbol of the Iroquois Confederacy) today is used in cough syrups. Terpin hydrate, a prescription drug used to treat coughs and colds, is derived from the sap of pine trees (turpentine). The Indians also were the first people to utilize caffeine as a stimulant.

Native American Vegetal Remedies

Balm of Gilead	Mixed with cream to form a balm for sores.
Blackberry	Root as tea; said to cure dysentery.
Black haw	Liquid boiled from bark; relieves stomach and menstrual cramps.
Black walnut	Tea boiled from bark relieves severe colds.
Catnip	Tea from the leaves may quiet a restless baby.
Corn silk	As tea, to combat pain caused by kidney trouble.
Dogwood	Tea from the roots serves as a general tonic.
Elder	Tea made from flowers relieves colic in children.
Elm (American or white)	Liquid from steeping the inner bark in water relieves symptoms of flu, such as coughs and chills. Elm is also used as a poultice for gunshot wounds. (General Washington's army used it during the Revolutionary War.)
Fish weed (Jerusalem artichoke)	A tea made from its leaves may rid children of worms.
Flannel mullein	Heated leaves in a compress provide relief from rheumatic pains.
Hog weed (ragweed)	The root is a strong laxative.
Hops	In a tea, leaves serve to relieve symptoms of a cold or, as a compress, to relieve pain.
Jimson weed	Heated leaves relieve the pain of burns; not to be taken internally.
Morning glory	A tea of the leaves relieves some types of stomach pain.
Peach	Crushed leaves used as a compress reduce swelling.
Peppermint	Boiled leaves sometimes relieve stomach pains.
Prickly ash	Tea made from the bark relieves the symptoms of colds; the bark and root can be used to relieve toothache pain.
Sassafras	A tea may reduce high blood pressure.
Tobacco	A soft wad of chewed tobacco will reduce the pain of a bee sting.
Watermelon	Tea from boiled seeds may relieve the pain of kidney trouble.
Wild grape	The juice conditions the hair and scalp.
Wild strawberry	Crushed fruit, applied to face, may improve complexion.
Yarrow	Crushed, boiled roots boiled as tea reduce excessive menstrual flow.
White oak	The liquid steeped from bark helps heal cuts and scratches.

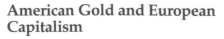

American Gold and European Capitalism

Jack Weatherford's *Indian Givers* (1988) takes the influence of Native American contributions to European capitalism beyond individual products. It begins with the birth of money capitalism, fueled by Indian gold and silver, which provided the necessary capital for the rise of industrial capitalism. Spain, England, and France did not set out to America as empires. Each acquired much of its riches in America and elsewhere around the world.

England's industrial revolution provoked urbanization, which also created a need for an agricultural revolution to feed the populations of burgeoning cities. Weatherford argues that, without Native American corn, potatoes, and other crops, many increasingly urbanized Europeans could have starved to death. Some scholars may argue that Weatherford has something of an intellectual love affair with the potato. How greatly any one contribution shaped history as a whole often has been a point of departure for debate. Regardless of possible differences regarding emphasis, Weatherford makes his point for the appreciation of Native precedents.

In Weatherford's *Native Roots* (1991), ancient Native ingenuity is described in ways that bear on present-day problems. Read, for example, how the Ancestral Puebloans fashioned their dwellings to take advantage of passive solar energy, as well as the shading of overhanging cliffs, blunting the seasonal extremes of the Southwest and reducing the amount of precious firewood they had to burn. Weatherford also describes how the Inuit created a kayak that fits its occupant like a wetsuit, a boat so watertight that its occupant can turn upside down, then right side up again, without getting wet.

Ideas of Freedom

Europe didn't discover America, but America was quite a discovery for Europe. For roughly three centuries before the American Revolution, the ideas that made the American Revolution possible were being discovered, nurtured, and embellished in the growing English and French colonies of North America. America provided a counterpoint for European convention and assumption. It became, for Europeans in America, at once a dream and a reality, a fact and a fantasy, the real and the ideal. To appreciate how European eyes were opened on the "New World," we must take that phrase literally, with the excitement evoked in our own time by stories of travel to other planets. There was one electrifying difference: The voyagers of that time knew that their New World was inhabited. They had only to look and learn, to drink in the bewildering newness and enchanting novelty of seeing it all for the first time.

The idea of personal equality in the societies of many Native peoples pervades both of Weatherford's books, especially as he contrasts Native concepts of liberty with European notions of hierarchy. Weatherford sometimes describes architecture to make his point: nowhere did Native peoples of the Americas create the cathedrals or palaces commissioned by European elites. Instead, the Ancestral Puebloans (for example) built relatively comfortable housing for the average person that European peasants might have envied. In the world of ideas, liberty and equality have a long American lineage: Over time and space, the roomy homes of the Ancestral Puebloans could be imagined as the precursor of Jefferson's freehold farmer in his snug log cabin and the tract housing suburbs of modern-day American urban areas. Could it be argued that the Ancestral Puebloans helped create the type of housing that characterizes the "American dream"?

Europeans didn't bring liberty and prosperity to America; they sought it here, meanwhile forcing on Native people its antithesis—slavery and indentured servitude. Weatherford, in *Native Roots*, reveals that Native Americans were forced into slavery in large numbers. The Spanish, French, and English all enslaved Native peoples. Indeed, the name of Labrador, for example, may have been handed down from a Portuguese term for "slave coast," Weatherford writes (1991, 138).

Who Invented Scalping and Introduced Syphilis?

Keoke and Porterfield also weigh into the debate regarding who invented scalping. Their verdict: Native Americans didn't do it. They rely on precontact records indicating that Europeans took scalps centuries before they offered money for Native American scalps. This book describes the practice as a well-established tradition for Europeans as early as 440 years before the common era, when the Greek historian Herodotus noted the practice. Much later, according to the authors of this book, the English paid bounties for Irish scalps because scalps were easier to transport and store than entire heads. They display records indicating that the English Earl of Wessex scalped his enemies during the eleventh century.

Something else that Native Americans did not introduce to the world was syphilis, according to Keoke and Porterfield. They point to archaeological evidence that they say provides strong evidence that syphilis was present in Europe before the voyages of Columbus. They describe excavations at a friary in Hull, England, that have uncovered at least a dozen skulls displaying evidence of syphilis that have been carbon dated to between 1300 and 1450. The authors write that pre-Columbian skeletons with syphilis also have been found elsewhere in Europe, including Ireland, Naples, and Pompeii, as well as Israel.

Names and Semantic Confusion

The communication of names between cultures goes both ways, of course, and often involves some semantic confusion. The names that we most often use to describe various Native tribes and nations are a linguistic mishmash. One could generally tell whose enemy was whose. "Iroquois" is French for people who called themselves Haudenosaunee, meaning People of the Longhouse. The Algonquians called the Iroquois the Nation of Snakes. It has been said that "Mohawk" is an Algonquian derivation for man-eater. "Sioux" is an archaic French derivation for snake or enemy. "Huron" is French for lout or ruffian, used to describe people who called themselves Wendat ("dwellers on a peninsula"). "Huron" actually comes from an archaic French term that describes the bristles on the snout of a wild boar—not the type of image that most peoples would cultivate for themselves.

Native American languages have left their linguistic tracks all over English, and not only in thousands of geographical place names. Many of the following words come from the Algonquian languages spoken over much of what is now the eastern United States: hickory, hominy, moose, succotash, terrapin, tomahawk, totem, woodchuck. "Blizzard" is a Native American word, although we don't know which language it came from. The first published reference to a blizzard was handed down to us by Davy Crockett, who, according to Weatherford, used it in 1834. Crockett himself was a walking cultural amalgam, of course, from his coonskin hat to his leggings and moccasins. He was not, however, in the habit of giving credit to Native peoples for much of what he borrowed from them.

As they acquired new foods and tools from Native Americans, early colonists also adopted Native American place names. Twenty-six of the states in the United States of America today bear names first spoken (at least in part) before non-Natives immigrated here in large numbers. Thousands of words have entered English and other European languages from American Indian sources; they are too numerous even to survey in this brief overview.

Non-Natives also adapted to their own needs many Indian articles of clothing and other artifacts, including hammocks, kayaks, canoes, moccasins, smoking pipes, dog sleds, and parkas. Most European and American arctic explorers borrowed extensively from the clothing of the Inuit, whose sleds often were pulled by the "husky," also an Inuit word. "Muckamuck" (applied in derision to someone in authority) comes from trading jargon Chinook, as does the slang term "hootch," for alcoholic beverages. Other Native words now used in English include cigar (Mayan), tobacco (Arawakan), potato (Taino), and tomato (Nahuatl).

Bruce E. Johansen

See also Albany Congress, Native Precedents; Cohen, Felix; Franklin, Benjamin, Native American Influences; Haudenosaunee Confederacy, Political System; Lacrosse; State Names, United States, Native American Derivations; Thanksgiving Holiday, Origins.

References and Further Reading
Abram, Charles. 1923. "Law of the Woman Chief, May 21, 1923." Hewitt Collection, BAE Manuscript No. 1636, NAA. Smithsonian Institution.
Allen, Paula Gunn. 1986. *The Sacred Hoop: Recovering the Feminine in American Indian Traditions.* Boston: Beacon Press.
Anthony, Susan B. 1985. *History of Woman Suffrage.* Edited by Elizabeth Cady Stanton and Matilda Joslyn Gage. North Stratford, NH: Ayer Company.
Axtell, James. 1981. *The Indian Peoples of Eastern America: A Documentary History of the Sexes.* New York: Oxford University Press.
Barreiro, José. 1992. "The Search for Lessons." In *Indigenous Economics: Toward a Natural World Order.* Edited by José Barreiro. *Akwe:kon Journal* 9, no. 2 (Summer): 18–39.
Birchfield, D. L. 1997. *The Encyclopedia of North American Indians.* Vol. 5. Tarrytown, NY: Marshall Cavendish.
Brown, Judith K. 1970. "Economic Organization and the Position of Women Among the Iroquois."

Ethnohistory 17, nos. 3–4 (Summer-Fall): 151–167.

Cameron, Kenneth W., ed. 1967. *The Works of Samuel Peters*. Hartford: Transcendental Books.

Carr, Lucien. 1884. *The Social and Political Position of Women Among the Huron-Iroquois Tribes*. Salem, MA: Salem Press.

Case, Nancy Humphrey. 2002. "Gifts from the Indians: Native Americans Not Only Provided New Kinds of Food and Recreation; They May Have Given the Founding Fathers Ideas on How to Form a Government." *The Christian Science Monitor*. November. Available at: http://www.turtletrack.org/Issues02/Co11302002/CO_11302002_Gifts.

Cohen, Felix. 1952. "Americanizing the White Man." *American Scholar* 21, no. 2: 177–191.

Cohen, Felix. 1960. *The Legal Conscience: Selected Papers of Felix S. Cohen*. Edited by Lucy Kramer Cohen. New Haven, CT: Yale University Press.

Corkran, David H. 1962. *The Cherokee Frontier: Conflict and Survival, 1740–62*. Norman: University of Oklahoma Press.

Cronon, William. 1983. *Changes in the Land: Indians, Colonists, and the Ecology of New England*. New York: Hill and Wang.

Crosby, Alfred W. 1972. *The Columbian Exchange: Biological and Cultural Consequences of 1492*. Westport, CT: Greenwood Press.

Edwards, Everett E. 1934. "The Contributions of American Indians to Civilization." *Minnesota History* 15, no. 3: 255–272.

Fenton, W. N. 1941. *Contacts Between Iroquois Herbalism and Colonial Medicine*. Washington, DC: Smithsonian Institution.

Foner, Philip S., ed. 1945. *Complete Writings of Thomas Paine*. New York: Citadel Press.

Forbes, Jack. 1964. *The Indian in America's Past*. Englewood Cliffs, NJ: Prentice-Hall.

Frachtenberg, Leo J. 1915. "Our Indebtedness to the American Indian." *Wisconsin Archeologist* 14, no. 2: 64–69.

Gipson, Arrell Morgan. 1980. *The American Indian: Prehistory to Present*. Lexington, MA: D. C. Heath and Company.

Grinde, Donald A., Jr., and Bruce E. Johansen. 1991. *Exemplar of Liberty: Native America and the Evolution of Democracy*. Los Angeles, CA: UCLA American Indian Studies Center.

Grinde, Donald A., Jr., and Bruce E. Johansen. 1995. *Ecocide of Native America: Environmental Destruction of Indian Lands and Peoples*. Santa Fe, NM: Clear Light Publishers.

Johansen, Bruce E. [1982] 1987. *Forgotten Founders: How the Iroquois Helped Shape Democracy*. Boston: Harvard Common Press, 1987.

Keoke, Emory Dean, and Kay Marie Porterfield. 2002. *Encyclopedia of American Indian Contributions to the World*. New York: Facts on File.

Kraus, Michael. 1949. *The Atlantic Civilization: Eighteenth Century Origins*. New York: Russell & Russell.

Moquin, Wayne. 1973. *Great Documents in American Indian History*. Westport, CT: Praeger.

Porterfield, Kay Marie. 2002. "Ten Lies About Indigenous Science—How to Talk Back." October 10. Available at: http://www.kporterfield.com/aicttw/articles/lies.html. Accessed January 9, 2007.

Public Broadcasting Service. No date. Africans in America: Revolution, Resource Bank, part 2: 1750–1805. "Crispus Attucks." Available at: http://www.pbs.org/wgbh/aia/part2/2p24.html. Accessed February 20, 2003.

Selsam, Millicent. 1959. *Plants That Heal*. New York: William Morrow & Co.

"Substance of the Speech of Good Peter to Governor Clinton and the Commissioners of Indian Affairs at Albany." 1814. Collections of the New York Historical Society, 1st Series, 2: 115.

Weatherford, Jack. 1988. *Indian Givers: How the Indians of the Americas Transformed the World*. New York: Fawcett Columbine.

Weatherford, Jack. 1991. *Native Roots: How the Indians Enriched America*. New York: Crown.

Ancestral Puebloan Culture

The American Southwest (the current states of Arizona, New Mexico, southern Utah, and Colorado) and northwestern Mexico (Sonora, Chihuahua, and parts of Sinaloa) have been the homes of indigenous peoples since time immemorial. Contemporary indigenous communities and societies recognize ancestors who correspond to archaeologically recognized and named cultures. The Ancestral Pueblos, agricultural peoples who resided on the Colorado Plateau, are the ancestors of the contemporary Puebloan groups (Acoma, Cochiti, Hopi, Hopi-Tewa, Isleta, Jemez, Laguna, Nambe, Pecos, Pojoaque, Picuris, Sandia, San Felipe, San Ildefonso, San Juan, Santa Ana, Santa Clara, Santo Domingo, Taos, Tesuque, Zia, Zuni). The Hopi say sites designated by archaeologists as Ancestral Pueblo are "the footprints of the ancestors." Most Puebloans prefer the term "Ancestral Pueblo" to Anasazi, an Anglicized Diné (Navajo) term that means enemy ancestors who resided in the area.

Archaeologists use the term "Anasazi" to designate three things: a culture (with internal variation), a geographical region, and a time period. This means that the label "Anasazi," like that of other major

Southwestern cultural configurations (Mogollon, Hohokam, and Patayan), reflect patterns of material culture remains or constellations of cultural traits (such as distinctive settlement patterns) that form a recognizable pattern different from similar configurations in time and space. They are recognizable tangible markers of cultural similarity and difference that reflect adaptations to specific geographical and ecological zones. Unfortunately, they do not and cannot mark all the spiritual and kinship features that Native peoples today use to define themselves as distinct peoples. The typological categorization terms thus obscure as much as they reveal.

Culture

Archaeologist Alfred V. Kidder first proposed the term "Anasazi" in 1936 as a solution to problems that had arisen from the 1927 Pecos Classification. The Pecos Classification was designed initially as a single cultural developmental sequence of stages that would apply to the entire Greater Southwest. It was based on changes in Puebloan architecture: from pithouses to aboveground structures to cliff dwellings to the contiguous multiroom settlements seen at the time of European contact. When archaeologists who were excavating extensively in lowland desert and mountain areas discovered that these regions showed strikingly different housing patterns, Kidder broke the region into three units: Anasazi, Hohokam, and Mogollon. The Pecos Classification had also delineated a break between Basketmaker and Pueblo periods to reflect the transition from pithouses to aboveground structures. Despite this bifurcation, Kidder felt that continuity rather than a dramatic break was the hallmark of all the Ancestral Pueblo peoples—agriculturalists who lived on the southern half of the upland Colorado Plateau (from southeastern Nevada near present-day Las Vegas, across southern Utah and Colorado to the Pecos River, from the Colorado River in Utah, south through northwestern New Mexico and communities along the Rio Grande and its tributaries, and northeastern and north central Arizona down to the Mogollon Rim and the San Pedro Valley). Groups on the northern Colorado Plateau have been distinguished as Fremont and Largo-Gallina peoples; groups to the south as Mogollon and Hohokam. Groups to the east are categorized under the Great Plains categorization.

Anasazi peoples are a heterogeneous mix of agriculturalists who have a marked cultural continuity to contemporary Puebloan peoples. Continuities can be seen in a broad material culture complex that includes architecture (pithouses transformed into contiguous masonry and adobe habitations and storage room); basketry; clothing; ceramics (coil-and-scrape technology, plain, corrugated gray utility wares, and black-on-white, black-on-red, and polychrome painted wares); community structure and settlement patterns (changing through time from small family-based settlements to large towns); iconographic symbolism; petroglyphs; specialized religious and social structures (kivas, great kivas, towers, and plazas); and textiles. Variability in the specifics of these basic patterns has led archaeologists to group the Anasazi into branches: Chaco, Cibola, Mesa Verde, Kayenta, Little Colorado, Winslow, Tusayan, Virgin, and Rio Grande. These branches flourished at slightly different times reflecting the migrations of different groups and the acceptance of culture change at any given time.

Geographical Region

One reason there has been regional variability was the need for flexibility in agricultural practices due to differences in local environments and the availability of permanent water supplies that could be used for irrigation and rainfall variations for dry farming. The Anasazi region is generally divided into three large physiographic provinces: the Great Basin, the Rio Grande Valley, and the southern Colorado Plateau. The Colorado Plateau is characterized by sandstone and shale sedimentary deposits that have been eroded into canyon-mesa topography. The regions become increasingly drier and lower in elevation as one travels south. These broad differences resulted in an east–west cultural dichotomy that can be seen archaeologically for over 6,000 years and resulted in different developmental histories. All these patterns can be seen in contemporary Puebloan communities, as can cultural distinctions based on local environmental adaptations.

Time Period

Anasazi as a time period is a designation that isolates ancestral indigenous peoples during certain times in their history. The region was occupied in the Paleo-Indian period (which is generally defined as before 8,000 BP (prior to 6000 BCE), followed by an Archaic period (8,000–3,000 BP/ 6000–1000 BCE). These designations reflect changes in tool types, economic/food procurement activities, settlement patterns, housing types, and group size. Following this, Anasazi history is divided into seven basic developmental stages, defined by the 1927 Pecos Classification, although there is variation by branch. These stages should be considered generalized approximations. Problems arise when these stages are given definitive chronological dates or time ranges. In general, it appears that recognizable changes that marked new stages occurred earlier in the eastern than in the western groups.

The Paleo-Indian period is sparsely represented in many regions, characterized by Clovis and Folsom projectile points that were used on spears to hunt game animals. More sites are known for the Archaic period, which some archaeologists have called the Oshara subtradition, a widespread cultural pattern of hunting and gathering that was remarkably stable. The Archaic time period is characterized by an emphasis on the local use of plants and the development of horticulture and ceramics. In many ways these two broad time periods correspond to Puebloan traditions of the first two worlds through which their ancestors traveled.

The first defined stage of Ancestral Pueblo/Anasazi cultures, Basketmaker I, is generally considered a hypothetical preagricultural stage. It is now subsumed into the Archaic. Early maize and squash cultivation, added to a seasonal subsistence base of hunting and plant gathering, marks the beginning of Basketmaker II, which is evident in sites dated around 2,950 BP (ca. 1000 BCE) to around 1,450 BP (500 C.E.) in the eastern areas and 1,250 BP (700 CE) farther west. This time period is considered by scholars to contain the first archaeologically recognizable transition to agriculturally based communities with the beginnings of regionally distinctive architectural styles. Housing shows a transition, over 1,000 years, from the intermittent occupation of rock shelters to dispersed hamlets housing a small group of related people. These were composed of one or two shallow pithouses and storage units or cists. The hamlets were not occupied year-round because mobility was needed to gain access to seasonal food sources. Because mobile peoples need light and nonbreakable containers, baskets and woven and hide bags were common. Pottery (brownware ceramics) was not developed until around 1,650 BP (300 CE). Most likely the first pieces came via trade with the Mogollon peoples to the south. The introduction of pottery marks the transition to the next developmental phase.

Basketmaker III (1,450–1,250 BP, 450–700 CE) is characterized by the appearance of cultural traits that indicate a food procurement strategy based on a greater reliance on farming and a more sedentary lifestyle. The items archaeologists use to make this assessment include the introduction of beans and domesticated turkey to the diet, ground stone axes, more efficient grinding stones, less reliance on basketry and more on pottery as containers. Hunting patterns also shifted, as reflected by new styles of bows and arrows. True circular pit structures (around 2–7 meters or 6.6–23 feet) are evident for living spaces. There are also surface structures to store food and goods as well as communal outdoor work areas. Archaeologists have surveyed and excavated a large number of these settlements. They vary in size from small housing clusters for an extended family (hamlets) to medium-sized villages of ten or more structures. In the east, the settlements are integrated around larger sites that include communal ceremonial structures, called kivas. There is now evidence of strong regional variability because this type of housing and village organization is absent in the west. There is also greater variability in pottery with distinctive ceramic styles emerging. For example, in the Mesa Verde region women produced primarily gray wares, some of which were decorated with black paint, while in southeastern Utah, women made orange pottery painted with red designs.

The Pueblo I stage began around 1,250 BP (700 CE) in the east and 1,100 (800 CE) in the west, evidenced by a marked increase in population and some migrations between river drainage systems. It was a time of increasing cultural and social diversity in the eastern region with evidence of greater social complexity. This pattern seems to be absent in the western region, which continues to follow the traditions of the Basketmaker III period. Change there appears to have been slower and less dramatic. In the east Pueblo I is first marked by a gradual transition to jacal surface houses. These were primarily rectangular rooms with slab-based foundations to support jacal walls. These rooms formed a linear or curved room block, some of which were quite long (up to 75 meters or 246 feet). Pithouses seem to be increasingly reserved for communal ceremonial activities. In both the eastern and the western regions, however, settlements varied in size from small hamlets to large villages. Some communities were quite large; the McPhee Village in the Dolores (Mesa Verde) region was home to over 100 households. In the east, villages were integrated into larger community systems by a network of great kivas. Great kivas were extremely large pit structures that probably served as sites of ritual integration for the dispersed communities. These seem to be absent in the western region. Ceramic types continued to vary by region with orange and red wares being produced in southern Utah, gray and white wares in the northern San Juan basin, and black-on-white pottery in the Cibola region around Zuni.

Archaeologists think that Pueblo I transitioned into Pueblo II around 1,050 BP (900 CE) in the east and 950 BP (1000 CE) in the west. This was a period of great population growth and geographical expansion for the Ancestral Puebloan peoples, manifested by a profusion of sites of many sizes. Peoples were now able to live in more elevation zones and on more types of land. Most communities in the Mesa Verde region built small, multi-unit pueblos (called Prudden sites after archaeologist T. M. Prudden), composed of a block of surface rooms, a kiva, and a trash area located to the south or southeast. Buildings now had both jacal and masonry architecture, and the kivas had more formal features and layout compared to earlier structures. Each unit pueblo probably belonged to a larger community of pueblos related through kinship ties.

Pueblo II is notable for the development of the Chacoan system, which encompassed most of the San Juan Basin and neighboring areas and culturally influenced other communities through trade. The Chaco system began around 1,000–1,050 BP (850–900 CE), growing out of the eastern Pueblo I cultures, possibly because the people needed to tap outside resources to maintain their large communities. They developed a regional system around 1,000 BP (900 CE) that dominated the eastern Puebloan area for several hundred years until it fell apart or transitioned to a less centralized system around 750 BP (1200 CE). At this time people from the Chaco Canyon area moved into the area near the Aztec and Salmon ruins in northern New Mexico. In the past archaeologists have labeled this a collapse and have speculated about why the people abandoned the region: drought, resource overuse, microenvironmental and climatic change in rainfall patterns, internal dissension and fighting, and incursions of nomadic raiders, i.e., the southern Athapascans. Pueblo peoples say the migrations reflect their ancestors' ongoing search for their proper places in this world.

The features that denote the Chacoan peoples include great houses (with hundreds of rooms and dozens of kivas), very large carefully planned settlements, great kivas, a complex system of engineered and maintained roads, well-designed masonry building styles, a wealth of exotic materials obtained through trade, and increased ritual activity with panregional implications. At its height, the Chaco system had large villages in the Chaco areas and in outlying local communities. Each had a hierarchy of settlements that were integrated by an intricate road system with signaling stations. Each community group was integrated around a great house in Chaco Canyon, which was evidently a center for the accumulation and distribution of goods and services for its community network and a spiritual and ritual center. The Village of the Great Kivas in the Nutria Valley is perhaps the best-known outlier community. There is also evidence of the long-distance trade of turquoise south into Mesoamerica, with parrot feathers and other goods flowing north in return. This extended community system required a greater coordination and formal political organization that archaeologists feel was never matched in subsequent time periods. Neo-evolutionists categorize this as the attainment of a chiefdom level of social complexity.

The western Anasazi were only minimally affected by the Chacoan phenomenon. There is little evidence for multiple, hierarchical settlements forming an intricate regional system or of a large-scale regional road system. Instead, the large Pueblo I pithouse villages were replaced by small, scattered, extended family settlements. These were composed of a block of living and storage rooms in front of a kiva and a trash mound. Such settlements are found across an extremely large region until 800 BP (1150 CE), when the population began to contract toward a center on the Little Colorado River Basin. People migrated from huge areas, like the Virgin River Basin, and again archaeologists have speculated about why, usually positing the same range of reasons that led to the eastern migrations. Most today think families and communities moved as a result of serious environmental deterioration that necessitated cultural adaptations. Hopi sacred origin texts, however, consider this further evidence of clan migrations in their search for their proper places in their homelands.

These population shifts in both the eastern and western regions mark the beginning of the Pueblo III phase. This phase is characterized by more regional variations but is best-known as the time of the cliff dwellers. The famous and well studied ruins in Mesa Verde and nearby Montezuma Valley draw hundreds of thousands of tourists a years. In the east, the Cibola and Mesa Verde regional systems blossomed (beginning 1,300 BP, 1100–1050 CE) as a result of significant population growth; each region became home to complex interaction networks evidenced by multifaceted hierarchies of settlement types. More intensive agriculture was practiced to support the aggregated villages, and there is an increase in the number and scale of water collection and water diversion features. In the west, there was a different pattern. After the Kayenta and Tusayan branches experienced a period of marked settlement flux, by 700 BP (1250 CE) a strong Tsegi-phase pattern emerged. Information from Tsegi Canyon sites points to hierarchical settlements that were comparable to those in the eastern ancestral pueblo area a 150 years earlier. At the same time, different patterns flourished in the middle Little Colorado River drainage, marked by distinctive ceramic styles and settlement patterns.

The Pueblo III phase is thought to have ended about 700 years ago (ca. 1300) following another series of migrations. The Mesa Verde, Chaco, and Kayenta peoples moved away from their areas; other communities left the San Juan Basin. Reasons for these moves probably included lowered rainfall levels from climatic change, a scarcity of resources like arable land, internal social problems that often arise in large villages, or a need for peoples and clans to continue to search for their proper homes. The people moved south and east to join other Puebloan groups; the people from Mesa Verde immigrated to the Rio Grande River Valley and were probably Keresan speakers. The Chacoans seem to have dispersed to the south, although there is little archaeological evidence of that to date; some probably joined the Cibola peoples in the Zuni region seen in the larger settlements in higher elevations in the El Morro Valley. In the western region some Kayenta people moved south to join Tusayan branch peoples in the Hopi area, while others traveled south into the Mogollon area of east central Arizona near present-day Safford.

Pueblo IV, the period between the migrations from the San Juan Basin to the arrival of the Spanish in the Rio Grande Valley, occurred around 1550–1600 (400 BP). The phase's primary characteristics include major population aggregations along the Rio Grande River (down to the Gulf of Mexico) and its western tributaries and along the Pecos River in the east and on the Hopi Mesa and along the Zuni River in the west. Traditions from the Pueblo II and Pueblo III time periods continued, but the large villages remained autonomous. There is no evidence of large regional systems of communities. Puebloan sacred origin texts describe this period as the one during which each community found its proper place, that is, the land where they should reside and over which they should serve as stewards. It was also a time of social and religious change, which may have been the result of increasing contact with peoples and influences from Mesoamerica on the south and groups residing on the north and east or from different Apachean groups continuing to move into the areas between Puebloan communities.

The last Anasazi period, called Pueblo V, is used to designate the Puebloan groups after the arrival of Spanish and other European and American colonists. Settlement patterns reflect the contemporary communities already noted, as well as groups of eastern Pueblos who were forced to abandon their villages due to Spanish colonial polices and raiding by other Native American groups. Communities continued to grow, although epidemics of communicable diseases lowered population figures significantly. Groups of Pueblos, like the seven major communities at Zuni, continued to coalesce into one group, in this case the village of Halona:wa. Each remained autonomous with continuations of the regional cultural variations expressed in earlier times. Some Pueblos, like Taos, became regional trade centers for groups on the Great Plains, and all participated in extensive trade networks.

Nancy J. Parezo

See also Agriculture; Archaeology and the First Americans; Basketry; Environment and Pollution; Hohokam Culture; Katsinas; Mogollon Culture; Pottery; Sacred Sites; Trade.

References and Further Reading

Cordell, Linda S., and George J. Gumerman, eds. 1989. *Dynamics of Southwest Prehistory.* Washington, DC: Smithsonian Institution.

Crown, Patricia, and W. J. Judge, eds. 1991. *Chaco and Hohokam: Prehistoric Regional Systems in the American Southwest.* Santa Fe, NM: School of American Research Press.

Doyel, David E., ed. 2001. *Anasazi Regional Organization and the Chaco System.* Albuquerque, NM: Maxwell Museum of Anthropology.

Ferguson, T. J., and E. R. Hart. 1985. *A Zuni Atlas.* Norman: University of Oklahoma Press.

Kanter, John. 2004. *Ancient Puebloan Southwest.* Cambridge and New York: Cambridge University Press.

Olson, John. 2005. *Bandelier National Monument: Home of the Ancestral Pueblo People.* Atglen, PA: Schiffer Press.

Preucel, Robert W. 2002. *Archaeologies of the Pueblo Revolt: Identity, Meaning, and Renewal in the Pueblo World*. Albuquerque, NM: University of New Mexico Press.

Reed, Paul F. 2000. *Foundations of Anasazi Culture: The Basketmaker-Pueblo Transition*. Salt Lake City: University of Utah Press.

Reid, J. Jefferson, and Stephanie Whittlesey. 1997. *The Archaeology of Ancient Arizona*. Tucson: University of Arizona Press.

Stuart, David E., and Susan B. Moczygemba-McKinsey. 2000. *Anasazi America: Seventeen Centuries on the Road from Center Place*. Albuquerque: University of New Mexico Press.

Varien, Mark, and Richard H. Wilshusen. 2002. *Seeking the Center Place: Archaeology and Ancient Communities in the Mesa Verde Region*. Salt Lake City: University of Utah Press.

Vivian, R. Gwinn. 1990. *The Chacoan Prehistory of the San Juan Basin*. San Diego, CA: Academic Press.

Anglicans

The Anglicans, the predominant Protestant denomination in Canada, played a major role in white–Indian relations, especially in western Canada.

Clergy as well as members of the Church of England (known generally as the Anglican Church) accompanied British imperial involvement throughout the world. In each country within the British empire, the colonial period laid the basis of an Anglican Church that emerged at independence as separate national churches reflecting different historical experiences but sharing common doctrinal principles. In the United States, Anglicanism was transformed into the Episcopal Church within a few years of national independence. Although this denomination retains membership in the worldwide community of Anglican churches, it developed an organizational structure different from England's model.

The closer ties between Canadian and English Anglicans are partly the reflection of the fact that Canada was a mission field of the Church of England until Canada became a self-governing dominion in 1867. This later, peaceful attainment of independence for Canada, the absence of a single, unified Canadian Anglican Church until the 1890s, and closer ongoing relations between Canada and England combined to create a denomination that closely paralleled the practices of the Anglican Church in England. Practical physical unification of Canada occurred only with the establishment of

Canada's transcontinental railway in 1885, which facilitated the creation of a national governing body for Canadian Anglicans in 1893. For all of these reasons, Anglicanism in Canada relied on missionary societies rather than on central, national coordination in its relations with the indigenous people of Canada until the late twentieth century.

A succession of mission societies dominated Anglican work with indigenous people. Prior to the American Revolution, Anglican missionary efforts throughout British North America rested in the hands of the Society for the Propagation of the Gospel (SPG), which worked with both white and Native peoples. When the United States became independent, SPG missionaries accompanied the exodus of Loyalists northward. Because the SPG sought to create self-sustaining churches, it began a withdrawal from Canada in the midnineteenth century in reaction to continuing Canadian reluctance to finance their own churches. This decision opened the door for the Church Missionary Society (CMS), whose interest was the implementation of a program to convert Native peoples. Their approach included the development of a cadre of ordained Indian clergy and education in residential boarding schools. The CMS left Canada in the early twentieth century when Canadians established the Missionary Society of the Church of England in Canada. Founded in 1902, it was Canada's first significant Anglican missionary society.

The reliance of missionary societies on government funding for residential schools was an intended result of the Davin Report of 1879. This report called for the "aggressive civilization" of Indian people and recognized that missionary societies had the experience to implement this plan. Government funding rather than charitable donation became the predominant financial source for the educational work of Anglican and many other missionary groups. In return for providing funds, the government hoped that the boarding schools would end the political problems inherent in the management of Indian affairs.

These residential schools had several impacts. The isolation of children from their families and traditional cultures, as well as the imposition of alien dress, routines, and ideas, often led to significant psychological damage. These practices were made public in a series of lawsuits in the 1990s that jointly blamed the government and the denominations that managed the residential schools. In 2003 Canadian Anglicans and the national government agreed to

legally cap Anglican liability at $25 million (Canadian) for abuses in their residential schools.

The other major effort of Anglican missionaries was the creation of Native clergy. This effort was successful in the nineteenth century in the sense that Anglicans developed a number of indigenous clergy for Native churches. The efforts failed, however, when measured by the subsequent incorporation of these clergy into the national Anglican clerical hierarchy. Hayes cites several accomplished Native clergy in the early twentieth century who were clearly suited to serve as bishops. Two of these men, Robert MacDonald (1829–1913) and Thomas Vincent (1835–1907), were not elevated to the position of bishop in part because they were of mixed-blood heritage. Anglicans did not select a bishop of Indian heritage until the 1980s.

In the 1960s, Anglicans modified the denomination's relationship with indigenous people by replacing the emphasis on civilization and conversion with a social work–based program to alleviate poverty and related social problems. This effort, based on the Hendry Report, was formally published as *Beyond Traplines*. This report itself met much criticism because it portrayed Indians as people separate from the rest of the society. A second edition of the report in 1998 called for the full incorporation of indigenous people into the Anglican Church in all roles.

David S. Trask

See also Canada, Indian Policies of.
References and Further Reading
Hayes, Alan. 2004. *Anglicans in Canada Controversies and Identity in Historical Perspective*. Urbana: University of Illinois Press.
Hendry, Charles. 1969. Rev. ed. 1998. *Beyond Traplines: Does the Church Really Care? Toward an Assessment of the Work of the Anglican Church in Canada with Canada's Native Peoples*. Toronto, ON: Anglican Church of Canada.
Rutherdale, Myra. 2002. *Women and the White Man's God: Gender and Race in the Canadian Mission Field*. Vancouver: University of British Columbia Press.

Athapaskan Languages

One of the largest of indigenous language families in North America, the Athapaskan language family, spans from Alaska through western Canada and into the American Pacific Coast and Southwest. The Athapaskan language family is a relatively cohesive group of languages spread out in distinct geographical regions of North America. The languages are known for being difficult to learn due to their rich and highly inflected verbs. One of the most well-known members of the family, the Navajo language, was used as a World War II code, which was never broken. Other linguistic features that Athapaskan languages are known for include the development of tone in some of the languages from syllables originally closed with glottalization, as well as incidents of sibilant harmony where *s*-like sounds affect the pronunciation of certain words. The languages are also known for a set of verb stems called classificatory verbs, which classify an object according to its shape or manner. Linguists tend to direct the greatest attention, however, to the complex verb morphology of Athapaskan, where numerous prefixes attach to the verb stem in a very specific way, which has been likened to a template.

The family comprises three geographic groupings within four cultural areas and includes the language of Navajo, the largest Native American tribe in the United States. The three general geographical groupings are referred to as Northern Athapaskan, Pacific Coast Athapaskan, and Apachean (aka Southern Athapaskan).

The Northern Athapaskan group consists of between twenty-three and thirty languages spoken in a large continuous area in western Canada and the interior of Alaska, through the western Subarctic and the northern Plains. The number of languages calculated depends on how divisions are made within the family. No Northern language or dialect has been completely isolated from the others for very long, and this constant contact creates mutual influence between languages.

The majority of the well-documented Athapaskan languages are among the Northern group. A number of the Athapaskan-speaking peoples in this area, especially those in Northern British Columbia and Southern Northwest Territories, prefer the term "Dene" to "Athapaskan" as a classificatory identity. The term "Dene" is recognized to mean "person" or "people" by most speakers of Athapaskan languages. The official body of the Dene nation belongs to the Northern Athapaskan group and includes the Gwich'in, Bearlake, Hare, Dogrib, Slave, Chipewyan, and Mountain people.

The other Athapaskan languages are found farther south on the continent. The Pacific Coast languages number about eight and are spoken by river-oriented peoples in southwest Oregon, on the coast of northern California, and in northwestern California. There was also a language spoken on the Columbia River on both the Washington and the Oregon sides. Many of the languages of this group are not as well documented as most other groups. A list of all the names of the languages in this group and the others is given at the end of this entry.

The Apachean languages make up the southern-most geographical division of the Athapaskan family. The languages of the Apachean group are spoken in the Southwest and in the southern Plains, and they number between four and eight. This group, including Navajo, Western Apache, Mescalero-Chiricahua, Kiowa Apache, Lipan, and Jicarilla, are thought to come from a common ancestral language that separated from the Northern group in approximately 1000 CE. These languages are relative new-comers to the Southwest.

The origin of the Athapaskan-speaking peoples is considered to be in the north, according to comparative studies of the languages. The mother language, Proto-Athapaskan, is thought to have been a single language until approximately 500 BCE, when splits and migrations diversified it. There is more diversity found among the Northern group than among the Southern languages, and so the Proto-Athapaskan homeland is likely to be in the specific areas of oldest differentiation: somewhere in the area of the eastern interior of Alaska, northern British Columbia, and the upper drainage of the Yukon River (Krauss and Golla, 1981, 68).

One theory about the splits of the mother language, Proto-Athapaskan, and the separation of the daughter languages, postulates an enormous volcanic eruption that may have created a considerable ashfall in the southern Yukon that spread east (Workman, 1979, 352). Oral traditions among the Northern peoples uphold this idea, although it is not yet supported archaeologically. Whether or not they were driven by natural disaster, three major migrations may explain the widespread distribution of the Athapaskan languages. The first migration was probably to the west, farther into Alaska, and south into central and southern British Columbia. The second was east into the McKenzie River drainage area and as far as Hudson Bay. The last migration was likely south along the eastern Rocky Mountains and into the Southwest (Krauss and Golla, 1981, 68). There is likely a connection between the two later movements, since there are closer ties between the Southern Apachean languages and the Albertan language, Sarcee, than with the Athapaskan languages in British Columbia. The movement into the Plains

by Kiowa and Lipan in the Southwest and the Sarcee in the North occurred within the last few hundred years.

Linguistic historical methods indicate the time of separation of the Apachean group from the Sarcee at approximately 1000, while archaeological evidence indicates that at least one Apachean group had arrived in the Southwest by 1500 (Young, 1983, 393). These ancestral peoples moved into the area slowly, eventually spreading to occupy much of southeastern Colorado, New Mexico, western Texas, northern Mexico, and central and southeastern Arizona.

Links between the Pacific Coast group and the most recent relations elsewhere in the family are not as clear. This suggests that these languages separated earlier from the Northern languages than the Apachean group. One possible route the ancestors of the Pacific Coast Athapaskans may have taken is across the Columbia River Basin through Oregon to northern California. Another possibility is a course along the eastern coastal ranges, which would have offered more environmental continuity. It is possible that Athapaskan speakers were the latest arrivals in prehistoric California, arriving around 1000–1300 (Foster, 1996, 75).

Athapaskan is a branch of an even larger genetic grouping of languages that also includes Eyak, a single language from the south coast of Alaska, called Athapaskan-Eyak. This grouping has also been linked to the Tlingit language, spoken along the Alaskan Panhandle, due to similarities in grammar and phonology. There is a possibility that Haida, a language isolate spoken off the northwest coast of British Columbia, may also be related to this group, in a grouping referred to as Na-Dene by Sapir in 1915. However, many linguists doubt this relationship, and even the relationship between Tlingit and Athapaskan-Eyak is still undetermined.

There are several spellings of the Athapaskan language family name, but the most common are Athapaskan and Athabaskan. The first was assumed by the Smithsonian Institute and the National Museum of Canada, and the second was adopted by the Alaska Native Language Centre, responsible for much of the documentation of the Northern languages.

The table on page 334 is a list of the languages in the Athapaskan language family (adapted from Mithum, 1999, 346).

Aliki Marinakis

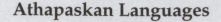

Athapaskan Languages

Northern Athapaskan
Alaska - Yukon
    Ahtna
    Tanaina (Dena'ina)
    Ingalik (Deg Xinag)
    Holikachuk (Innoko)
    Koyukon
    Upper Kuskokwim (Kolchan)
    Tanana
        Lower Tanana
        Tanacross
        Upper Tanana
    Tutchone
        Northern Tutchone
        Southern Tutchone
    Kutchin (Gwich'in)
    Han
Southern Yukon - Northern BC
    Tagish
    Tahltan
    Kaska
    Sekani
    Beaver
    Tsetsaut
Northwest Territories
    Slave-Hare
        South Slavey
        Mountain
        Bearlake (Sahtu Dene)
        Hare
    Dogrib (Tlicho)
    Chipewyan (Dene Suline)

Pacific Coast Athapaskan
    Kwalhioqua-Clatskanie
Oregon
    Upper Umpqua
    Tututni
    Galice-Applegate
    Tolowa
California
    Hupa
    Mattole
    Eel River
    Cahto

Apachean Athapaskan
Western Apachean
    Navajo
    Western Apache
    Mescalero
    Chiricahua
Eastern Apachean
    Jicarilla
    Lipan
    Kiowa Apache

See also Athapaskan Peoples; Language, Written in America, Pre-Contact; Na-Dene Peoples.

References and Further Readings
Able, Kerry. 1993. *Drum Songs: Glimpses of Dene History.* Montreal, QC, and Kingston, ON: McGill–Queen's University Press.
Foster, Micheal K. 1996. "Language and the Culture History of North America." In *Handbook of North American Indians.* Vol. 17: *Languages.* Edited by Ives Goddard, 64–110. General editor, William C. Sturtevant. Washington, DC: Smithsonian Institution.
Krauss, Michael E., and Victor K. Golla. 1981. "Northern Athapaskan Languages." In *Handbook of North American Indians.* Vol. 6: *Subarctic.* Edited by June Helm, 67–85. General editor, William C. Sturtevant. Washington, DC: Smithsonian Institution.
Mithun, Marianne. 1999. *The Languages of North America.* Cambridge: Cambridge University Press.
Workman, William B. 1979. "The Significance of Volcanism in the Prehistory of Subarctic Northwest North America." In *Volcanic Activity and Human Ecology.* Edited by P. D. Sheets and D. K. Grayson, 339–371. New York: Academic Press.
Young, Robert W. 1983. "Apachean Languages." In *Handbook of North American Indians.* Vol. 10: *Southwest.* Edited by Alphonse Ortiz, 393–400. General editor, William C. Sturtevant. Washington, DC: Smithsonian Institution.

Athapaskan Peoples

Athapaskan peoples dwell in a vast territory covering several ecological zones, both above and below the Arctic Circle, from tundra to boreal forest and subarctic mountains and plateaus, stretching across Alaska, the Yukon Territory, and the Northwest Territories, and south into northern British Columbia, Alberta, Saskatchewan, and Manitoba. The Apache and Navajo are Athapaskan-speaking peoples who live far to the south of the northern forests in California, Arizona, Utah, and New Mexico.

In Alaska, the various Athapaskan groups are known as the Koyukuk, Ingalik, Kolchan, Tanacross, Ahtna, Han, Tanana, Denaina, Gwich'in, Holikachuk, and Nabena; while in Canada they include the Dogrib, Sahtu, Kaska, Tagish, Gwich'in, Witsuwit'in, Dunne-za, Slavey, Dene Tha, and Chipewyan. Many northern Athapaskans call themselves Dene or Dena, which means "human beings," and speak languages that belong to the Athapaskan branch of the Na-Dene family of languages (in general usage, "Athapaskan," or "Athabascan," or "Athabaskan" is a linguistic label for these related languages). In the Northwest Territories, Dene nation has become the preferred self-designation to refer to Athapaskan peoples collectively.

Archaeologists generally say that Athapaskan-speaking peoples probably crossed the Bering Strait from Siberia to Alaska between 10,000 and 15,000 years ago. These people moved into North America as the great glaciers and ice sheets of the Pleistocene period receded. Most Athapaskan artifacts, however, can be dated to only about 2,000 years ago, and there are many gaps in the archaeological knowledge of Athapaskan prehistory. Much of what is known about Athapaskan origins comes from both archaeology and linguistic research.

The archaeological view of Athapaskan origins is at odds with Athapaskan oral traditions and religious beliefs, which express the view that all Athapaskan peoples emerged from the same spot at the beginning of time. Like the hazy archaeological knowledge as to the emergence of Athapaskan culture on the North American continent, the exact time of this creation is difficult to pinpoint. Athapaskans say this happened in the Distant Time. Although the Distant Time is a remote, ancient time, oral histories nonetheless recount its events in incredible detail, reflecting an immensely rich spiritual and cultural heritage. The stories of the Distant Time provide accounts of Athapaskan origins and the place of peo-

Athapaskan mother and children. (Library of Congress)

ple in relation to the world around them. Distant Time stories provide indigenous accounts of the origins of the world, the elements, and the animals. These stories also reveal how, like other northern peoples, the Athapaskans live in an aware world, where everything (humans, animals, rivers, lakes, trees, thunderstorms, etc.) has consciousness. Athapaskan oral history describes how features of the landscape or the elements—the wind, the sun, the moon, stars, and so on—were originally human beings whose spirits are now embodied in aspects of the natural world. The Raven (or Raven Man) is a central figure in Athapaskan origin stories: Before the beginning of time—in fact even before the beginning of Distant Time—there existed only darkness until Raven created the world by revealing the daylight. Having revealed the daylight, Raven then created the first people.

The forests, rivers, and lakes of Alaska and northern Canada have provided Athapaskan peoples with a rich variety of resources that have formed the basis for diverse economies and modes of subsistence. Traditionally and in modern times, life in Athapaskan communities has revolved around an annual seasonal round of hunting, fishing, and gathering. Athapaskan peoples have traditionally exploited a wide ecological niche and have hunted, when the need has arisen, almost every species of animal in their traditional areas. Moose and caribou are especially important animals for many communities in providing a source of meat for the entire year. Smaller animals, birds, and fish also provide an important part of the Athapaskan diet. In the Alaskan interior, especially for communities on the banks of the Yukon, Tanana, and other rivers, although the hunting of large animals is a vital part of local economies, fishing has given particular stability to the Athapaskan way of life throughout the year. The Gwich'in of northeast Alaska and northern Yukon have depended almost entirely on the porcupine caribou herd, while the Denaina of Cook Inlet and the Kenai Peninsula in southern Alaska have depended a great deal on sea mammal hunting. In the past, settlement patterns corresponded to the annual subsistence cycle, and even winter dwellings were either temporary or semipermanent. Today, although Athapaskan hunters and fishers travel great distances in search of game and often spend the summer in camps, they live in permanent villages and their daily lives are influenced heavily by the institutions of North American society.

Traditional social organization was based on kinship groups, with northern Athapaskans living in autonomous bands with their own hunting, fishing, and gathering territories. Athapaskans carried out potlatch-type ceremonies, similar to those of the Alaska and British Columbia coast. Athapaskan culture was affected initially by contact with Russians in Alaska and with British fur traders in the Canadian Northwest in the eighteenth century. As well as economic, cultural, and ideological influences, explorers and traders brought new diseases to Athapaskan lands to which the indigenous peoples had little or no immunity. The historical record shows that, in some places, entire communities were wiped out by diseases such as smallpox, influenza, tuberculosis, measles, and typhoid. Missionary activity also had a profound effect on the Athapaskan worldview. The lives of Athapaskan peoples changed as a result of their involvement with the fur trade; most noticeably, the trapping of fur-bearing animals meant that hunting became more specialized and concentrated on only a few species.

However, perhaps even more dramatic changes swept through Athapaskan communities during the twentieth century. Because of formal non-Native schooling, together with policies of modernization and assimilation into mainstream American and Canadian societies, many traditional skills and activities have been lost and the everyday use of Athapaskan languages has declined. Today, in Canada's Northwest Territories, major developments in the oil and gas industries, together with a proposed gas pipeline running up the Mackenzie Valley, dominate discussion over the future of Athapaskan communities. Cultural survival, however, has been made possible in part through land claim agreements in Alaska (the Alaska Native Claims Settlement Act of 1971) and Canada (comprehensive land claims agreements in the Northwest Territories and self-government agreements in Yukon). The rights and interests of Athapaskan peoples in Alaska and Canada are represented in the Arctic Council by the Arctic Athabaskan Council (AAC).

Mark Nuttall

See also Athapaskan Languages; Language, Written in America, Pre-contact; Na-Dene Peoples.

References and Further Reading
Arctic Athabaskan Council. No date. Available at: www.arcticathabaskancouncil.com.
Cruikshank, Julie. 1992. *Life Lived Like a Story.* Vancouver: University of British Columbia Press.
Nelson, Richard K. 1973. *Hunters of the Northern Forest.* Chicago: Chicago University Press.
Savishinsky, Joel. 1994. *The Trail of the Hare.* New York: Gordon and Breach.

Basketry

Native American basketry is an ancient art form with a 10,000-year history. If, as is likely, Indian people wove over 1,000 baskets each year, then at least 10 million baskets were made before contact with non-Native peoples. Only a tiny percentage of these survive, the best representing masterpieces of woven arts. Major collections of Native American baskets can be found at the National Museum of the American Indian, Smithsonian Institution, Harvard University's Peabody Museum, as well as at universities, museums, and state historical societies from coast to coast. The fine art of basketry remains very active

Baskets made by Mission Indians, photographed in 1924. (Library of Congress)

throughout Native America. A vast literature and over a quarter of a million Web sites exist for the avid student.

Fiber arts spread to almost every tribe in the western hemisphere. Each tribe developed unique styles that are identifiable by studying the weaving techniques, direction of weave, starts, finishes, decorations, and materials. The dating of baskets is determined in part by the rate at which plant fibers age and develop an amber patina over time.

Native American baskets can be divided into three main techniques: plaiting, twining, and coiling.

1. *Plaiting* involves the arrangement of splints in horizontal and vertical patterns, called plain and twill weaves. Natural plants are often dyed into designs using two or more colors. Plaited baskets were made throughout the Western Hemisphere. Basketry sandals and plaited sifter baskets were made at Mesa Verde, Chaco Canyon, and other ancient Southwest sites. Plaited

basketry in the Southwest continues at Hopi and Jemez Pueblo, with yucca being the most popular fiber. Plaited cedar mats, storage baskets, and hats are still being made in the Pacific Northwest. In the Northeast, the Iroquois, Penobscot, Passamaquoddy, and other eastern Woodland cultures have maintained dynamic basketmaking cultures. Their plaited baskets mostly are made from black ash splints and by twisting fibers like ribbon into designs. From the Southeast to Oklahoma, river cane and white oak baskets are plaited by the Cherokee, Choctaw, Coushatta, and Chitimacha tribes. One of their innovations is the double weave, featuring a double wall construction.

2. *Twining* and wicker techniques involve wrapping horizontal fibers, called wefts, around vertical or radiating fibers, called warps. In full-wrap twining, the design can be seen on the inside and the outside of a

basket. In half-wrap twining, the design can be seen only on the outside of the basket. Twined soft-fiber bags are among the most ancient and widespread type of basketry. Although once common in the ancient Southwest, soft-fiber bags are in need of cultural revival in this region. Wicker basketry is flourishing on Third Mesa at Hopi and to a lesser extent at Zuni Pueblo. Soft-fiber twined bags have best survived in the Plateau region among the Nez Percé, Yakima, Wasco, and Klamath tribes of Oregon, Washington, and Idaho. Twined basketry flourishes along the Pacific Coast from Alaska and British Columbia down through western Washington, Oregon, and the northern half of California.

3. *Coiling* techniques involve wrapping fibers around and around an inner foundation like a clock spring. The inner foundation may take the form of a bundle of grass, single rods, or, more commonly, three-rods, often from willow, sumac, or cottonwood shoots. An awl is used to poke a hole through the preceding coil. The sewing strand must be quickly poked through the hole and pulled tight. Basket collectors count the number of coils per inch times the number of stitches per inch to determine the total number of stitches per square inch—the higher the number, the finer the weave. This calculation helps to determine the value of a basket.

Almost 5,000 individual basketmakers have been identified in the literature. Basketweavers tend to follow family lines and can be traced through genealogical research. The history of Indian baskets represents family traditions carried forward and perpetuated often by family matriarchs and in rare instances by patriarchs. The ancient art form is passed on from generation to generation when children watch their parent and grandparent weaving. To encourage young ones, the elder encourages them to play with scraps of weaving materials.

Approximately 90 percent of the work in making a basket is in the preparation of the materials. Elders teach their offspring to respect the plants used in basketry. Each plant has a name, a history, and a spirit. Basketmakers often talk to the spirits of the plants and explain what good purpose they intend, taking care not to harvest more than is needed. An old cus-

tom advises not to take the first one found of the species, but to keep searching until a second is located, thus ensuring the preservation of the species.

The biggest challenge faced by thousands of contemporary Native American basketmakers is the preservation of, and access to, nontoxic plant material. The challenge has grown during the past fifty years with the introduction of toxic pesticides, herbicides, and chemical fertilizers. In response, Native American weavers have been organizing associations of basketmakers with resource protection programs. Existing organizations include the California Indian Basketweavers Association (CIBA), Southern California Indian Basketweavers Organization (SCIBO), Great Basin Native Basketweavers Association, Northwest Native American Basketweavers Association (NNABA), Great Lakes Indian Basket & Box Makers Association (GLIBBA), Oklahoma Native American Basketweavers (ONAB), Maine Indian Basketmakers Alliance (MIBA), Qualla Cooperative, Tohono O'odham Basketweavers Organization (TOBO), and many more.

No other group of Native American artists has organized more effectively than basketmakers. After years of negotiating with federal, state, and local government officials, as well as with private landowners, historic agreements are being forged to protect basketry environments and to provide access for contemporary weavers to existing sites. Vigilance is required to protect fragile wetlands and forests in the face of commercial development. Alliances have formed between Native American groups and environmental organizations to preserve and to expand endangered habitats.

To help make their case, basketmakers have learned the importance of documentation. A vast literature is growing, as books, articles, videotapes, DVDs, and other media are being developed. Their strategy for preserving basketry is very well thought out. Basketmakers in general are deep thinkers, often visionaries. The long process of weaving offers time for self-reflection and meditation. Perhaps reflecting the traditional nature of their art, basketmakers often have a communal orientation, organizing basketmaking parties, retreats, and special gatherings. These activities offer time to socialize, to share techniques, to discuss designs, to sing traditional songs, and to contemplate their traditional history.

The first major attempts to compile the long history of Native American basketry were made a century ago by Otis Tufton Mason and George Wharton James. The most comprehensive recent survey of

Indian baskets, *Indian Baskets*, was compiled by a husband and wife team from the Peabody Museum at Harvard University, Sarah Peabody Turnbaugh and William A. Turnbaugh (1997). This work has since been supplemented by a more informal collection of related stories by the same authors, *Basket Tales of the Grandmothers: American Indian Baskets in Myth and Legend* (2000). A three-volume compilation of 5,000 biographies of basketmakers, *American Indian Baskets* (Schaaf and Schaaf, 2005; volumes II and III due in 2007 and 2009), is now being completed by Gregory Schaaf and Angie Yan Schaaf. All artists need patrons, and the collectors of American Indian baskets play an important role in supporting the weavers. To create a basketry masterpiece takes much time. Three years were required to weave the largest basket in Hopi history (39 by 43 inches). Patrons of the arts sometime sponsor an artist, helping to support them during the long weaving process.

The transformation of Native American basketry from a utilitarian craft into a fine art form emerged between 1880 and 1930. A Washoe weaver from Carson City, Nevada, named Dat so la lee, became the most famous basketmaker in history. With support from merchant Abe Cohen, the value of her baskets soared from $30 to $3,000. Today, the same baskets are appraised at over $100,000. The world record for a single basket reportedly is over $1 million.

The future of Native American basketry is bright. Collectors and great museums from around the world vie for contemporary masterpieces. At Santa Fe Indian Market, the oldest and largest Indian art show, avid collectors sleep in the booths of their favorite artists to get a chance to buy one at dawn's first light. The opening of the National Museum of the American Indian on the Mall in Washington, D.C., is providing an important new showcase for basketmakers and other Native American artists from throughout the western hemisphere.

Gregory Schaaf

See also Economic Development.
References and Further Reading
James, George Wharton. *Indian Basketry, and How to Make Indian and Other Baskets*, 3rd rev. ed. New York: H. Malkan, 1903; Glorieta, NM: Rio Grande Press, 1970.

Mason, Otis Tufton. 1904. *Aboriginal American Basketry: Studies in a Textile Art Without Machinery.* Washington, DC: U.S. Government Printing Office.

Schaaf, Gregory, and Angie Yan Schaaf. 2005. *American Indian Baskets I.* Santa Fe, NM: CIAC Press.

Turnbaugh, Sarah Peabody, and William A. Turnbaugh. 1997. *Indian Baskets.* Atglen, PA: Schiffer Press.

———. Turnbaugh, Sarah Peabody, and William A. Turnbaugh. 2000. *Basket Tales of the Grandmothers: American Indian Baskets in Myth and Legend.* Seattle: University of Washington Press.

Whiteford, Andrew Hunter. 1988. *Southwestern Indian Baskets: Their History and Their Makers.* Santa Fe, NM: School of American Research Press.

Beadwork

Almost every Native American culture in the western hemisphere has a beadwork tradition, although few have been well documented. Contemporary beadwork artists can be divided into two main groups. Shell beadmakers are concentrated at Santo Domingo Pueblo in New Mexico, where fine shell heishi and rolled turquoise and coral beads are made, and are also among the Iroquois and eastern Woodland tribes, who still make wampum beads from Quahog clam shells. The second and larger group of beadworkers sew glass beads onto leather or cloth. Their art forms include beaded bags, shirts, leggings, moccasins, dresses, coats, belts, knife sheaths, awl cases, gun scabbards, headdresses, bow case and quiver sets, as well as necklaces, bracelets, and beaded jewelry.

Before the coming of non-Natives, Native American beads were handmade. Drilling holes in seeds represents an ancient technology that grew into drilling and hand-rolling freshwater and saltwater shells. Strings of beads were measured from hand to elbow to provide a rate of exchange. Trade routes formed throughout the western hemisphere, and beads were distributed from the northern Arctic to the tip of South America. Among the most valuable ancient beads are the 5,000-year-old jade necklaces of the Olmec from Central America and the steatite beads inlaid with shell produced by the Chumash of southern California.

One of the largest bead production centers was located on the islands off the coast of present-day Santa Barbara. Like an ancient Native American "mint," the Chumash distributed millions of beads made mostly from a half dozen species of seashells. Bead routes followed the coastlines and the inland waterways, then went from spring to spring across

Wolf Necklace (Harlish Washshomake), a Paloos chief wearing a bead necklace and a beaded purse, 1890. (National Archives and Records Administration)

beaded. Personal items included pipe bags, tobacco bags, teepee bags, paint bags, and strike-a-lites, small bags with tin cone dangles that held flint and steel for starting a fire. The Southwest and California show strong Plains Indian influences, while some adapted their own basketry designs. The Plateau region of eastern Washington, Idaho, and Montana developed flat bags, averaging 12-by-14-inch panels, decorated in contour beadwork in which the beads follow concentric outlines. Some artists paint pictures in beads that feature human figures, bears, deer, horses, and even full landscapes with mountains and waterfalls. Northwest and California beadworkers often add shell pendants, as well as creating unique forms of beaded bottles and baskets. Rainforest beadwork from Central and South America often incorporates feathers and plant fibers for elaborate and colorful displays.

Contemporary beadwork is made mostly for other Native Americans who need beaded outfits for ceremonial dances. Beaded belts, necklaces, and little bags are distributed through trading posts and galleries to the general public. Elaborate beaded dolls and cradles often are the blue-ribbon winners at Indian Market, the Heard Museum Show, Southern Plains Exposition, and other Native American art shows. The future of Native American beadwork looks bright.

Gregory Schaaf

See also Trade; Wampum.
References and Further Reading
Coe, Ralph. 1985. *Lost and Found Traditions: Native American Art 1965–1985.* Seattle: University of Washington Press.

Dubin, Lois Sherr. 1999. *North American Indian Jewelry and Adornment: From Prehistory to the Present.* New York: Harry N. Abrams.

Monture, Joel. 1993. *The Complete Guide to Traditional Native American Beadwork: A Definitive Study of Authentic Tools.* New York: Collier Books.

Penney, David. 1992. *Art of the American Indian Frontier: The Chandler-Pohrt Collection.* Detroit, MI: Detroit Institute of Arts.

the desert to the culture centers of Mesa Verde, Chaco Canyon, and thousands of other ancient villages that now are in ruins.

When Christopher Columbus and other Europeans arrived, they brought glass and metal beads that were mass-produced, mostly in North Africa, Holland, and Venice. Native Americans soon discovered creative ways to use the more colorful glass beads. They began decorating their clothing and household items with beads, sewing them on with a needle and thread. Each bead was carefully selected by color and size to create patterns and designs. Every tribe developed its own unique style.

In the Northeast, Iroquois beadworkers used larger pony beads and created three-dimensional effects called embossed beadwork, while loom beadwork flourished in the Great Lakes. In the Southeast, Seminole, Creek, and Cherokee women produced elaborate shoulder bags and sashes that are still highly prized. On the northern and southern Plains, production was greater than any other region. War shirts, dresses, and blanket strips were heavily

Berdaches

Found throughout most of Native North America, berdaches were individuals who assumed, to varying degrees, the mannerisms, appearance, and labors of the opposite gender. In most Native societies, berdaches were biological males who assumed a feminine (or in some cases, a somewhat feminine)

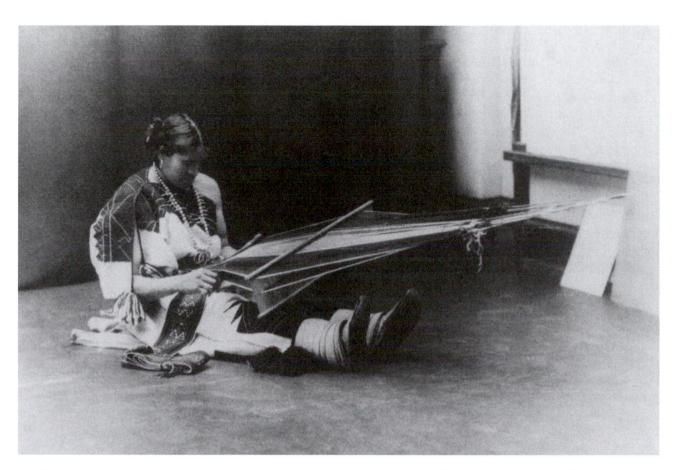

We-Wa, a Zuni man dressed as a woman, weaving a belt on a waist loom with reed heddle. (National Archives and Records Administration)

identity. Some scholars have argued that berdaches represent a third and in some cases, a fourth gender in Native American cultures.

The process of becoming a berdache varied from one Native society to another. Hidatsas believed that a young man became a berdache through the intervention of a female deity. While berdaches were accepted in Hidatsa society, parents did their best to prevent this particular "divine favor" from being bestowed on their sons by making sure that boys did not develop an interest in playing with girls' toys such as dolls. However, Hidatsa parents showed little concern—possibly because of the rarity of female berdaches—if their daughters developed a fascination with bows and arrows. Illinois peoples singled out young boys who played with women's tools, such as hoes and spindles, rather than bows and arrows, as eventual berdaches. The Illinois dressed them as girls and trained them to mimic the female ". . . accent, which is different from that of the men. They omit nothing that can make them like the women."

Europeans encountered berdaches during their earliest explorations of the Americas. Spanish explorer Cabeza de Vaca met berdaches during his eight-year sojourn through what is now much of the American Southwest, disapprovingly claiming that they were "impotent and womanish beings, who dress like women and perform the office of women." A few years later, berdaches attracted the notice of French explorer Jean Ribault in Florida, who erroneously concluded (as other Europeans would) that they were hermaphrodites.

Berdaches seem to have been prevalent among Illinois peoples. Louis Hennepin, a seventeenth-century French Recollet missionary, mentioned them, as did Jesuit Pierre Marquette. Marquette thought that some young men chose to become berdaches because they were regarded as spiritually powerful. He also noted that they were considered "persons of Consequence" and that " nothing is decided without their advice." French trader and soldier Pierre Liette had a very different opinion, noting that Illinois women "retain some moderation," making it impossible for young men to satisfy "their passions as much as they would like." To solve this problem (at least to Liette's understanding), the Illinois created a class of "men who were bred for this purpose since childhood."

To European and American observers, Native berdaches played a complex and, to them, confusing role in Native societies. A male berdache could cross the line between genders several times over the course of his lifetime. Among Miami peoples in the Northeast and Omaha peoples on the Great Plains, a male berdache normally performed women's day-to-day tasks. However, during times of conflict, they donned male clothing, picked up their weapons, and accompanied the other men to war. Upon returning, they again dressed as women and resumed their feminine pursuits.

Far rarer than male berdaches, female berdaches most often appeared in the northern Plains and the Plateau regions. Unlike the males, who in some societies could cross the line between gender lines several times in their life, female berdaches usually crossed it only once and never looked back. Berdaches became less common as Native peoples began adopting the mores of the larger American society in the late nineteenth and twentieth centuries. As European-American society imposed its values, respect for berdaches was diminished. Indeed, some anthropologists working among Native people had difficulty locating informants willing to talk about berdaches.

Roger M. Carpenter

References and Further Reading
Trexler, Richard C. 1995. *Sex and Conquest: Gendered Violence, Political Order, and the European Conquest of the Americas.* Ithaca, NY: Cornell University Press.
Roscoe, Will, ed. 1998. *Changing Ones: Third and Fourth Genders in Native North America.* New York: Palgrave Macmillan.

Black Hills (Paha Sapa)

An expansive area of wildly eroded granite, consisting of peaks that shelter narrow, winding valleys surrounded by a ring of carven limestone canyons, the Black Hills, also known as *Paha Sapa* or *He Sapa* ("hills that are black"), extend approximately fifty miles east and west and 100 miles north and south in western South Dakota. Covered by dark evergreens, predominantly Ponderosa Pine, the hills appear dark purple or black from a distance. This characteristic is reflected in their namesake, attributed to them by Siouan peoples who have inhabited the area from the late eighteenth century to the present.

Considered a sacred place and home to powerful spirits, western Siouan peoples have long regarded the Black Hills as the center of their cosmos, with some regarding the vicinity of Wind Cave National Park in the south as the site of their origin. Regarding the significance of the Hills to their indigenous inhabitants, newspaper accounts in 1874 reported that "the Black Hills are holy ground of the holiest sort," that they were "the most sacred spot on earth." Indeed, the geological ring of limestone that surrounds the Hills has been understood as the site of the primordial race between the birds, or two-legged beings—which represented humankind—and the animals, or four-legged beings. The birds won, thereby establishing the natural order, including the subsistence of human beings on bison and other animals.

During the midnineteenth century the Sioux were inhospitable to white encroachment onto their hunting grounds. As immigration to the area increased, so did conflict. Although the United States military established outposts nearby to monitor the situation, to avoid exacerbating what were already tense relations they seldom entered the Hills. As encroachment continued, however, various bands of Sioux reportedly raided settlements and then retreated to the Hills. Reports of these incidents resulted in military reconnaissance in the area.

As a result of growing reports of gold in the Hills, in 1865 residents of what is now eastern South Dakota requested permission from Congress for military reconnaissance to organize miners and prospectors to conduct a geological survey. Recognizing the strained character of the situation, in 1867 General William T. Sherman determined that the military was not in a position to assist and would therefore not provide protection to civilians who decided to pursue prospecting and mining.

Growing pressure to explore and move into the Hills was temporarily abated with the Fort Laramie Treaty of 1868. In an effort to constitute a lasting peace between the United States and indigenous peoples inhabiting the Plains, the treaty established what became known as the Great Sioux Reservation, encompassing all of present South Dakota west of the Missouri River and acknowledging the area of Nebraska north of the North Platte River and the eastern portions of Wyoming and Montana from the boundary of the reservation to the summit of the Big Horn Mountains as "unceded Indian territory." The treaty prohibited settlers or miners from entering the Hills without authorization and provided for the establishment of agencies to distribute food, clothes, and money. In turn, the Sioux agreed to cease hostilities toward transient pioneers and railroad workers.

Throughout the 1870s, stories about gold and other wealth in the Hills continued to circulate. Although the military and Department of the Interior discouraged any entry into the Hills, citizen pressure for a government-sanctioned expedition mounted. As citizen excursions into the Hills and retaliatory Sioux raids on settlements continued, the government launched an expedition led by Lieutenant Colonel George A. Custer in an effort to control growing hostilities as well as to locate a suitable fort site. Curiously, the expedition included a geologist and miners, and, when gold was found—regardless of government discouragement—word of it began to circulate and the rush was on. Agreements delineated

in the Treaty of 1868, therefore, continued to erode and the military proved ineffective at keeping prospectors, miners, and squatters at bay.

By 1875 Colonel Richard I. Dodge estimated that 800 men were prospecting and mining in the Hills. In an effort to solve the matter of ownership, the federal government invited Sioux leaders to Washington, D.C., where they refused all offers to relinquish claim to the Hills. Nevertheless, by 1876 approximately 10,000 people had taken up residence, and a contested agreement was exacted that ceded lands in the Black Hills to the government. Continued contention over the Hills led to a series of armed conflicts. In the spring of 1877 Sitting Bull and his followers escaped from the military into Canada while Crazy Horse and his followers surrendered at Camp Robinson, settling at the Red Cloud Agency. The effective end of armed resistance to white encroachment was marked on September 5, 1877, when Crazy Horse was killed in a scuffle with a soldier at Camp Robinson. His followers then fled north to join Sitting Bull or settled at other agencies.

The Black Hills of South Dakota are sacred to the Sioux Indians. (Phil Schermeister/Corbis)

The Black Hills remain a matter of contention. With an eight-to-one majority, on June 30, 1980, the Supreme Court determined that the United States had taken the Hills in violation of the "just compensation" clause of the Fifth Amendment. Although the federal government had the authority to take the Hills, the Court ruled that the Sioux had not received proper compensation. The Sioux were, in turn, awarded $17,553,484 (the calculated value in 1877) with interest at 5 percent from February 28, 1877, or approximately $105 million. Upon notification of the decision, Sioux leaders adopted a resolution disavowing any such settlement, as accepting the award would validate the position of the government and effectively end any hope of eventually reclaiming the Hills. The cash award remains in the U.S. Treasury earning interest, now in excess of $500 million.

Timothy J. McCollum

See also Battle of the Little Bighorn; Crazy Horse; Great Sioux Uprising; Red Cloud; Sacred Sites.

References and Further Reading

Lazarus, Edward. 1999. *Black Hills, White Justice: The Sioux Nation Versus the United States, 1775 to the Present*. Lincoln: University of Nebraska Press.

Sundstrom, Linea. 2000. "The Sacred Black Hills: An Ethnohistorical Review." In *American Indians*. Edited by Nancy Shoemaker, 164–191. Oxford, UK: Blackwell Publishing.

Black Seminoles

After the introduction of African chattel slavery in North America some runaway slaves, who became known as maroons, fled south to what is now Florida, establishing independent communities and alliances with indigenous peoples. In the meantime, in the late 1600s, a number of indigenous nations, each decimated by disease introduced by the Spanish, formed the Creek Confederacy in what is now Georgia and Alabama. By 1750, a sector of the confederacy declared itself independent of Creek authority and moved south to Florida. These Creeks united with indigenous peoples, including the Miccosukees, and maroons to form the Seminole nation. Thus, from its inception, the Seminole nation included persons of African descent, known in the Seminole language as the Estelusti.

The newly emergent United States wanted both the military and political benefits of treaties with American Indian nations, yet was unwilling to recognize a nation that included persons of African descent, for the Constitution protected the institution of slavery and, under most state law, those identified as "black" were presumed to be slaves. The 1790 Treaty of New York purported to be an agreement between all U.S. citizens and "all the individuals, towns and tribes of the Upper, Middle and Lower Creeks and Semanolies [sic] composing the Creek nation of Indians." In addition to ceding large tracts of land, the Creeks agreed to deliver all "prisoners and Negroes" in the nation. The Seminoles repudiated the treaty on the grounds that they were not Creeks, had not been represented in the negotiations, and lived in Spanish Florida.

Nonetheless, slaveholders in Georgia and South Carolina pressured the federal government to force Spain to turn over persons of African descent, some of whom had, by the early nineteenth century, been living freely in Florida for five or six generations. As pressure mounted to annex Florida, Congress secretly approved a series of invasions, each of which was repelled by Spanish and Seminole resistance. In May 1816 General Andrew Jackson authorized U.S. troops to attack a Seminole-controlled fort on the Apalachicola River, sixty miles inside Florida. U.S. forces killed 270 Seminoles, mostly women and children. They took the survivors to Georgia and turned them over to planters who, according to Ohio Congressman Joshua Giddings, "claimed to have descended from planters who, some three or four generations previously, owned the ancestors of the prisoners" (Giddings, 1858, 42).

Shortly thereafter, the Seminoles launched a retaliatory attack that was, in turn, used as a pretext by the United States to begin the First Seminole War. In 1819, the United States convinced Spain, drained by the Napoleonic Wars, to sell Florida, setting the stage for thirty years of warfare over the removal of the Seminoles. In 1821, the United States negotiated the Treaty of Indian Springs, under which the Creeks ceded 5 million acres of land. Despite their protests that the Seminoles were a separate nation, more than half of the payment for land was set aside to pay claims of slaveholders for "property" purportedly lost to the Creeks between 1775 and 1802. In exchange for this indemnification, title to this "property"—which included the black Seminoles—was transferred to the United States, to be held in trust for the Creeks.

Having been unsuccessful in controlling the Seminoles through the Creeks, the United States finally acknowledged the existence of the Seminole nation by entering into the Treaty of Moultrie Creek on September 18, 1823. Under its terms, which the U.S. negotiator candidly acknowledged the "Indians would never have voluntarily assented to," the Seminoles ceded their fertile land in northern Florida for a large but barren tract farther south and bound them to turn over any "absconding slaves, or fugitives from justice" (Prucha, 1994, 152).

By this time, "Seminole society had blacks of every status born free, or the descendants of fugitives, or perhaps fugitives themselves. Some were interpreters and advisers of importance, others were warriors and hunters or field hands." The Treaty of Moultrie Creek was signed by Abraham, a Seminole of African descent identified as "the prime minister and privy counsellor of Micanopy," and one of the six most influential chiefs involved in the negotiations was known as Mulatto King (Foreman, 1972, 319). Osceola, one of the nation's best-known leaders, was married to an Estelusti and engaged in some of his most daring exploits to retaliate for his wife having been kidnapped and sold into slavery.

Even General Thomas Jesup, commander of the U.S. forces in Florida, acknowledged the difficulty in distinguishing fugitive slaves from black Seminoles, writing in 1837, "I have some hopes of inducing both Indians and Indian negroes to unite in bringing in the negroes taken from the citizens during the war" (Giddings, 1858, 147). Similarly, after visiting several "Negro Villages" looking for runaways, a white planter complained that he could not determine the number of slaves living among the Seminoles because "of their being protected by the Indian Negroes" (Klos, 1995, 131–132).

After passage of the 1830 Indian Removal Act, the U.S. government attempted to move the Seminoles from Florida to land already occupied by the Creeks—the nation from which the United States had just taken more than $250,000 in exchange for "title" to a significant sector of the Seminole population. For many Seminoles removal thus equated not only to loss of land, but to being sold into slavery as well. Their resistance led to the Second Seminole War, which lasted from 1835 to 1842. Although military historians have described it as the "longest and most expensive Indian war" waged by the U.S. government, General Jesup insisted that it was "a negro and not an Indian war" (Porter, 1996, 107).

The United States never achieved a military victory over the Seminole nation, but, community by community, most Seminoles were eventually forced west, many living off the generosity of the Cherokees until assigned lands of their own. Some remained in the Everglades, living quietly until white settler pressure resulted in the Third Seminole War (1855–1858), which destroyed most of their remaining villages.

After the Civil War and the passage of the Thirteenth Amendment, the federal government imposed treaties on the Seminoles and on other Indian nations providing for the emancipation of any slaves and the incorporation of the "freedmen" on an "equal footing with the original members" (14 Stat. 755, Treaty with the Seminoles, March 21, 1866). In 1901, Congress unilaterally declared members of the Five Civilized Tribes, including the Seminoles, to be U.S. citizens and in 1906 effectively abolished the Seminole government and assigned a commission headed by Senator Henry Dawes to provide an accounting, or tribal enrollment, of members of the nation. The Dawes Commission created a list of approximately 3,000 Seminoles, about one-third of whom were of African descent. Although not required to do so, it divided the members between a Seminole Blood Roll and a Freedmen Roll. Reflecting the pervasive racial classifications of contemporaneous Jim Crow laws, the Commission put persons of visible African ancestry on the Freedmen Roll, identifying the remaining Seminoles by a "blood quantum" standard that reflected their degree of European ancestry.

In 1950 and 1951, the Seminole Nation of Oklahoma (SNO) and Seminoles still living in Florida filed claims for compensation for their Florida lands. In 1976 the Indian Claims Commission (ICC) finally awarded $16 million to the "Seminole Nation as it existed in Florida on September 18, 1823," the date of the signing of the Treaty of Moultrie Creek. Congress, however, did not pass an act to distribute the monies until 1990, by which time the judgment fund, with interest, had grown to $56 million.

In 1996 Sylvia Davis, an enrolled member of the Dosar Barkus band of the SNO, filed suit in federal court because the Bureau of Indian Affairs (BIA) denied her son a $125-school clothing allowance from the funds awarded by the ICC. The BIA, backed by the governing council of the SNO, denied members of the Dosar Barkus and Bruner bands, Seminoles of African descent, access to these funds by arguing that the Estelusti were not members of the Seminole nation as it existed in 1823. Contrary to the historical record of black Seminoles predating the existence of the United States itself, the BIA took

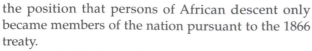

the position that persons of African descent only became members of the nation pursuant to the 1866 treaty.

The leadership of the SNO, apparently under the mistaken impression that all judgment funds would be frozen pending the outcome of the lawsuit, voted to expel the Dosar Barkus and Bruner bands from the SNO and in July 2000 the governing council approved amendments to its constitution to that effect. The BIA refused to recognize the results of SNO elections from which the Freedmen were excluded, a position upheld by a D.C. District Court [U.S. District Court for the District of Columbia] in 2002 (*Seminole Nation of Oklahoma v. Norton*), which subsequently awarded some governmental benefits to the excluded bands. The Tenth Circuit Court of Appeals dismissed Sylvia Davis's suit in 2003 because the SNO could not be joined as a party to the litigation, and the Supreme Court declined to consider the case (*Davis v. United States*). Today about 2,500 of the 14,000 members of the SNO are Estelusti. In 2005 representatives of the Bruner and Dosar Barkus bands, including Sylvia Davis, were elected to positions on the governing council, but the divisions induced by the federal government's long imposition of racialized identity on the Seminoles continue to take their toll.

Natsu Taylor Saito

See also African Americans; Creek War; Indian Removal Act; Relocation; Seminole Wars; Slavery; Trail of Tears.

References and Further Reading
Foreman, Grant. 1972. *Indian Removal: The Emigration of the Five Civilized Tribes of Indians*. Norman: University of Oklahoma Press.
Giddings, Joshua R. 1858. *The Exiled of Florida; Or, The Crimes Committed by Our Government Against the Maroons, Who Fled from South Carolina and Other Slave States, Seeking Protection under Spanish Law*. Columbus, OH: Follett, Foster and Company.
Klos, George. 1995. "Blacks and the Seminole Removal Debate, 1821–2835." In *The African American Heritage of Florida*. Edited by David R. Colburn. Gainesville: University of Florida Press.
Porter, Kenneth W. 1996. *The Black Seminoles: History of a Freedom-Seeking People*. Gainesville: University Press of Florida.
Prucha, Francis Paul. 1994. *American Indian Treaties: The History of a Political Anomaly*. Berkeley: University of California Press.

Blue Lake, New Mexico

The Taos Pueblo people tell a story, through song, of how they arose from the underworld at Shiabapu and emerged from a lake. From there they migrated to their present place of residence after countless centuries of roaming and guidance by the Great Spirit. In their land, the Pueblo people learned to live in harmony with their environment and prosper. Today, they still live at the site where the Spanish first encountered them in the sixteenth century, although on a much reduced land base, and they still practice their religious traditions handed down from time immemorial.

On November 7, 1906, President Theodore Roosevelt created the Carson National Forest in New Mexico from Pueblo lands and restricted the people of Taos in their use of their sacred Blue Lake. The proclamation stripped the Taos people of title and rights to the land. Many Americans traveled to the beautiful spot for camping and recreation and to boat and fish on the Blue Lake after the Forest Service built cabins and garbage pits there in 1928.

While the struggle for the return of title to Blue Lake was born, the effort continued for the right to conduct religious ceremonies at various shrines around Blue Lake. Indian religious ceremonies had been outlawed by the 1883 Religious Crimes Act. The 1934 Indian Reorganization Act finally abolished the government's control over religious ceremony, but the Taos people were having a difficult time convincing the federal government that their claim to exclusive use title to the Blue Lake was centered on religious issues.

On October 4, 1940, Congress passed a bill giving Taos Pueblo a fifty-year use permit for Blue Lake to continue their religious ceremonies there as well as for collecting food, water, and wood. However, the Forest Service continued to cut trails and issue permits for camping on the sacred land. Eventually the trash that accumulated at Blue Lake desecrated the sacred site.

Many people were involved in the struggle to return Blue Lake to the Pueblo. John Collier was an early and ardent supporter; Seferino Martinez, a Pueblo leader of the 1930s through 1960s, worked to battle against Forest Service timbering and the use of Pueblo lands; Paul J. Bernal, who became instrumental in negotiating between the government and his people; the author Oliver LaFarge, who joined the fight in 1955 and was later replaced by Corinne Locker as coordinator of the return effort; Querino

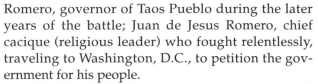

Romero, governor of Taos Pueblo during the later years of the battle; Juan de Jesus Romero, chief cacique (religious leader) who fought relentlessly, traveling to Washington, D.C., to petition the government for his people.

Initially, the Indian Claims Commission (ICC) offered $297,684.67, the 1906 valuation of the land, to Taos Pueblo for Blue Lake. By the mid-1960s, however, the ICC felt that the history and religious beliefs of Taos Pueblo supported their title to the land. Instead of payment, the ICC proposed a bill to return the lands.

Oklahoma Senator Fred Harris was instrumental in seeing the return of the lake through the Senate. Fred and his wife LaDonna (Comanche) convinced the Richard M. Nixon administration, including Spiro Agnew, of the centrality of Blue Lake to the Taos Pueblo's religion. The only opposition in the Senate came from Clinton P. Anderson of New Mexico, who feared the loss of the watershed on Carson National Forest lands.

On December 15, 1970, H.R. Bill 471, which had been introduced by Senators Harris and Ted Kennedy, passed by a vote of seventy to twelve. It returned Blue Lake and 48,000 acres to the Taos Pueblo. President Nixon supported the bill as a vehicle for American Indian self-determination and religious freedom. As he signed Public Law 91–550, Nixon stated that the event was not to be viewed as a gift to Taos Pueblo, but as long overdue justice.

The battle for Blue Lake became a major turning point in the American Indian self-determination movement. Not only did the Taos Pueblo receive their land, but they also gained an education in how to deal with the federal government. In addition, they achieved a sense of unity and support from American Indians all across the country.

Vera Parham

See also American Indian Religious Freedom Act; Sacred Sites; Tribal Sovereignty.

References and Further Reading

Forbes, Jack D. 1981. *Native Americans and Nixon: Presidential Politics and Minority Self-determination, 1969–1972.* Los Angeles, CA: UCLA American Indian Studies Center, 1981.

Gordon-McCutchan, R. C. 1991. *The Taos Indians and the Battle for Blue Lake.* Santa Fe, NM: Red Crane Books.

Sando, Joe S. 1976. *The Pueblo Indians.* San Francisco: Indian Historian Press.

Bole-Maru Religion

The *Bole-Maru* originated in the atmosphere of the late nineteenth century revitalization movement that arose out of Wodziwob's (Gray Hair, Paviotso Piaute, Nevada) apocalyptic vision depicting a great natural cataclysmic event destroying ("swallowing up") the living and the dead with only the Natives being resurrected to prosperity. The Pomo tribe, who developed Bole-Maru from the Earth Lodge or Kuksu cult, learned of the apocalyptic visions primarily through Wintun and Hill Patwin tribes when forced together through growing Euro-American encroachment. Bole-Maru became a more adaptive movement than the various versions of the Ghost Dance developed after Wodziwob. The Pomo integrated characteristics derived from different tribes in northern and central California along with increasing knowledge of Euro-American culture and its religions.

During the winter of 1871–1872, the medicine man Richard Taylor predicted that a flood would soon wash away the white people and that those who danced through the deluge in semisubterranean dance houses would survive. The predicted event failed to happen. Participants returned to their communities taking the hope of the prediction with them. Those who returned to their homes modified aspects of Kuksu practices, such as regarding Dreamers as prophets for the people, the use of dance houses, and a dualistic understanding of creation that later blended with Christian concepts of heaven and hell/God and the devil. Kuksu Dreamers were exclusive members of a secret society of men. As the Bole-Maru developed, this exclusivity diminished. Years of contact with the emerging dominant culture decreased Native population and social cohesion, presenting the need for adaptive changes in social life that minimized the loss of traditional values and understanding. Originating among the various communities, Bole-Maru developed as a religious/social political movement combining traditions from various communities. Variations spawned by each new community provided the catalyst for Bole-Maru to survive the conflicts surrounding increasing contact with the Euro-American culture.

In *Keeping Slug Woman Alive*, Greg Sarris (p. 66) says, "Where once there had been many private or secret cults within a tribe, now an entire tribe was united under one cult, the Bole-Maru." The name of the cult itself reflected the diverse influence, *Bole* (hill, Patwin) and *Maru* (eastern Pomo); both referred to the person leading the ceremonies, who, through dreams, received instruction on many levels. Dreams also influenced the dancing of the participants, their regalia, and the decorations of the dance house. The leaders designed clothing, instruments, dance patterns, feast patterns, and other aspects of the ceremonies, as well as retaining the cohesiveness of the traditional society.

Annie Jarvis, a Kashaya Pomo Dreamer between 1912 and 1943, strengthened Native identity during the time that Bole-Maru was losing influence among other Pomo and coastal Miwok. Mary Jean Kennedy (HRAF 2000 Computer File #24, p. 133) "simultaneously with the development of the Dreamer religion, the people became more involved economically in the dominant culture." Along with the benefits came damaging influences as well. As drinking, gambling, and other such influences became a concern, Kennedy strengthened Native identity by requiring sober participation in ceremonies and by standing against boarding school education and intermarriages. Through her influence and her Dreaming, she brought cohesion, as well as additional Christian influence, to dances and activities. She taught a belief in heaven and a resurrection. She instituted a naming ceremony, blessing a baby by naming it with an Indian name and announcing that name to the Father in heaven.

Assisting Kennedy, Essie Parrish (1903–1979) became the next influential Dreamer. Essie's dreams were more like visions, because they tended to occur while she was awake. She foresaw World War II, the atomic bomb, the coming of a black book, and the influence of a new religion. Throughout her life, she experienced resistance from Pentecostals, who declared that her visions came "from the Devil" and forbade their adherents to participate in Bole-Maru. Eliciting a more sympatric response from the Mormons, Essie converted to that religion, declaring her earlier vision about the black book as the coming of the Mormons.

The Bole-Maru Dreamers incorporated the healing aspects of their older beliefs. Innovations from their dreaming and the wisdom of the adaptation of nontraditional lifestyles created a new cosmology, just as traditional healers did before contact with the dominant society.

Arthur Robert Brokop II

See also California Indians, Genocide of; Dreamer Cult; Ghost Dance Religion; Wovoka.

Buffalo

On the High Plains of North America, the buffalo (or bison) was the economic basis of Native American life well into the nineteenth century. When non-Native settlement began to encroach on the area early in that century, an estimated 30 million buffalo lived in an area roughly bordered by present-day Texas, northern Alberta, western New York, to Alabama and Mississippi, and to Idaho and eastern Oregon. Within three quarters of a century, competition from non-Natives, including deliberate slaughter, reduced the buffalo population to about 100,000 animals. By 2004, a concerted effort to replenish buffalo herds had raised population to an estimated quarter of a million.

Most Native peoples worked nature into their rituals and customs because their lives depended on the bounty of the land around them. Where a single animal predominated in a Native economy (such as the salmon of the Pacific Northwest or the buffalo on the Plains), strict cultural sanctions came into play against killing the animals in numbers that would exceed their natural replacement rate. On the Plains, the military societies of the Cheyenne, Lakota, and other peoples enforced rules against hunting buffalo out of season and against taking more animals than a people could use. Many Plains societies had special police who maintained discipline before and during communal buffalo hunts. An individual who began the hunt early could be severely punished.

Before they acquired horses, Native bands sometimes hunted buffalo by herding them over "jumps," cliffs that were nearly invisible to the stampeding animals until they were crowded over the edge by animals behind them. Following such a stampede, the hunters and their wives worked quickly to preserve the meat, often by drying it in the sun to make jerky. In the heat of summer, when buffaloes were usually hunted, undressed meat could spoil in a day.

Native peoples on the Plains used nearly every part of the buffalo in their everyday economies. In addition to the meat that was eaten fresh or preserved as jerky, buffalo hides were tanned and used as teepee covers, moccasin tops, shirts, leggings, dresses and other clothing, bedding, bags, and pouches. Rawhide was used for moccasin soles, snowshoes, shields, rattles and drums, as well as for saddles, bridles, and other horse tack. Buffalo horns were fashioned into cups, spoons and other eating

Blackfeet Indians chasing buffalo, Three Buttes, Montana. Artwork by John M. Stanley, 1853–1855. (National Archives and Records Administration)

utensils, toys, and rattles. The bones became knives, arrowheads, shovels, hoes, war clubs, and ceremonial objects, while buffalo hair was used in headdresses and ropes. Buffalo tails became fly brushes, while the bladder could be fashioned into a watertight canteen. Buffalo chips (dung) were sometimes used as fuel when wood was unavailable.

Native acquisition of the horse had an immense impact both on the hunting of buffalo and on the economic behavior and social structure of society. A large number of Native societies transformed themselves into roving buffalo hunting bands. A male buffalo can weigh a ton, and can charge at thirty miles an hour. Elite societies of young men skilled at buffalo hunting emerged, forming the basis of the Plains warrior societies.

Before 1870, large buffalo herds still roamed the southern Plains, and many thousands of Native people still lived as they preferred, with the buffalo at the root of their economies. During the 1870s, however, non-Native hunters killed a million buffalo a year on the northern Plains. The railroads ran special excursions along their newly opened tracks from which self-styled sportsmen shot buffalo from the comfort of their seats.

General Phil Sheridan, one of the foremost Indian fighters in the U.S. Army, viewed the slaughter of the buffalo as a weapon in the Army's arsenal against the last remaining independent Native Americans: "I would not seriously regret the total disappearance of the buffalo from our western prairies, in its effect upon the Indians, regarding it rather as a means of hastening their dependence upon products of the soil," Sheridan said (Morris, 1992, 343). At one point, Sheridan suggested that buffalo poachers be given medals with a dead Buffalo engraved on one side and a discouraged-looking Indian on the other (Morris, 1992, 343). Sheridan, never a man to mince words, remarked that buffalo hunters had done more to defeat the Indians than the entire regular Army. Hunters of the dwindling herds were followed by skinners, who (depending on market conditions) might strip the hides or just remove the slain buffaloes' tongues. No one ever counted the number of buffalo that fell.

By the 1870s, non-Natives were killing more buffalo than were Indians. Of 1.2 million buffalo skins shipped east on the railroads in 1872 and 1873, about 350,000 (28 percent) were supplied by Indians. By that time, the Plains were swarming with unemployed railroad workers, would-be farmers whose homesteads would not sustain their families, and hopeful miners caught between gold rushes. By the time buffalo populations were reduced to levels that would no longer sustain the trade during the 1880s, an estimated 5,000 non-Indian hunters were chasing them.

By the early 1880s, the U.S. Army's version of total war against the Plains Indians had reached its goal: The buffalo were nearly extinct. Ten years earlier, some of the Plains Indians still had an ample supply of food; by the early 1880s, they were reduced, as General Sheridan had intended, to the condition of paupers, without food, shelter, clothing, or any of the necessities of life that had come for so long from the buffalo.

Bruce E. Johansen

See also Genocide; Great Sioux Uprising; Horse, Economic Impact.

References and Further Reading

Branch, Douglas E. 1973. *The Hunting of the Buffalo.* Lincoln: University of Nebraska Press.

Hodgson, Bryan. 1994. "Buffalo: Back Home on the Range." *National Geographic* 186, no. 5 (November): 64–89.

Homaday, William T. 1869. *The Extermination of the American Bison.* Washington, DC: Annual Report of the U.S. National Museum.

Johnson, Lowell, ed. 1984. *The First Voices.* Lincoln: University of Nebraska Press.

Klein, Alan M. 1993. "The Political Economy of the Buffalo Hide Trade: Race and Class on the Plains." In *Political Economy of North American Indians.* Edited by John H. Moore. Norman: University of Oklahoma Press.

Morris, Roy, Jr. 1992. *Sheridan: The Life and Wars of General Phil Sheridan.* New York: Crown.

Walker, James R. 1982. *Lakota Society.* Edited by Raymond J. DeMallie. Lincoln: University of Nebraska Press.

Cahokia

Between roughly 1100 and 1200—a time when settlements in the Americas rarely exceeded 400 or 500 inhabitants—the Native American center of Cahokia was as large as contemporary London, a size that no other city in the United States would attain until the nineteenth century. The well organized aggregation of mounds and residential districts had a population estimated at 10,000 to 30,000—some sources claim 40,000. Cahokia's distinctive earth mounds (there were a 120 of them) took three forms: conical, ridge top, and, most commonly, platforms, often crowned with ceremonial buildings or the houses of the powerful. At the heart of the city stood the huge ceremonial embankment (now known as Monks Mound) that was in itself a stupendous feat of planning and engineering.

The indigenous American civilization known as Mississippian—no one knows what they called themselves—sprang up in the American Bottom, an extensive fertile floodplain near the confluence of the Mississippi, Missouri, Illinois, Kaskaskia, and Meramec Rivers. Between about 1000 and 1250, they lived near what is now central and east St. Louis and where the Illinois towns of Fairmont City, Dupo, Lebanon, and Mitchell now stand. This suburban concentration was eclipsed by their greatest achievement: Cahokia, dubbed America's lost metropolis. Cahokia was named for the branch of the Illinois people who occupied the region in the seventeenth century, long after the builders had departed.

In terms of both agriculture and trade, Cahokia was perfectly located. The predictable annual flooding of farmland enabled planning and replenished the soil so that maize and other crops were sustainable for centuries. The river systems reaching out to much of North America facilitated trade, and there is evidence of commercial traffic over a network that extended from Minnesota in the north to Mississippi in the south; Cahokian traders reached west as far as Kansas and east to Tennessee. Raw materials such as copper, seashells, and mica were imported and processed in Cahokia to be exported as copper ornaments and shell beads—indications of a sophisticated manufacturing industry. It was once believed that this productive economic environment led to population growth, as Cahokian civilization slowly flowered.

Recently, archaeologist Timothy Pauketat has questioned this conclusion, claiming that there is no evidence for it. Although not all his peers agree, he suggests that Cahokia experienced an urban implosion in little more than a decade early in the eleventh century, growing from a village of only 1,000 people into a city ten times that size. Based on studies of wider Native American beliefs, that event may have been due to the emergence of a charismatic chief whose arrival prompted villagers to abandon their

settlements throughout eastern Missouri and southern Illinois and migrate to Cahokia.

It is now widely accepted that the middle Mississippian area of which Cahokia forms a large part was under some kind of chiefdom government. Each chief—a Brother of the Sun—seems to have ruled a territory that depended on a specific floodplain, and he managed food distribution between the central place and outlying settlements. Perhaps he had other roles, including matters of trade, administration of a civil service, and most probably religiopolitical duties. Little more is known.

However it came into being, the fact of Cahokia is staggering. Its earthen mounds extended over 6 square miles (15 square kilometers). At the heart of the city, defended by a wooden stockade, was the 200-acre (81-hectare) precinct of the ruling class, with the great ceremonial flat-topped mound at its center. The engineers and architects built to a master plan that was almost certainly based on Mississippian cosmology—a sort of model of the universe. Cahokians viewed their universe as Father Sky and Mother Earth, and the layout of streets and structures mirrored that. The northern half of the city rep-

resented Sky, the southern half Earth. They were defined by a long east–west street; another, running northeast, formed a cross symbolizing north, south, east, and west, its center point just in front of the central mound and at the end of a grand plaza. Archaeologists have uncovered four circular solar calendars built of large, evenly spaced red cedar posts at the outer limits of the two streets. These "wood-henges," so-called because they had the same purpose as Stonehenge in England, were essential to the Cahokians' agriculture-based economy, both in a practical and a ceremonial sense.

From about 1100 the central precinct, containing seventeen earth mounds, was protected by a 2-mile-long (3.2-kilometer) stockade, constructed from some 15,000 to 20,000 1-foot-thick (30-centimeter) oak and hickory logs. The wall was about 12 feet (3.6 meters) high, with projecting bastions every 70 feet (21 meters) along its length. Outside it, thousands of single-family houses clustered, organized in small groups around ceremonial poles. Although it may have served as a social barrier between the Cahokian elite and the general population, it is clear from its form and the evidence of some hastily built parts

This photo was taken in 1907, more than 500 years after the mound builders abandoned Cahokia. (Library of Congress)

that the palisade's main purpose was defense. It was rebuilt three times before 1300.

The inner city of Cahokia was dominated by an enormous platform mound, identified as the largest prehistoric earthwork in the Americas. Surviving today, Monks Mound was named after a Trappist monastery in the vicinity. Its base, measuring 1,037 by 790 feet (291 by 236 meters), extends over 14 acres (5.25 hectares), and the structure rises through four sloping-sided rectangular terraces to a height of 100 feet (30.6 meters). It contains 820,000 cubic yards (692,000 cubic meters) of earth, all of which was hand-excavated from large borrow pits and carried in woven baskets to the site. Monks Mound was built in several stages over about 200 years, with carefully designed strata of sand and clay and drains to deal with water saturation. Long ago, it was crowned with a 50-foot-high (15-meter) thatched roof building of timber-pole construction, 105 by 48 feet (31 by 14 meters). Some scholars identify it as a temple. It was certainly the chief's residence, in which the political and religious observances were conducted that ensured the nation's continuing prosperity. In effect, the mound was a means of lifting Mother Earth to Father Sky, bringing male and female together. That these ancient builders could set out their city with its streets aligned to the cardinal compass points and construct such a durable monument over generations, without having a written language or the wheel, makes their accomplishment the more marvelous.

Around 1200, for reasons that may only be guessed, Cahokia began to decline. Perhaps growth had placed too much burden on the agricultural hinterland or overloaded the urban infrastructure; perhaps deforestation had changed the local ecology. Or perhaps there was civil war over dwindling resources. Other scholars attribute the demise of the city to a mud slide on the great mound, which may have been construed as an omen. No one really knows. And no one knows where the Cahokians went. By 1400 their remarkable metropolis was abandoned. Arriving much later in the area, the first Europeans mistook the mounds, overgrown by then, for natural hillocks. Monks Mound was not discovered until the beginning of the nineteenth century.

Modern farming, expanding towns, highways, and pollution continue to threaten the smaller communities around Cahokia that have not already been destroyed. The 2,200-acre (890-hectare) Cahokia Mounds State Historic Site is administered by the Illinois Historic Preservation Agency. It was added to UNESCO's World Heritage List in 1982. Archaeological investigation continues. Following major slumps on the east and west sides of Monks Mound in the mid-1980s, attempts were made to reduce internal waterlogging. In January 1998 construction workers, drilling horizontally into the west side, struck a deep layer of limestone or sandstone cobbles 40 feet (12 meters) beneath the surface. Further tests were hampered by groundwater, but the find has excited scientists because stone does not naturally occur in the region. There is much more to be revealed at Cahokia.

C. S. Everett

See also Adena Civilization; Archaeology; Hopewell Culture; Mississippian Culture; Mound Cultures of North America; Natchez Culture; Trade.

References and Further Reading
Pauketat, Timothy R., and Thomas E. Emerson, eds. 1997. Cahokia: Domination and Ideology in the Mississippian World. Lincoln: University of Nebraska Press.
Young, Biloine Whiting, and Melvin L. Fowler. 1999. Cahokia, the Great Native American Metropolis. Urbana: University of Illinois Press.

Cannibalism

The ritually sanctioned consumption of human flesh by North American indigenous peoples is a widely debated subject among scholars in anthropology, ethnohistory, and Native studies. In fact, a vast amount of the secondary literature on the subject deals with debates regarding whether the practice ever occurred in the Americas. For decades ritual cannibalism (anthropophagy) was uncritically accepted either as an indicator of Native ferocity and savagery (and therefore justification for missionization and exterminative practices on the part of colonizers) or as one aspect of Native peoples' deeply ceremonial practice of warfare. William Arens' 1979 book, The Man-Eating Myth, called into question the anthropological assertion that cannibalism in Native North America was a frequent and large-scale socially sanctioned practice, and thus it opened up the discourse on the act of cannibalism as both practice and symbol. Other scholars contend that ritual or ceremonial cannibalism was a regular part of many indigenous American societies.

Many scholars maintain that, because the history of North America depends so heavily on written sources that largely represent the colonizer's point of view, any discussion of cannibalism must consider

This colonialist depiction of a group of Native Americans portrays the alleged "ceremonies and methods of killing and eating enemies" employed by the savage cannibals who populated the North American continent in the imaginations of those who settled the New World. Such sensationalized distortions of the Native population, along with their susceptibility to foreign diseases and lack of military technology, contributed to their eventual slavery and decimation. (Library of Congress)

the Eurocentric bias inherent to the primary sources from which much of our information is drawn. From Christopher Columbus's first writings in America onward, cannibalism appears to have been an act Europeans expected to find among the newly encountered indigenous peoples. While use of the word "anthropophagous" to refer to the consumption of human flesh dates to antiquity, "cannibal" has its origins during the invasion of the Americas. The term evolved from Carib/Canib, the name applied by the Arawaks to their apparently ferocious neighbors and subsequently used by Europeans. This idea spread, appearing in works from Columbus to Shakespeare, such that, by the early eighteenth century, "cannibal" and "anthropophagus" were synonyms (Hulme, 1986, 67–73). "Cannibal" came to denote any person or group who ate human flesh.

Some scholars, including Arens, agree that whatever actual cannibalism may have occurred in the Americas was very likely exaggerated by the European worldview that expected to find cannibalism everywhere (Barker et al., 1998, 42). Numerous books that were widely read in medieval and early modern Europe, including those by Augustine,

Pliny, John Mandeville, and Marco Polo, created a vast catalogue of grotesque qualities, placing cannibals alongside dog-headed men and amazons, labels ready to be applied to America's exotic indigenous "others" (Hulme, 1986, 21).

Arens suggests that no convincing first-hand eyewitness accounts of indigenous cannibalism exist in the historical or ethnographic record (Barker et al., 1998, 21). Further, Ward Churchill's (Cherokee/ Metis) 2000 review article in *American Archaeologist* asserts that institutionalized cannibalism among Native groups was an invention of Eurocentric scholarship meant to systematically defile preinvasion Native cultures (Churchill, 2000, 278–280). Alternately, opponents of Arens and Churchill suggest that ritual cannibalism was a regular part of many North American indigenous societies. Some scholars assert that the human flesh of warriors often was consumed in order to incorporate the warrior's bravery. Peggy Reeves Sanday suggests that the Hotinonshonni (Iroquois) "were indiscriminant in their search for torture victims to appease their war god" (Sanday, 1986, 127).

However, Wendat (Huron) historian Georges Sioui allows that some ritual cannibalism occurred among his Wendat and other Hotinonshonni (Iroquoian-speaking) peoples. Sioui maintains that this practice occurred only in cases of extreme grief, when a (usually male) captive would be executed and small amounts of the person were eaten, in order to both honor the captive and to engage in collective healing on the part of the captors (Sioui, 1999, 173–174). Sioui's indigenous perspective presents a useful middle ground on the historical debate surrounding cannibalism. Anthropological, ethnohistorical, and Native studies evidence suggests that cannibalism likely occurred in ritual settings to varying degrees across the Americas. However, the point that these occurrences may have been exaggerated in the European-authored literature to exaggerate Native ferocity and therefore to justify colonization remains a key issue, and something of the utmost importance when considering the veracity of primary sources.

Daniel Morley Johnson

See also Warfare, Intertribal; Worldview and Values.
References and Further Reading

Arens, William. 1979. *The Man-Eating Myth*. New York: Oxford University Press.
Barker, Francis, et al., eds. 1998. *Cannibalism and the Colonial World*. Cambridge: Cambridge University Press.
Churchill, Ward. 2000. *"Man Corn."* (Review) In *North American Archaeologist* 21, no. 3: 268–288.
Hulme, Peter. 1986. *Colonial Encounters: Europe and the Native Caribbean, 1492–1797*. London: Methuen.
Sanday, Peggy Reeves. 1986. *Divine Hunger: Cannibalism as a Cultural System*. Cambridge: Cambridge University Press.
Sioui, Georges. 1999. *Huron-Wendat: The Heritage of the Circle*. Translated by Jane Brierley. Montreal, QC: McGill-Queen's University Press.

Canoes

Aboriginal oral traditions in northeastern North America recall the significance of the canoe in Native American history. Early in the twentieth century, the hereditary chief Peterwegeschick recalled that, in the 1820s, the citizens of the Bkejwanong First Nation (also known as the Walpole Island First Nation) participated in extensive trade, among other places, at Detroit and that his father "went there to trade when he was very small. He told me [Chief Peterwegeschick] that the St. Clair was often black with canoes in their journeying to the trading post at Detroit." The canoe, especially its birchbark variety was, for at least five centuries, the most important aboriginal device of technology; it was an essential part of their knowledge and was shared with the European newcomers. The canoe, in war, diplomacy, and trade, was the principal means by which aboriginal autonomy and sovereignty were long secured.

The English word "canoe" is derived from the Arawak (Taino) word for boat. In the fifteenth century, the Spanish appropriated the Arawak word, and it became "canoa." The term was used at the time of Christopher Columbus's voyages to the Caribbean to indicate a hollowed-out log used by "uncivilized Nations" as a boat that is propelled by paddles through the water. The Ojibwa word for canoe is "chiimaan (an)" (boat[s]). Indeed the major water transportation from the southern Ontario mainland to Manitoulin Island and the north country is by the modern ferry aptly named the *Che-Chemaun*, or big canoe.

The history of aboriginal people has been traditionally maintained through oral traditions. Central to these stories are those of creation. Their focus is on water as an integral part of the four natural elements of earth, water, air, and fire, and the canoe links these elements. For aboriginal people the canoe is spiritual in its origin. Resting horizontally across a plane of water and with a paddle held vertically, the canoe represents the four sacred directions. As such, it is a holistic representation or symbol of life and the human journey through the mortal world to the world of the spirits. In yet another dimension, the canoe still is, as Blake Debassige has shown, a veritable "celestial craft of souls." It is a metaphor related to the creation of Turtle Island–North America. One example is that of the muskrat in the story from Ojibwa mythology. In this story, the canoe is the huge log on which the Anishinabe, or Original Man, managed to climb after the Great Flood covered the surface of the earth. Some of the earliest canoes on Turtle Island were, of course, hollowed-out logs. And so the water and the canoe came before the land. The canoe provides the vehicle for reaching the four directions and provides the principle of balance, connecting the four natural elements of earth, water, air, and fire. The canoe is spiritual; yet it is also a practical form of aboriginal science as well as art. Aboriginal technology and science are ecologically based on knowledge of the natural and supernatural worlds.

One of the greatest gifts from aboriginal people was the technology of the birchbark canoe. Birchbark was extremely light and plentiful in the Great Lakes watershed. Moreover, in addition to the making of canoes, birchbark was used for fuel, the making of lodges, and maps to guide travellers in the canoe to their destination, aided by the star maps at night. So valuable was this scientific invention that it was soon appropriated by the European visitors for use by missionaries, explorers, the military, professional artists, as well as fur traders. It can be found in the monumental canoe sculpture by Bill Reid, "The Spirit of Haida Gwaii," which stands now in front of the Canadian Embassy in Washington, D.C. James Tully has described it as follows: "Cast in bronze, it recreates a group of thirteen human, animal and bird figures interacting with each other as they head into the unknown in a Haida canoe, under the guidance of Chief Kilstlaai. Wrapped in the skin of the mythical sea wolf and holding a speaker's staff that tells the Haida story of creation."

The canoe is the central or focal point to the international relationship that is represented in the Haudenosaunee (Iroquois) Two Row Wampum belt. Made from wampum shells by aboriginal artists, the belt represented the main gift of Native diplomacy

Indians in North Carolina fishing with traps, spears, and nets. Artwork by John White, 1885. (National Archives and Records Administration)

to the European empires. There is a specific relationship characterized in the belt. The belt has two rows of purple wampum on a white background. One row represents the aboriginal nations; parallel to it is the other row symbolizing the European nations. The two rows are emblematic of two canoes being paddled down a river side by side but never meeting. This relationship was used in diplomacy and trade between Europeans and aboriginal people, in peace negotiations after warfare. It also was subsequently embodied in the treaty-making process, which included both peace and friendship as well as arrangements regarding the uses of lands and natural resources.

The Two Row Wampum embodied the relationship between the English imperial government and the aboriginal nations. The latter included the Iroquois Confederacy; the Abenaki, Malecite, Mi'kmaq

Confederacies; and the western confederacy of Algonquian-speaking peoples, such as the Ojibwa, Ottawa (Odawa), and Potawatomi, among others. The wampum itself represented the relationship as one of peace, respect, and trust. The Covenant Chain was continually renewed by both the English crown, the Haudenosaunee, and the Anishinabe. Later, other aboriginal nations entered into the Covenant Chain as well. For the Iroquoian and Algonquian-speaking aboriginal nations as well as the European nations, it continued to be an important fixture of international diplomacy, war, and trade throughout the shifting conflicts and realignments wrought by the European incursions in the seventeenth and eighteenth centuries. Above all, the Chain showed the continuing sovereignty and independence of aboriginal nations in an international context. The most famous of these events occurred in 1609, one year after Quebec was founded. The French alliance, which included a force of Algonquin, Huron, and Montagnais, was cemented militarily when Samuel de Champlain canoed into the very heart of the Iroquois territory in what is now New York State and defeated the Iroquois at Ticonderoga. Champlain, using European technology—an arquebus—killed two of the Iroquois chiefs, thereby at once consolidating the French alliance with these nations and also igniting a series of wars that lasted through the century. The Iroquois became the allies of the Dutch and then the English.

Champlain understood the significance of the canoe when he wrote back to his French superiors: "With the canoe of the savages, one may travel freely and quickly throughout the country as well as up the little rivers as up the large rivers. So that by directing one's course with the help of the savages and their canoes, a man might see all that is to be seen, good or bad, within the space of a year or two." To consolidate their presence, the French sent both explorers such as Etienne Brule and priests into the northern interior of the Great Lakes. French travel through what became known as Canada could have been accomplished only by using Anishinabe guides who were able to "read" the landscape, make birchbark maps, and possessed the technology of which the canoe was of paramount importance for most of the year. In the Canadian winter, canoes were replaced on the frozen land and waterways by Anishinabe toboggans and snowshoes, both of which enabled Europeans to adapt to the new land that they had encountered. Failure to use Anishinabe technology would have meant defeat for the Europeans, who

soon recognized the principle that the land is, as Gary G. Potts has frequently asserted, the boss. Failure to show proper respect would result in death. By the end of the seventeenth century, the Iroquois could only sue for peace with their Anishinabe and French enemies, and a treaty was entered into at Montreal among the Five Nations and the French in 1701. By its terms, the Iroquois were no longer a military factor north of the Great Lakes.

One of the major results of canoe warfare was to shift the French influence south and west and to consolidate the English empire's hold on James and Hudson Bays and the fur trade of that region. This was also a major factor in the demise of the French empire in the Seven Years Wars (ca. 1755–1763), when the French tried to take over the Ohio valley from the Seneca and the encroaching Virginians. The resistance movement, which began in May of 1763 and was led by Pontiac, was fought by the Anishinabe nations of northeastern North America against the British imperial government in the Great Lakes area to protect their traditional territories and cultures from "frauds and abuses." Two of the key battles fought in this war included a significant role for the canoe in Anishinabe victories against the English at Michilimackinac and at the siege of Detroit. In June, more than four hundred warriors arrived by birchbark canoe at Michilimackinac and, using the ruse of a game of baggawataway (lacrosse), were able to capture this English fort and trading station, killing seventy out of the ninety English troops and capturing the remainder. So successful was this victory that, using the speed of the canoe, the word of the battle reached Detroit and then another English fort soon thereafter. Again using their canoes, a number of the warriors were able to come from the northern lakes to lay siege to Detroit later that same summer. Although the fort did not fall, the Anishinabe nations initiated peace negotiations under the Covenant Chain of Silver and the resistance movement ended, successfully achieving its objectives. In this resistance movement the Anishinabe nations were not conquered. Even after the war, Sir William Johnson indicated that the English imperial government feared the military power of the Western Confederacy of nations and wished to come to terms with them in a treaty.

The Royal Proclamation of 1763 was promulgated by King George III after the Seven Years War, partly in response to the Anishinabe resistance movement. The proclamation was an English imperial document, among other things, that established the administrative framework for the new English colonies in Quebec and in the rest of North America. It also recognized and reaffirmed the "Indian territory." It established English imperial rules for the treaty-making process under the Covenant Chain as well as for aboriginal trade with nonaboriginal people. The proclamation also recognized the significance of the aboriginal trading system and, with it by extension, the canoe.

During the American Revolution, the canoe was dominated by the larger ships and cannon of the Royal Navy on the Great Lakes. One of the aboriginal objectives, intended to mitigate this "disaster" for themselves and enable them to survive into the twentieth century and beyond, was to try to dovetail their situation with English imperial strategies of trade, of land and emigration policies, and ultimately of white colonization. This they tried to do by entering into a renewed treaty-making process that would safeguard their hunting territories, their waters, and their economies built on the back of the birchbark canoe. For example, treaties were entered into in the 1780s and 1790s to lease or share certain areas with settlers while retaining Anishinabe sovereignty and water rights. The rights to the aboriginal trade and free trade were synonymous, and these rights were intended by British imperial policy to protect the aboriginal nations at a time when Britain was relinquishing its western posts (1796). They were also to be safeguarded in the treaty-making process. The primary motivating factor was the real English fear that, if these rights were not reaffirmed, there would be an "Indian war" in the Great Lakes that would have, they thought, resulted in the loss of upper Canada for the English imperial government. These treaties are still at issue today and the subject of major litigious battles in Canada's courts.

The canoe was the preeminent vehicle for transport and trade. The tradition of aboriginal trade and trading was primarily focused on the waterways flowing to the Atlantic and Arctic coasts, the Saint Lawrence River Valley, the Great Lakes, and the Ohio and Mississippi River Valleys, as well as to the Northwest. In Canada, land became a subject of trade largely through the treaty-making process. It was only much later when these empires, with their military capabilities became overwhelming in terms of manpower, sea power, and arms, that the aboriginal trade became severely disrupted. Gradually, throughout the nineteenth century, the aboriginal trading networks either went underground or shifted northward and north westward—but they

never disappeared. In the late eighteenth century, in response to the aboriginal control of the trade and the presence of Montreal peddlers, the Hudson's Bay Company's traders set up secondary posts inland to attempt to effect more control over the fur trade. The first permanent inland post was established at Cumberland House on Pine Tree Island on the Saskatchewan River in 1783. Thereafter the company did not succeed in controlling the trade, having less than 20 percent of its total. Even then, in the north and the west for much of the nineteenth century the role of canoes in this trade remained of considerable significance until World War II, when bush planes proliferated and became a new means of travel and when limited road networks were built into Canada's vast northern region.

This trade, out of Montreal and into the Great Lakes, Laurentian Shield, and the Ohio Valley, was carried on by aboriginal and Metis in conjunction with many Scottish and Irish traders, like Peter Pond and John Askin, Sr. (1738–1815) of Detroit, in the eighteenth and early nineteenth centuries. It spanned all parts of northeastern North America, a vast geographical area. It lasted for more than 400 years. Peter Pond has left us this description of the canoes and trade from 1774 when he arrived at Prairie du Chien for the annual rendezvous:

> [W]e saw a large collection from every part of the Mississippi who had arrived before us, even from Orleans eight hundred leagues below us. The Indian camp exceeded a mile and a half in length. Here was a sport of all sorts. The French were very numerous. There was not less than one hundred and thirty canoes which came from Mackinac, carrying sixty to eighty hundred weight apiece, all made of birchbark and white cedar for the ribs. These boats from Orleans and Illinois and other parts were numerous.

During the War of 1812, along with the famous role played by Tecumseh, Anishinabe warriors, using birchbark canoes, defended the Indian territory against another American invasion, assisting in the defense of upper Canada and thereby its maintenance as a colony in the British empire for their English allies. At first the Six Nations tried to remain neutral for the first few months of this war, causing much anxiety among the English military establishment. But soon they were heavily participating in the battle of Queenston Heights and later in the battle of Chippewa (where, ironically, Iroquois were also fighting on the American side). Farther west, the Three Fires Confederacy once again rose to the occasion and inflicted early and overwhelming defeats on the Americans using the birchbark canoe as the most important tried-and-true methods of the speed of forest warfare. During the summer of 1812, the Ojibwas and Ottawas captured Fort Michilimackinac by means of a canoe invasion, and this was followed by victories in the south at Brownstown, Magauaga, which led to the capture of Detroit in August of that year. Indeed, Detroit fell largely because the American commander, General William Hull, both feared the Indians and believed that he was surrounded by thousands of them. They also fought successfully at battles at York (Toronto), Beaver Dam, and Lundy's Lane (Niagara). Yet the War of 1812–1814, a "turntable in Canada's history"(Olive Patricia Dickason, in "A Concise History of Canada's First Nations", changed fundamentally the military balance of power in northeastern North America. From the perspective of the English imperial government, the aboriginal nations were no longer required as military allies. This war signalled a 150-year decline in the military significance of the birchbark nations in what is now seen as the southern Canada–Great Lakes basin.

The aboriginal nations—largely thanks to their indomitable spiritual values, of which the canoe is symbolic—have survived and have undergone a renaissance in the twenty-first century. In Canada's north and west, the canoe and the kayak have remained paramount. The indomitable spirit of Tecumseh remains to this day, like the birchbark canoe, personifying the will of the aboriginal nations to resist and to survive in the modern world.

David T. McNab and Ute Lischke

See also Environment and Pollution; Fur Trade; New France and Natives; Trade.

References and Further Reading

Jennings, John, Bruce W. Hodgins, and Doreen Small, eds. 1999. *The Canoe and Canadian Cultures*. Toronto Natural Heritage.

Kent, Timothy J. 1997. *Birchbark Canoes of the Fur Trade*, 2 volumes. Ossineke, MI: Silver Fax Enterprises.

McNab, David T., Bruce Hodgins, and S. Dale Standen. 2001. "Black with Canoes: Aboriginal Resistance and the Canoe: Diplomacy, Trade and Warfare in the Meeting Grounds of Northeastern North America, 1600–1820." In *Technology, Disease and Colonial Conquests, Sixteenth to Eighteenth Centuries. Essays Reappraising the Guns and Germs Theories*. Edited by George Raudzens, 237–292. Leiden, Netherlands, and Boston: Brill International.

Roberts, Kenneth G., and Philip Shackleton. 1983. *The Canoe: A History of the Craft from Panama to the Arctic*. Toronto.

Captivity Narrative

A captivity narrative is a story told by a white person who experienced capture by Indians and his or her return to white society. Sometimes, these accounts were dictated to another person, such as a minister, who oversaw the publication. Of the many such stories published in the late seventeenth and early eighteenth centuries by the captives and their ministers, some accounts bore heavy religious themes of Christian faith testing and redemption. The act of being taken captive by Native Americans was often seen as a sort of biblical punishment for failing to meet God's expectations as a Christian. Therefore, enduring hardship was a necessary element of the narrative. The captivity narrative genre was an autobiographical or, many times, a biographical account of a New England colonist's encounter with Indian cultures and eventual return to Puritan culture. However, for readers who read or heard them from the pulpits as part of sermons at New England meetinghouses, they were seen as a journey of the sinful soul to forgiveness and restoration to God and the Christian community. For the captives to return to and accept their own white community, the actual writers of the narratives made the Native American community appear monstrous and terrible, using language to demean them as agents of the devil to emphasize or exaggerate their conduct toward the white captives. Demonizing Indians gave the readers no doubt as to who possessed divine Christian virtue or on who it was bestowed.

While the attempt to equate captivity to Christian redemption overshadows the individual's actual experience among the Native Americans, the latter is still present. Another important element missing or lacking in the accounts is the fact that far more captives did not return to white society than did. Perhaps not surprisingly, non-Native America found it highly disturbing that their members could choose

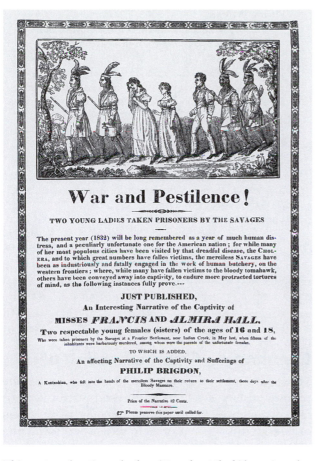

This poster advertises a book written about the kidnapping of two white women by Native Americans in the early nineteenth century. This genre of literature, called captivity narrative, was often sensationalistic and exploited white fears of Native Americans. (Library of Congress)

However, as the eighteenth century wore on, the form of the captivity narrative shifted away from redemption and restoration to become more of a metaphoric fable. After the Boston Massacre, newly added prefaces to republished accounts like Mary Rowlandson's manipulated the captivity narratives for political purposes, turning the story of a woman captured by Native Americans into a metaphor of the struggle of the American colonies (as the character of Mary Rowlandson) against the mother country, Great Britain (Indian captors). Hence, the military power of the Indians threatened the liberty of the Mary Rowlandsons. Through this fabled tale of perseverance, American colonists could overthrow the English tyrant, King George, and be restored to their liberty.

Later captivity narratives from the late eighteenth and into the nineteenth century focus less on Christian moralizing and more on the narrative quality of telling a story, complete with climactic drama. Some of these captivity narratives were so embellished by coauthors (not necessarily by the real captive) that they became more fiction than a factual account of the person's experiences. However, their emphasis remained centered on a white person being taken into captivity by indigenous people, and that emphasis fueled the expansionist policies of the U.S. government. As literacy levels rose, and as the territories of the United States expanded, Americans became increasingly intrigued by the idea of traveling to Indian lands to control and even destroy the Indian nations.

Captivity narratives may reveal important ethnographic information to the reader. Many of these accounts have left a textual record, however biased, of the cultures and mannerisms of some Native nations in the early contact period. Some accounts contradicted descriptions of Indians as the vile people depicted in other captivity narratives. Indeed, it was often the case that surviving captives were adopted into Native family situations, learning the kindness and generosity of their captors.

At other times, captivity narratives reveal the conflicted realities of being a witness to the intimacies of the policies on indigenous nations. For instance, in August 1812, James Van Horne was an infantry private, posted at Fort Dearborn, now modern-day Chicago. His garrison had been ordered to advance to Fort Wayne, approximately 250 miles southeast, to help defend Detroit against the British. Among the sand hills of western Lake Michigan, a mile south of the fort, his garrison met a strategic

to remain among indigenous nations rather than their white cultures. Of those captives who did return, their accounts were written to reaffirm their allegiance to the white community.

Beginning in 1682 with the publication of Mary Rowlandson's account of her capture and later return to white society in *The Sovereignty and Goodness of God, Together with the Faithfulness of his Promises Displayed being a Narrative of the Captivity and restoration of Mrs. Mary Rowlandson*, captivity narratives have long intrigued readers. Many of them became best sellers in their era and long after. Other noted early captivity narratives are *The Redeemed Captive* by John Williams (1704), as well as various captivity narratives authored by Cotton Mather about Hannah Swarton (1697), Hannah Dustan (1697), again John Williams (1706), Mary French (1706), and Hannah Bradley (1707).

ambush led predominately by 500 Potawatomi and Winnebago (Ho-Chunk) warriors. Within fifteen minutes of battle, according to his narrative, the Indian nations secured surrender and led the survivors back to the fort. From there, over the coming afternoon and night, prisoners were divided up among various tribes, and Van Horne was made a prisoner of a family led by an old man. The next morning, he journeyed southwest with his captors into the Illinois prairie in an area that is now Kane and Kendall Counties of Illinois.

As he entered the village, his master prevented fellow tribesmen from killing Van Horne. Over the coming weeks, he feared for his life but actually had a good deal of freedom to move around in the village. His master named him *Shessup*, meaning duck, which he attributed to his being short. It appears his master knew some English and was able to communicate with him to some degree. Soon, his American clothing was removed, his skin was rubbed with yellow clay, his beard was plucked out, and his head was shaved. Although he had met up with white traders along the way, asking them to ransom him, they all refused. In the meantime, he took on the tasks his master required of him, doing all he could to be compliant. In the late fall, he helped his master hunt. In February, he relates that they moved out of the village to go to the sugar camps. In April, along with packs of furs, he was bought by traders of French descent; he was then sent on to Detroit to be taken prisoner by the British.

Van Horne's account is interesting for the information, prior to white settlement, on the activities this particular Potawatomi village engaged in and the times of the year they engaged in them. He relates the unhappy fortunes of some of his fellow prisoners, but without language colored with demeaning adjectives and expletives toward the victors, as is found in earlier captivity narratives. Van Horne was a soldier, taken prisoner by his enemy, and exchanged. Such is this particular type of captivity narrative.

Sally Bennett

References and Further Reading
Axtell, James. 1975. "The White Indians of Colonial America." *The William and Mary Quarterly* 3rd ser., 32, no. 1 (January): 55–88.

Derounian-Stodola, Kathryn Zabelle. 1998. *Women's Captivity Narratives.* New York: Penguin.

Drinnon, Richard. 1972. *White Savage, the Case of John Dunn Hunter.* New York: Schoken Books.

Foster, William Henry. 2003. *The Captors' Narrative: Catholic Women and Their Puritan Men on the Early American Frontier.* Ithaca, NY: Cornell University Press.

Quaife, Milo M., ed. 1917. *The Indian Captivity of O. M. Spencer.* Cleveland, OH: Lakeside Press.

Sieminiski, Greg. 1990. "The Puritan Captivity Narrative and the Politics of the American Revolution." *American Quarterly* 42, no. 1 (March): 35–56.

Strong, Pauline Turner. 1999. *Captivating Selves, Captivating Others: The Politics and Poetics of the Colonial American Captivity Narratives.* Boulder, CO: Westview Press.

Van Horne, James. 1817. *Narrative of the Captivity and Sufferings of James Van Horne, Who was Nine Months a Prisoner of the Indians on the Plains of Michigan.* Middleboro, MA: Lawrence B. Romaine, Weathercock House.

Ceremonies, Criminalization of

The institutions of Christian religion are among the prominent forces that have eclipsed Native American sovereignty. Unfortunately, the most basic beliefs of Christianity—love of neighbor as self and the brotherhood of all mankind—were not fully practiced by many of the so-called believers when they made contact with Native Americans. Instead they were guided by other religious notions—that only believers could find eternal salvation, that nonbelievers must be converted, that those who rejected conversion were beyond the enjoyment of basic human liberties. The first Spanish conquistadors justified military conquests of the Native peoples on the basis of these "Christian" ideals. Missionaries stripped Native Americans of their cultural identities and even reduced some individuals to slavery and peonage in efforts to convert them. Certainly, conversions to Christianity were won with love and proper persuasion. However, most contacts between the European Christian world and the Native Americans lacked the true spirit of Christianity.

Cultural conflict and the degradation of sovereignty sprang from the fact that Christian institutions are not focused on specific places and specific people. Religious leaders felt a need to spread the belief system to all peoples everywhere. They interpreted the absence of Christianity among Native Americans as an absence of all religion. However, Native peoples did have developed religious belief systems and rituals well before the time of contact with Europeans.

Although traditional Native American religions shared many attributes that set them apart from Christianity, there were also religious distinctions among the tribes. Native nations that relied on hunting and gathering for their sustenance used animal ceremonialism; agricultural nations featured rain and fertility rituals in their religions. Hunting groups focused on a male supreme being, while the agricultural societies worshipped both gods and goddesses. The agricultural nations saw creation coming out of the ground, and spirits returned to the earth after death and burial. For this reason burial places are of central importance. Hunting societies looked toward the sky as the source of both creation and heavenly afterlife (Hultkrantz, 1993, 257–282).

The traditional Native American nations were tied to specific geographical places—even if they migrated as seasonal hunters or gatherers. Therefore, their religions are much more place specific than Christian sects. Christianity assigns sacred meanings to locations such as Bethlehem and Jerusalem; however, Native places are less the objects of worship than they are specific mountains or lakes or woods perhaps representing the place where a nation of peoples was created or ended a long migration. As the Jewish nation considers Israel to be a sacred land given to them by God, the Navajo Nation considers their Arizona and New Mexico lands to be sacred. The boundaries of their home are four sacred mountains: the Big Sheep Peak to the north, Mount Taylor to the south, the San Francisco Peaks to the west, and Peludo Mountain in the east. To have these mountains near

Cheyennes and Arapahoes perform a ghost dance, one of the first Indian ceremonies to be formally criminalized by the U.S. government. (Library of Congress)

and to be able to worship in the mountains is a critical factor in Navajo religion—much as the Wailing Wall of Jerusalem is a critical place for the Jewish faithful (Deloria, 1994, 267–282).

The historical hostility of Christians to Native American religions stemmed not only from a desire to convert but also from the desire to control the lands of the Native American nations. Conflict was inevitable as Euro-Americans recognized Native rituals not as the religious ceremonies they were but as elements in a power struggle for a continent. A misreading of a religious ceremony, confusing it for a desire for a political uprising against the Euro-Americans, led federal government officials—reservation agents and military commanders—into one of the most tragic episodes in the history of the United States.

On the first day of 1889 the Paiute prophet Wovoka had a vision in which he saw the Creator and was told to instruct Native peoples to live in peace with whites and to participate in a "dance in a circle." If they did this they would be able to travel to the other world where they would be reunited with their friends and relatives. Wovoka's teachings quickly spread and they became known as the Ghost Dance Religion. Although it was a ritual of peace, the federal government attempted to suppress the Ghost Dance. A band of Lakota Sioux under Big Foot persisted in the ceremony. A series of miscommunications and blunders by government officials culminated in disaster. In December 1890, federal troops opened fire on the band, killing several hundred men, women, and children. It was the worst mass killing of Native Americans by the military in U.S. history (Waldman and Braun, 1985, 158–159).

Other Native American ceremonies and rituals were also banned or suppressed by the government. The Sun Dance involved flesh piercing and long periods of gazing into the sun, during which time a tribal member would experience visions. The dance was included in a general ceremony of friendship and thanksgiving, but the U.S. government saw it differently. The dance was made a punishable offense in 1883. Tribes engaging in the ceremony could have supplies promised in treaties denied to them.

Northern Pacific nations had a ceremony called the potlatch. The ritual built tribal solidarity because individuals would give away their possessions to other members of their group. Christians also sought to suppress this ritual, although the ceremony did seem to reflect teachings of Christ. Nineteenth-century Christians, however, saw the potlatch as antithetical to their newfound capitalist value system, a system that had been successfully merged with their biblical teachings (e.g., the Protestant ethic). In Canada, the government made the practice of the potlatch a criminal offense (Waldman and Braun 1985, 192; Champagne, 1994b, 230).

Native Americans utilized the peyote plant for religious and medicinal purposes long before their first contact with Europeans. Peyote ceremonies became widespread among western and southwestern nations in the late nineteenth century. The active ingredient in peyote is a mind-altering stimulant called mescaline. During all-night prayer sessions the peyote is either chewed or ingested as a tea. Participants in the ceremonies may have visions, hallucinations, or even out-of-body experiences. They also may experience nausea.

As the peyote ceremonies became popular among tribes across the country, opposition to the use of peyote developed. Traditional tribal religious leaders—shaman and medicine men—opposed it. Some tribes passed rules against the use of peyote and the peyote ceremonies. Government officials—both federal and state—considered peyote to be an illegal substance. Several states passed laws against its use, and general federal drug laws were interpreted at times to include bans on its use. In an attempt to have its use brought under the protection of religious freedoms, members of several tribes established the Native American Church in 1918, to which only Native Americans could belong. Peyotism was incorporated into its beliefs and activities. Aside from holding peyote ceremonies, the Native American Church was similar to other Christian organizations. It advocated self-respect, brotherhood among Native Americans, morality, sobriety, and charity; today it has about 400,000 members (Stewart, 1987).

In 1954 a court ruling repudiated the idea that peyote use could be covered by the First Amendment's protections of the free exercise of religion. In 1970 peyote was classified as a hallucinogen under the Controlled Substance Act. At the same time, however, the Native American Church began to win support for its position. Several states recognized the ceremonies as proper religious activities and exempted them from their drug enforcement concerns. By 1990, twenty-eight states allowed peyote for Native American religious exercises, while twenty-two did not.

The uneven treatment of the ceremonies became a matter of serious debate after the Supreme Court ruled in *Employment Division, Department of*

Human Resources of Oregon v. Smith (1990) that a state could fire a civil servant for simply having participated in such a ceremony. Pressures on Congress were successful and in 1994 Native American religious use of peyote won a general exemption from all drug enforcement activities (Getches et al., 1993, 752–767; Peregoy, 1995, 1).

Native Americans also use eagle feathers in religious ceremonies, and they revere them as sacred objects. However, to get feathers, birds usually must be killed. The Bald Eagle Protection Act (1972) prohibited the killing of the birds. In recognition of the religious nature of the feathers, the Secretary of the Interior can issue permits to Native Americans allowing them to selectively take eagles as long as the overall conservation mandate of the legislation is met. The killing of the eagles must be strictly and solely for the purpose of gaining religious feathers for Native peoples (Getches et al., 1993, 765–766).

Native American medicine men have also won an exemption to customs searches of their sacred medicine bags. The medicine men would travel to Canada to gather herbs, rocks, shells, arrowheads, and other objects for their bags. The bags would then be used in healing rituals. However, if a bag was opened by a nonholy person, such as a government customs official, its religious powers would be wasted.

Recent decades have seen attempts by the federal government to reverse old policies of suppression of Native peoples and to replace them with policies supporting Native American lifestyles. This has been quite evident in the field of religion.

One decision of great symbolic and theoretical importance came with the passage of the Indian Civil Rights Act of 1968. This congressional action has also been called the Indian Bill of Rights. However, the practical impact of the Act has not been significant. The U.S. Bill of Rights (essentially provisions on habeas corpus and bills of attainder in the body of the Constitution as well as the first ten amendments and the Fourteenth Amendment) protects persons from arbitrary actions taken by federal and state (and local) governments.

Native American tribal governments have been in a kind of no man's land—being neither the U.S. government nor a state government. For more than 100 years, courts refused to impose the protections of the Bill of Rights to persons (for the most part Native Americans) in their relationships with tribal governments. As a practical matter, most of the tribal governments established since the Indian Reorganization Act of 1934 (and many before) had protective bills of rights in their own constitutions. Some did not.

The Act of 1968 specified that most of the protections of the Bill of Rights would apply to all Native American reservations. Of major importance was the provision establishing the right of habeas corpus. The Act also guaranteed that people would enjoy a free exercise of religion on reservation lands. However, one noticeable omission from the Act was the prohibition against the establishment of religion. The national government can do nothing about the establishment of a national church, and state governments are not permitted to establish religions. However, today a tribal government may take actions that would establish an official religion. Native American religions may receive tribal funds, even if the ultimate source of the funds is the federal government. Religious ceremonies may be sponsored by the tribes, unless the tribes themselves prohibit such religious establishments.

In 1978 Congress felt a further need to support the official quality of traditional Native American religion. Congress "affirmed" that "traditional religions" were an "indispensable and irreplaceable" part of Native American life. By resolution of the two houses—the House of Representatives and the Senate—Congress proclaimed that tribes would have religious freedom. As this was a two-house resolution instead of an Act, the matter did not require presidential action. The president could not veto the resolution. President Carter had indicated that he had major difficulties with having the U.S. government endorse particular types of religious activities.

The resolution directed all federal government agencies to explore their policies and actions to ensure that they did not deny Native Americans full access to religious sites and sacred lands. Agencies also had to guarantee that no policies were impeding the free practice of religions by Native Americans. Senator James Abourezk of South Dakota sponsored the resolution. He felt it was necessary to give Native Americans a statutory basis for lawsuits that could protect their religious sites and ceremonies. Supporters of the resolution argued that the U.S. government could give special treatment to Native American religions without violating the constitutional prohibition against the establishment of religions. By some manner of logic they suggested that the prohibition might not apply because Native American religions were not "proselytizing" religions. There was no fear of the conflict between church and state because Native Americans did not seek to spread their religions the way Christians did. By the same strange logic, Congress might appropriate funds for Jewish synagogues. Opponents worried that the resolution would require giving Native Americans access to sacred sites on private lands, allow Native Americans to use peyote (still considered illegal in much of the nation), and limit the protections of the Endangered Species Act.

Abourezk and the other supporters misinterpreted the resolution. The opponents had nothing to worry about. Several law cases took any "teeth" out of the resolution that the supporters might have wished it to have. The Cherokee Nation tried to stop the construction of a dam that would have flooded burial sites and sacred lands. In the case of *Sequoyah v. T.V.A.* (1980), the Supreme Court ruled against Native peoples because they did not own land in the area.

Another case arose after the National Park Service permitted private companies to send excursion boats to the Rainbow Bridge rock formation near Lake Powell, Arizona. Tourists visited the area and drank alcoholic beverages in excess. They were loud and abusive, and they threw beer cans under the natural rock formation. The Rainbow Bridge was the home of gods worshipped by the Navajo Nation. The high court recognized that the actions of the tourists impeded the Navajo's right to practice their religion. However, if the tourists were to be stopped by federal action, that action would in the eyes of the court amount to an establishment of religion. It would be prohibited by the first amendment. As with the Sequoyah case, the Navajo Nation lost the dispute because the land was outside of their reservation (*Badoni v. Higginson* 1981).

In the 1988 case of *Lyng v. Northwest Indian Cemetery Protective Association*, the Supreme Court again ruled against the Native Americans. The court gave its blessings to the construction of a logging road by the U.S. Forest Service. The project in the Six River National Forest of California disturbed sacred burial sites of three different Native nations.

William N. Thompson

See also American Indian Religious Freedom Act; Anglicans; Baptist Church; Black Hills; Blue Lake, New Mexico; Boarding Schools, United States and Canada; Bureau of Indian Affairs: Establishing the Existence of an Indian Tribe; Canada, Indian Policies of; Episcopal Church; Fishing Rights; Ghost Dance Religion; Mission System, Spanish; Missionaries, French Jesuit; Mormon Church; Native American Church of North America; Potlatch; Praying Villages of Massachusetts; Pueblo Revolt; Sacred Sites; Sun Dance; Worldviews and Values.

References for Further Reading

Champagne, Duane. 1994. *Chronology of Native North American History.* Detroit: Gale Press.

Deloria, Vine, Jr. *God Is Red,* 2d ed. 1994. Golden, CO: Fulcrum Publishing.

Getches, David, Charles Wilkinson, and Robert A. Williams Jr. *Federal Indian Law,* 2d ed. 1993. St. Paul, MN: West Publishing.

Hultkrantz, Ake. "Native Religions of North America" in H. Byron Earhart, ed. *Religious Traditions of the World.* 1993. San Francisco: Harper-Collins.

Peregoy, Robert M. "Congress Overturns Supreme Court's Peyote Ruling." *NARF Legal Review* 20, no. 1 (January 1995).

Stewart, Omer. *Peyote Religion.* 1987. Norman: University of Oklahoma Press.

Walman, Carl and Molly Braun. *Atlas of the North American Indian.* 1985. New York: Facts on File.

Code Talkers, Navajo

During World War II, Navajo soldiers created an unbreakable code that was based on their Native language, and more than 400 Navajos served in the U.S. Marine Corps as radio operators. Working in pairs as transmitter and receiver, they frustrated the repeated attempts of Japanese cryptographers and were credited with helping to shorten the war and saving thousands of lives. They used Navajo words adapted for war, like "hummingbird" for fighter plane, "eggs" for bombs, and "rabbit trail" for road. At the battle of Iwo Jima, the Navajo code talkers handled more than 800 messages in forty-eight hours.

Following the crippling attack on Pearl Harbor in December 1941, the American armed forces continued to suffer setbacks at the hands of the Japanese. One of their biggest problems was communication. Many of the Japanese code breakers had been educated in the United States and were familiar with American slang and idioms. They were thus able to break any military code the Americans created.

Philip Johnston, a middle-aged civil engineer living in Los Angeles, read about the problem the military was having and suggested an unusual solu-

A two-man team of Navajo code talkers attached to a Marine regiment in the Pacific relay orders over the field radio using their native language. The Navajo language was a particularly effective code during World War II, as it is not a written language and only a relatively small number of people understand it. (Corbis)

tion. Johnston, the child of missionaries, had grown up on the Navajo reservation and spoke the language fluently. At the early age of nine, he had served as the interpreter for President Theodore Roosevelt during a meeting with Navajo elders (Paul, 1973, 8). He understood the complexity of the Navajo language and saw its possible use.

While other Native languages, like Choctaw and Comanche, had been used for battlefield communication, there had been problems with their inadequacy in describing modern military terms. Johnston's proposal was to use the Navajo language to create a secret military code. The Navajo language had many advantages as a code. Few outside the Navajo reservation spoke or understood it. There was no written form for others to study, and a slight variation in inflection could radically change the meaning of a word. In short, to outsiders it was unintelligible.

Johnston convinced Lieutenant Colonel James E. Jones, the Marines Signal Corps Communications Officer, that his idea was worth a try, and together they set up a test. Two teams of Navajos were sent to separate rooms and given a typical field order to transmit, in their own language, to their companions several rooms away. When translated back into English, the message received proved to be an accurate copy of the original field order. The Marines were amazed at the speed and accuracy, and the test was pronounced a rousing success.

Johnston initially proposed to recruit 200 Navajos. The Marines were more cautious. They suggested recruiting thirty. That way, if things didn't work out, they weren't out that much time and money (Wilson, 1997, 7). Eventually twenty-nine Navajos were selected and sent to San Diego for basic training. They were told they would be "specialists" and were officially designated as the 382nd Platoon, U.S. Marine Corps. Following their basic training, the Navajo Marines were moved to Camp Pendleton in Oceanside, California.

In addition to their regular duties, the Navajo soldiers began to create a new military code. The code's words had to be short, easy to learn, and easy to remember. The men devised a two-part code. The first part was a twenty-six-letter alphabet that used the Navajo names for animals and birds, plus a few other words for unusual letters like "q," "x," and "z." The second part was a 211-word English vocabulary and their Navajo equivalents like "iron fish" for submarine and "buzzard" for bomber.

In August 1942, the first group of Navajos was sent to join the First Marine Division at Guadalcanal. Major General Alexander Vandegrift was so impressed with their performance that he immediately requested eighty-three more Navajos be assigned to his division. By August of 1943, nearly 200 Navajos had gone through the code talker program. The staff sergeant in charge was Philip Johnston, who had originated the idea.

The code talkers soon won a reputation for bravery and the ability to do their job under the worst of conditions. One of the code talkers recalled a combat experience:

> One night we held them [the Japanese] down. If you so much as held up your head six inches you were gone, the fire was so intense. And then in the wee hours, with no relief on our side or theirs, there was a dead standstill. Anything—any sound from anywhere—called for fire. If there was any movement—the breaking of a little twig—maybe there would be a hundred shots there. You just sat or lay there, gun cocked. It must have gotten so that this one Japanese couldn't take it anymore. He got up and yelled and screamed at the top of his voice and dashed over to our trench, swinging a long samurai sword. I imagine he was shot from 25 to 40 times before he fell.
>
> There was a buddy with me in the trench. For four days we had no relief . . . hardly anything to eat; but we had to stay on the line. I had a cord tied around my wrist and to my

buddy's hand. If I pulled the string and he pulled back there in the dark, I knew he was still alive. But that Japanese cut him across the throat with that long sword. He was still gasping through his windpipe. When he exhaled, blood gushed. And the sound of him trying to breathe was horrible. He died without help, of course. When the Jap struck, warm blood spattered all over my hand that was handling the microphone. I was calling [in code] for help. They tell me that in spite of what happened, every syllable of my message came through (Paul, 1973, 2).

The code talkers served with all six Marine divisions in the Pacific. They participated in major Marine assaults on the Solomons, the Marianas, Peleliu, and Iwo Jima. Major Howard Connor, the Fifth Marine Division's Signal Officer, said that "The entire operation was directed by Navajo code. . . . During the two days that followed the initial landings I had six Navajo radio nets working around the clock. . . . They sent and received over 800 messages without an error. Were it not for the Navajo Code Talkers, the Marines never would have taken Iwo Jima" (Wilson, 1997, 20).

The code talkers were among the first to hear the Japanese had surrendered and the war was over. They helped to spread the word to their fellow Marines. By the end of the war, more than 400 Navajos had completed training at Camp Pendleton, and most had been placed with combat units overseas. After the war, they returned to anonymous lives on the reservation. They had a hard time obtaining the few jobs that existed, in part because of the secrecy of their war mission. When asked by prospective employers about their experience in the Marine Corps, they couldn't tell them. They were honored by their own people, but their story was virtually unknown to most Americans.

The exemplary service of the Navajo code talkers did help to earn Native Americans some basic rights. Native Americans had been granted citizenship in 1924, but in states like Arizona, New Mexico, and Utah, they were still not permitted to vote. In response to a 1944 letter from a Navajo soldier, James M. Stewart, Superintendent of the Navajo Indian Service, wrote, "While you are fighting on the battlefront, a fight must be waged here on the home front to obtain for you the right accorded to all free peoples." In 1948, New Mexico and Arizona gave Native

Americans the right to vote. Utah followed in 1953 (Newmiller, 2005, 7).

The Navajo code was not declassified until 1968 and a year later, the Navajo code talkers were officially honored at a Marine convention in Chicago. A special medallion was struck for all members of this unique unit. There is now a Code Talkers Association that holds regular meetings on the Navajo Reservation in Window Rock, Arizona. In 2002, a hit movie called *Wind Talkers,* starring Nicolas Cage, brought the story of the Navajo code talkers to the big screen. While perpetuating some myths, it finally brought these warriors the recognition their meritorious service had earned (Miller, 2002, 3).

Hugh Reilly

References and Further Reading

Jevec, Adam, and Lee Ann Potter. 2001. "The Navajo Code Talkers: A Secret World War II Memorandum." *Social Education* 65, no. 5: 262–269.

Miller, Samantha, and Inez Russell. 2002, "The Word Warriors." *People* 57, no. 23: 111–112.

Nichols, Judy. 1995. "Navajo 'Code Talkers' Were Vital Link in Pacific War." *Christian Science Monitor* 87, no. 137: 9

Newmiller, William. 2005. "The Navajo Code Talkers and Their Photographer." *War Literature & the Arts: An International Journal of the Humanities* 17, nos. 1–2: 6–11.

Papich, Bill. 2000. "Cheeseburgers and Code Talkers." *American Heritage* 51, no. 8: 11–12.

Paul, Doris A. 1973. *The Navajo Code Talkers.* Philadelphia, PA: Dorrance & Company.

Wilson, William R. 1997. "Code Talkers." *American History* 31, no. 6: 16–22.

Confederacies

Introduction

Confederacies have been identified as a method of governance among indigenous peoples in North America both before and after contact with Europeans. The confederacies that will be considered here are the Blackfoot Confederacy, Council of the Three Fires, Creek Confederacy, Old North-West (Delaware) Confederacy, Huron-Wendat (Wyandot) Confederacy, Iroquois (Haudenosaunee) Confederacy, Seven Nations of Canada, Wabanaki Confederacy, and Wabash Confederacy.

Not every conceivable regrouping labeled as a confederacy is discussed here. For example, it is possible to find references to the Illini Confederation and the Neutral Confederacy. The Illini Confederation, however, is most likely to have been one large, segmented tribe rather than an example of distinct nations joined together (Fester, 2004). The Neutral Confederacy was also not truly a confederacy. The Neutrals were one nation, living in several villages along the western shore of Lake Ontario, Canada, and were an Iroquoian-speaking people who farmed the land much like the Huron and the Iroquois. They were given the name Neutral or Neutral Confederacy by the French because they chose to stay out of the Huron-Iroquois wars (Halton, 2004).

A confederacy can be defined as a league or agreement between two or more independent nations who unite for their mutual welfare and the furtherance of their common aims. A confederacy usually involves political connections by which a central government is created to govern the nations; however, each nation retains its sovereign powers for domestic purposes (Nolan and Nolan, 1990, 296).

Among indigenous peoples in North America, confederacies were not uncommon. Alliances developed primarily out of a need for mutual assistance and cooperation. Indigenous nations understood that there was strength in unity and that it was beneficial to have the support of other neighboring nations for trade and in times of difficulty and warfare. Although a number of confederacies were and are enduring, the general interpretation of a confederacy does not take into account the fact that membership was not always static and, in some cases, that alliances of a more temporary nature were formed as the need arose and dissolved when the need was no longer there. The issue of whether a temporary alliance constituted the creation of an entirely new confederacy or merely an extension of an already existing one has been often debated by historians, anthropologists, ethnologists, and even indigenous nations themselves and remains a question of interpretation.

Blackfoot Confederacy

The term "Blackfoot" is generally used in Canada and the term "Blackfeet" is used in the United States. However, as these people preceded the postcontact political entities, they remain connected, regardless of terminology or the existence of the forty-ninth parallel. "Blackfoot" is the term used in this article.

The Blackfoot Confederacy includes the Piikani/Peigan, North Piikani/Peigan, Kainai/Blood, and Siksika /Blackfoot nations. Until 1861, the confederacy also included the Gros Ventres (Samek, 1987, 11). While the original Blackfoot territory included present-day Alberta, Saskatchewan (Canada), and northern Montana (United States), the Blackfoot people eventually settled on reservations in Alberta and Montana (Samek, 1987, 12).

The member nations of the Blackfoot Confederacy shared a common culture and language and were known for their military prowess. They were a nomadic people who lived on the plains, hunting the vast buffalo herds. The member nations were also involved in the trade of buffalo robes, guns, and horses, sometimes trading as far as the northeastern coast of North America (MNSU, 2005).

The confederacy was at the height of its power in the middle of the nineteenth century when smallpox epidemics, the massacre of the buffalo herds, and battles with European settlers and gold prospectors began decimating the population and encroaching on Blackfoot territory. The Blackfoot continued to travel back and forth, as they always had, across what came to be the Canada–United States border. Samek believes that the signing of Treaty No. 7 with Canada created a separation within the Confederacy to a certain extent, since some people were now looking to the Canadian government to correct past wrongs, honor treaty provisions, and settle the question of territory, while others were looking to the United States government (Samek, 1987, 13–14).

In the United States, the American government entered into three treaty processes with some of the Blackfoot residing in Montana. The first treaty, in 1855, included other indigenous nations as well and resulted in the cession of large portions of Blackfoot territory for use by settlers. In 1865 and 1868, the U.S. government attempted to settle the land question, but both times, the U.S. Senate failed to ratify the treaties due to violence and fighting between Blackfoot and settlers. Many have questioned whether the indigenous nations really understood these "treaties" (essentially land cessions) and whether they knew that they were giving up their lands forever. It has been argued that the member nations of the Blackfoot Confederacy believed they were signing peace treaties (Samek, 1987, 15).

Council of the Three Fires

Although not formally a confederacy, the Council of the Three Fires, composed of the Pottawatomis, Ottawas (Odawas), and Ojibways (Chippewas), conducted themselves as such and allied themselves for political and military purposes. The Pottawatomi chiefs were known as the Firekeepers and their central meeting place was generally at Michilimackinack (Union of Ontario Indians, 2004). This confederacy also maintained relations, during the 1600s and 1700s, with others such as the Iroquois Confederacy and the Sauk, Fox, Menominees, Hurons, Winnebagos, Sioux, and British and French Nations. Again, relations between nations were not always static and changes such as the rise of the fur trade brought competition and fighting to once friendly nations (Fester, 2004). By the mid-1700s, the Council of the Three Fires became the founding group for what Sir William Johnson called "the Western Lakes Confederacy," a union of Algonquin, Nippissing, Sauk, Fox, Menominees, Winnebagos, Crees, Hurons, and Toughkamiwons (Union of Ontario Indians, 2004).

While the original Three Fires territory was quite expansive and included large portions of the states of Indiana, Illinois, Michigan, and Wisconsin (Potawatomi, Ottawa, and Chippewa) and the Province of Ontario, Canada (Ojibway/Chippewa), the Council of the Three Fires was severely handicapped by the U.S. government removal policies of the 1800s, as were many indigenous nations and confederacies. A large number of Pottawatomis were removed to Kansas and Oklahoma, while some sought refuge in the northern Wisconsin Territory and others settled with confederacy relatives in Ontario, Canada, specifically Walpole Island, Kettle Point, and Manitoulin Island (ITCMI, 2001). The remaining member nations of the Three Council Fires were forced to settle on small reservations in Michigan, Indiana, and Ontario.

Creek Confederacy

The Creeks were one of the largest nations in the southern United States in terms of population and territory, residing in what is now present-day Georgia, Alabama, Florida, and South Carolina, and they were part of the cultural tradition identified by anthropologists as the Mound Builders. Confederacy territory by the end of the eighteenth century spanned approximately 62,130 square miles

(Ethridge, 2003, 23), from the Oconee River in Georgia (the upper Creeks) to the Tombigbee River in Alabama (the lower Creeks), and included seventy-three towns for a total of about 15,000 to 20,000 people (Ethridge, 2003, 31).

When the Creeks joined together in a confederacy, their system of governance had changed significantly from that of the Mound Builders. European diseases and slave trading devastated the Creek population, and the surviving people, forever changed by their experience, allied themselves together as a means of protection and survival (Ethridge, 2003, 23–24).

Nevertheless some argue that the Creeks themselves did not constitute a homogeneous nation (Ethridge, 2003, 278, n. 1) and were not a true confederacy because they were not united with other distinct nations. There was no permanent central government for the Creek Confederacy, and the focus of Creek life was the village rather than the nation. Each Creek tribe lived in an independent village with its own political structure, and there was no obligation for a village to act in accordance with a decision from the national council. It is the union of these independent villages that is said to have constituted the Creek Confederacy (Muscogee [Creek] Nation, 2005). Interestingly, there was a common Creek language across the villages, in addition to a tribal village language. This common language was also known to the Chickasaws and the Choctaws (Golden Ink, 2005).

In 1814, the Creek signed a treaty with the United States in which they ceded approximately two-thirds of their land. Later cessions further reduced their territory and, between 1836 and 1837, over 20,000 Creeks were forcibly removed by the U.S. Army to Indian Territory (Oklahoma) (Muscogee [Creek] Nation, 2005).

Old Northwest Confederacy

The Old Northwest Confederacy, which is sometimes called the Delaware Confederacy, was composed of the Delawares, Wyandots, Chippewas, Ottawas, Pottawatomis, Shawnees, and Miamis. The Wyandots were elected as the Keepers of the Council Fire, where all matters of importance were discussed. It is interesting to note that the Chippewas, Ottawas, and Pottawatomis were also members of the Council of the Three Fires around the same time period, a fact that reveals the fluidity of relations between nations. The confederacy contin-

ued until the member nations were forcibly removed by the United States from the northeastern United States (the old northwest) to Indian Territory. The member nations continue to live on reservations in Kansas and Oklahoma to this day. Some Delaware moved north into Canada to avoid the removal. Their descendents continue to live on two small reserves in Moraviatown and Munsee, Ontario (Hahn, 2005). Eventually, around 1848, the Council Fire was rekindled and the Wyandots were again appointed as Keepers of the Council Fire (Hahn, 2005).

Huron-Wendat (Wyandot)

The Huron Confederacy is thought to have originated in the 1600s. It consisted of five nations, known in the Huron language as the Attignawantans, Attigeenongnahacs, Arendaronons, Tahontaenrats, and the Ataronchronons. Although the Hurons dominated central and eastern Ontario and developed alliances with the Tobacco and Neutral nations, as well as with the neighboring Ojibways, the Huron Confederacy was in constant battle with the Iroquois Confederacy, to whom they eventually lost much of their territory. While principal, or peace, chiefs were chosen to tend to civil affairs and participate in the national and confederate councils, other chief titles existed for addressing specific issues. For example, war chiefs were responsible for defense in times of war (Sioui, 1999, 129–131).

The confederacy Council met several times a year and addressed issues of concern to all member nations, such as political developments, trade, important feasts, major expeditions for hunting, fishing, or trading, in addition to the replacement of chiefs who had passed on. The Councils also served to reinforce and renew ties among the nations (Sioui, 1999, 132). The Hurons eventually settled in Wendake, Quebec, Canada. Some Hurons who were removed by the United States settled on reservations in Kansas, Oklahoma, and Michigan.

Iroquois Confederacy

The Iroquois Confederacy (Haudenosaunee or Rotinohshonni) is also referred to as the Five Nations Confederacy or the Six Nations Confederacy. This confederacy was originally composed of five nations: Mohawks, Oneidas, Onondagas, Senecas, and Cayugas. In the early eighteenth century, when the Tuscaroras were forced to leave their lands in

North Carolina by settlers and the U.S. government, they became the sixth nation to join the confederacy.

The Iroquois Confederacy represents one of the more static confederacies in the sense that the five (and then six) nations remained members throughout its existence. This was in keeping with the general policy of the Iroquois Confederacy to adopt other people and sometimes entire nations that were smaller and weaker—the adoptees taking on the language and culture of the Iroquois, reflecting the dominance of the Iroquois Confederacy in the 1600s and 1700s.

There are similarities between the Huron and Iroquois Confederacies in that both were matrilineal societies that grouped individuals into clans. An individual's clan was inherited from the mother and all individuals within a clan were considered to be one large family. Certain clans (the Bear, Turtle, and Wolf Clans among the Iroquois) were found in all of the nations. This helped to unify the nations in the confederacy, because family members were present in each of the nations. Chiefs were selected by the clan mothers, and a chief could also be deposed by the women if he did not behave in an honorable, selfless manner.

Each nation selected its chiefs, as representatives of each clan, to govern its own internal matters. When the nations joined together to discuss issues affecting all nations, each would first come to a decision on the matter before submitting its views to the confederacy Council. At the Council, matters would be discussed, sometimes for several days, and there was a concerted effort to consider all views and arrive at a solution that was acceptable to all.

The Iroquois Confederacy continues to exist and function to this day, although, like most indigenous governments, U.S. and Canadian policies of removal or relocation, extermination, and assimilation have severely affected its ability to function as it did in the past.

Seven Nations of Canada

The Seven Nations of Canada, also sometimes referred to as the Seven Fires, represents an alliance between the Iroquois (including the Mohawks of Akwesasne, Kahnawake, Kanesatake, and the Onondagas of Oswegatchie), Hurons, Abenakis, and Anishnabes (Algonquin and Nippissing). The Seven Nations initially allied themselves with the French and had for the most part adopted the Catholic religion. However, during the American Revolution and the War of 1812, the Seven Nations of Canada were an important ally of Britain in the wars between that country and the United States.

Some have argued that the Seven Nations of Canada is not a true confederacy, in the sense that it was merely an extension of the Iroquois Confederacy, representing a group of individuals who branched off from the main Confederacy due to differing views and beliefs. An important point to keep in mind is that the Seven Nations of Canada were really seven communities joined together, rather than seven entire nations. Even within each community, individuals might consider themselves to be loyal to the Iroquois Confederacy, while others might consider themselves loyal to the Seven Nations. One explanation for this confusing designation is that the term Seven Nations of Canada was primarily a European designation that may have been applied more out of a need to impress on enemies the strength of their Native allies, rather than a recognition that each community of this alliance was a separate nation (Bonaparte, 1999).

Wabanaki Confederacy

The Wabanaki Confederacy grouped together several Algonquian nations, namely the Mi'kmaq, Maliseet, Passamaquoddy, and Penobscot nations. These nations lived along the eastern seaboard in what is now the state of Maine and the Canadian provinces of New Brunswick, Nova Scotia, Prince Edward Island, and Newfoundland (Leavitt and Francis, 1990, 1).

The confederacy broadened its ranks in the mideighteenth century (Leavitt and Francis, 1990, 12) by bringing in other nations and communities. Although Speck seems to suggest that this created a confederacy all of its own, it would appear that this was rather just an extension of the original Wabanaki Confederacy. In either case, the Wabanakis extended their ranks to include the Ottawas (who acted as an advisory body) and the Mohawks of Kahnawake and Kanesatake. At one time, according to Speck, the capital of the Wabanaki Confederacy was at Kahnawake (Leavitt and Francis, 1990, 12).

Speck also argues that the presence and influence of the Mohawks and of the Iroquois Confederacy generally is reflected in the similarities in the system of governance and that the Wabanaki modeled their system of government on the existing Iroquois system (Leavitt and Francis, 1990, 12). In addition, Speck suggests that the Wabanaki Confederacy was more or less a regrouping of Christianized tribes acting under the influence of the Mohawks ". . . who found themselves recasting in their own way under new conditions the old original principles of the Iroquois League" (Leavitt and Francis, 1990, 12).

Interestingly, Speck indicates that while the "eastern members" of the confederacy (the four main member nations) continue to speak of the existence of the Wabanaki Confederacy, the "western members" (namely the Mohawks of Kahnawake and Kanesatake and the Ottawas) seem to have all but forgotten their participation in the Wabanaki Confederacy (Leavitt and Francis, 1990, 14–15). Although the reasons for this remain unclear, it would appear that ties with the western members seem to have been ruptured in the late 1800s (Leavitt and Francis, 1990, 15). The alliances between member nations of the Wabanaki Confederacy continue to be respected to this day.

Wabash Confederacy

Compared to other alliances, the Wabash Confederacy was fairly short-lived. It is said to have existed between 1785 and 1795. This confederacy included the Hurons, Shawnees, Council of the Three Fires, Delawares, Miamis, and the Six Nations of the Grand River, Kickapoo, and Kaskaskia. The Wabash Confederacy was a purely military alliance for the purpose of fighting in the so-called "Indian wars" of the United States. The informal alliances that had existed among these nations since the French colonial era were renewed with vigor during the American Revolution (Mississippi Biographies and History, 2005).

By virtue of the Treaty of Paris (1783), the United States government acquired control of the land east of the Mississippi and south of the Great Lakes. The indigenous nations living in these areas, however, were not included in the discussions. The nations, joined together in the Wabash Confederacy, wanted to deal with the United States as a collectivity, rather than individually (Mississippi Biographies and History, 2005).

The Battle of Fallen Timbers, on August 20, 1794, is said to have brought an end to the Wabash Confederacy and victory to the United States for control of the disputed territory. In 1795, confederacy members signed the Treaty of Greenville, which had the effect of ceding much of present-day Ohio to the United States. One young man who refused to sign the treaty was a Shawnee named Tecumseh. He would later become known for renewing Indian resistance (Mississippi Biographies and History, 2005).

Conclusion

Many of the confederacies described here continue to exist, albeit in a somewhat modified form. As the European presence grew in North America, indigenous nations were forced to adapt their traditional structures and procedures. As North America became more and more settled, the need for military prowess and power declined. Government policies across North America forced indigenous nations to perform traditional ceremonies and conduct political discussions in secret. Entire nations were relocated far from their traditional territories, and children were taken from their parents and placed in schools where they were severely punished for speaking their own languages and trying to carry on their cultures. The Bureau of Indian Affairs in the United States and the Department of Indian Affairs in Canada ensured that government policies were carried out and that indigenous people would remain on the small parcels of land allocated to them. It is not surprising, therefore, that contact with Europeans took a heavy toll on the system of governance identified as confederacies. Nevertheless, the continued existence of several of the confederacies described here reflects the tenacity and adaptability of indigenous governments.

Lysane Cree

See also Blackfeet Confederacy; Haudenosaunee Confederacy, Political System; Tecumseh; Tungavik Federation, Nunavut.

References and Further Reading

Bonaparte, Darren. 1999. "The Seven Nations of Canada: The Other Iroquois Confederacy." Available at: http://www.wampumchronicles .com/ sevennations.html. Accessed January 9, 2007.

Cornell, George. 1986. *People of the Three Fires*. Grand Rapids, MI: Grand Rapids Inter-Tribal Council.

Ethridge, Robbie. 2003. *Creek Country: The Creek Indians and their World*. Chapel Hill: University of North Carolina Press.

Fester, Robert. 2004a. "The Illini: Lords of the Mississippi Valley." Available at: http:// members.tripod.com/~RFester/index.html. Accessed January 9, 2007.

Fester, Robert. 2004b. "The Iroquois Wars." Available at: http://members.tripod.com/~RFester/ iroq.html. Accessed January 9, 2007.

Golden Ink. "Our Georgia History: The Creek Indians of Georgia, Parts I–III." Available at: http://www.ourgeorgiahistory.com/indians/Creek/creek01.html. Accessed January 9, 2007.

Hahn, Thomas Swiftwater, ed. 2005. "A Brief History of the Lenape-Delaware: An Algonkian People." Available at: http://www.lenapedelawarehistory.net/mirror/briefhistory.htm; http://www.lenapedelawarehistory.net/mirror/oldconfederacy.htm. Accessed January 9, 2007.Halton Region Museum. 2004. "The First People." Available at: http://www.region.halton.on.ca/museum/Exhibits/HaltonsHistory/firstpeople.htm. Accessed January 9, 2007.

ITCMI (Inter-Tribal Council of Michigan). 2001. "Profile of the Inter-tribal Council of Michigan." Available at: http://www.itcmi.org/thistories percent5Cpokagon.doc. Accessed January 9, 2007.

Leavitt, Robert M., and Francis, David A., eds. 1990. *The Wampum Records: Wabanaki Traditional Laws.* Fredericton: University of New Brunswick.

MNSU (Minnesota State University). 2005. "Blackfoot Confederacy." Available at: http://www.mnsu.edu/emuseum/cultural/northamerica/blackfoot.html. Accessed January 9, 2007.

Muscogee (Creek) Nation of Oklahoma. 2005. "Muscogee (Creek) History." Available at: http://www.muscogeenation-nsn.gov/. Accessed 1/27/07

Nolan, Joseph R., and Jacqueline M. Nolan-Haley. 1990. *Black's Law Dictionary,* 6th ed. St. Paul, MN: West.

Samek, Hana. 1987. *The Blackfoot Confederacy 1880–1920: A Comparative Study of Canadian and U.S. Indian Policy.* Albuquerque: University of New Mexico Press.

Sioui, Georges E. 1999. *Huron-Wendat: The Heritage of the Circle.* Vancouver: University of British Columbia Press.

Trigger, Bruce G. 1987. *The Children of Aataentsic: A History of the Huron People to 1660.* Montreal, QC, and Kingston, ON: McGill-Queen's University Press.

Union of Ontario Indians. 2004. "Council of the Three Fires: A History of the Anishnabek Nation." Available at: http://www.anishinabek.ca.

Counting Coup

Counting coup was a method of combat developed by Native Americans to humble their enemies in battle without taking their lives. Derived from the French word, *coup,* meaning a "stroke" or "blow," counting coup was considered a more prestigious and heroic act than killing. Gaining personal honor in battle was the greatest achievement a warrior could attain.

Coup could be counted in a number of ways. The most notable method was to touch the enemy by hand, knife, or elaborately decorated coup stick. Other means of counting coup were leading a successful war party, stealing a horse in a daring manner, taking a weapon from an enemy in hand-to-hand combat, or saving a fellow warrior in battle.

Counting coup, also known as war honors, had to be publicly announced and accepted. These honors were reflected in various articles of dress, such as feathers and types of shirt fringe. Eagle feathers were the highest display of war honors. War bonnets were worn only in ceremony or parade with other highly decorated items. Many tribes developed a complex system of rankings based on particular acts of bravery. Winning honor in battle was so important in Native American society that few warriors dared lie about their exploits. Once a coup was attained, warriors would often paint a symbol of their coup on their tepees or buffalo robes. Others expressed their deeds by designs on their faces or clothes.

Counting coup is generally associated with the Native peoples of the Great Plains. As Spanish explorers moved north from Mexico into the southwest region of the present-day United States, Native Americans became very adept at acquiring their horses. By the late seventeenth to mideighteenth centuries, the acquisition of horses allowed many Indians of the Great Plains to adopt a nomadic lifestyle. These peoples considered daring and bravery, especially during the hunt or warfare, the most important of virtues. Military leadership was usually provided by young men seeking glory and personal honor. Boys were usually trained for war at an early age because much of their ceremonial life would later be validated by their status as warriors.

Warfare in aboriginal North America was not necessarily a political act. In some instances, Native Americans elevated warfare to ritualistic contests of great spiritual significance. However, they did not develop warfare to its most destructive potential until the continued mass migration of white settlers offered no other alternatives. The few intertribal massacres that resulted in substantial loss of life occurred when a small camp or hunting party was overwhelmed by a vastly superior force. In general, Native peoples raided or engaged in battle to obtain material goods, take revenge, seize captives, or merely to vent aggression.

A Peigan man dressed in his war bonnet and holding his feathered coup stick. (Library of Congress)

were made. At some point, a daring warrior might ride perilously close to the other side instigating a full charge. War clubs and coup sticks smashed against shields as each side struggled for advantage. Most of these conflicts ended quickly with little loss of life unless one side was able to exploit a weakness or a vast numerical superiority. Regardless of the overall results, the objective was obtaining personal honor by counting coup rather than killing the enemy.

One school of thought maintains that counting coup was the confluence of European influences and Native American culture. The introduction of the horse and gun allowed tribal warfare to become far-ranging and deadly. Epidemics and the constant search for food kept populations low. Heavy casualties in battle were unacceptable. The goal of personal honor among Native Americans persisted, however. The role of counting coup permitted warriors to obtain status without disastrous battlefield losses.

Charles W. Buckner

See also Warfare, Intertribal.
References and Further Reading
McGinnis, Anthony. 1990. *Counting Coup and Cutting Horses: Intertribal Warfare on the Northern Plains, 1738–1889*. Evergreen, CO: Cordillera Press.
Hoig, Stan. 1993. *Tribal Wars of the Southern Plains*. Norman: University of Oklahoma Press.

For example, during the 1850s and early 1860s, the Pawnee declined in power as the Sioux dominated. Although Pawnee losses in some battles were overwhelming, most conflict between the two consisted of large displays of bravado and little loss of life. Generally, at dawn, several hundred Sioux would appear on the outskirts of a Pawnee village. Often, first coup was obtained from a few unlucky Pawnee women getting water from the river. Coup could be counted on a man, woman, or child as long as the warrior dared to attack an enemy at close quarters. Pawnee warriors reacted quickly, mounting their horses and confronting the enemy. The Sioux would wait patiently until both sides faced each other almost formally at a distance of a few hundred yards. Insults were hurled back and forth. Warriors declared their opponent's women ugly. Mocking and insulting hand and arm gestures

Dams, Fishing Rights, and Hydroelectric Power

Hydroelectric development projects involve a wide range of interconnected environmental manipulations. While constructed mainly out of public concern for flood control, dams may entail many associated changes, including waterway modification and navigation improvement, riverbank stabilization, and soil conservation. Given paramount federal authorization through major congressional and executive-level policies, these projects often involve comprehensive development plans, vast endeavors that include hydroelectric power generation, the development of recreational mixed-use areas, and irrigation projects. As they involve Native people, these projects have ultimately proven a crucible of transitioning political trends concerning land, resource, and development issues; Indian civil rights generally; and tribal self-determination and the evolution of their communities' relationship with the federal government through its subagencies. The following case studies demonstrate how Native people are consistently burdened with water, land, and resource conflicts and how, although they are called on to make significant sacrifice toward their resolution, they are frequently denied an equitable share of the benefits that such endeavors promise.

One public works project is notorious for its subversion of Indian land rights and callous treatment of the involved Indian communities: the Missouri River Basin Development Program, commonly known as the Pick-Sloan Plan after, respectively, General Lewis A. Pick of the U.S. Army Corps of Engineers and William G. Sloan of the Department of the Interior's Bureau of Reclamation. These rival designers were forced to merge radically different engineering plans to ensure the project's political success. The plan relied on the perceived relative ease of "resettlement" of the populations along the upper Missouri valley, rather than the lower basin, apparently because the upper valley had far more Indian communities and lands, and the lower valley had sizable non-Indian towns. The project, initially authorized in 1944, called for 107 dams, with the largest-scale dams located close to the Sioux reservations in the upper Missouri, the Dakotas, and northern Nebraska. The project would flood over 200,000 acres of Sioux territory and require the removal of over 550 Indian families (Lawson, 1994, 29). Agitated by historical animosities between the Sioux and the U.S. Army, here in the form of the Army Corps of Engineers, who held dominating control throughout the project, the stage was set for arguably the most severe confrontation between Plains Indians and the United States since Wounded Knee.

In successive stages involving the communities of the Affiliated Tribes of Fort Berthold, the Sioux of Crow Creek and Lower Brulé, the Standing Rock and Cheyenne River Sioux, and the Yankton Sioux, the Corps moved forward with its standard procedure of condemning the needed land through federal district courts. Under the assumption of eminent domain and with authority over compensation values, there was no consultation with tribal authorities prior to commencement of the construction on the first of the projects segments. These actions stood in clear violation of the 1851 Fort Laramie Treaty (and the 1858 Yankton Treaty in the case of the Yankton Sioux) and, because the Corps is a division of the federal government, in clear conflict with the federal obligation as trustee of American Indian lands. Congress had earlier debated the merits of breaking Indian treaties for public works projects: In 1936 it first considered breaking the Canandaigua Treaty with the Seneca nation to build Kinzua Dam upstream from Pittsburgh. Though it decided then that the merits of the project did not warrant this action, with the Pick-Sloan era behind it, it would change its mind in the late 1950s and force the resettlement of Allegheny Senecas from towns inundated when the dam was eventually built. But by 1944, the Bureau of Indian Affairs, as the administrator of trust obligations, was weakened by its burdensome bureaucracy and was clearly overshadowed in its task of representing the involved Indian communities amid the larger federal agencies.

The Affiliated Tribes of Fort Berthold were the most devastated community, by virtue of being the first to be annexed by the project. The plan's call for over 150,000 acres of their land to be deluged under the reservoir that Fort Garrison Dam would create would flood one-fourth of their land base—the most valued river bottomlands (Lawson, 1994, 59). Concentrated near the river lands, 80 percent of these traditionally agricultural people were forced to resettle, losing over 90 percent of their best farmlands. The Sioux of Crow Creek lost over 9,000 acres of valuable river bottomland, one-third of which was rich forestland; a third of their community was slated for resettlement (Lawson, 1994, 47). At Lower Brule, fully half of the primary community was displaced. One-third of the Standing Rock and Cheyenne River Sioux were also forced to relocate when the massive reservoir of the Oahe Dam flooded over 160,000 acres of their lands, including 90 percent of timberlands prized as traditional hunting areas (Lawson, 1994, 50). The social and cultural costs were even more exacting: In addition to the loss of remaining traditional foods and medicines supportive of cultural identity, the Sioux suffered the ignobility of having their ancestors' graves exhumed to be moved along with other community sites, including agency service sites and hospitals, to remote locations dislocated from the reservation population. Critically, federal agencies failed to acknowledge a legal precedent for Indian preferential rights to water access, established by court precedent in 1907 (*Winters v. United States,* 1907), a principle thereafter known as the Winters doctrine.

Only retroactively did Congress consider the violations of Indian land rights. Not until 1950, when all the communities were already heavily impacted by their respective dislocations, were administrative means proposed in Congress to negotiate final settlements with tribal representation. The affected tribes were extraordinarily diplomatic in offering alternatives to the plan that might ameliorate the effects on their communities; still, they struggled well into the second decade of the project to achieve a level of compensation that could remotely be labeled as adequate, and some issues have never been resolved.

Earlier dam projects initiated under New Deal policies of the mid-1930s also resulted in the cultural trauma of dislocation, primarily as they affected traditional fisheries of Native people. The impact of these projects was in many cases difficult to determine in the immediate aftermath of reservoir creation, and their long-term damage has proven the subject of another protracted era of dispute and negotiation among Indian tribes, the United States, and its agents. The Indians of the Columbia River basin had long been known as Salmon People, and their reliance on access to river fishing sites was both a cultural necessity and a right that they did not relinquish to the United States when these tribes signed treaties in the mid-1850s. The tribes of the Yakama, Warm Springs, and Umatilla Reservations lived under the assumption that their access to fishing sites (and thus the basis of their economy and spirituality) was a permanent right they would enjoy forever, as their treaties stated. When the Army Corps of Engineers began to build dams on the Columbia in the 1930s, such as the enormous Bonneville Dam, Grand Coulee, and later Dalles Dam, it created a new era of Indian rights struggles due to the numerous traditional fishing sites that were inundated by the new dams and uncertainties over the impact on the sensitive cycles of upstream migration through which the salmon population regenerates itself. Though the Columbia River dams proceeded without any consent from the tribes who frequented the river for fishing, it was irrefutable that Indians retained rights in their treaties to fish in the "usual and accustomed places." Due to the Indian Reorganization Act's principles of promoting economic self-determination, the Corps was obligated to make a pledge by 1939 (over two years after the dam waters rose) that it would undertake to replace the lost traditional sites with new ones it would develop

in consultation with the tribes—"in-lieu sites" amounting to 400 acres of access. State and commercial fisheries, representatives, pursuing their supposed vested interests, delayed the replacement process measurably. In the end, the Corps provided only about 10 percent of the 400 acres it promised (Ulrich, 1999, 137).

All these issues came to a dramatic climax after the significant federal circuit court ruling in 1974 of Judge George Boldt, which reaffirmed treaty fishing rights and arbitrated a rule that Indians were entitled to 50 percent of the catch. The result was the pressure required to bring state and non-Indian fishery representatives to the table to negotiate such contentious issues as catch limits, season terms, and enforcement of fishing regulations by tribal authorities rather than agencies. These trends led to a template for the current model in the region, that of intertribal fisheries coalitions such as the Columbia River Inter-Tribal Fish Commission (CRITFC), which aided the resolution of differing tribal resource management practices and continued to bring pressure to bear on the completion of the original pledge of 400 acres of access, which after over sixty years is still in process.

More recent trends in hydroelectric development involving Native people and lands have brought increasing attention to bear on the environmental impact of such projects. In Quebec, the Cree, Inuit, and Innu (Naskapi) have struggled since the 1970s to reduce the impact of the largest hydroelectric endeavor to be proposed in North America. In no way conceivable as a single dam project, the James Bay Development Corporation and Hydro-Quebec began, in the early 1970s, a two-phase manipulation of the entire James Bay region to serve the presumed energy interests of Canada and the United States. Impact testing since the first phase of the project has already shown that some of their concerns for the ecosystem were critically correct: The reservoir creation and the reduction of flow around the bay have created toxic conditions resulting from mercury conversion and PCB concentration; Native people have been told not to eat fish from many of their former traditional subsistence areas. Since 1990, the second phase of the project has seen a more coalition-based opposition, between Native people and environmental groups, resulting in increasing reluctance of American utilities to accept the energy product produced under such conditions.

Christopher Lindsay Turner

See also Bureau of Indian Affairs: Establishing the Existence of an Indian Tribe; Columbia River Inter-Tribal Fish Commission; Dalles Trading Area; Fishing Rights; James Bay and Northern Quebec Agreement; Land, Identity and Ownership of, Land Rights; Reservation Economic and Social Conditions; Sacred Sites; Salmon, Economic and Spiritual Significance of; Trust, Doctrine of; Water Rights; *Winters v. United States.*

Reference and Further Reading

Bilharz, Joy A. 1998. *Allegeheny Senecas and the Kinzua Dam: Forced Relocation Through Two Generations.* Lincoln: University of Nebraska Press.

Grinde, Donald A., and Bruce E. Johansen. 1995. *Ecocide of Native America: Environmental Destruction of Native Lands and Peoples.* Santa Fe, NM: Clear Light Publishers.

Lawson, Michael L. 1994. *Dammed Indians: The Pick-Sloan Plan and the Missouri River Sioux, 1944–1980.* Norman: University of Oklahoma Press.

Richardson, Boyce. 1991. *Strangers Devour the Land.* White River Junction, VT: Chelsea Green Publishing.

Ulrich, Roberta. 1999. *Empty Nets: Indians, Dams, and the Columbia River.* Corvallis: Oregon State University Press.

Democracy and Native American Images among Europeans

European philosophy has been profoundly influenced since 1492 by perceptions of the people by explorers in the Americas, Africa, Asia, and the Pacific. Montesquieu, in his *Spirit of the Laws,* made use of African, Arab, Persian, East Indian, and Chinese concepts in his discussions of forms of government. During the Age of Discovery, Europeans were not only exploring a world new to its people, they were also opening their eyes to other peoples' ways of thinking (as well as helping themselves to their material riches). Because of these intellectual imports, the Old World changed. Born of European wish fulfillment, the image of the noble savage was created from the cloth of this imagery, fashioned by European philosophers and often returned to the lands of its birth. Native societies, especially in America, reminded Europeans of imagined golden worlds known to them only in folk history.

As the seventeenth century ended, about 200,000 European colonists lived in widely scattered settlements along the eastern seaboard of North America. Travel narratives from America, each with its own mixture of fact and speculation, reality and desire, flooded Europe at that time and influenced its intellectual currents. Shakespeare's plays were being staged for the first time in England. John Locke had just published his most influential work describing relations between the individual and the state under natural law. From the street, to the stage, to the salon, America was the talk of the day.

In this new environment, the colonists of English North America were influenced by Native American ideas of confederation and democracy. But the story does not begin or end there. The assumption that American democracy evolved from the English parliament or from a perusal of European political thinkers must be tempered with the realization that writers such as John Locke and Jean Jacques Rousseau derived ideas about democracy in a workable form from travelers' accounts of American Indian governmental structures. American Indian societies were working democracies that drew the attention, and often the admiration, of Europeans from the time of the first contacts.

The way European thinking was shaped by its "discovery" of the New World (as well as of Africa and parts of Asia) also outlines some of its confusing contradictions. From the beginning, the noble savage was idealized in philosophy as his real-life counterparts were slaughtered to make way for "progress." This concept was an apparition of the European imagination, of course, but, like any racial stereotype, it said as much about the very real drives, perceptions, dreams, and desires of its creators as about the newly "discovered" Americans themselves. The influence of the concept on European thought was likewise very real, especially during the Enlightenment years that culminated with the American and French revolutions. The idea that people deemed expendable could so profoundly shape European (and colonial American) thinking was, and remains, an intellectual challenge to people who take European and Euro-American assumptions for granted.

Like most stereotypes, that of the noble savage simplified a complex reality. It also created an image that was, paradoxically, both more and less than reality. More, because it ascribed to the Natives more life, liberty, and happiness than many of them actually possessed, creating a myth that imagined an autonomous wild man of the woods and ignoring the very real social conventions and traditions by which Native Americans ordered their lives.

Less, because the image of the noble savage combined many dozens of peoples and belief systems into one generic whole.

And, as with most stereotypes, distance distorted the reality of the image. Thus, the image of the Indian created by Rousseau or Locke seems utterly more fantastical than that of Franklin, Jefferson, and other influential founders of the United States, who did diplomatic business with American Native people in the course of their daily lives. These days, the noble savage is usually dismissed merely as a figment of imagination, ignoring the power the image held in the Enlightenment mind and the impact of its appeal to influential thinkers of the time. What we, in the late twentieth century, take as reality mattered not one whit to John Locke or Benjamin Franklin. They saw with their own eyes, not ours.

Europeans came to America, in reality or only in imagination, seeking degrees of material well-being ranging from subsistence to extravagance—and more intangible benefits, most having to do with some incarnation of freedom. Conveniently, the immigrants found America and its Native peoples rich in both. It also found opposition to its taking, of course, and so the image of the noble savage (like most stereotypes) also engendered its opposite, the "bad Indian," who stood in the way of the Europeans' destruction of the naturalness its philosophers so admired. They built churches in a place that was described to them as the Garden of Eden.

The image of the noble savage was abstracted from real human beings who became larger than life in European imagination, their mental photographs airbrushed of every pimple inflicted by a complex and sometimes contradictory reality. Many of the most prominent thinkers in Europe and America drank at this well in one way or another during the three centuries following Columbus's voyages—all according to their own conceptions of the past and their own designs for the future. Memory outlasted image, and image outlived changing American realities, which themselves had been reworked by desirous imagination, taking what had been real to its most logical (and often patently absurd) extreme. As a vehicle of dreams, the noble savage helped reawaken in Europeans a passionate desire for the liberty and happiness that so suffused Enlightenment thought, helping to ignite revolution on both sides of the Atlantic. Images can do such things to reality.

William Brandon finds Voltaire laughing at any talk of noble savages, "but his fake Huron in *L'Ingenu* (1767) sometimes echoed, and not always ironically, both Lahontan and Delisle, in spite of all Voltaire's efforts to keep him from doing so." To Brandon, "Voltaire mocked at himself for falling victim to such nonsense—'My muse calls to you from America, [he complained]. . . . I needed a new world. . . . But I tremble that I'll be taken for a savage." At the same time, on the other side of the Atlantic, the ultimate pragmatist Benjamin Franklin often found himself called by the same ironic muse (Brandon, 1986, 104).

The French philosopher and essayist Montaigne has been most often credited with introducing the image of Native America to the European world of letters, although a reading of literature produced by Spain's Golden Century can provide earlier precedents. Montiagne, like Thomas More, penned his vision of Utopia after hearing the stories of a traveler. Montaigne's essay, "Of the Cannibals," was written after the traveler had been in the New World roughly a decade and had resided in Montaigne's home; More's informant was more of a chance meeting. More's work is fiction, with New World overtones; Montaigne's is philosophy, based on purported fact, but the results seem strangely similar. "Of Cannibals" sets a culturally relativistic tone as Benjamin Franklin would more than a century later in his "Remarks Concerning the Savages of North America": "There is nothing that is either barbarous or savage, unless men call barbarism which is not common to them" (Florio, 1910, 218). To Montaigne, America's Native people were civilized, in the purist way, in the original state of humankind, the state of nature, embodying "the most true and profitable virtues" (Florio, 1910, 218).

Montaigne also helped set a standard for Enlightenment assumption when, as he measured natural man in America against Europe's imagined Golden Age, wishing that Plato and Lycurgus could see it for themselves: "For me seemeth that what in those nations we see of experience, doth not only exceed all the pictures herewith licentious Poesie hath profoundly embellished the golden age . . . but also the conception and desire of Philosophy. They could not imagine a genuine so pure and simple, as we see by experience" (Florio, 1910, 218).

Pure, simple, and free: Three short but potent words sketched the Native American to the eye of the European Enlightenment. In our time recognized as a rather simplistic stereotype of humankind in America, these notions framed the terms of debate that spawned revolutions. Whether founders of the

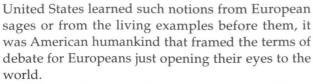

United States learned such notions from European sages or from the living examples before them, it was American humankind that framed the terms of debate for Europeans just opening their eyes to the world.

Wrote Montaigne: "It is a nation, would I answer Plato, that hath no kind of traffick, no knowledge of magistrates, no knowledge of Letters, no intelligence of numbers, no name of magistrate, nor of politike superiorite; no use of service, of riches, or of poverty, no contracts, no successions" (Florio, 1910, 220). And so forth. These words, in numerous variations, become very familiar—they echo in time to Shakespeare's Gonzalo, who nearly steals Montaigne's lines thirty years later, thence to Roger Williams, Jefferson, Franklin, Paine, and Engels. Peter Martyr said much the same thing before Montaigne, as did Columbus. The portrait is overdrawn, of course, but some stereotypes grow out of a kernel of reality, and in this case, Native societies in America provided the perfect vehicle by which to criticize contemporary European society—and to help shape the images, desires, and dreams of those rebelling against it.

Bruce E. Johansen

References and Further Reading
Brandon, William. 1986. *New Worlds for Old: Reports from the New World and Their Effect on the Development of Social Thought in Europe, 1500–1800.* Athens: Ohio University Press.
Florio, John, trans. [1910]1965. *Montaigne's Essays.* New York: Dutton.
Kennedy, J. H. 1950. *Jesuit and Savage in New France.* New Haven, CT: Yale Universit, Press.
Secondat, Charles de, ed. 1777. Baron de Montesquieu, *The Complete Works of Montesquieu.* London: Printed for T. Evans & W. Davis.

Diabetes

For thousands of years before contact with Europeans, indigenous peoples lived off the resources that could be obtained from the land and water around them. Since contact, the lifestyles and diet of indigenous peoples have for the most part changed significantly. Diabetes is one of the consequences of that change.

Diabetes, or diabetes mellitus, refers to a group of diseases characterized by high blood glucose lev-els. A disease that was once rarely seen among indigenous peoples, diabetes has grown to epidemic proportions among Native Americans in the United States (including Native Hawaiians and Alaska Natives) and among indigenous peoples globally during the past fifty to sixty years. Diabetes is a significant part of the social and health crises faced by Native Americans and is interlinked with poverty, alcoholism, and drastic changes in diet, exercise, and eating habits.

There are three types of diabetes mellitus, commonly known as Type 1, Type 2, and gestational diabetes. Type 1 (where the pancreas makes little or no insulin) is usually seen in children and teenagers. Type 2 occurs when the pancreas is not releasing enough insulin or the insulin that it releases is ineffective. Gestational diabetes arises in some women during pregnancy and generally resolves following birth of the child. Women who develop gestational diabetes, however, have been found to be at a higher risk of developing Type 2 diabetes later. Their child also may be at an increased risk (NDIC, 2002; NADA, 2005). The type of diabetes that is most frequently seen among indigenous populations around the world is Type 2 diabetes, which is a preventable type of diabetes.

The Association of American Indian Physicians (AAIP) estimated in 2001 that at least 12.2 percent of Native Americans over the age of nineteen have Type II diabetes (AAIP, 2001). The American Diabetes Association states that 107,775 Native Americans and Alaska Natives (or 14.5 percent of the population) currently receiving care from Indian Health Services (IHS) have diabetes. In the southeastern United States this figure is 27 percent (ADA 2005). The Pima tribe of Arizona, for example, has the highest incidence of diabetes in the world with about 50 percent of Pimas between the ages of thirty and sixty-four having diabetes (AAIP, 2001). Type 2 diabetes, also sometimes referred to as adult-onset diabetes, is also increasingly prevalent among Native American children ten years and older (NDIC, 2002).

Some researchers have determined that one of the reasons diabetes is prevalent among indigenous populations is that its occurrence has been linked to substance abuse and chronic stress (which includes post-traumatic stress disorder [PTSD], abuse, oppression, and genocide), all of which reflect the drastic impact of colonialism and assimilation experienced by indigenous populations since the time of first contact with Europeans. It has been suggested as well that Native Americans experience intergenerational PTSD, thereby reflecting a continuation of the vicious cycle of substance abuse, violent behavior, child abuse, and suicide (Dapice, Inkanish, Martin, and Brauchi, 2005, 3).

Another significant factor, reflecting the daily reality of the foods available to indigenous peoples, is the important link between diabetes and obesity. Among the factors that increase a person's risk for developing Type 2 diabetes are obesity, lack of exercise, and a diet high in sugar and fat (NADA, 2003).

Traditional activities of hunting, fishing, gathering, trapping, and farming have been drastically disrupted, reduced, and in some cases eradicated, as Native Americans witnessed their traditional territories being reduced to small parcels of land to make way for settlers and gold prospectors. Often the lands set aside for reservations had the poorest soil and devastated wildlife. Native Americans living on reservations are among the poorest in society. Even today in many cases they are forced to eat government rations of flour, sugar, and lard. Modern-day fast food has replaced the flour, lard, and sugar of the past, in some cases, but its nutritional value is little better.

Traditional diets were adapted to their environment and consisted of a variety of wild game, fish, marine mammals, and vegetable matter (berries, fruits, and other edible plants and root vegetables). Wild game, marine mammals, and fish do not contain the cholesterol and fat content of modern-day grain-fed farm animals. In fact, the fat contained in wild animals is often quite beneficial and contains vitamins useful to the human body (Health Canada, 1995).

Given the high rates of diabetes among indigenous peoples, it is not surprising that they are also at a much higher risk than the general population for developing complications related to diabetes. The Association of American Indian Physicians estimated in 2001 that between 10 and 21 percent of all people with diabetes develop kidney disease. This percentage rate is six times higher among Native Americans with diabetes. While the risk of amputation of a lower limb increases significantly for any person with diabetes, the amputation rates among Native Americans are three to four times higher than among the general population (AAIP, 2001).

Failure to diagnose the disease promptly, as well as failure to follow a doctor's recommendations, can give rise to serious complications, including diabetic retinopathy (a deterioration of the blood

vessels in the eye affecting vision and often leading to blindness), cataracts, diabetic nephropathy (kidney failure), amputation of the lower extremities, periodontal disease, infections, and death. Diabetes is also a serious risk factor for the development of cardiovascular disease, stroke, and hypertension (high blood pressure) (NDIC, 2002). Diabetes retinopathy has been found to occur in 18 percent of Pima Indians and 24.4 percent of Oklahoma Indians (AAIP, 2001). In Hawai'i, approximately 70,000 to 90,000 Native Hawaiians have Type 2 diabetes. Native Hawaiians have a diabetes-related mortality rate that is six times that for the general U.S. population (Young, 1998)

As mentioned, Native Americans living in the United States are not alone in their struggle with diabetes. Indigenous peoples around the world are being diagnosed at alarming rates with Type 2 diabetes. In Canada, as part of the Canadian Diabetes Strategy, $58 million was allocated by the federal government of Canada over a five-year period to specifically target the problem of diabetes among indigenous people. This program, managed by the Department of Indian and Northern Affairs Canada, is called the Aboriginal Diabetes Initiative. The department estimates that the rate of diabetes among indigenous people in Canada is three to five times higher than for non-Native Canadians (Health Canada, 2003). More than half (53 percent) of indigenous people in Canada who live on-reservation with diabetes are forty years old or less and 65 percent are forty-five years old or less (Health Canada, 2000, 11).

What is more surprising is that Type 2 diabetes is even showing up among children, as young as five to eight years old, something that was once considered quite rare (Health Canada, 2000, 11–12). In addition, the government of Canada believes that, for every person diagnosed with diabetes, there is an undiagnosed case of impaired glucose tolerance (IGT). IGT describes a person whose plasma glucose levels are higher than normal, but not yet high enough to result in a diagnosis of diabetes. A person with IGT has a risk of developing diabetes and cardiovascular disease (Health Canada, 2000, 14). In Canada, the province of Manitoba alone estimates that the number of cases among First Nations can be expected to triple over the next twenty years. This will also lead to increased numbers of diabetes-related complications—stroke, kidney failure, lower limb amputations, and blindness (Health Canada, 2000, 22).

Statistics from Australia reflect a similar picture. Aboriginal people in Australia are two to six times more likely to suffer from Type 2 diabetes. In some Aboriginal communities in Australia, the prevalence of diabetes among adults over the age of thirty-five is 33 percent. The same grim statistics are being reported among indigenous peoples in New Zealand, Western Samoa, Fiji, Kiribati, and the Cook Islands (Young, 1998).

The realization over the years of the growing epidemic of Type 2 diabetes among indigenous populations has been reflected in an expanding awareness and search for solutions in most indigenous communities. Since Type 2 diabetes is preventable and treatable through proper diet and exercise, communities are developing diabetes prevention programs to encourage young children to follow the right path in regard to food selection, nutrition, and adequate exercise. Community programs also seek to educate adults to make good choices both to prevent diabetes as well as to minimize its impact on those who are already affected by it. Indigenous people are also strongly encouraged to have their blood sugar levels tested, whether or not they are experiencing symptoms.

Lysane Cree

See also Disease, Historic and Contemporary.
References and Further Reading
American Diabetes Association (ADA). 2005. *Diabetes Statistics for Native Americans.* Available at: http://www.diabetes.org/diabetes-statistics/native-americans.jsp.
Association of American Indian Physicians (AAIP). 2001. *Diabetes Facts: Diabetes Among Native Americans.* Available at: http://www.aaip.com/resources/diabetesamongna.html.
Dapice, Ann N., Clark Inkanish, Barbara Martin, and Pam Brauchi. 2005. *Killing Us Slowly: When We Can't Fight and We Can't Run.* Available at: http://www.traditionalhealth.org/healtharticle detail.asp?articleid=14.
Gardner, Amanda. 2004. "Diabetes Rampant Among Native Americans." Available at: http://www.medicinenet.com/script/main/art.asp?articlekey=38767.
Health Canada. 1995. *Native Foods and Nutrition: An Illustrated Reference Manual.* Ottawa, ON: Minister of National Health and Welfare.
Health Canada. 2000. *Diabetes Among Aboriginal People in Canada: The Evidence.* Ottawa, ON: Aboriginal Diabetes Initiative.
Health Canada. 2003. "Aboriginal Diabetes Initiative: Introduction." Available at: *http://www.hc-sc.gc.ca/fnihb/cp/adi/.* Accessed January 9, 2007.
National Aboriginal Diabetes Association (NADA). 2003. "Prevention." Available at: http://www.nada.ca/diabetes/ prevention.php. Accessed January 9, 2007.
National Aboriginal Diabetes Association (NADA). 2005. *About Diabetes.* Available at: http://www.nada.ca/diabetes/definitions.php. Accessed January 9, 2007.
National Diabetes Information Clearinghouse (NDIC). 2002. "Diabetes in American Indians and Alaska Natives." Available at: http://diabetes.niddk.nih.gov/dm/pubs/americanindian/#23. Accessed January 9, 2007.
Young, Robert S., Ph.D. 1998. "Type 2 Diabetes: A Threat to Indigenous People Everywhere." Available at: http://www.ahsc.arizona.edu/nartc/articles/ young98.htm. Accessed January 9. 2007.

Dreamer Cult

Known as *waasaní* (Washani, meaning "dancers" or "worship") in the Sahaptin language, the Dreamer Cult emerged among the Indian peoples of the Columbia Plateau in response to the pressures of Euro-American colonization during the second half of the nineteenth century. Like earlier religious revitalization movements, such as those led by the Delaware prophet Neolin (mideighteenth century) and the Shawnee prophet Tenskwatawa (early nineteenth century), the Washani mingled traditional spirituality with Christian beliefs and ritual forms. Dreamer prophets rejected non-Indian culture and advocated returning to indigenous traditions, which made their teachings a significant obstacle to the policies of removal and assimilation pursued by the U.S. government. Indian agents and missionaries blamed the Dreamers for obstructing Native American "progress," but their efforts to suppress the faith largely failed, even though its promise of world renewal never came to pass.

The Dreamer Cult both reflected and reacted against the influences of Christianity and Euro-American culture. Prior to contact, Plateau Indian spirituality revolved around a complex of winter dances, personal vision quests, and seasonal feasts tied to the annual subsistence cycle and the acquisition of guardian spirit powers. Starting in the 1820s, fur traders and missionaries introduced Christian doctrines and symbols that Indians selectively adapted and incorporated into the evolving Washani religion. Among the most visible influences were the ringing of hand bells during ceremonies, the use of the numbers three and seven in a sacred context, and the performance of services on Sundays. Interaction with whites also spread devastating diseases, however, while the growing non-Indian population generated pressure for land cessions. By the early 1850s, a number of nativistic prophets had begun exhorting their people to shun the newcomers and return to traditional ways. Most scholars attribute the revitalization of the Washani to the Wanapam prophet Smohalla, but there is evidence that he developed the creed in concert with the Yakama prophet Kotiakan. Together with a host of disciples, they carried a powerful message of hope up and down the Columbia River.

The Dreamer faith appealed to Indian communities reeling from the impact of American colonization. In visions received during deep trances, Smohalla foresaw the disappearance of the whites, the resurrection of the Indian dead, and the restoration of the world to a pristine state. This millennial transformation required no acts of violence—indeed, most Dreamers counseled pacifism—but to achieve it the Indians had to obey the instructions of the Creator as conveyed through the prophets. In addition to performing the *wáashat* (Washat), or Prophet Dance, they were exhorted to cast off white culture and show respect for the land. The earth was sacred and not to be bought, sold, or torn up for agricultural and extractive uses. As the Yakama chief Owhi explained at the 1855 Walla Walla treaty council, "God made our bodies from the earth as if they were different from the whites. What shall I do? Shall I give the lands that are a part of my body and leave myself poor and destitute? Shall I say I will give you my lands? I cannot say. I am afraid of the Almighty." Such sentiments, though laced with Christian imagery, helped spark the Plateau Indian wars of 1855–1858 as well as inspiring passive resistance to federal policy well into the twentieth century.

To the government's dismay, the Dreamer Cult spread far beyond Smohalla's winter village near Priest Rapids. Although some of his disciples modified Washani symbols and ceremonies, all retained the basic belief that Indians must honor their own traditions. "Their model of a man is an Indian," cursed one exasperated official. "They aspire to be Indian and nothing else." Accordingly, many Dreamers stayed off the reservations and refused to take allotments or send their children to school. Agents and missionaries, acting with the support of sympathetic Christian Indians, responded with a crusade to crush the Washani. In 1878, for example, the Walla Walla prophet Homli complained that the agent and the Roman Catholics on the Umatilla reservation persecuted his followers, "which makes their hearts sore, and [they] cannot stay on the reservation if they are not left alone, and allowed to worship God in their own way." Seven years later, numerous Yakama families abandoned their reservation farms after the agent clapped Kotiakan in irons and imprisoned him at hard labor for six weeks. Far from suppressing the Washani, however, government coercion merely drove it underground or off the reservations, where agents and Indian police had little power.

The Dreamer Cult remained strong until the early 1890s, when Kotiakan and Smohalla passed away and their followers began to lose faith in the promise of a world free of whites. The Washani's nativistic edge also dulled over time, as Plateau Indian culture continued to evolve, but many of the Dreamers' songs, dances, and ritual innovations survive as part of the contemporary Seven Drums Religion.

Andrew H. Fisher

See also Seven Drums Religion; Smohalla; Tenskwatawa; Wovoka.

References and Further Reading

Relander, Click. 1956. *Drummers and Dreamers.* Caldwell, ID: Caxton.

Ruby, Robert, and John A. Brown. 1989. *Dreamer Prophets of the Columbia Plateau: Smohalla and Skolaskin.* Norman: University of Oklahoma Press.

Spier, Leslie. [1911, 1935] 1979. "The Prophet Dance of the Northwest and Its Derivatives: The Source of the Ghost Dance." In *General Series in Anthropology* No. 1: AMS Press.

False Face Society

A Haudenosaunee (Iroquois) curing society, the False Faces heal ailments of the head, neck, shoulders, and joints, such as nosebleeds, ear and tooth aches, sore or inflamed eyes. and paralysis. Explorer Samuel de Champlain may have been the first European to witness the rituals of the society during his seventeenth-century visit to the Huron, an Iroquoian-speaking people south of Lake Huron; Jesuits and other missionaries, naturalist John Bartram, and captive Mary Jemison later described the society among the Huron and the Six Nations (Haudenosaunee).

While anthropologists disagree over its antiquity, the Haudenosaunee possess origin stories of the society that suggest an ancient beginning. According to tradition, the Creator met a being who walked across the earth carrying a turtle rattle and a wooden staff. Called the Great Doctor, the Hunchback, Gagohsa, the Face, or Hadui, this being lived on the rim of the world and controlled the winds and disease. Both the Creator and Hadui claimed to be more powerful than the other. Agreeing to a contest to decide, each commanded a nearby mountain to move toward them. The Creator was so successful that Hadui struck his face on the rock. As a result, he consented to give humans the ability to call upon his power to cure illnesses by blowing hot ashes over patients. In return, the Haudenosaunee carve and wear False Face masks in his likeness, prepare feasts and conduct ceremonies that include singing, dancing, and tobacco offerings. Masks are to be treated with respect, and they are periodically offered corn mush and tobacco. In another story, a group of hunters met several beings called Common Faces in the forest who taught them these rituals to heal the sick.

The regalia of the society includes turtle shell and bark rattles, wooden staffs, and False Face masks. Carved from basswood or other soft woods, the masks often depict Hadui with a broken nose, a wrinkled forehead, and a twisted mouth, symbolizing his pain when he hit his face against the mountain during his competition with the Creator. Common Face masks have mouths that are often pursed to represent them whistling for tobacco or blowing ashes. Animal hair or fur is often attached to serve as hair, and shell or metal plates around the eyes catch the firelight at ceremonies. The Haudenosaunee consider these masks to be alive and believe that disrespect toward them can cause serious consequences such as illness and death.

Society membership consists of those who have been cured by or who have dreamt of Hadui or the Common Faces. Although the protocols may vary locally, the society conducts and participates in three main ceremonies: the Traveling Rite, or the purging of towns of disease in the spring and fall; rituals hosted in private homes; and the Midwinter or New Year's Festival held in January or February. In the Traveling Rite, the society visits each house, rubbing turtle rattles over the outside, and whisking the inside with pine boughs to rid the residence of illness. Those who are ill are cured with hot ashes. Afterward, the community gathers at the Longhouse, the spiritual center of the village, for tobacco offerings, songs, dances, feasting, and speeches that thank Hadui and the Common Faces for their protection. Medicine is distributed to all, but individuals who are ill or need their society membership renewed ask to have ashes blown over them. Throughout the year, the society conducts private ceremonies in the home to heal the sick or to renew membership as required each year. At Midwinter, the society visits each house, asks for tobacco, cures the sick, renews membership, and participates in dancing and feasting. In the early 1800s, Handsome Lake, a Haudenosaunee prophet who reformed their religion, unsuccessfully attempted to suppress these ceremonies.

In the nineteenth and twentieth centuries, the False Face Society attracted the attention of many anthropologists, including William Beauchamp, A. A. Goldenweiser, J.N.B. Hewitt, Arthur C. Parker, David Boyle, Harriet M. Converse, M. R. Harrington, Frank G. Speck, and in particular, William N. Fenton, a central figure in Iroquoian studies. They collected society regalia for museums, recorded its songs and dances, and photographed its ceremonies. (Photography of the masks is frowned on by traditionalists; the sale of the masks also is forbidden.)

Today, the False Face Society is active in Haudenosaunee communities in New York State and Canada. Several groups, such as the Haudenosaunee Standing Committee on Burial Rules and Regulations and the Grand Council of the Haudenosaunee, visit museum collections to conduct ritual offerings to masks and are working toward the repatriation of society regalia to their communities for spiritual and ceremonial use.

Michelle A. Hamilton

References and Further Reading
Fenton, William N. 1987. *The False Faces of the Iroquois.* Norman: University of Oklahoma Press.
Shimony, Annemarie Anrod. 1994. *Conservatism Among the Iroquois at the Six Nations Reserve,* 2nd ed. Syracuse, NY: Syracuse University Press.
Speck, Frank G. 1949. *Midwinter Rites of the Cayuga Long House, by Frank G. Speck.* Philadelphia: University of Pennsylvania Press.
Tooker, Elisabeth. 1970. *The Iroquois Ceremonial of Midwinter.* Syracuse, NY: Syracuse University Press.

Feminism, Native American Influences

When European-American women began to organize for their rights in upstate New York in the late 1840s, they found a model for the position they envisioned in their closest neighbors. Economic independence, rights to their bodies and children, spiritual authority, and a political voice: All these and more were held by Haudenosaunee (Iroquois) women.

Suffrage leaders Matilda Joslyn Gage and Elizabeth Cady Stanton were aware that, within the ancient Iroquois confederacy, women had responsibility for the land, selecting the hereditary chiefs, and making final decisions on issues of war and peace. While men hunted, women were the agriculturalists and determined food distribution.

United States women, on the other hand, came from a religious tradition that ordered them to keep silent in the churches, obey their husbands, and stay in the home. The tradition gained legal standing when canon (church) law became the basis for common law. Women—once they married and became one with their husbands—ceased to have a legal existence. They lost their property, wages, and children to their husbands, who could dispose of any of them as they wished, even willing away unborn children. Women could not vote, being under the authority of their fathers or husbands, who represented them in the political arena.

Told by church, government, and society that woman's subordination to man was divinely inspired, natural, and legal, leaders of the nineteenth-century woman's rights movement took courage and vision from Haudenosaunee (Iroquois) women who had political, social, economic, and religious equality with the men of their nations.

How did the suffragists know about the Haudenosaunee? While they lived in very different cultural, economic, spiritual, and political worlds during the early 1800s, Euro-American settlers in central and western New York were, at most, one person away from direct familiarity with people of the six nations: Onondaga, Mohawk, Seneca, Cayuga, Oneida, and Tuscarora. The Haudenosaunee continued their ancient practice of adopting individuals of other nations, and many European-American residents of New York (including Matilda Joslyn Gage) carried adoptive Indian names. Friendships and visiting were common between Natives and non-Natives. Newspapers routinely printed news from Iroquois country. Each local history book began with

Susan B. Anthony (left) and Elizabeth Cady Stanton were pioneers in the fight for equal suffrage and women's rights. They were strongly influenced by Native American attitudes toward women. (Library of Congress)

a lengthy account of the first inhabitants of the land. Three leaders of the woman's rights movement, Elizabeth Cady Stanton, Matilda Joslyn Gage, and Lucretia Mott, were among those who had a personal connection to the Haudenosaunee.

Lucretia Mott and her husband James were members of the Indian Committee of the New York and Philadelphia Friends (Quaker) Yearly Meetings, which provided schooling and support for the Seneca at Cattaraugus. The Motts visited the Cattaraugus community in June 1848, where they observed the Seneca women plan the strawberry ceremony and take part in the deliberations over a possible change in the Seneca form of governance. The month after their visit, Mott organized the first woman's rights convention with Stanton and three Quaker friends in nearby Seneca Falls.

"I received the name of Ka-ron-ien-ha-wi, or 'Sky Carrier,' or *She who holds the sky*. It is a clan name of the wolves," wrote Matilda Joslyn Gage (Wagner, 2001, 32). Gage, who was recognized as the third member of the suffrage leadership "triumvirate" with Stanton and Susan B. Anthony, wrote about the superior position of Haudenosaunee women while supporting Native sovereignty and treaty rights.

Elizabeth Cady Stanton's second cousin, Peter Skenandoah Smith, was named for an Oneida friend of the family, Chief Skenandoah. On visits to Peter's brother, Gerrit Smith, Stanton frequently encountered Oneida guests. In addition, her nearest Seneca Falls neighbor, Oren Tyler, came from Onondaga, where he "had friendly dealings" with the people there and was adopted by them. He spoke their language fluently, and parties of Onondagans passing through Seneca Falls to sell their beadwork and baskets "sought out their 'brother,' as they called Capt. Tyler, who always befriended them" (Wagner, 2001, 32).

Gage and Stanton, the major theorists of the woman's suffrage movement radical wing (the National Woman Suffrage Association [NWSA]), became increasingly disenchanted with the inability and unwillingness of Western institutions to change and embrace the liberty of not just women, but all disfranchised groups. They became students of the Haudenosaunee and found a cosmological worldview that they believed to be superior to the patriarchal one of the European-American–dominated nation in which they lived. They read Lewis Henry Morgan, whose *League of the Ho-De-No-Sau-Nee* is often credited with being the first anthropology text, but he was only one of many sources used by Gage. Describing the matrilineal system, Gage cited "Lafitte and other Jesuit missionary writers" along with "[Henry Rowe] Schoolcraft, [George] Catlin, [Joshua V. H.] Clark, Hubert Bancroft of the Pacific coast, and many students of Indian life and customs" (Wagner, 2001, 35).

Personal and scholarly knowledge of their Haudenosaunee friends and neighbors was reinforced by the daily news. These suffragists regularly read newspaper accounts of everyday Iroquois activities—the sports scores when the Onondaga faced the Mohawks at lacrosse; a Quaker council called to ask Seneca women to leave their fields and work in the home (as the Friends said God commanded); and a condolence ceremony to mourn a chief's death and to set in place a new one. The average nineteenth-century upstate New York newspaper reader was assumed to have the kind of knowledge of Iroquois history and government that today is possessed, among Euro-Americans, only by scholars.

New York newspaper readers, like Stanton and Gage, discovered from printed interviews with white teachers at various Indian nations the wonderful sense of freedom and safety felt by Haudenosaunee women, because rape was virtually nonexistent on the reservations. These front-page stories admonished big city dandies to learn a thing or two from Native men's example, so that European-American women too could walk the streets without fear. An April 10, 1883, description of life on the Onondaga nation for a white woman was published in the *Skaneateles Democrat*, a paper to which Gage was a sometime contributor:

It shows the remarkable security of living on an Indian Reservation, that a solitary woman can walk about for miles, at any hour of the day or night, in perfect safety. Miss Remington often starts off, between eight and nine in the evening, lantern in one hand and alpenstock in the other, and a parcel of supplies strung from her shoulder, to walk for a mile or more up the hillsides (Beauchamp, 1883).

Miss Remington had long been in charge of the mission house at Onondaga. Adopted into the Snipe clan of the Onondaga nation, she was given the name *Ki-a-was-say*, or "A New Word."

Harriet Maxwell Converse, a friend of Gage's who wrote numerous articles about the Haudenosaunee for the New York papers, published this account:

Rev. M. F. Trippe, long a missionary on the Tonawanda, Cattaraugus and Alleghany reservations, said to me:—"Tell the readers of the *Herald* that there is absolutely no profanity, no 'swear words' in the Native language of these people. The use of bad language, like the use of liquor they learn from the whites, but they do not practice either as much as their white neighbors. They have a sincere respect for women—their own women as well as those of the whites. I have seen young white women going unprotected about parts of the reservations in search of botanical specimens best found there, and Indian men helping them. Where else in the land can a girl be safe from insult from rude men whom she does not know (Wagner, 2001, 44–45).

Just as feminists 100 years later learned from Margaret Mead's research among the Arapesh that rape is not universal, so did the suffragists learn from their research, newspapers, and neighbors that men in some societies do not rape women. They understood that rape is socially structured behavior. Violence against women had its origins, they analyzed, in the absolute authority—religiously and legally sanctioned—that husbands had over wives and men had over women.

Attorney Carrie Burnham, a coworker of Gage and Stanton in the National Woman Suffrage Association, explained:

> By marriage, the husband and wife are one person in law; that is, the legal existence of the woman is "merged in that of her husband." He is her "baron," or "lord," bound to supply her with shelter, food, clothing and medicine and is entitled to her earnings—the use and custody of her person which he may seize wherever he may find it (Wagner, 2001, 73).

One implication of the legal nonexistence of married women was, English Chief Justice Matthew Hale pronounced in 1736, that husbands could not be held legally responsible for raping their wives. Subsequent rape laws in the states were based on this legal sanction of marital rape, rape generally being defined as the forcible penetration of the body of a woman, not the wife of the perpetrator. When federal legislation in the 1870s put authority for determining what was "obscene" in the United States in the hands of religious fundamentalist Anthony Comstock, Stanton and Gage saw allies like Moses Harmon imprisoned for simply raising the issue of marital rape in his newspaper, *Lucifer the Lightbearer.*

Euro-American men had the spiritual responsibility to enforce the obedience of their wives, and the legal system upheld a husband's right to "moderate correction," since he was responsible for her behavior. A North Carolina court ruled in 1864 that the state should not interfere in cases of domestic chastisement unless "permanent injury or excessive violence" was involved. By contrast, Haudenosaunee men were spiritually and socially prohibited from striking women—be they mother, wife, or child.

Alice Fletcher, suffragist and early ethnographer, addressed this issue at the International Council of Women, held by the NWSA in 1888. With the leaders of the woman's rights movement from around the world gathered for the first time, she shared the concern of her Native women acquaintances that, once they came under U.S. law, they would lose the traditional protection they had against male violence. Traditionally, the men of a woman's clan family would punish any man—husbands included—who violated or beat her. Under U.S. law, the brother who defended his sister "would himself become liable to the law and suffer for his championship," Fletcher worried (Wagner, 2001, 66).

Husbands also had absolute control of their offspring—even to having the legal authority of naming a guardian other than the mother for an unborn child in the event of his death. Gage documented such a case and contrasted the Euro-American mother's lack of say in the lives of her children with that of Haudenosaunee women, whose children followed her line:

> So fully to this day is descent reckoned through the mother, that blue-eyed, fair-haired children of white fathers are numbered in the tribe and receive both from state and nation their portion of the yearly dole paid to Indian tribes. The veriest pagan among the Iroquois, the renowned and important Keeper of the Wampum, and present sole interpreter of the Belts which give the most ancient and secret history of this confederation, is Ephriam Webster, descended from a white man, who, a hundred or more years since, became affiliated through marriage with an Indian woman, as a member of the principal nation of the Iroquois, the Onondagas (Wagner, 2001, 69–70).

Not just the Haudenosaunees, but generally, Gage asserted, Indians of North America trace descent in the female line. One implication of this, Gage's friend Harriet Maxwell Converse wrote, was that "in a divorce or separation, the children are taken by the mother, the family descent being from the maternal line."

In a speech before the National Council of Women in 1891, Elizabeth Cady Stanton celebrated Haudenosaunee-style divorce, pointing to it as a model:

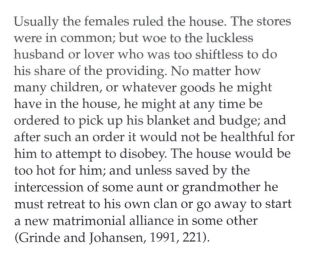

Usually the females ruled the house. The stores were in common; but woe to the luckless husband or lover who was too shiftless to do his share of the providing. No matter how many children, or whatever goods he might have in the house, he might at any time be ordered to pick up his blanket and budge; and after such an order it would not be healthful for him to attempt to disobey. The house would be too hot for him; and unless saved by the intercession of some aunt or grandmother he must retreat to his own clan or go away to start a new matrimonial alliance in some other (Grinde and Johansen, 1991, 221).

Stanton was especially sensitive to the issue of divorce. Among suffragists, she was uniquely courageous in advocating that the laws be changed to allow women the right to leave unacceptable marriages. For this stand she was labeled an infidel, since traditional Christianity generally held at the time that marriage was a covenant with God that no woman had a right to break, even if her life was in danger from a violent husband.

Underlying female autonomy among the Haudenosaunee nations was economic authority. Women, the creators, were the farmers, responsible for everything in Mother Earth, whereas men were responsible for hunting and everything on the surface of the land in the gender balance at the foundation of Haudenosaunee culture. Haudenosaunee women were extraordinary agriculturalists, Gage reported. In a published newspaper report on the 1875 Onondaga County Indian Fair, she noted that:

Forty-eight kinds of beans were on exhibition . . . this confederacy, with its wonderful government and customs and its fixed dwelling places, had in its own steps of progress developed a science of agriculture. Corn, beans, potatoes, and plants of the gourd family, including squash and a species of pumpkin, and tobacco, were all regularly cultivated, and together with vast quantity of nuts, were stored in pits or cellars for winter use (Gage, 1875).

Gage recognized that Native women farmers used methods unknown to white men.

Their method of farming was entirely different from our own. In olden Iroquois tillage there was no turning the sod with a plough to which were harnessed a cow and a woman, as is seen today in Christian Germany; but the ground was literally "tickled with a hoe" and it "laughed with a harvest." Corn hills three or four times larger than those seen to-day remained in use successive years, and when the country was first settled the appearance of those numerous little mounds created great wonder. Slightly scratched with a stick or piece of bone, maize was there planted, and but little labor attended its cultivation (Wagner, 2001, 53).

Married women in the United States, by state laws, were denied the right to control and possess their own property; it passed to their husbands upon the words "I do." It took tremendous political effort for nineteenth-century feminists slowly to change these state laws and claim the right to economic independence. Alice Fletcher at the 1888 International Council of Women informed her audience that the situation was completely different, not only for Native women but also for children. Everyone—men, women, and children—had their own possessions that no other family member could control. "A wife is as independent in the use of her possessions as is the most independent man in our midst," she declared, telling this story:

When I was living with the Indians, my hostess . . . one day gave away a very fine horse. I was surprised, for I knew there had been no family talk on the subject, so I asked: "Will your husband like to have you give the horse away?" Her eyes danced, and, breaking into a peal of laughter, she hastened to tell the story to the other women gathered in the tent, and I became the target of many merry eyes. I tried to explain how a white woman would act, but laughter and contempt met my explanation of the white man's hold upon his wife's property (Grinde and Johansen, 1991, 232).

Economic independence and authority, control of their property, rights to their bodies and children, and rights to divorce when a marriage became untenable, the ensured protection of their relatives, the spiritual authority with the responsibility of planning ceremonies—these were privileges Haudenosaunee women took for granted. They assumed, until they met European-American women, that this was the natural, universal condition of women. And they assumed that their political authority was a reality for all women.

The cultural contrast was dramatic. Women citizens of the United States, until they began to organize and slowly—school board by municipality by state—accomplished the Herculean task of creating a political voice, had no say in their own lives, from family to country. While Haudenosaunee women had full participation in their government, European-American women faced state laws making it a crime for them to vote, and Susan B. Anthony was arrested, tried, and found guilty for exercising her right of citizenship. They did not gain recognition of their inherent right to the ballot—in a republic based on the consent of the governed—until 1920. Haudenosaunee women, on the other hand, had possessed a political voice equal to men since the founding of the Iroquois Confederacy, before Columbus arrived on these shores. They called their own councils and determined their own issues, which were then heard by the grand council. The chiefs who represented the clans in council were nominated by the women and, as Stanton told the National Council of Women in 1891, "They did not hesitate, when occasion required, 'to knock off the horns,' as it was technically called, from the head of a chief and send him back to the ranks of the warriors" (Wagner, 2001, 82). The clan mother alone had the authority to remove the chief, as Stanton understood. Women were the great power among the clan, as everywhere else, she maintained. Mott wrote about listening to speeches of their chiefs, when she visited the Seneca in 1848.

"Division of power between the sexes in this Indian republic was nearly equal," Gage enthused, and it wasn't just Haudenosaunee women who had a political voice: "among some tribes women enjoy almost the whole legislative authority and in others a prominent share." Haudenosaunee women also have the final say in whether their men would go to war. Writing in her capacity as president of the National Woman Suffrage Association, Gage told readers of *The New York Evening Post* in 1875: "Its women exercised controlling power in peace and war, forbidding at will its young braves to enter battle, and often determining its terms of peace" (Wagner, 2001, 48, 71).

Henry Schoolcraft, one of Gage's sources, wrote in 1847, that the war authority of women "exists to-day as incontestably as it did centuries ago. They were entrusted with the power to propose a cessa-tion of arms. They were literally peace-makers" (Schoolcraft, 1847, n.p.). When the Wolf Clan adopted Gage in 1893, her Mohawk sister told her that the Council of Matrons would decide "as to my having a voice in the Chieftainship" (Gage, 1893). How amazing this must have been to a woman who went to trial the same year for voting in a school board election in her upstate New York village. Considered for decision-making authority in her adopted nation, she was arrested for voting in her own nation—and lost her case.

Alice Fletcher summarized the contrast between Native and non-Native women for suffragists in her 1888 International Council of Women speech in this way:

> As I have tried to explain our statutes to Indian women, I have met with but one response. They have said: "As an Indian woman I was free. I owned my home, my person, the work of my own hands, and my children could never forget me. I was better off as an Indian woman than under white law." Men have said: "Your laws show how little your men care for their women. The wife is nothing of herself. She is worth little but to help a man to have one hundred and sixty acres. . . . She has fallen under the edge of our laws" (Fletcher, 1888, 238).

Sally Roesch Wagner

References and Further Reading

Beauchamp, Mary Elizabeth. 1883. Letter to the Editor. *Skaneateles Democrat*, April 10. Beauchamp File, Syracuse, NY: Onondaga Historical Association.

Fletcher, Alice. 1888. "The Legal Conditions of Indian Women." *Report of the International Council of Women, Assembled by the National Woman Suffrage Association . . . 1888.* Washington, DC: Rufus H. Darby.

Gage, Matilda Joslyn. 1875. "The Onondaga Indians: Their Recent Agricultural Fair—How the Ancient Iroquois Tilled the Ground—Further Evidence of the Importance of Women Among the Allied Tribes of New York State—The Origin of Hasty Pudding." *New York Evening Post*, 3 November 11. Reprinted in Fayetteville, New York, *Weekly Recorder*.

Gage, Matilda Joslyn. 1893. "To My Dear Helen[daughter]." December 11. Matilda Joslyn Gage Collection, Schlesinger Library, Radcliffe College. Cambridge, MA.

Grinde, Donald A., Jr., and Bruce E. Johansen. 1991. *Exemplar of Liberty: Native America and the Evolution of Democracy.* Los Angeles, CA: UCLA American Indian Studies Center.

Schoolcraft, Henry R. 1847. *Notes on the Iroquois.* New York: Bartlett & Welford.

Wagner, Sally R. 2001. *Sisters in Spirit: Haudenosaunee (Iroquois) Influence on Early American Feminists.* Summertown, TN: Native Voices.

Fishing Rights

Control of and access to natural resources has been a contentious issue throughout American Indian history. While conflicts over fur trapping and big game hunting characterized much of the period of westward expansion, in the latter half of the twentieth century the most serious conflicts in the United States have involved Native American fishing rights.

The nature of American Indian fishing can be traced through four historical periods that occurred similarly throughout Native North America but at different periods of time and of different durations.

Initially the traditional use of fisheries resources was part of the traditional round of subsistence activities. Access to, control of, and distribution of fisheries resources were vested in the kinship group and varied according to cultural custom. For example, in some areas of the Pacific Northwest, fishing locations were owned by extended families (kindreds) or clans, whereas in the Great Lakes area fishing locations were open access. During the early phase of European contact, these traditional systems of access persisted. Even when the European colonizers were interested in exploiting the fisheries resource, traditional American Indian systems of allocation and European concepts of fisheries as common property coexisted.

As the European and later the European-American populations increased, in step with demands on the fisheries resources, Native Americans were initially incorporated as producers and workers in the burgeoning fishing industries. This second period lasted only a few years in some areas, whereas in other areas it is evident to this day. This period was generally ushered in with the commercialization of fisheries resources, and Native Americans were often

Native Americans protest violations of tribal fishing rights along the Columbia River in Washington state in 1971. (Corbis)

in a position as fishers and processors to provide the knowledge and skilled labor necessary to effectively develop the resource on a large scale.

The third period of American Indian fisheries can be characterized as a time of marginalization. In most areas, increasing technological sophistication and increased capitalization worked to exclude small-scale producers from participation in the fisheries for commercially valuable species. Combined with federal policies designed to shift Native Americans from participation in traditional pursuits to settled agriculture, Native peoples were directed away from the developing fishing industries. Finally, American Indians brought about a fourth period by gaining reentry into the fisheries through legal channels. This has resulted in some of the most controversial court decisions in the history of the United States.

In the Pacific Northwest, the tribes of western Washington and the Columbia River have been actively pursuing fishing rights assured by treaty since the 1890s. It was not until the 1960s and 1970s, however, that favorable court decisions specifically guaranteed a Native allocation. The Native American fishers had been largely excluded from the salmon fisheries of the Pacific Northwest by the early 1900s. Increased commercialization and environmental degradation caused the salmon stocks to decrease dramatically so that by 1960 Native American fishers were taking less than 3 percent of the total harvest.

Salmon are an essential part of the economic and religious life of the Native peoples of the Pacific Northwest, and the fear that access might disappear altogether prompted several tribes to go to court to argue for a specific treaty Indian allocation. This resulted in two landmark cases. *Sohappy v. Smith* (1969), or the Belloni decision, stipulated that state regulatory agencies must provide an opportunity for treaty Indians to harvest a "fair share" of the salmon resource. *United States v. State of Washington* (1974], or the Boldt decision, went further to specify an allocation. Based on treaty wording, the court decided that the allocation should be established at 50 percent of the harvestable salmon resource. Since 1974, the treaty allocation has been extended to other commercially valuable species as well, such as herring, halibut, and shellfish. Especially controversial is the "fisheries clause" in the Treaty with the Makah, which enabled the 1999 harvest of a gray whale, the first in nearly eighty years. The fisheries clauses in the treaties with tribes in the Pacific Northwest have been at the heart of the controversies. All of the treaties with tribes in western Washington and along the Columbia River contain wording securing the right of taking fish at all usual and accustomed places and to hunt and gather on open and unclaimed lands; some of the treaties contain further rights specific to the signatory tribes, such as whaling, the taking of shellfish, or the pasturing of horses.

The Great Lakes fishery followed a similar course of events. Commercialization of the resource started as early as 1836, and Native people were an essential part of this early development but were gradually squeezed out of the industry. By the late 1800s, the Native people of these areas were primarily involved in a subsistence fishery, marginalized as the commercial fishery developed. Overutilization eventually caused the collapse of the commercial fishery, and in the 1960s state efforts were focused on rejuvenating the Great Lakes fishery to attract tourism dollars into economically depressed areas. American Indian fishers also sought participation in the revived fishery based on treaty rights to the resource. After several state court cases, Native groups eventually won favorable decisions in federal court. Among others, *United States v. Michigan* (1979), the Fox decision, *Lac Courte Oreilles v. Voight* (1983), the Voight decision, and *Minnesota v. Mille Lacs Band* (1998) established treaty rights to fish in the Great Lakes and other waters of Michigan, Wisconsin, and Minnesota. Unlike the Pacific Northwest treaties the Great Lakes treaties do not limit the traditional right. In the aftermath of these decisions there was a rash of anti-Indian activism.

Native American fishing rights in the United States are generally of two types: those on reservation lands and those on off-reservation lands. Off-reservation lands are usually ceded lands, but in the Pacific Northwest treaty fishing rights are expanded to "usual and accustomed areas," which may extend beyond lands ceded by treaty. On-reservation fishing rights are generally exclusive, whereas off-reservation fishing rights are generally shared with citizens of the United States.

Fishing rights controversies entered the courts as early as the 1880s, and throughout the early 1900s a long series of state and federal court decisions dealt with singular issues. For example in *United States v. Winans* (1905) the U.S. Supreme Court ruled that Yakama fishers could not be excluded from their traditional off-reservation fishing locations by a non-Indian landowner. The treaty right to access usual and accustomed areas superseded the right of a nontreaty fisher to place a fishing device on the

Subsistence Language in Northwest Coast Treaties

Treaty	Date	Subsistence Clause
Medicine Creek	12/24/1854	The right of taking fish, at all usual and accustomed grounds and stations, is further secured to said Indians in common with all citizens of the Territory, and of erecting temporary houses for the purpose of curing, together with the privilege of hunting, gathering roots and berries, and pasturing their horses on open and unclaimed lands. Provided, however, That they shall not take shellfish from any beds staked or cultivated by citizens, and that they shall alter all stallions not intended for breeding-horses, and shall keep up and confine the latter.
Point Elliott	1/22/1855	The right of taking fish at usual and accustomed grounds and stations is further secured to said Indians in common with all citizens of the Territory, and of erecting temporary houses for the purposes of curing, together with the privilege of hunting and gathering roots and berries on open and unclaimed lands. Provided, however, That they shall not take shell-fish from any beds staked or cultivated by citizens.
Point No Point	1/26/1855	The right of taking fish at usual and accustomed grounds and stations is further secured to said Indians, in common with all citizens of the United States; and of erecting temporary houses for the purpose of curing; together with the privilege of hunting and gathering roots and berries on open and unclaimed lands. Provided, however, That they shall not take shell-fish from any beds staked or cultivated by citizens.
Makah Treaty	1/31/1855	The right of taking fish and of whaling or sealing at usual and accustomed grounds and stations is further secured to said Indians in common with all citizens of the United States, and of erecting temporary houses for the purpose of curing, together with the privilege of hunting and gathering roots and berries on open and unclaimed lands. Provided, however, That they shall not take shell-fish from any beds staked or cultivated by citizens.
Quinalt Treaty	1/25/1856	The right of taking fish at all usual and accustomed grounds and stations is secured to said Indians in common with all citizens of

traditional location. In *Winans* the U.S. Supreme Court further determined not merely that the state could not regulate a treaty fishery except for conservation but also that the treaties must be interpreted "in accordance with the meaning they were understood by the tribal representatives" and in "a spirit which recognizes the full obligation of this nation to protect the interests of a dependent people," thereby applying the canon of Utmost Good Faith to treaty fishing rights. In *Tulee v. State of Washington* (1942) a

Yakama fisher who was arrested for fishing without a state license argued that treaty fishing rights could not be regulated by the state.

During the 1960s several western Washington treaty tribes began to organize protests and legal proceedings to draw attention to how the commercial fishery had come to exclude treaty Indians. Numerous fish-ins were organized at conspicuous locations, most frequently in south Puget Sound, resulting in a series of courts cases known as Puyallup I, II, and III.

		the Territory, and of erecting temporary houses for the purpose of curing the same; together with the privilege of hunting, gathering roots and berries, and pasturing their horses on all open and unclaimed lands. Provided, however, That they shall not take shell-fish from any beds staked or cultivated by citizens; and provided, also, that they shall alter all stallions not intended for breeding, and keep up and confine the stallions themselves.
Yakama Treaty	6/9/1855	The exclusive right of taking fish in all the streams, where running through or bordering said reservation, is further secured to said confederated tribes and bands of Indians, as also the right of taking fish at all usual and accustomed places, in common with the citizens of the Territory, and of erecting temporary buildings for curing them; together with the privilege of hunting, gathering roots and berries, and pasturing their horses and cattle upon open and unclaimed land.
Walla Walla Treaty	6/9/1855	That the exclusive right of taking fish in the streams running through and bordering said reservation is hereby secured to said Indians, and at all other usual and accustomed stations in common with citizens of the United States, and of erecting suitable buildings for curing the same; the privilege of hunting, gathering roots and berries and pasturing their stock on unclaimed lands in common with citizens, is also secured to them.
Nez Percé Treaty	6/11/1855	The exclusive right of taking fish in all the streams where running through or bordering said reservation is further secured to said Indians; as also the right of taking fish at all usual and accustomed places in common with citizens of the Territory; and of erecting temporary buildings for curing, together with the privilege of hunting, gathering roots and berries, and pasturing their horses and cattle upon open and unclaimed land.
Middle Oregon Treaty	6/25/1855	That the exclusive right of taking fish in the streams running through and bordering said reservation is hereby secured to said Indians; and at all other usual and accustomed stations, in common with citizens, of the United States, and of erecting suitable houses for curing the same; also the privilege of hunting, gathering roots and berries, and pasturing their stock on unclaimed lands, in common with citizens, is secured to them.

By 1971 this opposition had developed to the point where thirteen western Washington tribes were ready to pursue the issue in court. The tribes brought suit in 1973 with the federal government intervening on their behalf.

On February 14, 1974 Federal District Court Judge George Boldt decided that the subsistence clause of the 1854–1856 western Washington treaties must be interpreted to mean that treaty tribes are entitled to a guarantee of half of the harvestable allocation of salmon because the state of Washington had been "either unable or unwilling" to ensure an allocation for treaty fishers. The immediate response of non-treaty fishers was one of indignation and violent resistance. The state of Washington initially balked at enforcing the adjudicated allocation and for four years the salmon fishery of Washington was in a state of chaos. A number of violent altercations ensued, a fourteen-year-old Indian fisher was shot at by a sniper on one occasion, and in another incident a fisheries patrol officer wounded a nontreaty fisher with a shotgun. In July 1978 Judge Boldt assumed control of management of the fishery and called on the U.S. Coast Guard to enforce management decisions.

The Boldt decision has been one of the most controversial issues in American Indian history. Based on similar wording in articles contained in the five ratified western Washington treaties, the decision legally defined the phrase "in common with" that was part of the wording in the treaty subsistence clauses.

By dictionary definition and as intended in the Indian treaties and in this decision, the phrase "in common with" means *sharing equally* the opportunity to take fish at "usual and accustomed grounds and stations"; therefore, non-treaty fishermen shall have the opportunity to take up to 50 per cent of the harvestable number of fish that may be taken by all fishermen, and treaty right fishermen shall have the opportunity to take up to the same percentage of harvestable fish . . . " (*United States v. State of Washington*, 384 F Supp. 312 [1974]).

An important determination of the courts was the interpretation that fishing rights were *reserved* by treaty, whereas fishing was a *privilege* extended to nontreaty fishers. This interpretation of treaty language argues that treaty fishers owned the resource traditionally and through treaties relinquished a share of it. The public and the media generally do not understand that the Boldt decision did not "give" half of the fishery to the treaty tribes; rather, the legal interpretation is that they reserved half of what they originally owned in its entirety.

The Boldt decision was appealed and upheld by the U.S. Court of Appeals in 1975. In 1976, the U.S. Supreme Court declined review of the case. The controversy surrounding the implementation of the decision and the state and federal attention it received compelled the Supreme Court to hear the appeal, the first time in the history of the U.S. Supreme Court that it reversed a decision not to hear a case. In 1979 the U.S. Supreme Court upheld the Boldt decision in a six-to-three ruling. Since 1979 the state of Washington has resumed management of the fishery and has implemented a management regime that has enabled the treaty tribes to reap their share of the harvest. The tribes have also assumed management of much of the treaty share of the fisheries. In 1974 the western Washington treaty tribes organized the Northwest Indian Fisheries Commission to "assist and coordinate the development of an orderly and biologically sound treaty fishery in the Northwest." Elsewhere, similar organizations were founded in the wake of sympathetic court decisions, including the Columbia River Inter-Tribal Fish Commission and the Great Lakes Indian Fish and Wildlife Commission.

In a repeat performance of the Boldt decision, the Fox decision in *United States v. Michigan* (1979) found that the treaty fishing rights of the Chippewas and Ottawas are protected by treaty and that these "tribes have unique, exclusive, off-reservation rights to engage in gill net fishing in waters of Lake Michigan, despite Michigan laws to the contrary . . . these treaties grant the Indians an absolute right to engage in gill net fishing in these waters free from any regulation by the State of Michigan or any limitations of time, place or manner generally applicable to other citizens . . . " The state of Michigan appealed the decision, and the U.S. Supreme Court declined to review it. Subsequently, similar decisions extended fishing rights to treaty tribes in Wisconsin and Minnesota.

Access and control of natural resources continues to be one of the most contentious issues for indigenous peoples and the states wherein they reside. With the universal problem of declining resources and increasing American Indian influence in management decisions, the repercussions extend beyond traditional rights of access to fish. A second component of the Boldt decision, known as Phase II, extends some influence over the environmental impacts to concerned Native American tribes. The Boldt decision reasoned that without fish there would be no fishing rights. Environmental concerns, such as development in watersheds, offshore oil drilling, and the breaching of antiquated dams will become the dominant issues in the near future as Native Americans continue their role as stewards of the environment and attempt to protect the natural resources on which they depend.

Daniel L. Boxberger

See also Ceremonies, Criminalization of; Columbia River Inter-Tribal Fish Commission; Dalles Trading Area; Dams, Fishing Rights, and Hydroelectric Power; Economic Development; Great Lakes Intertribal Council; Red Power Movement; Salmon, Economic and Spiritual Significance of; Sohappy, Sr., David; Treaty Diplomacy, with Summary of Selected Treaties; Tribal Sovereignty; Water Rights.

References and Further Reading

Boxberger, Daniel L. 1989. *To Fish in Common: The Ethnohistory of Lummi Indian Salmon Fishing*. Lincoln: University of Nebraska Press.

Boxberger, Daniel L. 2000. *To Fish in Common: The Ethnohistory of Lummi Indian Salmon Fishing.* Lincoln: University of Nebraska Press. Seattle: University of Washington Press.

Cohen, Fay. 1986. *Uncommon Controversy: The Continuing Controversy Over Northwest Indian Fishing Rights.* Seattle: University of Washington Press.

Columbia River Inter-Tribal Fish Commission. No date. Available at: http://www.critfc.org. Accessed March 25, 2006.

Doherty, Robert. 1990. *Disputed Waters: Native Americans and the Great Lakes Fishery.* Lexington: University Press of Kentucky.

Great Lakes Indian Fish and Wildlife Commission. No date. Available at: http://www.glifwc.org. Accessed March 25, 2006.

Nesper, Larry. 2002. *The Walleye Wars: The Struggle for Ojibwe Spearfishing Treaty Rights.* Lincoln: University of Nebraska Press.

Northwest Indian Fisheries Commission. No date. Available at: http://www.nwifc.org. Accessed March 25, 2006.

Ulrich, Roberta. 1999. *Empty Nets: Indians, Dams and the Columbia River.* Corvallis: Oregon State University Press.

Whaley, Rick, and Walt Bresette. 1999. *Walleye Warriors: The Chippewa Treaty Rights Story.* Warner, NH: Silver Brook Press.

Wilkinson, Charles. 2000. *Messages from Frank's Landing: A Story of Salmon, Treaties and the Indian Way.* Seattle: University of Washington Press.

Fur Trade

The North American fur trade comprised an important episode in the continent's history and had far-reaching consequences for the course of European-American westward expansion. Fur traders were the advance guard of European and American society and were typically the first Europeans to encounter Native Americans. The concept of trapping animals and selling their fur to distant consumers introduced a market economy to the Native Americans' world. In the process, the trade hunted many animals to extinction. Moreover, the fur trade was truly an international venture, including not only Native Americans but also the British, French, Russians, Spanish, Dutch, and Americans.

Before Europeans arrived in North America, Native Americans traded furs among themselves. The trade, however, occurred on the local level and served relatively small populations. Also, because many Native groups had migratory habits, Native Americans did not accumulate more furs than

Engraving of fur traders socializing with Native Americans in the seventeenth century. (Library of Congress)

could immediately be put to use or traded for other goods.

When Europeans arrived on the North Atlantic coast in the sixteenth century, they encouraged Native Americans to assist them in conducting a fur trade on a much larger scale. Presented with abundant and seemingly inexhaustible supplies of fur-bearing animals, Europeans desired sable, mink, otter, ermine, and especially beaver to use in the finest coats, clothes, and hats, establishing a trade both to Europe and to parts of Asia. For their part, Native Americans wanted iron tools and other items that only Europeans could provide.

The beginning of the fur trade exchange transformed Native American culture in the Northeast, as it would elsewhere later. After the French explorer Jacques Cartier found an abundant beaver population in the Saint Lawrence River Valley during his expeditions between 1534 and 1543, Paris hatmakers eagerly imported North American beaver pelts, setting a fashion trend that spread quickly to the rest of Europe and driving an even larger demand for furs.

Native Americans usually obtained the pelts for French, British, and Dutch employers, because they knew the land and had experience hunting. As the profits from the trade increased and animal pelts began to grow scarce, competition over trading territory among Native groups intensified and led to a number of Iroquois wars in the midseventeenth century. The Iroquois and their British and Dutch trading partners virtually annihilated the Hurons, who had served as the region's largest fur brokers. This initial phase of the fur trade frequently pitted Native Americans against each other as various groups struggled to achieve or maintain dominance in a particular region.

Meanwhile, another rivalry developed between the European powers to protect their profitable trading empires. Although the French had established a stronghold in Montreal early in the seventeenth century, the British challenged French dominance in the northern and western fur trade by chartering the Hudson's Bay Company in 1670. The French responded by putting more traders in the field. By 1680, 800 French traders worked in the backcountry and had established strong economic bonds with several Native American groups. The French aggressively continued to establish trading posts throughout the Great Lakes region until the end of the French and Indian War in 1763, which ended in their defeat at the hands of the British.

After the French had been swept from the North American continent, the Hudson's Bay Company faced competition from the North West Company, a combination of former French companies, and British, Scottish, and New England merchants. The Hudson's Bay Company and the Nor'westers, as the traders and trappers of the North West Company were called, moved aggressively throughout the interior of North America.

In the Ohio Valley and the region around the Great Lakes, the fur trade created a unique society. As in the colonial Northeast, Native Americans played a significant role in the interior fur trade, serving as guides when Europeans pushed into new regions and working as trappers. They were also an eager market for European goods, contributing to the trade's profitability, as Europeans not only made money trading with the Indians but also reaped significant rewards when the furs were sold in Europe. Each group, then, needed the other.

Native Americans often paid a high price for their involvement in the trade, however. American traders and trappers introduced alcohol and diseases to Native Americans, with devastating consequences. Epidemics of measles, mumps, influenza, and especially smallpox decimated tribal populations. The resultant decline in Indian populations further opened the door for white settlement, making the fur traders vanguards of the American empire.

This capitalistic relationship also forged more personal ties between Europeans and Native Americans. European traders frequently married Native women. In fact, historians now estimate that as many as 40 percent of trappers may have married Native Americans. These unions generally benefited both parties, as European men desired companionship, and Native women often gained power among their own people and usually a level of material comfort. European traders also used their marriages to gain access to traditional Native lands and knowledge, as well as gaining hardworking partners for the arduous labor of the fur trade.

The children that resulted from these marriages were known as Métis, who paradoxically fit in both European and Native American societies but who were sometimes ostracized from both. Métis served as a cultural bridge to these separate populations, but ultimately such intermarriage undermined Native family patterns.

As trappers moved west, they pushed into the land of the Louisiana Purchase and the Mexican-controlled Rocky Mountain region. Here, such famous trappers as Jedediah Smith and Jim Bridger captured the imagination of the American public as they spent years in the mountains trapping beavers and other fur-bearing animals.

The Rocky Mountain trapping system differed substantially from the fur-trapping practices of the Hudson's Bay Company and other colonial traders. Rather than establishing a trading post and having Native American or British trappers periodically go to the post to exchange hides for goods, an American merchant named William Ashley created the annual rendezvous system in 1825. Every year, Ashley sent a supply train to a spot in the Rocky Mountains where American trappers, Native Americans, and Mexicans came to trade. The only social event of the year for these trappers, the rendezvous assumed something of a carnival-like atmosphere, with a variety of entertainments, storytelling, drinking, and dancing. The rendezvous became an important part of the culture of the Rocky Mountain fur trade.

The most successful of the traders was an American named John Jacob Astor. A German by birth, Astor had immigrated to America in the 1780s and shortly thereafter, opened his own fur-trading firm in New York City, naming it the American Fur Company. From there, he financed an army of trappers who spread out over the North American interior. By 1820, he had nearly established a monopoly on the American fur trade, the profits from which he famously reinvested in Manhattan real estate. Wisely, he foresaw the decline of the fur trade in the mid-1830s and sold his interest in the business.

By that time, fur-bearing animal populations were seriously suffering, hovering on the brink of extinction in many areas of North America. The situation was so poor that in 1838 Mexico, which ruled much of the Rocky Mountain region at this time, declared a moratorium on trapping the animals to allow the populations a chance to recover. It marked the end of the trade in the interior, and by 1840 the Rocky Mountain trapping system had significantly declined. The fur trade in central North America was replaced by a thriving industry in buffalo hides, which would ensure the buffaloes' almost complete extinction by the end of the nineteenth century.

As some trappers explored the interior of the continent, others extended the trade along the Pacific Coast. Since the 1740s, the Russian-American Company had been taking sea otter pelts, which they dubbed "soft gold," in Alaska. Between 1743 and 1800, 100 separate business ventures, all sponsored by the Russian-American Company, obtained more than 8 million silver rubles worth of pelts. The Spanish empire also engaged in some fur trading activities along the Pacific Coast.

The trade along the Pacific Coast vastly accelerated at the close of the eighteenth century, after Great Britain's Captain James Cook anchored in Nootka Sound on Vancouver Island in 1778. While on the island, Cook obtained sea otter pelts from the Native Americans, and, when his ships reached China, the crew found that the otter pelts were worth a fortune. When news of this exchange spread, American and British merchants flocked to the Pacific Northwest to join in the trade, quickly out-harvesting Russian and Spanish traders. In fact, they were so successful that the sea otter population had dwindled to dangerously low levels by about 1815. The trade thus faltered, as too few sea otters remained to sustain a profitable business.

In 1811, however, the Pacific Fur Company, a subsidiary of Astor's American Fur Company, established a fur trading post at Astoria, Oregon, to counter British dominance in the region, which served as the basis for later settlements of American trappers. Undeterred, the Hudson's Bay Company then pursued a policy to make the rich Columbia River region a "fur desert." This strategy, pursued by Peter Skene Ogden beginning in about 1834, involved hunting fur-bearing animals to near extinction, making it unprofitable for American fur traders to trap in the region and slowing American migration. For another decade or more, the British remained the dominant force in the Northwest, until the diplomatic maneuverings of President James K. Polk forced the British to relinquish their hold on the region.

By midcentury, the fur trade was exhausted in most of the United States. Only in Alaska did it continue to flourish. Although the U.S. purchase of Alaska in 1867 essentially expelled Russian traders from the region, it did not end the fur trade. Picking up where the Russians had left off, British, Canadian, and American entrepreneurs began trapping aggressively in Alaska. The Pribilof Islands, for example, generated more than 100,000 seal pelts per year until 1890, when scientific authorities recognized the fur seal population was dangerously low.

In response, representatives from the United States and Great Britain signed the Convention for the Protection of Fur Seals in Alaska (1892), which placed a limit on the number of seals that could be killed in the course of a year. Because Russia and Japan, two of the most aggressive fur-hunting countries, were not involved, however, the convention did not prove as effective as its proponents had hoped. Not until 1911 did representatives from the four countries gather and hammer out a more comprehensive agreement that significantly restrained the fur trade in Alaska.

Throughout the twentieth century, furs have remained popular in the fashion world, although hunting for fur has been prohibited in the United States. In the 1980s and 1990s, Americans became increasingly concerned with fur hunting in the Arctic Circle, most of which is conducted by trappers from other countries. Outrage over the practice of clubbing baby seals to death for their fur led to the emergence of a widespread movement to ban the wearing of animal furs. In several well-publicized incidents, protestors of the fur trade poured buckets of red paint on women wearing fur coats. Environmental groups in the United States have also organized large public rallies to protest the continuing fur trade. However, because most of the trade is conducted by trappers from other countries, American public opinion has had little effect.

Adam Sowards

See also Beaver Wars; Canoes; Disease, Historic and Contemporary; French and Indian War; Hudson's Bay Company; New France and Natives; North West Company; Northwest Ordinance; Russians, in the Arctic/Northwest; Trade; Warfare, Intertribal.

References and Further Reading
Cronon, William. 1983. *Changes in the Land: Indians, Colonists, and the Ecology of New England.* New York: Hill and Wang.
DeVoto, Bernard. 1947. *Across the Wide Missouri.* Boston: Houghton-Mifflin.
White, Richard. 1991. *The Middle Ground: Indians, Empires, and Republics in the Great Lakes Region, 1650–1815.* New York: Cambridge University Press.
Wishart, David. 1979. *The Fur Trade of the American West, 1807–1840: A Geographic Synthesis.* Lincoln: University of Nebraska Press.

Ghost Dance Religion

What non-Indian observers deemed the Ghost Dance was a much older belief and ceremony among various Numic-speaking peoples that emerged as a pan-Indian faith in two movements; 1869–1870 and 1889–1890. Both movements began among the *Numu* (northern Paiutes) of the Walker River Reservation in western Nevada and promised the reunification of the living and the dead on a reborn earth, the return of game animals, and, by varying accounts, the elimination of non-Indians or nonbelievers. Both movements found adherents far beyond the Numu homeland. There were, however, important differences between the two movements, with the latter being more widespread and exhibiting much greater Christian syncretism. "Ghost Dance" is a non-Indian term; each American Indian people has its own specific name for the ceremony.

The Ghost Dance religion is a pan-Indian movement that exhibited similarities to pan-Indian religions stretching back to the eighteenth century. During the French and Indian War, the Delaware prophet Neolin preached that Native peoples must wean themselves of dependence on the Europeans in order to clear a path to heaven. His teachings were the spiritual underpinning of Pontiac's coalition of Native peoples that for a time stalled British expansion in the Ohio country. A half-century later, the Shawnee prophet Tenskwatawa announced a similar prophecy, which played a similar role in his brother Tecumseh's attempt to create a pan-Indian political and military alliance. On the Columbia Plateau, the Prophet Dances and the Dreamer Religion of the Wanapum Prophet Smohalla also proposed a millennial vision of a pan-Indian future and identity.

The first pan-Indian Ghost Dance movement emerged from the vicinity of the Walker River Reservation around 1869. The 1870 Ghost Dance has remained far more obscure than the religious movement that followed two decades later. Contemporary non-Indian observers did not even recognize the larger pattern within scattered reports of religious excitement among Native peoples. The 1870 Ghost Dance prophet was Wodziwob (Gray Hair or Gray Head), a Fish Lake Valley Paiute who lived at Walker River, where he was also known as Hawthorne Wodziwob and Fish Lake Joe. Announcing his initial prophecies at communal gatherings, Wodziwob told his followers that Indian people could radically transform the present through supernatural means by practicing the prescribed ceremonies. He prophesied a return of the old ways with all the Indians living and dead reunited on a renewed earth.

The ceremonial base of both Ghost Dance movements was the Great Basin Round Dance, a rite that served a number of important ritual purposes during communal gatherings such as rabbit drives and fish runs. Men, women, and children all participated. Within the circle, they alternated sexes, interlocked fingers, and shuffled slowly to the left, all the while singing songs revealed to individual dancers in visions. The dances occurred five nights in succession, and the cycle could be repeated up to twenty times a year.

The 1870 Ghost Dance spread north and west to the Washoes, Pyramid Lake Paiutes, Surprise Valley Paiutes, Modocs, Klamaths, Shastas, Karoks, Maidus, and Patwins. In California, the dances inspired revivals of preexisting religions (the Kuksu or God Impersonating cult) or were transformed into new belief systems (the Bole-Maru and Dream religions). Contrary to established historical opinion, the 1870 Ghost Dance spread at least as far east as the Rocky Mountains where Shoshones, Bannocks, and Utes all practiced the religion continuously throughout the last three decades of the nineteenth century.

The second Ghost Dance movement also began on the Walker River Reservation. The prophet Wovoka (also known as Jack Wilson) experienced his first vision on New Year's Day, 1889. He reported traveling to heaven and meeting God. He was instructed to return to earth and to tell the people to

A Paiute Ghost Dance during the late nineteenth century. The Ghost Dance was a messianic movement started by the Paiute prophet Wovoka in the late nineteenth century that promised the return of a pre-contact golden age, including the return to life of deceased Indians. (Library of Congress)

lead good and loving lives and to follow a ritual that, if faithfully obeyed, would reunite them with their deceased loved ones and friends in a world without "death or sickness or old age." The first dances took place at Walker River shortly thereafter, and word of the prophecy spread rapidly to reservations across the West. Native peoples from across the Great Basin attended the second series of dances later that spring, and by the end of 1889 a delegation had arrived from the Lakotas and other Plains peoples.

Broad similarities notwithstanding, several aspects of Wovoka's doctrine marked important departures from the earlier movement. First, the 1890 Ghost Dance was as "redemptive" as it was "transformative." Wovoka did prophesy a radical transformation of the existing order—a renewal of the earth and the reunification of all American Indian people—but he also preached a gospel of peace, love, and accommodation that, by eliminating many of the causes of internal discord, served to strengthen Indian communities. Caspar Edson, an

Arapaho who visited Wovoka in August 1891, was the only Native person to record a written version of the doctrine: the famed Messiah Letter. Wovoka told his followers to live at peace with the non-Native immigrants: "Do not fight. Do always right." On the other hand, his words also could be interpreted to suggest that non-Indians, or even Native nonbelievers, would not survive the coming cataclysm. Secondly, Wovoka's doctrine exhibited far greater Christian influence than the earlier movement. As a young child, he had been exposed to Christian teachings (acquiring the name Jack) while working on the Mason Valley ranch of David and Abigail Wilson. By several accounts, Wovoka claimed he was Jesus and even reportedly showed the stigmata of crucifixion to a number of Native seekers including the Cheyenne holy man Porcupine.

In most accounts, the Ghost Dance of 1890 has been inextricably linked to the tragic events that took place on the Lakota reservations. The popularity and perceived militancy of the religion among the

Lakotas (many Lakota dancers wore Ghost Shirts, which were reputed to be bullet-proof) panicked non-Indian settlers and elicited an overwhelming military response. Following Sitting Bull's assassination at Standing Rock, the Minneconjou Lakota headman Bigfoot led his band south toward a hoped-for refuge at Pine Ridge. Instead they were intercepted by the U.S. Seventh Cavalry and on December 29 1890, along the banks of Wounded Knee Creek, Bigfoot and well over 150 of his people died as the soldiers' attempt to take them into custody degenerated into a slaughter.

Contrary to popular understanding, the Ghost Dance religion was not a short-lived phenomenon. In many cases, it inspired cultural revitalization among Indian peoples. The Lakotas continued to practice the religion for at least two years after the massacre at Wounded Knee. In 1902 the Lakota apostle Kicking Bear once again visited the prophet Wovoka and later introduced the religion to the Fort Peck Reservation in Montana. From there, an Assiniboine man named Fred Robinson took his interpretation of the doctrine—emphasizing Wovoka's admonition to lead a "clean, honest life"—to the Wahepton Sioux of Saskatchewan, where it survives as the New Tidings religion. The Ghost Dance religion also facilitated the revitalization of Pawnee culture in the 1890s and early twentieth century, while the Kiowas practiced a modified version of the dance from 1894 to 1916. Moreover, the Ghost Dance continues to be practiced today among Paiutes, Shoshones, Bannocks, and Utes, where it was a customary religious practice long before the movements of 1870 and 1890.

Gregory E. Smoak

See also Assimilation; Bole-Maru Religion; Dreamer Cult; Smohalla; Wovoka.

References and Further Reading
Hittman, Michael. *Wovoka and the Ghost Dance,* expanded ed. Lincoln: University of Nebraska Press, 1997.
Mooney, James. *The Ghost Dance Religion and the Sioux Outbreak of 1890,* reprint ed. Lincoln: University of Nebraska Press, 1991.

Graham, Mount (Dzil Nchaa Si An), Controversy over

Mount Graham, at 10,720 feet, is one of the tallest mountains in Arizona; it is also a sacred pilgrimage and ceremonial site for the Apache Indians. Also known as Dzil nchaa si an, Mount Graham is the central source of Apache spiritual guidance and home to the Gaahn, tribal spiritual deities to whom prayers are offered. Atop the sacred mountain Apache Indians procure medicinal plants, bury medicinal leaders, and perform religious rituals.

Because of Mount Graham's unique height and location, its ecology possesses more life zones and vegetative communities than any other solitary mountain range in North America. Specifically, the sacred mountain is home to at least eighteen species and subspecies of plants and animals found nowhere else on the planet, including the endangered Red Squirrel. Yet, despite the unique ecosystem of Mount Graham, and its sacred and cultural significance to the Apache Indians, the site has been designated as a preeminent location for astronomy and the construction of a new astrophysical complex, which would contain the most powerful telescope multiplex in the world.

Beginning in the 1980s, University of Arizona astronomers and an international group of researchers proposed the construction of eighteen advanced-technology telescopes on top of Mount Graham. Characterizing the telescope construction as cultural genocide, the San Carlos Apaches immediately initiated a campaign to halt construction. Similarly, national and international environmentalists became involved arguing that construction of the telescope complex would destroy Mount Graham's unique ecosystem. Radical environmentalists staged road blockades and stole or destroyed equipment intended for the telescopes. Subsequently, lawsuits were filed and a public relations offensive was launched.

Although the U.S. Fish and Wildlife Service's Draft Environmental Impact Statement recommended limiting the project to five telescopes, the University of Arizona demanded a new evaluation for a proposal of at least seven telescopes. In anticipation of project disapproval if a public hearing was conducted under the National Environmental Policy Act (NEPA), the University of Arizona lobbied and convinced Congress to grant exemptions from NEPA for construction of the first three telescopes.

Currently, construction of the Max Planck and Vatican telescopes has been completed and construction of the Columbus Scope has been started; however, due to relentless opposition from American Indians, grassroots organizations, and environmental groups, the University of Arizona is having difficul-

Mount Graham and the Gila River are seen at sunset. Apache Native Americans vigorously opposed building a telescope on the mountain, which they consider a sacred site. (David Muench/Corbis)

ties in securing sufficient funds to complete the large binocular telescope. Controversy surrounding the construction has labeled Mount Graham a national symbol for religious intolerance and disrespect of American Indian spiritual practices and sacred sites.

J. Landon K. Schmidt

See also Ceremonies, Criminalization of; Sacred Sites.

References and Further Reading

HighCountryNews.org. "Making a Mountain into a Starbase: The Long, Bitter Battle over Mount Graham." Available at: http://www.hcn.org servlets/hcn.Article?article_id=1149. Accessed March 29, 2005.

Minnesota Public Radio., "Commentary: Is it Sacred Enough?" Available at: http://news .minnesoat.publicradio.org/feeatures/2003/08 /18_gundersond_spiritladuke. Accessed March 29, 2005.

Student Environmental Action Coalition. "Mount Graham, Sacred Mountain, Sacred Ecosystem." Available at: http://seac.org/seac-sw/ mtg.htm. Accessed March 29, 2005.

Taylor, Bron, and Joel Geffen. 2004. "Battling Religions in Parks and Forest Reserves: Facing Religion in Conflicts over Protected Places." *The George White Forum* 21, no. 2: 57–59.

Native American students, supporters, and community leaders take part in a song of blessing at the start of a 24-hour vigil at the University of Minnesota in 2002 protesting the Mount Graham observatory. (AP Photo)

Hohokam Culture

The Hohokam occupied an ecologically and geologically diverse environment that extended from the low desert country of northern Sonora and southern Arizona northward up to the Mogollon Rim escarpment and onto the Colorado Plateau's southwestern edge. Rainfall in this region averages only around seven to ten inches per year. Hohokam culture flourished from the first millennium to approximately 1450. Archaeologists divide the Hohokam culture into four major periods. The first, called the Pioneer phase, extends from 300 to 550 CE; the Colonial era runs from 550 to 900; the Sedentary phase goes from 900 to 1100, with the final stage of Hohokam culture, termed the Classic, spanning the years from 1100 through 1450. The origin of the Hohokam culture is uncertain. Some archaeologists argue that the Hohokam were immigrants from Mesoamerica, while others theorize that the culture developed from local hunting and gathering groups who lived in the Sonoran Desert since 7000 BCE.

During the Pioneer phase, Hohokam people settled in small villages near the Salt, Gila, and Santa Cruz Rivers. Their settlements consisted of small clusters of wattle-and-daub pithouses arranged around a common plaza with spaces set aside for work sites and for cemeteries. In the work areas they processed food, produced well made plain clay bowls and jars and manufactured tools. The cemeteries were used for the interment of human remains and also for cremation.

To survive in the harsh desert, the Hohokam developed the most advanced canal irrigation system in the Americas. They built dams of brush and logs to divert water from nearby rivers into irrigation canals. Using log-and-brush headgates, they were able to direct the flow of water into networks of distribution ditches to fields or to village cisterns and reservoirs. Within a 1,400-year period they built over 1,000 miles of canals using wedge-shaped stone hoes, stone axes, and wooden tools. They irrigated thousands of acres of farmland on which they grew maize, lima and tepary beans, squash, tobacco, cotton, barley, and amaranth.

During the Colonial phase, villages increased in size, extensive trade networks developed, and the Hohokam culture spread beyond the Salt, Gila, and Santa Cruz Rivers. The people improved their farming and irrigation techniques, and canals were cut deeper to minimize surface evaporation. The plain pottery of the Pioneer phase was replaced by buff pottery with red designs. Cremation became the standard mortuary practice; the ashes of the deceased were gathered, placed into a ceramic jar, and then buried in a small pit.

In the Sedentary phase, villages continued to increase in size, and platform mounds dominated the landscape. The largest platform mounds were located at the head of major canal systems and were spaced approximately every three miles along the canals. Many researchers believe that the mounds were tied to the organization and operation of the canal systems. Artisans made far more elaborate red-on-buff pottery, and stone and clay figurines appear. Mortuary practices began to change, as cremation became less common and inhumation became the preferred custom.

Another interesting feature of the Hohokam culture appearing in the Sedentary period is the ball court. The oval bowl-shaped courts varied in size, averaging 80 to 115 feet long and 30 to 50 feet wide. The playing surface was smoothed caliche and surrounded by a nine-foot-high embankment. Unfortunately, the exact nature of the game played in the courts is not known.

During the Classic period, some villages disappeared while others increased in size. The people continued to build pithouses but they also constructed multistoried adobe surface structures, called big houses. The bottom floor was a platform mound with three to four additional stories built on

A canal built by the Hohokam peoples is excavated at Pueblo Grande Museum and Park in Arizona. The Hohokam was a civilization of Native American farmers who lived in present-day southern Arizona from ca. 300 BCE to 1400 CE. (Jan Butchofsky-Houser/ Corbis)

top. There were several rooms on each floor, and the interior rooms were covered with a fine white plaster. Some of the walls were etched with depictions of humans, animals, or lightning, which possibly had religious or ceremonial significance. The purpose of the big houses is unclear. Some researchers argue that the structures served as astronomical observatories while others believe they served as watchtowers for defensive purposes.

Artisans continued to make red-on-buff pottery and to develop redware polished ceramics in a variety of shapes and sizes. Toward the end of the Classic period, the people ceased building ball courts and the quality of their pottery diminished. By 1450 the Hohokam abandoned their villages. Hypotheses regarding the disappearance of the Hohokam include soil salinization, disease, warfare, floods, droughts, and climatic changes.

Joyce Ann Kievit

See also Archaeology and the First Americans.
References and Further Reading
Andrews, John P., and Todd W. Bostwick. 2000. *Desert Farmers at the River's Edge: The Hohokam and Pueblo Grande.* Phoenix, AZ: City of Phoenix Parks, Recreation and Library Department.
Gumerman, George J., ed. 1995. *Exploring the Hohokam: Prehistoric Desert Peoples of the American Southwest.* Albuquerque: University of New Mexico Press.

Members of the Hopewell culture gather crops of maize and squash. The Hopewell were the first Native American people fully committed to agriculture. (North Wind Picture Archives)

Hopewell Culture

Also referred to as one of the cultures known as the Mound Builders as well as the "Woodland culture," Hopewell refers to a Native American culture that grew out of the earlier Adena culture and that existed from 200 BCE to 400 CE in the eastern Woodlands of the United States. The Hopewell culture is characterized by its monumental earthen structures, complex mortuary rituals, diversified art forms, and vast trade networks known as the Hopewell Interaction Sphere that stretched from the Dakotas and Canada to Florida and Louisiana. Well-known Hopewell sites include Mound City, Ohio; Mound House, Illinois; the Effigy Mound, Iowa; and the Serpent Mound, Ohio. Smaller Hopewell sites are found across the eastern United States. Reasons for the collapse of the Hopewell culture are still unknown: Some scholars attribute it to the evolution of cultural ideas and sole reliance on agriculture, while others state that famine, warfare, and plague destroyed the Hopewell people.

Warren King Moorehead, one of the first archaeologists to work on Hopewell sites, coined the term "Hopewell." It refers to Captain C. M. Hopewell, the owner of the property on which the first excavations of the cultural group occurred. There is no known single point of origin for the Hopewell culture. The universal features shared by all Hopewellian settlements include complex mortuary rituals associated with large mortuary mounds, diversified art, and extensive trade networks. The Hopewell people are considered hunter-gatherers as well as agriculturists, although it is believed that they placed a greater reliance on agriculture than on hunting and gathering. Evidence indicates that the Hopewell exploited a great number of local domesticates, including squash, marsh elder, goosefoot, sunflower, erect knotweed, may grass, little barley, sump weed, and chenopod. The Hopewell people also exploited local game and riverine resources.

The Hopewell culture is believed to have been made up of multiple chiefdom settlements, the majority of which were clustered around major waterways and areas with plentiful resources. These settlements varied in size, though an average settlement had a population density between 1,290 and 4,500 people. Permanent settlements were created around the periphery of a central ceremonial complex and were often made up of single-family or extended-family communities. There is evidence of social stratification within Hopewellian societies, as illustrated through their mortuary rituals.

The Hopewell people are known for their complex mortuary rituals consisting of monumental earthen mounds as well as funerary rituals that took a couple of months to years to complete. Hopewell people also had various types of funerary customs that appear to be reserved for certain status groups. Excavations of mortuary mounds have yielded information illustrating this practice as related to the status of the deceased through the evidence of differing burial treatment. The dead were interred in a variety of ways: primary burials, burial shortly after death, laid out in either an extended or flexed, or fetal, position; secondary bundle burials, burial after the removal of the flesh from the bones, be it from an extended period of time or intentional removal of the flesh from the bones; and cremations.

Social stratification is illustrated in Hopewell burials through the diversity of burial goods, or the lack there of, found with the deceased. Many burials have been found with a rich assortment of grave items, including clothing, fabrics, costuming, household items such as cooking pots and grinding stones, and occupational items such as bone needles and projectile points of varying degrees of craftsmanship and material types. Items that are formed from rare or exotic materials are believed to be associated with higher-status individuals, and the lack of grave goods in a burial is believed to be associated with lower-status individuals, which is evidence of social stratification within the Hopewell culture. There is also a notable gender difference in the distribution of burial goods, with household items associated with women and hunting items associated with men. There do not appear to be any patterns associated with age and gender for burial type that are universal for the Hopewell culture.

Burial mounds are geometric structures with a charnel house at the summit. The charnel houses were the locations for ritualized cremation ceremonies. It is also believed that both the charnel houses and the mounds were aligned with an astronomical body such as the moon. Given the diversity of mortuary rituals utilized by the Hopewell people, it is believed that it may have taken months to years for these rituals to be completed and they were undertaken by groups of people. It is further believed that the family of the deceased may have helped with these mortuary rituals.

The monumental earthworks of the Hopewell are associated not just with mortuary ritual but with general ceremonial practices as well. Religion may have played a role in the creation of these earthworks. These mounds take the shape of various geometric designs and span wide areas. The most famous of these geometrically shaped mounds is Serpent Mound in Adams County, Ohio, although it is unclear if the Hopewell peoples or a previous cultural group built this mound structure. Other shapes include squares, circles, ovals, semicircles, and combinations of these.

There is evidence outside of the mounds themselves that points to the presence of shamanistic religious practices within Hopewell culture. Such evidence includes animal effigies, the use of animal symbolism in Hopewell artworks, and household artifacts. A number of sacrificial caches have been found within Hopewell settlements that are associated with the dominant religious practice. These sacrificial caches included effigy pipe, flint disk, shell bead, pearl and copper celt caches. The effigy pipe and shell bead caches showed evidence of intentional ritual sacrifice as they were "killed"—that is, rendered useless by holes punched through them.

Artifacts common in Hopewell culture include ceramic vessels, various types of smoking and effigy pipes, clay human figurines, conch shell artifacts, mica mirrors, panpipes, flint bladelets, nonutilitarian celts, awls, projectile points, modified human remains, jewelry, weaponry and armor, fabrics, buttons, beads, cutouts, and tinklers. These artifacts were created out of a variety of local and nonlocal materials, including animal and human bone, vegetation, and minerals such as copper, iron, galena, hematite, silver, gold, mica, quartz crystal, chalcedony, hornstone, pipestone, sandstone, steatite, gypsum, and cannel coal. Animal and human motifs are illustrated in many of the commonplace artifacts and are not limited to ceremonial artifacts. Hopewell pottery is known to have been cord-marked (imprinted with rope while the clay was

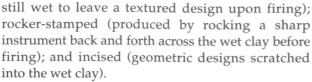

still wet to leave a textured design upon firing); rocker-stamped (produced by rocking a sharp instrument back and forth across the wet clay before firing); and incised (geometric designs scratched into the wet clay).

Although it appears that local resources were exploited most often, the use of nonlocal resources (such as obsidian, silver, and mica) for the creation of various artifacts supports the long-distance trading network that the Hopewell culture is known for: the Hopewell Interaction Sphere. The term was first coined by archaeologist Joseph R. Caldwell in 1964 and is defined as being a long-distance trade network that spanned from the Dakotas and Canada to Florida and Louisiana. This trade network is also credited for being the reason for the spread of Hopewell culture throughout the eastern Woodlands. It is also from this vast trade network that it is believed that the Hopewell peoples spoke either various dialects of the same language or different languages. This is unclear as there is no evidence of the Hopewell having any form of written language.

Evidence of the fall of the Hopewell culture indicates that it started around 200 CE in some areas and that the culture had completely fallen everywhere by 400. Various hypotheses exist to explain the decline. One hypothesis states that the culture evolved into a more advanced version of itself due to the emergence and acceptance of maize agriculture. Another hypothesis states that the Hopewell peoples disappeared due to plagues, warfare, or drought. Presently there is not sufficient evidence to support either of these hypotheses.

Christine Elisabeth Boston

See also Adena Civilization; Archaeology and the First Americans; Mound Cultures of North America; Pottery; Trade.

References and Further Reading

Dancey, William. 2005. "The Enigmatic Hopewell of the Eastern Woodlands." In *North American Archaeology.* Edited by Timothy R. Pauketat and Diana Dipaolo Loren, 108–137. Malden, MA: Blackwell Publishing.

Dancey, William S., and Paul J. Pacheco. 1997. "A Community Model of Ohio Hopewell Settlement." In *Ohio Hopewell Community Organization.* Edited by William S. Dancey and Paul J. Pacheco, 3–40. Kent, OH: Kent State University Press.

Milner, George. 2004. *The Moundbuilders: Ancient Peoples of Eastern North America.* London: Thames and Hudson.

Romain, William F. 2000. *Mysteries of the Hopewell: Astronomers, Geometers, and Magicians of the Eastern Woodlands.* Akron, OH: University of Akron Press.

Horse, Economic Impact

Before horses diffused into Indian Country from Spanish settlements, the only beast of burden used by American Indians was the dog, which could pull small loads on a travois (a frame slung between trailing poles). Not surprisingly, horses were first greeted as a larger, stronger kind of dog. Native peoples who acquired horses usually affixed travois to them before learning to ride. A number of Native peoples gave horses names based on their earlier nouns for dogs: The Assiniboines called them sho-a-thin-ga and thon-gatch-shonga, both meaning "great dog." The Gros Ventures called horses it-shou-ma-shunga, meaning "red dog." The Blackfeet called them ponokamita, for elk dog. The Crees called horses mistatim, meaning "big dog." The Sioux called their newly domesticated beasts honk-a-wakan, meaning "mystery dog" or "amazing dog" (Roe, 1955, 61), or tesunke, "big dog."

Horses may have been introduced to some Native American peoples by the Coronado expedition of the early 1540s, but the most likely genesis of Native American horse culture probably sprang from the herds the Spanish kept at Santa Fe following the Oñate expedition a half century later. Some horses escaped Spanish herds and bred wild in New Mexico and Texas. These were "Indian ponies," averaging less than 1,000 pounds in weight, smaller than modern-day riding horses. These agile, fast horses were interbred with larger animals acquired from Spanish (and later Anglo-American) herds. The Pawnees, especially, had access to these horses and to others traded to them by Native merchants who tapped supplies in Mexico (Wissler, 1914, 2, 10), and they became among the most prolific and best horse traders on the Plains.

By 1659, Spanish reports indicate that the Apaches were stealing horses from them, despite their best efforts to keep the valuable animals out of Indian hands. At roughly the same time, the Apaches and Pueblos traded for horses; by shortly before 1700, the Utes and Comanches had acquired mounts. After that, Native peoples' use of horses diffused throughout the continent. Ethnohistorian Dean Snow described the diffusion of the horse

The Battle between the Blackfeet and Peigans, *a painting by Charles M. Russell, ca. 1897. Russell's painting shows how much of a necessity horses had become to some Native Americans in battle, hunting, and travel. (Corel)*

throughout the Plains: "The Shoshones adopted Spanish horses quickly, taking them north and east, introducing them to the Indian societies of the Great Plains. Algonquians such as the Blackfeet, Gros Ventres, and Arapahos, as well as some Crees and Ojibways, abandoned forest hunting and gathered to become mounted nomadic hunters on the Great Plains. . . . Later, the horticultural Cheyennes (Algonquians) entered the Plains as well, quickly becoming the quintessential American Indian nation in the eyes of many" (Snow, 1996, 193). By 1750, the horse was recognized as far north as Montana as transportation and as a unit of barter and wealth. By roughly 1700, the horse frontier had reached a line stretching roughly from present-day eastern Texas, northward through eastern Kansas and Nebraska, then northwest through Wyoming, Montana, Idaho, and Washington. Horses became such an essential part of many North American Indian cultures that the Apaches, for example, incorporated them into their oral history as gifts of the gods.

Having acquired horses, a number of Native peoples migrated to the Plains because mounts made economic life there, especially the buffalo hunt, more tenable. Some of these peoples also were being pressured westward by the European-American settlement frontier. The various Lakota-Nakota-Dakota bands moved westward before widespread white contact, as did the Omahas and many others. The horse extended Native peoples' ranges, as well as control over their environment. A Native group on foot was limited to a few miles a day, while, with horses, a camp could be moved thirty miles or more in the same period. A small party of warriors on horseback could cover 100 miles of rough country in a day or two.

Native Americans explored different ways of training horses. Unlike the English and Spanish, the Cheyennes, for example, did not usually "break" their horses. Instead, they "gentled" them. Boys who tended horses stroked them, talked to them, and played with them. An owner of a horse might sing to it or smoke a pipe and blow smoke in its face. At age eighteen months, the horse would begin more intense training, but was still sung to, smoked over, and stroked with eagle wing fans. Gradually, the horse was habituated to carrying a human being, saddle, and bridle. Horses meant for war or hunting were trained specifically in those skills.

The horse shaped economic behavior in many ways. One was the productivity of raiding, which acquired considerable status. By the early nineteenth century, raiding on horseback was the Apaches' major economic activity; the greatest fame a Crow could earn came when he was able to snatch a tethered horse from under the nose of an enemy. "What must certainly be considered a really remarkable feature in the Plains Indian horse culture is the almost phenomenal rapidity with which they mastered their early fears and developed into one of the two or three foremost equestrian peoples on earth," commented historian Frank Gilbert Roe (Roe, 1955, 56).

The horse also turned a subsistence lifestyle on the harsh High Plains of North America into a festival of ornamentation for a few decades, until diseases also imported from Europe killed a large majority of Native peoples there. Maximilian described the Sioux in 1833: "Many of the Sioux are rich, and have twenty or more horses, which they obtained originally from the Spanish . . ." (Roe, 1955, 90). Many Native nations on the Plains and adjacent Rocky Mountains, such as the various divisions of the Lakota, Nakota, and Dakota, the Crow, and the Nez Percé, became rich in horses. The wealth in horses and the wealth produced by them affected ceremonialism as well, which among many Plains groups became more lavish than in preequine days.

Horses changed some peoples' housing styles from fixed lodges to mobile teepees. They also allowed the size of the average teepee to increase, because a horse could haul a teepee as large as eighteen to twenty feet in diameter, much larger than a dog or a human being could carry. Some teepees weighed as much as 500 pounds and required three horses to carry. The horse reduced economies of scale in hunting, especially of buffalo, making hunting parties smaller. The increased mobility brought by horses energized trade, as well as intertribal conflict, because ease of transport brought more contact between diverse peoples, friendly and not (Anderson, 1995, 59–61).

Bruce E. Johansen

See also Buffalo; Spanish Influence; Trade; Warfare, Intertribal.

References and Further Reading

Anderson, Terry L. 1995. *Sovereign Nations or Reservations? An Economic History of American Indians*. San Francisco: Pacific Research Institute for Public Policy.

Calloway, Colin. 1997. *New Worlds for All: Indians, Europeans, and the Remaking of Early America*. Baltimore, MD: Johns Hopkins University Press.

Denhardt, Robert M. 1975. *The Horse of the Americas*. Norman: University of Oklahoma Press.

Holder, Preston. 1970. *The Hoe and the Horse on the Plains*. Lincoln: University of Nebraska Press.

Moore, John H. 1997. *The Cheyennes*. London, UK: Blackwell Publishing.

Roe, Frank Gilbert. 1955. *The Indian and the Horse*. Norman: University of Oklahoma Press.

Saum, Lewis O. 1965. *The Indian and the Fur Trader*. Seattle: University of Washington Press.

Snow, Dean. 1996. "The First Americans and the Differentiation of Hunter-Gatherer Cultures." In *The Cambridge History of the Native Peoples of the Americas*. Edited by Bruce G. Trigger and Wilcomb E. Washburn, 125–199. Cambridge, UK: Cambridge University Press.

Wissler, Clark. 1914. "The Influence of the Horse in the Development of Plains Culture." *American Anthropologist* 16 :1–25.

Humor, as Value

Humor is a ubiquitous aspect of human interaction. It smooths relationships, enhances communication, moderates behavior, assists with managing emotions, and delineates identity. Given the trials and tribulations American Indians have suffered and continue to face, humor in the context of Indian life might be considered by some a hard-pressed value. In his manifesto, *Custer Died for Your Sins* (1969), Vine Deloria, Jr. regards knowing what makes a people laugh as one of the best ways to understand them. He observes that in humor life is redefined and accepted and that irony and satire often provide keen insights into the collective psyche and values of a group; he advises that, when a people can both laugh at themselves and at others, then it would seem that they can survive.

Although public imagination often envisions and expects stereotypic "wooden Indians"—solemn and stoic—humor is in abundance in Indian country. Some American Indians have even wondered how anything is accomplished because of the apparent overemphasis on the comedic in Indian life. Regarding past and present injustices, Indians have found a humorous side to nearly every problem, with life experiences often so well-defined through jokes and stories that they become things unto themselves. This should not, however, suggest that American Indians do not take serious things seriously, only that humor often serves as a salient mode of communication through which the serendipitous and somber are negotiated.

This negotiation can be performed in numerous ways. In addition to jokes and storytelling, it includes the practice of "razzing" or "ribbing," which may occur in normative contexts defined by intragroup relations as well as in larger, less normative intergroup or pan-Indian contexts. Though usually employed among Indians, given the situation, non-Indians may also be recipients. Serving both constructive and instructive purposes, razzing is usually conducted in good fun, thus enabling the situation, or as a public corrective concerning improper social behavior, therefore disabling the situation. Even though it can be quite cutting and may even offend, it is rarely very serious.

Other practices might appear more standardized in form and function, directed internally toward the group and externally toward those considered foreign, however defined. An example can be found in the ceremonial buffoonery, or tradition of "clowning," found most prominently among the Pueblo groups of the Southwest, as well as among groups on the Great Plains, in California, and throughout the Pacific Northwest. Although group-specific themes certainly exist, the most common themes are those that possess greatest emotional appeal or human interest in variance across groups. One such theme involves the derision and burlesque of things, persons, and activities otherwise deemed sacred, including the mockery of lifeways and mores considered essential to the function of society. Other common themes include sexuality and obscenity, misfortune and daily life, and the caricature and burlesque of those deemed foreign to the group.

Another example of standardized humor is found among the Kwakwaka'wakw (Kwakiutl), a group indigenous to the central coast of British Columbia in the Pacific Northwest, who have staged a type of "play potlatching" involving elaborate skits in which both neighboring Indian groups and those of European heritage are impersonated and in this manner lampooned or derided. Likewise, the western Apaches residing on the Fort Apache Reservation in southeastern Arizona have performed stereo-

Oneida tribe member Charlie Hill is a successful Native American comic. (Christopher Felver/Corbis)

typic caricatures of "the white man," understood and employed as models for dealing with whites and the concomitant problems they represent. As a symbol of what "the Apache" is not, these humored portraits express as much about Apaches' conceptions of themselves as they do about Apaches' conceptions of whites and the values of society at large.

In recent years so-called "Indian humor" has entered the mainstream. The exhibition, *Indian Humor,* was organized in 1995 by American Indian Contemporary Arts and traveled for several years throughout the United States. It featured eighty-seven works in various media by thirty-eight contemporary Indian artists addressing the issue of Indian humor from different perspectives. Award-winning authors, including Louise Erdrich (Ojibwe) and Sherman Alexie (Spokane/Coeur d'Alene), have captured the imaginations of readers with their charm and wit. Indeed, an Alexie short story was adapted for the first all-Indian cinematic production, *Smoke Signals* (1998), a tragicomedy that garnered both critical and audience acclaim. And stand-up comedians like Charlie Hill (Oneida) continue to emerge and amuse through their comedic insights and social critique.

In the face of hardships and inequities, humor can serve as a social vent as well as a survival mechanism through reinforcement of group orientation, cohesion, and solidarity. More often than not, humor emerges from puns, word play, allusions, insults, irony, miscues, exaggeration, conflicts, mistakes, and misunderstandings borne from the experience of being human. As in most human groups, the fundamental value of American Indian humor is rooted in its role as a social lubricant witnessed not only in the aforementioned fun making, but in everyday, ordinary social interaction.

Timothy J. McCollum

See also Identity; Worldviews and Values.
References and Further Reading
Basso, Keith H. 1979. *Portraits of "the Whiteman": Linguistic Play and Cultural Symbols Among the Western Apache.* New York: Cambridge University Press.
Lincoln, Kenneth. 1993. *Indi'n Humor: Bicultural Play in Native America.* New York: Oxford University Press.

Identity

An American Indian may be identified in three ways: One is through self-identification; another is by tribal identification and definition; and a third is by legal definition, as defined by the U.S. government. Legal definition has created many issues for American Indians regarding their identity, affecting their abilities to receive federal benefits such as health and education benefits, their rights for leadership in Indian nations, and their cultural heritage. American Indians are the only minority group in the United States whose members carry an identifying card with a number, tribal affiliation, and blood quantum attached to it to receive recognition for federal benefits.

History has often portrayed America as a "melting pot" of cultures and ethnic groups. Only in recent years has that version of identity definition been challenged. In 1971, Hazel W. Hertzberg wrote a 362-page book on *The Search for an American Indian Identity* (1971). In this book, she discussed the issue of how the indigenous people of the United States defined themselves as part of American society and whether they embodied the melting pot theory or some other form of pan-Indianism, the amalgamation of various Indian groups to share cultural similarities.

Society has treated people from distinct cultures as having pureblood stock. Even immigrants who came to this country were treated as being either pure German, Italian, Spanish, French, English, Dutch, or whatever. It has been assumed as well that, when those of European stock came to North America and intermarried with the indigenous people, their pure European bloodlines and those of the indigenous people became diluted. When intermarriage produced children, they became identified as "half-breeds," a term that also becomes an issue of identity. One has only to read Maria Campbell's book *Halfbreed* (1982) to get a picture of the issues associated with the label of being a half-breed Indian.

Prior to 1887 and the passage of the Dawes Allotment Act, most American Indian people were easily identifiable. They lived in separate communities and identified themselves as such. They lived a different lifestyle vis-à-vis European immigrants. They ate different foods and dressed in a different manner. Their entire cultures and religions were based on a subsistence lifestyle directly connected to the land. They identified themselves by their nations: Dakota, Cheyenne, Anishinabe, Dine, Absaalooke, Mohawk, Huron, Delaware, and so on. It was the Europeans who identified them as Indian. This would be not only the name applied to them across the board, but also a name that would be applied to them all for 500 years. Then in the 1970s this name would be changed to American Indian or Native American. Even today there is confusion as to what to call the indigenous people of this country. Most American Indian people identify themselves as Indian or by their tribal affiliations. Some like to say that they had the name "Indian" for 500 years, and then it was changed to "Native American." Some have explained that the name "Indian" came from the Spanish term *indios*, which means "of God," in which case the term may be preferable to "Native American."

It is only when money, land, or some other benefit is legislated for the indigenous people of America that the United States became involved in developing a legal definition of an Indian. When land allotments had to be made to individual Indians, the federal government wanted to make sure that only "American Indian" people were getting the allotments, not

non-Indians who either had married into the tribal groups or had been adopted into the tribal groups.

This problem came from the American Indian tradition of "adopting" outsiders into their cultures and it caused politicians much concern. The adoption of outsiders meant that individuals from other cultures and ethnic backgrounds who had befriended American Indians could be invited to become full-fledged members of a given tribe. An elaborate ceremony could take place within the tribal community during which the invited person would be adopted into the tribe with full participation and benefits. If a non-Indian had been adopted into a tribal group, most politicians believed that it was not legal for non-Indians, so adopted, to receive any benefits from the federal government through reparations to Indian tribes. The government was faced with trying to identify legal members of tribal groups.

Indian nations exercise a sovereign right to determine their own membership qualifications. As a community that was confined to a specified area of land (reservations), a tribe knew who the members of their community were. As the twentieth century approached and the movement to urban areas of many tribal members became a reality, the identification process became difficult. Yet, tribes still have the sovereign right to identify their own tribal members. Many tribes who are federally recognized were encouraged under the Indian Reorganization Act of 1934 to adopt the federal definition of Indian identity. Books such as Felix Cohen's *Handbook of Federal Indian Law* (1941) and David H. Getches' *Federal Indian Law: Cases and Materials* (1979) are good sources of discussion of the legal definition and the Indian Reorganization Act.

The federal and legal definition of an Indian has wreaked havoc on Indian people and will forever impact American Indians in some negative way. Felix Cohen said: "If a person is three-fourths Caucasian and one-fourth Indian, it is absurd, from the ethnological standpoint, to assign him to the Indian race. Yet legally such a person may be an Indian" (Cohen, 1941, 2). The federal (legal) definition is that a person must be an enrolled member of a federally recognized tribe and have at least one-quarter Indian blood. Further, in the lower forty-eight states, a person can be enrolled in only one tribal group. Once enrolled in one tribal group, the identifying blood quantum of other tribal groups disappears. Adding to that confusion is the discussion of what happens when marriage takes place between two people of

two different tribal groups. Parents are forced to pick a tribe for their children. What happens to their other tribal blood? It disappears.

Which tribes are federally recognized and how did they get federal recognition? A tribe became federally recognized when its members made their identity known to the U.S. military in some fashion. Throughout American history, "recognition" often happened through confrontation of some kind. Currently more than 500 federally recognized Indian tribes exist in the United States, as well as roughly 300 nonfederally recognized tribes.

How does a parent decide where to enroll children? This is not a simple matter. Some Indian nations are matrilineal, meaning that the children belong to the clan of the mother. Some Indian nations are patrilineal, meaning that their children belong to the clan of the father. Depending on the family dynamics, the decision to enroll one's child will depend a great deal on internal discussion with the birth parent, with the grandparents, and with the extended family. It would be easy if decisions could be based on lineal clanship alone, but with so many intermarriages between different tribal groups as well as intermarriage with "whites," the process becomes complicated. What if the married couple belong to tribes that were traditional enemies? This can create a lot of animosity among families.

Some parents in today's society have chosen to go with the Indian nation that has the strongest economic prospects. For example, a tribe may have developed a natural resource, such as coal, oil, or natural gas, or may be building a casino. The potential for economic sustainability in a tribe with such prospects can be enormous, and young parents in particular may opt to align the future of their children with the economic development of one tribe over another.

Alaska Natives and Native Hawaiians are not under the same constraints as the Indians of the lower forty-eight states. For example, an Alaska Native can be identified with several tribal groups should their parents be from different tribal groups. Therefore the blood of two tribes is included in their identity.

What good does it do a person to have federal recognition? Treaty rights become a factor. Many of the traditional elders signed treaties fully aware that they were signing them as representatives of sovereign nations who were negotiating with another sovereign nation and were to receive education and health benefits forever as well as certain sovereign rights.

Lastly, self-identification is an ideal that will always exist regardless of federal or legal definitions. A person who grows up with an Indian identity and takes it on as his or her own believes that he or she is an Indian, regardless of the law. If a grandparent is enrolled and the adult parents are not enrolled, then the grandchildren may not be eligible for enrollment. Despite that, the grandparent may raise the grandchildren with the cultural traditions. Is that grandchild any less "Indian" than one who meets the legal and tribal definitions?

American Indian people today stand at a crossroads on the issue of identification. They see that their numbers are decreasing, and the decrease is all due to the complexities of the legal definitions versus their own rights to identify their members. Parents have intermarried with non-Indians but their children may be just as "Indian" as the grandparents. Why is the federal government still insisting on its definition?

Jeanne Eder

See also Bureau of Indian Affairs: Establishing the Existence of an Indian Tribe; Canada, Indian Policies of; Cohen, Felix; Kennewick Man; Osage, and Oil Rights; Pan-Indianism; *Standing Bear v. Crook.*

References and Further Reading
Campbell, Maria. 1982. *Halfbreed.* Lincoln: University of Nebraska Press.
Canby, William C., Jr. 2004. *American Indian Law,* 4th ed. St. Paul, MN: West .
Cohen, Felix S. 1941. *Handbook of Federal Indian Law.* Washington, DC: United States Government Printing Office.
Garroutte, Eva. 2003. *Real Indians: Identity and the Survival of Native America.* Berkeley: University of California Press.
Hertzberg, Hazel W. 1971. *The Search for an American Indian Identity: Modern Pan-Indian Movements.* Syracuse, NY: Syracuse University Press.
Jackson, Deborah Davis. 2002. *Our Elders Lived It: American Indian Identity in the City.* DeKalb: Northern Illinois University Press.

Indian Shaker Movement

The Indian Shaker movement is a Native American religion that originated in northwestern North America and the first pan-Indian religious movement to establish itself legally under state law. It is not related to non-Indian eastern Shakerism. The Indian Shaker Church is a fusion of indigenous spiritual practices, Catholicism, and Protestantism that originated among the Salish people of Washington State during the early 1880s. It continues to have an active membership among Native peoples in the western United States and Canada.

The movement was founded by a Squaxin tribal member, John Slocum in 1882, who, at forty years of age, came back to life after a logging accident with a revelation that Native peoples could achieve salvation by turning away from drinking, gambling, and smoking and by rejecting the ministrations of shamans and traditional healers. Slocum, a charismatic man who was baptized Catholic, claimed that God would give his followers greater medicine than was held by the shamans.

The name of the movement originated with Slocum's wife, Mary. A year after Slocum revealed his vision, he suddenly fell very ill. Mary, who shared a strong faith in Slocum's vision, went to the river to pray and while praying was overcome by an uncontrollable trembling. She entered the house and continued to shake while she prayed over her husband's head. John Slocum began to recover, and Mary's shaking was deemed the medicine God had promised. Thus Mary is known as the bearer of "the shake," which is believed to bring healing to those spiritually or physically ill.

People from all over the Puget Sound region came to hear the prophet's message, and many experienced shaking similar to Mary's. Early converts included Luis Yowaluck (Mud Bay Louis) and his brother, Mud Bay Sam. Missionaries and Indian Agents made attempts to squelch the movement, but the Shakers defied or avoided restrictions as the movement gained momentum, spreading outward from the Skokomish Reservation, east to Idaho, south to California, and north to British Columbia.

In 1892, the Shakers legally constituted themselves as a church to protect their religious freedom, on the advice of lawyer James Wickersham. John Slocum became a church elder, and Mud Bay Louis became leader (Amoss, 1990, 633). In 1897, Slocum died, as did Mud Bay Louis in 1905. In 1910, the church was incorporated under Washington State law. The structure of the Shaker Church involved a bishop and a board of elders who elected the bishop every four years. Mud Bay Sam was elected the first bishop.

A disagreement over the role of the *Bible* created a split in the Shaker movement. Some members wanted to read from the *Bible* during services, while others believed that Shakers had no need for a written text and that their inspiration came from "the Spirit" (Amoss, 1990, 634). Eventually, a formal separation occurred. The pro-*Bible* group became known as the Indian Full Gospel Church and the more conservative Shakers retained the title of the Indian Shaker Church.

General Shaker beliefs involve an all-powerful God, Jesus, and the Spirit of God. It is believed that the Spirit provides the power to heal and to exorcise evil. The Spirit also brings the "shake." The faithful believe that sin interferes with the ability to receive the power of the spirit and that sickness can be caused by sin, sorrow, or supernatural factors. Some elements of Guardian Spirit beliefs stem from the Puget Sound traditions (Amoss, 1990, 636).

Formal Shaker rituals include Sunday meetings, "shakes," funerals, weddings, and dedications, and they are often held in a modest and extremely clean church. Candles and handbells used in healing ceremonies and prayer are kept on the prayer tables. Charity is a basic element in Shaker practice, and members readily minister to the sick whenever asked. The church is respected outside the membership for its success in teaching against the use of alcohol.

Aliki Marinakis

See also Assimilation.

References and Further Reading

Amoss, Pamela T. 1990. "The Indian Shaker Church." In *Handbook of North American Indians.* Volume 7: *Northwest Coast.* Edited by Wayne Suttles, 633–639. General editor, William C. Sturtevant. Washington, DC: Smithsonian Institution.

Castile, George P. 1982. "The Half-Catholic Movement: Edwin and Myron Eells and the Rise of the Indian Shaker Church." *Pacific Northwest Quarterly* 73: 165–174. Center for the Study of the Pacific Northwest

Harmon, Ray. 1971. "The Indian Shaker Church, the Dalles." *Oregon Historical Quarterly* 72: 148–158. Portland, OR: Oregon Historical Society.

Ruby, Robert H., and John A. Brown. 1996. *John Slocum and the Indian Shaker Church.* Norman and London: University of Oklahoma Press.

Iroquois Great Law of Peace (Kaianerekowa)

The Great Law of Peace is the oldest constitution in North America defining a system of participatory democracy that has sustained the Iroquois Confederacy for perhaps 1,000 years. At a time of terrible war, say tribal elders, a Great Peacemaker emerged to inspire the warriors to bury their weapons of war (the origins of the saying, "to bury the hatchet"). The Peacemaker planted on top of the weapons a sacred Tree of Peace and established a code of laws called *Kaianerekowa,* the Great Law of Peace.

Mohawk Wolf Clan Chief Jake Swamp explained: "The powerful story of the birth of democracy began long, long ago. In the beginning, when our Creator made humans, everything needed to survive was provided. Our Creator asked only one thing: 'Never forget to appreciate the gifts of Mother Earth.' Our people were instructed how to be grateful and how to survive" (Schaaf, 2004, 7).

"During the dark age of our history 1,000 years ago, humans no longer listened to the Original Instructions. Our Creator became sad, because there was so much crime, dishonesty, injustice, and war. So the Creator sent a Peacemaker with a message to be righteous and just, and make a good future for our children seven generations to come," said Swamp (Schaaf, 2004, 7).

Six historic accounts of the Great Law of Peace exist. The versions exhibit minor variations. The Newhouse edition was the first published account. The Chiefs' edition was a joint collaboration by the chiefs of the Six Nation Council. Linguists at the Smithsonian Institution translated the Gibson edition. The Wallace, Buck, and Mohawk editions included the highlights of the Peacemaker's life.

Iroquois elders widely agree that the Great Peacemaker was a divine being who was sent by the Creator to make peace on Mother Earth. The Great Peacemaker is said to have been the result of an immaculate birth on the shores of the Great Lakes. As a child, he displayed extraordinary talents thwarting early attempts to take his life.

War raged for generations 1,000 years ago around the Great Lakes and present-day upstate New York. The Peacemaker and Hiawenthe (Hiawatha) bravely marched into the middle of the battle. No one harmed the holy men, but the warriors at first did not stop fighting. Armed only with logic, reasoning, and their spiritual message, they conducted Condolence Ceremonies with the battleworn warriors. They convinced the original five Iroquoian nations, one by one, to make peace and to unite as the Iroquois Confederacy.

The Peacemaker then unveiled a new form of government—participatory democracy—and a legal system called the Great Law of Peace. The core teaching of the Great Law is that "peace was the law, and the law was for peace." Under the Great Law, fifty chiefs and clan mothers were organized in a three-part system of government, with executive, legislative, and judicial divisions. The Onondaga nation became like an "executive branch." The "legislative branch" was formed when the Mohawk and Seneca were organized like the U.S. Senate, and the Oneida and Cayuga (later joined by the Tuscarora) formed a sort of U.S. House of Representatives. The "judicial branch of government" was turned over to the clan mothers; thus the women gained veto power over war and the power to nominate the chiefs.

Mohawk Bear Clan Chief Tom Porter described how chiefs are raised: "Women deserved 90 per cent of the credit in raising the children. Oh, we men do a little. We might change a diaper or two, but in the middle of the night, when a baby cries and we men are sound asleep, momma gets up and rocks the babies back to sleep. The mothers watch the children carefully as they are growing up. The ones who are greedy and push around the weaker children will never be chosen to be a chief. The ones who are kind, unselfish, and always helping others are considered for future leadership positions. Honesty is the first requirement for leadership" (Porter, 1986).

The Iroquois Grand Council provided a model for the American colonists. As early as 1754, Benjamin Franklin proposed: "One general government may be formed in America, administered by a President General . . . and a Grand Council to be chosen by representatives of the people of the several colonies . . ." (Franklin, 1754). The main difference in the original Iroquois system as compared with the U.S. Constitution is that the Women's Council constitutes the Supreme Court and the judicial branch of government. Under the Great Law of Peace, the women nominate the chiefs and have the power to impeach any chief who violates the Great Law of Peace or the dignity of leadership. The Women's Council retained veto power over war. The men could not go to war if the women said no. Women also held in trust the title to the land and the property in their homes. If the delegates to the U.S. Constitutional Convention had embraced all facets of the Great Law of Peace, then there would be Founding Mothers, as well as Founding Fathers.

Another main difference exists between the Great Law of Peace and the U.S. Constitution. The U.S. system is a form of "elective" democracy versus the Iroquois form of "participatory" democracy. Iroquois citizens must actively participate in their governance. Their system encourages direct citizen involvement.

To better analyze the similarities and differences between the Great Law of Peace and the U.S. Constitution, a project began in 1980 to organize the two documents in two columns showing the parallel passages side by side. The comparison clearly illustrated similarities and differences in the two founding documents. In 1987, the evidence was submitted as testimony before U.S. Senate hearings on the origins of the Constitution. For the first time in history, Congress officially recognized that the U.S. government was "explicitly modeled" after the Iroquois Confederacy (Congressional Record, 1987).

Mohawk Chief Jake Swamp further commented: "Our Iroquois chiefs and clan mothers have long said that the Great Law of Peace served as a model for the U.S. Constitution. We know that our ancestors met personally with Benjamin Franklin, Thomas Jefferson, James Madison and others involved in drafting the U.S. Constitution" (Swamp, 1983).

Comparisons with the Great Law of Peace allow students to see the U.S. Constitution in a new light. Featuring high qualifications for leadership, political rights for women, and a remarkable system of justice, the Great Law of Peace may inspire people to reconsider the founding principles of the United States. For example, why were the rights of women guaranteed in the Great Law of Peace, but denied under the original U.S. Constitution? The logical conclusion would be a difference in philosophy regarding fundamental human rights. Under the Iroquois system slavery was illegal. There were no taxes or prisons. The recognition of equal rights for all was the law.

Iroquois women to this day hold greater rights in accordance with the Great Law of Peace, than their non-Indian female counterparts under the U.S. Constitution. Interviews with Iroquois clan mothers revealed their Native philosophy. Women choose the leaders, because they devote the most time to raising the babies. Women have veto power over war, because they give birth and respect the sanctity of life in a special way. Land title is passed down through the women, because one always knows for certain who the mother is. Iroquois social structure is matrilineal and land title is passed down through the women.

The women nominate men for leadership positions based on the following qualities: "The Chief Statesmen shall be mentors of the people for all time. . . . Their hearts shall be full of peace and good will,

and their minds filled with a yearning for the welfare of the people. . . . With endless patience they shall carry out their duty, and their firmness shall be tempered with a tenderness for their people. Neither anger nor fury shall find lodgment in their minds, and all their words and actions shall be marked by calm deliberation" (Schaaf, 2004, 22–23).

The clan mothers explained why warriors and war chiefs were forbidden from being civil leaders: If you choose a war leader to be a leader in your civil government and your country is constantly at war, whom do you have to blame but yourselves?

Gregory Schaaf

See also Albany Congress, Native Precedents; Deganawidah; Haudenosaunee Confederacy, Political System; Hiawatha.

References and Further Reading

Barnes, Barbara Kawenehe, ed. 1984. *Traditional Teachings.* Cornwall Island, ON: North American Indian Travelling College.

Congressional Record–Senate. 1987. *Senate Concurrent Resolution 76, To Acknowledge the Contribution of the Iroquois Confederacy,* 100th Cong. 1st Sess.133 Cong Rec S 12214. September 16. Washington, DC: U.S. Government Printing Office.

Fadden, John Kahionhes. 1999. *Kaianerekowa Hotinonsionne: The Great Law of Peace of the Longhouse People.* Berkeley, CA: Oyate.

Fenton, William Nelson. 1998. *The Great Law and the Longhouse: A Political History of the Iroquois Confederacy.* Norman: University of Oklahoma Press.

Franklin, Benjamin. 1855. "Albany Plan of Union" (Albany, NY, July 10, 1754). Queen's State Papers Office, British Museum, London, "New York Papers," Bundle Kk, No. 20. Edited by E. B. O'Callaghan. Albany, NY, v. VI, 853–892.

Parker, Arthur Caswell. 1916. *The Constitution of the Five Nations or the Iroquois Book of the Great Law.* Albany: New York State Museum.

Porter, Tom. 1986. Personal communication.

Schaaf, Gregory, and Chief Jake Swamp. 2004. *The U.S. Constitution and the Great Law of Peace.* Santa Fe, NM: CIAC Press.

Scott, Duncan C. *Traditional History of the Confederacy of the Six Nations.* Ottawa: Proceedings and Transactions of the Royal Society of Canada, 1911.

Swamp, Jake. 1983. Personal communication.

Tehanetorens, Ray Fadden. 2000. *Roots of the Iroquois.* Summertown, TN: Book Publishing Company.

Thomas, Chief Jake. 1994. *The Great Law.* Grand River, ON: Six Nations Council.

Wallace, Paul. [1946] 1998. *The White Roots of Peace.* Santa Fe, NM: Clear Light Publishers.

Katsinas

Katsina, also spelled *Kachina* or *Katcina,* is a Hopi word that has three definitions: (1) a spiritual "friend," one of more than 300 deities who help keep the world in balance; (2) a ceremonial dancer who represents one of the spiritual "friends"; (3) a wooden carved doll used to teach children about the spiritual world.

The Katsina Society is a religious organization of both men and women who carry on the spiritual function of their religion. Perhaps 1,000 years ago, the Katsina Clan, a group of extended families, moved from Mexico into the American Southwest. They are believed to have walked with the Parrot Clan upstream along the Rio Grande into central New Mexico. They visited many hundreds of Keresan- and Tewa-speaking pueblos, where they established their religious societies. Their religion still

Hopi masked dolls represent the katsinas, ancestral spirits who dwell in the clouds and serve as intermediaries between humans and the spirit world. (Corel)

exists in the Rio Grande pueblos, although they are hidden in secret societies. Reference to them is whispered as the "K Society." Only rarely do they emerge from their kivas, religious chambers that symbolize the womb of Mother Earth.

Members of the Katsina Clan and Society spread westward to the Acoma, Zuni, and Hopi pueblos. The Acoma Katsina Society is secret, like those along the Rio Grande. At Zuni, the Katsina Society is very revered, even as they come out of the kivas and dance in the plazas. The largest Zuni ceremony is called Shalako; it occurs during the winter solstice when eight-foot-tall spiritual deities are fed at designated homes. At Hopi, the Katsina Societies remain very strong and well attended. Each village sponsors a Katsina Society where children are initiated during the spring Powowmu, or Purification Ceremony. At the end of summer, hundreds of Katsinas gather in the plazas for the Home Dance, a beautiful and awe-inspiring ceremony. The Katsinas then depart for their winter home atop the San Francisco Peaks near Flagstaff, Arizona.

In 1894, Smithsonian anthropologist Jesse Walter Fewkes published the first of three major studies on Katsinas. Thousands of people began attending the Katsina dances. Among the throngs were individuals who were excited to collect Katsina dolls, as well as paintings, baskets, pottery, and other Hopi arts and crafts. The finest Katsina dolls now sell for more than $100,000 at Sotheby's and other international auction houses.

In 1906, a split occurred at Hopi over the issue of whether children should be removed from homes to attend government boarding schools. At Old Oraibi, the dispute resulted in a tug-of-war. The traditionals lost and were forced to establish a new village. At the boarding schools, Hopi children were forbidden to speak their language. However, when some teachers secretly allowed Hopi children to paint freely, they created colorful paintings of Katsinas and sacred clowns. Fred Kabotie, Waldo Mootzka, Raymond Naha, and others became successful fine art Katsinas painters.

In 1959, Harold S. Colton first published a book that allowed collectors to identify hundreds of different Katsina figures by name and attributes. He described the unique features and color combinations that distinguish each Katsina doll. The book became a best seller by Indian art standards, being reprinted over and over again.

In the 1970s, two distinctive styles emerged: traditional dolls with or without feathers and realistic dolls featuring finely carved wooden sculptures of Katsinas. Walter Howato, Jimmy Koots, and Orin Pooley were among the most popular traditional doll makers. Cecil Calnimptewa, Ronald and Brian Honyuti, Dennis Tewa, Loren Phillips, and Ros George emerged as popular realistic carvers. They studied books of Michelangelo's sculptures and *Gray's Anatomy* to perfect their renditions of the human form. To demonstrate their mastery of carving, top artists began to make "one-piece dolls." A new category was created for them at Indian Market in the Heard Museum Show in Santa Fe, Phoenix, and at the Hopi Show at the Museum of Northern Arizona in Flagstaff. The prize ribbons won by top Hopi carvers attract major collectors who compete with passion for the best dolls.

Gregory Schaaf

References and Further Reading
Colton, Harold. 1987. *Hopi Kachina Dolls: With a Key to Their Identification.* Albuquerque, NM: University of New Mexico Press.
David, Neil, Sr., et al. 1994. *Kachinas: Spirit Beings of the Hopi.* Albuquerque, NM: Avanyu Publishing.
Fewkes, Jesse Walter. 1897. "Tusayan Katcinas." In the *Bureau of American Ethnology Annual Report.* Vol. 15. Washington, DC: Smithsonian Institution.
Secakuku, Alph. 1995. *Following the Sun and Moon: Hopi Kachina Tradition.* Flagstaff, AZ: Northland Press.
Wright, Barton. 1977. *Hopi Kachinas: The Complete Guide to Collecting Kachina Dolls.* Flagstaff, AZ: Northland Press.

Kennewick Man

Kennewick man—also known as The Ancient One—is the name given to the human skeletal remains discovered in the Columbia River at Kennewick, Washington, on July 28, 1996. The remains exhibited features of Caucasian populations and became the subject of contention, legal and otherwise, among Indians, scientists, and other interest groups. Indian groups were interested in reburying the skeleton, whereas scientists and others wanted to study and preserve the remains. The scientists' quest for access was ultimately victorious and the remains continue to be held at the Burke Museum in Seattle, Washington.

The events began when two young men discovered a skull protruding from the Columbia River and called the police. The local coroner, Floyd Johnson, contacted James C. Chatters, owner of Applied Paleoscience, to perform forensic skeletal analysis. Chatters and Johnson unearthed what turned out to be a nearly complete intact male skeleton.

The completeness and unusually good condition of the remains, led Chatters to believe that the skeleton was that of a relatively recently deceased European settler. Controversially, however, Chatters also used forensic methods of racial classification (such as nose shape, mandible shape, and cranial index) to identify the skeleton as Caucasoid (exhibiting characteristics typical of Caucasian populations) rather than Mongoloid (exhibiting characteristics of Asian populations)—a group to which American Indians are most often classed. The physical characteristics of Kennewick man/The Ancient One are said to most closely resemble those of the Ainu indigenes of Japan.

Chatters questioned this classification when a Cascade projectile point was found embedded in the skeleton's right illium (upper hip). Cascade projectile points are typical of southern Plateau assemblages from 8500 years BP to 4500 BP, though similar styles were used up to the nineteenth century in parts of the western United States. Adding to the confusion were the physical characteristics (such as the shape of the eye orbits) of the remains that are associated with neither European nor Indian populations.

After discovering these ambiguities, Johnson ordered radiocarbon and DNA testing. Radiocarbon dating performed on the left fifth metacarpal (the pinky finger) returned an isotopically corrected age of 8,410 +/− 60 years BP (7300–7600 BCE). Although DNA from the skeleton remained intact, testing was inconclusive.

Four days after the radiocarbon dates were returned, the Army Corps of Engineers, the group with authority over the federal lands where the remains were found, halted any further scientific research on the remains and took possession of the skeleton. The Corps published their intention to repatriate the remains in the local *Tri-City Herald* on September 17 and 24, 1996, to a group of five tribes—the Umatillas, Yakamas, Nez Percé, Wanapums, and Colvilles—as outlined by provisions of the Native American Graves Protection and Repatriation Act (NAGPRA). These groups, filing a joint claim, intended to immediately bury the remains in an undisclosed location.

A group of eight high-profile archaeologists, physical anthropologists, and other scientists launched a lawsuit on October 17, 1996, to gain access to the remains for study. Likewise, the California-based Asatru Folk Assembly, a group practicing a Norse religion, launched a lawsuit on October 26, 1996, to prevent the Corps from repatriating the remains. This group argued that the skeleton could be their ancestor and represent a European presence on the continent at a much earlier time than is generally believed.

U.S. Magistrate Judge John Jelderks presided over the cases and rebuked the Corps strongly for their intention to repatriate and their secretive contact with the tribes. On September 3, 1998, Jelderks ordered the remains transferred from a Richland, Washington, lab to the Burke Museum at the University of Washington, where the Department of the Interior studied the remains to determine cultural affiliation. In September 2000 the department decided that the remains should be repatriated to the tribes—a decision without much force.

After much legal wrangling and testimony, Jelderks eventually ruled in favor of the scientists on August 30, 2002. In his decision he criticized the government for their hasty decision to repatriate and their slow movement throughout the ordeal. Further, he cited the insufficiency of oral tradition and geography in attempts to repatriate material as old as the remains.

On October 29, 2002, four tribes—the Nez Percé, Umatillas, Colvilles, and Yakamas—launched an appeal of Jelderks' decision. Similarly, the U.S. Justice Department filed an appeal of Jelderks' decision on October 29, 2002. On February 4, 2004, the Ninth Circuit Court of Appeals upheld Jelderks' decision, citing the lack of adequate means or evidence to establish cultural affiliation. The court subsequently refused a request by the tribes to have the case reheard in front of a full court on April 20, 2004. Shortly after the tribes declared that they would not continue their legal battle, the U.S. Justice Department declared that it would not appeal the decision on July 22, 2004; scientists subsequently began to study the remains.

The battle for Kennewick man/The Ancient One is often viewed as one for control of the past. It also represents one of the most recent struggles between American Indians and academics, lawmakers, and the wider sociopolitical system. This confrontation has multiple antecedents in various events throughout the historical relationship between Indians and the wider power structures: Thus it is not viewed in isolation by most Indians.

The use of population-based racial identification and its frequent portrayal in the popular media as racial essentialism remains one of the most controversial aspects of the ordeal. This is particularly true for those groups—including many Indians—who reject the value and relevance of notions such as race. These concepts could have significant political implications at a time when race has significant social and political relevance in the United States.

Adding to this controversy have been the claims of groups like the Asatru Folk Assembly of a European presence on the continent for a significant period of time. Similarly, Kennewick man/The Ancient One and several other skeletons of great antiquity have led scientists to question their traditional migration theories and suggest that there have been multiple "waves" of migration by distinct populations who came to inhabit North America. Efforts of Indians to assert sovereignty and a political presence in the contemporary United States could be hampered by assertions that they lack claims to the land and rights through descent and prior inhabitation.

These migration theories have also proved controversial in that they are contrary to the traditional beliefs of Indian groups who believe that they have lived on the continent since time immemorial. Individuals who perceive this as a marginalization of Indian tradition find further evidence in the court rulings of Jelderks as well as the appeals court that denies the relevance of oral tradition and prior habitation in asserting legal and political claims. Many find offensive the notion that the relevant Indian tribes cannot rebury the remains in accordance with their customs. All of these circumstances explain why the struggle has been frequently and inaccurately portrayed as one of "science" versus "religion"—labels that appear to have hurt the image of tribal groups in the United States, casting them as timeless and antiscientific.

The struggle over Kennewick man/The Ancient One has important ramifications elsewhere. Within academic disciplines like archaeology, physical anthropology, and cultural anthropology, the issue divided colleagues along ethical fault lines as well those between science and humanism. Legally and politically, many felt that NAGPRA was antiscientific, and some, including Congressman Doc Hastings (Republican, Washington), have attempted to change legislation in a way that would allow for the study of the remains. This move was opposed by the

Clinton administration. Others, however, felt that Jelderks' ruling and the appeals court upholding of it were contrary to the spirit of NAGPRA in that it did not balance interests and marginalized the desires of Indian groups. Senator John McCain (Republican, Arizona), an individual who played a key role in the drafting and passing of NAGPRA in 1990, introduced a bill in April 2005 to amend the legislation (Senate Bill 536 §182) so as to allow for the increased ability of Indians to rebury their remains. This move was opposed by the administration of George W. Bush and many in the scientific community.

Though Kennewick man/The Ancient One has faded from news headlines, the implications are still tangible and many are unknown. Academics and Indians are attempting to rebuild damaged relationships, while others in each camp continue to lobby for legal reform and access to skeletal remains. What this ordeal has proved most, however, is the fragility of relationships between Indians and the wider society and that there are significant political implications to the study of and access to the past.

Christopher A. J. L. Little

See also Archaeology and the First Americans; Bering Strait Theory; Identity; Native American Graves Protection and Repatriation Act (NAGPRA).

References and Further Reading

Bonnichsen et al. v. United States, Civil Action No. 96–1481-JE (District of Oregon, 2000).

Chatters, James C. 2000. "The Recovery and First Analysis of an Early Holocene Skeleton from Kennewick, Washington." *American Antiquity* 65, no. 2: 291–316.

Chatters, James C. 2001. *Ancient Encounters: Kennewick Man and the First Americans.* Toronto: Simon & Schuster.

Downey, Robert. 2000. *Riddle of the Bones: Politics, Science, Race, and the Story of Kennewick Man.* New York: Copernicus.

Dewar, Elaine. 2001. *Bones: Discovering the First Americans.* Toronto: Random House Canada.

Hurst, David Thomas. 2000. *Skull Wars: Kennewick Man, Archaeology, and the Battle for Native Identity.* New York: Basic Books.

Johansen, Bruce E. 1999. "Great White Hope? Kennewick Man, the Facts, the Fantasies and the Stakes." *Native Americas* 16, no. 1: 36–47.

Mihesuah, David A. 2000. *Repatriation Reader: Who Owns American Indian Remains?* Lincoln: University of Nebraska Press.

The Tri-City Herald. "Kennewick Man Virtual Interpretive Center." Available at: http://www.kennewick-man.com/. Accessed January 11, 2007).

Lacrosse

The name "lacrosse" refers to a number of indigenous games played by teams using a ball and sticks. It undoubtedly has become the most popular sport native to North America. In amateur clubs, intercollegiate competitions, professional leagues, and international matches, thousands play, watch, and enjoy modern renditions of the traditional ball game. Importantly, lacrosse remains a vital element in some American Indian communities, nurturing ethnic identity, social relations, and cultural traditions.

Aboriginal lacrosse was concentrated around and to the east and southeast of the Great Lakes. Two teams, often numbering in the dozens and occasionally in the hundreds, faced off in a huge playing field. Ostensibly, the object of the sport was to score more goals than the opposing team. For indigenous participants and spectators, however, lacrosse was more than a recreational activity; the game possessed important spiritual components, reinforced local, kinship-based social organization, and had deep associations with physical combat.

In some Native societies, lacrosse was considered sacred. Individual Potawatomis convened matches to honor their guardian spirit. Other Native groups, like the Iroquois League, played the game in connection with key religious rites. Lacrosse was frequently associated with funerary and memorial ceremonies. Further, medicine men and conjurers played a key role in the sport, blessing players and equipment alike, while often engaging in combat with one another through spells. Finally, some people viewed its medicinal powers as evidence of the sacred character of lacrosse. Some tribes, like the Hurons, believed lacrosse could cure diseases, whereas others, such as the Potawatomis, thought it could prevent illness.

Beyond its spiritual significance, lacrosse had profound social importance as well. Matches were grand gatherings of people, encouraging economic activity and cementing social relations. Moreover, games were the occasion of intense gambling.

Choctaw Indian men and boys play a game similar to lacrosse in the 1840s near Fort Gibson, Oklahoma. (Library of Congress)

Lacrosse also provided a means for individual distinction and culturally sanctioned competition. In fact, many American Indian communities understood the game to be a surrogate for warfare, often speaking of the two in similar terms, employing shared rituals and designing lacrosse sticks after war clubs.

In the seventeenth century, French missionaries offered the first written description of the sport. For much of the next century, largely in New France, Europeans watched and wagered on matches between Native Americans, sometimes engaging in competitions against them. Beginning in the early nineteenth century, Euro-Canadians, particularly in the vicinity of Montreal, began playing the game among themselves, systemizing it in 1867. Although indigenous peoples outside Canada played lacrosse, it did not capture much public attention in the United States until after the Civil War, when it become an established intercollegiate sport in the northeast by the 1880s. As lacrosse was systematized in the United States and Canada, American Indians were excluded and marginalized. More recently, an indoor version of lacrosse, known as box lacrosse, has served as the basis for the professionalization of the sport.

The institutionalization of lacrosse in the United States eclipsed, but did not eradicate, indigenous forms of the sport. Throughout the twentieth century, indigenous communities continued to play local versions of the ball game and began to embrace modern lacrosse as well. Importantly, for many Native Americans, the ball game has fostered the rediscovery of cultural heritage and the validation of ethnic identity. Indeed, the formation of the Iroquois Nationals team in 1983 marked a pivotal moment in indigenous activism and sport. In 1990, the Iroquois Nationals team played the U.S. team in the Lacrosse World Cup.

At the start of the twenty-first century, lacrosse remains a vital sport summarizing the Native American experience: a powerful tradition replete with religious and social meanings; a cultural complex taken from indigenous peoples, then modified to fit the ideals of western sport and society; a game in which American Indians were discouraged from further play and banned from participation in established leagues; and, most recently, a sport repossessed as a resource of ethnic identity and an emblem of indigenous resurgence.

C. Richard King

See also Haudenosaunee Confederacy, Political System.

References and Further Readings
Blanchard, Kendall. 1981. *The Mississippi Choctaw at Play*. Urbana: University of Illinois Press.
Fisher, Donald M. 2002. *Lacrosse: A History of the Game*. Baltimore, MD: Johns Hopkins University Press.
Lipsyte, Robert. 1986. "Lacrosse: All-American Game." *New York Times Magazine*, June 15: 29–38.
Vennum, Thomas. 1994. *American Indian Lacrosse: Little Brother of War*. Washington, DC: Smithsonian Institution.

Language and Language Renewal

Linguists estimate that nearly a thousand languages were spoken in North, Central, and South America before the arrival of European colonists. In North America about 300 languages were spoken, but because of assimilation pressures only about half of these languages still have speakers, and fewer and fewer children are learning them. A number of factors have led to this language loss. Since 1492, most colonial governments and missionaries have actively worked to keep children from speaking their indigenous languages in schools. However, in the twenty-first century, when languages are less suppressed in schools, it is mass media, particularly television and movies, that are moving Native children in the Americas rapidly away from their heritage languages toward international languages such as English and Spanish.

As fewer and fewer children speak their Native languages, many parents and grandparents are becoming increasingly concerned that their languages soon will lose fluent speakers, and with the language their culture will be lost. In response, efforts are being made across the Americas to revitalize indigenous languages. One of the problems with revitalization, however, is that there are so many languages and they can be very dissimilar. Linguists have divided North American indigenous languages into six or more major language phyla (large related groups of languages). The following is a list of widely accepted phyla with some sample languages from each group:

1. Eskimo-Aleut includes the "Eskimo" family of languages, such as Inuit and Yupik and the Aleut family.
2. Na-Dené, or Eyak-Athabaskan, includes more than forty Athapaskan (Athabaskan) languages, extending from Tanaina in Alaska, Dogrib and Sekani in Canada, to Apache, Hupa, Navajo (Diné), and Umpqua in the Southwest of the United States.
3. Salishan encompasses Pacific coastal groups from British Columbia to Oregon, as well as Flathead, Kalispel, and Spokane in Idaho and Montana.
4. Cochimí-Yuman, in Upper and Lower (Baja) California and Arizona, takes in Havasupai, Walapai, Yavapai, and Mojave.
5. Aztec-Tanoan is made up of Uto-Aztecan, one of the largest language families spoken from Oregon to Panama (some members are Comanche, Paiute, Shoshoni, Hopi, Pima, Tarahumara, and Náhuatl), as well as the Kiowa-Tanoan family.
6. Macro-Siouan is made up of the Siouan family of Assiniboine, Catawaba, Dakota, Ho Chunk (Winnebago), Crow, and Mandan; the Iroquoian family, including Cherokee, Tuscarora, Huronian, Seneca, and Mohawk; and the Caddoan family, including Caddoan, Pawnee and Wichita.
7. Macro–Algonkian is made up of the Algonquian family, spread from California to the East Coast and from Canada to Mexico (some of this family's members are Arapahos, Blackfoot, Cheyennes, Crees, Fox, Kickapoos, Menominees, Ojibwas, Shawnees, Miamis, and Yuroks), and the Gulf Branch families, including Alabama, Chickasaw, Choctaw, and Seminole (adapted from Midgette 1997 and Campbell 1997).

In addition, isolates exist, such as Zuni, that resist classification into the larger American Indian language groups. While there have been attempts to link some American Indian languages to current European and Asian languages, including Welsh and Japanese, these efforts have been uniformly rejected by the vast majority of linguists for lack of evidence.

James Estes (1999) lists 154 indigenous American languages still spoken in the United States with Navajo having the most speakers (148,530), followed by Ojibwa with 35,000 speakers, Dakota with 20,355, Choctaw with 17,890, Apache with 12,693, and Cherokee with 11,905 speakers. Seven languages are listed with only one speaker. They include Coos and Kalapuya in Oregon, Eyak in Alaska and Coast Miwok, Plains Miwok, Pomo and Serrano in California. In Canada, the Summer Institute of Linguistics' *Ethnologue* estimates that Cree has 80,550 first language speakers, and in Mexico Náhuatl has 1,376,898 speakers (Gordon, 2005). The various dialects of Quechua, the language of the Incas, still have millions of speakers in Peru, Bolivia, Equador, and other South American countries.

Linguists who study American Indian languages see the many languages of today as having evolved from one or more early languages that began to differ as groups of people repeatedly divided and went their separate ways, populating the Americas. Linguists even try to roughly date when separations occurred by the degree of difference between languages. Because some groups are more ready to borrow words from their neighbors' languages than others, it is difficult to date these hypothesized separations. However, the vast differences that occur even in one language phylum indicate that the people who spoke these languages have lived in the Americas for many thousands of years. English is one language that has borrowed words from hundreds of languages, including many Indian languages, especially the names of animals and plants that were new to Europeans. Some of these words were first loan words into Spanish and French and then were borrowed into English. In addition, many place names in the Americas are of Indian origin.

While most indigenous languages lacked any system of writing before the European invasion, the Aztecs, Mixtecs, Zapotecs, Epi-Olmecs, and Mayans had hieroglyphic writing systems. After 1521, the Spanish burned most of the Mayan codices (ancient bark paper books), because they were seen as pagan. During colonial times interested amateurs such as Thomas Jefferson made word lists in different indigenous languages. These lists can be compared to check their similarities, but vocabulary is only one measure of a language's uniqueness. Looking at word order (syntax) is another way to compare the differences and similarities between languages.

Missionaries went even further than compiling lists. They developed writing systems for various indigenous languages and worked with tribal informants to translate Christian texts. John Eliot worked with Indian informants to translate the *Bible* while others translated catechisms and prayer books. Eliot's *Indian Bible* in the Massachusetts dialect of the Algonquian language was printed at Harvard University in 1663. Other missionaries produced dictionaries that are still useful today, such as Stephen Riggs' 1852 *Grammar and Dictionary of the Dakota Language* and the Catholic Franciscan Fathers' 1919 *An Ethnologic Dictionary of the Navajo Language,* printed at their St. Michael's mission. In some cases, the word lists of early amateur scientists and later linguists, as well as the translations and dictionaries produced by missionaries, are all that remains of languages that no one speaks today, and these remnants are being used by descendents to reawaken their ancestral languages.

While most of the missionaries' early writing systems for Indian languages were attempts to phonetically spell Indian words using a European alphabet, in sharp contrast a non-English–speaking Cherokee, Sequoyah, independently developed a unique syllabary of eighty-five symbols representing the sounds in his language. Sequoyah, who moved westward to avoid whites, hoped his writing system would help preserve Cherokee culture. A missionary, Samuel Worcester, printed Sequoyah's syllabary in 1821, and the Cherokees used it in their bilingual newspaper, the *Cherokee Phoenix,* started in 1828, and in private correspondence. Unfortunately, the Georgia Guard soon destroyed the *Cherokee Phoenix's* printing press, and the Cherokees were forcibly removed to Indian Territory on the Trail of Tears. There, between 1835 and 1861, Worcester's new mission printed almost 14 million pages, many in Sequoyah's syllabary. John B. Jones, the Indian agent at Tahlequah in Indian Territory, wrote in 1872 that, "Almost the whole of those Cherokees who do not speak English can read and write the Cherokee by using the characters invented by Sequoyah" (Reyhner and Eder, 2004, 54).

John Wesley Powell, the explorer of the Grand Canyon, published in 1877 *An Introduction to the Study of Indian Languages* and in 1879 became the first director of the U.S. Bureau of Ethnology. In 1891 he published *Indian Linguistic Families of America North of Mexico,* listing fifty-eight separate language families, which became a foundation for future research by anthropologists and linguists such as Franz Boas, Roland Dixon, Alfred Kroeber, Edward Sapir, J. P. Harrington, Robert Young, Kenneth Hale, Akira Yamamoto, and Leanne Hinton.

Sapir was able to reduce the number of major language groups down to six. These linguists used Native speakers as informants.

Linguists have moved from merely studying Indian languages to helping keep remaining languages alive by developing writing systems (orthographies), helping schools develop bilingual education programs, training tribal linguists, and improving language teaching techniques. For example, University of California linguist Leanne Hinton (Hinton, 1994; Hinton and Hale, 2001; Hinton, Vera, and Steele, 2002) is helping to develop the master-apprentice training program to help young adults to learn languages spoken only by a few elderly tribal members, a situation all too common in California.

While linguists tend to see languages as evolving, as English has evolved from the time of Chaucer, to the time of Shakespeare, to today with pronunciations changing and new words being added over time, traditionally American Indians have viewed their languages as sacred gifts from the Creator. For example, the Northern Arapaho Language and Culture Commission has stated that its language is the foundation of Arapaho culture and spiritual heritage. Without it, the Arapahos believe that they would not exist in the manner that the Creator intends.

The connection between language and culture and how and if language shapes the way people understand the world they live in has received much discussion. Many see language as embodying culture. This point of view was expressed by a Cheyenne elder who said, "Cheyennes who are coming toward us are being denied by us the right to acquire that central aspect of what it means to be Cheyenne because we are not teaching them to talk Cheyenne. When they reach us, when they are born, they are going to be relegated to being mere husks, empty shells. They are going to look Cheyenne, have Cheyenne parents but they won't have the language which is going to make them truly Cheyenne" (Reyhner, 1997, vii).

Some linguists have argued that languages determine how we think about and see the world. The Sapir-Whorf hypothesis argues for this determination, while other researchers see languages as having only an influence. One can do a good job of translating from one language to another, although sometimes it takes a whole phrase in one language to get at the meaning of a single word in another language. Some words are very hard to translate.

Sally Midgette (1997, 40) gives the example of "the Navajo word *hózhó,* which lies at the heart of their worldview. This word can only be translated by three separate English words: peace, harmony, and beauty. Some languages do not use verbs to mark past, present, and future as English does, but that does not mean, as some have contended, that speakers of these languages cannot express those concepts.

Using another example of how languages can differ, Midgette (1997, 33) describes how Navajo and other Athapascan languages use different verbs to express whether an action is instantaneous, repeated, or takes a long time. Navajo is a polysynthetic language unlike English, which is an analytic language. In an analytic language, sentences are made up of relatively short and simple words while a polysynthetic language uses very complex words, with roots, prefixes, and suffixes occurring in a fixed order. One complex polysynthetic word can express the meaning of a whole sentence in English. An example Midgette gives is the Navajo word *Naa'ahélgo'* that translates into the English as "I pushed them and made them fall over one after another." These words are always verbs with the noun incorporated into the verb, such as "we are going berry-picking" (verb) instead of "we are going to pick berries" (verb plus noun).

While linguists who study Indian languages quickly see how sophisticated they are. Yet the popular view of Indian languages by many non-Indian Americans in the nineteenth century was that they were "barbarous" primitive dialects incapable of expressing complex ideas. The U.S. government's Peace Commission reported in 1868 that "between Indian and white it was, the difference in language, which in a great measure barred intercourse and a proper understanding each of the other's motives and intentions. Now, by educating the children of these tribes in the English language these differences would have disappeared, and civilization would have followed at once. . . . Through sameness of language is produced sameness of sentiment, and thought; customs and habits are moulded and assimilated in the same way, and thus in process of time the differences producing trouble would have been gradually obliterated" (Reyhner and Eder, 2004, 74).

This attitude toward the role of language ignored the fact that, in the bloody Civil War that ended only three years before, both the North and the South had spoken English.

Commissioner of Indian Affairs J.D.C. Atkins in his 1887 annual report ordered only English to be used in schools on Indian reservations:

Every nation is jealous of its own language, and no nation ought to be more so than ours, which approaches nearer than any other nationality to the perfect protection of its people. True Americans all feel that the Constitution, laws, and institutions of the United States, in their adaptation to the wants and requirements of man, are superior to those of any other country; and they should understand that by the spread of the English language will these laws and institutions be more firmly established and widely disseminated. Nothing so surely and perfectly stamps upon an individual a national characteristic as language (Reyhner and Eder, 2004, 76).

Some missionaries who effectively used bilingual education to first teach reading and writing in their students' Native language before teaching English vigorously opposed Atkins' approach. For example, Stephen Riggs found teaching English "to be very difficult and not producing much apparent fruit." It was not the students' lack of ability that prevented them from learning English, but rather their unwillingness. "Teaching Dakota was a different thing. It was their own language." Riggs's son at Santee Sioux School in Nebraska found that learning to read in their Dakota language and then using illustrated bilingual books "enables them [the children] to master English with more ease when they take up that study; and he thinks, also, that a child beginning a four years' course with the study of Dakota would be further advanced in English at the end of the term than one who had not been instructed in Dakota" (Reyhner and Eder, 2004, 79). Dartmouth College's president wrote in 1887, "The idea of reaching and permanently elevating the great mass of any people whatever, by first teaching them all a foreign tongue, is too absurd ever to have been entertained by sane men" (Reyhner and Eder, 2004, 77).

Various methods were used in schools to keep students from "talking Indian," including washing student's mouths out with lye soap if they spoke their Native languages. When these students became parents, they sometimes did not teach their children their language so that they would not be punished in school like their parents. Over time, some languages ceased to be spoken. It was thought that once American Indians spoke only English, they would do well in school, but in the many Indian communities in the twenty-first century where children no longer know how to speak their ancestral language, the academic achievement gap between Indian and middle-class white students is still wide. Recent research (Reyhner, 2001) has shown that students who still speak their Native language and practice traditional activities do as well or better in school as those who do not. This fact, along with the breakdown of families and the increase in gang and other antisocial activities in Indian communities, led to a movement in the late twentieth century to teach Indian languages in locally controlled schools.

American Indian languages are not the only ones that have been suppressed in U.S. schools. Spanish-speaking students were prevented from and punished for speaking Spanish in schools for more than a century in the Southwestern United States, and as a group they had poor academic achievement. In 1968, at the height of the Civil Rights Movement and the War on Poverty, President Lyndon B. Johnson, who had taught Mexican-American students in Texas as a young man, signed the Bilingual Education Act. American Indians quickly took advantage of this new source of funding to establish bilingual education programs of their own. However, there was a lack of trained teachers who were fluent in Indian language, and students often ended up learning only a few words in their Native languages.

Ironically, as direct efforts to suppress American Indian language through schooling decreased with the Civil Rights Movement during the 1960s, language loss actually accelerated among many Native peoples, as paved roads reduced isolation and English-language radio and then television entered Indian homes in North America. The recognition of the accelerating rate of language loss led some tribes to pass language policies. The Navajo Tribal Council passed educational policies in 1984 supporting local control, parental involvement, Indian hiring preference, and Navajo language instruction. It declared:

> The Navajo language is an essential element of the life, culture and identity of the Navajo people. The Navajo Nation recognizes the importance of preserving and perpetuating that language to the survival of the Nation. Instruction in the Navajo language shall be made available for all grade levels in all schools serving the Navajo Nation. Navajo language

instruction shall include to the greatest extent practicable: thinking, speaking, comprehension, reading and writing skills and study of the formal grammar of the language (Reyhner and Eder, 2004, 310).

These policies also required Navajo history and culture courses. In his preface to the policies, Tribal Chairman Peterson Zah wrote, "We believe that an excellent education can produce achievement in the basic academic skills and skills required by modern technology and still educate young Navajo citizens in their language, history, government and culture" (Reyhner and Eder, 2004, 310). The Northern Ute Tribal Business Committee passed a similar resolution the same year declaring that Ute is the official language of the Northern Ute Nation and may be used in the business of government—legislative, executive and judicial—although in deference to, and out of respect to speakers of English, it may be utilized in official matters of government. "We declare that the Ute language is a living and vital language that has the ability to match any other in the world for expressiveness and beauty. Our language is capable of lexical expansion into modern conceptual fields such as the field of politics, economics, mathematics and science," the statement said (Reyhner and Eder, 2004, 310–311).

Fears of a proposed constitutional amendment to make English the official language of the United States and a desire for language revitalization, especially by Native Hawaiians, led to the passage in the United States of the Native American Languages Act in 1990. This act declared that, "the status of the cultures and languages of Native Americans is unique and the United States has the responsibility to act together with Native Americans to ensure the survival of these unique cultures and languages." The Act made it U.S. policy to "preserve, protect, and promote the rights and freedom of Native Americans to use, practice, and develop Native American languages. . . . The right of Indian tribes and other Native American governing bodies to use the Native American languages as a medium of instruction in all schools funded by the Secretary of the Interior" is recognized. In addition, "the right of Native Americans to express themselves through the use of Native American languages shall not be restricted in any public proceeding, including publicly supported education programs" (Reyhner and Eder, 2004, 309).

Multilingualism is more common than monolingualism outside the United States, and researchers

(Baker, 2002) have found that knowing more than one language is an asset rather than a handicap. One does not have to cease speaking their mother tongue to learn a second language or one of the "global" or "international" languages spoken widely around the world. Researchers (Baker, 2002) indicate that an average of one to two years is required to acquire speaking ability in a second language, compared to about six years to master reading it (and writing in a new language and to do well academically in it). Unfortunately, voters in the United States have been seduced with "English for the children" propaganda, starting in 1998 in California, Arizona, and Massachusetts. These initiatives largely ban the use of bilingual education in public schools. While aimed at speakers of Spanish, this legislation is affecting negatively indigenous language programs in public schools.

During the last quarter of the twentieth century many indigenous peoples became more aware of the dire straits their languages had encountered. The Maori in New Zealand realized that, if nothing was done soon, no one would be speaking their language in a few years. In addition, their English-speaking children were not doing well in school. In 1982, they started Maori language preschools, called *Te Kohanga Reo* (language nests), staffed by elders who spoke only Maori with the young children in their care. The number of these preschools increased rapidly. By 1991, 700 had been started, with 10,000 students. The Maori originally came from Hawai'i, and the Hawaiian language was in the same imperiled condition as Maori. Native Hawaiians quickly saw the success of the Maori and started their own language nests, called *Punana Leo*, in 1984. Their mission statement reads:

> The *Punana Leo* Movement grew out of a dream that there be reestablished throughout Hawai'i the mana of a living Hawaiian language from the depth of our origins. The *Punana Leo* initiates, provides for and nurtures various Hawaiian Language environments, and we find our strength in our spirituality, love of our language, love of our people, love of our land, and love of knowledge (Reyhner, 2003, 3).

According to parents and staff, the *Punana Leo* embody "a way of life . . . you have to take it home" that is bringing back the moral values of the culture and mending families. Parents were asked to learn Hawaiian along with their children and provide vol-

unteer help to the preschools, and in 1986 they were able to get the 1896 state law outlawing the use of their language in schools repealed so that their children graduating from the language nests could continue their Hawaiian language education in the public schools. In 2003, there were twenty-three public schools with Hawaiian-immersion classes, and the first immersion students graduated from high school in 1999. Both in New Zealand and Hawai'i students can also now take university-level teacher education courses in their indigenous language, and they are working to Hawaianizing the curriculum they teach rather than just translating it from English. Immersion programs like the one in Hawai'i are still in their infancy in the continental United States.

Throughout most of history in the United States, Indian education has been English-only and assimilationist. However, after World War II, many Native peoples experienced the Civil Rights Movement, demanding more self-determination, including the right to run their own schools. One of the first Indian-controlled schools was Rock Point Community School on the Navajo Nation. Rock Point tried to raise test scores through using English as a second language (ESL) teaching techniques in the early 1960s, with only limited success. They then tried bilingual education starting with two-thirds of a day of Navajo immersion kindergarten in 1967, then adding one grade a year until they had a K–12 bilingual program. Students were immersed in Navajo one-half of the school day in grades one through three and then about one-fourth of the day through high school. While not reaching national averages, the bilingual program raised students' English-language test scores substantially. Children at this time were still coming to school as Navajo speakers in this isolated community and, with the bilingual program, math was taught emphasizing understanding with manipulatives and science was taught as a hands-on process. In high school the students were taught applied Navajo literacy and social studies (Reyhner and Eder, 2004).

As more and more students came to school with Navajo as their first language, the Rock Point model of Native-language maintenance and English-language development needed to be changed to a language-revitalization model. In 2005, the Window Rock School District's Diné (Navajo) immersion program exemplified this new type of program. Located at the capitol of the Navajo Nation in Arizona, Window Rock's immersion program provides for the unique cultural and academic related needs of

Navajo children by bringing back traditional Diné cultural values.

Parents must choose to put their children into the *Tséhootsooí Diné Bi'ólta'* (Diné Language Immersion School) where in kindergarten and first grade the language of instruction is Navajo. Starting in second grade, English instruction is added until in sixth grade, half of the instruction is in English. The Navajo Nation's *Diné Cultural Content Standards* are used along with Arizona state academic standards for reading, writing, math, foreign language, science, and social studies as the framework for instruction, resulting in students who are speakers and thinkers in Diné while meeting Arizona's academic and English language expectations. The district's goal is to revitalize the Diné (Navajo) language among school-age children through a culturally and linguistically relevant educational program. The school enrolls some 200 students taught by fifteen teachers instructing only in Diné and three English language teachers. The Navajo's tribal college offers teacher education courses taught in Navajo.

The district's vision is to be "an exemplary student centered learning organization reflecting the Diné values of life-long learning." Test data show that Diné language immersion students outperform in most subject areas Navajo students who are getting their instruction in English. Contrary to what many people commonly believe, bilingual education research (Francis and Reyhner, 2002) has found that learning to speak, read, and write a Native language can help students increase their English language skills. In addition, the use of the Diné language and integrating the Diné culture validate students' identity. Window Rock's immersion students are gaining Diné language proficiency at a time when fewer and fewer Diné children are speaking Navajo, and they are staying in school to graduate at a higher rate than other Navajo students.

Window Rock's efforts are supported by various studies (Reyhner, 2001) showing that students who speak their tribal language and participate in traditional activities do as well as in school or better than students who have lost their tribal language. Today, language revitalization programs working to keep Native languages alive are part of a larger process seeking to heal the wounds of colonial oppression that often sought to stamp out all aspects of Native culture. Sally Midgette writes, "I have heard several Native Americans speak about their sense of rootlessness and despair, and how they recovered when their grandmothers taught them to speak Tolowa, or Navajo, and they regained a sense of themselves and their heritage" (1997, 39). Evangeline Parsons Yazzie found in her doctoral research that, "Elder Navajos want to pass on their knowledge and wisdom to the younger generation. Originally, this was the older people's responsibility. Today the younger generation does not know the language and is unable to accept the words of wisdom." She concluded, "The use of the native tongue is like therapy, specific native words express love and caring. Knowing the language presents one with a strong self-identity, a culture with which to identify, and a sense of wellness" (Reyhner 1997, vi). Richard Littlebear, president of Chief Dull Knife College, concluded that his Northern Cheyenne language can be an antidote to the forces pulling the youth of his tribe into joining gangs.

Jon Reyhner

See also Language, Written in America, Pre-Contact; Sequoyah.

References and Further Reading

Assembly of Alaska Native Educators. 2001. *Guidelines for Strengthening Indigenous Languages.* Anchorage, AK: Alaska Native Knowledge. Available at: http://www.ankn.uaf.edu/standards/Language.html. Accessed May 11, 2005.

Baker, Colin. 2002. *Foundations of Bilingual Education and Bilingualism,* 3rd ed. Clevedon, UK: Multilingual Matters.

Campbell, Lyle. 1997. *American Indian Languages: The Historical Linguistics of Native America.* Oxford: Oxford University Press.

Cantoni, Gina, ed. 1996. *Stabilizing Indigenous Languages.* Flagstaff, AZ: Northern Arizona University.

"Endangered Languages, Endangered Lives." 2001. *Cultural Survival Quarterly* 25, no. 2 (special issue). Available at: http://www.cultural survival.org/publications/csq/index.cfm?id=25.2. Accessed May 11, 2005.

Estes, James. 1999. "How Many Indigenous American Languages Are Spoken in the United States? By How Many Speakers?" Washington, DC: National Clearinghouse for Bilingual Education.

Fishman, Joshua A. 1991. *Reversing Language Shift: Theoretical and Empirical Foundations of Assistance to Threatened Languages.* Clevedon, UK: Multilingual Matters.

Fishman, Joshua A, ed. 2000. *Can Threatened Languages Be Saved? Reversing Language Shift, Revisited: A 21st Century.* Clevedon, UK: Multilingual Matters.

Francis, Norbert, and Jon Reyhner. 2002. *Language and Literacy Teaching for Indigenous Education: A Bilingual Approach.* Clevedon, UK: Multilingual Matters.

Gordon, Raymond G., Jr. 2005. *Ethnologue: Languages of the World,* 15th ed. Dallas, TX: Summer Institute of Linguistics. Available at: http://www.ethnologue.com//web.asp. Accessed May 11, 2005.

Hinton, Leanne. 1994. *Flutes of Fire: Essays on California Indian Languages.* Berkeley, CA: Heyday Books.

Hinton, Leanne, and Kenneth Hale, eds. 2001. *The Green Book of Language Revitalization in Practice.* San Diego, CA: Academic Press.

Hinton, Leanne, Matt Vera, and Nancy Steele. 2002. *How to Keep Your Language Alive: A Guide to One-on-One Language Learning.* Berkeley, CA: Heyday Books.

Midgette, Sally. 1997. "The Native Languages of North America." In *American Indian Studies.* Edited by Dane Morrison, 27–45. New York: Peter Lang.

Reyhner, Jon. No date. "Family, Community, and School Impacts on American Indian and Alaska Native Students' Success." Available at: http://jan.ucc.nau.edu/~jar/AIE/Family.html. Accessed May 11, 2005.

Reyhner, Jon. 2003. "Native Language Immersion." In *Nurturing Native Languages.* Edited by Jon Reyhner, Octaviana Trujillo, Roberto Carrasco, and Louise Lockard, 1–6. Flagstaff, AZ: Northern Arizona University. Available at: http://jan.ucc.nau.edu/~jar/NNL/ (accessed May 11, 2005).

Reyhner, Jon, and Jeanne Eder. 2004. *American Indian Education: A History.* Norman: University of Oklahoma Press.

Reyhner, Jon, Louise Lockard, and J. Rosenthal. 2000. "Native American Languages." In *Handbook of Undergraduate Second Language Education.* Edited by Judith W. Rosenthal, 141–163. Mahwah, NJ: Lawrence Erlbaum Associates.

Reyhner, Jon, Gina Cantoni, Robert St. Clair, and Evangeline Parsons Yazzie, eds. 1999. *Revitalizing Indigenous Languages.* Flagstaff, AZ: Northern Arizona University.

Silver, Shirley and Wick R. Miller. 1997. *American Indian Languages: Cultural and Social Contexts.* Tucson: University of Arizona Press.

"Teaching Indigenous Languages." Available at: http://jan.ucc.nau.edu/~jar/TIL.html. Accessed May 11, 2005.

Language, Written in America, Pre-contact

Written languages existed throughout the Americas during the long pre-contact period, albeit in nonalphabetic form. Stories and messages have been encoded in the Aztec and Mayan codices, in wampum belts, and in petroglyphs and pictographs, as well as on rocks, hides, teepees, clothing, and ledger books. The nomadic Blackfeet and Shoshone peoples used Writing-on-Stone Provincial Park, located in a canyon on the Milk River in southern Alberta, as a campground for centuries. Consequently, many messages were left there, some of which detail hunting, warfare deeds, and daily life; others, the introduction of horses, guns, and metal. Some may represent ceremonial information. This writing dates back as far as about 1,800 years and as recently as around 1730. Some of the petrogylphs in the Southwestern United States, such as those found at the Ancestral Puebloan settlements at Chaco Canyon, are connected with calendrical counts and may have been used in conjunction with the astronomically aligned buildings to determine the proper solar, lunar, and stellar alignments used in ceremony. These glyphs date back nearly a thousand years. The petroglyphs and pictographs, using the same symbol systems, are distinguished by scholars from one another by their manner of creation. Pictographs are made using paints or pigments, often red ochre (pulverized iron ore and water), or drawn with a small piece of limestone. Petrogylphs are cut into rock with antlers, bones, other rocks, or, in more recent times, metal tools.

The documentary film, *The American Indian's Sacred Ground,* reveals that sign languages used in intertribal communication directly correspond to the corresponding written forms. The sign for snow, for instance, made by extending both arms from the elbow slightly above the waist with the fingers loose and making a wavy motion downward, relates to the petroglyph made by applying paint to the fingers and making the sign over the surface of the rock. This correspondence suggests an ingrained system, one that had been used for an extensive period of time, highly organized and systematic, pervasive across many tribal lines. In her article "On the Probable Origin of Plains Indian Sign Language," Patricia Kilroe, like the documentary film , notes the connection found by some archaeologists between North American petroglyphs and Plains

PICTURE WRITING

Pictographs on birch bark recording a chant used in religious ceremonies. (Library of Congress)

Sign Language (PSL)—particularly a Tule River, California, glyph that includes the signs for rain, for nothing here, and for hunger; an Alaskan woodcarving from the late nineteenth century that shows the signs for nothing and for winter lodge, made by two men in a boat; and Dakota petroglyphs with an ear of corn representing the Arikara, signed in PSL as corn shellers and a figure making the sign for Kiowa (rattle-brained), made by circling the hand or hands horizontally on one or either side of the head.

Kilroe also lists at length correspondences between PSL and Mayan and Mixtec pictography. As opposed to some of the glyphs found in the continental United States and Canada, the Mayan and Mixtec figures all seem to be of the same sort as for the preceding sign for Kiowa—a figure gesturing the sign rather than a reproduction of the pattern of the sign, like that for snow or sacred place. The Dresden

codex includes a figure signing the PSL for yes and one signing the same; one Mixtec figure makes the PSL for fire; another makes the sign for to give; and connections exist between the signs for sun, moon, accession, and water or drink. Kilroe further points out Helen Neuenswander's 1981 finding that some contemporary Mayans seem to use signs, at least in regard to lunar cycles and seasons, that bear a correspondence to ancient lunar series glyphs.

Not only do these correlations suggest a once extensive network of a widely used, visually based linguistic system, but the Mayan codices and other ancient Meso-American "writings" themselves demonstrate remarkable evidence for the extent to which a semipermanent visual recording of knowledge might have been part of the pre-contact past, with perhaps as much cultural import as the alphabetic system of recording has for contemporary cultures. As Zelia Nuttal says in the introduction to *The Codex Nuttal, A Picture Manuscript from Ancient Mexico*, "Ancient Mexican screenfolds are remarkably versatile as forms of information storage. It is possible to view several pages simultaneously and even to consult the obverse at the same time as the reverse. Clearly, the screenfold format was devised as a solution to the need of non-Western, non-lineal patterns of thought" (O'Neill et al., n.d.). These once plentiful codices were stored in vast repositories, but only a few were saved by Catholic monks and smuggled to Europe, escaping burning by the other Spaniards.

Due to the nature of their complexity, however, anything included here about the scope of Meso-American writing systems must be hugely oversimplified; an overview of these systems is necessary to understanding the history of the visual recording of thought in the Americas. Ancient writings—almost twenty of which are in the form of the folding screen books and others of which appear on walls, on vases, on individual sheets, and on a variety of other artifacts—are extant from several cultures: Mayan, Aztec (or, more properly, Mexica, pronounced Me-shi-ka), Mixtec, and Zapotec. The Mayan system, though it is glyphic, is fundamentally agreed on by scholars to have developed into a phonetic system of sorts, while the Mexica, Mixtec, and Zapotec systems appear to be pictographic. These pictographic screenfolds in particular are thought to have been intended to accompany, not necessarily to replace, the spoken word, as PSL often does in contemporary Plains discourse.

A more recent sort of pictographic writing in terms of indigenous cultures can be found in the Plains ledger books. Though Plains peoples had recorded pictographs prior to this period on a variety of surfaces—notably hides, teepees, and clothing in addition to the petroglyphs—between 1860 and 1900, a number of pictographic books were created in accountants' ledger books with crayon, colored pencil, and sometimes watercolor. The books first recorded war exploits and later ceremonial information and details from daily life. The accurate accounting of war deeds was extremely important in Plains cultures, because warfare had important ceremonial implications. The ledger books continued a long tradition by the warrior/artists of the Plains. They recorded their deeds pictographically to aid in their preservation in the oral tradition of the people. An old saying goes, "The picture is the rope that ties memory solidly to the stake of truth" (*Cheyenne Dog Soldiers*, 1999).

One of the earliest of these books was created by the Cheyenne Dog Soldiers in the years following the Sand Creek Massacre of 1864. The book was given to the Colorado Historical Society (CHS) on November 30, 1903. Though the book originally was produced with 144 blank pages, one 114 pages remain in the book as it is. The CHS has determined that the book is the work of fourteen author artists. Several issues, including sequencing and a seemingly patterned order of blank pages, complicate interpretation for scholars. The CHS states that the largest problem, however, is that they are "severely limited by an incomplete oral tradition," a complication that arises from the fact that, again, these recordings are pictographic and meant to accompany, not replace, the oral. The pictographic method, if not the symbols themselves, is very close to that found in the codices, containing figures for both the names of the warriors whose deeds are recorded in it and for objects associated with the deeds.

Like the other media written of in this section, the Plains ledger books provide ample evidence of a strong visual recording tradition in the Americas, a tradition in accordance with the right-hemispheric tendencies of cultures that revered and still revere the visual receiving of knowledge. With differences in media, origin, geography, and symbol systems, pre-contact Americans found ways to write and transmit information about important historical events, territorial boundaries, sacred spaces, hunting, ceremony, trading, and their daily lives all over these lands in ways far more permanent than books.

Kimberly Roppolo

See also Language and Language Renewal; Sand Creek Massacre.

References and Further Reading

American Indian's Sacred Ground. 1991. Narrated by Cliff Robertson. Freewheelin' Films Ltd. and Wood Knapp Video.

Cantor, George. 1993. *North American Indian Landmarks: A Traveler's Guide*. Detroit, MI: Gale Research

Cheyenne Dog Soldiers: A Courageous Warrior History. 1999. Denver: Colorado Historical Society. CD-ROM.

Gibbon, Guy, ed. 1998. *Archaeology of Prehistoric Native America: An Encyclopedia*. New York: Garland Publishing.

Kilroe, Patricia. No date. "On the Probable Origins of Plains Sign Language." In *Search of Language Origins: Selected Papers from the Seventh Meeting of the Language Origins Society, Dekalb, Illinois*. Edited by Edward Callary. Available at:

http://baserv.uci.kun.nl/~los/Meetings/
Dekalb/Accessed December 30, 2001.

O'Neill, Maureen, et al. No date. "Images in
Practice." Available at: http://www.envf
.port.ac.uk/illustration/images. Accessed
January 2, 2002.

Roppolo, Kimberly. 2002. "Collating Divergent
Discourses: Positing the Critic as Culture-
Broker in Reading Native American Texts."
Ph.D. dissertation, Baylor University.

Longhouse Religion

The Iroquois Confederacy (or Haudenosaunee, meaning "people building a longhouse") represents the coming together of five Iroquois nations—the Mohawks, Oneidas, Onondagas, Senecas, and Cayugas—for the purposes of political and military cohesion and strength. By 1722, a sixth nation—the Tuscaroras—joined the confederacy. While there are some differences between nations in regard to language and traditions, overall the nations of the confederacy followed the same practices and traditions and could understand the language of one another without much difficulty.

Initially, the longhouse was a building in which Iroquois families lived. In modern times, the longhouse building has become a place for people who continue to follow the traditional Iroquois ways to gather for social, political, and ceremonial events. Many of these more traditional Haudenosaunee people refer to themselves in everyday language as being "Longhouse," that is, belonging to one of the six Iroquois nations that constitute the confederacy and following the traditional customs and traditions of the people of the longhouse. This does not necessarily exclude people who are "Longhouse" from embracing other religious traditions. While some purists may argue that these people are somehow less authentic in their beliefs, it is a reflection of the reality of different cultures interacting and sometimes clashing for several hundred years.

The phrase "longhouse religion" is a term most often used in the United States to describe the Iroquois people who follow the Handsome Lake Code. As with many indigenous peoples, the nations that were known as the Iroquois Confederacy were affected in all aspects of their lives by the arrival of Europeans on their lands. After contact with Europeans, a Seneca man by the name of Handsome Lake spoke about a system of rules and guiding principles that he believed were given to him by the Creator to pass on to others for their benefit, to lead a better life. These principles became known as the Handsome Lake Code (*Gai'wiio*, good words). It has been argued by some traditionalists that this code was merely a melding of traditional Haudenosaunee ways with Judeo-Christian principles (such as those found in the Ten Commandments) and therefore does not reflect the "authentic" beliefs and traditions of the Iroquois. The debate continues to this day and in many communities there are two branches reflecting traditional Haudenosaunee beliefs: the more purist or traditionalist longhouse and the Handsome Lake longhouse.

Handsome Lake, of the Seneca nation, was born in 1735 and was the half-brother of the renowned Chief Cornplanter. Throughout his life, Handsome Lake had problems with alcohol and was very ill for several years from excessive drinking. It was during this time of illness that he began to seriously contemplate life, and he experienced visions or revelations that would change his life (Parker, 1913, 9). Handsome Lake's teachings came at a time when the Seneca and other Iroquois nations were experiencing severe hardships, poverty, and loss of their traditional lands, and Handsome Lake gave people hope and faith for a better future. He was even commended for his teachings and efforts by President Thomas Jefferson (Parker, 1913, 10).

Initially despised and belittled for his teachings, even by Cornplanter himself, Handsome Lake was at times quite discouraged. Some individuals continued to remind him of his alcoholism and former ways and could not believe that such an imperfect person could be a true prophet. In time, however, a significant group of followers developed.

Through his code, Handsome Lake encouraged his followers to reject alcohol, witchcraft, charms, abortion, and gossip against other people. He also encouraged couples to remain together, to not divorce or separate, to not have children outside of marriage, and to not physically abuse one another. While he rejected many of the traditional practices of the Iroquois nations, he maintained that certain specific traditional dances and activities should continue: the Great Feather Dance, the Harvest Dance, the Sacred Song, the Peach Stone game, and the Midwinter Festival (Parker, 1913, 27–81).

Handsome Lake continued to teach these principles for sixteen years, until his death on August 10, 1815, in Onondaga, New York (Parker, 1913, 6, 81).

After his death, Chief Cornplanter, who had come to accept the Handsome Lake Code, said of his half-brother:

> He made mistakes, many mistakes, so it is reported, but he was only a man and men are liable to commit errors. Whatever he did and said of himself is of no consequence. What he did and said by the direction of the four messengers is everything—it is our religion. [Handsome Lake] was weak in many points and sometimes afraid to do as the messengers told him, He was almost an unwilling servant. He made no divine claims, he did not pose as infallible nor even truly virtuous. He merely proclaimed the Gai'wiio' and that is what we follow, not him. We do not worship him, we worship one great Creator. We honor and revere our prophet and leader, we revere the four messengers who watch over us—but the Creator alone do we worship (Parker, 1913, 14).

Lysane Cree

See also Cornplanter; Haudenosaunee Confederacy, Political System; Handsome Lake.

References and Further Reading
Carnegie Museum. 1998. "The Iroquois of the Northeast." Available at: http://www.carnegiemuseums.org/cmnh/exhibits/north-south-east-west/iroquois/. Accessed January 11, 2007.
Garraty, John.,ed. "Peacemaker Hero: Handsome Lake." Available at: http://myhero.com/myhero/hero.asp?hero=handsomelake. Accessed January 11, 2007.
Kanatiiosh. 2001. "The Longhouse." Available at: http://www.peace4turtleisland.org/pages/longhouse.htm. Accessed January 11, 2007.
Lord, Rebecca, and David Ratcliffe. 2002. "The Six Nations: Oldest Living Participatory Democracy on Earth." Available at: http://www.ratical.org/many_worlds/6Nations/. Accessed January 11, 2007.
Parker, Arthur C. 1913. "The Code of Handsome Lake, the Seneca Prophet." Available at: http://www.harvestfields.ca/ebook/NativeTribal/04bk/tch00.htm. Accessed January 11, 2007.
Six Nations. "Culture: What Are the Values, Beliefs and Traditions That the Haudenosaunee Seek to Maintain?" Available at: http://www.sixnations.org. Accessed January 11, 2007.
Thomas, Jacob E. 1994. *Teachings from the Longhouse.* Toronto, ON: Stoddart Publishing Company.

Mascots

For more than a century, non-Natives have used names, symbols, and material culture associated with or built on their stereotypes of indigenous peoples to create mascots for high school, college, and professional sport teams. Although such imagery remains common in the United States, increasingly, over the past thirty years, Native American leaders and educators, advocates for social justice, and a variety of professional and political groups have called for an end to the misappropriation and misrepresentation central to Native American mascots. The movement against the misuse of Indian symbols in sports has been ignored or even resisted by some schools, sports fans, and athletic organizations, but it has had a noticeable and positive impact across the United States.

History

Native American mascots are a common feature of sports in the United States. Although it is difficult to arrive at an exact count, most scholars agree that several thousand schools have used names, symbols, and/or cultural artifacts associated with indigenous peoples, referring to their teams as Warriors, Braves, Indians, Redskins, or others. At the collegiate level, according to the National Coalition on Racism in Sports and Media, more than eighty institutions have Native American mascots. Dozens of professional and semiprofessional teams have employed images of Indians. Significantly, indigenous peoples stand alone as the only racial or ethnic group to be misappropriated and misrepresented in this mass fashion, more than a half century after false and psychological injurious images of blacks, Latinos and others became problematic.

Educational institutions, professional franchises, and amateur clubs have used American Indian symbols for a variety of reasons. Some, like Dartmouth College, chose Native American mascots to reflect an historical link between an institution and indigenous people (Dartmouth was founded as an Indian school). Others, like the University of Illinois or the University of Utah, selected such symbols to enshrine regional history and legitimately claim territory occupied by indigenous peoples. Still other uses are largely accidental, hinging on school colors (often red), the team play (described as savage or wild), or the enthusiasm of an individual (whether a coach, band leader, student, or alumnus) for Indians and Indianness.

Native Americans protest the Washington Redskins' mascot name in 1991. (Wally McNamee/Corbis)

Whatever their specific origins, Native American mascots crystallized in an historical context that made it possible, pleasurable, and powerful for Euro-Americans to incorporate images of Indians in athletic contexts. First, beginning with the Boston Tea Party, Euro-Americans crafted identities for themselves by "playing Indian." Second, the conquest of Native America simultaneously empowered Euro-Americans to appropriate, invent, and otherwise represent Native Americans and to aspire for aspects of the cultures damaged by conquest. Third, countless spectacles, exhibitions, and other sundry entertainments centered on Indianness proliferated during the last quarter of the nineteenth century. Native American mascots built on these patterns and traditions.

Not surprisingly, given these sociohistorical foundations, while Native American mascots have afforded many Euro-American individuals and institutions a means to fashion identity, to many indige-

nous peoples these athletic icons perpetuate inauthentic and injurious images. Halftime performances, fan antics, and mass merchandizing transform somber and reverent artifacts and activities into trivial and lifeless forms that simultaneously reduce Native Americans to a series of well-worn clichés, effacing the complexities of Native American cultures and histories.

Stereotypes and More

Mascots stereotype American Indians for pleasure and profit. They offer misleading, flat, and fictional renderings of Native Americans, frequently trapping them in the past, while reducing them to stereotypical bellicosity, wildness, and savagery. Sports teams and educational institutions have used clichéd elements associated with Indians and Indianness, often borrowed without permission from tribes or, worse, copied directly from Hollywood westerns, to rearticulate values important to them, such as pride, valor, aggression, strength, and tradition.

Native American mascots do more than stereotype; they also reveal much about the unequal position of American Indians. Indeed, such imagery reflects and contributes to the denial of cultural self-determination for Native Americans. The acceptance of misleading and injurious images, such as Chief Wahoo of the Cleveland Indians, makes it impossible for American Indians to be recognized as fully human social actors and to exercise the rights and protections accorded them under the law. Consequently, it is difficult for American Indians to be recognized as Indians and heard as meaningful actors; they must contort themselves to fit white stereotypes. Significantly, Native American mascots negatively impact American Indian youth.

Even as they dehumanize indigenous peoples, Native American mascots empower Euro-Americans, allowing them to fashion identities, histories, and communities. Indianness in sports lays the foundation for the construction of intimate networks, powerful spaces, and meaningful traditions. It is not simply defined in white terms, but through individualism that presumes that individuals can choose who they are, fashion their own identities, and opt to choose or reject stereotypical imagery and the identities that come with it.

Indian imagery in sports does more than recreate Native American identity in a white cast. It also contributes to the production of nationalism, gender bias, and social hierarchy. Native American mascots

reflect core ideas of what it means to be traditionally American, white, and male. On the one hand, such renderings of Indianness are best understood in a broader, comparative framework that connects indigeneity with whiteness and blackness. On the other hand, the true meaning of Native American mascots cannot be appreciated without reference to gender: Predominantly white institutions create images of savage warriors that affirm accepted connections among masculinity—aggressiveness, violence, bravery, and honor—while confirming the righteousness of conquest.

Schools using Native American mascots contribute to stereotyping and the mistreatment of American Indians. They miseducate students, teaching them the dominant culture's perceptions of history, culture, and power. As a consequence, American Indian nicknames and symbols transform schools and stadiums into hostile environments for indigenous peoples. Perhaps because of their centrality to miseducation and the maintenance of problematic ideas about race, history, and nation, such imagery increasingly has become the site of social struggle.

Change

Although indigenous peoples long have protested popular misrepresentations and impersonations, beginning in the late 1960s, energized by a political, cultural, and social resurgence throughout Indian Country, Native Americans critiqued the tradition of playing Indian at halftime, demanding its end. Although initially successful, forcing retirements at Dartmouth College and Stanford University, as well as changes at Marquette University and the University of Oklahoma, the movement encountered strong resistance among fans, alumni, and boosters, failing to make much progress for the following two decades. Then, during the early 1990s, activists confronted mascots with renewed energy, fostering public debates and policy changes. During the subsequent decade several universities retired mascots, including St. John's University and the University of Miami, or revised their uses of Indianness, among them Bradley University and the University of Utah. A number of school districts (notably in Los Angeles and Dallas) and state boards of education encouraged or required the end of Indian mascots; countless political, social, and professional organizations (from the National Congress of American Indians and the National Association for the Advancement of Colored People to the American Anthropological Association and the National Education Association) condemned such symbols and spectacles; and the federal Trademark Trial and Appeal Board voided the trademark rights of the Washington Redskins of the National Football League, finding that the name and logo used by the team were disparaging and hence violated the law. The ruling was voided by a higher court on a technicality, however, and the imagery continued to be used.

More recently, two important developments have occurred at the national level. First, the United States Civil Rights Commission has held that Native American mascots infringe on the basic human rights of American Indians, encouraging discrimination and prejudice. Second, in 2004, the National Collegiate Athletic Association issued a prohibition on teams using American Indian imagery in postseason tournaments. While it has granted exceptions to schools that it deems have the support of specific Native nations or tribes, this marks an important move toward a more proactive agenda outside of Indian Country to challenge Native American mascots.

Despite these trends, it is unlikely that Native American mascots will disappear from American sports anytime in the near future. For the most part, Euro-Americans have failed to grasp the significance of playing Indian at halftime, refusing to appreciate the implications of Euro-American privilege or the pain caused by their casual abuse of ethnic imagery. Indeed, the continued use of Indians and Indianness in sports will likely serve as a barometer of the extent to which Americans have come to terms with racism, the conquest of North America, and the humanity and sovereignty of Native America. At the same time, the persistent protests of American Indian imagery in sports offer forceful reminders of the insistence of indigenous peoples to be understood as citizens worthy respect and inclusion.

C. Richard King

See also American Indian Movement; Myth of the Noble Savage.

References and Further Readings

Davis, Laurel. 1993. "Protest Against the Use of Native American Mascots: A Challenge to Traditional, American Identity." *Journal of Sport and Social Issues* 17, no. 1: 9–22.

King, C. Richard, ed. 2004. "Re/Claiming Indianness: Critical Perspectives on Native American Mascots." *Journal of Sport and Social Issues* 28, no. 1 (special issue).

King, C. Richard, and Charles F. Springwood, eds. 2001. *Team Spirits: The Native American Mascot Controversy*. Lincoln: University of Nebraska Press.

Spindel, Carol. 2000. *Dancing at Halftime: The Controversy over American Indian Mascots*. New York: New York University Press.

Mississippian Culture

The Mississippian peoples were hierarchical mound builders who occupied much of the eastern part of North America between 700 and 1550. Connected culturally and technologically, these eastern Woodland Native Americans lived along the Mississippi River, on its tributaries, and in the riverine basins along the Gulf of Mexico and Atlantic Oceans. Their domain stretched from Florida through the Appalachian Mountains and extended to the eastern part of the Great Plains.

Although early Spanish conquistadors, such as Hernando de Soto and others, left descriptions of the Mississippians as they existed at the end of the era, archaeology provides most of what we know about these cultures. The Spanish and archaeological sources both describe densely populated centers in the Mississippian era. Population estimates vary, but the Mississippians probably numbered in the millions.

The intense cultivation of maize enabled Native Americans to produce the surpluses necessary to support the growing populations and political hierarchy. Although men continued to hunt and women still gathered nuts and fruits, the introduction of cleared-field corn agriculture in about 800 provided the means for the rise of large Mississippian chiefdoms. Women primarily controlled the fields in Mississippian society, and eventually their corn, beans, and squash provided most of the food.

The Mississippian chiefdoms spoke mutually unintelligible languages, competed for trade and hunting grounds, and waged wars of conquest with one another. Warfare was the norm in Mississippian society, providing both the means for territorial expansion and the threat of conquest. As the palisades at Cahokia attest, Mississippians lived with an omnipresent fear of invasion. Other evidence points to the esteem afforded to those warriors who proved themselves in battle. Other social and cultural similarities likewise connected the chiefdoms into a complex network of competing chiefdoms. They shared the technology that allowed shell-tempered pottery, lived in similar forms of circular housing, hunted with bow and arrows, used short-handled hoes made of stone or shells, and lived in hierarchical societies where chiefs from elite lineages received tribute. Trading networks also connected the chiefdoms, allowing elites to create goodwill with neighbors as well as to obtain the exotic goods required to maintain one's social and sacred position.

Mississippian societies also shared the Southeastern Ceremonial Complex. This artistic tradition contained a shared set of symbols and iconography that reveals aspects of the Mississippian cosmology and social structure. Many scholars assert that the paramount chiefs were believed to have had spiritual powers and were expected to use them to benefit their communities. Chiefs also were believed to have possessed a special relationship with the sun, perhaps explaining the construction of the mounds to bring them closer together.

Mound building was the most distinguishable characteristic of the Mississippian people. The mounds were usually pyramidical and most often (but not always) part of large urban centers. Cahokia, located in Illinois near today's St. Louis, Missouri, was the largest of these centers. Monk's Mounds was the largest of its mounds, measuring about 100 feet high and 1,000 feet in length. This rectangular mound had several flat tiers with sacred buildings on top. Cahokia had more than 100 other significantly smaller mounds across its two hundred acres. Mississippians built various public buildings and houses for their paramount chiefs and other elites on top of these mounds, while other mounds contained the graves for their leaders. The grave goods at this site contain items from as far away as the Great Lakes, Rocky Mountains, and Gulf of Mexico. At its height, wooden palisades surrounded Cahokia, and it served as the centerpiece of a theocratic chiefdom containing tens of thousands of residents. Cahokia collapsed by 1150, prior to the arrival of the Europeans, and other smaller chiefdoms took control of their territory. The other excavated mounds have tended to be smaller, but similarly the center of large concentrations of people. In total, the Mississippians built more than a thousand mounds in the United States.

Instability characterized the Mississippian era. Warfare and conquest created some instability, but the rise and fall of chiefdoms likely had more to do with the internal problem of succession. The death of paramount chiefs may have resulted in the renewed competition of different networks of kin to replace deceased leaders. Disagreements resulted in migrations and the splintering of communities. Even when a successor was found, the Mississippian structure remained fragile. If followers feared that their successor lacked the spiritual power to protect the community, some societies collapsed, while others simply became depopulated as a result of massive migrations. The arrival of the Europeans and their diseases in the sixteenth century brought disruptions that the Mississippian chiefdoms could not withstand.

Andrew K. Frank

See also Agriculture; Natchez Culture.
References and Further Reading
Galloway, Patricia, ed. 1999. *The Southeastern Ceremonial Complex: Artifacts and Analysis.* Lincoln: University of Nebraska Press.
Hudson, Charles M. 1975. *The Southeastern Indians.* Knoxville: University of Tennessee Press.
Smith, Bruce D., ed. 1990. *The Mississippian Emergence.* Washington, DC: Smithsonian Institution.

Mogollon Culture

Mogollon is one of four major cultural areas archaeologists recognize in the American Southwest. The others are Ancestral Puebloan, Hohokam, and Patayan, each of which has subregional variations (see Ancestral Puebloan for a discussion of archaeological designations). The Mogollon people resided in the mountainous areas of western and southern New Mexico and eastern Arizona. Their neighbors to the north, the Ancestral Pueblos, resided on the Colorado Plateau and along the Rio Grande River and its tributaries, and their neighbors to the south and west, the Hohokam, resided in the lowland desert regions. The Mogollon peoples lived primarily at higher elevations, but some groups also resided in the adjacent lower desert regions to the south and east. The Mogollon region is generally bounded by the Little Colorado River on the north, the Verde River on the west, and the Pecos River on the east. Mogollon peoples also lived in the Mexican states of Sonora and Chihuahua, but few surveys have been undertaken to establish how far south the culture area extended. Some researchers have suggested that the Mogollon peoples are the ancestors of the Tarahumara (Ramamuri).

The Mogollon as a cultural, temporal, and regional concept was introduced by archaeologist Emil W. Haury in 1936 based on work he and others conducted at the Mogollon Village and Harris Village sites and from extensive survey in the region. The idea was initially met with great skepticism by archaeologists who did not want to distinguish the region from the Ancestral Puebloan cultural sphere or question the sweeping Pecos classification (see Ancestral Puebloan Culture), but by the mid-1950s it had become accepted.

Archaeologists today consider the Mogollon cultural traditions to have flourished from the end of the Archaic phase (1,800 BP/200 CE) until the arrival of the Spanish about 1540 CE. Some archaeologists, however, think that the Mogollon lost their distinctive identity as a regional culture around 1,000 BP/1000 CE and that the people amalgamated into the Ancestral Puebloan cultures, especially in the Cibola region (near Zuni); others feel they remained distinct until peoples migrated from the region in large numbers around 600 BP/1400 CE. The differences probably reflect regional variation between northern and southern peoples. There are still extensive scholarly debates as to the direct descents of the group. Some communities are definitely ancestral to the Hopi and Zuni, as documented in clan migration stories; other groups probably merged with O'odham and Sobaipuri communities, western Apache bands, and peoples in northern Chihuahua.

Culturally, Mogollon is characterized by pithouses, distinctive burial patterns, head deformation, and coil-and-scraped brown pottery that changed over time and had regional variations. The brown wares were generally corrugated with incised or painted designs, although some types were polished redwares or decorated red-on-brown ceramics. In terms of settlements, Mogollon communities are characterized by Pueblo villages that focused inward on a plaza and rectangular kivas found within the room blocks. Archaeologists distinguish six basic regional variations that express long, continuous occupation: San Francisco Valley (Pine Lawn and Cibola) and Mimbres in New Mexico, Point of Pines, San Simon Valley and Forestdale in Arizona, and Jornado near present-day El Paso, Texas. There is also evidence of extensive intermingling of peoples in these groups so that the branches are not as distinct as those noted for the Ancestral Puebloans.

Archaeologists divide Mogollon history into three basic time periods: Early Pithouse, Late Pithouse, and Mogollon Pueblo (some others conceptualize five phases of continuity and graduate change). These are further subdivided by regional variation. The Early Pithouse period dates from 1,800 BP/200 CE), growing out of the late Archaic in the desert areas, and is marked by the introduction of plain brown pottery followed later by red-slipped wares with simple geometric designs. Lifeways exhibit great continuity from earlier times as well as evidence of seasonal mobility of households. Most easily recognized are small, circular or bean-shaped pithouse villages sited on hilltops and ridges, which were occupied for only part of the year since the people moved often to gather wild foods. A few villages were larger, with up to fifty houses. This settlement pattern would reflect an adaptation to life in the mountains and its seasonal and scattered food resources as well as the need for communities to come together for social and religious activities. There is also evidence of limited agriculture at lower elevations reflecting a longer growing season.

The Late Pithouse phase begins around 1,400–1,350 BP/600–650 CE, marked by the appearance of red-on-brown pottery and an increase in population. There is also more regional variation, reflecting greater trade and communication with different Hohokam and Ancestral Puebloan peoples. All groups began to use their local environments more intensely, including the valley floors adjacent to lands they were cultivating, especially in areas with rivers. Peoples still needed hunting and gathering, but the greater reliance on horticulture may explain the larger population size. Seasonal mobility is still evident in the range of settlement types. All communities reflect a change in pithouse styles seen in the development of rectangular rooms with lateral ramp entrances and interior hearths. Special pottery types were also developed. The people in the Mimbres Valley, for example, began to use a cream slip with red decorations and increasingly complex designs; later in the period they experimented with oxidizing firing and produced black-on-red or white designs.

The Pueblo period began with the construction of aboveground, masonry villages, first seen in the Mimbres Valley of New Mexico about 1,000 BP/1000 CE and in communities in the Arizona (Point of Pines and Grasshopper) mountains a hundred to

three hundred years later. Continued contact with outside groups is reflected in regional variations in settlement, housing, and pottery styles. In general, villages are larger and suggest greater aggregation of peoples. Villages of 100 to 250 rooms were built over the ruins of older pithouse villages. Around 700 BP/1300 CE communities of up to 800 to 1,000 rooms are seen. These consist of several blocks of contiguous, surface roomblocks built of unshaped masonry stone around plazas. Large subterranean ceremonial rooms are located between roomblocks or on the edges of the pueblos while surface ceremonial chambers are incorporated into the roomblocks. Point of Pines Village, for example, had 800 rooms, a large rectangular great kiva, two plazas, and a surrounding wall set in a grassland plain in the mountains. There is evidence of a great deal of building, rebuilding, and remodeling, suggesting changes in uses for rooms and common areas. Interspersed in some areas are smaller sites, which may have been seasonal farm hamlets for extended families. There is also an influx of population, probably a result of clan migrations of Ancestral Puebloan peoples into the area. The migrants lived in Mogollon villages and established their own communities. For example, at Point of Pines Village, Kayenta Ancestral Puebloan migrants built a small, seventy-room addition to the main pueblo with a D-shaped kiva. The same subsistence patterns of seasonal hunting and plant gathering and dry-farming horticulture in the mountains and irrigation farming in the valleys continued but with evidence of more intensive agriculture and deforestation as farmers cleared the land.

This pattern continued with significant regional variation in periods of smaller and larger sites, as well as the introduction of cliff dwellings and adobe structures, until around 500 BP/1400–1450 CE. At this time, some groups moved from the central Arizona mountains to look for better farmlands elsewhere, and others established a lifestyle less dependent on farming. Some groups merged with the widespread Salado peoples (700–650 BP/1300–1450 CE) and lived in cliff dwellings with adobe structures, large rooms, and formally walled plaza areas. Some of these communities were very short-lived, with people moving often. At the end of this period, Apachean groups moved into the area and established it as their homeland.

Of all the Mogollon subregions, the Mimbres branch stands out because of its significant artistic achievement: decorated black-on-white pottery that was traded extensively throughout the Southwest,

Texas, and northern Mexico. Unfortunately, it is also distinguished because Mimbres sites have been the most looted and all but obliterated as pothunters search for the Classic styles (1,000–820 BP/1000–1180 CE), which fetch large sums in the antiquity and fine art markets. Classic Mimbres pottery dates from the Pueblo period and has stylized animals and humans in black designs painted on a white slip before the pottery is fired in an oxidizing atmosphere. In addition to the figurative designs, Mimbres potters produced nonfigurative ware noted for its symmetry and use of negative and positive space. Archaeologists speculate that this reflects an ideological statement about life and death. The pottery is so specialized that archaeologists suspect that some potters were specialists. Some pottery was ceremonially "killed" during funerals; the bowls were placed over the head of the deceased as they were buried beneath the floors of habitation rooms or in the plazas. The pottery ceased being produced by 800 years ago, most likely a result of the collapse of the economic system due to overpopulation and worsening climatic conditions. Smaller groups remained and reorganized themselves into more flexible and mobile groups. New trading centers like Casas Grandes formed in northern Chihuahua.

Nancy J. Parezo

See also Ancestral Puebloan Culture; Pottery.
References and Further Reading
Anyon, Roger, and Steven A. LeBlanc. 1984. *The Galaz Ruin: A Mimbres Village in Southwestern New Mexico.* Albuquerque: University of New Mexico Press.
Brody, J. J. 1977. *Mimbres Painted Pottery.* Albuquerque: University of New Mexico Press.
Cordell, Linda S. 1984. *Prehistory of the Southwest.* Orlando, FL: Academic Press.
Haury, Emil W. 1985. *Mogollon Culture in the Forestdale Valley, East-Central Arizona.* Tucson: University of Arizona Press.
Kabotie, Fred. 1982. *Designs from the Ancient Mimbreños: With a Hopi Interpretation.* Flagstaff, AZ: Northland Press.
LeBlanc, Steven A. 1983. *The Mimbres People: Ancient Pueblo Painters of the American Southwest.* New York: Thames and Hudson.
Reid, J. Jefferson, and Stephanie Whittlesey. 1997. *The Archaeology of Ancient Arizona.* Tucson: University of Arizona Press.
Reid, J. Jefferson, and Stephanie M. Whittlesey. 1999. *Grasshopper Pueblo: A Story of Archaeology and Ancient Life.* Tucson: University of Arizona Press.

Mound Cultures of North America

For both the scholar and the general reader, the Native American mound cultures of North America linger in relative obscurity, compared to the renown of Central and South American cultures. However, the North American mounds are monumental works of human ingenuity, with some—including the City of Cahokia, at the confluence of the Missouri, Mississippi, and Illinois Rivers; the 10.4-square-kilometer ceremonial complex, at Newark, Ohio; and the Poverty Point Earthworks, in northeastern Louisiana—rivaling the Pyramid of Giza and Stonehenge as wonders in the ancient world (as noted in Mann, 2005, 252; Fagan, 1998). These cultures are, as yet, only tentatively dated by archaeologists but are placed between 3000 BCE and 1400 CE, depending upon the culture.

The ancient mound centers of North America coalesced primarily along important waterways, particularly the Mississippi and Ohio River valleys, although mounds dot the landscape throughout much of North America. North American mounds come in a variety of types:

- *Platform mounds.* High mounds, flat on top, were primarily ceremonial and/or living space for elite leaders, with the houses of ordinary folk ringed around their bases, although, according to Native tradition, everyone could scramble up to the platforms for safety during emergencies such as floods.
- *Conical burial mounds.* Burial mounds might be large or small, depending on both the area of the country and the nation that built them. These were heavily plundered, bulldozed, and plowed under in the nineteenth, and well into the twentieth, centuries. Hundreds of thousands of sets of human remains were carted off to universities and museums, large and small, including the Smithsonian, to serve as the bases of racial studies (Mann, 2003, 7–8, 29–46).
- *Planting mounds.* These mounds were waist high, round-topped (Parker, 1968, 27, who envisioned the hills as breasts ["bosoms"] of Mother Earth, 36, 37) or square (Lindeström, 1925, 179, and n 15), depending on the nation that built them, and used exclusively by women, who were the farmers of Native North America. Planting mounds formed the

centerpiece of the massive agriculture practiced by, especially, woodlands cultures. Mound cultures might have been abandoned for the most part between 1100 and 1400, but women's planting mounds continued into modern times. To this day, some Natives plant in mounds.

- *Loaf mounds.* These occurred either in connection with ceremonial sites, in which case they were long, narrow ovals, or in connection with graded highways. In conjunction with wide highways, they marked the sides of the road, much as white striping edges the highways of today. The best-known example of roads is the so-called Great Hopewell Road, which runs nearly 60 miles (90 kilometers) south from Newark to Chillicothe, Ohio, connecting its circle-octagon observatory with the only other circle-octagon observatory still in existence, at nearby High Bank (Lepper, 1995).

- *Geometrical ceremonial mounds.* Specifically ceremonial sites existed, whose mounds outlined geometrical shapes. Simple circles, concentric circles, and concentric semicircles existed throughout the Mississippian cultures. In the Ohio River valley, circle-square mounds were also common. As traditional iconography, these designs referenced the twinned cosmos of Native North America, the complementary halves of Earth and Sky (often described west of the Mississippi as Water and Air, respectively, and sometimes given as Blood and Breath, respectively). For concentric circles, in the Woodlands, the innermost circle was the back of the turtle (of Turtle Island fame, i.e., Earth), with water around, often as a middle concentric circle. The outer circle was Sky. In the semicircles, the same intention applied, with the lower hump being the back of turtle, and the higher rise, the dome of sky. With the circle-square design, the circle indicated Sky, and the square, the four directions holding down Earth (Mann, 2003, 197–212). The spectacular circle-octagon complexes at Newark and High Bank, Ohio, are a variation on the circle-square theme. They hosted sophisticated observatories, capable of tracking the standstills of the moon, an event that occurs but every 18.61 years (Hively and Horn, 1982, 1984).

- *Animal effigy mounds.* Effigies are mounds in the shape of Earth or Sky animals. Perhaps the best-known is the extensive and long Great Serpent Mound of Adams County, Ohio. He is the Horned Serpent of tradition, standing as the male symbol of Earth (Mann, 2003, 169–238). Contrary to popular archaeological belief, Ohio Natives hold that it is not "an egg" in his mouth but rather his medicine bag, slung between the horns he shows only when he travels. He is an observatory, too, although Western scholars are still debating this (Fletcher and Cameron, 1988). Just as his scales (mica sheets) and horn (flint chips) were used to bring rain and make other Earth medicine, so were the humps of his form used as sighting lines for astronomical events, Sky medicine. (Pulling Sky and Earth together this way makes for very strong medicine.)

Based on both the historical traditions of North American Indians and archaeological research, the cultures that produced the mounds were agricultural and hierarchical. Native traditions from the Ohio valley recount that massive wars were fought in the time of the Mound Builders, including revolutions to overthrow what became oppressive governments, leading to the participatory democracies common to the Eastern Woodlands. There are even traditions discussing how to build mounds (Mann, 2003, 112–168).

From the eighteenth century until nearly through the twentieth, archaeology handled the mounds quite poorly, leading to two centuries' worth of the "slaughter" of, particularly, the burial mounds (Prufer and McKenzie, 1967, 267). Until the 1940s, archaeologists and hobbyists (it was sometimes hard to tell the difference) ripped the mounds open for little more than idle curiosity's sake. As archaeology became more sophisticated in the midtwentieth century, the destruction continued apace, despite archaeologist William Lipe's pointing out in 1974 that ancient sites were "non-renewable resources" (Lipe, 1974, 213).

For their part, farmers plowed the mounds flat in many places, often selling artifacts and human remains taken from them for a secondary source of income. A magnificent burial mound in present-day Columbus, Ohio, was dismantled so that workers could use its clay to make bricks to build the original state capital. Meantime, highway and railroad engineers simply blasted their way through any inconvenient mounds, oblivious of or indifferent to their significance. The work crews building the Ohio Canal in 1848 and the Ohio Railroad from 1852 to 1855 destroyed the burial mounds, a square, and a large platform mound at the Newark Complex. The remaining circle-octagon complex is currently leased until 2088 to a members-only golf club by the Ohio Historical Society (Fagan, 2000; Mann, 2003, 102–103, 306–307).

Most unfortunately, workers and farmers quickly plundered the impressive stone mounds of Ohio, taking them down to bare earth to use the worked stones to build their cellars and reservoirs. A splendid sandstone mound outside tiny Thornville, Ohio, was plundered to build the unnecessary Licking Reservoir between 1831 and 1832. Between ten and fifteen *thousand* wagonloads of worked stones were carted from that one mound, which measured 183 feet in diameter at its base and 55 feet at its apex (Fowke, 1902, 2: 389). Outside Jasper, Ohio, archaeologist Gerald Fowke destroyed a Shawnee mound built of 150–pound stones for his 1902 survey (1902, 1: 375). Due to such wanton destruction, many people, including many modern scholars, are ignorant of the fact that large stone mounds were built in Ohio, continuing the false impression that Native North Americans did not build in stone.

The results of such extensive manhandling were devastating to the mounds. For example, Ohio sported 12,000 mounds of various types in 1870. By 1951, the total number of Ohio mounds was down to 5,000, with some fairly spectacular sites, including a third circle-octagon complex, wiped clean from the earth.

The destructiveness of Euro-Americans toward the mounds was exceeded only by the lunacy of their explanations of the mounds and their builders. For political reasons, non-Natives were reluctant to attribute clear signs of civilization, including agriculture on a massive scale, to the same North American Natives they had defined as "savages," ripe for extermination. Strong Native American traditions of Mound Builder cultures were studiously ignored throughout the nineteenth century. As a result, bizarre theories, seriously propounded, identified the "lost civilization" of Mound Builders as variously Carthaginian, Chinese, Roman, Egyptian, Hindu, Persian, Phoenician, Spanish, Welsh, and Atlantean, among other candidates (Mann, 2003, 53–86; Silverberg, 1968; Williams, 1991). After Cyrus Thomas finally and conclusively identified the Mound Builders as Native North Americans in 1894, interest in them almost ceased.

Now that scholars are noticing the disastrous effects of racial bias on intercultural studies and are taking steps to erase old biases, scholarly interest is on the increase regarding the remaining mound sites. At the same time, Native American descendents of the Mound Builders are pressing their cases for, first, being consulted in discussions of their own history and, second, having the hundreds of thousands of Mound Builder remains that were so casually disinterred by museums and universities through the 1980s returned to them for proper reburial. As political agendas sort themselves out, a wider and better appreciation of mound cultures is emerging.

Barbara Alice Mann

See also Cahokia; Hopewell Culture; Ohio Valley Mound Culture.

References and Further Reading

Atwater, Caleb. 1820. "Description of the Antiquities Discovered in the State of Ohio and Other Western States." *Archaeologia Americana: Transactions and Collections of the American Antiquarian Society* 1: 105–267.

Bieder, Robert E. 1986. *Science Encounters the Indian, 1820–1880: The Early Years of American Ethnology.* Norman: University of Oklahoma Press.

Bieder, Robert E. 1990. *A Brief Historical Survey of the Expropriation of American Indian Remains.* Bloomington, IN: Native American Rights Rund.

Fagan, Brian M. 1998. *From Black Land to Fifth Sun: The Science of Sacred Sites.* Reading, MA: Helix Books.

Fagan, Brian M. 2000. "Golf and Archaeology: The Only Ancient Site with a Golf Course Faces More Destruction." *Discovering Archaeology* November/December: 8–10.

Fletcher, Robert, and Terry Cameron. 1988. "Serpent Mound: A New Look at an Old Snake-in-the-Grass." *Ohio Archaeologist* 38, no. 1: 55–61.

Fowke, Gerald. 1902. *Archaeological History of Ohio: Mound Builders and Later Indians.* 2 volumes. Columbus: Ohio Archaeological and Historical Society.

Gibson, Jon L. 1998. "Elements and Organization of Poverty Point Political Economy: High-Water Fish, Exotic Rocks, and Sacred Earth." *Research in Economic Anthropology* 19: 291–340.

Hively, Ray, and Robert Horn. 1982. "Geometry and Astronomy in Prehistoric Ohio." *Archaeoastronomy* 4: 1–20.

Hively, Ray, and Robert Horn. 1984. "Hopewellian Geometry and Astronomy at High Bank." *Archaeoastronomy* 7: 85–100.

Lepper, Bradley Thomas. 1993. "Ancient Astronomers of the Ohio Valley." *Timeline* 15, no. 1 (January/February): 2–11.

Lepper, Bradley Thomas. 1995. "Tracking Ohio's Great Hopewell Road." *Archaeology* 48, no. 6 (November/December): 52–56.

Lindeström, Peter. 1925. *Geographia Americae with an Account of the Delaweare Indians, Based on Surveys and Notes Made in 1654–1656.* Translated by Amandus Johnson. Philadelphia: Swedish Colonial Society.

Lipe, William D. 1974. "A Conservation Model for American Archaeology." *The Kiva* 39, no. 3–4: 213–245.

Mann, Barbara Alice. 2003. *Native Americans, Archaeologists, and the Mounds.* New York: Peter Lang.

Mann, Charles. 2005. "Ten Thousand Mounds." In *1491: New Revelations of the Americas Before Columbus,* 252–267. New York: Alfred A. Knopf.

Parker, Arthur. [1913] 1968. "The Iroquois Uses of Maize and Other Food Plants." In *Parker on the Iroquois.* Edited by William N. Fenton. Syracuse, NY: Syracuse University Press.

Pauketat, Timothy R. 1994. *The Ascent of Chiefs: Cahokia and Mississippian Politics in Native North America.* Tuscaloosa, AL: University of Alabama Press.

Pauketat, Timothy R. 1997. "Refiguring the Archaeology of Greater Cahokia." *Journal of Anthropological Research* 6: 45–89.

Prufer, Olaf H., and Douglas H. McKenzie. 1967. *Studies in Ohio Archaeology.* Cleveland, OH: Press of Western Reserve University.

Romain, William F. 2000. *Mysteries of the Hopewell: Astronomers, Geometers, and Magicians of the Eastern Woodlands.* Akron, OH: University of Akron Press.

Shaffer, Lynda Norene. 1992. *Native Americans Before 1492: The Moundbuilding Centers of the Eastern Woodlands.* Armonk, NY: M. E. Sharpe.

Silverberg, Robert. 1968. *Mound Builders of Ancient America: The Archaeology of a Myth.* Greenwich, CT: New York Graphic Society, Ltd.

Squier, Ephraim George, and E. H. Davis. [1848] 1965. *Ancient Monuments of the Mississippi Valley: Comprising the Results of Extensive Original Surveys and Explorations.* Smithsonian Contributions to Knowledge. Vol. 1. New York: Johnson Reprint Corporation.

Thomas, Cyrus. 1891. *Catalogue of Prehistoric Works East of the Rocky Mountains.* Washington, DC: Government Printing Office.

Thomas, Cyrus. 1894. *Report on the Mound Explorations of the Bureau of Ethnology.* Bureau of Ethnology Report no. 12. Washington, DC: Smithsonian Institution.

Ward, Heather D. 1998. "The Paleoethnobotanical Record of the Poverty Point Culture: Implications of Past and Current Research." *Southeastern Archaeology* 17, no. 2: 166–174.

Williams, Stephen. 1991. *Fantastic Archaeology: The Wild Side of North American Prehistory.* Philadelphia: University of Pennsylvania Press.

Woods, William I. 2001. "Monks Mound: A View from the Top." Paper presented at the 66th Annual Meeting of the Society for American Anthropology. April 19. New Orleans.

Woods, William I. 2000. "Monks Mound Revisited." In *Terra 2000: 8th International Conference on the Study and Conservation of Earthen Architecture.* Edited by N. Sterry, 98–104. London: James and James, Ltd.

Woods, William I. 2004. "Population, Nucelation, Intensive Agriculture, and Environmental Degradation: The Cahokia Example." *Agriculture and Human Values* 21: 151–157.

Muskogean Language

The parent of several tribal languages originally spoken in what is today the Southeastern United States, the remnants of Muskogean language now exist primarily in Oklahoma and, to a much lesser extent, in Florida and Alabama. The Muskogean language family evolved over thousands of years to a point that it was the primary language spoken among the people of the southeastern Woodlands until the arrival of Hernando de Soto in 1540. Modern descendents of the Muskogean-speaking peoples include the Muscogee (Creek), Seminole, Chickasaw, and Choctaw peoples, as well as smaller groups in independent towns who had treaties with the U.S. government prior to the removal and the formation of those contemporary nations, such as the Alabamas, Apalachees, Hitchitis, Mikasukis, and Koasatis.

Subsequent to the war between Creek traditionalists, known as the Red Sticks, and the U.S. government that culminated in the Battle of Horseshoe Bend (1814), many Muscogee speakers migrated to Florida, where other Creek and Hitchiti speakers already had moved due to disenchantment with Native leaders who had sided with colonial agents or due to European encroachment on aboriginal lands. These people became collectively known as the Seminoles, itself a word derived from the Spanish *cimarrón,* meaning "wild" or "untamed."

By 1828, many Muscogee (Creek) people realized that removal from their Alabama and Georgia homelands was inevitable, causing roughly three thousand Creeks to move to Indian Territory and establish homes in the contemporary area of Tulsa. In 1836 and 1837, the United States enforced the removal of the remaining Creeks to Indian Territory on what became known as the Long Walk, in which nearly 40 percent of the 24,000 people who were compelled to make the journey died. A second group of forced migrants settled in the lower Creek nation of Indian Territory, which remains a relatively rural area in the early twenty-first century. In this area, the Muscogee language was still used widely at churches and ceremonial grounds by speakers beyond the age of forty. However, due to attempts to erase Native cultures during the twentieth century, the number of Muscogee (Creek) speakers has been dwindling. By 2000, the language was being taught at Oklahoma State University and the University of Oklahoma, and several materials are available in the Muscogee (Creek) language.

Following the Second Seminole War (1835–1842), roughly 4,000 Seminoles were deported via boats across the Gulf Mexico and up the Mississippi River to Indian Territory, where land for them had been set aside by the United States adjacent to the Muscogee (Creek) people. The Third Seminole War (1855–1858) proved too costly for the United States to continue, leaving about 300 Seminole people in the Florida Everglades as the remaining speakers of Muscogee in the area. Today, the Muscogean language is still spoken by some Seminole elders in Oklahoma, but by the Seminoles' own admission, the language is slowly slipping away. Hopes of rejuvenating the language now rely on local public schools that are introducing Seminole children to the language.

The Choctaw nation of Oklahoma has also placed a significant emphasis on preserving its branch of the Muskogean language. By 2005, the tribe was offering courses by certified teachers in high schools, colleges, and community centers, as well as via Internet and satellite distribution. The Choctaws were the first of the five major Southeastern groups removed to Indian Territory from their traditional homelands in Alabama and Mississippi. Choctaws who did not move are now known as Mississippi Choctaw and are the keepers of much traditional culture, including the language that has been lost by the Oklahoma Choctaws. Very close to the Choctaw language branch of the Muskogean linguistic family is the Chickasaw language, at one time the language of commerce along the lower portion of the Mississippi River where the Chickasaws resided before their removal to Oklahoma beginning in 1837. In 2005, the Chickasaws paired a fluent speaker with a learning facilitator at sites throughout the Chickasaw nation in Oklahoma to teach the language.

Hugh W. Foley, Jr.

See also Language and Language Renewal; Seminole Wars; Trail of Tears.

References and Further Reading

Chickasaw Nation of Oklahoma. "Language." Available at: http://www.chickasaw.net. Accessed May 28, 2005.

Choctaw Nation of Oklahoma. "Culture" and "History." Available at: http://www .choctawnation.com. Accessed May 28, 2005.

Gouge, Earnest. 2004. *Totkv Mocvse (New Fire)*. Norman: University of Oklahoma Press.

Innes, Pamela, Linda Alexander, and Bertha Tilkens. 2004. *Beginning Creek: Mvskoke Emponvkv*. Norman: University of Oklahoma Press.

Martin, Jack B., and Margaret McKane Mauldin. 2000. *A Dictionary of Creek/Muskogee: With Notes on the Florida and Oklahoma Seminole Dialects of Creek*, xiii – xiv. Lincoln: University of Nebraska Press.

Mississippi Band of Choctaw Indians. "Language." Available at: http://www.choctaw.org. Accessed May 28, 2005.

Muscogee Creek Nation of Oklahoma. "Creek History." Available at: http://www .muscogeenation-nsn.gov. Accessed January 11, 2007.

Seminole Tribe of Florida. "Culture." Available at: http://www.seminoletribe.com/culture/ language.shtml. Accessed May 28, 2005.

Seminole Nation of Oklahoma. Available at: http://www.seminolenation.com/. Accessed May 28, 2005.

Myth of the Noble Savage

One of the most enduring, ironic, and perhaps damaging of the concepts used to describe American Indians is represented both by the idea of a "noble savage" and by the phrase, "myth of the noble savage." In the first instance, the oxymoronic pairing of words and the myth that has surrounded them put Native peoples in an untenable social position. In the second instance, the myth idea has been used to dismiss the legitimate contributions, worldviews, and qualities of indigenous people.

Christopher Columbus may have started the concept of the noble savage with his first reports about the islanders he "discovered" in the new world. He described them as being generous, innocent, peaceful, and easy to make servile while rationalizing his treatment of them because they were nonetheless savages. Throughout European and American literature, poetry, paintings, and film, the noble savage was depicted as being totally innocent, physically perfect, always fearless, highly instinctive (without thinking or emotional skills), peaceful, free of social restraints, and an extremely brutish part of nature when provoked. In literature, such attributes made for good fantasy. They also played to European audiences as they set the stage for showing how the stronger, more realistic characteristics of Europeans could be used to conquer the weaker, "outdated" primitives. Historically and politically, such images of indigenous people may have helped rationalize genocidal atrocities on the one hand and assuage guilt for such crimes on the other.

Although the phrase "noble savage" was first used to describe the Natives of Mexico in the fictional writings of John Dryden around 1672, Jean-Jacques Rousseau and others gave significance to the idea in political discourse. Rousseau used it to criticize dominant European political and educational assumptions and as a backdrop for his own political agenda in the mid-1700s. In so doing, he mentioned authentic indigenous approaches to democracy and equality that would later be used by the founding fathers of the United States to develop its constitution. However, like Thomas Hobbes and John Locke, he also dehumanized and disenfranchised the American Indians by placing them in a state of evolution to which "civilized" humans could not return. These writers wrongly promoted the idea that indigenous people merely wandered freely in nature and did not have social institutions that might otherwise cause them to be less equitable in their lifestyles and cultures.

The Jesuit missionaries also contributed to the noble savage myth. Wanting to achieve martyrdom, they described the danger and savagery of the indigenous people. Wanting to rationalize their Christian missions, they also had to convey that the people were nonetheless children of God and deserving of being saved by their missionary agenda. Thus, they gave the indigenous populations the noble attributes of innocent children, as were favored in the noble savage myth, simultaneously with those of the brute savage with whom they took great risks for God's work.

After the conquest and submission of American Indians, many people subscribed to the ideas about

their nobility and strengths to legitimize their own right to the land and to challenge new immigrant "invaders." The settlers themselves now could claim to be Native to the land. In so doing, they could rationalize their right to resist the migration of new settlers who brought their foreign, ignorant, and threatening ways with them. Later, in the 1800s, American pioneers may have used similar appropriations about indigenous virtues in their stories about such "heroes" as Red Cloud, Sitting Bull, and Crazy Horse to convey their own strength and their own claims to the land.

The myth of the noble savage has been but one of the European ideas that served to colonize and oppress American Indians. Even in contemporary times, the media has made American Indians appear as anything but who they really are: a perfect sidekick for a white hero, a dangerous foil for the military might of other white heroes, or a romantic artifact of the past.

Throughout history, this ironic phrase has been used to rationalize physical and cultural genocide against indigenous people. It supported manifest destiny. Scholars employed the concept in discussions about human nature and social progress. Politicians refer to it as a way to promote Euro-centric superiority. And it continues to be used to dismiss legitimate potential contributions that might offer a proven challenge to the worldview, policies, and practices of the dominant Western culture.

Four Arrows–Don Trent Jacobs

See also Democracy and Native American Images among Europeans; New Agers, "Indian" Ceremonies and.

References and Further Reading

Alfred, Geral Taiaiake. No date. "The Idea of the Noble Savage." Conversation with Michael Enright on CBC Radio One, Canada.

Na-Dene Peoples

"Na-Dene" is the name of a language stock that includes the Athapaskan language family, Tlingit and Eyak, and possibly Haida. The Na-Dene peoples (also called Proto-Na-Dene) are hypothesized to be the ancestors of today's Athapaskan, Tlingit, Eyak, and possibly Haida peoples. Na-Dene is a grouping that posits a genetic relationship among these languages. Eyak and Athapaskan form a language group called Eyak-Athapaskan. Tlingit is also related to this group, and together they form the language stock Na-Dene. Haida was once thought to be a member as well, but many linguists dispute this today.

The languages of Tlingit, Haida, and Eyak are spoken along the northwest coast of British Columbia and Alaska, whereas the Athapaskan languages are spread throughout the west of Canada and the U.S. Pacific coast and Southwest. Eyak is northernmost of the three, spoken in traditional territories on the northern part of the Alaskan Panhandle. The traditional territories of the Tlingit reach below the Eyak to the coast just north of the Queen Charlotte Islands of British Columbia, now known as the Haida Gwaii, home to the Haida people.

The term "Na-Dene" is sometimes used to refer to the Athapaskan peoples specifically, which includes groups like the northern Dene and the Navajo. The term "Athapaskan" is not universally endorsed by peoples of that heritage; "Na-Dene" presents a more generalized but relevant term because it includes the common linguistic root for the word "people" or "person."

The Na-Dene peoples are also believed to have been the second wave of migration into North America, which occurred approximately 8,000 years ago. They are believed to have emigrated from Asia, possibly in boats. Migrations from the Northwest of Canada took populations south, eventually distributing Na-Dene peoples throughout the continent. About 1,500 years ago, the ancestors of the Navajo and Apache peoples reached the southern United States.

Edward Sapir coined the term "Na-Dene" in 1915 as a reference to a grouping of Tlingit, Haida, and Athapaskan. It is coined from the Haida name for house (na) and the Athapaskan and Tlingit word for person (dene). When Sapir gained access to Eyak language data, he recognized its relationship to Athapaskan and included it in the grouping as well. His theory was met with skepticism, but Michael Krauss later undertook a study that supported the relationship between Eyak and Athapaskan. The relationship between Tlingit and Eyak-Athapaskan is remote, but now considered well established. Whether Haida is related as well is still unclear due to the considerable time separating it from the other languages.

The Na-Dene grouping was supported by Joseph Greenberg in 1987 when he published an article containing a controversial assertion that all of the languages in the Americas belonged to three major groups, with Na-Dene being one of them. Although many linguists maintain that Old World and New World language stocks are not related, Greenberg postulated three migration waves that began at least 11,000 years ago with the Amerind, followed 6,000 to 8,000 years ago by the Na-Dene, and 3,000 years ago by the Eskimo-Aleut.

Greenberg's model supports the prominent Clovis first model of American aboriginal origins. According to this theory, the North and South American continents have been populated for approximately 12,000 years. Similar technology of Siberian populations and the Proto-Na-Dene group offered the link of timing and origins of the second Na-Dene migration.

The complexity and number of Native languages are an important indicator of how long the Americas have been occupied by human beings. Today, new evidence from archaeology and linguistic theory suggests a much longer human occupation in the Americas than previously thought. Prominent models by Joanna Nichols and Richard Rogers lend support to the archaeological evidence of human occupation in South America from about 30,000 years ago.

Aliki Marinakis

See also Archaeology and the First Americans; Language and Language Revival.

References and Further Reading

Fagan, Brian. 1995. *People of the Earth: An Introduction to World Prehistory*, 8th ed. New York: Thames and Hudson.

Greenberg, Joseph. 1987. *Languages of the Americas*. Stanford, CA: Stanford University Press.

Gruhn, Ruth. 1997. "Language Classification and Models of the Peopling of the Americas." In *Archaeology and Linguistics: Aboriginal Australia in Global Perspective*. Edited by Patrick McConvell and N. Evans, 99–110. Oxford: Oxford University Press.

Krauss, Michael. 1964. "Proto-Athapaskan-Eyak and the Problem of Na-Dene I: Phonology." *International Journal of American Linguistics*, Vol. 30 No. 2:118–131.

Nichols, Johanna. 1990. "Linguistic Diversity and the First Settlement of the New World." *Language*, Vol. 66, No. 3 (Sept. 1990), 475–521.

Rogers Richard A., Larry Martin, and T. D. Nicklas. 1990. "Ice-Age Geography and the Distribution of the Native North American Languages." *Journal of Biogeography*, Vol. 17, No. 2 (March 1990), 131–143.

Sapir, Edward. 1915. "The Na-dene Languages, a Preliminary Report." In *American Anthropologist, New Series*, Vol.17, No. 3 (July–Sept. 1915), 534–558.

Natchez Culture

The Natchez were a temple-mound people who survived, atypically, into the period of sustained contact with Europeans. Their culture was thus something of a living window on other similar ones that had vanished or changed markedly by the time non-Natives arrived.

The Natchez were ruled by a man called the Great Sun, whose pronouncements regarding individuals were absolute and despotic. In decisions regarding the nation, however, he was subject to the consensus of a council of respected elders. Unlike the Pueblos, whose houses were egalitarian, the Natchez gave their ruler a large house, twenty-five by forty-five feet, built atop a flat-topped earthen mound eight to ten feet high.

A French observer said that, when the Great Sun "[g]ives the leavings [of his meal] to his brothers or any of his relatives, he pushes the dishes to them with his feet. . . . The submissiveness of the savages to their chief, who commands them with the most despotic power, is extreme. . . . If he demands the life of any one of them he comes himself to present his head" (Champagne, 1989, 59–60). Nearby, on another mound, stood a large building, with two carved birds at either end of its roof—the temple in which reposed the bones of earlier Great Suns. Only the Great Sun (who was also head priest as well as king) and a few assistants could enter the temple.

The sons and daughters of the Great Sun, the younger members of the royal family, were called Little Suns. Below the royal family in status was a class of Nobles, and below them a class of Honored Men. The rest of the people occupied the lower orders and were called the Stinkards. The term was not used in the presence of Stinkards themselves because they considered it offensive. Into this hierarchical society, the Natchez introduced marriage customs that included real class mobility. A Great Sun had to marry from among the Stinkards. The male children of Great Suns became Nobles, who were also obliged to marry Stinkards. The male children of Honored Men became Stinkards. Descent followed the female line, and children of female Suns

Engraving of a Natchez Indian from a French history of Louisiana, ca. 1758. (Library of Congress)

became Suns themselves. The system was matrilineal, but in the household the man's word was law.

The Natchez military was hierarchical, with different warrior grades, including apprentices (at the bottom), ordinary warriors, and warrior chiefs. The whole was governed by a council comprised of the most experienced warriors. People of Stinkard status could rise in rank through valor in war. Another way to rise in status was by means of meritorious religious action. When a king died, a father and mother could sacrifice a child in the king's honor. A person also could sacrifice him- or herself upon a king's death. Thus were remaining family members elevated in class. By the time the first English colonists established themselves on the eastern seaboard of

North America, Spanish explorers had crossed the Mississippi Valley and the regions southeast and southwest of it, fruitlessly seeking gold and other riches, meanwhile meeting the Natchez people. In 1540, the Spanish explorer Hernando de Soto became the first European to visit the area. In 1673, Father Jacques Marquette and trapper Louis Joliet traveled down the Mississippi River and landed near the Natchez Trace; in 1682, René-Robert Cavelier, Sieur de La Salle, claimed the land along the Mississippi River for France.

In the late 1720s, the Natchez chaffed under French colonialism in the newly established Louisiana Colony and rebelled against the growing French presence. The war resulted in the defeat of the Natchez, many of whom were sold into slavery and sent to the Caribbean islands, while some remnants escaped to live with the Chickasaw and Creek nations.

Bruce E. Johansen

See also Archaeology and the First Americans; Mound Cultures of North America.

References and Further Reading

Champagne, Duane. 1989. *American Indian Societies: Strategies and Conditions of Political and Cultural Survival.* Cambridge, MA: Cultural Survival.

MacLeod, William Christie. 1924. "Natchez Political Evolution." *American Anthropologist* 26, no. 2: 201–229.

MacLeod, William Christie. 1926. "On Natchez Cultural Origins." *American Anthropologist* 28, no. 3 (July): 409–413.

New Agers, "Indian" Ceremonies and

Prior to the 1960s, very few white Americans, other than anthropologists and other scholars, paid much attention to Native American spiritual and religious practices. What little most Americans knew (or thought they knew) about Native beliefs, was dismissed as paganism or superstition. But a profound change took place in the 1960s with the advent of the counterculture. Many young Americans felt dissatisfied with what they regarded as a spiritually deadened, materialistic popular culture, and they sought alternatives to the mainstream Judeo-Christian tradition. Many of these young people became curious about Eastern religions and other alternatives to traditional mainstream religions, including Native American spiritual practices. While some of these young Americans were sincere in their desire for a more satisfying religious and spiritual experience, many were merely experimenting.

While young Americans were becoming interested in Native spiritual beliefs, another movement, usually dubbed New Age by the media, appeared in the 1980s and attracted the notice of spiritual seekers. New Age practices cannot be easily defined, since the term refers to a hodgepodge of individualized spiritual practices and the appropriation of religious observances from a variety of cultures. Some New Age practices involve environmentalism, channeling, and the use of tarot cards as well as quartz crystals. Eschewing formal religions and religious doctrines, New Agers tend to choose whatever spiritual practices they feel most comfortable with and gravitate toward religions that are little known and somewhat exotic to most Americans. A number of New Agers have adopted what they believe to be Native spiritual practices. The notion that Native Americans have a special relationship with the earth permeates popular American culture. As a consequence, New Agers with an ecological bent often set out to adopt Native religious beliefs.

One prominent feature of the New Age movement is syncretism, and some practitioners often combine Native (or what they think are Native American beliefs) and non-Native beliefs, with little regard for Native people's sensibilities. The result has been a bastardization of Native spirituality, which has outraged many Native people, who object to the use of sacred dances, sweat lodges, and sage being used in ways that were never intended and by New Agers who do not understand their true meaning.

The New Agers' quest for an "authentic" Native American spiritual experience has led to a proliferation of entrepreneurs who bill themselves as shamans and medicine men, who for a fee will help enlighten or provide a customer with a spiritual quest of some sort. Many of these entrepreneurs claim to have had training from Native people; however, in most cases they are unable to provide proof to back up their claims.

Many Native people have been upset with what they view as the cultural misappropriation of their spiritual practices and ceremonies for profit. Many of the so-called shamans and medicine men are in reality businesspeople who recognize the potential for profit.

Most New Age practitioners are content to purchase books for their spiritual fix. Taking as their model John Neihardt's *Black Elk Speaks* from the 1930s, authors of these tomes often claim to have been trained by Native clan mothers, medicine men, and sorcerers. Many of these works tend to blend small elements of some Native spiritual traditions with others. Nor is it unusual to find the spiritual practices of disparate Native groups mixed in with Buddhism and Druidism. Some of the claims in these works are clearly in the realm of fantasy. For example, one book mentions a flying horse that transforms itself into a dolphin, while another (perhaps with a nod to *Chariots of the Gods*?) claims that Pueblo katsinas came to earth in a flying saucer.

With the advent of the Internet, many of these marketers are able to reach a wider audience. For example, a search on the Internet reveals a number of individuals who sell "authentic" Cherokee tarot cards.

Native people have objected vigorously to the appropriation, commercialization, and bastardization of their sacred practices by non-Native people who often do not understand (or care to understand) the significance behind Native ceremonies and spiritual practices. Some Native activists have confronted peddlers of Native spirituality at their workshops. Some New Agers argue that their appropriation of Native American spiritual practices is justified as a form of free speech and as freedom of religion.

Roger M. Carpenter

See also Black Elk; Katsinas.

References and Further Reading

Aldred, Lisa. 2000. "Plastic Shamans and Astroturf Sun Dances: New Age Commercialization of Native American Spirituality." *The American Indian Quarterly* 24, no. 3: 329–352.

Deloria, Philip J. 1998. *Playing Indian*. New Haven, CT: Yale University Press.

Ohio Valley Mound Culture

Ancient Native North Americans created vibrant and long-lived cultures throughout the Eastern Woodlands, but especially along the Ohio and Mississippi River Valleys. One major seat of culture, dating back to 2450 BCE, was in Ohio and along its portion of the Ohio River (Webb and Baby, 1975, 103). In the year 1908, even after two centuries' worth of destruction by settlers, 12,000 mounds still existed in Ohio (Randall, 1908, 16). By 1951, between "developers" and archaeologists, that number was down to 5,000 (Shetrone, 1951, 6).

There were four consecutive Mound cultures in the Ohio Valley. Archaeologists call the first Adena, the second Hopewell, the third Erie, and the fourth Fort Ancient. Natives reject as racial slurs the terms Adena and Hopewell, and, since 2004, they have forced Ohio Historical Society personnel to stop using these terms to name Native peoples, not the least because tradition names exactly who the Mound Builders were. Of the first two, the so-called Adena were the Moon-Eyed People, and the Hopewell the Cherokees. The Eries—a true, Iroquoian name—were western Senecas. Simultaneous with the Iroquois (the Eries) in the north were the Lenápes in the southeast. Somewhat later, the Shawnees came into the southwest of the Ohio Valley to form the so-called Fort Ancient culture.

Mounds are artificial hills or mountains created by hand, in various shapes. There are planting mounds, platform mounds, conical burial mounds, animal effigy mounds, geometric "ceremonial" mounds, and long, straight loaf mounds running along either side of wide, straight, depressed highways that connect ceremonial centers. Mounds often tower sixty or seventy feet in the air, although the tallest have since been dismantled by the settlers. According to Ohio tradition, since Mother Earth is a woman, it was the women who carried and packed high the dirt of the mounds, often transporting basket loads of it from their home villages to the mound sites.

Ohio oral tradition does not agree with archaeologists that anyone lived atop the platform mounds in Ohio, although it does say that civic centers existed there for governmental reasons. There is a lot of flooding in Ohio, and some oral traditions claim that, in case of floods, people sought temporary refuge in the large council houses on the platform mounds while awaiting the water to recede. Otherwise, people did not live in the ceremonial centers, but merely visited them at certain times of the year. Towns were located at a safe distance from so many collected spirits.

Ceremonial complexes featured burial mounds in the vicinity of circle-and-square designs, which stood for Sky (circle) and Earth (square), the two living halves of the cosmos, which must be kept in balance through ceremony. Alternative (and almost certainly earlier) designs used the circle of Sky in combination with animal effigies of Earth, such as the Great Horned Serpent effigy in Adams County, Ohio, who carries his medicine pouch slung between his horns. Like the Octagons at Newark and High

Bank, the Great Horned Serpent is also an observatory. Bringing together Sky and Earth this way produced powerful medicine (Mann, 2003, 169–238).

The ancient mounds are sacred sites; so protecting the remaining mounds from further depredation is a prominent issue for Natives in Mound Builder states. This is not always easy. One major ceremonial site, the Newark Earthworks in Newark, Ohio—categorized worldwide as one of the wonders of the ancient world (Fagan, 1998)—covered 10.4 square kilometers (Lepper, 1998, 130). Included in its structures were a massive circle-and-square combination, numerous burial mounds, effigy mounds, and a rare circle-octagon mound, since shown to have been a very sophisticated observatory, capable of tracking the 18.61-year lunar cycle (Hively and Horn, 1982). In addition, the Great Hopewell Road connects this complex to the only other extant circle-octagon, also a sophisticated observatory, ninety kilometers southwest, at Chillicothe (Hively and Horn, 1984; Lepper, 1995; Squire and Davis, 1848, 67).

A major burial mound at the center was dismantled to build the Licking Reservoir in the 1830s, while the Ohio Canal demolished still more of the center in 1848, and the Ohio Railroad ran through it from 1852 to 1855, using burial mound dirt for its pilings. By 1854, the square was destroyed and the great circle was first turned into the Licking County Fairgrounds and then used as a boot camp during the Civil War, before finally being "developed" as Idlewild Park, an amusement park, in 1896. Nearly destroyed by the twentieth century, the Great Circle was finally set aside as Mound Builders State Memorial Park in 1933 (Mann, 2003, 99–100).

The all-important circle-octagon complex fared even worse. After being granted to the Ohio Historical Society (OHS) in 1910, it was leased by OHS to the Mound Builders Country Club in 1911, for use as a members-only golf course (Mann, 2003, 103). In 2001, the Ohio Historical Society, in a secret meeting, extended the country club's lease on the sacred site to 2088 (Mann, 2003, 306). Today, the country club's heavy mowing equipment is shoving the earthworks level with the ground, even as its golfers regularly slice chunks out of the sides of the sacred mounds. Although the original 1910 lease required the land to be open to the public, the country club refuses to allow visitors, especially Native Americans. When Grandmother Barbara Crandell, the head mother of the Ohio Cherokees, went to the circle-octagon created by her own Cherokee ancestors to pray on June 26, 2002, she was arrested (Shaw, 2002).

This sorry saga echoes what happened to other mounds. Settlers seemed remarkably unconcerned about disturbing sacred places, regularly plundering burial mounds to gather materials for their own building projects. Modern Ohio Natives do not find it accidental, therefore, that the first capital building of Ohio burned to the ground. Its bricks had been made from the clay of a massive burial mound that, standing on the site of modern-day Columbus, was dismantled as a "resource" for the project (Randall, 1908, 18).

In addition to dirt mounds, the Lenápes and Shawnees of Ohio constructed stone mounds, which were promptly taken down by early settlers, partly to remove the evidence of Native engineering skills, and partly to use the stones in their own building foundations. The great sandstone mound at Flint Ridge, Ohio, standing up to 55 feet in the air with base diameter of 183 feet, was plundered of its flat stones, weighing up to 60 pounds, between 1831 and 1832, to build the unnecessary Licking Reservoir (Hill, 1881, 489). Work crews dragged off from ten to fifteen *thousand* wagonloads of stones. Those left behind as too small to bother with were then plundered through the 1890s by local farmers, who used them to build their cellars (Fowke, 1902, 2: 389; Morris, 1871, 126; Powell, 46–47).

If the mounds themselves have been treated with almost no consideration by the settlers, the cultures that spawned them were (and continue to be) misrepresented by Western archaeologists, historians, and hobbyists. Since racist settler mythology posited Natives as "savages" incapable of either intellect or organized culture, settlers hatched fevered theories throughout the nineteenth and into the twentieth centuries concerning the *true* architects of the mounds. Seriously put forth as the "lost race" of Mound Builders were (among other equally ludicrous candidates) the: Ten Lost Tribes of Israel, Ancient Greeks, Ancient Romans, Hindus, Phoenicians, and Atlanteans. Joseph Smith's *Book of Mormon* rests on, and is a direct expression of, these overheated speculations (Brodie, 1971, 35–58, *passim*; Mann, 2003, 51–89; Silverberg, 1968, 94–96; Williams, 1991, 159–67).

What all of these wild-eyed theories had in common was the stubborn refusal to admit that Native North Americans were the creators of American Mound Culture. Once the monumental work of Cyrus Thomas in the 1890s conclusively demolished these harebrained notions, archaeologists began downplaying the mounds, so that modern students of Native American history are hard-pressed even to hear of 4,000 years' worth of Mound Cultures. Moreover, modern archaeologists dismiss clear evidence that the mounds of Ohio were built by the direct ancestors of the Cherokees, Lenápes, Iroquois, and Shawnees. Natives believe much of this dismissal is politically motivated, for, given such an admission, the Native American Graves Protection and Repatriation Act of 1990 (NAGPRA) would kick in, forcing the immediate repatriation of hundreds of thousands of skeletons and grave items seized from the mounds and held by modern universities, historical societies, and museums—importantly including the Smithsonian.

Although either ignored or, worse, mixed and matched in irresponsible ways by archaeologists, much oral tradition exists from the Iroquois, Shawnees, Lenápes, and Cherokees concerning the history of the Mound Builders of the Ohio Valley. Ohio Valley Natives insist that their Mound traditions be differentiated by nation, and that traditions of more westerly or southerly nations (such as the Miamis and Lakotas) not be interpolated into theirs.

Of those nations whose traditions claim tenure in ancient Ohio, the earliest were the Moon-Eyed People (Barton, 1976, xliv). Moon-Eyes tracked time by watching the night sky (Shaffer, 1992, 42). When the old Cherokees first came into Ohio around 200 BCE, the Moon-Eyed culture combined with theirs in a new flowering that continued until around 500 (Duncan, 1998, 199).

According to the Cherokees and the Iroquois, they were once the same people speaking the same language and living in towns only a three-day walk from one another, far to the southwest of Ohio. When the area became too crowded, the Cherokees stood up and walked east, causing the two groups to develop distinct languages (Norton, 1970, 46), a split that modern linguists date at 3,500 to 3,800 years ago (Lounsbury, 1961, 11). The Cherokees eventually traveled into Ohio, where they met and absorbed the Moon-Eyed People, becoming the Tsalages, the Great Mound Builders of Ohio (Adair, 1930, 3; Barton, 1976, 9; Duncan, 1998, 199; Haywood, 1823, 236–237; Mann, 2003, 154–156).

The Cherokee's relatives, the Iroquois, lingered in that far southwestern place for another 1,500 to 1,800 years, until they, too, stood up and walked east, as they recalled their relations had done, so long before. When the Iroquois reached the Mississippi River, they encountered the Lenápes, also

walking east, to a place their scouts had already visited and named Dawnland. Much confusion exists among Western scholars regarding this portion of tradition, because they do not understand that, for woodlanders, the Allegheny, Ohio, and lower Mississippi are one river, the Mississippi of oral tradition (Hale, 1883, 14). After feeling one another out, the Lenápes and Iroquois formed an alliance, as they both walked east (Beatty, 1768, 27–28; Barton, 1976, 29; Clinton, 1811, 92; Haywood, 1811–1859, 215; Heckewelder, 1971, 47–48; Mann, 2003, 144–145; Schweinitz, 1870, 32–33).

To reach Dawnland, which lay on the mid-Atlantic coast, the Lenápes and Iroquois had to cross through Ohio, which they easily saw was heavily populated already by people the Lenápes called Talligewi (i.e., Tsalages, or Cherokees). Although refused permission to settle along the Ohio River, the newcomers were granted safe passage across Ohio on their trek east. Once they began crossing the Ohio, however, they were attacked by the Tsalages, whose priests took alarm at the size of the force crossing the river. Many Lenápes and some Iroquois, mostly women and children, were killed in the Tsalages' unprovoked attack. Angered, the Lenápes and Iroquois retaliated in a massive assault of their own, which began a prolonged war for the Land of the Three Miamis (Ohio) (Cusick, 1892, 10–11; Heckewelder, 1971, 47–48; Schweinitz, 1870, 32–37; Mann, 2003, 145–149). Hostilities raged for at least two centuries, until the Iroquois invented bow-and-arrow technology, between 300 and 550, which quickly overcame the old atlatl weapons of the Tsalages (Cusick, 1892, 10–11; Shaffer, 1992, 50).

Having deposed the Tsalages, the Lenápes and Iroquois banished them from Ohio, pushing them first into present-day Tennessee and then—that not being far enough south to suit the Iroquois—to North Carolina, where they continued their Mound Builder culture. The victors then split Ohio between them, the Iroquois taking the northern half of the state, and the Lenápes the southeastern portion, with both becoming Mound Builders in their own right. Around the 1300s, Ohio became too crowded, so the Lenápes stood up and walked the rest of the way east to Dawnland (Heckewelder, 1971, 50–51; Mann, 2003, 147–52). Eventually, for the same reason, many of the Iroquois spread out into Ontario, western Pennsylvania, and New York, although they always maintained a presence in Ohio as the Eries, who were western Senecas (Cusick, 1892, 31; Johnson, 1978, 176; Thwaites, 1959, 33: 63).

The last Mound Builders in Ohio were the Shawnees, linguistic isolates in North America, whose original tongue was lost by the early nineteenth century. They most probably came from Mexico, in one wave, coming during the time of the Spanish conquest, for Shawnee traditions speak of the people desperately fleeing a monstrous new enemy by making a dangerous voyage across the open sea to reach Florida. After sojourning in North Carolina, where they learned to build mounds, groups traveled to southwestern Ohio, where they continued as Mound Builders (Barton, 1976, 3; Johnston, 1820, 273; Mann, 2003, 121–127; Spencer, 1908, 383; Spencer, 1909, 320; Townbridge, 1939, 2–3, 9, 57–59).

Barbara Alice Mann

See also Cahokia; Hopewell Culture; Mound Cultures of North America.

References and Further Reading

Adair, James. [1775] 1930. *History of the American Indians.* Edited by Samuel Cole Williams. Johnson City, TN: Watauga Press.

Barton, Benjamin Smith. [1798] 1976. *New Views of the Origin of the Tribes and Nations of America.* Millwood, NY: Kraus Reprint.

Beatty, Charles. 1768. *The Journal of a Two Months Tour.* London: William Davenhill and Geroge Pearch.

Brodie, Fawn. [1945] 1971. *No Man Knows My History: The Life of Joseph Smith, The Mormon Prophet,* 2nd ed. New York: Alfred A. Knopf.

Clinton, De Witt. 1811–1859. "A Discourse Delivered before the New-York Historical Society, at Their Anniversary Meeting, 6 December 1811." *Collections of the New-York Historical Society for the Year 1811.* Vol. 2, 37–116. New York: I. Riley.

Cusick, David. [1825] 1892. "Sketches of Ancient History of the Six Nations." In *The Iroquois Trail, or, Footprints of the Six Nations in Customs, Traditions, and History.* Edited by William Martin Beauchamp. Fayetteville, NY: H. C. Beauchamp.

Duncan, Barbara R. 1998. *Living Stories of the Cherokee.* Chapel Hill, NC: University of North Carolina Press.

Fagan, Brian. 1998. *From Black Land to Fifth Sun: The Science of Sacred Sites.* Reading, MA: Helix Books.

Fowke, Gerald. 1902. *Archaeological History of Ohio: The Mound Builders and Later Indians.* 2 volumes. Columbus, OH: Ohio State Archaeological and Historical Society.

Hale, Horatio. [1883] 1963. *The Iroquois Book of Rites.* Toronto, ON: University of Toronto Press.

Haywood, John. 1823. *The Natural and Aboriginal History of Tennessee, up to the First Settlements Therein by the White People, in the Year 1768.* Nashville: George Wilson.

Heckewelder, John. [1819, 1976] 1971. *History, Manners, and Customs of the Indian Nations Who Once Inhabited Pennsylvania and the Neighboring States.* The First American Frontier Series. New York: Arno Press and New York Times, 1971.

Hill, Normal Newell. 1881. *The History of Licking County, Ohio: Its Past and Present.* Newark, OH: A. A. Graham.

Hively, Ray, and Robert Horn. 1982. "Geometry and Astronomy in Prehistoric Ohio." *Archaeoastronomy* 4: 1–20.

Hively, Ray, and Robert Horn. 1984. "Hopewellian Geometry and Astronomy at High Bank." *Archaeoastronomy* 7: 85–100.

Johnson, Elias. [1881] 1978. *Legends, Traditions, and Laws of the Iroquois, or Six Nations.* New York: AMS Press.

Johnston, John. 1920. "Account of the Present State of the Indian Tribes Inhabiting Ohio." *Archaeologica Americana: Transactions and Collections of the American Antiquarian Society* 1: 271–298.

Lepper, Bradley T. 1995. "Tracking Ohio's Great Hopewell Road." *Archaeology* 48, no. 6 (November/December): 52–56.

Lepper, Bradley T. 1998. "The Archaeology of the Newark Earthworks." In *Ancient Earthen Enclosures of the Eastern Woodlands.* Edited by Robert E. Mainfort, Jr., and Lynne P. Sullivan. Gainesville: University Press of Florida.

Lounsbury, Floyd G. 1961. "Iroquois-Cherokee Linguistic Relations." *Bulletin of the Bureau of American Ethnology.* Vol. 180, 11–1. Washington, DC: Smithsonian Institution.

Mann, Barbara Alice. 2003. *Native Americans, Archaeologists, and the Mounds.* New York: Peter Lang.

Mann, Barbara Alice. 2006. *Land of the Three Miamis: A Traditional Narrative of the Iroquois in Ohio.* Toledo, OH: University of Toledo, Urban Affairs Press.

Morris, C. 1871. "The Extinct Races of America." *The National Quarterly Review* 24 (December): 121–144.

Native American Graves Protection and Repatriation Act (NAGPRA). 1990. Public Law 101–601.

Norton, John [Teyoninhokarawen]. 1970. *The Journal of Major John Nortion, 1816.* Edited by Carl F. Klinck and James J. Talman. Toronto, ON: Champlain Society.

Lindestrom, Peter. 1925. *Geographia Americae with an Account of the Delaware Indians, Based on Surveys and Notes Made in 1654–1656.* Translated by Amandus Johnson. Philadelphia: Swedish Colonial Society. [This 1925 edition added a footnote, "Square and round hills had a wide distribution and were found in South America, also," Lindestrom, *Geographia Americae,* 179 (n. 15).]

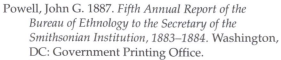

Powell, John G. 1887. *Fifth Annual Report of the Bureau of Ethnology to the Secretary of the Smithsonian Institution, 1883–1884.* Washington, DC: Government Printing Office.

Randall, Emilius Oviatt. 1908. *The Masterpieces of the Ohio Mound Builders: The Hilltop Fortifications, Including Fort Ancient.* Columbus, OH: Ohio State Archaeological and Historical Society.

Schweinitz, Edmund de. 1870. *The Life and Times of David Zeisberger, the Western Pioneer and Apostle to the Indians.* Philadelphia: J. B. Lippincott Co.

Shaffer, Lynda Norene. 1992. *Native Americans Before 1492: The Moundbuilding Centers of the Eastern Woodlands.* Armonk, NY: M. E. Sharpe.

Shaw, Julie. 2002. "Mounds Home to Varying Opinions: Earthworks the Site of a Curious Dilemma." *The Advocate,* August 11. Available at: http://www.newarkadvocate.com/news/stories/20020811/topstories/409718.html. Accessed March 10, 2005.

Shetrone, Henry Clyde. 1951. *Primer of Ohio Archaeology: The Mound Builders and the Indians,* 5th ed. Columbus, OH: Ohio State Archaeological and Historical Society.

Silverberg, Robert. 1968. *Mound Builders of Ancient America: The Archaeology of a Myth.* Greenwich, CT: New York Graphic Society.

Spencer, Joab. 1908. "The Shawnee Indians: Their Customs, Traditions and Folk-Lore." *Transactions of the Kansas State Historical Society* 10: 382–402.

Spencer, Joab. 1909. "Shawnee Folk-Lore." *Journal of American Folk-Lore* 22 : 319–326.

Squire, Ephraim George, and E. H. Davis. [1848] 1965. *Ancient Monuments of the Mississippi Valley: Comprising the Results of Extensive Original Surveys and Explorations.* Smithsonian Contributions to Knowledge. Vol. 1. New York: Johnson Reprint Corporation.

Thomas, Cyrus. 1894. *Report on the Mound Explorations of the Bureau of Ethnology.* Bureau of Ethnology Annual Report no. 12. Washington, DC: Smithsonian Institution.

Thwaites, Reuben Gold, ed. and trans. 1959. *The Jesuit Relations: Travels and Explorations of the Jesuit Missionaries in New France, 1610–1791.* 73 volumes. New York: Pageant Book Company.

Trowbridge, Charles Christopher. [1824] 1939. *Shawnee Traditions.* Edited by Vernon Kinietz and Erminie W. Voegelin. Ann Arbor: University of Michigan Press.

Webb, William S., and Raymond S. Baby. [1957] 1975. *The Adena People, No. 2.* 4th printing. Columbus, OH: Ohio Historical Society.

Williams, Stephen. 1991. *Fantastic Archaeology: The Wild Side of North American Prehistory.* Philadelphia: University of Pennsylvania Press.

Osage, and Oil Rights

In the 1920s, with oil prices at record highs, the Osage became known as the richest people in the world. Between 1907 and 1929, when tribal mineral revenues were their highest, the tribe received $233 million in mineral income.

Although the first producing oil well was drilled on Osage land in 1897, tribal oil revenues remained negligible for another twenty years. By 1918, the reservation was dotted with nearly four thousand productive oil wells, and the tribal council had negotiated favorable lease and royalty agreements to maximize tribal profits. Leases to establish wells on 160-acre tracts were auctioned by the tribe to the highest bidder, with some oil companies paying bonuses of more than $1 million dollars to lease a single tract.

The majority of the tribe's original 15-million acre Oklahoma reservation was allotted in severalty, or parceled out, to individual tribal members based on the allotment provisions of the Osage Act of 1906. Within a few decades, most of the land had been sold to non-Osage ranchers. Today, the Osage nation is a federally recognized tribe with 18,000 members and several town-site reservations located in Osage County in north central Oklahoma. A small number of enrolled Osage live on the diminished reservation, while most tribal members are scattered throughout the United States and abroad.

The tribe retains surface rights to several hundred acres of land as well as subsurface mineral rights to the entire one and a half million acres of the original reservation. Oil and gas companies lease from the tribe the right to drill for and extract minerals from specified tracts of land on the former Osage reservation. Although non-Osage now own the surface rights to most of this land, the tribe owns the minerals beneath the ground and the right to erect oil derricks and other structures on the surface in order to reach the minerals beneath. Most, if not all, of the oil companies that lease Osage mineral rights are not Osage owned. Thus, the tribe profits from owning the minerals but is not involved in extracting them. Tribal profits are derived from the leasing fees, bonuses, and royalties that oil companies pay the tribe.

The 1906 Act, as negotiated by the tribe, provides for almost all of this tribal mineral income to be distributed annually on a per-capita basis to individual tribal members. The members to whom revenues

Osage meeting with President Calvin Coolidge at the White House in 1925. (Library of Congress)

were initially to be distributed were the 2,229 Osages listed on the 1906 tribal roll. As these people passed away, their right to a share of the mineral income passed to their spouses and descendents. This right to an equal portion of tribal mineral income has come to be known as an Osage headright.

Annual headright income can be considerable. From March 2000 through March 2006, headright owners received on average $12,000 per year. The Department of the Interior, which maintains contact information for all headright owners, distributes headright income quarterly. Although royalties are distributed equally among the 2,229 headrights, not all headright owners receive equal payments. Headright owners of more than 50 percent Indian blood, whose affairs are managed by the Department of the Interior, are paid just $1,000 per quarter, with the remainder of the payment placed in an account for the Indians' benefit. In addition, some shareholders own multiple headrights, while others own only a fraction of a single headright; mineral income is paid out to these individuals according to the percentage of the headrights they own.

Although most headrights are owned by the Osage descendents of the individuals listed on the 1906 roll, today most tribal members do not own headrights. Further, not all headright owners are Native American. Several hundred headrights are currently owned by non-Indians who purchased or inherited them. Before 1978, it was not uncommon for headrights to be sold or inherited by non-Indians. These practices have since been severely curtailed. Today, Indian headright owners may not sell their shares and non-Indian shareholders may sell shares only after first offering them to the tribe. In addition, only a life estate in a headright—not a permanent, heritable interest—may be willed to or inherited by a non-Osage.

A small portion of the tribe's mineral income is reserved for tribal government use and to pay the federal government's administrative costs. In addition to mineral income, the tribe derives additional revenue from other enterprises, including several tribal casinos.

For almost a hundred years from the enactment of the 1906 Osage Act, membership in the tribe and participation in tribal government were reserved to headright holders of Osage blood. During this time, only headright owners qualified for the benefits accorded members of federally recognized tribes, and only headright owners could vote or run for office in tribal elections. Although for years the tribe struggled against these rigid prescriptions and made several attempts to expand tribal membership and suffrage, the Bureau of Indian Affairs (BIA) and the courts invalidated the efforts on the grounds that they violated the 1906 Act. It was not until the 2004 passage of Public Law 108, also known as the Osage Membership Act, that the tribe regained control over its membership and government. With the passage of the 2004 Act, tribal enrollment swelled to 18,000 members, all of whom now qualify for federal Indian programs and will have the opportunity to participate in tribal government.

The 2004 Act resolved some, but not all, of the inequalities among tribal members caused by the headright system. Today all members can equally partake of the benefits of tribal membership, but only a few share in the tribe's mineral wealth. Today, the thousands of cubic feet of natural gas and gallons of oil extracted annually from beneath the tribe's former reservation are of little benefit to the tribe or most tribal members. Instead, the system of headright ownership has created among the Osage a group of haves and have-nots. While the haves receive a substantial mineral income, the have-nots receive little or nothing.

Wealth has been a source of both prosperity and suffering for the Osage. Several hundred years before the discovery of oil beneath the tribe's Oklahoma reservation, the Osage were a powerful and wealthy tribe with a vast territory that included much of the present-day states of Kansas, Missouri, Oklahoma, and Arkansas. The Osage drove competing tribes from the area and leveraged their geographic position to monopolize the European fur and weapons trades.

By 1825, the expansion and growing strength of the U.S. government had reduced the tribe's territory to an 8 million-acre reservation in southern Kansas. Although the Osage used their land primarily for hunting, the reservation contained fertile agricultural land that white emigrant settlers wanted for homesteads. Groups lobbied Washington to open the reservation to white settlement, while intruders invaded the reservation, stole livestock, forced Osages from their homes, and established illegal settlements. Eventually the U.S. government acceded to the settlers' demands and in 1870 forced the Osage to sell their Kansas reservation and relocate to a new reservation in Indian Territory—now the state of Oklahoma.

Stinging from the loss of their Kansas reservation and desiring a permanent homeland safe from the predations of white settlers, the Osage chose for their new reservation land that they felt would be undesirable to farmer-homesteaders. In this manner, they were able to keep the land to themselves for a number of years. The next invasion of Osage territory came in the form of trespassing cattle grazing on the reservation's rich fields of bluestem grass. Tribal members quickly made the best of this situation by selling grazing leases to white cattlemen.

As a result of income from grazing leases and interest from the proceeds of the sale of the Kansas reservation, by the time reservation oil wells began to produce, the Osage were already in a better financial position than most tribes. The tribe had proved incredibly resilient in responding to rapidly changing circumstances, but in coping with its oil wealth, it was to face its greatest challenge.

When tribal leaders arranged for per-capita distribution of mineral royalties, they were acting to keep tribal resources in the hands of tribal members. But the incredible wealth generated by oil profits led to exploitation at every level. Government agents took kickbacks and oil companies underreported output. Common criminals flocked to the reservation along with lawyers eager to represent Osage for ridiculously high fees. Merchants left their merchandise unmarked, then charged the Osage higher prices than other customers or sold items on credit for 10 percent interest. Most of the Osage, who were considered incompetent to manage their own affairs, were appointed legal guardians, who collected high fees for their services while misusing their influence to cheat their wards.

National media coverage focused on the Osages' sudden wealth. Racially charged comic photos depicted extravagant spending, such as traditionally dressed Osages parking Pierce Arrow limousines outside their wickiups. Such depictions fed white resentment and paved the way for the worst of the depredations—whites who married Osage for money, then murdered their spouses to inherit their headrights.

Amy L. Propps

See also Economic Development.
References and Further Reading
Baird, W. David. 1972. *The Osage People*. Phoenix, AZ: Indian Tribal Series.
McAuliffe, Dennis, Jr. 1999. *Bloodland*. San Francisco: Council Oak Books.
"Osage Nation." 2005. In *Cohen's Handbook of Federal Indian Law*. Albuquerque, NM: American Indian Law Center.
Wilson, Terry P. 1985. *The Underground Reservation*. Lincoln: University of Nebraska Press.

Paleo-Indians

The term "Paleo-Indians" describes the earliest inhabitants of North America (ca. 10,000–8,000 BCE). According to one version of events (many Native peoples describe their origins differently), these hunter-gatherers originated in northeast Asia and colonized North America sometime around 10,000 BCE, crossing a now submerged land bridge that connected Russia to Alaska during the last Ice Age. Clovis people, the first widespread North American cultural group, rapidly colonized much of the continent between about 10,000 to 9000 BCE, suggesting that they were highly mobile and adaptive to changing environments. Around 9000 BCE, the cultural uniformity of the Clovis period fragmented into regional hunter-gatherer groups. Paleo-Indians in each region were uniquely adapted to their respective environments, each developing distinctive tool kits and lifeways.

The timing, route, and process of the first colonization remain contentious issues in North American archaeology. Nonetheless, most archaeologists subscribe to the land bridge theory. Indeed, some of the oldest evidence of Paleo-Indians can be found in northwestern North America. Sites in Alaska have yielded tools and other cultural remains, including small teardrop-shaped projectile points called Chindadn points. Archaeologists call this group the Nenana complex (Hamilton and Goebel, 1999). They hunted sheep, elk, and birds. About 1,000 years later,

a new technology developed in the Arctic based on microblades, which are specialized stone flakes used to make composite hunting tools. Little is known about the lifeways of these later Paleo-Indians, named the Denali complex. They likely hunted both land and marine animals (e.g., caribou and fish).

While Alaska was mostly ice-free during the last Ice Age, much of Canada was covered by a thick ice sheet that blocked early Paleo-Indian migration into the contiguous United States. There were two possible migration routes from Alaska to the continental interior. The first is called the Ice-Free Corridor route, which was an opening east of the Rockies between the two large ice sheets that covered Canada. Paleo-Indians may have followed migrating animals southward through this corridor into the United States (Wilson and Burns, 1999). Some archaeologists, however, have questioned the Ice-Free Corridor theory. Archaeological sites south of the ice sheets, which may be older than the Ice-Free Corridor, suggest that another route may have been used. Early Paleo-Indians may have traveled down the West Coast, either on foot or by boat. Unfortunately, very early sites have not been found in this region, so the presence of early Paleo-Indians cannot be confirmed (Dixon, 1999).

In any discussion of prehistoric North America, two other perspectives should be mentioned. Some archaeologists propose that North America was colonized long before 10,000 BCE, perhaps as early as 30,000 BCE (Dixon, 1999). They point to the presence of a few archaeological sites in North and South America that appear to predate Clovis times. Two of the best-known are Monte Verde in Chile, which has evidence for a Paleo-Indian occupation about one thousand years before Clovis times, and Meadowcroft Rockshelter in Pennsylvania, which may date as early as 16,000 BCE. The validity of these early sites is passionately debated among scientists. Alternatively, many Native Americans take issue with these archaeological theories because their oral histories state that their ancestors have lived in North America since the time of creation.

Although the specific route and timing of the first Paleo-Indian colonization remain contentious, there is widespread agreement that by 9500 BCE Paleo-Indians occupied much of North America. The oldest archaeological sites often contain Clovis spear points, associated with the remains of now extinct animals like mammoth, megabison, and horses. Clovis spear points are distinguished by their flutes, which are large channel-like flake scars that typically reach from the point's base to its midsection. Because of this feature, they are often called fluted points. The extensive occurrence of Clovis sites has led some archaeologists to suggest that the distribution indicates a single widespread cultural group, while others maintain that the distribution results from the rapid transfer of a new technology (the Clovis projectile point) from group to group.

Clovis hunter-gatherers were very proficient at killing large mammals, though they also utilized a wide range of smaller animals and plants. The first appearance of Clovis hunters in North America coincided with the extinction of many large mammal species (e.g., mammoth, horse, and camel). This has led some to argue that the first Paleo-Indians hunted these animals to extinction. Although there is little doubt that early Paleo-Indians were highly skilled hunters, it is likely that the rapidly changing climate of the last Ice Age contributed to these extinctions.

Paleo-Indians in the Great Basin region of western North America used two different technologies between 10,000 and 8000 BCE. Some of the earliest sites contain projectile points similar to the Clovis-style, whereas others contain stemmed points. These different technologies may represent multiple Paleo-Indian groups living in the region at the same time or a cultural change over time. Unlike their neighbors on the Great Plains, Paleo-Indians from the Great Basin appear to have focused their diet on waterfowl, fish, and small mammals rather than big game.

The Great Plains region has some of the best evidence for early Paleo-Indian lifeways, with abundant Clovis sites dated between 10,000 and 9000 BCE. Distinctive Clovis fluted points are often found associated with the remains of large mammals. Between 9000 and 6000 BCE several other Paleo-Indian groups inhabited the Great Plains, including Folsom, Agate Basin, Hell Gap, Alberta, and Cody. Because many large mammals went extinct during the Clovis period, these later Paleo-Indians focused instead on bison hunting. They used natural and constructed traps to contain large herds of bison to kill dozens of animals at once. Most aspects of Plains Paleo-Indian lifeways were connected to the bison.

Eastern North America was home to different groups of Paleo-Indians. Since environments in the east differed from those in the west, Paleo-Indians in this region used different hunting methods and toolkits (Storck, 2004). Early projectile points found in the east are similar to their western counterparts (often fluted) but include small differences in overall shape. Some common types of eastern Paleo-Indian projectile points include Gainey, Parkhill, Crowfield (in the northeast), and Cumberland and Suwannee (in the southeast). Unfortunately, the cultural chronology is not as well understood in the east as it is in the west. Eastern Paleo-Indians were proficient hunters, able to kill mastodon, caribou, and other large mammals. They were probably more generalized than their Great Plains counterparts, using a wide range of animals and plants in their diets.

Much of what we know about Paleo-Indian lifeways comes from their stone tools and hunting methods. The presence of tools made from stone originating over 1,000 kilometers away indicates that Paleo-Indians were highly nomadic. They lived in small bands comprised of several families, although they periodically formed larger social groups. They were highly skilled hunter-gatherers able to adapt quickly to new environments (Anderson and Gillam, 2000). Their main hunting technology was the spear and atlatl (spear thrower), which was tipped by specialized projectile points. We know little of their religion and beliefs, although there is some evidence for possible religious activity (Storck, 1991).

Jason David Gillespie

See also Archaeology and the First Americans; Mound Cultures of North America; Ohio Valley Mound Culture.

References and Further Reading

Anderson, David G., and J. Christopher Gillam. 2000. "Paleoindian Colonization of the Americas: Implications from an Examination of Physiography, Demography, and Artefact Distribution." *American Antiquity* 65: 43–66.

Dixon, E. James. 1999. *Bones, Boats and Bison: Archeology and the First Colonization of Western North America*. Albuquerque: University of New Mexico Press.

Hamilton, Thomas D., and Ted Goebel. 1999. "Late Pleistocene Peopling of Alaska." In *Ice Age Peoples of North America: Environments, Origins, and Adaptations*. Edited by Robson Bonnichsen and Karen L. Turnmire, 156–199. Corvallis: Oregon State University Press.

Storck, Peter L. 1991. "Imperialist Without a State: The Cultural Dynamics of Early Paleoindian Colonization as Seen from the Great Lakes Region." In *Clovis: Origins and Adaptations*. Edited by Robson Bonnichsen and Karen L. Turnmire, 153–162. Corvallis: Center for the Study of First Americans.

Storck, Peter L. 2004. *Journey to the Ice Age: Discovering an Ancient World*. Vancouver: University of British Columbia Press.

Wilson, Michael Clayton, and James A. Burns. 1999. "Searching for the Earliest Canadians: Wide Corridors, Narrow Doorways, Small Windows." In *Ice Age Peoples of North America: Environments, Origins, and Adaptations*. Edited by Robson Bonnichsen and Karen L. Turnmire, 213–248. Corvallis: Oregon State University Press.

Pipes, Sacred

Probably the most commonly used ceremonial object throughout Native North America, both historically and contemporaneously, the sacred pipe was and is used during prayer and healing and to make binding agreements. It is this last function, smoking to unite those present and in the spiritual realm in harmony regarding peace, war, or confederacy, that gave rise to the popular term "peace pipe," though its history and use are far more varied. The French termed the sacred pipe *calumet*, their word for reed pipe, and it is sometimes listed by this term in texts.

Archaeological evidence shows that pipes have been in use in the Americas for at least four thousand years and have been made in various forms from several different materials. Constructed from the leg bones of animals such as deer or antelope, tubular pipes are the oldest known form, varying in length from several inches to over a foot. The mouth

Taos man seated, holding peace pipe. (Library of Congress)

end of a tubular pipe is slightly smaller than the open end in which tobacco was placed. Later stone pipes, known as monitor or platform pipes, had a central bowl and evolved among eastern Woodlands tribes into effigy pipes with bowls in the shapes of animals, humans, and spirits. Keel pipes and disc pipes were also used, and one-piece elbow pipes were used by some California tribes and by Iroquoian peoples.

Two-piece elbow pipes with separate bowls and stems, the stem carved of wood and the bowl usually of catlinite, are the most commonly used today. Catlinite, or pipestone, comes exclusively from one site in Minnesota on Pipestone Creek, which flows from the Big Sioux River. Under the maintenance today of the National Park Service, this site has been used for quarrying since around 1600 and can still be accessed by Native peoples for this purpose. Pipes are "carried," or owned, by ceremonially qualified people who follow specific tribal traditions regarding their use and origins. Stems and bowls are typically kept separately wrapped in a buckskin or cloth pipe bag. The male stem and female bowl are brought together only in preparation for smoking and prayer. Often, a series of rituals precedes smoking, usually involving the offering of tobacco to the Spirits in the Sacred Directions as well as to the Creator and Mother Earth.

Tobacco blends vary among Native peoples, incorporating such various ingredients as sumac, red willow, bearberry leaves, kinnikinnick (hence the Algonquian word *kinnikinnick* for a smoking mixture), sage, mullein, mint, or osha. Despite the misconception in mainstream culture, no pipe mixture used in sacred pipes throughout Native America is hallucinogenic or mind altering. According to the eldest living Cheyenne Sun Dance Priest, Eugene Blackbear, Sr., the smoke from the pipe carries the prayers and thoughts of those smoking to the Creator, Mother Earth, and the Spirits. Mr. Blackbear suggests that those breaking agreements made during the smoking of a pipe, such as Custer did after smoking with the Cheyenne, are visited by difficulty and sometimes death. For the southern Cheyenne, or Tsis-tsis-tas, pipes are used ceremoniously by Sun Dance and fasting supplicants, qualifying the supplicant after the completion of his or her vow to keep and use a pipe.

Several pipes, pipe ceremonies, and pipe bundles are particularly well-known. The Sacred Calf Pipe of the Lakota was brought to them by White Buffalo Calf Woman. All pipes used by the Lakota today, known as *chanupa*, have had their power transferred to them through contact with this pipe, held today by bundle keeper Arvol Looking Horse. The Pawnee have a tradition of a complex pipe ceremony known as the Hako. The Arapaho have a sacred flat pipe, the Säeicho, which is also part of a sacred bundle kept and opened according to ritual regulations. In recent times, Christians, such as Catholic priest Father Paul Steimetz, have attempted to fuse the use of the pipe with Christian theology. However they are used, pipes are held in respect as sacred and living beings throughout Native America.

Kimberly Roppolo

See also Archaeology and the First Americans.
References and Further Reading

Blackbear, Eugene Sr., 2004. Personal interview.
Hirschfelder, Arlene, and Paulette Molin, eds. 2000. *Encyclopedia of Native American Religions*, updated ed. New York: Facts on File.
Lyon, William S. 1996. *Encyclopedia of Native American Healing*. Santa Barbara, CA: ABC-CLIO.
Markowitz, Harvey, ed. 1995. *Ready Reference: American Indians*. Vol. 1. Pasadena, CA: Salem Press

Potlatch

The peoples of the Northwest Coast of North America have proved themselves to be exceptional on several counts, one of which was their ceremonial potlatch. The potlatch, which included the ritual squandering of goods (including slaves in some cases), illustrated the wealth of their societies.

The Northwest Coast peoples produced a genuinely high culture (ranking with that of the Pueblos of the Southwest or the temple-mound people of the Southeast) without benefit of agriculture, a very rare event in the history of humankind. Instead of pottery and agriculture, the Northwest Coast peoples, extending along the coast from the Alaskan Panhandle to coastal Oregon and northern California, created exquisite baskets and wood bowls that they filled with the bounty of the forests and the sea. The Saskatoon berry, which they harvest, for example, contains three times as much iron as prunes and raisins. The bounty of the ocean and forests was so abundant and so skillfully exploited by the Northwest Coast peoples that most were able, during the summer, to lay up enough food (much of it dried) to

Indian dancers during a potlatch at Chilkat, Alaska in 1895. (Library of Congress)

last the winter. The major sources of protein for the Northwest Coast peoples were fish and sea mammals. Among the Makah, the word for fish is the same as the word for food.

The social and economic lifeways of Northwest Coast peoples evolved very differently compared to those of Native peoples across the rest of North America. While many other American Indian peoples were democratic in their political orientation, the Northwest Coast peoples maintained a very strict caste system. They also maintained an economy that was not communal, like those of many other Native peoples in North America. In a Northwest Coast village, everyone had a class, and everything had an owner.

Because the chiefs controlled access to food, shelter, and even spiritual sustenance, the societies of the Northwest Coast peoples were more hierarchical than even that of the Aztecs or the monarchical societies of Europe during the period of first contacts with Native America. No councils of chiefs existed to exercise restraint on them. Customs did exercise restraint on unbridled power, however. A good chief gathered power by being generous to those "under the arm." The ceremonial potlatch was an expression of this ethic: On one level, it was a display of wealth by the chief or chiefs hosting it; on another level, the intricate gift giving of the ritual bespoke an inherent desire to distribute the bounteous wealth of Northwest Coast Native American societies. The potlatch thus consolidated the power and authority of its hosts by reminding lesser nobles and commoners that the high chiefs controlled every aspect of village life.

The mild, rainy winters of the Northwest Coast are a time of elaborate socializing and ceremonies. The potlatch often became a festival of wealth squandering between rival chiefs. Everything about the potlatch bespoke ostentation. Guests arrived in ornately carved canoes, flanked by assistants, all dressed in their best clothes. Once at the potlatch, which might have been planned for years, guests were expected to feast until they became ill from overindulgence. Competing chiefs wore headgear topped with special rings that indicated the number of potlatches they had held. In a social and economic context, the potlatch indicated the value the Northwest Coast peoples placed on status. The ostentation of the ritual also bespoke a society of surplus—one so successful at adapting to its environment that its members virtually had resources to burn or otherwise consume with reckless disregard for necessity.

Northwest Coast ceremonies, including the potlatch, were not usually concerned so much with the economic motives of getting and giving as with enhancing social status, honoring ancestors, and sealing personal relationships. According to Duane Champagne, the potlatch "should be understood from within its own cultural and institutional framework, and not be too easily compared with self-interested materialism" (1989, 110). Similarly, the emphasis on rank in Northwest Coast societies was not simply an imitation of Western hierarchical societies. Instead, the Tlingit concept of rank was integrated into that people's belief that proper behavior in the present (such as contributing to potlatches, fulfilling one's clan obligations, and submitting to the collective will of the house group) could cause a person to be reborn into a more aristocratic lineage.

The word "potlatch" is anglicized from *patshatl*, meaning "giving." Such giving could take many forms. At a grease feast, for example, precious oil sometimes was splashed on fires until erupting flames burned members of competing households. Sometimes the spattering oil set their cedar clothing aflame. As a potlatch continued, the value of gifts usually rose steadily. After the rival chiefs had given away valuable cedar boxes and other expensive items, one chief might up the ante by sacrificing a slave with a special club called a slave killer. The "giving" chief might then hurl the scalp of the slain slave at his rival. Slaves also could be freed at potlatches. Another act of potlatch oneupmanship was the giving and destruction of large copper plates that served as currency of very high denomination, in the thousands of dollars if converted into U.S. currency.

Like most other aspects of life among Northwest Coast peoples, the potlatch was carried out with rigid, time-honored formality. Parts of the ritual were rehearsed insults, in which one chief often dared the other to give away ever more precious objects, such as large canoes that were carved out of huge tree trunks and used to hunt whales. Some of the insults were very personal. The Kwakiutl may have been adopting a European custom from the Hudson's Bay Company when they complicated the potlatch by demanding 100 percent interest on gifts, a postcontact wrinkle in the ritual in which the act of giving now incurred a debt at twice the value of the original gift.

The Northwest Coast peoples hosted a number of other ceremonies and rituals in addition to the potlatch. Some of these rituals were associated with secret societies (exclusive groups of genetically unrelated individuals, sometimes called sodalities by anthropologists). Perhaps the most important such ritual among the Kwakiutl-speaking peoples of the British Columbia coast was the cannibal dance, in which an individual, seized by an emotional frenzy, pretended to consume the flesh of another person. Illusions and fakery enjoyed a high degree of prestige among the Northwest Coast peoples, and a small bear might be cooked in such a way that it resembled a human being, to be consumed during the cannibal dance. The person doing the cannibal dance might enliven the atmosphere by seizing bits of skin and flesh from members of the audience.

Bruce E. Johansen

See also Agriculture; Fishing Rights; Seattle; Slavery and Native Americans.

References and Further Reading
Champagne, Duane. 1989. *American Indian Societies: Strategies and Conditions of Political and Cultural Survival.* Cambridge, MA: Cultural Survival.
Drucker, Philip. 1955. *Indians of the Northwest Coast.* New York: McGraw-Hill.
Gibson, Arrell Morgan. 1980. *The American Indian: Prehistory to Present.* Lexington, MA: D. C. Heath and Company.
Gunther, Erna. 1972. *Indian Life on the Northwest Coast of North America.* Chicago: University of Chicago Press.
Maxwell, James A. 1978. *America's Fascinating Indian Heritage.* Pleasantville, NY: Readers Digest.
Moore, John H. 1993. "How Giveaways and Pow-wows Redistribute the Means of Subsistence." In *The Political Economy of North American Indians.* Edited by John H. Moore, 240–269. Norman: University of Oklahoma Press.
Oberg, Kalervo. 1973. *The Social Economy of the Tlinget Indians.* Seattle: University of Washington Press.
Pascua, Maria Parker. 1991. "Ozette: A Makah Village in 1491." *National Geographic,* October: 38–53.
Ruby, Robert H., and John A Brown. 1993. *Indian Slavery in the Pacific Northwest.* Spokane: Arthur H. Clark.

Pottery

The term "pottery" refers to jars, bowls, and other items that are made out of clay. Native Americans in most of the United States have made pottery for over 2,500 years. Historically, pottery was a part of everyday life because it was utilized for cooking and storing. Also, pottery was important in ceremonies and rituals because many effigy, or religious, figures were made out of clay. Archaeologists trace back pottery shards, or the broken pieces from a once complete pot, to about 2300 BCE in the southeastern United States, 1000 BCE in the Northeast, and 600 BCE in the Southwest (Wirt, 1984, 13). A shift in the use of pottery occurred in the 1880s, when potters started manufacturing souvenirs for tourism. Many collectors and travelers recognized women potters as artists. Today many potters use historical patterns and techniques along with their own expressions to create pottery for exhibits and galleries. They have also come to see their pottery as artwork and as an expression of their experiences and identities.

The historical process of preparing the clay for sculpting was similar across North America, and it is still practiced by many contemporary potters. First, clay has to be gathered. Potters find clay in rivers and streambeds and by other bodies of water. In arid regions, the clay can be found in soil deposits (Wirt, 1984, 15). Once the potters or their families collect the clay deposits, they have to remove any impurities, such as pebbles or twigs. If the clay is already moist, these impurities can be pulled out. If the clay is dry the process takes a lot longer. The clay has to be made into a texture similar to coarse flour. The potter does this first by pounding it with a larger hammer or stick (or by stomping on it) and then grinding it with a mortar and pestle (Peterson, 1997, 44). Then the potter sifts it, allowing the clay to fall or blow upwind into a blanket while the impurities stay in the basket or screen (Peterson, 1997, 43; Wirt, 1984, 16). Once the potter deems the clay free of impurities, she adds water to it and starts kneading the clay into a putty or dough consistency. While working the clay, the potter adds bits of temper, or material used to strengthen the clay and keep it from cracking during the firing process. Depending on location, temper materials usually consist of finely ground volcanic rock, quartzite, sandstone, sand, vegetable matter, and sometimes old pottery shards (Wirt, 1984, 16). The potter has to be careful to add just the right amount because too little or too much could ruin the pot during firing.

Once the potter finishes preparing the clay, she turns her attention to creating the jars, bowls, water jugs, or whatever else she plans on making. Two techniques of creating pottery obtain in North America. One technique, coiling, consists of creating long, round strips of clay that are layered on top of each other while the potter pitches and smoothes the new layer with the ones below (Peterson, 1997, 45; Wirt, 1984, 17). For larger pots, the maker starts with a flat clay base, allowing it to dry and then adding the coils. Potters sometimes also place these bases into a shallow bowl or basket for support during the coiling process (Peterson, 1997, 45). A second technique for pottery making is called the paddle and anvil (Penney, 2004, 81), or sometimes modeling and paddling (Whiteford, 1983, 13). Potters again make coils, but, instead of having the coils build from each other, the makers press the clay with an anvil or other tool into the side of a container to create the shape of the pot (Penney, 2004, 81; Whiteford, 1983, 13). The clay stays inside the container until it dries, at which time the potter carefully removes it for firing. This latter technique is mainly practiced by some Southeastern tribes and by the Tohono O'odham and Yuma in the Southwest (Whiteford, 1983, 13).

For both techniques, the dried pot goes through a series of steps before it is fired. First, the potter smoothes the sides of the pot with a knife or another scraping tool (Whiteford, 1983, 14). If the potter wants to decorate the pottery, instead of just letting the gray color of the clay be the surface, she or a member of her family will then add layers of slip to the outside of the pot. Slip is a thick, paint-like mixture of clay and water that gives the pot an evenly colored surface (Whiteford, 1983, 14). If the potter does not intend on painting the pot after firing, it is polished at this point.

After this process, the pot is ready for firing. This has to be done carefully, because a balance needs to be struck between too much heat and not enough from the fire. Potters usually place multiple pots onto a grill and place firewood underneath. They then cover the entire structure with dried cakes of animal dung, which burn at a hotter and more consistent rate then wood (Whiteford, 1983, 15). The pots are usually fired for between forty-five minutes and three hours, depending on the size of the pottery and the intensity of the fire. Upon their removal from the fire, the pots are polished again to ensure an even finish (Peterson, 1997, 59; Whiteford, 1983, 15). Once the pot is cooled, the potter or a member of her family paints the design on it.

While pottery was once made over much of the United States, today some of the most famous potters live in the Southwest and the Southeast. One of the major factors behind this is the rise of Southwestern tourism in the 1880s with the creation of the Santa Fe Railroad. Potters would go up to the windows of the trains and sell to the passengers during stops, and the railroad also had a line of track that went directly to the Laguna Pueblo in New Mexico (Penney, 2004,101). Furthermore, the Fred Harvey Company did much to market Native American products, and many potters found a way to provide incomes for themselves through their skills (Peterson, 1997, 17).

The first potter to gain individual recognition was Nampeyo of Hano in Hopi First Mesa, Arizona (Peterson, 1997, 54). Nampeyo is credited with revitalizing a historical pattern called Sikytaki, which has designs painted in black, orange, and white (Penney, 2004, 102; Whiteford, 1983, 31). Tourists were extremely interested in buying this Sikytaki decorated pottery, and traders recruited Hopi women to make pottery. By the late nineteenth century, almost half of all Hopi women created pottery for tourist markets (Penney, 2004, 102). Maria Martinez of San Ildefonso Pueblo in New Mexico was also instrumental in the revival or popularization of Native American pottery. Martinez and her husband, Julian, are credited with rediscovering how to make another style of pottery decoration (Penney, 2004, 103; Peterson, 1997, 62; Whiteford, 1983, 29). This style is called black-on-black, and the name derives from the look of the finished pot. The pot is turned black during the firing process, and then a matte, black design is painted onto the shiny black surface after it is polished and cooled (Penney, 2004, 103). The pot blackens during firing when the potter places moist manure directly on the fire, causing it to create a dense smoke that surrounds the pottery with carbon (Whiteford, 1983, 15). Maria and Julian Martinez also demonstrate how Pueblo families worked together to make the pottery. It was common for wives to make the pots, while the husbands decorated them (Penney, 2004, 102–103). In the case of the black-on-black pottery, Maria would make the pots and fire them, while Julian painted the matte designs. After Julian's death, Maria's daughter-in-law, Santana, stepped into the position as painter (Peterson, 1997, 121).

Nampeyo and Martinez were not the only potters who were influential in the early twentieth century. Many women can be credited with taking historical patterns and adding their own creativity to them, such as Lucy Martin Lewis, Margaret Tafoya, Helen Cordero, and Blue Corn (Peterson, 1997, 74–106). It was from these women that many contemporary potters gained their first training and education. Like their teachers, these potters are also taking the older designs and building on them. For instance, Barbara Gonzales, the great-grandchild of

Maria and Julian Martinez, has taken her great-grandparents' shiny black finish and altered it so that red hues are also present. Gonzales also places turquoise and coral beads on the surfaces of her pottery (Peterson, 1997, 126). Other contemporary potters have risen out of their own training and ingenuity as well. One such artist is Anita Fields, who is of Osage descent. Influenced by clothing that her grandmother gave her, Fields creates pottery that captures the designs and patterns of historical Osage and other Native American societies' clothing and textile traditions.

Carolyn Speros Baughman

See also Archaeology and the First Americans; Women in Native Woodlands Societies.
References and Additional Reading
Feest, Christian. 1980. *Native Arts of North America.* New York: Oxford University Press.
Penney, David. 2004. *North American Indian Art.* New York: Thames and Hudson.
Peterson, Susan. 1997. *Pottery by American Indian Women: The Legacy of Generations.* New York: Abbeville Press.
Schaaf, Gregory. 2000. *Pueblo Indian Pottery: 750 Artist Biographies.* Volume 2. American Indian Art Series. Santa Fe, CA: Center for Indigenous Arts and Culture Press.
Whiteford, Andrew Hunter. 1983. *North American Indian Arts.* New York: Golden Press.
Wirt, Sharon. 1984. *American Indian Pottery.* Blaine, WA: Hancock House Publishers.

Sacred Sites

Sacred sites, according to many American Indians, are places from which spiritual power emanates and at which traditional ceremonies and important rituals occur. In contrast to Western religions, which teach that land is a resource that produces commodities, American Indians conceive of land as sacred and living. Characterizing themselves as caretakers of the earth, many Native peoples believe that all of nature is comprised of conscious beings who must be treated with respect and care. To Indians, each plant, stream, and mountain has its own spirit and life.

Numerous sacred sites are located throughout North America; unfortunately, most are threatened with tourism, recreation, resource extraction, and development. For instance, the Zunis' Salt Lake in New Mexico (home to *Ma'l Oyattsik'I*, an Indian deity) and Bear Lodge (Mato Tipi, also known as Devil's Tower, a sacred butte in the Black Hills,)

Devil's Tower National Monument in Wyoming, also called the Bear Lodge, is a sacred site to several Native American tribes, including the Lakota Sioux, Cheyenne, and Kiowa. (Corel)

both are places where different tribes come together to perform traditional ceremonies and rituals. However, in 1996, Salt Lake became threatened with a coal-mining project. Similarly, Bear Lodge plays host to rock climbers searching for the preeminent climbing experience. Such religious intolerance and cultural disrespect leaves many American Indians searching for various ways to protect their sacred sites. Congressional legislation, the courts, and international law, which are increasingly favoring American Indian claims, are finding ways to protect and preserve these culturally significant properties.

Currently, several legislative acts provide some protection for sacred sites. For instance, the Antiquities Act of 1909 allows sacred properties to be protected from human destruction through presidential declaration. Similarly, the Historic Sites, Buildings, and Antiquities Act of 1935 enables the Secretary of the Interior to protect, preserve, and maintain historic sites by establishing historic preservation programs and contracting with states to protect such properties.

Likewise, the Federal Lands Policy Management Act and the National Forest Management Act of 1976 require public and forest lands to be managed in a manner that protects the quality of historical, archaeological, and cultural values of such lands. Accordingly, the Acts mandate that management programs minimize damage to any cultural values and grant the secretary authority to take necessary action to prevent undue degradation of lands.

Similarly, in recognition of the impact of private destruction to Indian lands, Congress passed the Archaeological Resources Protection Act of 1979, which requires federal land managers to notify and consult with affected Indian tribes, prior to the issuance of a permit that may result in harm to, or destruction of, any religious or cultural site.

Perhaps the foremost legislation utilized for the protection of sacred sites is the National Historic Preservation Act, which was enacted in 1966 to preserve historical and cultural properties. According to the Act, once the secretary identifies a property as significant in American history, archaeology, or culture, then all federal undertakings affecting such property must take into account their effect on the site and recommend to an advisory council any measures to avoid, minimize, or mitigate adverse effects on it.

However, despite congressional intent to afford protection to tribal sacred sites, American Indians remain unable to adequately protect the integrity of such properties, including tribal access. Consequently, American Indians have judicially attempted to preserve and protect their traditional cultural properties by asserting constitutional religious violations.

Religious free exercise claims have consistently been rejected. Specifically, despite American Indian complaints that any proposed federal undertaking on, adjacent to, or near a sacred site would make it difficult to practice religious ceremonies, because there is no governmental threat of fines, incarceration, or the loss of governmental benefits, the courts have determined that no religious constitutional burden exists and have therefore rejected the Indians' free exercise claims.

American Indians have succeeded in protecting sacred sites under the Establishment Clause (First Amendment) of the U.S. Constitution. Specifically, the courts have determined that federal agency plans, which remove barriers to Indian religious worship and are noncoercive and secular in purpose, do not advance or inhibit religion. Consequently, agency decisions to deny oil and gas leasing, limit timber sales, and issue climbing management plans for religious accommodations at sacred sites do not violate the Establishment Clause.

Nevertheless, American Indians continue to struggle to protect sacred sites, and lobbying Congress to enact legislation that specifically addresses sacred site protection may be a viable solution. In recent years, Congress has favored protecting Indian religious practices. For instance, Congress enacted the American Indian and Religious Freedom Act to protect and preserve the inherent right of American Indians to believe, express, and exercise their traditional religions including access to sites and the freedom to worship through ceremonies and traditional rites. In addition, Congress passed the Native American Graves Protection and Repatriation Act to protect Indian graves and repatriate cultural items to tribes. Furthermore, Congress exempted Native American Church practitioners from federal laws criminalizing the possession of peyote.

Similarly, the executive branch has recognized the importance of American Indian religious practices and access to sacred sites. For instance, President Clinton issued Executive Order 13007, which requires all federal agencies, in the management of federal lands, to "accommodate access to and ceremonial use of Indian sacred sites by Indian religious practitioners" and avoid adverse effects to the physical integrity of such sites. Likewise, the Department of Interior recently promulgated secretarial orders that require agencies to identify the potential effects of governmental activities on Indian trust lands and to consult with tribes when such activities affect tribal resources.

In accordance with such agency directives, federal land management agencies have developed programs preserving American Indian access to sacred sites. Specifically, in 1994, the Fish and Wildlife Service issued a policy requiring the agency to respect American Indian cultural values when planning and implementing programs. Similarly, the National Park Service developed a climbing management plan for Bear Lodge in 1995, which requests rock climbers to refrain from climbing the butte during the month of June so that American Indians may peacefully perform sacred religious ceremonies.

However, if legislation and executive policies fail, an international appeal may be a more workable solution. The economic development of sacred and cultural sites of American Indians and of other indigenous peoples throughout the world has prompted an international debate concerning the destruction of such properties. Accordingly, the United Nations drafted the Declaration on the Rights of Indigenous Peoples, which requires nation-states to preserve and allow a right of access to the properties and sites of religious and cultural significance for indigenous peoples. Although the declaration mandates that states should "take effective measures, in conjunction with the indigenous peoples concerned, to ensure that indigenous sacred places, including burial sites, be preserved, respected, and protected," the document lacks enforcement provisions. Nevertheless, the United Nations has brought indigenous sacred site claims to the forefront of international policy that may lead to stronger protection of such sites in the near future.

In this manner, American Indians may protect sacred sites under international cultural property law, which would provide international protections for properties of significant cultural value. Because sacred sites define a group's culture, assist in the

members' understanding of the past, and reflect the group's visualization of themselves, such properties necessarily fall within the definition of cultural property. Thus, inclusion of sacred sites in cultural property theories would allow for their protection in the international arena.

Current sacred site legislation is limited and judicial support of agency decisions can adversely affect sacred sites and access to them. However, because recent U.S. congressional, executive, and agency policies favor the protection of American Indian religious practices, national and international enforcements specifically protecting sacred sites from desecration and destruction may be in the near future.

J. Landon K. Schmidt

See also Archaeology and the First Americans; Native American Graves Protection and Repatriation Act (NAGPRA).

References and Further Reading
Archer, Heather S. 1999. "Effect of United Nations Draft Declaration on Indigenous Rights on Current Policies of Member States." *Journal of International Legal Studies* 5: 205–241.
Bear Lodge Multiple Use Ass'n v. Babbitt, 2 F. Supp. 2d 1448 (Wyo. Dist. 1998), *affirmed on other grounds*, 175 F.3d 814 (10th Cir. 1999), *cert. denied*, 529 US 1039 (2000).
Fisher, Louis. 2002. "Indian Religious Freedom: To Litigate or Legislate." *American Indian Law Review* 20: 1–39.
Griffin, Rayanne J. 1995. "Sacred Site Protection Against a Backdrop of Religious Intolerance." *Tulsa Law Journal* 31: 395–419.
LaDuke, Winona. "The Salt Woman and the Coal Mine." Available at: http://www.sierraclub .org/sierra/200211/winona_printable.asp. Accessed March 28, 2005.
Stern, Walter E., and Lynn H. Slade. 1995. "Effects of Historic and Cultural Resources and Indian Religious Freedom on Public Lands Development: A Practical Premier." *Natural Resources Journal* 35: 133–183.
Suagee, Dean B. 1996. "Tribal Voices in Historic Preservation: Sacred Landscapes, Cross-Cultural Bridges, and Common Ground." *Vermont Law Review* 21: 145–224.
Suagee, Dean B. 1999. "The Cultural Heritage of American Indian Tribes and the Preservation of Biological Diversity." *Arizona State Law Journal* 31: 483–538.
Tatum, Melissa L. 1999. *The Black Hills: Are They Cultural Property?* 1999 Annual Meeting, Michigan Academy of Science, Arts & Letters, Law Section.
Tsosie, Rebecca. 1996. "Tribal Environmental Policy in an Era of Self-Determination: The Role of Ethics, Economics, and Traditional Ecological Knowledge." *Vermont Law Review* 21: 225–333.
Winslow, Anastasia P. 1996. "Sacred Standards: Honoring the Establishment Clause in Protecting Native American Sacred Sites." *Arizona Law Review* 38: 1291–1343.

Salmon, Economic and Spiritual Significance of

For the peoples of the Pacific Northwest, which includes the western slope of the Rocky Mountains, as well as northern California, Oregon, Washington, Idaho, western British Columbia, and Alaska, the salmon has played a significant role in defining their culture. In pre-contact times salmon contributed to the organization of the peoples of this region into political groups.

The people of this region spoke many languages that in some cases were the common factor that bound them together, but often there were other ties such as family and relationships based on shared labor, including fishing, the basis of their diets. These two features held in common were key elements in determining political relationships at the village level. The village consisted of a group of people with a shared desire to follow a particular headman while performing specific tasks essential to survival. Salmon fishing was such an important activity to the survival of these people that their sociopolitical organization was often based upon task grouping. This was a method of forming their communities based on specific tasks and the skills necessary to perform the tasks (Miller, 2003, 10, 11).

Usually village residents were related by bloodlines, to some extent, but also were interrelated with residents of other villages. The villagers usually remained with their village while it suited them—politically, socially, or economically—but were free to move from village to village at will. For example, if a village fell on hard times due to a shortage of roots or berries in a specific area, many of the villagers might find fault with the local headman and migrate to a more prosperous village. One might also move to be nearer a close friend or relative. The size and makeup of the village were generally determined by the needs of cooperative labor to perform a specific task. The interaction of a number of

A Hupa Indian fishes for salmon with a spear. (Library of Congress)

villages made up a tribe, and tribes often allied themselves for survival. The larger units were more loosely arranged and less permanent (Miller, 2003, 10, 11).

As a staple food, salmon were so important to the Native peoples of this region that the fish was held in high spiritual esteem. As a way of guaranteeing that the fish would return in abundance, the First Fish ceremony was performed throughout the Northwest by the peoples who depended on the return of the annual salmon runs. Daniel Boxberger, an anthropologist who has done extensive studies on the Lummi of northern Puget Sound offered this description:

> The first salmon was treated as a special guest in the village. After it had been honored and every member of the village had partaken of a small portion of its flesh, its bones would be returned to the water, where it would resume its previous form and go tell the other salmon how well it had been treated. The salmon

would then allow the Lummis to capture them (Boxberger, 1989, 18).

Andy Fernando describes the First Fish ceremony of the Skagit Indians of northwestern Washington State in detail, explaining the role of the villagers who participated and the First Fish as having " . . . fulfilled their duty, prescribed by the great spirit. The salmon had returned to the appointed time and place, the villagers had faithfully honored the salmon in sharing and ceremony. The people thereby assured themselves of a good season, and the harvest could begin" (Hurtado, 1994, 529–530).

Social status and social interaction were linked to salmon fishing as a method of exhibiting skill and of generosity by providing the food for social and religious gatherings. In Fernando's description of the First Fish ceremony, he explains that "[t]he entire village would gather together and appoint fishermen to each catch one salmon—no more [for the purpose of the ceremony]." Prior to the ceremony being performed and the salmon being honored, no one was allowed to participate in any fishing activities purely for the sake of catching fish (Fernando, 1998, 529).

In his discussion of the receiving of a *guardian spirit* by a member of a task group, Miller gives an example of the importance of that member's ability to catch fish and how that individuals' contribution affected the band in the task-group system:

> . . . if a band had a large number of people who were granted strong fishing powers, this would be its predominant activity in the task group system . . . [T]hus, [that group was] most likely to play a leading role in economic and social life. Even such social activities as gift giving played a part in identifying the economic role of the host group. Not only did the giving of gifts indicate that a host band was capable of generating a surplus; the nature of the gifts (baskets, dried fish, etc.) identified the group's particular economic strengths (Miller, 2003, 20).

Most of the technology of the Indians of the Pacific Northwest was based on a need to catch fish—mainly salmon. Salmon were undoubtedly the most important food staple and economic resource of the Straits Salish, who inhabited the Puget Sound area. One estimate of the pre-contact, per-capita consumption of salmon is as high as 600 pounds annually among the Lummis (Boxberger, 1989, 13). This level of fish consumption required very efficient fishing technology, intense cooperation of labor, and private property boundaries. Boxberger explained this system:

> The precapitalist fishing economy of the Straits Salish was a complex interaction between free-access resources and locations held in trust by individuals for a larger kin group. A man was guaranteed access to fishing locations as far as his (and his wife's) kinship networks extended. . . . The two most productive forms of traditional Straits Salish salmon fishing, reef netting and weir fishing, both required a great deal of labor and organization. Both reef net and weir sites were owned and controlled by individuals on behalf of a larger kin group . . . [A]lthough a weir might be owned by a kin group, everyone had a right to take fish from it (Boxberger, 1989, 13).

Boxberger uses the Lummis to illustrate the economic dilemma of most Native peoples when it comes to commercial salmon fishing:

> In the western Washington fishery the massive capital outlays and subsequent technological advances displaced the small operations and increasingly restricted Indian access to the resource. Though the tribal resources were developed, the Lummi tribe became underdeveloped. As fisherfolk, the Lummis were incorporated into the capitalist system to provide raw materials for the processors and labor for the processing sector. Once they entered the dominant economy there was no turning back, for when their labor and resources were no longer needed they were still dependent on the dominant economy though no longer able to participate (Boxberger, 1989, 6).

In modern times, many Indians of the Pacific Northwest fish with modern fishing gear and, after decades of court battles having finally won rulings in their favor, fish in the "usual and accustomed" fishing areas guaranteed them by the treaties of the 1850s. The Lummis, for example, now fish Puget Sound and its tributary streams using modern gill nets and purse seine boats requiring a high capital investment on a commercial basis, as well as using traditional methods of fishing for subsistence use (Boxberger, 1989, 167). Either way, salmon has retained its social, economic, and spiritual significance for most Indians in the Pacific Northwest.

Daniel R. Gibbs

See also Fishing Rights.

References and Further Readings

Boxberger, Daniel L. 1989. *To Fish in Common: The Ethnohistory of Lummi Indian Salmon Fishing.* Columbia Northwest Classics. Lincoln: University of Nebraska Press.

Evans, Sterling, ed. 2002. *American Indians in American History: 1870–2001. A Companion Reader.* Westport. CN: Praeger.

Fernando, Andy. 1994. "On the Importance of Fishing Rights in the Northwest, 1984." In *Major Problems in American Indian History.* Edited by Albert L. Hurtado and Peter Iverson. Lexington, MA: D. C. Heath and Company

Iverson, Peter. 1998. *We Are Still Here: American Indians in the Twentieth Century.* The American History Series. Wheeling, IL: Harlan Davidson

Miller, Christopher. 2003. *Prophetic Worlds: Indians and Whites on the Columbia Plateau.* Seattle: University of Washington Press.

Nikel-Zueger, Manuel. 2003. *Saving Salmon the American Indian Way.* A case study in a series. Bozeman, MT: Property and Environment Research Center.

Scalping in the Colonial Period

The removal of all or a portion of the scalp was a custom practiced by various Native American groups and later by European settlers. The current consensus is that the practice of scalping was an indigenous creation. The males of many Native American groups wore their hair in a certain manner that lent itself to this practice. Both groups utilized this practice, which was often fatal, as a component of warfare. The scalp could be removed in several ways. Likewise, scalping held a number of symbolic meanings, both positive and negative.

Many Native American tribespeople wore their hair in a specific fashion, with a lock of hair braided and hanging. This distinct lock of hair came to be known as the scalplock. For many Iroquois and Algonquian speaking tribes, the warrior's soul was believed to reside in the scalplock. Though Europeans did not wear their hair in the same fashion, once hostilities arose between the two groups, they too could become victims of the process.

Misunderstanding the significance of scalping to Native Americans, the Europeans perceived the practice as simply an atrocity and responded to it

Drawing of an American Indian holding a scalp. Although Native Americans were thought to have created the practice indigenously, Europeans also took part in scalping. (Library of Congress)

the warrior prowess of one Native American to another. By the same token, taking a warrior's scalp after death served as a tribute to the martial ability of the fallen. It acknowledged that the slain had been a worthy opponent. If captured, a warrior could sometimes expect gruesome torture to the death (that within eastern Indian cultures was regarded as a sacrifice to restore balance to the world). Part of this torture might include the removal of the scalplock as a sign of the removal of masculinity or the soul prior to death.

As time passed and traditions eroded, especially among the Iroquois due to the practice of mourning war, scalping became a tactic employed against all of their victims, regardless of gender. Most historians link the degeneration of the practice to the frequency and intensity of the wars in the late seventeenth and early eighteenth centuries, the period encompassing the conflicts over the fur trade. These conflicts, along with disease epidemics, ravaged the elders of the various tribes, especially in the Northeast. These were the members of the tribe who served as the transmitters of their people's culture.

While scalping among American Indians served a number of purposes, all of these were vital in the creation of a young warrior's identity. Primarily, the acquisition of an enemy's scalplock in battle presented a concrete testament to the young man's martial prowess. At the same time that the captured lock of hair gave evidence of increased status, it simultaneously provided a means to salute the abilities of the vanquished. Thus the removal of the scalplock from the head of a dead warrior did honor to both contestants in the engagement.

James R. McIntyre

accordingly. As time passed, both the French and British took scalps of Native Americans. These Europeans saw the taking of scalps as a means of gaining proof that Native Americans had been killed on an expedition. By the same token, Europeans sometimes paid money for scalps collected by Indians, the payment being known as a scalp bounty. The most infamous figure known in connection with this practice was the Lieutenant Governor of Canada during the American War of Independence, Henry "the Hair Buyer" Hamilton.

Among some Native Americans, scalping served a number of significant, symbolic purposes. It added to the prestige of a young warrior to gain the scalp of another in battle. It transmitted tangible evidence of a warrior's ability. Likewise, it was often believed that it transferred the masculinity or even

See also Beaver Wars; Disease, Historic and Contemporary; Fur Trade; Identity; Warfare, Intertribal.

References and Further Reading

Axtell, James, and William C. Sturtevant. 1980. "The Unkindest Cut or Who Invented Scalping?" In *William and Mary Quarterly* 37: 451–472.

Brooks, Robert L. 1994. "Warfare on the Southern Plains." In *Skeletal Biology in the Great Plains: Migration, Warfare, Health, and Subsistence.* Edited by Douglas W. Owsley and Richard L. Jantz, 317–324. Washington, DC: Smithsonian Institution.

Eid, Larry V. 1998. " 'A Kind of Running Fight': Indian Battlefield Tactics in the Late Eighteenth Century." In *Western Pennsylvania Historical Magazine* 71: 147–171.

Gleach, Frederick W. 1997. *Powhatan's World and Colonial Virginia: A Conflict of Cultures.* Lincoln: University of Nebraska Press.

Richter, Daniel K. 1983. "War and Culture: The Iroquois Experience." *William and Mary Quarterly,* 3rd ser., no. 40: 528–559.

Seven Drums Religion

The Seven Drums Religion has many names. Called *wáashat* (Washat, meaning "dance") or *waasaní* (Washani, "dancers" or "worship") in the Sahaptin language of the Columbia Plateau, it is also known as the Sacred Dance Religion, the Longhouse Religion, or simply the Indian religion. The latter label reflects the contemporary view that Washat is the most "traditional" of the various faiths practiced in Plateau Indian communities, even though it exhibits some Christian parallels. Many practitioners avoid the term "religion" altogether because of its narrow, compartmentalized connotation. "To non-Indians, the longhouse represents religion," explained Lewis Malatare, the leader of a Washat congregation on the Yakama reservation. "To Yakamas, we prefer not to use the word religion but more a way of life—a life that was dictated to us by the natural surroundings of our environment." Wilson Wewa, a drummer from the Warm Springs reservation, suggested "spirituality" as a better way to describe Washat "because it's about honoring the Creator in everything we do." Whatever it is called, the Seven Drums Religion has long provided a central venue for the expression of Indian culture and identity among Plateau peoples. Washat's close association with tribal traditionalism also made it a target of government repression until the 1930s, but today more than a dozen longhouse congregations carry on the traditions of their ancestors.

Like most modern religions, Washat has changed significantly over time as Plateau Indians interacted with outsiders and adapted to shifting circumstances. Its spiritual roots extend nearly 10,000 years into the aboriginal past, when the native inhabitants of the Columbia Basin developed the seasonal round of fishing, gathering, and hunting that characterized their culture at the time of European contact. Their subsistence cycle led to the identification of five sacred foods—salmon, roots, berries, deer, and water—which Plateau Indians propitiated through an annual series of first food feasts conducted to show respect for the resources and ensure abundant harvests. Catholic and Protestant missionaries first observed these ceremonies in the 1830s, and their efforts to convert the Indians set in motion a process of religious borrowing and blending that continued into the late nineteenth century. The bells obtained from fur traders and Jesuit priests quickly made their way into Washat rituals, where the sound of the bell came to represent the heartbeat of all life. Similarly, Indians adopted Sunday as a regular day of worship and attached spiritual meaning to the numbers three and seven. While five retained its ritual importance, appearing frequently in Washat songs and dances, seven became the standard number of drummers for most ceremonies (though fewer often serve now if enough are not available).

The popularity and power of the Seven Drums Religion peaked during the latter half of the nineteenth century, the era of the so-called Dreamer Cult. Riding a wave of Indian anxiety over the effects of American colonization, the Dreamers temporarily infused Washani with a strong millenarian and nativistic message. Their greatest prophet, Smohalla, promised his followers divine deliverance from their oppressors if the Indians would cast off white ways and return to their own traditions. Because this creed interfered with federal assimilation policies and encouraged the retention of "savage" customs, the Office of Indian Affairs tried to suppress Washat services using the Indian police and the courts of Indian offenses on each reservation. Agency authorities banned traditional dancing, spied on tribal meetings, arrested religious leaders, confiscated or destroyed drums, and directed Indians to attend Christian churches. Such measures persisted into the early 1930s, long after the prophets and their visions had faded away, but the faithful kept Washat alive by holding their ceremonies in secret, moving them off reservation, or cloaking them in approved holidays such as the Fourth of July.

The Seven Drums Religion remains active today, although its membership has declined significantly due to Indian acculturation and competition from various Christian denominations as well as the Indian Shaker Church. Washat is not an exclusive sect, however, so many people who participate in it also attend other churches. Currently, there are fifteen permanent longhouses located on five reservations and in several off-reservation communities across the Columbia Plateau. Besides holding Sunday services and seasonal first food feasts, they provide gathering places for naming ceremonies, weddings, funerals, and other community events that define "traditionalism" for contemporary Plateau Indians. Some longhouses are thought to be especially powerful for certain purposes, such as the first salmon feast held at Celilo, and ritual practices vary from congregation to congregation. "Everybody does different things in different longhouses, just like Protestants and Catholics," noted elder Ella Jim, "but we're all worshipping the same Creator."

Andrew H. Fisher

See also Handsome Lake; Indian Shaker
   Movement; Sohappy, Sr., David.
References and Further Reading
Hunn, Eugene S., with James Selam and Family.
   1990. *Nch'i-Wána, "The Big River": Mid-Columbia
   Indians and Their Land.* Seattle: University of
   Washington Press.
Relander, Click. 1956. *Drummers and Dreamers.*
   Caldwell, ID: Caxton.
Ruby, Robert, and John A. Brown. 1989. *Dreamer
   Prophets of the Columbia Plateau: Smohalla and
   Skolaskin.* Norman: University of Oklahoma
   Press.

Slavery and Native Americans

Generalizations about the history of slavery in the New World are becoming increasingly difficult to accept as more complete and complex information is revealed. Still, it is well-known that Columbus encountered Caribbean Natives when his first voyage reached the shores of Hispaniola, but it was during his second arrival that he ordered every Indian over the age of fourteen to be placed into bondage. Columbus was well within legal parameters, as nearly fifty years earlier Pope Nicholas V had legitimized slavery by authorizing Catholic nations to sell into servitude heathens and "foes of Christ." Later, this concept was expanded to include all captives taken in religious wars, including everyone who was "unconverted," and the Native islanders met that definition. Within a few decades, however, the numbers of indigenes in the circum-Caribbean region were greatly reduced due to forced labor, imported diseases, and harsh treatment by religious and military European-American immigrants. This catastrophe would be repeated many times. Centuries later in the United States, poor white Europeans of any religious affiliation became indentured servants in some of the thirteen original colonies; others, such as Massachusetts, outlawed servitude in 1712. Virginia colonists, on the other hand, had tried

enslaving Indians but a deadly retaliation occurred and the effort was abandoned. Ultimately, the disastrous effect of communicable diseases prevented Indian slavery from becoming a major institution in the colonies because many Natives would die from imported ailments within fifty years after contact with the Puritans. Years later in the American South, the Seminoles also owned African slaves who, when they escaped, took refuge among the occupying Spaniards in Florida. Cherokees too held slaves and were themselves enslaved by mixed-blood plantation owners. Half-Indian proprietors of vast estates forcibly brought Chickasaw Indians from Mississippi to Indian Territory to work for free. The Creeks were both slaves and slave owners. The best example of continuous Indian slavery occurred on the Spanish colonial frontier of northern Mexico. Conquistadors, heirs to a long history of forcing work and other forms of tribute from conquered peoples in Europe, brought the tradition to Mexico in 1521. For example, explorer Hernan Cortes took a fourteen-year-old girl as his slave and concubine shortly after arriving (Brooks, 2002, 25). Soon, Spanish ships were docked at Mexican West Coast ports like Guaymas, awaiting hunters who tracked, caught, and transported Indians into slavery in the central area of the country. "Throughout the entire seventeenth century [Spaniards] paid fifty to one hundred pesos to go out into the wilds and enslave groups of Indians on the pretext of bringing them into Hispanic society" (Cuello, 1988, 688). Male captives, worth over one hundred pesos in 1575 when sold privately or at public auctions, were expected to serve their purchasers for twenty years. Women and older children, in high demand as house servants, received a sentence of ten to fifteen years. Younger children were "deposited" with Spanish masters for indefinite periods (Cuello, 1988, 687).

In the late 1500s and well into the following centuries, northern Mexico fell under the authority of Jesuit and Franciscan missionaries. These religious pioneers' dual task was to introduce Christianity to the Indians, convert them, and prepare the new Christians to become tax-paying citizens of the empire; enslaving the indigenes was the result. To meet the goals, priests relied on a policy of *reducción-congregación*, procedures that *reduced* populations in Indian villages, through violence if necessary, and then *congregated* the natives in strictly controlled settings where their labor was forced and their culture nearly obliterated through punishment, reeducation, involuntary religious instructions, and renaming

Native Americans working in salt mines under Spanish rule. (Bettmann/Corbis)

(Stockel, 2004, 58–59). The Indians' initial obligation in the mission environment was to construct the entire compound, beginning with the center of the community: the church. To build the long, rectangular adobe foundation, workers were forced to cut timber and haul the heavy tree limbs to a designated area at the future mission's home. Under armed guard and at the direction of a priest, the laborers created square wooden frames, cut from the tree limbs as molds for adobe bricks. They dug out the rocky caliche soil, so characteristic of the region, mixed it with water, small stones, and slivers of wood, and poured it into the shells. Days later, when the sun had thoroughly dried and baked the mud, the Indians lifted each weighty brick and carried it to the proposed sacred site. They piled one brick on top of the other or two beside each other, sometimes to a width of thirty-six inches, to raise the church's walls. Roof construction began by boiling and then peeling bark from other tree limbs, lifting them, and setting them across the open width between the walls from one side to the other. Next, skinny wooden braches

of willow, saguaro cactus ribs, or similar materials were also boiled and peeled and placed at right angles atop the beams. Mud, cow manure, grass, and other natural flora sealed the roof. To prevent deterioration, the slaves hauled, pushed, and pulled tons of limestone boulders to a pit they dug, heated them in roaring fires until they exploded, and then pulverized and blended the residue with water. Other Indians stood ready to smear the mixture by hand onto church walls, frequently standing on shaky scaffolds that could collapse and plunge the men to earth. If the workers hesitated or sat down to rest without permission, soldiers were ordered to discipline them on the spot.

Daily regimentation controlled the field workers. Each day began with religious services followed by a small breakfast after which the slaves walked under guard to the field to work all day at planting, tending, and raising crops. At sunset each day the tired Indians returned to the mission complex and were required to stop at the church to say the doctrina and pray before eating supper. Collecting tribute was the responsibility of crown-appointed trustees called *encomenderos*. Beginning in 1562, these few privileged individuals, having exhibited impressive loyalty to the crown, held a specified number of Indians in trust, or in *encomienda*, a remnant of a feudal institution through which loyal subjects to the king were rewarded. Tribute consisted of gifts of goods, crops, hides, blankets, and anything the *encomendero* requested from his Indian slaves. Even after the crown prohibited the practice, taxes in the forms of direct labor or personal service persisted, with officials looking the other way and justifying *encomienda* as necessary because a scarcity of non-Indian agricultural workers existed (Weber, 1992, 124). *Repartimiento* (Weber, 1992, 126) replaced *encomienda* and became another legalized form of slavery even though it has been defined as a "time honored institution by which Spanish officials distributed native men to work on a rotating basis at tasks deemed to be for the public good" (Weber, 1992, 126). Participation was compulsory, but in contrast with the common understanding of slavery, the Indians were supposed to receive wages. Although the length of their servitude was controlled by laws, as was the type of labor they were expected to do, Indians were "unpaid, underpaid, paid in overvalued merchandise, unfed, underfed, and kept for longer periods of time than regulations permitted" (Weber, 1992, 126).

Control through a well-defined hierarchical structure and disciplinary actions for disobedience were essential both in *encomienda* and *repartimiento*, religious and political officials rationalized, if managing a large group of Indian slaves was to be even moderately successful in creating a stable community. They thus gave themselves permission to disregard the laws. Simultaneously, soldiers and settlers also wanted free slave labor to tend herds, till fields, cut firewood, serve in Hispanic households, and haul cargo as pack animals. Competing needs eventually caused a conflict between the religious and secular frontier Spaniards. Civil authorities charged that the missionaries forced the Indians to work for free. The missionaries responded that appointees demanded that the indigenes work for them purely for individual profit. Importantly, allegations also involved the priests' severe disciplinary methods for misbehavior, countered by the missionaries' similar allegations against their accusers. The continuing enslavement of Indians by Europeans was interrupted by a series of external events beginning in 1810 when stirrings of independence from Spain altered funding and supplies to northern Mexico. Later, the successful war further disrupted the frontier, as did war with America in 1846. In the final analysis the occupation and subjugation of Mexico's indigenous populations cast the conquerors, especially the missionaries, into the role of aggressors, demanding and imposing cultural and religious changes through violence when necessary. That this massive colonial endeavor was successful is apparent today in the Spanish surnames and Christian affiliations of Native peoples in northern Mexico and the American Southwest. That the attempt was unsuccessful is evident in the Indians' continuous public and private practice of ancestral ceremonies and traditional celebrations (Stockel, 2004, 268).

H. Henrietta Stockel

See also Dalles Trading Area; Mission System, Spanish; Potlatch; Seminole Wars; Spanish Influence.

References and Futher Reading
Bailey, L. R. 1996. *Indian Slave Trade in the Southwest.* New York: Tower Publications.
Brooks, James F. 2002. *Captives & Cousins: Slavery, Kinship, and Community in the Southwest Borderlands.* Chapel Hill: University of North Carolina Press.
Cuello, José. 1988. "The Persistence of Indian Slavery and Encomienda in the Northeast of Colonial Mexico, 1577–1723." *Journal of Social History* 21 (Summer): 683–700.
Spicer, Edward H. 1962. *Cycles of Conquest: The Impact of Spain, Mexico, and the United States on the Indians of the Southwest, 1533–1960.* Tucson: University of Arizona Press.
Stockel, H. Henrietta. 2004. *On the Bloody Road to Jesus: Christianity and the Chiricahua Apaches.* Albuquerque: University of New Mexico Press.
Weber, David J. 1992. *The Spanish Frontier in North America.* New Haven, CT: Yale University Press.

State Names, Native American Derivations

Roughly half the states in the United States of America have names that derive, in some way, from Native American languages. Most are English or French adaptations of the original Native American words. Sometimes, more than one meaning has been attributed to a name, in which case both are listed.

Alabama: From *alipama* or *alibamu*, a Muskogee tribal name meaning "Those who clear the land."

Alaska: From the Aleut word for their homeland on the Alaska peninsula, *Alakhskhakh;* also Aleut for "great land."

Arizona: A Pagago word, *airzonac*, probably meaning "small springs."

Arkansas: From the Illinois name for the Quapaw, *akansea*. The same word has been said to mean "downstream people."

Connecticut: Mohegan or Pequot for "long tidal river" or "wind-driven river."

Dakota (North and South): A Dakota Sioux term for themselves (*dahkota*), meaning "friends" or "allies." It is interesting that the immigrants expropriated the Sioux's own name for themselves, with its friendly connotations, meanwhile assigning the Dakota a corruption of an old French word *Sioux*, meaning "snake" or "enemy."

Idaho: The Native language from which this state name is derived is unknown; it is said to have meant "gem of the mountains"; some say it means "The sun is coming up."

Illinois: The name of an Algonquian confederation, meaning "original people" or "superior men," after a term that the Illinois Indians used for themselves. The name originated with the Algonquian *iliniwak*, modified by French traders as Illinois.

Iowa: For the Ioway Indians, modified through French, from the Fox language, as *aayahooweewa* (possibly from the Sioux *ayuhba*). Both words mean "sleepy ones."

Kansas: Kansa for "people of the south wind."

Kentucky: From *kenta*, possibly an Iroquois word for "planted field." Some say the word is Cherokee for "meadowland."

Massachusetts: Meaning "people of the big hill," this name was used to describe an Algonquian people who lived near a steep hill near Boston.

Michigan: Meaning "great water" (*michigamea*) or "big lake," the name is probably derived from the Algonquian or Ottawa language.

Minnesota: From *minisota*, a Dakota word meaning "sky-tinted water."

Mississippi: A combination of two Algonquian or Ojibway words: *misi*, meaning "great" or "large" and *sipi*, meaning "water," usually taken to mean "big river."

Missouri: A French adaptation of an Illinois (*Iliniwak*) word meaning "people with dugout canoes." This is also the name of a tribe that lived near the river and also may be taken to mean "big muddy river," after the Missouri Indians' name for it, *Pokitanou*, which carries that meaning. To this day, inhabitants of cities along the river customarily call it The Big Muddy.

Nebraska: From the Omaha name *Nibdhathka*, meaning "flat river" or "flat water," named for the shallow but wide Platte River. Some sources say the word is from the Oto language; it may be from both.

New Mexico: As a province of New Spain, New Mexico's name was derived from *Mexica*, the Aztecs' name for themselves.

Ohio: Derived from a Seneca word meaning "beautiful river."

Oklahoma: "Red men" in Choctaw, a translation of "Indian Territory" into the Choctaw language.

Tennessee: From *Tanasi*, a Cherokee name for the Little Tennessee River, as well as a principal Cherokee town by the same name. It is said to mean "area of traveling waters."

Texas: First a Spanish (*Tejas*), then an English derivation from *taysa*, a word used among members of the Caddo tribal confederacy meaning (like "Dakota") "friends or allies."

Utah: From the tribal name Ute, anglicized from *yuuttaa*, the Utes' name for their homeland, "the land of the sun."

Wisconsin: The name of a tribal confederacy living near the Wisconsin River, the English name is probably derived from the Ojibway *Wees-kon-san*, "gathering of the waters" and "grassy place."

Wyoming: This name, meaning "big meadows" or "big river flats," originated with the Delaware (Leni Lenápe) of present-day Pennsylvania and New Jersey, and was carried by non-Indian migrants to the state that now bears the name. "Wyoming" is anglicized rather liberally from the Leni Lenápe *maughwauwame*, a name given first to the Wyoming valley of Pennsylvania.

Bruce E. Johansen

See also Albany Congress, Native Precedents; Cohen, Felix; Franklin, Benjamin, Native American Influences; Haudenosaunee Confederacy, Political System; Lacrosse; State Names, United States, Native American Derivations; Thanksgiving Holiday, Origins.

References and Further Reading

Abram, Charles. 1923. "Law of the Woman Chief, May 21, 1923." Hewitt Collection, BAE Manuscript No. 1636, NAA. Smithsonian Institution.

Allen, Paula Gunn. 1986. *The Sacred Hoop: Recovering the Feminine in American Indian Traditions.* Boston: Beacon Press.

Anthony, Susan B. 1985. *History of Woman Suffrage.* Edited by Elizabeth Cady Stanton and Matilda Joslyn Gage. North Stratford, NH: Ayer Company.

Axtell, James. 1981. *The Indian Peoples of Eastern America: A Documentary History of the Sexes.* New York: Oxford University Press.

Barreiro, José. 1992. "The Search for Lessons." In *Indigenous Economics: Toward a Natural World Order.* Edited by José Barreiro. *Akwe:kon Journal* 9, no. 2 (Summer): 18–39.

Birchfield, D. L. 1997. *The Encyclopedia of North American Indians.* Vol. 5. Tarrytown, NY: Marshall Cavendish.

Brown, Judith K. 1970. "Economic Organization and the Position of Women Among the Iroquois." *Ethnohistory* 17, nos. 3–4 (Summer-Fall): 151–167.

Cameron, Kenneth W., ed. 1967. *The Works of Samuel Peters.* Hartford: Transcendental Books.

Carr, Lucien. 1884. *The Social and Political Position of Women Among the Huron-Iroquois Tribes.* Salem, MA: Salem Press.

Case, Nancy Humphrey. 2002. "Gifts from the Indians: Native Americans Not Only Provided New Kinds of Food and Recreation; They May Have Given the Founding Fathers Ideas on How to Form a Government." *The Christian Science Monitor.* November. Available at: http://www.turtletrack.org/Issues02/Co11302002/CO_11302002_Gifts.htm. Accessed January 9, 2007.

Cohen, Felix. 1952. "Americanizing the White Man." *American Scholar* 21, no. 2: 177–191.

Cohen, Felix. 1960. *The Legal Conscience: Selected Papers of Felix S. Cohen.* Edited by Lucy Kramer Cohen. New Haven, CT: Yale University Press.

Corkran, David H. 1962. *The Cherokee Frontier: Conflict and Survival, 1740–62.* Norman: University of Oklahoma Press.

Cronon, William. 1983. *Changes in the Land: Indians, Colonists, and the Ecology of New England.* New York: Hill and Wang.

Crosby, Alfred W. 1972. *The Columbian Exchange: Biological and Cultural Consequences of 1492.* Westport, CT: Greenwood Press.

Edwards, Everett E. 1934. "The Contributions of American Indians to Civilization." *Minnesota History* 15, no. 3: 255–272.

Fenton, W. N. 1941. *Contacts Between Iroquois Herbalism and Colonial Medicine.* Washington, DC: Smithsonian Institution.

Foner, Philip S., ed. 1945. *Complete Writings of Thomas Paine.* New York: Citadel Press.

Forbes, Jack. 1964. *The Indian in America's Past.* Englewood Cliffs, NJ: Prentice-Hall.

Frachtenberg, Leo J. 1915. "Our Indebtedness to the American Indian." *Wisconsin Archeologist* 14, no. 2: 64–69.

Gipson, Arrell Morgan. 1980. *The American Indian: Prehistory to Present.* Lexington, MA: D. C. Heath and Company.

Grinde, Donald A., Jr., and Bruce E. Johansen. 1991. *Exemplar of Liberty: Native America and the Evolution of Democracy.* Los Angeles, CA: UCLA American Indian Studies Center.

Grinde, Donald A., Jr., and Bruce E. Johansen. 1995. *Ecocide of Native America: Environmental Destruction of Indian Lands and Peoples.* Santa Fe, NM: Clear Light Publishers.

Johansen, Bruce E. [1982] 1987. *Forgotten Founders: How the Iroquois Helped Shape Democracy.* Boston: Harvard Common Press, 1987.

Keoke, Emory Dean, and Kay Marie Porterfield. 2002. *Encyclopedia of American Indian Contributions to the World.* New York: Facts on File.

Kraus, Michael. 1949. *The Atlantic Civilization: Eighteenth Century Origins.* New York: Russell & Russell.

Moquin, Wayne. 1973. *Great Documents in American Indian History.* Westport, CT: Praeger.

Porterfield, Kay Marie. 2002. "Ten Lies About Indigenous Science —How to Talk Back." October 10. Available at: http://www.kporterfield.com/aicttw/articles/lies.html. Accessed January 9, 2007.

Public Broadcasting Service. No date. Africans in America: Revolution, Resource Bank, part 2: 1750–1805. "Crispus Attucks." Available at: http://www.pbs.org/wgbh/aia/part2/2p24.html. Accessed February 20, 2003.

Selsam, Millicent. 1959. *Plants That Heal.* New York: William Morrow & Co.

"Substance of the Speech of Good Peter to Governor Clinton and the Commissioners of Indian Affairs at Albany." 1814. New York City: Collections of the New York Historical Society, 1st Series, 2: 115.

Weatherford, Jack. 1988. *Indian Givers: How the Indians of the Americas Transformed the World.* New York: Fawcett Columbine.

Weatherford, Jack. 1991. *Native Roots: How the Indians Enriched America.* New York: Crown.

Sun Dance

The Sun Dance is the central ceremony of the year for many of the Plains tribes. It is held among the Arapahos, Arikaras, Assiniboines, Blackfoot (Blackfeet), Comanches, Crows, Eastern Dakotas, Gros Ventres, Hidastas, Kiowas, Lakotas, Mandans, plains Crees, plains Ojibwas, Sarsis, Shoshones, Sisetons, Suhtais (northern Cheyenne), Tsis-tsis-tas (southern Cheyenne), and Utes. Recently, some Navajos have put on the Sun Dance as well. Moreover, because of the questionable practice of selling Sun Dances, splinter groups of intertribal Indians, unaffiliated mixed-bloods, and whites have been putting on Sun Dances in places such as Colorado and Texas. This practice is highly controversial.

From 1881 to 1934, Sun Dances were held secretly because they had been banned in both Canada and the United States. The Canadian Indian Act made it illegal in that country, and in the United States it was proscribed under the Court of Indian Offenses after 1883. Even prior to government prohibition, Sun Dances had been discouraged by other means. The agent among the Blood band of the Blackfoot withheld rations and rendered other food ceremonially useless as well as preventing a traditional leader from getting employment to discourage the ceremony. Sun Dances without piercing began to be held more openly after the Indian Reorganization Act of 1934 with its Circular No. 2970 on American Indian religious freedom, and those including piercing became less secret in the late 1950s. The tribal council at Pine Ridge even advertised a Sun Dance to tourists for a Fourth of July Fair.

The Sun Dance has been practiced the longest by the Arapahos, Cheyennes, Crows, and Sioux, having come later to the others who practice it. For the Lakotas, the Sun Dance was brought by White Buffalo Calf Woman; for the Suhtai, by Erect Horns. For the Tsis-tsis-tas, Sweet Medicine brought the dance from the teachings given to him by the spirits inside Bear Butte. Sun Dances are traditionally held among these peoples in the summer, usually either around the end of June or beginning of July or around the end of July and beginning of August. This is the time of year when berries ripen or chokecherries darken to fullness, the time the buffalo was traditionally hunted and preserved.

The Sun Dance arbor is constructed each year anew around a central pole, the Tree of Life, often ritually hunted and brought in by one of the warrior societies. Shades made of tarps or other cloth cover the

Cheyenne Sun Dance pledgers. (Library of Congress)

beams that fan out around the center pole, creating the sacred circle in which the dancers will make their sacrifice. Around and on the central pole are highly sacred objects and sometimes prayer cloths. Buffalo, the lifeblood of the Plains, are essential to the ceremony for most participating tribes, at least in some way. The Blackfoot include the use of Sacred Tongues in the food blessed in the ceremony. Buffalo skulls are used both for prayer and for a piercing weight.

Some peoples who hold the Sun Dance do not pierce for various reasons. The Tsis-tsis-tas, who once engaged in this Sun Dance practice, no longer do so because, as Eugene Blackbear, Sr., oldest living Tsis-tsis-tas Sun Dance leader, says, "Once a way has been lost, we cannot bring it back without someone who is qualified to do it," to act as an instructor who has engaged in the practice as a dancer. For the Kiowa, piercing would violate a prohibition against shedding blood during the time of the ceremony. Among peoples who pierce, skewers are put under the flesh and either tied to the central pole, to scaffolds, or to the buffalo skulls some supplicants drag behind them. Dancers who pierce often have to ultimately remove the piercing through a flesh offering, by dancing up to and away from the pole until the skin rips and the skewer flies free. During the ritual, dancers often do without food and water for up to four days. Led by their instructors, they dance intermittently for days on end, blowing sacred eagle bone whistles at times. They may not leave the arbor except when given permission by their instructors for a break to urinate or for ceremonial purposes. In some tribes, only men dance. In others, dancing is done by both male and female supplicants. Among the southern Cheyenne, women may fast but do not dance.

The dance's central purpose is for the renewal of life for the next year for the people, so that they might overcome the obstacles to their survival and have plentiful food for the next year; it is a thanksgiving, a giving back to the Creator for the blessings of the past year. The ceremony commemorates the creation of the world and acts to recreate it and the relationships within it annually. However, preparation for an individual Sun Dance supplicant begins with a vow to undertake the ceremony. Often, a vow is taken so that a relative might be healed from an ailment or safely returned from war or other separations. This vow might vary from one year to four years of Sun Dancing. The dancer, or faster, in the case of a female, must find an instructor qualified to lead him or her in the ceremony. The instructor gives up some of the medicine given to him or her in their years as a dancer or faster.

According to Blackbear, Cheyenne instructors keep back "one paint" or transfer for themselves. Because of the notion of reciprocity in ceremony and in life that is an ideal in many tribes, those taking vows offer gifts to the instructors, both upon taking the vow and in the ritual itself. Often, the entire extended family of the dancer spends nearly a year gathering and making the gifts; these include blankets, shawls, guns, horses, moccasins, and enamelware dishes and pots, among other items. A dancer often has to find someone to cook during the ceremony for him as well, often several female relatives. Elaborate meals are given to the instructor and his or her family several times a day during the ceremony itself, and a larger feast is held after the dance ends, including both the dancer's and the instructor's families. In other tribes, cooking for those encamped and the instructors is done on the community level, with women from various families chosen or volunteering to prepare food for all who attend.

Dancers often abstain from sexual activity for a period of time before the ritual; in some tribes, celibacy is practiced for a month to four months. In traditional Tsis-tsis-tas ways, the period at one time was four years. Moreover, some peoples acquire a pipe for praying and observe taboos that they must follow for the rest of their lives that accompany the medicine they are given through the dance. Often, dancers and instructors pray prior to the dance in a sweat lodge for the purpose of purification. Another sweat follows in some tribes at the dance's conclusion. In some nations and tribes, the Sun Dance is preceded by other bundle ceremonies, such as Arrow Worship among the Tsis-tsis-tas, a men's ritual that women know nothing about. In others, such as the Lakota, individual supplicants go out on the hill seeking a vision prior to dancing.

For many who take part in the ceremony, the Sun Dance is a homecoming, just as it was a gathering of the bands in the prereservation era. The camp life of the ceremony provided time for traditional games, council meetings, and the passing of information to those one seldom saw. Young people traditionally and today see the Sun Dance as an opportunity for courtship. Tents and recreational vehicles today help form the outer circle along with the teepees and bough-covered cooking shades that once formed it alone. Those about the camp who support dancers, visit old friends and relatives, and engage in various preparatory activities often must observe taboos as well, such as not wasting water or tossing it out carelessly. Drug and alcohol use is strictly prohibited and constitutes a major violation of the ceremonial space and the camp.

Menstruating women might be sent to a "moon lodge" in some ceremonies, while in others they should avoid the campground entirely as their power can interfere with that of the instructors. In some tribes, the Sun Dance is a time to bring those born during the year into tribal life formally, some piercing children's ears and others conducting formal naming ceremonies. Despite the changes brought by time and colonization, the Sun Dance religion remains vitally important to all aspects of life for the tribes that practice it. It perpetuates life and ideals such as generosity, bravery, and honesty, weaving the tribe together as a people and sustaining them.

Kimberly Roppolo

See also American Indian Religious Freedom Act; Identity.
References and Further Reading
Blackbear, Eugene, Sr. 2004. Personal interview.

Hirschfelder, Arlene, and Paulette Molin, eds. 2000. *Encyclopedia of Native American Religions,* updated ed. New York: Facts on File.

Hoxie, Frederick E., ed. 1996. *Encyclopedia of North American Indians: Native American History, Culture, and Life from Paleo-Indians to the Present.* Boston: Houghton-Mifflin.

Markowitz, Harvey, ed. 1995. *Ready Reference: American Indians.* Vol. 1. Pasadena, CA: Salem Press.

Sweat Lodges

Used both by itself as a ceremony and as a purification ritual in preparation for and/or following other ceremonies, the sweat lodge is known throughout Native America and has or had variants from tribes as geographically diverse as the Aztecs and Mayans to the Inuit. Today, it is most common among the Plains peoples, but it is practiced both in urban and reservation Native communities, often using the Lakota model of Inipi, one of the seven Lakota sacred rites. Sweats are also used by traditional healers in "doctoring" (Blackbear, 2004).

Sweat lodges are most often constructed using a rounded framework of bent willow saplings tied together and covered prior to using the sweat with blankets, tarps, or carpets, replacing the animal hides used historically, leaving a small area covered with a flap for a doorway. Most lodges, or sweats, as they are commonly called, are between six and twelve feet in diameter, though a six-foot sweat would be unusually small and some are even larger than twelve feet. A pit is dug in the center of the sweat, lined in some traditions with stones and in

Three Native American men pose outside a Crow village sweat lodge in Montana. (Bettmann/Corbis)

others left as bare earth. Lakota tradition incorporates the use of prayer or tobacco ties, small bundles left tied to the underside of the central portion. Some lodges have east and west doorways, while others have only east doorways.

In some traditions, only men sweat. In others, men and women sweat separately. In some contemporary circumstances, men and women sweat in the same lodge, often with men to one side and women to another, with the sweat lodge leader seated either in the honor seat, or hot seat directly across the way from the door or in the seat next to the door. Attire varies, with some tribes such as the Crow sweating only in segregated groups because of the lack of it, and others allowing shorts for men and T-shirts and shorts for women. In some tribes, such as the Blackfoot and Lakota, women wear long cloth dresses for sweats, whether they are integrated with the men or not.

Prior to the sweat, rocks, varying in number greatly from tribe to tribe and from one sweat lodge leader to another, are heated in a large pit outside the lodge near the door. After the lodge has been covered to ensure no light can enter once the door has been closed, participants line up, sometimes cedaring, also known as brushing off or smudging, with sage, sweetgrass, cedar, or a combination thereof prior to crawling into the lodge. Other sweat lodge leaders will have participants cedar once the rocks are brought in during all or the first of the four rounds of which a ceremony typically consists. Once the door is closed, water is poured on the hot rocks, creating steam and temperatures that can reach 200 degrees Fahrenheit. Prayers and songs are offered, and they help many to reach the state of mind necessary for withstanding these temperatures. The process is repeated for each round, between which the door is usually opened to allow the participants to recover briefly. Sweats are often followed by a meal and socializing. Before socializing and/or meals, some nations' sweats are followed by a dip in a cold stream or lake.

Though much scholarship has been done on sweats, particularly in regard to the details of the Lakota tradition, only those qualified to run a sweat through their ceremonial experiences should lead a ceremony. Eugene Blackbear, Sr., a highly regarded and experienced southern Cheyenne ceremonial leader, points out that several deaths have been inadvertently caused by unqualified and untrained Native and non-Native people running sweats in Texas and California. Run correctly by qualified sweat lodge priests, however, sweats have been one of the ceremonies most accessible to Natives isolated from their communities through urbanization, and they have proven helpful to those incarcerated and those in alcohol and drug rehabilitation. Though the sweat and other ceremonies were prohibited by the U.S. government for a time, the ceremony has persisted and offers what Mr. Blackbear considers to be one of the most accessible ways for young people to return to their traditions and seek help.

Kimberly Roppolo

See also American Indian Religious Freedom Act; Identity.

References and Further Reading

Blackbear, Eugene, Sr. 2004. Personal interview.
Hirschfelder, Arlene, and Paulette Molin, eds. 2000. *Encyclopedia of Native American Religions*, updated ed. New York: Facts on File.
Lyon, William S. 1996. *Encyclopedia of Native American Healing*. Santa Barbara, CA: ABC-CLIO.
Markowitz, Harvey, ed. 1995. *Ready Reference: American Indians*. Vol. 1. Pasadena, CA: Salem Press.

Thanksgiving Holiday, Origins

Ceremonies of thanksgiving for the bounty of nature are a common element in many Native American cultures. Feasts of gratitude and giving thanks have been a part of these cultures for several thousand years. In Lakota culture, a feast of thanksgiving is called a *Wopila;* in Navajo, it's *Hozhoni;* in Cherokee, it's *Selu i-tse-i;* and in Ho Chunk (Winnebago), it's *Wicawas warocu sto waroc.* Thanksgiving in many cases is a yearlong event, celebrated, for example, after the safe birth of a baby, a safe journey, or the construction of a new home.

Native peoples introduced their thanksgiving celebrations to English colonists near Plymouth Rock in 1621. A fall thanksgiving holiday, usually accompanied by feasting on traditional Native American foods (turkey, corn, yams, squashes, cranberry sauce, etc.) has been widely practiced since about 1800 by most non-Native people in the United States and Canada. President Abraham Lincoln's 1863 Thanksgiving Proclamation led directly to Thanksgiving being declared a national holiday in the United States. Canada declared an official Thanksgiving holiday in 1879, which is celebrated six weeks before its counterpart in the United States.

In this painting of the first Thanksgiving feast, members of the Wampanoag tribe are treated as honored guests by the Pilgrims of Plymouth Colony as they celebrate their survival in 1621. Though the image depicts a commonly held perception, the reality of the relationship between the Pilgrims and the Wampanoag was more complex and less congenial. (Library of Congress)

Thanksgiving is part of an annual cycle. Many Native American peoples celebrate a number of seasonal thanksgivings each year, of which general American culture has adopted only one. At each season, thanks are given for nature's provision of an economic base, whether it is corn, buffalo, or salmon. According to José Barreiro, editor of *Native Americas*, "The Thanksgiving tradition requires that human beings place themselves in a humble position relative to the natural, plant, and animal elements and to consider, in one mind, the contributions of these other species to our well-being and survival . . . Among the Iroquois and other traditionalists, the 'wish to be appreciated' is the fundamental shared perception—the first principle—of existence (Barreiro, 1992, 28).

Mohawk Nation Council Subchief Tom Porter offered a traditional thanksgiving prayer, "Words before all else," that is used for all of the Iroquois' nine thanksgiving celebrations:

[Before] our great-great grandfathers were first born and given the breath of life, our Creator at that time said the Earth will be your mother. And the Creator said to the deer, and the animals and the birds, the Earth will be your mother, too. And I have instructed the earth to give food and nourishment and medicine and quenching of thirst to all life. . . . We, the people, humbly thank you today, mother earth.

Our Creator spoke to the rivers and our creator made the rivers not just as water, but he made the rivers a living entity . . . You must have a reverence and great respect for your mother the earth. . . . You must each day say "thank you" [for] every gift that contributes to your life. If you follow this pattern, it will be like a circle with no end. Your life will be as everlasting as your children will carry on your flesh, your blood, and your heartbeat (Grinde and Johansen, 1995, 34–35).

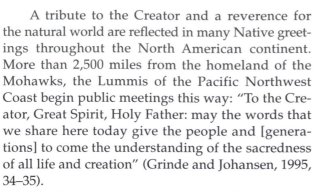

A tribute to the Creator and a reverence for the natural world are reflected in many Native greetings throughout the North American continent. More than 2,500 miles from the homeland of the Mohawks, the Lummis of the Pacific Northwest Coast begin public meetings this way: "To the Creator, Great Spirit, Holy Father: may the words that we share here today give the people and [generations] to come the understanding of the sacredness of all life and creation" (Grinde and Johansen, 1995, 34–35).

The domesticated fowl that would come to be called turkey in English was first eaten by Native Americans in the Valley of Mexico; the Aztecs introduced it to invading Spaniards. By the time the Pilgrims reached Plymouth Rock in 1620, turkey had been bred in Spain and exported to England for almost a century. The passengers of the Mayflower had some turkeys on board their ship, so when they prepared for the first Thanksgiving, the English immigrants were familiar with the wild turkeys that were hunted by Native peoples in eastern North America. Wild American turkeys seemed larger and better tasting to many colonists than their European-bred brethren. They were also easy to hunt. Thomas Morton said that a hunter in early seventeenth-century New England could shoot one turkey while others nearby looked on, "The one being killed, the other sit fast everthelesse . . ."

(Cronon, 1983, 23). By the late twentieth century, wild turkeys were scarce in much of New England.

Native Americans gathered the seeds of corn when it was a wild grass, and selected yields for the most productive, hardiest varieties. By the time European immigrants made landfall in North America, corn was more productive per acre than any cereal crop in the Old World. Corn, along with squashes, beans, fish, venison (deer meat), and various "fowls" (probably turkeys, ducks, and geese) were consumed during the first Anglo-American Thanksgiving. The abundance was welcomed by the Pilgrims, who had arrived in the New World with English seeds, most of which did not sprout in American soil. They nearly starved during their first winter. William Bradford, governor of the small colony, wrote in his diary that Squanto, who was able to teach the immigrants in their own language how to survive, was "a special instrument sent of God for [our] good" (Case, 2002).

Bruce E. Johansen

See also American Indian Contributions to the World; Environment and Pollution.

References and Further Reading

Barreiro, Jose. 1992. "The Search for Lessons," in Jose Barreiro, ed.
Indigenous Economics: Toward a Natural World Order. *Akwe:kon Journal* 9:2(Summer, 1992): 18–39.

Examples of Foods Native to the Americas

Asparagus
Avocados
Blueberries
Cassava (tapioca)
Chewing gum (Chicle)
Chocolate (Cacao)
Corn
Corn products, such as hominy, corn starch, and corn meal
Cranberries
Cucumbers
Currants
Green and yellow beans
Leeks
Maple sugar and syrup

Mint and mint flavorings
Peanuts and peanut products
Green and red peppers
Pecans
Popcorn
Potatoes and potato products
Sassafras tea
Squashes, including pumpkins, watermelon, yams, and cantaloupe
Sunflower seeds
Turkey
Vanilla
Venison
Wild rice

Case, Nancy Humphrey. 2002. "Gifts from the Indians: Native Americans Not Only Provided New Kinds of Food and Recreation; They May Have Given the Founding Fathers Ideas on How to Form a Government." *Christian Science Monitor,* November 26. Available at: http://www.csmonitor.com. Accessed January 13, 2007.

Cronon, William. 1983. *Changes in the Land: Indians, Colonists, and the Ecology of New England.* New York: Hill and Wang.

Grinde, Donald A., Jr., and Bruce E. Johansen. 1995. *Ecocide of Native America: Environmental Destruction of Indian Lands and Peoples.* Santa Fe, NM: Clear Light Publishers.

Totem Poles

The totem pole has always been associated with Native Americans, even though other indigenous peoples make totem poles as well, such as the Maori of New Zealand, the Ainu of Japan, and many African tribes, particularly in Madagascar. Although the reasons and educational context of different cultures contrast greatly in their development, the totem poles of the Native American people of the Northwest Pacific Coast, where many historians believe the first totem pole originated (before those in Alaska, British Columbia, Canada, and the United States), have very specific traditions related to the creation and use of totem poles, including the deeply institutional meanings behind each symbol presented. Commonly, totem poles are like a coat of arms or a great seal, a way that the pole's owner says, "This is who I am."

The use of totem poles in the Northwest predate European-Americans' arrival in the early eighteenth century. The antiquity of totem pole construction is not known because they were made of wood and decayed easily in the rain forest environment of the Northwest Coast. Thus, examples of totem poles carved before 1800 do not exist today.

To be authentic, a totem pole needs to be sanctioned, that is, it must pass certain tests. First, it must be made by a trained Northwest Pacific Native person or, in rare cases, by a non-Native apprentice who has been approved by a Northwest Pacific Coast band from Coastal British Columbia or Alaska. Second, it must be raised and blessed by Northwest Natives or elders who are part of the totem pole tradition.

House and totem pole of Tlingit Chief Sou-i-hat in Alaska. (Library of Congress)

Only after a meeting of elders, sponsors, and a master carver, is a totem pole carved, usually from a clear, red, mature cedar tree with few knots and imperfections. The master carver sculpts a small model of the design, after which the tree is debarked and tested for blemishes, and the wood is smoothed. The master carver begins at the bottom and works toward the top. Traditionally, as carvers work, they sing a variety of ceremonial songs, as the figures begin to emerge. The bottom is carefully detailed because the most important figures are at the bottom and observers see these figures close up. The story or theme of the totem pole is at the top.

Most totem poles range in size between three and seven feet in height, although, some much larger poles have been found. As the master carver cuts out the rough forms, he discusses the overall concept of the pole with each apprentice carver. Small poles usually take two to three months to complete, and large poles require eight to nine months.

The decision to paint the pole comes last. The carver chooses whether to paint it. Usually, the pole is painted with a series of family or clan crests or with figures representing mythic beings and then erected, usually outside a dwelling. The colors are usually bright and customarily made from animal oils, blood, salmon eggs, charcoal, graphite, and other natural and mineral dyes. The brushes were traditionally made from animal fur, and, according to history, the colors also help to tell a story associated with the various faces carved in the wood.

Many symbols and legends have been incorporated into the making of totem poles. Animals have been carved into totem poles because of Native peoples' belief that animals have spirits, as well as special talents. In many instances, Native Americans grew up hearing stories and fables about animals. The Raven, for example, is identified by its straight beak and is generally alleged to be a power trickster, curious and defiant, but likable. The Eagle has a downward, curved beak and is part of the Sky Realm. The Bear is often portrayed with large paws and sometimes a protruding tongue and as an animal that can transform into human forms. The Copper Woman, a god from Native American mythology, grants wealth to her favorites and is the friend of the Frog.

A totem pole can be very difficult to decode by outsiders, because each symbol has many stories and legends associated with it. The true and deep meaning of a pole may be known only to the family, the carver, and others familiar with its history. In addition, the totem pole has been surrounded by popular myths, such as that they were the objects of worship, they were used to ward off evil spirits and thus heeded the remains of dead ancestors, and they were always "serious" in nature. The poles were also sometimes used for public ridicule and called shame poles, erected to shame individuals or groups for unpaid debts. Shame poles today are rarely discussed, and their meanings have in many places been forgotten.

Totem poles of all types share a common graphic style with carved and painted containers, house fronts, canoes, masks, ceremonial dress, weapons, and armor. Most figures are two- or three-dimensional. This artistic system was developed by Northwest Coast Native peoples over many thousand of years, as evidenced by stone and bone artifacts uncovered in archaeological studies, which display clear examples of the same design.

The craft of making totem poles is slowly disappearing, and old totem poles are becoming scarce. Almost no nineteenth-century or early twentieth-century totem poles remain in their Native settings or in Native American ownership. Most have disappeared, and only a few have been preserved in museums or for international exhibits.

Totem poles have been called the most "iconic" of Native American arts and crafts, and the symbols presented on a given pole say a great deal about the family who owned it, a person, or the reason for creating it. These columns were once used as a form of communication and to relate narratives about Native American history, but they came to symbolize the belief of various Native American groups that forces of nature were their spiritual brethren. Fundamentally, totem poles were raised to represent the Native kinship systems, rights, prestige, accomplishments, sense of dignity, adventures, major events, and clan histories. A totem pole could be raised to honor a deceased elder, to show the name of an important person, to record an encounter with a spiritual being, or to symbolize generosity. Scholars have acknowledged that the meanings of the designs on totem poles are as varied as the cultures that produce them.

The popularity of carving poles increased with the growth of trade with non-Natives. As such, carvers began using the stronger, easier-to-use iron tools brought from overseas to increase their productivity. The art of totem pole carving almost died out between the 1880s and the 1950s because the potlatch was forbidden.

At one time, potlatch ceremonies celebrated important events, with guests coming from afar to feast and to be a part of communal rituals. The ceremonies included the celebration of a marriage or an accession at which the host distributed gifts according to each guest's rank or status. Over time the potlatch evolved to the representation of a family and clan in its place in the First Nation hierarchy. When the potlatch was again allowed, tribes resumed carving totem poles. Freshly carved totem poles are being erected up and down the Northwest Coast to create a renewed interest in their artistic production.

In later periods, totem poles were also raised to keep a record of the privileges of a person acquired within the society over a lifetime or to record an encounter with a supernatural being. Some poles embodied one-of-a-kind stories or unusual symbols. These stories or symbols are known in entirety only to the pole's owner and to the carver of the totem pole. The unusual meanings became known only if the pole's owner or carvers gave an account to a relative, granted interviews to academics, or left a written record. Otherwise, the hidden or special meanings were lost.

Today, totem poles are carved for both Natives and non-Natives. They have come to represent Northwest Pacific Natives and their traditions and pride, but also they are being made for "big money." Authentic, full-sized totem poles cost $25,000 to $100,000 each. Outsiders usually commission them to commemorate a great event or a coming of age, to symbolize a pact between nations, or to illustrate some sort of bond between Native people and a corporation or government entity that has commissioned the pole. The selling of totem poles is not new, nor is it a part of the old totem tradition. The practice has become a part of the modern tradition and is usually considered legitimate.

In recent years, Northwest Coast carvers have been commissioned to carve full-sized poles for many museums, corporations, and private collectors worldwide. Today, Native Americans throughout the Northwest Coast are carrying on their traditions by raising new poles to honor their deceased relatives, to celebrate their family histories, and to make totem poles for anyone who can afford them.

Fred Lindsey

See also Potlatch.
References and Further Reading
Barbeau, Marius. 1944. "Totemism: A Modern Growth on the North Pacific Coast." *Journal of American Folklore*, 57, no. 233 (March): 51–58.
Malin, Edward. 1986. *Totem Poles of the Pacific Northwest*. Portland, OR: Timber Press.
Stewart, Hillary. 1993. *Looking at Totem Poles*. Seattle: University of Washington Press.

Wakashan Languages

The Wakashan language family consists of seven languages that are spoken on the Northwest Pacific Coast. Specifically, the Wakashan languages are spoken in Canada on Vancouver Island and on the coastal mainland of the British Columbia coast, east and north of Vancouver Island. One language in the family, Makah, is spoken in the United States, on the Olympic Peninsula. Most of the languages in the Wakashan family are endangered.

The Wakashan language family is divided into northern and southern groups, which are quite different from each other. Languages within the two branches, however, are very closely related. The Northern Wakashan branch includes Haisla-Henaksiala, Heiltsuk (or Bella Bella), Oowekyala (or Oowekeeno), and Kwakw'ala (formerly called Kwakiutl). Southern Wakashan includes the languages Nuuchalnulth (formerly known as Nootka), Ditidaht (or Nitinaht), and the Makah language (or Qwiqwidicciat). The Southern Wakashan group is sometimes referred to as the Nootkan branch, and the Northern Wakashan is sometimes referred to as the Kwakiutlan branch.

"Kwakuitl" is the name of a particular village in Fort Rupert, British Columbia, whose name has long been used as a reference for all the distinct groups of Kwakw'ala-speaking people. Collectively, those who come from Kwakw'ala-speaking people refer to themselves as Kwakwaka'wakw. Anthropologist and linguist Franz Boas wrote extensively on the Kwakwaka'wakw people, their language and their potlatch ceremonies.

The most northern of the Northern Wakaskan languages is Haisla, which is traditionally spoken at the head of Douglas Inlet, near Kitimat. The Hieltsuk language, spoken around Bella Bella, is closely related to the Oowekyala language, which is traditionally spoken around Rivers Inlet. The Kwakwaka'wakw traditional territories include the northern half of Vancouver Island and extend east and north on the mainland of British Columbia. There are two main dialects recognized within the Kwakwaka'wakw group, one along the outer coast of the traditional territories, from Cape Cook to Smith Sound, and the other inner dialect within the Queen Charlotte and Johnson Straits.

The most prominent language in the southern branch is the Nuuchalnulth, which encompasses many different groups and dialects, extending along the northwestern coast of Vancouver Island from Quatsino Sound to Barkely Sound. Dialect groups include the Kyuquot, Ehattisaht, Nuchatlaht, Mowachaht, Hesquiat, Ahousaht, and Tla.o.qui.aht. Nuuchalnulth is the best documented of the southern group as well. The languages of Ditidaht and Makah are distinct, but closely related to Nuuchalnulth. In the past, reference was made to the West Coast Language, which included Nuuchalnulth, Ditidaht, and Makah, but the three languages are not mutually intelligible. Ditidaht territory is near the southern tip of Vancouver Island and surrounds Nitinaht Lake. The Makah language is traditionally spoken across the Strait of Juan de Fuca in Washington State, at the northwest tip of the Olympic Peninsula.

Some of this language family's distinctive features include extensive suffixing, infixing, and reduplication. Wakashan languages also are known for their large number of consonants, many of which do not exist in English. The languages are considered polysynthetic, and there is debate over whether a difference exists between noun and verb roots in the language, apart from their use and inflection. Some of the languages in this family also are notable for specific ceremonial styles and baby language.

Makah and Ditidaht are distinct within the family due to a specific sound change. Like neighboring but unrelated languages, and unlike the rest of the Wakashan languages, they have no nasal consonants. This characteristic is extremely rare cross-linguistically. This current lack of nasal consonants explains why Ditidaht is called Nitinaht by other groups on Vancouver Island.

It is thought that Vancouver Island is the homeland of the Wakashan-speaking peoples and that their presence precedes that of Salish-speaking peoples on the island.

Aliki Marinakis

See also Language and Language Renewal; Potlatch.
References and Further Readings
Foster, Micheal K. 1996. "Language and the Culture History of North America." In *Handbook of North American Indians*. Vol. 17: *Languages*. Edited by Ives Goddard, 64–110. General editor, William C. Sturtevant. Washington, DC: Smithsonian Institution.

Jacobsen, William. 1979. "Wakashan Comparative Studies." In *The Languages of Native America: A Historical and Comparative Assessment*. Edited by Lyle Campbell and Marianne Mithun, 766–791. Austin: University of Texas Press.

Mithun, Marianne. 1999. *The Languages of North America*. Cambridge, UK: Cambridge University Press.

Thompson, Laurence, and M. Dale Kinkade. 1990. "Languages." In *Handbook of North American Indians*. Vol. 7. Edited by Wayne Suttles, 30–52. General editor, William C. Sturtevant. Washington, DC: Smithsonian Institution.

Wampum

Contrary to general interpretations, wampum was not money, but rather a means of remembering solemn agreements and treaties. The first wampum—cylindrical shell beads—was made over a thousand years ago. Iroquois elders in upstate New York still recite stories and sing songs of the Great Peacemaker who first created wampum to heal a grieving man. Today, the Condolence Ceremony survives as an essential part of Iroquois cultural tradition and religion. The old wampum belts have been judged objects of cultural patrimony, national treasures so important they cannot be separated from their society. Several wampum belts have been returned in compliance with the Native American Grave Protection and Repatriation Act (NAGPRA, 1999).

The origins of wampum are woven into the life story of the Great Peacemaker, who inspired the unification of the Iroquois Confederacy long before the coming of Europeans. Although the young Peacemaker exhibited remarkable talents, he was born with one handicap: He struggled with a speech impediment. When he departed on his mission in life, he encountered a man who was sobbing beside a lake. He stopped and inquired into the source of the man's grief. He said that his name was Hiawenthe (not the Hiawatha of Longfellow's famous poem). He was mourning the death of his wife and seven daughters. An evil wizard, he said, had tried "to have his way" with Hiawenthe's wife and daughters. As each of them refused, the wizard murdered them one by one (Shenandoah, 1979).

To heal Hiawenthe's broken heart, the Great Peacemaker created a Condolence Ceremony. He gathered clam shells along the water's edge and formed seven strings of cylindrical tubes called wampum beads. He designed patterns by stringing different sequences of white and purple beads from the purplish-blue base of quahoag clam shells. The Great Peacemaker raised the first string and said, "Now, Hiawenthe, with this string I take the softest skin of the fawn and wipe the tears from your eyes. With this next string, I take the lightest feather that falls from the heavens and open your ears, so that you may hear clearly once again" (Swamp, 1981).

After four more verses, the Peacemaker said on the seventh string, "Now I take those medicine waters, those soothing cool medicine waters, and I open your throat, so that you might speak clearly once again" (Swamp, 1981). Hiawenthe was healed, and he became the spokesperson of the Great Peacemaker. They inspired the formation of the Iroquois Confederacy by uniting the original five nations: the Onondagas, Mohawks, Senecas, Oneidas, and Cayugas (later joined by a sixth nation, the Tuscaroras).

So that they might never forget the Great Law of Peace, the Iroquois wove a special wampum sash called the Hiawatha Belt. Woven into the center of the design is the Tree of Peace, a great white pine planted atop the weapons of war. This act has been recognized in the United Nations as the "oldest effort for disarmament in world history." The Great Tree also symbolizes the center of their council fire, the Onondaga nation. Four squares flank the Tree of Peace symbol, and the tree and the squares together represent the original five nations. The Great Peacemaker explained, "Each nation is like an arrow. Alone it is easily broken. But if five arrows, like the confederation of five nations, are bound together, they cannot be broken. There is strength in unity." The Hiawatha Belt exists today (Swamp, 1981).

With the coming of Europeans, early colonial records are filled with entries related to wampum diplomacy. Strings and belts of wampum were exchanged at meetings between the Europeans and the Iroquois, as well as among other Iroquoian- and Algonquian-speaking nations along the Atlantic seaboard and inland to the Ohio River Valley. Indian orators were observed breathing their solemn commitments into strings and belts of wampum "so our promises might never be forgotten."

One of the first agreements between the Iroquois and the Euro-American settlers was called the Kahswenhtha, or Two Row Wampum. The design features two parallel horizontal bands with purple backgrounds stretching the length of the belt. An Iroquois chief explained the symbolism: "The white

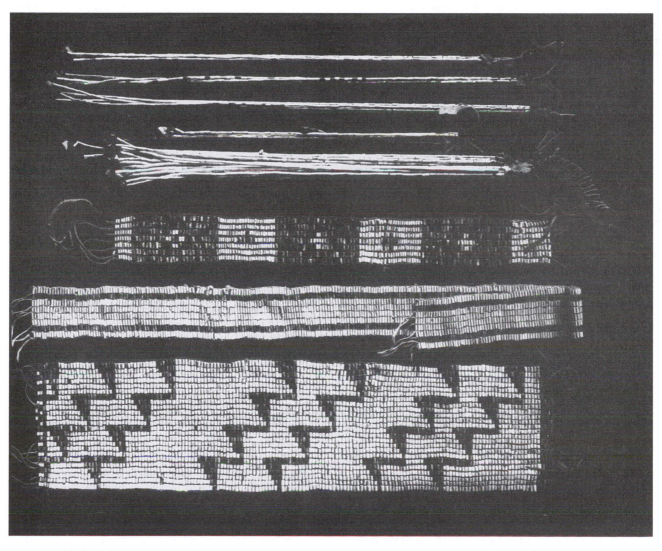

Wampum (shell beads) were used as currency, jewelry, and as bonds between nations by Native Americans. (National Archives and Records Administration)

bands represent our agreement never to try to convert one another, but rather to accept a promise that our two cultures will go together into the future side-by-side as equals" (Shenandoah, Swamp, Thomas, and Lyons 1977–1981).

A contemporary Mohawk chief further explained, "Imagine that the two white bands are like two canoes flowing down the river of life. In the Indian canoe we have placed our languages, cultures, and ways of life. The European canoe holds their languages, cultures, and ways of life. No man can go down the river of life with one foot in two canoes. The result would be disaster." This is why the Iroquois resisted assimilation policies. When government officials attempted to force Iroquois children to attend boarding schools, to stop speaking their languages, and to stop practicing their religious ceremonies, Iroquois chiefs were quick to point out that such policies were a violation of the Two Row Wampum Belt (Swamp, 1981).

A wampum belt dated 1610 has been preserved at the Vatican archives in Italy. It represents a "Concordat between the Holy See and the Mi'kmaq Nation" of Nova Scotia, Canada. By this wampum belt, diplomatic relations were established and maintained. In 2010, the Mi'kmaq nation and the Vatican will celebrate the 400th anniversary of their agreement, which remains in effect to this day.

A 1710 wampum belt was depicted in a painting of Tyanoga, whom the English called King Hendrick, a Wolf Clan leader of the Mohawk nation. The belt displays thirteen crosses that may relate to the Iroquois alliance with the English in the French and Indian War. Hendrick was one of four chiefs who traveled to London on a diplomatic mission. Queen Anne arranged to have their portraits painted, and Hendrick is portrayed holding the thirteen-cross wampum belt.

Just seventy-six days before the signing of the Declaration of Independence, John Hancock and the Continental Congress instructed Indian agent George Morgan to take a great wampum Peace Belt to the "warriors and sachems of the Western Indian nations." With the birth of the United States in 1776, this wampum belt, featuring a thirteen-diamond design symbolizing the thirteen original states, represented the original promises made by U.S. officials to Indian nations. The first promise was that the United States would never force Indian people to get involved in the "white man's wars." The second was that Indian tribes would be recognized as nations and their national lands would be respected. Many other promises were made "for as long as the sun shines and the waters flow." Congress ratified over three hundred and fifty Indian treaties, many of them sanctified with wampum belts. While many of the wampum belts survived, most of the treaties were broken in violation of Article 4 in the U.S. Constitution that states, "Treaties are to be judged the supreme law of the land" (Schaaf, 1990, 161).

In 1787, Thomas Jefferson penned the Northwest Ordinance and stated in part: "The utmost good faith shall always be observed toward the Indians; their land and property shall never be taken from them without their consent; and in their property rights and liberty they never shall be invaded or disturbed . . ." (Jefferson, 1787).

Seven years later in 1794, the famous Covenant Chain Wampum Belt was made to remember the Canandaigua (or Pickering) Treaty between the United States and the Iroquois Confederacy. The design on this wampum belt portrays thirteen men representing the thirteen United States. In the center stands the Grand Council, a phrase borrowed from the Iroquois to describe the U.S. Congress (Jemison, Schein, and Powless, 2000).

During the bicentennial of the Constitution in 1987, the U.S. Senate unanimously passed Senate Concurrent Resolution 76 that essentially renewed the Covenant Chain wampum belt. The Senators acknowledged in part:

> Whereas, the Confederation of the original thirteen colonies into one Republic was explicitly modeled upon the Iroquois Confederacy as were many of the democratic principles which were incorporated into the Constitution itself; and,
>
> Whereas, since the formation of the United States, the Congress has recognized the sovereign status of Indian Tribes . . .
>
> The Congress also hereby reaffirms the constitutionally recognized government-to-government relationship with Indian Tribes which has historically been the cornerstone of this nation's official Indian policy . . . (*Congressional Record–Senate*, 1987).

Gregory Schaaf

See also Haudenosaunee Confederacy, Political System; Hendrick; Hiawatha; Northwest Ordinance; Treaty Diplomacy, with Summary of Selected Treaties.

References and Further Reading

Congressional Record–Senate. 1987. "Senate Concurrent Resolution 76, To Acknowledge the Contribution of the Iroquois Confederacy, 100th Congress, 1st Session, 133 Congressional Record S 12214." September 16. Washington, DC: United States Government Printing Office.

Fenton, William. 1998, *The Great Law and the Longhouse: A Political History of the Iroquois Confederacy.* Norman: University of Oklahoma Press.

Grinde, Donald, and Bruce Johansen. 1991. *Exemplar of Liberty: Native America and the Evolution of Democracy.* Berkeley: University of California Press.

Jefferson, Thomas. "Ordinance for the Government of the Northwest Territory." United States Congress, July 13, 1787. National Archives, M247, r72, i59, b. I, pp. 229–230.

Jemison, G. Peter, Anna M. Schein, and Irving Powless, Jr., eds. 2000. *Treaty of Canandaigua 1794: 200 Years of Treaty Relations Between the Iroquois Confederacy and the United States.* Santa Fe, NM: Clear Light Publishers.

Johansen, Bruce. 1987. *Forgotten Founders: How the American Indian Helped Shape Democracy.* Boston: Harvard Common Press.

Native American Graves Protection and Repatriation Act (NAGPRA). 1999. 25 USC, Chapter 32, 3001 et seq., Native American Graves Protection and Repatriation Act, effective July 22.

Schaaf, Gregory. 1990, *Wampum Belts & Peace Trees.* Golden, CO: Fulcrum Publishing.

Shenandoah, Leon. 1979. Personal communication.

Shenandoah, Leon, Chief Jake Swamp, Chief Jake Thomas, and Faithkeeper Oren Lyons. 1977–1981. Personal communications.

Snow, Dean. 1996. *The Iroquois.* Malden, MA: Blackwell Publishing.

Swamp, Jake. 1981. Personal communication regarding the Iroquois Condolence Ceremony.

Tehanetorens, Ray Fadden. 1999. *Wampum Belts of the Iroquois.* Summertown, TN: Book Publishing Company.

Wallace, Paul. [1946] 1986. *The White Roots of Peace.* Philadelphia, PA: Chancy Press.

Warfare, Intertribal

Intertribal warfare consists of the conflicts between various Native American groups, as opposed to warfare between Native Americans and Europeans. With the notable exception of rich oral historical accounts, a good deal of the information on this topic remains conjectural, due primarily to the dearth of evidence left by indigenous sources in many instances and by the fact that the arrival of non-Natives in any region altered the manner and the purpose of intertribal conflicts. Native groups fought for many reasons. Moreover, while there was not one overarching form of warfare among all American aboriginal cultures, there were certain commonalities. These encompassed, but were not limited to, the tactics employed and the desired ends of most conflicts. A full treatment is beyond the scope of the present article, so all that will be presented here is a general overview.

Among the reasons various Native American tribes fought against one another were security, revenge, honor, pride, and the capture of booty. Making war for security's sake could be either defensive or preemptive. Revenge entailed the counterattack of the aggrieved tribe and could spawn a whole cycle of violence as in the case of the Mourning War among the Iroquois. In this type of warfare, attacks and reprisals were made to fill the gap made by losses in the community. Likewise, captives taken in raids could be adopted into the tribe as a means to fill the gap as well. Numerous Native American groups made war on one another as a means for their younger warriors to gain honor and to prove their abilities as leaders. The acquisition of honor worked to complement the gain of pride. Warriors might take the scalps of those they had killed in battle, both for spiritual purposes and as a token of their martial abilities. Likewise, booty, captured on a raid, both provided material support for the tribe and demonstrated the prowess of the warrior who had taken it. Wars could also be fought over territory and resources, as was the case in the Beaver Wars. Tokens of martial ability stand as one of the commonalities of intertribal warfare.

Tactics were an area in which there was a great deal of commonality among Native American societies. The basic tactical unit in intertribal warfare was the raiding party or war party, although there is evidence of massed armies as well. The main differentiating factor is size. Raiding parties were small groups that went out to settle petty issues between individuals of different tribes. War parties comprised at least the entire force of a single tribe and often its allies.

A raiding party often, but not always, consisted of the members of a tribe who voluntarily chose to follow a warrior when he sent out the call to go to war. The call to arms could be issued in many ways, including striking the war post with a war club or tomahawk. The warrior initiating the call could do

Painting of battle between Sioux and Blackfeet. (Library of Congress)

so simply by placing his weapons at a prominent space in the village, facing in the direction of the chosen enemy. If the call was sent out to a number of tribes, such as in the Iroquois Confederacy and its affiliated tribes, war belts were used to transmit the appropriate message.

Actual membership in a raiding party could range anywhere from ten to 100 warriors. The leader was sometimes referred to as a war chief, though not all raiding parties required the leadership of such a prominent figure. Once the party assembled, it moved with as much stealth as possible, traveling only at night, resting during the daylight hours, with guards posted, and avoiding the use of fire in camp. The members marched single file to avoid disclosing numbers. Likewise, the last men in line would try to cover the tracks of the group.

Once in the neighborhood of their designated target, the members of the attacking force usually attempted to bring on hostilities at dawn. The party chose this time in the hope that the target could be taken unawares and would therefore be more vulnerable. Weather conditions, such as fog, that could conceal and disorient were advantageous to attackers for many of the same reasons. Some historians have suggested that catching opponents off guard and cutting

them off from the support of the rest of their community were important as well. In achieving surprise in this manner, the attackers demonstrated their ability as cunning warriors, which added a definite morale component to their physical aggression. Surprise held a concrete value because many Native American groups utilized some form of fortification, and thus it was important to catch opponents before they could reach the safety of their defensive works. Ambush and guerilla warfare comprised other common tactics of raiding parties. Direct, head-on combat was something various groups sought to avoid, because it lacked the psychological advantage of stealth and therefore was seen as actually denigrating the capabilities of the aggressors.

For the Iroquois and other groups, the goal was to kill the other warriors and take their scalps. Women and children were taken captive and sometimes adopted in accordance with their culture's practice of mourning war. Still, warfare between different Native American groups could be quite lethal. In some cases, the goal stood as the complete destruction of an opponent, to such a degree that it could be considered akin to an act of genocide. Such was the case between the Creeks and the Tuscaroras, as well as between the Sioux and the Illini.

By the same token, if the element of surprise were lost, or if an attack met with stiffer resistance than expected, retreat, either in stages or by head-long flight, stood as an acceptable practice. In a staged retreat, some members would break off their attack, fall back, and take up a new position in the rear. They would then put down a covering fire as their brethren to the front followed suit.

The preferred weapons utilized in intertribal warfare included the war club, the bow and arrow, and the spear. Projectile weapons were favored in the initial attack. Once foes joined combat at close range, warriors often preferred clubs and axes. While guns were not part of intertribal warfare originally, as they became available to the different tribes through the growing trade in firearms, they were utilized as well.

Intertribal warfare both embraced a complex web of motivations and possessed certain commonalities. The motivations varied from the acquisition of honor and resources to the fulfillment of a blood debt incurred by one group on another. Tactically, the aggressor placed a great deal of stock in achieving some form of surprise. These tactics were later adapted, to varying degrees, by the various Europeans who made contact with the Native Americans of North America. A hybrid form of warfare thus evolved. This evolution is exemplified by the incorporation of firearms into intertribal warfare as well as the Europeans' adopting the practice of scalping and guerilla warfare. Intertribal warfare could inflict proportionally very high casualties, even to the point of destroying an opponent's ability to live as an independent people.

James R. McIntyre

See also Beaver Wars; Fur Trade; Scalping in the Colonial Period; Wampum.

Suggestions for Further Reading

Ferling, John. 1980. *A Wilderness of Miseries: War and Warriors in Early America*. Westport, CT: Greenwood Press.

Gleach, Frederick W. 1997. *Powhatan's World and Colonial Virginia: A Conflict of Cultures*. Lincoln: University of Nebraska Press.

Grenier, John. 2005. *The First Way of War: American War Making on the Frontier*. Cambridge, UK: Cambridge University Press.

Hunt, George T. 1940. *The Wars of the Iroquois: A Study in Intertribal Trade Relations*. Madison: University of Wisconsin Press.

Lee, Wayne E. 2004. "Fortify, Fight, or Flee: Tuscarora and Cherokee Defensive Warfare and Military Culture Adaptation." *Journal of Military History* 86 (July): 713–770.

Malone, Patrick M. 1991. *The Skulking Way of War: Technology and Tactics Among the New England Indians*. New York: Madison Books.

Richter, Daniel K. 1938. "War and Culture: The Iroquois Experience." *William and Mary Quarterly* 3d ser., 40 (1983): 528–559.

Weaving

The textile arts of Native American weaving include blankets, rugs, clothing, bags, and other similar art forms. Weaving involves the manipulation of strands of fibers to create a smooth surface. The purposes of weaving include warmth, dress, and other utilitarian functions. The finest weavings are appreciated and collected as fine art. The world auction record for a single textile weaving is $535,000, the price paid at Sotheby's for a midnineteenth-century Navajo First Phase Chief's Blanket.

According to the Navajo, the world was woven into existence by a female deity named Spider Woman. Many traditional weavers pray to this female spirit. Because the weavers put their whole soul or spirit into the textile, some weave a little line to the edge of the textile called a Spirit Release Line. A vast literature exists on their legends and stories that span the centuries.

Archaeologists have found fragments of weavings that have been scientifically dated as many thousands of years old. The exact date of the earliest known weavings in the western hemisphere is still being debated, but may be over 10,000 years ago. Weavings were made long before the advent of looms.

Native weaving materials included plant and animal fibers. Some materials were collected and used in their natural forms, but most were made stronger by spinning multiple fibers together like yarn. Designs were created by dying the yarns different colors or by using two or more different fibers to make patterns. Relief designs also were created by mathematically calculating the sequences of fibers to go over or under, as in twill plaiting. Some very sophisticated ancient weavings preserved in caves have survived nearly intact. After the advent of pottery, some weavings were kept sealed and found in nearly perfect condition.

The longest, continuous weaving traditions have survived in certain cultures throughout the western hemisphere. In North America, the Hopi, Zuni, and Rio Grande pueblos maintain a 2,000-year-old

This photograph shows a Navajo rug weaver. Najavos are well-known for their weaving skills. (National Archives and Records Administration)

weaving tradition. Before the coming of the Spanish conquistadors, Pueblo weavers clothed hundreds of thousands of people in the American Southwest. Their favorite fiber was cotton grown from seeds developed in southern Mexico. Traditional ceremonies accompanied the planting, tending, harvesting, processing, and weaving of cotton.

One type of ceremonial sash belt, woven in a technique called float warp, is created from Taos Pueblo in the north, through Mexico and Central America, to the tip of South America. Ancient weaving traditions have survived, especially among the Zapotec in Mexico, the Mayans in Guatemala, and the Andean weavers of Peru and Bolivia, where some of the most sophisticated hand weavings in the world were developed. The thread count on the finest wearing blankets tops 200 stitches per inch. Their pictorial designs are narrative scenes from legends and tribal traditions that help illustrate rich and varied cultural histories.

Great textiles sometimes emerged even during times of great turmoil or revolution. In the 1680s, when the Pueblo Indians of the American Southwest were fighting for their freedom and independence from the Spanish, a group of Navajo women married Pueblo men, who taught their wives to weave. Thus the Navajo textile tradition was given a tremendous boost, because the ancient techniques spread quickly through matrilineal family lines. Eventually over 10,000 Navajo weavers, mostly women, developed dynamic weavings on a vertical loom using wool from Spanish Churro or Moreno sheep.

During the nineteenth and twentieth centuries, perhaps no other tribe promoted textiles as fine art more than the Navajo. From the 1850s, a First Phase Chief's Blanket was one of the most highly valued items. Woven so fine it would repel water, this Navajo wearing blanket became increasingly more complex in color and design. Eye-dazzling serrated diamonds and zigzag patterns became popular. Their yarns were dyed of indigo blue, and reds of cochineal.

From 1880 to 1920, the so-called Transitional Period of Navajo textiles reflected the changing times for Indians, from freedom to reservation life. The weaves became looser, except for tapestries woven of fine Germantown yarn. During the first half of the twentieth century, regional styles developed named after the local trading posts. Today, Two Grey Hills tapestries are woven over eighty stitches per inch, as fine as the best contemporary weavings in Central and South America.

Gregory Schaaf

See also Archaeology and the First Americans;
  Paleo-Indians; Trade.

References and Further Reading
Schaaf, Gregory. 2002. *American Indian Textiles: 2,000 Artist Biographies*. Santa Fe, NM: CIAC Press.
Whitaker, Kathleen. 2002, *Southwest Textiles: Weavings of the Pueblo and Navajo*. Seattle: University of Washington Press.
Winter, Mark. 2004, *Dances with Wool*. Santa Fe, NM: Toadlena Trading Post.

Worldviews and Values

American Indians enjoy a rich diversity of worldviews, values, philosophies, spiritual concepts, mythologies, and ceremonies, both as individuals and as nations. However, American Indian cultures had and have certain characteristic ideas in common. Indeed, the recognition of an indigenous worldview as a philosophical system is gaining momentum in academic circles, though still in its infancy as a field outside the boundaries of traditional anthropology or New Age literature. Such generalized values and ways of experiencing the world offer positive alternatives to contemporary Western assumptions. Unlike the myth of the noble savage, the following concepts deserve serious study as an opportunity to restore the health and balance in all living systems.

Perhaps the most obvious consideration that runs through all or most indigenous worldviews is a strong sense of relatedness. The idea of interconnectedness between animals, rocks, rivers, people, and all things informs many of the values and ways of thinking and being in the world that are typical to American Indian people. This sense of relatedness naturally leads to avoiding dualistic thinking, that is, looking at the world as a detached observer. It emphasizes cooperative engagement over competi-

tion. It focuses on living in harmony with nature rather than attempting to conquer it. It underlies the basic American Indian regard for reciprocity as a cornerstone for decision making and relationships of all sorts.

Dovetailing also with the concept of relatedness are four other typically American Indian values: the acceptance of mystery, the honoring of alternative paths, an authentic sense of humility, and a belief that the highest form of courage is in the expression of generosity. These four concepts underscore American Indian spirituality, which might be defined as a life that gives sacred significance to all things. Perhaps an understanding that everything is related and significant, coupled with a learning style that emphasizes keen observation, has led to cultures that maintained a close relationship with the earth toward realizing that humans cannot possibly have all of the answers to the complex mysteries regarding life.

Although indigenous cultures are unique in their widespread adherence to such realizations about life, philosophers from all cultures have expressed similar ideas and values throughout time. Interestingly, however, many of these seem to refer to their own indigenous traditions.

A prime example is found in the worldview of the father of India's independence, Mahatma Gandhi, which parallels American Indian thinking. Gandhi often referred to the "primordial traditions" of India in describing the worldview that he called *swaraj* and that might be interpreted as fearless action and selfless suffering. *Swaraj* included selfless action in behalf of community welfare; complete individual freedom to seek truth in light of a deep understanding of relatedness with others; a nonanthropocentric understanding of self in relation to nature; sustainable lifestyles; shared wealth; fearlessness in pursuit of truth; and an understanding of pain and suffering in terms of a healing, integrative force for social welfare.

When such ideas are organic manifestations of the lived life of an entire community, rather than idealism advocated or practiced by a few individuals, a number of perspectives tend to emerge as behaviors in a culture that seem to oppose Western assumptions and behaviors. For example, taking care of others (not just one's self) guides all action. Recognizing the present becomes more important than preparing for the future, as long as actions do not create harm for "the seventh generation." Place becomes more important than time. Age is honored for its wisdom, and, balanced with the virtues of youth and beauty, patience is more easily accommodated than aggression. Listening becomes more prevalent than speaking up. Giving and sharing are a priority over taking and saving. Intuition is trusted as much or more than logic. Humility and modesty overshadow arrogance and ego. Aesthetics and creativity outshine the idea of a work ethic. And women are seen as equal to or even superior in their ability to contribute to society than are men.

Finally, the indigenous worldview includes an approach to conflict resolution that may explain why American Indian people were and are less warlike than those with more Indo-European worldviews. Peace making is rooted in transformative theory rather than in retributive, hierarchical, adversarial, punitive, or codified assumptions. Responsibility is emphasized over rights, and, when parties reach consensus for restoration and accountability, opposing parties are seen as being back in good relationship with one another, seeing the world more with their hearts than with their heads.

Four Arrows–Don Trent Jacobs

See also Environment and Pollution; Warfare, Intertribal.

References and Further Reading

Cajeti, Gregory. 1993. *Look to the Mountain*. Durango, CO: Kaveti Press.

Grim, John, ed. 2001. *Indigenous Traditions and Ecology: The Interbeing of Cosmology and Community*, Cambridge, MA: Belknap/Harvard University Press, 2001.

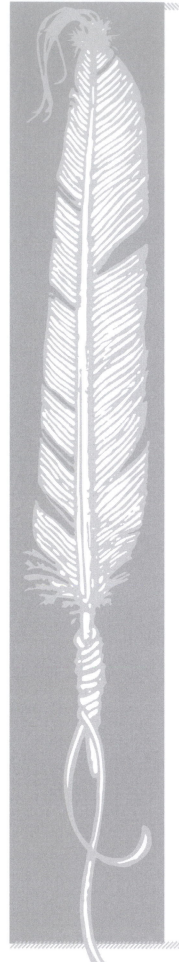

Alaska Native Claims Settlement Act

Alaska Natives, including the Aleut, Athabaskan, Inupiat, and Yup'ik Eskimos and the Tlingit and Haida Indians, settled their aboriginal land claims with the United States in 1971 under the Alaska Native Claims Settlement Act (ANCSA) Public Law 92–203. Unlike the Native American tribes of the lower forty-eight states, who entered into treaties with the federal government and whose lands are held under trust by the federal government, Alaska Natives pursued a legislative settlement that required them to establish profit-making corporations and to hold their land under fee simple title. Congress and the Richard M. Nixon Administration saw ANCSA, with its major features of land, money, and corporations, as a means to assimilate Alaska Natives into the larger society. Natives, on the other hand, largely viewed ANCSA as a vehicle of economic self-determination.

The 1867 Treaty of Cession, under which Russia sold Alaska to the United States, held that "uncivilized tribes" were to be subject to the same laws as other American Indians. In subsequent legislation, the federal government recognized the use and occupancy land rights of Alaska Natives first in the Organic Act of 1884 and then in the Alaska Statehood Act of 1958, which allowed the state to select 103 million acres of land. Although the statehood act stipulated that Native lands were exempt from selection, the state began to select lands used and occupied by Native villages and to claim royalties from federal oil and gas leases on Native lands. Alaska Natives began to organize regional associations to protect their land ownership. As Natives protested the actions of the state, Secretary of the Interior Stewart Udall ordered the suspension of federal oil and gas lease sales and adopted a "land freeze" on the disposition of all federal lands in Alaska. The freeze served to protect Native land rights and to block the construction of the 800-mile oil pipeline from Prudhoe Bay in the north to Prince William Sound.

With political pressure mounting to settle the land claims and to develop the oil resources of Alaska, Natives seized the opportunity to lobby Congress for a land claims settlement. Led by the Alaska Federation of Natives (AFN), they were successful in securing legislation that has been heralded as the largest aboriginal land settlement. It also diverged dramatically from earlier historic land models with Indian tribes. However, in the haste to secure a settlement and with the focus on the size of the land settlement, structural issues that should have been analyzed were overlooked and ignored in the legislation.

Under ANCSA, Alaska Natives received a total of 44 million acres of land including surface and subsurface rights. These lands were to be conveyed to twelve regional corporations and 203 village corporations that were organized under the laws of the state of Alaska. ANCSA also authorized the payment of $962 million for the extinguishment of all aboriginal claims.

Village corporations were entitled to receive 22 million acres of land, which were divided on a population basis. The regional corporations received full title to 16 million acres of land and the subsurface estate in the 22 million acres patented to the villages. The regional corporation land was divided among the twelve regional corporations on the basis of the total acreage in each region rather than population. The southeast Alaska Indian communities were allowed to receive only a single township or 23,040 acres. They had received a $7.5 million award in 1968 under the Tlingit and Haida judicial settlement for the federal withdrawals of 20 million acres of lands in southeast Alaska.

Two million acres were set aside for other purposes, including cemeteries and historical sites. Four Native urban corporations, which had formerly been historic Native communities but were predominantly non-Native cities in the 1970s, were allowed to select land from the 2 million acres. Native communities with populations less than twenty-five residents received land from this acreage. The total acreage for allotments, which had been filed before the passage of the Act, was also deducted from this entitlement.

Four million acres, which had been held by five reserves as trust lands by the federal government, were revoked by ANCSA. The Natives of these reserves formed corporations to hold their lands, including both surface and subsurface lands under fee simple title, but they were not entitled to the monetary benefits under ANCSA. Ironically, the only remaining reservation in Alaska was for the Tsimshian Indians, who had emigrated from Canada. They were granted the Annette Island reservation in southeast Alaska by Congress in 1891.

Natives who were not permanent residents of Alaska organized a thirteenth regional corporation. It received its pro rata share of the financial settlement, but it did not receive land, nor was it entitled to receive revenues from mineral or timber development of the regional corporations.

The Secretary of the Interior was authorized to prepare a roll of all Natives who were of one-quarter or more Alaska Native, who were born on or before the date of enactment of ANCSA, and who were living on or before December 18, 1971. The secretary's roll was to also include the village and region of each enrollee. Both regional and village corporations issued one hundred shares of stock to each Native enrolled in their region and village. Some Natives were enrolled as at-large shareholders, that is, shareholders only in regional corporations because their permanent homes were away from villages that were certified to participate in ANCSA. The number of shareholding Alaska Natives enrolled to Native corporations totaled more than 78,000.

The hunting and fishing rights of Alaska Natives were extinguished under ANCSA. However, Congress adopted a subsistence priority for rural Alaskans in 1980 within the Alaska National Interest Land Conservation Act.

ANCSA is unique in many aspects and one provision is the antithesis of profit-making corporations. Under Section 7(i), regional corporations are required to distribute 70 percent of their profits from mineral and timber development to other regional corporations. A minimum of 50 percent of 7(i) revenues must be distributed to village corporations and at-large shareholders. The intent of Congress was to equalize the resource revenues between regions that were resource rich and those that were resource poor.

Initially, Natives had assumed that their tribes, clans, or communities would be the recipient of lands, but by 1968 corporations were proposed as the vehicle to implement the land settlement. Many Natives had had experience with the ineptness of the Bureau of Indian Affairs and did not want to have their land held under trust and subject to the control of the federal government. The idea of Native control of their lands had gained prominence. Acceptance of the corporate model was clearly evident by the 1971 AFN Convention theme, "In the White Man's Society, We Need White Man's Tools."

Congress wanted to avoid creating any reservations or "racially defined" organizations and supported corporations as the vehicle to implement ANCSA. With this objective in mind, Congress limited the restrictions on the transferability of ANCSA stock for twenty years, or until 1991. Congress also rejected any possibility of keeping the enrollment open for those children born after 1971.

The conflict between for-profit corporations and Native values emerged as 1991 approached. Natives became alarmed that the expiration of the restrictions on the sale of stock could lead to non-Native control and ownership of Native lands. At the 1982 AFN Convention, Natives voted to make the "1991" issue its top priority and to seek amendments to ANCSA to protect Native land.

AFN was successful in securing the amendments that provided the legal authority to protect ANCSA land and control of their corporations. The 1991 amendments provided automatic protections for land and Native corporation stock. The stock would remain restricted unless shareholders voted to remove the restrictions. Undeveloped land was also automatically protected. The law also allowed for the issuance of stock to Natives born after 1971 and to those who missed the initial enrollment upon approval of a shareholder vote. In recognition of the cultural value of caring for elders, the amendments also allowed for special benefits to elders or those shareholders who were sixty-five years or older.

AFN was not successful in securing a tribal option, which would have allowed for the transfer of ANCSA lands to tribal governments. ANCSA did not extinguish the two hundred tribal governments in Alaska, but those governments effectively lost their land base. A few village corporations transferred their land to tribes, but concern that the lands would not be treated as trust lands and protected by the federal government deterred the movement.

ANCSA corporations are different from other profit-making corporations. They pursue both economic and social goals seeking to protect their Native way of life and traditions. They have been variously successful; some corporations have expanded into the national and international markets, while others teeter on the brink of bankruptcy. They are also unique in that Congress recognizes Native corporations as federally recognized tribes for special statutory purposes in over a hundred federal legislative statutes that offer special benefits and protections.

Daniel R. Gibbs

See also Alaska Native Brotherhood; Assembly of First Nations; Economic Development; Land, Identity and Ownership of, Land Rights; Pan-Indianism; Tribal Sovereignty.

References and Further Reading

Alaska Federation of Natives. 1991. "Making It Work: A Guide to Public Law 100–241 1987 Amendments to the Alaska Native Claims Settlement Act." Anchorage, AL: Alaska Federation of Natives.

Arnold, Robert D. et al. 1978. *Alaska Native Land Claims.* Anchorage, AL: Alaska Federation of Natives.

Case, D. S., and David A. Voluck. 2002. *Alaska Natives and American Laws.* Fairbanks: University of Alaska Press.

Jones, Richard S. 1981. *Alaska Native Claims Settlement Act of 1971 (Public Law 92–203): History and Analysis Together with Subsequent Amendments.* American National Government Division. Report No. 81–127 GOV. Washington, DC: Library of Congress, Congressional Research Service.

Worl, Rosita. 2003. "Models of Sovereignty and Survival in Alaska." *Cultural Survival Quarterly* 27, no. 3 (Fall).

Albany Congress, Native Precedents

On the eve of the 1754 Albany Conference, Benjamin Franklin was already persuaded that the Haudenosaunee leader Canassatego's advice advocating colonial unity was good counsel, and he was not alone in these sentiments. James DeLancey, acting governor of New York, sent a special invitation to Hendrick (Tiyanoga) to attend the Albany Conference, where the Mohawk sachem provided insights into the structure of the League of the Iroquois for the assembled colonial delegates. In letters convening the conference from the various colonies, instructions of the delegates were phrased in Iroquois diplomatic idiom. From colonist to colonist, the letters spoke of "burying the hatchet," a phrase that entered idiomatic English from the Iroquois Great Law. DeLancey also spoke of "renewing the covenant chain," another Haudenosaunee diplomatic idiom.

The Albany Congress convened June 19, 1754, five days after its scheduled opening, because many of the Iroquois and some of the colonial commissioners arrived late. Roughly 150 to 200 Iroquois and about twenty-five colonists attended the meeting, according to official accounts. Most of the sessions of the congress took place at the Albany Courthouse; many of the speeches to the Indians (and their replies) occurred in front of the governor's residence. Albany at the time straddled the border between colonial settlement and Iroquois country at the "eastern door" of the Six Nations' symbolic longhouse. The town was still dominated by the architecture of the Dutch, who had founded the town before the English replaced them in 1675.

On June 28, 1754, the day after Hendrick arrived with the Mohawks, James DeLancey met with him. The two hundred Indians in attendance sat on ten rows of benches in front of the governor's residence, with colonial delegates facing them in a row of chairs, their backs to the building. According to Theodore Atkinson's account of the conference, this gathering was held on a warm day, after a morning rain. Governor Delancey read a speech approved by the delegates paragraph by paragraph, as New York's interpreter relayed his words to the Indians. The speechmaking also stopped briefly for the presentation of belts to the Indians, following Iroquois diplomatic custom.

DeLancey's speech began with a condolence using Iroquois diplomatic language. ("I wipe away your tears, and take sorrow from your hearts, that you may open your minds and speak freely.") Then the governor gave "A String of Wampum" in a fashion similar to what Franklin had observed a year earlier at the Carlisle Treaty Council. As the governor proceeded, the assembled Indians "Signifyed [sic] their understanding of each paragraph by a kind of Universal Huzzah" (O'Callaghan, 1853, 6: 567). And "When the great Chain belt was Dil[i]vered [sic] on this occasion, they Signifyed [sic] their understanding or Consent by Such a Huzzah repeated Seven Times over for every Tribe" (McAnear, 1953, 736). Holding the chain belt given him by the colonial delegates, Hendrick made the belt a metaphor of political union, as he advised DeLancey that the colonists should strengthen themselves and "In the mean time we desire, that you will strengthen yourselves, and bring as many into this Covenant Chain as you possibly can" (O'Callaghan, 1849, 869). It is likely that Hendrick remarked on this subject several days later, when the Indians and delegates assembled again in front of the governor's residence.

Hendrick was openly critical of the British at the Albany Congress. He hinted that the Iroquois would not ally with the English colonies unless a suitable form of unity was established among them. In talking of the proposed union of the colonies and the Six Nations on July 9, 1754, Hendrick stated, "We wish this Tree of Friendship may grow up to a great height and then we shall be a powerful people" (Colonial Records, 1851, 6: 98). In effect, Hendrick was repeating the advice Canassatego had given colonial delegates at Lancaster a decade earlier, this time at a conference devoted not only to diplomacy, but also to drawing up a plan for the type of colonial union the Iroquois had been requesting. The same day, at the Courthouse, the colonial delegates were in the early stages of debate over the plan of union.

Hendrick followed that admonition with an analysis of Iroquois and colonial unity, when he said, "We the United Nations shall rejoice of our strength" as we will "have now made so strong a Confederacy." In reply to Hendrick's speech on Native American and colonial unity, DeLancey said: "I hope that by this present Union, we shall grow up to a great height and be as powerful and famous as you were of old" (Colonial Records, 1851, 6: 98). These words of Hendrick and DeLancey are significant in that they go beyond Covenant Chain rhetoric and talk of the symbol of the Great Law (the Great Tree). Franklin was commissioned to draw up the final draft of the Albany Plan the same day, two months to the day after his Pennsylvania Gazette had published the "Join or Die" cartoon.

On July 10, 1754, Franklin formally proposed his Plan of Union before the congress. Franklin wrote that the debates on the Albany Plan "went on daily, hand in hand with the Indian business" (Bigelow, 1868, 295). In drawing up his final draft, Franklin was meeting several diplomatic demands: the Crown's for control; the colonies' desires for autonomy in a loose confederation; and the Iroquois' stated advocacy for a colonial union similar (but not identical) to their own in form and function. For the Crown, the plan provided administration by a president-general, to be appointed by England. The individual colonies were to be allowed to retain their own constitutions, except as the plan circumscribed them. The retention of internal sovereignty within the individual colonies closely resembled the Iroquois system and had no existing precedent in Europe.

Franklin chose the name "Grand Council" for the plan's deliberative body, the same name generally applied to the Iroquois central council. The number of delegates, forty-eight, was close to the Iroquois council's fifty, and each colony had a different number of delegates, just as each Haudenosaunee nation sent a different number of sachems to Onondaga. The Albany Plan was based in rough proportion to tax revenues, however, while the Iroquois system was based on tradition.

The Albany Plan of Union called for a government under which each colony could retain its present constitution (Bigelow, 1868). Basically, the plan provided that Parliament was to establish a general government in America, including all the thirteen colonies, each of which was to retain its present constitution except for certain powers (mainly mutual defense) that were to be given to the general government. The king was to appoint a president-general for the government. Each colonial assembly would elect representatives to the Grand Council.

The president-general would exercise certain powers with the advice of the Grand Council, such as handling Indian relations, making treaties, deciding upon peace or war, raising troops, building forts, providing warships, and finally to make such laws and levy such taxes as would be needed for its purposes. Through this plan colonial leaders embraced a plan for union that Indian leaders such as Canassatego and Hendrick had urged upon them for a decade or more. Thus, the roots of intercolonial unity are in the Indian-white relations of the early eighteenth century. During this time, men such as Benjamin Franklin saw in the Iroquois Confederacy a model on which to build.

Bruce E. Johansen

See also American Indian Contributions to the World; Canassatego; Franklin, Benjamin, Native American Influences; Haudenosaunee Confederacy, Political System; Hendrick.

References and Further Reading

Bigelow, John, ed. 1868. *Autobiography of Benjamin Franklin*. Philadelphia, PA: J. B. Lippincott Co.

Colden, Cadwallader. 1902. *History of the Five Nations*. New York: New Amsterdam Book Company.

Colonial Records of Pennsylvania. 1851. Volume 6. Harrisburg, PA: Theo Fenn & Co.

Grinde, Donald A., Jr., and Bruce E. Johansen. 1991. *Exemplar of Liberty: Native America and the Evolution of Democracy*. Los Angeles, CA: UCLA American Indian Studies Center.

Jacobs, Wilbur R. 1966. *Wilderness Politics and Indian Gifts*. Lincoln: University of Nebraska Press.

Johansen, Bruce E. 1982. *The Forgotten Founders: Benjamin Franklin, the Iroquois and the Rationale for the American Revolution*. Ipswich, MA: Gambit.

McAnear, Beverly. 1953. "Personal Accounts of the Albany Congress of 1754." *Mississippi Valley Historical Review* 39, no. 4: 736–737.

O'Callaghan, E. B., ed. 1849–1851. *The Documentary History of the State of New York*. Albany, NY: Weed, Parsons and Company.

O'Callaghan, E.B., ed. 1853–1887. *Documents Relative to the Colonial History of New York*. Vol. 6. Albany, NY: Weed, Parsons and Company.

Van Doren, Carl, and Julian P. Boyd, eds. 1938. *Indian Treaties Printed by Benjamin Franklin 1736–1762*. Philadelphia: Historical Society of Pennsylvania.

American Indian Religious Freedom Act

The American Indian Religious Freedom Act (AIRFA, Public Law 95-341), was signed into law by President Jimmy Carter on August 12, 1978. President Carter defined the intention of AIRFA well when he stated at the signing ceremony

It is the fundamental right of every American, as guaranteed by the first amendment of the Constitution, to worship as he or she pleases. . . . This legislation sets forth the policy of the United States to protect and preserve the inherent right of American Indian, Eskimo, Aleut, and Native Hawaiian people to believe, express, and exercise their traditional religions.

The Act was introduced in the Senate on December 15, 1977, by Senator James Abourezk (Democrat, South Dakota) and later in the House of Representatives by Representative James Udall (Democrat, New Mexico). The Senate held hearings on AIRFA but the House did not. Testimony in the Senate hearings came primarily from Native Americans and representatives of various government entities. AIRFA was considered and passed in the

Senate on April 3, 1978, and in the House on July 18, 1978.

President Carter and Secretary of Agriculture Bob Berglud were enthusiastic supporters of AIRFA, as were several senators and congresspersons. The Department of Justice expressed concerns about the effect of AIRFA on existing state and federal laws but was reassured by Representative Udall, who stated that it had "no teeth in it" and was not intended to override existing state laws. President Carter echoed this sentiment and stated that the "act is in no way intended to alter . . . or override existing laws." With those concerns addressed, AIRFA passed with very little resistance in the House or Senate. Congress passed AIRFA with the intent of eliminating federal interference with the exercise of Native American religious traditions and to compel government agencies to consider AIRFA in the institution and administration of policies and procedures.

AIRFA is divided into two sections. The first section addresses the right of Native Americans to practice their traditional religions. The relevant language states:

> Whereas, the freedom of religion for all people is an inherent right, fundamental to the democratic structure of the United States and is guaranteed by the First Amendment of the United States Constitution . . .Whereas traditional American Indian ceremonies have been intruded upon, interfered with, and in a few instances banned: Now therefore, be it resolved by the Senate and House of Representatives of the United States of America in Congress assembled, that henceforth it shall be the policy of the United States to preserve for American Indians their inherent right of freedom to believe, express, and exercise the traditional religions . . . including but not limited to access to sites, use and possession of sacred objects, and the freedom to worship through ceremonial and traditional rites.

This section of AIRFA is important because it was the first federal legislation specifically addressing Native Americans' inherent right to freedom of religion.

Section 2 requires that the president direct federal departments and agencies responsible for administering relevant laws to evaluate their policies and procedures in consultation with traditional Native religious leaders and report back to Congress with any recommended changes in one year's time.

The AIRFA Report

The report committee formed to satisfy Section 2 of AIRFA was chaired by Secretary of the Interior Cecil B. Andrus. The report was submitted to Congress in August of 1979 and detailed the government's overall failure to protect Native Americans' religious freedoms. It stated that the failure had primarily stemmed from the "ignorance and misunderstanding on the part of the non-Indian" of Native American religions. The report called for the need for improvements in several areas, including access to sacred objects such as eagle feathers and peyote, access to sacred sites, protection of sacred sites, and the overall double standard in terms of the treatment of European-American versus Native American human remains. The response of government agencies and departments was sporadic and generally dismal. Because AIFRA lacked a clear interpretation of Congress's intent, primarily due to the use of convoluted language on the lack of penalties for noncompliance, there was little incentive for government response.

The Suppression of Native American Religious Traditions

Native Americans have had their free practice of religion suppressed by every Western nation that sought to colonize the New World. Throughout history, suppressing Native religious practices has been a common practice of those seeking to subjugate a people. It was thought that through the denial of a people's own culture, they would be easily assimilated into their suppressor's culture. France, Britain, Spain, and the United States all suppressed Native Americans' free practice of religion and supported, and often funded, efforts to convert Native Americans to Christianity. Freedom of religion has been the law of the land since the birth of the United States as a nation; however, this basic right, guaranteed to all by the Constitution, has repeatedly been denied to Native Americans.

It is ironic that the first Europeans who would become known as Americans settled here because they were fleeing religious persecution. The United States continued the policy of the earlier colonial governments by actively promoting Christianity to Native Americans. Christian missionaries were hired as Indian agents, tribal administrative control was often placed in the hands of religious denominations, and tribal-held land was repeatedly given away to organizations that promised to build religious schools or churches on it. In 1869, the Board of Indian Commissioners was established with the intended purpose of educating Native Americans in the principles of Christianity. In 1879, the Carlisle Indian Industrial School was established in Carlisle, Pennsylvania, by the U.S. government for the education of Native American children. The school's director, Richard Pratt, stated that his goal was to "[k]ill the Indian and save the man." The school punished children for wearing Native dress or speaking their own languages and forbade any practice of their Native religious traditions.

Interior Secretary Henry M. Teller holds the distinction of being the first U.S. government representative to order official restrictions on the practice of Native American religious customs. In an 1882 directive Teller ordered an end to all "heathenish dances and ceremonies" on reservations due to their "great hindrance to civilization." In 1883, Commissioner of Indian Affairs Hiram Price codified the practice of officially restricting Native American religious freedom by creating the Indian Religious Crimes Code. In his 1883 annual report to the secretary of the interior, Price stated

> there is no good reason why an Indian should be permitted to indulge in practices which are alike repugnant to common decency and morality; and the preservation of good order on the reservations demands that some active measures should be taken to discourage and, if possible, put a stop to the demoralizing influence of heathenish rites.

In 1892, Commissioner of Indian Affairs Thomas J. Morgan sought to further suppress Native religions by ordering penalties of up to six months in prison for those who repeatedly participated in religious dances or acted as medicine men.

The government's attempts to suppress and in many instances outright ban Native American religious practices led to one of the bloodiest events in the history of the United States: the Massacre at Wounded Knee. To enforce the ban on the Ghost Dance in accordance with the Indian Religious Crimes Code, the Seventh Calvary was sent into the Lakota Sioux's Pine Ridge and Rosebud Reservations to stop the dance and arrest the participants.

General Armstrong Custer's former unit, in response to a dispute over a firearm, attacked and killed approximately 150 Native American men, women, and children on December 29, 1890. Charges of killing innocents were brought against members of the Seventh Calvary, but all were later exonerated. The massacre marked the effective end of the Ghost Dance movement and, according to many historians, signified the end of the Indian Wars.

The Start of a Change in U.S. Policy

The shift toward acknowledging Native American religions, the government's obligations to the tribes, and their rites as citizens of the United States began in 1933 when President Franklin D. Roosevelt appointed John Collier as commissioner of Indian Affairs. Collier issued Bureau of Indian Affairs Circular 2970, "Indian Religious Freedom and Indian Culture," on January 3, 1934. The circular was sent to all federal agencies and read in part "no interference with Indian religious life or ceremonial expression will hereafter be tolerated." Collier also guided, with the support of President Roosevelt, the Indian Reorganization Act, commonly known as the Indian New Deal, through Congress. This act dramatically changed U.S. policy by allowing tribal self-government and consolidating individual land allotments back into tribal hands.

In the 1960s, partly in response to a nationwide wave of discontent and a trend toward active protesting of government policies, a renewed movement of Native American activism resulted in the passage of several acts, including AIRFA. Native Americans began to cooperate and organize a pan-Indian movement to push for change through political channels. While there is a long history of pan-Indian movements, many feel that this one had its roots in the forced boarding school programs and the Bureau of Indian Affairs relocation programs. Both programs brought Native Americans from several tribes together in situations in which their common hardships and interests led to increased intertribal communication and cooperation.

One of the first politically active Native American groups to form was the National Indian Youth Council (NIYC), created in 1961. NIYC participated in a series of protests calling for the recognition of treaty-granted fishing rights in the state of Washington. The American Indian Movement (AIM), the most vocal and well-known of the Native American activist groups, was formed in 1968 by George Mitchell and Dennis Banks in Minneapolis. AIM participated in the 1969 occupation of Alcatraz, the November 1972 occupation of the Bureau of Indian Affairs building in Washington, D.C., and the 1973 occupation of Wounded Knee.

Largely in response to Native Americans' well publicized calls for change, a large number of acts were passed by Congress in the late 1960s and 1970s: the Indian Civil Rights Act (PL90-284) in 1968; the Alaska Native Claims Act (PL92-208) in 1971; the Indian Education Act (PL92-318) in 1972; the Indian Self-Determination and Education Assistance Act (PL93-638) in 1974; the Indian Health Care Improvement Act (PL94-437) in 1976; and the Indian Child Welfare Act (PL95-608) in 1978. The Archaeological Resources Protection Act (PL96-95) was passed in 1979 and prohibited the excavation, removal, defacing, or sale of human remains or burial items unless done in accordance with the law.

The increased public awareness of the Native American's plight led to the creation of the American Indian Policy Review Commission in 1975. Consisting of three senators, three representatives, and five Indian commissioners, the commission oversaw thirty-three task forces reviewing Native American grievances and conditions. The final report was issued in May 1977 and concluded that the government had often interfered in and obstructed the efforts of Native Americans to practice their traditional religious customs. The report was instrumental in the struggle to convince Congress of the need for AIRFA.

Legislation Following AIRFA and AIRFA Amendments

Since 1978, a relatively steady progression of executive orders, memorandums, and legislation has addressed problems with AIRFA and clarified Congress's intent to the courts. Issues such as access to sacred sites, the ceremonial use of peyote, the rights of Native American prisoners to practice their religions, and the repatriation of human remains and ceremonial objects have all been specifically addressed. The efforts made in addressing the issue of Native Americans' free practice of religion have not satisfied all, but most would concur that there has been a significant amount of progress made in the nearly three decades since the passage of AIRFA.

President George H. W. Bush signed MAIA, the Museum of the American Indian Act (PL101-185) in 1989 and NAGPRA, the Native American Graves Protection and Repatriation Act (PL101-601) in 1990. MAIA called for the creation of the Museum of the American Indian and the repatriation of 18,500 Native American remains held by the Smithsonian. NAGPRA calls for museums and federal agencies to return Native American human remains, funerary objects, sacred objects, and objects of cultural importance to lineal descendents, affiliated tribes, and Native Hawaiian organizations.

In 1993, the Religious Freedom Restoration Act (PL103-141) was passed and signed into law by President William Jefferson Clinton. On signing the Act, President Clinton stated that it "reestablishes a standard that better protects all Americans of all faiths . . . in a way that I am convinced is far more consistent with the intent of the Founders of this nation." In 1994, President Clinton issued a memorandum to every executive department and agency of the government, titled "Policy Concerning Distribution of Eagle Feathers for Native American Religious Purposes." In his remarks to Native American and Native Alaskan tribal leaders, he said that the memorandum directed the agencies and departments to "cooperate with tribal governments to accommodate whenever possible the need for eagle feathers in the practice of Native American religions."

The AIRFA amendments (PL103-344) were passed in 1994 to correct the inadequacies of the original Act. The 1978 version of AIRFA was seen by the courts as a policy for executive agencies and as such was not given extensive weight in court decisions. The courts have always distinguished between religious beliefs and religious practices. People are free to choose their religious beliefs, but practices have been repeatedly prohibited by the courts. Polygamy, human sacrifice, and religious customs such as those allowing rape as a penalty for a violation of religious code are all illegal based on the overriding good of the public and existing state and federal laws. In *Employment Division, Department of Human Resources of Oregon v. Smith* (1990), the Supreme Court ruled that Oregon was within its legal right to fire a Native American employee for the use of peyote in a religious ceremony. The court failed to recognize the religious significance of the peyote use and instead viewed it as an illegal substance not protected under the First Amendment or AIRFA.

Many Native American groups and individuals pushed for amendments to AIRFA, which clarified the legality of peyote use for religious purposes and the distinction between its traditional use and use as a recreational drug. In the hearings held by the Senate Select Committee on Indian Affairs, the late Professor Vine Deloria testified that "We need to make clear that peyote is a sacramental plant used by American Indians in a sacramental way, going back long before the memory of man. Once that clarification is made, there is no possible way to link it to those other drugs."

The amendments were considered and passed in the House of Representatives on August 8, 1994, and in the Senate on September 26, 1994. The amendments state that "Non-withstanding any other provision of law, the use, possession, or transportation of peyote by an Indian for bona fide traditional ceremonial purposes in connection with the practice of a traditional Indian religion is lawful, and shall not be prohibited by the United States or any state." The amendment includes a list of several common sense exceptions and a section prohibiting discrimination based on a Native American's use of peyote in a religious context.

On May 24, 1996, President Clinton issued Executive Order 13007, "Protection and Accommodation of Access to Indian Sacred Sites." The order states that executive agencies and departments should "accommodate access to and ceremonial use of Indian sacred sites by Indian religious practitioners and avoid adversely affecting the physical integrity of such sacred sites. Where appropriate, agencies shall maintain the confidentiality of sacred sites." It was issued largely in response to the Supreme Court ruling in the *Lyng v. Northwest Indian Cemetery Protective Association*. The case resulted from the U.S. Forest Service's desire to build a road near a Native American religious site. Several tribes were joined by various parties, including the state of California, in seeking a court order to bar the project under AIRFA. The Supreme Court, as stated by Justice Sandra Day O'Connor, decided that "Whatever rights the Indians may have to use of the area those rights do not divest the Government of its right to use what is, after all, its land."

The Religious Land Use and Institutionalized Persons Act (PL106-274) was signed into law in 2000 by President Clinton. The legislation guarantees access for Native Americans to religious sites located on government property. Section 2 regards the right of Native American prisoners to practice traditional religions. It states, "No government shall impose a substantial burden on the religious exercise of a person residing in or confined to an institution, . . . even if the burden results from a rule of general applicability, unless the government demonstrates that imposition of the burden on that person is in furtherance of a compelling governmental interest; and is the least restrictive means of furthering that compelling governmental interest."

James Thull

See also Ceremonies, Criminalization of; Graham, Mount (Dzil Nchaa Si An), Controversy over; *Lyng v. Northwest Indian Cemetery Protective Association;* Native American Church of North America; Native American Graves Protection and Repatriation Act; Sacred Sites; Tribal Sovereignty.

References and Further Reading

American Indian Religious Freedom Act. 1978. Public Law 341, 95th Cong., 2d sess. July 18.

American Indian Religious Freedom Act Amendments. 1994. Public Law 344, 103rd Cong., 2d sess. September 26.

Andrus, Cecil, Secretary of the Interior, Federal Agencies Taskforce. 1979. *American Indian Religious Freedom Act Report, P.L. 95–341*. August.

Batzle, Peter, and Melanie Oliviero. 1980. "The Congress." *American Indian Journal* 6, no. 1: 16–20.

Lee, Irwin. 1997. "Freedom, Law, and Prophecy: A Brief History of Native American Religious Resistance." *The American Indian Quarterly* 21, no. 1: 35–56.

U.S. Senate Committee on Indian Affairs. 1992. *Oversight Hearing on the Need for Amendments to the American Indian Religious Freedom Act*, 102nd Cong., 1d sess., March 7.

U.S. Senate Committee on Indian Affairs. 2004. *Oversight Hearing on American Indian Religious Freedom Act*, 108th Cong., 2d sess., July 14.

Vecsey, Christopher, ed. 1991. *Handbook of American Indian Religious Freedom*. New York: Crossroad Publishing Company.

Venables, Robert W. 2004. *American Indian History Five Centuries of Conflict and Coexistence*, Vol. II. Santa Fe, NM: Clear Light Publishers.

Bureau of American Ethnology

The Bureau of American Ethnology (BAE), established in 1879 by Congress, is the sponsoring body that supported the most extensive early research program on North American cultures. It performed that task as a semiautonomous unit under the secretary of the Smithsonian between that year and 1965, when it merged with the Department of Anthropology at the Smithsonian. Though the activities of the BAE are varied, its most recognizable contributions are its *Annual Reports*, the *Contributions to North American Ethnology* series, and particularly the *Bulletins*, easily identified by the original large, green and gold trim volumes, with the imprint of the BAE logo—a "cliff dwelling" complete with rock art figures in the foreground—on the frontispiece. Published by the Government Printing Office (GPO), these were free and widely distributed and are still readily accessible today in many libraries that are government depositories.

The history of the BAE is intertwined with that of the development of American anthropology, its relationship with American Indians, and issues of the role of government in sponsoring research activity. The earliest ethnologists were not trained as such, but were in the service of the U.S. Geological Survey and found themselves in intimate contact with American Indians in their regions of activity. Among them was John Wesley Powell, who had worked extensively in the Southwest. Powell was responsible for lobbying for the establishment of the Bureau of Ethnology; he was made its first director in 1879. Under Powell, the BAE grew to become one of the most significant archival collections of ethnological information about Native Americans through the activity of its staff ethnologists. As a training ground for the field of anthropology, it supported the work of some of the most well-known early field anthropologists: Frank Hamilton Cushing, Franz Boas, Otis T. Mason, James Mooney, among others, were all contributors to the bureau's collections.

Classic monographs, such as Boas's *Tsimshian Mythology*, Mooney's *Myths of the Cherokee* and *The Ghost-Dance Religion*, and Cushing's *Zuni Fetishes*, were all, in their original form, contributions made with BAE support for the *Annual Reports* or the *Bulletins* series. These are surviving relics of an era sometimes called "salvage ethnography," after the apparent motivation of Congress and anthropological scholars to document Native American life in its perceived twilight, and they were notable for a division that was not conceived as a permanent institution. Nevertheless, the ethnologists involved with the BAE were increasingly well-trained figures, producing narratives with intensive ethnographic detail, which are still valued for the material they preserved.

As it evolved, the bureau engaged itself in shaping public awareness of anthropology through exhibitions and at international expositions. With this increasing notoriety, it became a repository of varied material from additional nonstaff sources (including military personnel, missionaries, and amateur scholars), drawing an extensive manuscript, map, and document archive, as well as an illustrative and photographic collection. Other major endeavors of the bureau included, under the direction of ethnologist-in-charge W. Frederick Hodge (1910–1918), the first *Handbook of American Indians*, published as *Bulletin 30* in 1907 as two volumes. Still widely valued for reference today, John Swanton's compendia, *The Indians of the Southeastern United States*, was published as *Bulletin 137* and *The Indian Tribes of North America* as *Bulletin 1945*. Also a major BAE project was the *Handbook of South American Indians*, edited by Julian Steward under his Institute for Social Anthropology and published as *Bulletin 143*, between 1946 and 1959.

In 1965, the BAE catalogue and materials were incorporated into the National Anthropological Archives, where they are housed today. In 1970, the last bulletin under the bureau name was issued, an index to authors and titles of all preceding BAE publications. Two current trends are also notable with respect to the history and significance of the BAE. Of late, the National Museum of Natural History has been sequentially closing the old Halls of Ethnology, remembered by many as hallmarks of the Smithsonian experience. Thus, the era of public exhibits that were shaped and informed by the long tradition of ethnological work at the Institution has come to a close. With respect to American Indian cultures and peoples, that mantle has passed to the National Museum of the American Indian. However, lest the collection become valued only by researchers and archivists, the NAA and the Smithsonian Institution Libraries have endeavored to begin the digitization of the publications of the BAE.

Christopher Lindsay Turner

See also Boas, Franz.
References and Further Reading
Glenn, James R. 1996. *Guide to the National Anthropological Archives, Smithsonian Institution.* Washington, DC: Smithsonian Institution.
Hinsley, Curtis M., Jr. 1978. *The Development of a Profession: Anthropology in Washington, D.C., 1846–1903.* Ann Arbor, MI: University Microfilms.

Smithsonian Institution, Bureau of American Ethnology. 1971. *List of Publications of the Bureau of American Ethnology with Index to Authors and Titles, Bulletin 200.* Washington, DC: U.S. Government Printing Office. Available at: http://www.sil.si.edu/DigitalCollections/BAE/Bulletin200/200title.htm. Accessed January 13, 2007.

Bureau of Indian Affairs: Establishing the Existence of an Indian Tribe

The Bureau of Indian Affairs (BIA) is the branch of the federal government charged with organizing and carrying out governmental policy relating to American Indians. While the original purpose of the BIA was to liquidate Indian lands, over the course of its history, the BIA has become an institution that attempts to manage Indian affairs and to act as the federal government's liaison with American Indian peoples on and off the reservations. Originally called the Office of Indian Affairs (OIA), the bureau was established by President James Monroe in 1824 as part of the Department of War for the purpose of supporting and, it was hoped, eventually assimilating American Indians.

In the beginning, the Office of Indian Affairs was dominated by the individual Indian agents, most often apolitical appointees placed on reservations. The Indian agents directed the distribution of food, goods, and other treaty annuities, oversaw education and missionary work, and policed various activities such as the prohibition of liquor as well as controlling the payroll of tribal police. The lack of direct supervision of Indian agents opened the door for corruption and mistreatment.

The Office of Indian Affairs was run by the Secretary of War until July 1832, when Congress established the position of the commissioner of Indian Affairs and appointed Elbert Herring to the post. The OIA was conceived as a temporary institution that would manage Indian affairs until the Native peoples were settled enough on the reservations to create new governments or had assimilated into mainstream society. On May 20, 1834, the House Committee on Indian Affairs reported that the activities of the OIA were being carried on in violation of law and without any legally recognized authority. The committee advised that the OIA be shut down and its work passed on to the Native peoples. After the committee's initial admonishment, they passed a bill on June 30, 1834, that effectively gave the Office of Indian Affairs branch status and legal status. In 1849, the renamed Bureau of Indian Affairs was transferred to the new Interior Department where it would more efficiently be able to liquidate Indian lands. The BIA was not a part of any treaty plan, but, as the federal government began to tighten its hold on reservation life, due to increased Western migration and demands for Indian lands, the bureau gained power and became unwieldy, often resulting in actions that reflected the government's rather than the Indian's interests.

After the Civil War, the BIA began to focus on breaking up traditional forms of tribal governments on reservations in order to harness political and decision-making powers. The BIA also began to search for a more effective means of eradicating Indian cultural practices. The General Allotment Act of 1887 changed the relationship between the BIA and Indian tribes. With the Allotment Act and the introduction of individual ownership of reservation property, the government found it easier to acquire more Indian lands as well as to exploit those lands for their natural resources. Indian agents were encouraged to force their charges to give up their property and traditional ways. The BIA policy toward American Indians was that of assimilation, the preferred method of assimilation was through education, and the preferred method of education was the boarding school, which separated children from their families and traditional culture. From 1900 through the 1970s, at least half of the BIA budget went toward schooling. And in 1908, Commissioner Francis E. Leupp eradicated the post of Indian agent and passed the administrative powers of the BIA onto the school teachers and educators on the reservations. After years of assimilation policies, the Bureau of Indian Affairs endured a public setback in 1928 with the publication of the Meriam Report. This report chastised the BIA for the poor reservation conditions American Indians suffered under and for the lack of programs for their economic, educational, and political development. The report also proposed that the BIA become an agency that worked to protect and encourage American Indian traditions. Beginning with Commissioner Charles Rhoads in 1929, policies began to turn more toward Indian self-determination.

In 1934, during the Great Depression, Commissioner John Collier took government policy

The twenty-fourth commissioner of Indian Affairs, Thomas J. Morgan, with a Sioux delegation. Morgan enunciated a clear program of education for Native American children and was a principal force in the effort to assimilate Native Americans into U.S. society. (Library of Congress)

significantly closer to self-determination, at least when compared with the past. Collier is, perhaps, the best-known commissioner of the Bureau of Indian Affairs. He believed that the purpose of the BIA was to protect Indian rights and lands and to bring greater cultural understanding of American Indians to the larger American population. He worked to preserve Indian traditions and to bring power back to Native polities with the Indian Reorganization Act of 1934. The so-called Indian New Deal attempted to create tribal governments with administrative power and democratic elections, but it failed to provide these governments with enough control due to the continued veto authority of the Secretary of the Interior over reservation laws. The Indian Reorganization Act has also been viewed as contributing to the destruction of traditional forms of power on reservations due to its enforcement of a uniform system of governance.

By 1950, the relationship between the BIA and American Indians had become increasingly strained due to the federal policy calling for the Termination of tribal status. Dillon S. Meyer, a supporter of termination, was appointed Indian commissioner in 1950 and began to install a policy of scattering Indian peoples in order to reduce their ties to the land. The launching of termination came with the passage of House Concurrent Resolution 108 and aimed to remove all federal services to American Indian tribes. Through strong agitation and protest, however, the termination policy was disbanded in 1960. The BIA also derived the relocation program from its Termination predecessor with the intent of moving Indians off poverty-stricken reservations and into cities where they could find work and a place to live. However, due to lack of funding and services for the new urban migrants, the program fell short of its goals.

The 1960s and 1970s saw an increase in non-BIA–controlled programs for American Indians and the weakening of BIA power. President Lyndon B. Johnson's Great Society included a place for independent autonomous reservations and began to flow money into housing programs, health care, education, and work training. The successes of these programs led President Richard M. Nixon to declare a policy of self-determination for Indian tribes and nations in which the Bureau of Indian Affairs would play a reduced role on reservations, and tribes would eventually host their own administrative governments. In 1975, the Indian Self-Determination and Education Act called for more Indian control over the BIA by giving tribes the ability to gain the contracts for reservation programs in order to manage the programs themselves. In addition, the 1960s saw the appointments of Indian commissioners to the BIA like Robert Bennett (Oneida) and Louis Bruce (Mohawk-Sioux.) These new commissioners were willing to challenge the bureaucracy of the BIA and refashion it into a governmental agency that would work for American Indians. Hiring practices also changed and by 1980, 78 percent of BIA employees were of American Indian descent.

From approximately 1908 to 1949, the BIA consisted of a central office, located in Washington, D.C., and field offices located on various reservations. In 1949, the BIA was reorganized in an attempt to increase communication and to reduce bureaucratic red tape. New area offices were added to coordinate between central and field offices. For the most part, this three-tiered BIA structure is still in place today. Currently the BIA is under the direction of the assistant secretary of the interior and is a suborganization of the Department of the Interior. Under the secretary of the interior is the commissioner of Indian affairs who is responsible for the execution of congressional laws, as well as Department of the Interior orders, rules, and regulations.

Today the BIA attempts to promote self-determination, and American Indian tribes and nations administer over 50 percent of all BIA programs. However, the BIA still retains power over many of the educational and management opportunities on reservations through financial control. In September 2000, Assistant Secretary for Indian Affairs Kevin Gover (Pawnee) issued an official apology on behalf of the Bureau of Indian Affairs for the policies of land theft and assimilation that had been practiced by the agency. His statement is an effort to reconcile the past with the present and to lead the BIA in a firmly Indian direction.

Vera Parham

See also Ceremonies, Criminalization of; Collier, John; Domestic Dependent Nation; Economic Development; General Allotment Act (Dawes Act); Genocide; Indian Claims Commission; Indian Reorganization Act; Indian Self-Determination and Education Assistance Act; Individual Indian Monies; Leupp, Francis Ellington; Parker, Ely; Reservation Economic and Social Conditions; Termination; Trail of Broken Treaties; Treaty Diplomacy, with Summary of Selected Treaties; Tribal Sovereignty; Trust, Doctrine of; Wardship Doctrine.

References and Further Reading
Deloria, Vine, Jr. 1984. *The Nations Within: The Past and Future of American Indian Sovereignty.* New York: Pantheon.
Forbes, Jack D. 1981. *Native Americans and Nixon: Presidential Politics and Minority Self-determination, 1969–1972.* Los Angles, CA: UCLA American Indian Studies Center.
Galli, Marcia J., and Curtis E. Jackson. 1977. *A History of the Bureau of Indian Affairs and Its Activities Among Indians.* San Francisco: R&E Research Associates.
Hirschfelder, Arlene, and Martha Kreipe de Montaño. 1993. *The Native American Almanac: A Portrait of Native America Today.* Upper Saddle River, NJ: Prentice Hall.
Prucha, Francis Paul. 1984. *The Great Father: The United States Government and the American Indians.* Vol. 2. Lincoln: University of Nebraska Press.
Taylor, Theodore W. 1984. *The Bureau of Indian Affairs.* Boulder, CO: Westview Press.

Canada, Indian Policies of

Policy is multidimensional and multifaceted. As J. W. Cell has noted it "as being something rather less fixed, something rather more historical," saying that, at any moment in time, there is "not so much policy as policy formation, an unsettled and changing set of responses by government to the continual interaction among men [and women], forces, ideas, and institutions." As such, the Indian policies of Canada as a nation-state have their origin in the history of the treaty-making process of Canada as a place. Canadian Indian policies as they developed in the eighteenth century owe their development to a mistaken European view and representation of how Europeans came to view and represent aboriginal peoples, including First Nations, Métis, and Inuit peoples. However, First Nations have no need for such policies and do not have any regard for them, except insofar as they impinge upon First Nations' sovereignty and self-determination.

The Covenant Chain of Silver literally means "to link one's arms together" and signifies a nation-to-nation relationship. Yet the nation-state of Canada misinterpreted the First Nations and the meaning of the Covenant Chain and especially the Two Row Wampum that symbolized the Covenant. As a result it misconstrued what the relationship should have been between the Dutch, English, and the French imperial governments on the one hand and the

aboriginal nations on the other: namely, peace, mutual respect, and trust.

Initially given by the English to the Haudenosaunee to cement the treaty entered into at Albany in 1664, the Covenant Chain's components were known as least by the early seventeenth century, when the very first treaties of peace and friendship were entered into between the French and the Mi'kmaq nations in Acadia (present-day Atlantic Canada). The significance of the Covenant Chain of Silver as a basis for the treaty-making process and Indian policies cannot be underestimated in terms of land and sovereignty. Sir William Johnson, the English Crown's Imperial appointee to the Indian Department in 1755, highlighted its magnitude in 1764 when he wrote that

> Tis [It is] true that when a Nation find themselves pushed, their Alliances broken, and themselves tired of a War, they are verry

[very] apt to say many civil things, and make any Submissions which are not agreable [agreeable] to their intentions, but are said meerly [merely] to please those with whom they transact Affairs as they know they cannot enforce the observance of them. But you may be assured that none of the Six nations, Western Nations [including the Western Confederacy] &ca. ever declared themselves to be Subjects, or will ever consider themselves in that light whilst they have any Men, or an Open Country to retire to, the very Idea of subjection would fill them with horror.

This statement by Johnson links the basis of this process with one of the early views also integral to Canada's Indian policies: the notion that aboriginal peoples were subject to the nation-state. This notion of subjects rather than First Nations was a direct result of the ideology of European empires, notably

King George VI and Queen Elizabeth visit a Native American encampment in Canada. (Hulton-Deutsch Collection/Corbis)

the French and the British empires, which sought to control and dominate the natural world of North America and the peoples who resided there. However, initially outnumbered and without sufficient technology to dominate aboriginal peoples (the canoe was one of the primary modes of resistance), the French and then the British empires recognized aboriginal peoples as nations and sought out and entered into treaties of peace and friendship.

One of the first statements of imperial policy toward the First Nations was the promulgation of the Royal Proclamation of 1763, partly in response to the Anishinabe and Seneca resistance movements earlier that year. Owing much to the treaty-making process, the Royal Proclamation was an English imperial document, among other things, that recognized and reaffirmed the "Indian territory" to be their "absolute property," established English imperial rules regarding the treaty-making process under the Covenant Chain, and recognized the significance of the sovereignty of aboriginal trade and trading. It would be reaffirmed one year later in a Grand Council of Nations at Niagara in 1764 and in subsequent treaties, indicated by the following First Nations' perspective:

> While the treaties are like stones marking a spot in time, the relationship between the Nations is like two equals, respecting each of their differences but supporting each other for a common position on peace, order and justice for all. The brotherhood created by the Twenty Four Nations Belt represents a relationship of both sharing and respect. The sharing is reciprocal: as the First Nations shared land and the knowledge in the past, now that situation is reversed, the generosity of spirit and action is expected to continue. The respect is also reciprocal: respect for each other's rights, existence, laws and vision of the future.

By the late eighteenth century, the balance of power was beginning to shift and increasingly the treaties came to be seen as land surrenders by the aboriginal peoples as subjects of the imperial crowns. These promises were not inconsequential at a time when the English imperial foothold on the North American continent was, at best, precarious. After Sir William Johnson died in 1774, things began to fall apart. By the 1790s, the solemn promises of the crown were forgotten by the Indian Department.

After the American Revolution, the new colony of Upper Canada became important to the English imperial government for a strategic reason: to protect the English colony from the United States as an aboriginal buffer state. The land was also seen to be, in the long term, of great value as a place for the second British empire to promote commercial agricultural settlement and colonization. Lieutenant John Graves Simcoe's plan for Upper Canada (1791) outlined this plan:

> There are but a very few Indians who inhabit within it, the greater part of the soil has been purchased & the whole ought to be before it will become of value, as the Indians will not want for suggestions to inhance [enhance] its price. I consider the Country to be of immense value, whether it be regarded to its immediate advantages, the future prospect of Advantage, or the probable grounds for supposing it will remain the most important foreign possession of Great Britain.

Based on the Royal Proclamation of 1763, a misconstruction of the treaty-making process, and Simcoe's land policy, a number of land surrenders in Upper Canada occurred from the 1790s to the Confederation of Canada (1867) and in the west and north by means of the numbered treaties.

These treaties were not entered into without resistance by First Nations' citizens. Despite the spirit of the Two Row Wampum and, later, the ostensible promise of protection of subject peoples, the treaty-making process became a landgrab filled with corruption and land speculation, as was the case in the United States. Conflict, rooted in imperial and colonial aspirations as well as in cultural disparateness of the First Nations and the White Settlers, grew apace as a part of Canadian aboriginal policies within regional frameworks. There were treaties of peace and friendship in Atlantic Canada, no treaties in Quebec, and land loss treaties in Upper Canada that became a model of the subsequent numbered treaties (1871–1930) in the west and north. The principle of protection gave way to assimilation, and with it came European scientific racism as part and parcel of Canada's Indian policies.

The War of 1812–1814 fought in the British North American colonies and in the United States was a "turntable" for Canadian Indian policies. Although they fought for the British in that war, the First Nations were no longer needed militarily when it was over. The result was that the United States and Britain agreed on a boundary that split the First

Nations' territories, literally carving it up along the survey of the international boundary and, more seriously, effectively taking away jurisdiction and governance (but not sovereignty) from the First Nations.

Relocation and attempted extinguishment of aboriginal title and reserve lands in Upper Canada occurred after the War of 1812–1814. Gradually, a full-blown British imperial policy of civilization was established and in effect by the 1820s. Many more requests came for land surrenders from the English crown, but the land surrenders were not followed. Most of the monies were not deposited to trust fund accounts, and more lands were taken than outlined in the written treaty documents. Even without the overt use of force, the British government sometimes used another process—one based on nonconsultation with aboriginal peoples and lacking their consent, all in violation of the spirit and intent of the Royal Proclamation and the treaties—to achieve the end of extinguishment.

Beginning in the 1820s, with increasing British immigration to Upper Canada, agricultural settlement by white settlers on a large scale began. Requests came for more land surrenders. In the 1820s under Lieutenant Governors Sir Charles Henry Darling, John Colborne (Baron Seaton), and then Sir Francis Bond Head, the British imperial government embarked on its policy of "civilization" in Upper Canada since it had already been deemed a success by English imperial officials in Lower Canada. While this policy was primarily designed with a hard edge to purposefully assimilate aboriginal people, it also promised monies for education and training and economic opportunities, for example, commercial agricultural opportunities, for the citizens of the First Nations. Another less desirable approach of the policy was a conscious plan of removal, developed by Head in the mid-1830s. The idea was to remove and to centralize aboriginal people into two geographical areas: primarily Manitoulin Island and Walpole Island. Once centralized, they could better be, according to the government view, "civilized" and then assimilated. This was strenuously resisted by the First Nations. The only group that became enfranchised as "white people" by the 1880s under this policy were the Wyandots of Anderdon.

The so-called civilization policy was not predicated on the surrender of Indian lands, at least initially, to pay for the policy. Rather, the monies for it would come from a general parliamentary grant from the crown. Subsequently, the policy became one of assimilation, which was financed crudely by selling Indian lands and using the funds raised to pay for their own assimilation. This policy was anathema to the First Nations. By 1840, the policy had already failed at Coldwater and other places. Yet the Indian Department, confronted by wholesale squatting and trespassing on First Nation lands, continued to implement it by taking land surrenders. This policy was codified in the late 1850s in the first Indian Act of 1857. The import of this new approach to civilization was not lost on the First Nations' leadership, who rejected it and bluntly stated that it was an attempt "to break them to pieces."

Partially responding to the attempted encroachments and the alienation of the Indian Territory, the English imperial government took action, flowing from the Royal Proclamation, to protect parts of it. In 1839 it passed legislation to protect crown lands, especially the Indian Territory, which had been the subject of considerable concern because of trespassing, squatting by nonaboriginal people, illegal land use (such as the taking of timber from Indian lands), and outright fraud. However, this legislation proved not to be strong enough in the decade following its passage, and the thefts or other depredations on aboriginal lands continued. On August 10, 1850, the government of the Province of Canada passed further legislation, an act for the "protection" of the "property occupied or enjoyed" by aboriginal people in Upper Canada "from Trespass and Injury." This legislation strengthened the provisions of the 1839 Act but the legislation still appears not to have been effective since the squatting and the process of dispossession continued unabated.

In 1861 Herman Merivale (1806–1874), an astute British imperial commentator and a consummate bureaucrat, observed that British imperial aboriginal policy had been a failure. His commentary could well be a description of Canada's aboriginal policy more than 144 years later:

> The subject, in short, is one which has been dealt with by perpetual compromises between principle and immediate exigency. Such compromises are incidental to constitutional government. We are accustomed to them: there is something in them congenial to our national character, as well as accommodated to our institutions; and on the whole, we may reasonably doubt whether the world is not better managed by means of them than through the severe application of principles.

But, unfortunately, in the special subject before us, the uncertainty created by such compromises is a greater evil than errors of principle.

Merivale's description of the vacillating nature of Canada's perpetual compromises between principle and immediate exigency is a significant observation about the failure of Canada's aboriginal policies. The policies only created great uncertainty and extreme frustration with the failure of the crown to uphold the Covenant Chain of Silver and the concomitant solemn treaty promises. This situation goes far to explain its failure of Canada's Indian policies.

One of the primary events of Canada's racist and colonial Indian policies was the Confederation of Canada. In 1867 the British North America Act was passed by the British imperial government, thereby establishing the Dominion of Canada. The First Nations effectively lost recognition and respect for their rights of aboriginal governance over their lands and waters. The new federal government assumed responsibility for "Indians, and Lands reserved for the Indians" by Section 91 (24), subject to any liabilities, which the government of the Province of Canada had, to the First Nations. This legislation allowed the federal government to pass the first consolidated Indian Act, thereby establishing a colonial relationship of the federal government to the First Nations. It also stated that the provinces had control over all other lands within the boundaries of each province (Section 109). Although this imperial statute was subject to any outstanding interests, including reserve lands as well as the aboriginal territory, much of which was still unceded, neither the interests nor the lands were specified. If the lands were not referred to, then the assumption was that the First Nations' land rights did not exist.

Originally, the Confederation of Canada was conceived of and was supposed to have been a treaty among the founding nations of Canada, including all of the First Nations based on the Two Row Wampum. But it soon became a means of carrying forward the policy of extinguishment, including the surrender or relinquishment of the Indian Territory as well as the implementation in the late nineteenth century of the residential school system with its horrific cultural and sexual abuses, which lasted well into the 1980s.

The negotiation of the so-called numbered treaties was a clear example not only of the divergence in thinking of the treaty makers in the 1870s but also of the weaknesses of Canada's regional Indian policies at that time and thereafter. Mawe-dopenais, a Mide chief of the Ojibwa, spoke to the crown's commissioner and chief negotiator, Alexander Morris (1826–1889), at the third treaty negotiations in October of 1873. As a spokesperson for the Rainy Lake and Rainy River people in this treaty-making process, he was clear on the position of aboriginal nations and the title to their lands: "I lay before you our opinions. Our hands are poor but our heads are rich, and it is riches that we ask so that we may be able to support our families as long as the sun rises and the water runs." Morris replied, disingenuously, indicating that he did not understand what aboriginal title and the treaty-making process meant for the aboriginal nations: "I am very sorry; you know it takes two to make a bargain; you are agreed on the one side, and I for the Queen's Government on the other. I have to go away and report that I have to go without making terms with you. I doubt if the Commissioners will be sent again to assemble this nation." This threat, implying the government approach of divide and conquer was not, as may be expected, well received by the Ojibwa nation. Treaty 3 was eventually negotiated and signed, but not on the basis of the spirit and the terms of the treaty as understood by the Ojibwa Nation. He did not believe, as many people do to this day, that the aboriginal nations were ready to share in the treaty-making process with the riches in their heads. There was no balance in the "bargain" before or after the treaty was signed. Morris and the federal government took too much away from the life of the Ojibwa. It has continued to do so here and elsewhere in Canada.

This nonconsultative treaty-making approach became central and pivotal to the development of the top-down policy approach of the federal government inherent in the Indian Act of 1876 and its successors, making the government both colonial and racist. Under this Act, the federal government alone, in a process that is neither consultative nor community-based, decides who is an aboriginal person and who is not under the registration process. Nonstatus and Métis persons are not recognized as aboriginal, and they cannot be registered under the Act, notwithstanding that they are recognized in Canada's Constitution as aboriginal peoples. In fact, it was not until the 1930s that the Inuit of Canada's north were recognized through a court ruling as having equal status as "Indians." Yet there is no Inuit Act today. Moreover, except for one substantial revision to that legislation in 1951, essentially the Indian Act remains a cornerstone of Canada's aboriginal policies. Canadian Indian policies have been and still are in complete disarray.

There remains a wide cultural gulf in the treaty-making process that has become intensified and that has led to the abrogation of aboriginal title and treaty rights and to the events of the summer of 1990 at the Oka and nearby Mohawk reserves. But the events at Oka were broader than those at Kahnesatake and Kahnawake. Similar situations also occurred in Ontario and in British Columbia, all involving unresolved land claims, a problem across Canada and one that resurfaced in 2006 with the conflict at Caledonia, Ontario.

What accounts for these Canadian Indian policies and the reality of Indian existence in Canada? The answer lies in the disparate histories of aboriginal and nonaboriginal people in Canada. The European, so-called scientific Western tradition of history has seen, sometimes in its crudest forms, the relationship between people and the land and its uses as a separate category and process. From the viewpoint of aboriginal traditions, these categories are wholly artificial and do not really exist. The aborigine has a holistic view, seeing land and man and nature and the uses that one makes of the lands and waters as one within a circle of time. They come from a single source—from a Creator who made all living things and nature. It is not enough to analyze each separately. The sum of the parts does not, in this instance, comprise the whole. The aboriginal way of seeing the world is simple, yet profound. Aboriginal people have protected and conserved their homelands—their territories—since time immemorial. This is understood and told by their elders, from the perspective of the First Nations. They tell who they are and, in spiritual terms, what their lands and waters mean to them. They have used the land and have shared in the harvesting of the fruits of the land for thousands of years.

The primary objective of aboriginal people is spiritual: to protect the land—Mother Earth—and the waters of Turtle Island. This is a sacred trust, a trust to protect the land. The continuity and integrity of the lands are important to the survival of indigenous people. Generations of First Nations members have used the land and have shared in its bounty and its uses. Moreover, they will continue to use this land and teach their children about the Creator and the land. So this relationship is all-important. They owe their very survival to it. It is both simple and profound. The events of the summer of 1990 at Oka and elsewhere across Canada occurred in our time at the initiative of aboriginal people to protect their lands and waters. To do this, they had no choice but to resist those who wished to destroy the land and themselves. Not to do this meant their destruction as well as the destruction of their children and grandchildren. It would have meant the end of their cultures and of their survival as aboriginal people. They will continue to protect their lands and waters.

In the twenty-first century we are witnessing profound structural changes in the history of the world. The world of nineteenth-century European imperialism is over. Decolonization is continuing apace. This process has been characterized by the forces of both construction and destruction. In Canada, as one example, aboriginal peoples are reaffirming their inherent right to governance through diverse approaches and a variety of means. Their lands are ever so slowly being recovered, if not always respected. Aboriginal title is beginning to be understood and recognized. One watershed in the twentieth century was the *Calder v. Attorney General of British Columbia* case of 1973. This decision of the Supreme Court of Canada found that aboriginal title and rights did exist in the white justice system of Canada. It opened the legal doors for the prosecution of aboriginal title and rights cases in Canada. *Calder* was followed by many constructive Supreme Court decisions that affirmed aboriginal title and land rights and treaties, including *Guerin, Simon, Sioui,* and *Sparrow* in the late 1980s and 1990s, and most recently, *Delgamuukw* (1997), to name but a few.

Calder opened the door to new land claims policies of the federal government in 1974, only one year after the case was decided by Canada's Supreme Court. It has brought about an undermining of Canada's historic Indian policies and their replacement with various forms of aboriginal governance that has led to the creation of the territory of Nunavut in 1999 and then the first modern treaty: the Nishga Treaty in British Columbia in 2003. This new Indian policy is not based on land claims processes, because there are no aboriginal land claims, only land rights. There are only aboriginal title and treaty rights to the land, and these must be protected. Among the land grievances flowing from the treaty-making process is that—unrecognized by the Euro-Canadian land tenure system or by government legislation, such as the Indian Act—the spiritual foundation is lost. And it is lost not only in the reserves, places of special and specific protection, but also in any of the strategic areas of land that aborigines used. Such lands were a major consideration for both the crown and the aboriginal people, but the antithetical concepts regarding land ownership and use still intensify conflicts over treaty areas and reserves.

For example, the people of the Bkejwanong First Nation submitted a small land claim regarding three hundred acres to the Specific Claims Branch of Indian Affairs in 1977, thirty years ago. After years of review and analysis, it was rejected in 1986, and now its rejection is being reviewed by the Indian Specific Claims Commission, which was established by the Mulroney Tories as a partial response to Oka in 1991. The hearings on the rejection of this claim were scheduled to take place in April of 1994, seventeen years after the claim was submitted. To date, federal officials are still reviewing the claim. Land claims exhibit too much process, very little substance, and too few settlements. This example is not at all unusual, because the Indian Specific Claims Commission, established after the events of the summer of 1990 at Oka and elsewhere, can only publish its findings and recommendations to the federal cabinet, but the government does not have to implement its recommendations.

Likely due to differing views between the government and aboriginal nations over land rights, the government's procedure for handling what it regards as land claims seems to be aimed at delaying resolution for as long as possible. From the aboriginal nation's point of view, a land claim is a statement of the land rights in reference to a specific geographical area. It is a claim based on whether the aboriginal users of the land and its resources ever entered into a treaty for it under the rules set out in the Royal Proclamation of 1763. A claim is not a court action; it is not litigation. It is a policy (actually two—one for comprehensive claims and the other for specific ones) and a program of the federal government administered by the Department of Indian and Northern Affairs. The federal government, in other words, forces First Nations into a policy that does not reflect the nation-to-nation treaty-making process. If a First Nation disagrees with this policy, its only recourse is to begin an expensive, decades-long litigation process on each of its claims.

From the government's policy and program point of view, the purpose is to extinguish "claims." When a claimant decides on litigation, the file wends its way slowly through the federal bureaucracy to the Department of Justice, where, in time, the claimant is seen to have withdrawn the claim. First, an application for a claim must be accompanied by a statement of facts that includes a summary statement of the historical research findings on the aboriginal people and their lands. It includes events that have been recorded either by oral traditions or by the written record since time immemorial. Legal argument and conclusions are often present as well. Lastly, copies of the historical documents are included. The government, or more correctly governments, since in Canada provincial governments have constitutional jurisdiction over lands and natural resources, while the federal government has responsibility for Indian land and people, begins to assess the claim based on its perception of its validity, its (often limited) understanding of the interpretation of the history of the aboriginal people, and pure political considerations.

The actions of previous governments are also taken into account from the time of the British empire in the eighteenth century through to the successive colonial governments, the provinces, and Ottawa. Also significant in any bureaucratic and political judgment is the role of legal and legislative precedents with similar claims. For example, a previous Supreme Court of Canada decision in a claimant's favor has an enormous impact on a claim with a similar fact situation because it likely has the same legal issues at stake. The difficulty is that there are still relatively few legal precedents. Thus, decisions on validity are often determined by the Department of Justice's lawyers whose job entails a conflict of interest. This system of deciding the claims by having a federal lawyer be the judge, jury, and executioner is not at all fair, and, moreover, it has failed. Only a truly independent claims commission, such as an independent tribunal, can protect the claims process and the federal government from disrepute.

Land claims are significant only if they can add to the land and the economic base of First Nation communities. Indian reserves were initially strategic economic areas that were excepted from the treaty-making process. Later they were transformed and designed by British imperial policy makers as special areas of "civilization" with the specific objective of assimilating the First Nations. Soon they became mere "half-way houses" that were to be appropriated whenever they were needed for the purposes of the crown or for nonaboriginal uses. Thus, the federal government held the First Nations' land in a kind of British imperial trusteeship, which gave way on a path leading to gradual and then, it was hoped, complete assimilation. This is a vestige of a pure colonial relationship. Even this misguided basis for aboriginal "claims," distorted as it is by twentieth-century lenses, has been rendered illegitimate through time by the alienation of the land and labor of aboriginal people. First Nations' land and labor were effectively or formally expropriated by the federal or provincial governments. Land surrenders, as well as the loss of the commons (their non-Reserve areas) for natural resource usage by governments and by private interests, assisted the process. What was seen to be legitimate was rendered both unlawful and unfair from an aboriginal perspective. The Temagami case, in particular the building of the Red Squirrel Road extension in 1988–1989, is a prime, but not a solitary, illustration. Only on October 2, 1990, at a conference on aboriginal sovereignty and self-determination in Toronto, as a result of many years of aboriginal resistance movements, has there been a recognition in Canada of the inherent right of aboriginal self-governance.

Fifteen years of constitution making since 1982 have collapsed into disunity, separatism, and regional antagonisms among the white visitors to Canada. The former Meech Lake Accord, the epitome of the old British imperial centralist model of confederation, stylishly referred to as "executive federalism," was defeated in 1990 and never ratified as part of Canada's constitution. The same was true for the second attempt with the Charlottetown Accord of 1992. This was a clear constitutional victory for aboriginal people: They are in the Canadian Constitution. Although the Charlottetown Accord of 1992 was also a failure, the inherent right of aboriginal people to self-governance, as well as their title and land rights, has since been reaffirmed. Gradually, Canada is becoming similar in structure to what it was in preconfederation days. At that time, British North America was a series of communities located along the Great Lakes and adjacent waterway systems. It comprised Euro-American and aboriginal communities in an alliance of nations within both aboriginal and British imperial confederacies. It was a true meeting ground of diverse languages, cultures, and communities. This is an illustration of how the past is an integral part of the present. Aboriginal title, time, and resistance movements may well be common themes in Canada's disparate histories of its founding nations.

The foundation exists now for a constructive approach to the making of Canada by means of treaty making. The Constitution of Canada recognizes aboriginal people as "Indian, Inuit and Métis." It also shows grudging respect for "existing Aboriginal and treaty rights." Why, then, did aboriginal people oppose the Meech Lake Accord, contributing dramatically to its failure in June 1990? Why did we have, some few weeks later, the violence and the blockades at Kahnesatake, Oka, and Kahnawake in Quebec, or the blockades of roads and railway lines in Ontario and British Columbia?

The answer lies in the First Nations' disparate histories and cultures. To put it simply, aboriginal people and the rest of Canada speak to one another from differing historical and cultural assumptions and experiences, including those regarding languages, customs, governance, lands, and waters, as well as time and progress. This also helps to explain the repeated failures of Canada's aboriginal policy or policies.

This reversal of English imperial policy was only altered in 1982 when Canada's Constitution was brought home from England in written form. Hitherto, it had been an unwritten document, essentially an embodiment of British imperialist legislation in 1867. With this act, "existing Aboriginal and treaty rights" (but not self-governance or sovereignty) were admitted as part of the Charter of Rights and Freedoms under that Constitution. Today the larger business of the treaty-making process and various land claims policies remains incomplete and unfulfilled. The land claims issues are currently being defined by Canada's Constitution on an issue-by-issue basis by the Supreme Court of Canada.

The validity of aboriginal oral history and traditions was reaffirmed in 1996 by the Royal Commission on Aboriginal Peoples and again in 1997 by the Supreme Court of Canada in its ruling in the case of *Delgamuukw v. British Columbia*, also known as the Gitksan and Wet'suwet'en comprehensive claim. That legal ruling stated that oral traditions are "not simply a detached recounting of factual events but, rather, are 'facts enmeshed in the stories of a lifetime.'" Moreover, they are "rooted in particular locations, making reference to particular families and communities." As a result, aboriginal oral history is in fact "many histories, each characterized in part by how a people see themselves, how they define their identity in relation to their environment, and how they express their uniqueness as a people." The Supreme Court stated that the laws of evidence in the Canadian justice system must accommodate aboriginal oral history and tradition such that it "be placed on an equal footing with the types of historical evidence that courts are familiar with, which largely consists of historical documents. This is a long-standing practice in the interpretation of treaties between the Crown and aboriginal peoples." Not to recognize and accept this history as an equally valid way of viewing the past is to invalidate aboriginal people and their land rights.

Without pen or ink, the First Nations remember and understand, through their stories, their internal and external landscapes of being and becoming. There are no boundaries and no beginning or end points. In short, there is no periodization of history. Their history is both separate and parallel to the history of Canada, as understood by nonaboriginal people—the history of the newcomers. In this way, aboriginal oral traditions also evoke and speak to the European past and have much to teach us about ourselves. They provide a necessary corrective, a balance as well as a deeper understanding of what we know today as Canada. For aboriginal people, circles of time are part of the natural world and nature, of life and living. Every living thing has a relationship to every other, and the events that occur in one's lifetime have an immediate impact on one's children and grandchildren. The seventh generation is immediate and close. We are, then, within circles of time.

Yet much of Canada's modern aboriginal land policy is still viewed one-dimensionally as primarily assimilative, as a form of directed cultural change. This has been seen as originating in the nineteenth century and culminating in the federal government's White Paper of 1969. Canadian historians have concentrated more on the origins and development of that policy and less on the resistance to it by the First Nations, especially on aspects of it in the twentieth century. Aboriginal policies must also be viewed from the perspective of the First Nations' citizens and their governments. It must not be forgotten that nonaboriginal people and their governmental institutions have been visitors to aboriginal homelands.

Canada's aboriginal policies have developed gradually and consist of two primary components that are diametrically opposed to each other. Thus they become built-in obstacles. The first is that the federal government has been largely indifferent to aboriginal title and land rights, taking a legalistic approach overall, acting only when it is forced to do so by Canada's courts. The second component is that the provinces continue to use their hegemony, through legislation and regulations, over lands and natural resources in self-serving ways. Canada's aboriginal policies since 1867 have been an artificial creation, both negative and destructive, for aboriginal people and their relationship to the rest of the country. Federal policies have always been driven by other more prominent national agenda items—western settlement, protective tariffs, free trade, and the Constitution. Witness, for example, the failure of the Meech Lake and the Charlottetown Accords in the early 1990s. Canada's aboriginal policy, through a long process of denial, has created institutional racism and corresponding resistance movements that culminated in violence and death. The events of the summer of 1990 at Oka have not been erased. The initiative for change in aboriginal history has always come from the First Nations. Government policy has always been characterized by reaction, crisis management, and denial. Encountering policy words with no substance and a benign, passive policy, the First Nations have always chosen to act; they had no choice but to resist these polices if they wished to survive.

David T. McNab and Ute Lischke

See also Assembly of First Nations; Boarding Schools, United States and Canada; Constitution Act; Cree-Naskapi Act; Department of Indian Affairs and Northern Development; Indian Act; James Bay and Northern Quebec Agreement; Nunavut Land Claims Agreement; Royal Commission on Aboriginal Peoples; Tribal Sovereignty; Tungavik Federation, Nunavut.

References and Further Reading

Lischke, Ute, and David T. McNab, eds. 2005. *Walking a Tightrope: Aboriginal People and Their Representations.* Waterloo, ON: Wilfrid Laurier University Press.

McNab, David T. 1999. *Circles of Time: Aboriginal Land Rights and Resistance in Ontario.* Waterloo, ON: Wilfrid Laurier University Press.

McNab, David T., Bruce W. Hodgins, and Ute Lischke, eds. 2003. *Blockades and Resistance: Studies in Actions of Peace and the Temagami Blockades of 1988–89.* Waterloo, ON: Wilfrid Laurier University Press.

Canandaigua (Pickering) Treaty

United States Secretary of War Timothy Pickering negotiated the Canandaigua Treaty with the Haudenosaunee, represented mainly by the Seneca, in

Timothy Pickering, while U.S. secretary of war, negotiated the Canandaigua treaty with the Haudenosaunee, represented mainly by the Seneca, in 1794. (Library of Congress)

1794. The treaty called for peace, as well as noninterference in the affairs of the Six Nations by the United States, quitclaims for lands already ceded, and an annuity of $4,500 a year. Hardly had the ink dried on the guarantee of noninterference, however, when the United States commissioners, hearing of General "Mad Anthony" Wayne's victory at Fallen Timbers (near Maumee and Toledo, Ohio), demanded portage rights at Niagara.

The Canandaigua Treaty is important today because it defines Seneca sovereignty specifically and Haudenosaunee sovereignty by implication. Specifically, the treaty says that the United States would "never claim the same [Seneca territory], nor disturb the Seneca nation . . . in the free use or enjoyment thereof; but it shall remain theirs until they choose to sell the same to the people of the United States" (Foster, 1984, 117).

To the Haudenosaunee, the important issues at Canandaigua were familiar: Several frontier murderers of Indians by whites were going unpunished.

Jurisdiction over major crimes was a common issue in treaty negotiations. The Iroquois also maintained that land cessions required by the Fort Stanwix treaty, negotiated in 1784, had been unfairly extensive, encroaching on their hunting grounds. The proposed settlement at Presque Isle was at issue as well. The Seneca insisted that the warrior chiefs who had negotiated the peace at Fort Stanwix had failed to submit the treaty to the Grand Council for ratification. Pickering proposed that the Seneca relinquish a strip of land four miles wide along the south of the Niagara River from Cayuga Creek to Buffalo Creek. Red Jacket replied that this was not acceptable because it would constitute a threat to Seneca fisheries and their settlement at Buffalo Creek. Pickering dropped the issue and settled for construction of a road, to be owned by the Seneca, from Fort Schlosser to Buffalo (Fenton, 1998, 695).

The negotiations continued until the parties achieved a general consensus that they had achieved all they could. On November 9, however, the Seneca Chief Cornplanter complained of past dealings with the United States and offered that the sachems alone, and not the warriors, should sign the treaty. Pickering was unwilling to do this. He felt that if the warriors did not sign, divisions would rise among the Indians that would undo the treaty (Fenton, 1998, 699).

Cornplanter's behavior significantly diminished his reputation as a friend of the United States in Pickering's eyes. The treaty was signed on November 11, 1794, and went into effect under U.S. law on January 21, 1795. The primary objectives of the United States were to settle the question of the Six Nations' claims to lands in Ohio and the Erie Triangle and to embark on a policy of sincere negotiations and fair payment in land transactions.

Today, the people of the Six Nations believe the U.S. government has not kept several promises made in this treaty. The Six Nations believe the United States recognized that the lands of the Six Nations belong to them, not to the United States. The U.S. and New York State governments have since acted contrarily to any reasonable interpretation of the promise not to claim the land or disturb the Six Nations in any way. And they do so despite the fact that the United States and New York State do not collect taxes or enforce a variety of laws and regulations on lands they have acknowledged as having status as a sovereign domain distinct from their own.

Finally, many Iroquois believe that the treaty recognizes parallel legal jurisdictions to a much greater degree than those that have evolved since 1794. The treaty states, for example, that in the event of a crime, the two parties will pursue prudent measures involving the president or the superintendent until some other "equitable" provision shall be made. Some U.S. representatives assert that transferring jurisdiction to New York State fulfilled the requirement for equitable or equal provision, involving both parties in resolution of problems. However, many Iroquois, most notably the traditional chiefs, have long complained that there was nothing equitable in either the spirit or practice of the U.S. legal system as it relates to this treaty.

The treaty, signed by George Washington on January 21, 1795, remains a seminal document in Iroquois–U.S. relations. Following the construction of the Kinzua Dam, the Senecas whom it displaced were compensated with $18 million because the eviction violated the Canandaigua Treaty. The Canandaigua Treaty was being used in the late twentieth century to prod federal government bodies, such as the Environmental Protection Agency, to act on environmental problems that damage Haudenosaunee living conditions from sources in the United States. Pollution from off-reservation sources is most serious at Akwesasne, which has been ranked as the most expensive toxic cleanup in the United States by the U.S. Environmental Protection Agency. The Senecas' Tonawanda reservation near Niagara Falls is close to Love Canal, one of North America's best publicized toxic sites. The Onondagas also invoked sovereignty guaranteed under the Canandaigua Treaty in 1983 when they granted sanctuary to American Indian Movement leader Dennis Banks and his family as he was being pursued by federal law enforcement authorities.

Bruce E. Johansen

See also Canada, Indian Policies of; Citizenship; Cornplanter; Hazardous Waste; Red Jacket; Tribal Sovereignty.

References and Further Reading

Fenton, William N. 1998. *The Great Law and the Longhouse: A Political History of the Iroquois Confederacy.* Norman: University of Oklahoma Press.

Foster, Michael K., Jack Campisi, and Marianne Mithun. 1984. *Extending the Rafters: Indisciplinary Approaches to Iroquoian Studies.* Albany: State University of New York Press.

Carlisle Treaty Council

The Carlisle Treaty Council between the Pennsylvania colony and the representatives of various Indian groups met at Carlisle, Pennsylvania, for one week beginning October 1, 1753. Ever the entrepreneur, Benjamin Franklin printed an account of the negotiation in his newspaper.

The chief reason for calling the conference lay in the growing tensions between the French and British and their respective Indian allies. Realizing that a war loomed on the horizon, the Pennsylvania Assembly called the conference and sent a delegation to negotiate for the renewal of alliances with various Ohio and Iroquois groups. The Pennsylvania delegation was composed of Franklin, in his first appearance as an Indian negotiator; Richard Peters, the secretary of the Provincial Council; and Isaac Peters, the secretary of the Pennsylvania Assembly. These three were the chief diplomats sent to the conference. Conrad Weiser, a local Indian trader who acted as interpreter, assisted the three delegates in their negotiations. George Croghan assisted Weiser in these activities.

Native American groups present included the Delawares, the Twightwees, the Shawnees, and the Wyandots. These last three were Ohio Indians. The Twightwees in particular were mentioned in Governor James Hamilton of Pennsylvania's announcement calling for the conference since the French attacked them in 1752. Also present were the Iroquois, who claimed suzerainty over the Delawares. The negotiator for the Iroquois was Scarrooyady.

Many of the normal issues of the colonial–Indian relations arose in the discussions at the conference. The various Indian groups sought restrictions on the increasing numbers of white settlers coming across their borders illegally and squatting on their lands. They therefore sought assurances that the Pennsylvanians would guarantee their lands. A paramount issue for the Indians—and one Scarrooyady became very outspoken on—was the use of rum in the fur trade. The chiefs called for a stop to this practice, and Franklin agreed. His conviction on the matter was reinforced when he witnessed the effects of alcohol on the Native Americans on the night following the conclusion of the conference.

For their part, the Pennsylvanians sought clear assurances that, should another conflict between Great Britain and France erupt in the backcountry, the Indians would at least remain neutral and at best join on the British side.

At one point during the conference proceedings, the Delawares attempted to assert their independence from the Iroquois Confederacy. This

nearly brought an end to the conference when Scarrooyady flatly rejected the claim.

In the end, Franklin signed a treaty whereby the Pennsylvania colony pledged to respect the boundaries with the various Indian groups and to hold back the flow of settlers. Likewise, he pledged to raise the matter of regulating the Indian trade, and more specifically removing liquor from the trade, with the Pennsylvania Assembly. The Indians likewise pledged their neutrality should a conflict break out with the French. In the long run, both sides failed to live up to their pledges when the French and Indian War broke out.

It is quite clear that a number of the issues that arose at the Carlisle Conference influenced Franklin's thinking as he prepared to attend the Albany Congress the following year. Among the concerns of Native Americans that certainly affected Franklin's thinking were the desires of the chiefs that white settlement be restricted and that alcohol be removed from the fur trade. Likewise, it is clear that Franklin was already thinking along the lines of mutual colonial defense as he prepared for the meeting in Albany in 1754 and that ideas along these lines developed as he negotiated with the chiefs at Carlisle. Finally, the successful conclusion of the Carlisle conference and treaty marked the beginning of nearly three decades of diplomacy on the part of Franklin with Native Americans, among the colonies, and with various European states.

James R. McIntyre

See also Albany Congress, Native Precedents; Franklin, Benjamin, Native American Influences; French and Indian War; Fur Trade.

References and Further Reading

Anderson, Fred. 2000. *Crucible of War: The Seven Years War and the Fate of Empire in British North America, 1754–1766*. New York: Alfred A. Knopf.

Bands, H. W. 2000. *The First American: The Life and Times of Benjamin Franklin*. New York: Anchor Books.

Wainwright, Nicholas B. 1959. *George Croghan, Wilderness Diplomat*. Chapel Hill: University of North Carolina Press.

Ward, Matthew C. " 'The European Method of Warring Is Not Practiced Here': The Failure of British Military Policy in the Ohio Valley, 1755–1759." *War in History* 4, no. 3 (1997): 247–263.

Cherokee Nation v. Georgia

Following the discovery of gold there in 1829, Georgia attempted to assert authority over the Cherokee Nation, which comprised several economically self-sufficient towns with their own farms, mills, animal herds, and government. Cherokees also used a written language, devised by Sequoyah. The assertion of political authority by the state of Georgia set the stage for a key test of federal–state relations in the decades before the Civil War, as the Cherokees resisted removal to Indian Territory, in *Cherokee Nation v. Georgia* (1831) and *Worcester v. Georgia* (1832).

The term "Marshall Trilogy" is used to describe the group of Chief Justice John Marshall's rulings in *Johnson v. McIntosh* (1823), *Cherokee Nation v. Georgia*, and *Worcester v. Georgia*. In these three cases, Marshall developed legal doctrines that defined the relationships among the United States, the individual states, and Native American nations. In these opinions, according to legal scholar Charles F. Wilkinson, "Marshall conceived a model that can be described broadly as calling for largely autonomous tribal governments subject to an overriding federal authority but essentially free of state control" (1987, 24).

The Marshall Trilogy is so important in American Indian law because the key precepts of Marshall's three opinions have been interpreted by lawyers, judges, legal scholars, and government officials in many different ways. The Bureau of Indian Affairs, for example, used the phrases "dependent," "pupilage," and "ward" to construct a cradle-to-grave social and political control system in which even adult Indians were regarded legally as incompetents, much like children.

President Jackson's adamant support of Indian removal placed him on a direct constitutional collision course with Chief Justice John Marshall, who was in the process of evolving legal doctrines vis-à-vis Native American land rights on which he had been working before Jackson was elected. The Cherokee cases, which came before Chief Justice Marshall's U.S. Supreme Court between 1823 and 1832, would display, in broad and emphatic relief, how closely much of early nineteenth-century American life was connected to the land speculation machine that helped propel westward movement.

In *Cherokee v. Georgia*, the Cherokees sued in federal court under a clause in the Constitution (Article III, section 2) that allows foreign citizens or states to seek legal redress against states in the union. In this case, the Cherokees were suing as an independent

An 1866 map of the state of Georgia shows county boundaries, roads, settlements, and topographical features. Also depicted is a large reservation for the Cherokee Indians. (Michael Maslan Historic Photographs/Corbis)

nation seeking redress because the state of Georgia had extended its power over Cherokee territory, extinguished the authority of the Cherokee government, and executed one of its citizens. Chief Justice Marshall skirted the issue by deciding that the Cherokees were not an independent country, but instead a "domestic dependent nation." Marshall thus threw the case out of court, deciding that the Cherokees had no grounds on which to sue under the Constitution.

Georgia replied, citing a clause in the Constitution that prohibits the establishment of a state within the borders of another state. Marshall found, however, that the Cherokees had a legal relationship with the federal government through treaties; Georgia's assertion of unilateral control was said by Marshall to be "repugnant to the said treaties, and . . . therefore unconstitutional and void" (Baker, 1974, 743). Writing for the majority in *Cherokee Nation v. Georgia*, Marshall said that the Cherokees possessed a limited sovereignty: "They may, more correctly, perhaps be denominated domestic depen-

dent nations . . . Their relation to the United States resembles that of a ward to his guardian." These phrases, as interpreted by the Bureau of Indian Affairs, became the legal justification for the colonial system that was being imposed on Indians as Anglo-American settlement exploded across North America in the nineteenth century. Whether he intended it or not, the government used Marshall's conception of the relationship to justify placing Indians in state of "wardship" in which their lives were placed under control by government agents. More than a century later, the "self-determination" movement aimed to dismantle this system.

The doctrine of wardship (as it has been applied to Native Americans) often is said to have grown out of Marshall's rulings, although he may not have intended such an application. As the legal scholar Felix Cohen wrote:

> . . . [T]he doctrine of Indian wardship arose out of a misunderstanding of Chief Justice Marshall's holding, in 1831, that an Indian tribe was not a foreign nation but was rather a "domestic dependent nation," and that its position toward the United States *resembles* that of a ward toward a guardian. This did not mean that an Indian tribe is a ward; even less did it mean that an individual Indian is a ward. But the opinion and several later opinions popularized the term wardship (Cohen, 1960, 331).
>
> Under the reign of these magic words ["wardship" and "trust"] nothing Indian was safe. The Indian's hair was cut, his dances forbidden, his oil lands, timber lands, and grazing lands were disposed of by Indian agents and Indian commissioners for whom the magic word "wardship" always made up for lack of statutory authority . . . (Cohen, 1960, 131–132).

In *Cherokee v. Georgia*, the justices of the Supreme Court took a variety of positions on the issue of Native American sovereignty that reflected societal attitudes toward the issue. While Justices Marshall and John McLean held that Indians lived in domestic dependent nations, Justices Smith Thompson and Joseph Story held that the Cherokees were a sovereign nation. Justice Henry Baldwin wrote that they had no sovereignty at all, and Justice William Johnson believed that the Cherokees had no sovereignty in his time but that they possessed an inherent political power that might "mature" into more complete independence in the future.

Removal of the Cherokees and several other Native nations during the 1830s allowed the expansion of Anglo-American populations south and west through parts of Georgia, Alabama, Mississippi, and neighboring states. At roughly the same time, the industrial application of Eli Whitney's cotton gin created a mass market in moderately priced cotton clothing. Within a decade after their removals, the Indians' homelands were replaced, in large part, by King Cotton and a revival of slavery.

The removal of the "civilized tribes" from their homelands is one of the most notable chapters in the history of American land relations. Jackson's repudiation of John Marshall's rulings, which supported the Cherokees' rights to their homelands, was contempt of the Supreme Court (an impeachable offense under the Constitution). The subject of impeachment was not seriously raised, however. During the incendiary years before the Civil War, the removals became intertwined with the issue of states' rights vis-à-vis the federal government. Had Jackson followed Justice Marshall's rulings, the Civil War might have started during the 1830s.

Jackson did not seek the removal of the Cherokees and other civilized tribes—the Cherokees, Choctaws, Chickasaws, Creeks, and Seminoles—because they did not productively use the land. On the contrary, the civilized tribes were making exactly the kind of progress that the Great White Father desired of them: becoming farmers, educating their children, constituting governments modeled on the United States. Immigrants, many of them Scots and Irish, had married into Native families. Some of them owned plantations and slaves.

The issue was not the Indians' degree of civilization. It was ownership of the best agricultural land in the area. Land was the largest type of wealth in the United States during Andrew Jackson's lifetime. Slaves who worked the land of the South—human capital—were the second most widely held type of financial asset. The entire financial superstructure of stocks, bonds, and various forms of fungible cash so familiar in the late twentieth century lay largely in the future.

Michael Paul Rogin wrote of the period: "Land in America was not only a symbol of national identity, but also—in a more thoroughgoing fashion than anywhere else in the world—a commodity. . . . Land was the nation's most sought-after commodity in the first half-century of the republic, and the effort of men to acquire it was one of the dominant forces of the period" (1975, 79). Rogin quoted a contemporary source: "Were I to characterize the United States, it would be by the appellation of the land of speculators" (1975, 80). Land, once ownership had been wrested from Native owners, became the largest "futures market" available at the time, its value determined by its hoped-for future use in a newly evolving non-Indian society. As a general, and later as president, Jackson represented the values and interests of the land speculation industry.

Removal as an idea was not Jackson's creation. Nearly three decades before Jackson executed it, in 1802, the state of Georgia signed an agreement with the U.S. government (the Cherokees were not consulted), stating its intent to work toward extinguishment of all Cherokee land titles within state borders as early as the land could be "peaceably obtained, and on reasonable terms" (Moulton, 1978, 24). By the time the Removal Act was passed by Congress in 1830, most white Georgians regarded the United States to be "seriously delinquent in the bargain" (Moulton, 1978, 24).

As President Jackson ignored Chief Justice Marshall's opinion in *Worcester v. Georgia,* he also showed his frontier constituencies that he supported a belief popular among states' rights advocates of the time: that the Supreme Court should be stripped of its power to review the rulings of state courts. Marshall repudiated the states' rights advocates' belief that Section 25 of the Judiciary Act of 1789 prohibited the Supreme Court from hearing the case. A bill that would have repealed that section (which gives the U.S. Supreme Court the power to rule on appeals from state courts) was debated on the floor of the House of Representatives, voted on, and defeated January 29, 1831.

The purported limits on the Supreme Court's authority based on states' rights stirred substantial controversy during the 1830s; when *Worcester v. Georgia* was heard before the Court on February 20, 1832, fifty members of the House of Representatives (about a quarter of the body) were in attendance. Marshall stepped into the maw of the states' rights firestorm by turning aside a ruling of the Georgia Superior Court. Jackson, in turn, all but created his own law by ignoring Marshall's ruling.

As a result of Jackson's action, Georgia proceeded with its plan to evict Indians living within its borders and transfer the Indians' land to non-Natives. Between one-third and one-fourth of the sixteen thousand Cherokee people who were removed during 1838 died on the march to Indian Territory (now Oklahoma) or shortly thereafter. The Cherokees' name for the march (*nuna-daa-ut-sun'y*, "the trail where they cried") provided its English name, the Trail of Tears.

Bruce E. Johansen

See also Domestic Dependent Nation; Forced Marches; Indian Removal Act; Jackson, Andrew; Land, Identity and Ownership of, Land Rights; Relocation; Trail of Tears; Wardship Doctrine; *Worcester v. Georgia*.

References and Further Reading

Baker, Leonard. 1974. *John Marshall: A Life in Law.* New York: Macmillan.

Cohen, Felix. 1960. *The Legal Conscience: The Selected Papers of Felix S. Cohen.* Edited by Lucy Kramer Cohen. New Haven, CT: Yale University Press.

Moulton, Gary E. 1978. *John Ross: Cherokee Chief.* Athens: University of Georgia Press.

Rogin, Michael Paul. 1975. *Fathers and Children: Andrew Jackson and the Subjugation of the American Indian.* New York: Alfred A. Knopf.

Wilkinson, Charles F. 1987. *American Indians, Time, and the Law: Native Societies in a Modern Constitutional Democracy.* New Haven, CT: Yale University Press.

Columbia River Inter-Tribal Fish Commission

The Columbia River Inter-Tribal Fish Commission (CRITFC) is a cooperative resource management organization composed of the Confederated Tribes of the Umatilla Indian Reservation, the Confederated Tribes of Warm Springs, the Confederated Tribes and Bands of the Yakama Nation, and the Nez Percé tribe. Founded in 1977, following a string of tribal court victories, its stated mission is "to ensure a unified voice in the overall management of the fishery resources, and as managers, to protect reserved treaty rights through the exercise of the inherent sovereign powers of the tribes." CRITFC operates on the principles of consensus and collaboration, working through the fish and wildlife committees of its constituent tribes and in consultation with various state and federal agencies to harmonize indigenous traditions with the best modern science and the realities of the modern river. Together with the Northwest Indian Fisheries Commission, its counterpart among the tribes of Puget Sound, CRITFC has become an important player in the ongoing effort to protect and restore the endangered salmon runs of the Pacific Northwest.

The indigenous communities of the Columbia Basin struggled for more than a century to have their voices heard by the Euro-American interests and institutions that dominate the river. By treaties signed in 1855, the tribes reserved "the right of taking fish at all usual and accustomed places, in common with the citizens of the Territory." Starting in the 1860s, however, the commercialization of salmon and other forms of economic development (especially dam construction) began to decimate fish populations, destroy spawning habitat, and obstruct Indian access to the river. Declining salmon runs and increasing competition for fishing sites at Celilo Falls compelled the Umatilla, Warm Springs, and Yakama tribes to establish the Celilo Fish Committee (CFC) in 1936. This organization, which also included representatives from local Columbia River Indian communities, constituted the first intertribal effort to settle disputes and prevent outside interference. The CFC tried for twenty years to resolve conflicts and regulate harvests, but internal strife and limited authority hindered its effectiveness until the backwaters of The Dalles Dam flooded Celilo Falls in 1957. The tribes continued to assert their sovereignty, however, and federal court rulings in *U.S. v. Oregon* (1968) and *U.S. v. Washington* (1974) finally established their right to participate in fisheries management.

CRITFC emerged from a 1976 Memorandum of Understanding among the four treaty tribes with the help of the Bonneville Power Administration, which agreed to fund tribal participation as part of its legal obligation to mitigate the effects of federal dams. The tribes then passed resolutions authorizing the commission, and by March 1977 they had adopted its constitution and bylaws. CRITFC's structure reflects the determination of its founders to overcome tribal differences and practice cooperative management. The four tribal fish and wildlife committees comprise the commission's governing body, and they must reach consensus before it can act on their behalf. Each tribal committee appoints several commissioners, who annually select three officers (vice chair, secretary, and treasurer) and a chairperson from among their ranks, with each tribe holding the chair on a rotating basis. The position of executive director also rotates among the tribes to avoid charges of bias. Although disagreements occasionally arise within the commission, it remains committed to "unity of action in service of the salmon."

CRITFC has expanded greatly in size and expertise since the late 1970s. At first, it employed only two fish biologists and depended heavily on state and federal fishery agencies for advice and support. Over the years, as the tribes gained confidence and clout, CRITFC's staff grew to include additional biologists, fish passage specialists, policy analysts, attorneys, public relations officials, and law enforcement personnel. Some tribal fishers initially resented the imposition of another layer of management, but most now view the enforcement program as essential to their own safety and protection as well as to the preservation of the salmon. CRITFC has also earned the respect (if not always the affection) of state and federal agencies, which soon discovered that the tribes had their own management objectives. Commission staffers are active in gathering scientific data, setting fishery seasons and harvest quotas, carrying out habitat restoration projects, offering technical support to tribal hatcheries, conducting legal research, and lobbying policy makers. In the late 1990s, CRITFC developed its own management plan, called *Wy-Kan-Ush-Mi Wa-Kish-Wit* ("Spirit of the Salmon"). Much bolder than the measures favored by state, federal, and private interests, the tribal plan seeks quite simply "to put fish back in the rivers and protect the watersheds where fish live." "We have to take care of them so that they can take care of us," explained former executive director Ted Strong (Yakama). "Entwined together inextricably, no less now than ever before, are the fates of both the salmon and the Indian people."

Andrew H. Fisher

See also Boldt Decision; Dams, Fishing Rights, and Hydroelectric Power; Economic Development; Fishing Rights; Great Lakes Intertribal Council; Land, Identity and Ownership of, Land Rights; Salmon, Economic and Spiritual Significance of; Sohappy, Sr., David; Treaty Diplomacy, with Summary of Selected Treaties.

References and Further Reading

Cohen, Fay G. 1986. *Treaties on Trial: The Continuing Controversy over Northwest Fishing Rights.* Seattle: University of Washington Press.

Columbia River Inter-Tribal Fish Commission. No date. Available at: http://www.critfc.org. Accessed January 13, 2007.

Dompier, Douglas W. 2005. *The Fight of the Salmon People: Blending Tribal Tradition with Modern Science to Save Sacred Fish.* Philadelphia, PA: Xlibris Corporation.

Constitution Act

In 1980, then Canadian Prime Minister Pierre Trudeau announced his intention to repatriate the Canadian Constitution from Britain, complete with a Charter of Rights and an amending formula. Two years of intensive negotiations between the federal government and the provinces followed. One contentious issue threatened to stall the negotiations a number of times: the inclusion of Section 35. This section and its four subsections provided for the recognition of existing aboriginal and treaty rights, defined who the aboriginal people of Canada were, and recognized existing treaty rights and those that may in the future be obtained vis-à-vis land claims, while indicating that treaty rights were guaranteed equally to both sexes.

Originally, the British North America Act of 1867 listed Indians under Section 91 (federal responsibility), subsection 24, "Indians and lands reserved for Indians." Section 91(24) did not define what "Indian" meant or what the federal responsibilities to Indians were. The term "Indian" took on legal significance under the auspices of the Indian Act of 1876, which legally defined who an Indian was and, in particular, how to gradually do away with that status until Indians no longer existed, legislatively, in Canada. The Indian Act, which is still the prevailing piece of legislation guiding the federal government in its day-to-day interactions with Indians, did not legally reconcile the unique cultural status of Canada's Métis and Inuit populations, nor did it accept nations such as the Anishinaabes, the Haudenosaunees, or the Niitsitapis, to name a few, as distinct cultural groups. This failure to accept the unique political statuses of different groups of Indians resulted in the government's ignoring the Inuit or Métis and therefore renouncing any responsibility for their well-being. This changed in 1939 with a Supreme Court decision that interpreted the federal government's power to make laws affecting "Indians, and Lands reserved for the Indians" as extending to the Inuit. The Métis did not achieve similar recognition.

Prior to the Constitutional discussions of the late 1970s, the aboriginal population in Canada began aggressively to object to the continued use of the term "Indian." Historically utilized by Europeans and the British to identify North American indigenous populations, many "Indian"' organizations of the late 1970s changed their names to include the word "Native" or the phrase "First

Nation." Many aboriginal leaders also began to describe their ancestors as founding members of Canada, perhaps a "third tier" of confederation. The political influence of aboriginal leaders of the 1970s led federal officials in 1978 to invite the National Indian Brotherhood, the Native Council of Canada, and the Inuit Committee on National Issues to participate in the constitutional discussions. Not satisfied to watch from the periphery, eleven additional aboriginal organizations initiated an influential lobbying effort, the goal being to secure, among other things, the constitutional recognition of aboriginal people and their rights.

Aboriginal leaders sought distinct status for these groups within the proposed Canadian Constitution. Section 35 was the product of bilateral discussions between the federal government and the aboriginal leaders that excluded provincial involvement. Section 35 contains four subsections. Section 35(1) recognizes and affirms existing aboriginal rights arising from both common law and treaties. Thus this section grants constitutional protection of aboriginal rights. Section 35(2) recognizes aboriginal people as consisting of the "Indians, Inuit, and Métis" peoples of Canada. Section 35(3) specifically includes modern land claim agreements in treaty rights. Section 35(4) guarantees that the aboriginal and treaty rights referred to in subsection (1) are guaranteed equally to male and female persons. In theory, Section 35(2) provides the description of Canada's aboriginal people, permitting a greater definition and understanding of subsections (1), (2), and (4). However, the ambiguous nature of the definition often means that the Canadian court system is employed to provide clarification, an expensive and time-consuming process.

For instance, in 1993, a Métis father and his son, Steve and Roddy Powley, were charged with hunting moose without a license and unlawful possession of moose meat, contrary to Ontario's *Game and Fish Act*. A two-week trial in 1998 resulted in the judge's determining that the Métis community at Sault Ste. Marie had an existing aboriginal right to hunt, a decision that was upheld by the Supreme Court of Canada. The case took nearly one decade to complete. In the end, Métis people were recognized as aboriginal people according to Section 35(2) and as possessing aboriginal rights according to Section 35(1).

Yale D. Belanger

See also Assembly of First Nations; Canada, Indian Policies of.

References and Further Reading
Belanger, Yale, and David Newhouse. 2004. "Emerging from the Shadows: The Pursuit of Aboriginal Self-Government to Promote Aboriginal Well-Being." *Canadian Journal of Native Studies* 24, no. 1: 129–222.
Walkem, Ardith, and Halie Bruce, eds. 2003. *Box of Treasures or Empty Box: Twenty Years of Section 35*. Penticton, BC: Theytus Books.

Cree-Naskapi Act

The Cree-Naskapi Act, signed in 1984, is a constitutionally protected treaty that represents the first aboriginal self-government legislation in Canada. The Act is a direct result of the James Bay and Northern Quebec Agreement (JBNQA, 1975) and the Northeastern Quebec Agreement (NQA, 1978), which enabled the province of Quebec to carry on with its construction of the James Bay Hydroelectric Project. Under the James Bay and Northern Quebec Agreement, the Crees and the Inuits ended their northern Quebec land claims in return for $225 million, special dispensation for Native hunting and fishing rights over 45,000 square miles of land, and greater prospects for self-government (Niezen, 1998, 71). The Northeastern Quebec Agreement followed a similar format, with the Naskapis of Quebec receiving $9 million and land rights similar to those outlined in the James Bay and Northern Quebec Agreement. In return, the Crees surrendered all their claims, rights, titles, and interest in the land.

The JBNQA forced on federal Parliament responsibility for enacting legislation enabling local government for the Crees and subsequently for the Naskapi. Pursuant to this commitment, the Canadian government enacted the Cree-Naskapi Act on July 3, 1984. The JBNQA and the NQA involved the government of Canada, the government of Quebec, three provincial crown corporations, and the Crees, Inuits, and Naskapis of Quebec. The two agreements resolved the outstanding land claims of the aboriginal people inhabiting their traditional territories, as outlined in the Quebec Boundaries Extension Act of 1912. The two agreements were sanctioned and legislatively enabled at both the federal and provincial levels of government. Consequently, the Cree, Naskapi, and Inuit people halted the progress of their claims in exchange for rights and benefits specified in the two agreements. These agreements changed the social, political, and cultural lives of these peoples, while inevitably altering their relationship with the rest of Canada.

The Cree-Naskapi Act applies to Kobac Naskapi-aeyouch (the Naskapi band) and to eight Cree bands. The Act replaces the Indian Act, in return adopting a bilateral approach through consultation in determining relationships between the federal government and the Crees and Naskapis. The Minister of Indian and Northern Affairs Canada (INAC), by virtue of this act, has been stripped of his ability to exercise control over the Crees and Naskapis. This authority instead was assigned to the bands. The Cree-Naskapi Act established new legal and political regimes in the form of local governments accountable to the Cree and Naskapi people. According to the Act, the Crees and Naskapis were recognized as having differing titles and interests in addition to descending degrees of access to and control over resources, as well as varied powers of self-government. These powers include, but are not limited to, the administration of band affairs and internal management, public order, taxation for local purposes, and responsibility for local services, including fire protection.

The major weakness of the Cree-Naskapi Act is in its failure to confer legislative authority on the Cree and Naskapi bands, even though they possess local government-type powers that are inextricably tied to a constitutionally protected treaty. Further concerns include the facts that the Crees and Naskapis do not have the power to create their own constitution and that the Minister of Indian Affairs possesses the power to disallow or create bylaws relating to local taxation, hunting and trapping, elections, special band meetings, land registry system, long-term borrowing, band expropriation, and fines and penalties for breaking band bylaws. In addition, the Cree-Naskapi bands do not retain title to their traditional lands. They are ultimately subservient to Parliament and to the Quebec National Assembly. The Crees or Naskapis may, however, choose to challenge Canadian authority and further strengthen local sovereignty through the courts.

Nevertheless, the Cree-Naskapi Act was the first aboriginal self-government legislation that provided for a level of self-determination previously unattainable under the Indian Act and INAC structure. It has also provided the Cree-Naskapi bands with influence over land use that requires the federal and provincial governments to confer with community leaders and elders prior to enacting policies or legislation that could negatively influence the people.

Yale D. Belanger

See also Canada, Indian Policies of; Department of Indian Affairs and Northern Development.

References and Further Reading

Cree-Naskapi Commission. 1986. *Report of the Cree-Naskapi Commission*. Ottawa, ON: Cree-Naskapi Commission.

Isaac, Thomas. 1991a. "Aboriginal Self-Government in Canada: Cree-Naskapi (of Quebec) Act." *Native Studies Review* 7, no. 2: 15–42.

Isaac, Thomas. 1991b. "Authority, Rights and an Economic Base: The Reality of Aboriginal Self-Government." *Native Studies Review* 7, no. 2: 69–74.

Isaac, Thomas. 1992. "The 1992 Charlottetown Accord and First Nations Peoples: Guiding the Future." *Native Studies Review* 8, no. 2: 109–114.

Niezen, Ronald. 1998. *Defending the Land: Sovereignty and Forest Life in James Bay Cree Society*. Boston, MA: Allyn & Bacon.

Department of Indian Affairs and Northern Development

The Department of Indian Affairs and Northern Development (DIAND) was established in 1966 with the intent of administering to the varying needs of Native people in Canada, a culturally, economically, and geographically diverse clientele to be sure. DIAND's responsibility for administering Indian Affairs in Canada involved reconciling the socioeconomic interests of an increasingly suspicious and militant Indian leadership with a myriad of legislation and the agendas of federal, provincial, and territorial bodies.

Responsibility for colonial Indian affairs in British North America was originally vested with the British imperial parliament. In 1755, Sir William Johnson and John Stuart were appointed the first two superintendents of the British Indian Department in British North America. The department was established to maintain peaceful relations between settlers and Indian populations of the Ohio Valley. This relationship was codified in the Royal Proclamation of 1763, an edict passed by King George III that also reserved the lands west of the Appalachian Mountain chain as Indian hunting territory. American colonists intent on opening up western settlement were prohibited from entering this territory and from engaging Native leaders in land negotiations due in part to the history of "great Frauds and Abuses" that had been perpetrated against Indians. The new Indian bureaucracy for all intents and purposes remained in operation until Canada's birth in 1867.

The Fathers of Confederation accepted responsibility for "Indians and lands reserved for Indians" according to Section 91(24) of the Constitution Act (1867). They also effectively dovetailed the British colonial model with the new federal bureaucracy by establishing the Indian Affairs Branch in 1868, one of the four branches under the jurisdiction of the Department of the Secretary of State for the Provinces. This would not be the home of Indian affairs for long, however. In 1873, responsibility for Indian Affairs was transferred to the Minister of the Department of the Interior, when the department was created that year. This commenced a long history in which the responsibility for Indian affairs was shunted from one department to another.

The Indian Act of 1876 created the legislative framework enabling Indian Affairs to promote its Indian policy (read "civilization" policy) uniformly across the country. The Indian Act granted considerable powers to the Superintendent General of Indian Affairs and his Indian agents. It also ensured that Indians in Canada were increasingly subject to the Indian Affairs regime. An amendment to the Indian Act in 1880 elevated the branch to departmental status, albeit still under the direction of the Minister of the Interior, who now held the secondary title of Superintendent General of Indian Affairs. An 1881 amendment to the Indian Act amplified the Indian agents' powers, making them justices of the peace while permitting them to prosecute and deliver sentences for violations of the Indian Act's provisions.

During the next five decades, the department was restructured numerous times, as federal officials attempted to facilitate the assimilation of Indians into mainstream Canadian society. Promoted as a cost-cutting measure, the departmental restructuring resulted in the creation of several distinct branches, reflecting the expanded nature of the department's activities. Then, in 1936, the department was dissolved as a cost-cutting measure, and responsibility for Indian Affairs transferred to the Department of Mines and Resources, where a subdepartment was established: the Indian Affairs Branch (IAB). The branch included the following components: field administration, medical welfare and training service, reserves and trust service, and the records service. During the next three decades, responsibility for Indian affairs was transferred a number of times, including its relocation to the Department of Immigration and Citizenship in 1949, where it remained until an independent Department of Indian Affairs and Northern Development was established in 1966.

In 1964, R. F. Battle was appointed the Assistant Deputy Minister of Indian Affairs in the Department of Citizenship and Immigration, and he immediately spearheaded a significant reorganization of the Indian Affairs Branch followed by the formation of three new directorates: the Development Directorate, responsible for establishing and coordinating social, industrial, and resource development; the Education Directorate, responsible for establishing and carrying out educational policy; and the Administration Directorate, responsible for dealing with Indian lands and estates, membership, records management, field administration and the provision of a secretariat and support services.

The complexity of Indian affairs led to the decision once again to elevate the Branch to departmental status. On June 16, 1966, the Department of Indian Affairs and Northern Development (DIAND) was established by the Government Organization Act. DIAND was assigned responsibility for the development of the national parks, the administration of Indian and Eskimo affairs, and the management of Canada's wildlife resources. Arthur Laing (Progressive Conservative) was appointed minister, while E. A. Cote was appointed deputy minister to oversee the five DIAND branches. Legislation made the minister also responsible for Indians and Inuits, the residents of the Yukon and Northwest Territories, and their resources. In an attempt to improve accountability to their clientele, nine regional Indian affairs offices were established across Canada. Two years later, DIAND's announcement that it was again restructuring operations was followed by the creation of the Indian-Eskimo Bureau to provide advisory services for and to liaise with field staff responsible for departmental programs. Within the DIAND, four directorates were created: policy and planning, administration, development, and education.

By 1970, the Economic Development Branch was created to assist Indians in achieving economic self-sufficiency, and the Indian Economic Development Fund was established. That year, the Membership Division began transferring local administration of membership functions to Indian bands, and the federal government began funding Indian groups and associations specifically for research into treaties and Indian rights. In 1972, spurred on by the National Indian Brotherhood's (NIB) demands for greater autonomy to deliver education programs, DIAND initiated its devolution program by transferring responsibility for education to Native communities. The devolution program became central to the DIAND, a program that, with minor modifications during the last three decades, is still officially responsible for aboriginal people in Canada.

Commonly known today as Indian and Northern Affairs Canada (INAC), the department is responsible for two separate mandates: Indian and Inuit affairs and Northern affairs. Primarily responsible for meeting the federal government's constitutional, treaty, political, and legal responsibilities to the First Nations, Inuit, and Northerners, INAC's mandate is all-encompassing and derived from the Indian Act, territorial acts, and legal obligations arising from Section 91(24) of the Constitution Act (1867). This comprehensive approach results in a significant level of responsibility that encompasses a wide range of services and in turn requires that INAC officials work closely with the First Nations, the Inuit and the Northerners, the Métis, and other federal departments and agencies, provinces, and territories that are responsible for issues affecting Indians.

INAC delivers basic services such as education, social assistance, housing, and community infrastructure to status (officially recognized) Indian and Inuit communities. The department also administers Indian reserve lands, oversees elections of First Nation councils, registers entitlement to Indian status and First Nation membership, and administers First Nation trust funds and the estates of certain individual Indians, in addition to negotiating the settlement of accepted land claims. According to the INAC Web site, some of the department's priorities include the recognition of greater program and political authority of First Nations and territorial governments by establishing a framework for the effective implementation of the inherent right of self-government; specific initiatives to implement self-government; continued devolution to territories of program administration; and assisting First Nations and Inuit peoples in strengthening their communities.

In many respects, the current INAC mandate reflects the basic Indian policy of the late 1860s when the first federal political branch was assigned responsibility to facilitate the physical and cultural absorption of status Indians, Inuits, and Métis into mainstream Canadian society. Paternalism remains the operating philosophy. INAC, for example, still oversees band council elections while guiding program delivery at the community level. Using the Indian Act as its guide, INAC has significant control over Canada's First Nations. For instance, Section 6 of the Indian Act enables INAC to determine who is or is not to be considered an Indian in Canada, which has the impact of alienating a number of Native people from government programs. Through Section 81 of the Indian Act, INAC is able to limit the powers of band councils. In all, despite INAC's self-professed interest in seeing self-government develop, its control over most aspects of First Nations life in Canada continues.

Yale D. Belanger

See also Assembly of First Nations; Canada, Indian Policies of; Constitution Act; Indian Act.

References and Further Reading

Leslie, John. 1985. *Commissions of Inquiry into Indian Affairs in the Canadas, 1828–1858: Evolving a Corporate Memory for the Indian Department*. Ottawa, ON: Treaties and Historical Research Centre, Department of Indian Affairs and Northern Development.

Leslie, John. 1993. *A Historical Survey of Indian-Government Relations, 1940–1970*. Ottawa, ON: Department of Indian Affairs and Northern Development, Claims and Historical Research Centre, prepared for the Royal Commission on Aboriginal Peoples.

Leslie, John F. 1999. "Assimilation, Integration, or Termination? The Development of Canadian Indian Policy, 1943–1963." Ph. D. dissertation, Carleton University, Ottawa, ON.

Milloy, John Sheridan. 1979. "The Era of Civilization: British Policy for the Indians of Canada, 1830–1860." Ph. D. dissertation, Oxford University.

Shewell, Hugh. 2004. " '*Enough to Keep Them Alive': Indian Welfare in Canada, 1873–1965*." Toronto, ON: University of Toronto Press.

Domestic Dependent Nation

This term refers to the status of Indian tribes in U.S. federal law, recognizing a government-to-government relationship with the United States and based on an inherent, though limited, sovereignty. The term was coined by Supreme Court Chief Justice John Marshall in *Cherokee Nation v. Georgia* (1831), the second case in the seminal Marshall Trilogy. These cases provided foundational principles for determining the federal–tribal relationship and tribal sovereignty and guided future debate about Native American treaties.

After the discovery of gold there, Georgia began extending its own laws to Cherokee land, annulling Cherokee laws in the process. In *Cherokee Nation*, the Cherokee sought to prevent the state of Georgia from appropriating land guaranteed under the Treaty of Hopewell (signed with the federal government in 1785) and subsequent treaties. While the Court split evenly in the case, the decisive opinion was provided by Chief Justice Marshall, who dismissed the case on jurisdictional grounds. He found the matter could not be heard because the Cherokee were not a foreign nation; therefore their action did not fall under the grant to the federal authority to hear disputes between the states and foreign states. In a new formulation, Marshall found that while the Cherokee had an "unquestionable" right to the land they occupied unless it was ceded voluntarily to the federal government, "yet it may well be doubted, whether those tribes which reside within the acknowledged boundaries of the United States can, with strict accuracy, be denominated foreign nations. They may, more correctly, perhaps, be denominated domestic dependent nations. They occupy a territory to which we assert a title independent of their will, which must take effect in point of possession, when their right of possession ceases. Meanwhile they are in a state of pupillage. Their relation to the United States resembles that of a ward to his guardian" (*Cherokee Nation v. Georgia*, at 17).

In his decision, Marshall achieved a compromise that reaffirmed the independent nature of Indian tribes while avoiding a constitutional confrontation between the state and the Supreme Court. The decision recognized the Cherokee Nation as "a distinct political society separated from others, capable of managing its own affairs and governing itself." While they were not "foreign," they were "a state." Their independence was limited in only two matters: the alienation of land and the ability to treat with foreign powers.

The decision's guardian/ward language underpins the doctrine of the federal trust responsibility for Indians. The ambiguity of a status at once "independent" and resembling a "ward" has allowed the Supreme Court in later cases to restrict Indian sovereignty with the trust relationship seen as a source of congressional power over Indians. In declining to view the Cherokee as a "foreign" nation, Marshall originally relied on the U.S. Constitution's Indian Commerce clause (Article I, 8, clause 3), in which Congress is recognized to have the power "to regulate commerce with foreign Nations and among the several states and with the Indian tribes." In fact Congress has legislated well beyond the bounds of "commerce" into all aspects of Indian life.

While some scholars recognize conflicts with internal law, others see no legal (as opposed to political) barriers on Congress's limiting tribal sovereignty (or treaties), so long as it makes that intent clear. Fifty years after *Cherokee*, the Supreme Court stressed that "[t]hese Indian tribes *are* the wards of the nation. They are communities *dependent* on the United States . . ." (*United States v. Kagama*). The view of Congress's plenary power over Indians was reinforced in *Lone Wolf v. Hitchcock.* In that case, a number of tribal members challenged the distribution and sale of tribal lands as inconsistent with a prior treaty. The Court found that to agree with that contention would be to ignore "the status of the contracting Indians and the relation of dependency they bore and continue to bear towards the government of the United States." The treaty was found in no way to qualify the "controlling authority of Congress" (*Lone Wolf v. Hitchcock*, 564–565). This authority still includes the power to modify or repeal Indian treaties.

Whereas Marshall's reasoning implied an assumption of sovereignty in the absence of statutes or treaties that negate this presumption, more recent interpretations of the phrase "domestic dependant nation" status have seen inherent tribal sovereignty diminished. The focus has been on the "domestic dependant" rather than the "nation" aspect of Marshall's term. Nonetheless, this status continues to underpin important protections for tribal governments, particularly against intrusions on their power by states.

Stuart Bradfield

See also *Cherokee Nation v. Georgia;* Wardship Doctrine.
References and Further Reading
Burke, Joseph C. 1969. "The Cherokee Cases: A Study in Law, Politics and Morality." *Stanford Law Review* 21:500–531.
Cherokee Nation v. Georgia, 30 U.S. (Pet.) 1 (1831).
Getches, David H., Charles F. Wilkinson, and Robert A. Williams, Jr., eds. 1998. *Cases and Materials on Federal Indian Law*, 4th ed. St. Paul, MN: West.
Lone Wolf v. Hitchcock, 187 US 553 (1903).
United States v. Kagama, 118 US 375 (1886).

Elk v. Wilkins

The U.S. Supreme Court held in *Elk v. Wilkins* (112 U.S. 94 [1884]) that the Fourteenth Amendment to the U.S. Constitution does not confer citizenship on Indian people. This position held even if the individual lives in an urban area, apart from his or her nation or band. The court also ruled that acts of Congress do not generally apply to Indians unless they are specifically mentioned. Ironically, this ruling was handed down three years before the Allotment Act (1887) bestowed U.S. citizenship on Native Americans who gave up their title to communal lands in exchange for individual plots.

At issue was the constitutional status of American Indians for purposes of citizenship and voting. The Fourteenth Amendment granted citizenship to "all persons born or naturalized in the United States, and subject to the jurisdiction of the United States." Did American Indians fall under this definition? A federal district court ruled that it did not apply to Indians who had not been "born subject to its jurisdiction—that is, in its power and obedience" (*McKay v. Campbell* 16 Fed. Cas. 161 [1871] [No. 8840]).

John Elk had been born on a reservation outside U.S. jurisdiction, but moved to Omaha as an adult and lived what the court described as a "civilized" life. He sought to become a citizen and exercise the right to vote in Omaha elections during 1880.

The Supreme Court ruled that the Fifteenth Amendment (which grants the right to vote to all persons regardless of race) did not apply in Elk's case, because he was not born in an area under U.S. jurisdiction. Therefore, Elk was not a citizen within the meaning of the Fourteenth Amendment. The fact that Elk had abandoned his Indian relatives and lifeways did not matter to the court. Elk's citizenship and voting rights were denied because the court held that an affirmative act was required of the United States before an Indian could become a citizen. The Supreme Court's opinion cited a dozen treaties, four court rulings, four laws, and eight opinions of the U.S. Attorney General requiring "proof of fitness for civilization" as a precondition of granting Indians citizenship and voting rights.

Six years after John Elk's request for citizenship was denied, Congress passed the Indian Territory Naturalization Act (26 Stat. 81, 99-100), which allowed any Indian living in Indian Territory to apply for citizenship through the federal courts. The aim of this Act was to break down communal loyalties among Native Americans in Indian Territory as it moved toward statehood as Oklahoma.

The Standing Rock Sioux scholar Vine Deloria, Jr., commenting on *Elk v. Wilkins,* noted that, while federal courts were busy maintaining the plenary power of Congress over Indians and classifying Indian tribes as wards of the federal government, as well as denying an international dimension to Indian political existence, individual Indians seeking to exercise their constitutional rights were being told that they were, in effect, no more than the children of (foreign) subjects.

The ruling is notable more for historical irony than for having any substantial effect as a legal precedent. In addition to contradicting the Allotment Act's selective award of citizenship later in the same decade, this ruling was effectively annulled by the general grant of U.S. citizenship to Native Americans by an act of Congress in 1924.

Bruce E. Johansen

See also Citizenship; Plenary Power; *Standing Bear v. Crook;* Tribal Sovereignty; Wardship Doctrine.

References and Further Reading

Deloria, Vine, Jr. 1974. 1985. *Behind the Trail of Broken Treaties: An Indian Declaration of Independence,* 2nd ed. Austin: University of Texas Press.

Johansen, Bruce E., ed. 1998. *The Encyclopedia of Native American Legal Tradition.* Westport, CT: Greenwood Press.

Factory System

Through legislation beginning in 1796 and renewed every three years thereafter, the United States of America established the factory system (1796–1822), which was to construct trading houses mainly on the unsettled U.S. frontier where a factor, appointed by the president, could trade goods for furs with the members of given Native nations or tribes located in the district of the factory. The factory system was a forerunner to the trust relationship between Indian tribes and the federal government as established by the commerce clause in the U.S. Constitution.

The Secretary of War, through the Superintendents of Indian Affairs, oversaw the day-to-day operations of purchasing goods and transporting them to the factories as well as overseeing the selling of furs. The sites for the factory trading houses were located in the westward territories and the south. The United States' intention was to control who traded with the Indians and to build and maintain friendly relations, while making them dependent on American goods instead of British goods.

Dating back to the first white presence on the North American continent, the colonial powers recognized the necessity of establishing ground rules for trading with the Indians. Not until after the French and Indian War ended did the control shift completely to Great Britain and in particular to London. After the American Revolution, the newly formed American government issued acts to regulate the intercourse of trade with the Indians under their jurisdiction. British traders continued to trade with Indians in what was considered American lands. Following the end of the Northwest Territory Frontier Wars in 1795, the Jay Treaty required all British traders to cease operations in the United States and its territories.

In most cases, the U.S. Army established a garrison on or near the site of a factory trade house. The construction of the factory buildings, as well as the garrison, was often done by the soldiers, though sometimes workers such as sawyers and carpenters had to be brought in. Factory trade houses were built of local materials, mostly logs, and included a trade room; it was similar to a store whose shelves were filled with trade goods. Often the factory building was also a residence for the factor, though sometimes another house would be built for him and his family, if he had one. In addition to the trade house, other buildings were constructed to store the overstock of goods, a residence for the interpreter, and storage for the traded furs. In the outbuildings, the furs would have to undergo further cleaning, and, depending on the climate or time of the year, they would have to be frequently turned and beaten to get rid of worms.

The trade goods often were manufactured not only in the United States, but also in Great Britain, Germany, France, India, and China, and other nations. They were sold or traded to Indians at a small percentage over cost to keep the prices low. Some of the goods were clearly items that were of no interest to the Indians, things such as china teapots, Queensware dishes, and ladies' parasols. Regulations stipulated that whites were not allowed to purchase goods from the factory, but they often did. In this middle ground where the two cultures met, soldiers and their wives charged against the promise of future pay just as individual Indians did in the hope of successful trapping. Often, the absence of sutlers located in or near the peace establishment army posts necessitated members of the garrison to charge

at the factory or trade furs from hunting. Soldiers often racked up more credit than Indians.

At first, issuing credit to Indians was forbidden, but soon it became a necessity before the winter hunting and trapping seasons. Furthermore, it was learned that, if they could not pay or failed to pay with furs, the government could then take the money from other sources such as annuities or force the tribe as a whole to sell land to pay off the debts. This appears to have been an aim of Thomas Jefferson in February 1803 when he informed William Henry Harrison, governor of Indiana Territory, that the government would "push" their trading houses, enjoy getting the more important leaders heavily into debt, and then trade the debt for ceding land (Esarey, 1922, 71). By selling the trade goods so low, Jefferson assumed the Indians would not want to go to anyone else, especially private traders who could not afford to sell goods so low.

The Indians trapped from the late fall through the winter, and in the spring they brought in their dressed furs to be traded. The types of furs ranged from bear, mountain lion, deerskin, beaver, and muskrat. The goods offered in trade to the Indians ran the lot of cloth like woolens (baize, blanket, and shroud), cottons (calico and homespun), linen, and silk ribbons. Other goods included fishing equipment; knives, tomahawks, guns, gun powder, and shot; brass, copper, and even sheet iron kettles; sewing implements; snuff boxes, bridles, saddles, looking glasses, silk stockings, hats; and much more. At least once a year, the factor shipped furs to the East to be auctioned to manufacturers. These manufactures would make sundry articles of the furs, including hats from beaver, breeches from deerskins, and hat coverings from bear fur for the U.S. Army. Some furs were shipped to other parts of the world, including Europe and China.

One of the projects of the factory system was to encourage agriculture and education among the Indians. Religious organizations, like the Moravians and Quakers, became the agents of the government to work among the tribes to teach them farming, animal husbandry, and domestic sewing arts as well as to convert them to Christianity. The U.S. government factories issued the farming implements, payment coming out of annuities and presents to the tribes, and often paid the salaries of religious men and women working among the tribes. At first, many Indians did not take to the concept of their males farming because, culturally, it was female work. Fines could be levied against annuities if an Indian was found to be trading or selling government-issued farm implements to other Indians or whites. After the War of 1812, Baptists and Presbyterians were offered government funds to commence Indian schools in Kentucky, Missouri, and Kansas. At these schools, Indians were taught reading, writing, arithmetic, and gender-specific occupations; females learned to spin, weave, and sew while the males learned carpentry and farming. They were also instructed in the Christian religion. In the beginning, permission of the parents was sought and no one was forced to attend. However, after the closure of the factory system, this would change.

Criticism of the factory system was most intense from private fur-trading companies. In particular, John Jacob Astor of the American Fur Company lobbied congresspeople, presidents, and others with influential connections to close down the factory system. By 1820, with Lewis Cass, the governor of Michigan Territory and Chouteaus, a prominent fur trade family from St. Louis, Astor pressured Congress to see that the government had no business regulating the trade with Indians. First, it failed to build and keep friendly relations with the Indians, resulting in the outbreak of the War of 1812; second, the trade goods were inferior; next, factors did not go out to tribal villages to trade with the Indians, rather they were required to stay at their factories; and lastly, despite the best efforts of the factories, the illegal selling of alcohol by small private traders continued to increase. Despite all the efforts of the factory system officials, the private traders won out and the system was closed down in 1822.

Sally Colford Bennett

See also Assimilation; Fur Trade; Trade.
References and Further Reading
Esarey, Logan, ed. 1974. *Governors Messages and Letters, Messages of William Henry Harrison, Vol. I 1800–1811.* New York: Arno Press. [Originally printed 1922. Indianapolis: Indiana Historical Commission.]
Lavender, David. 1964. *A Fist in the Wilderness.* Lincoln: University of Nebraska Press.
Madsen, Axel. 2001. *John Jacob Astor: America's First Multimillionaire.* Hoboken, NJ: Wiley.
Peake, Ora Brooks. 1954. *A History of the United States Factory System, 1795–1822.* Denver, CO: Sage Books,
Richards, James K. 1988. "Destiny's Middlemen, Astor's American Fur Company." *Timeline* 5, no. 29: 30–39.

Fletcher v. Peck

The decisions of Chief Justice John Marshall in the U.S. Supreme Court cases of *Cherokee Nation v. Georgia* and *Worcester v. Georgia* have been basic to subsequent arguments advanced both to support and to suppress the autonomy of indigenous peoples. These cases refined a Euro-centric doctrine regarding aboriginal rights following two earlier cases, *Fletcher v. Peck* and *Johnson v. McIntosh.* Unlike the Cherokee Nation cases, which actually involved a controversy between an indigenous nation and an American state, in *Fletcher v. Peck* aboriginal rights issues were litigated in the absence of any conflict between indigenous people and Euro-Americans. Tried in 1810, *Fletcher v. Peck* is important because of the part it played in establishing a legal doctrine used to limit the rights of indigenous peoples.

The question of aboriginal title was brought before the U.S. Supreme Court under the feigned controversy of *Fletcher v. Peck* to force the federal judiciary to address specific issues presented by land speculators who claimed a patent by virtue of a 1795 legislative act to appropriate land for the purpose of payment to state troops. It was argued that Georgia possessed the right to convey property rights to the Georgia Land Company even though the land in question was still claimed by an indigenous nation. This case represented the first time that the Court was called to deliberate on the question of absolute title to soil existing apart from the rights of "Indian ownership" in the land.

In addressing what would become a very crucial issue, arguments in this case exhibited distortion and error. When examining the question of ownership, John Quincy Adams and Robert Goodloe, representing the majority opinion, noted that aboriginal concepts did not resemble European concepts of land tenure and advised the Court to not hold any regard for the intrinsic values of indigenous culture. Presenting arguments that reflected an overriding belief that the values of Euro-American culture were superior to those of Indian cultures, the defense stated that Indians had "no idea of a title to the soil itself. It [the land] is overrun by them, rather than inhabited . . ." and thus any claim of Indian title to the land could not represent a true and legal possession. This opinion, however, overlooked the facts. When European settlers first landed in America, they encountered innumerable stretches of cultivated fields, some of which were reported to reach

almost two hundred acres. Because the majority of settlers coming over from Europe were merchants, tradespeople, and seekers of fortune, possessing little or no knowledge of an agrarian lifestyle, many colonists had to rely on the knowledge and skills of the indigenous people for instruction in the manner of planting, culling out the best seed, observing "the fittest season, keeping distance for hoes and fit measure for hills, to worm . . . and weed . . . and prune . . . and dress . . ." as the occasion required.

The defense further argued that the United States possessed "a right not in the individual, but national. This is the right gained by conquest . . . Europeans always claimed and exercised this right of conquest." The defense also erroneously asserted that all "treaties with the Indians were the effect of conquest, all the extensive grants have been forced from them by successful war. The conquerors permitted the conquered tribes to occupy part of the land, until it should be wanted for the use of the conquerors." The defense even credited William Penn with having obtained Quaker land under the right of conquest.

In delivering the opinion of the Court, Justice Marshall affirmed that Georgia did indeed possess the power of disposing of land within the limits of its borders in whatever manner it saw fit. Marshall's comments regarding Indian title came at the very end:

> The majority of the court is of the opinion that the nature of the Indian title, which is certainly to be respected by the court, until it be legitimately extinguished, is not such as to be absolutely repugnant to . . . on the part of the State.

Dissenting Justice William Johnson delivered the most straightforward statements pertaining to Indian title that the case offered, arguing that the correctness of his opinion relied on a just and unbiased view of the state of the Indian nation. Pointing out that innumerable treaties formed with North American Indians acknowledged them to be an independent people, Johnson was persuaded by evidence he believed clearly indicated that the Indians held an absolute right to the soil for themselves and their heirs.

> In fact, if the Indian nations were the absolute proprietors of the soil, no other nation can be said to have the same interest in it. What, then

. . . is the interest of the states in the soil of the Indians within their boundaries? Unaffected by particular treaties, it is nothing more than what it was assumed at the first settlement of the country . . . a right of conquest or of purchase, exclusive of all competitors, within certain defined limits. All the restrictions upon the right of soil in the Indians, amount only to an exclusion of all competitors from their markets . . .

The Court's reluctance to clearly articulate a legal definition of aboriginal title most likely stemmed from a realization that, if aboriginal nations were legally acknowledged to possess an absolute title to the land, the United States would be hindered by additional obstacles as it pursued a course toward national expansion.

Although the Court ruled that Georgia was empowered with a fee simple (i.e., unencumbered) title in the land, the soundness of the decision was challenged by the dissenting opinion of Justice Johnson. In Johnson's opinion "the interests of Georgia . . . amounted to nothing more than a mere possibility. . . ."

> If the interest in Georgia was nothing more than a preemptive right, how could that be called a fee simple, which was nothing more than a power to acquire a fee simple by purchase, when the proprietors should be pleased to sell. And if this ever was anything more than a mere possibility, it certainly was reduced . . . when the state of Georgia ceded to the United States, by constitution, both the power of pre-emption and of conquest . . .

For all the rhetoric regarding American absolute sovereignty, when the Court delivered its opinion in *Fletcher v. Peck*, there still existed numerous groups of indigenous peoples who, having never signed a treaty with the American government, continued to exist in absolute sovereignty on their ancestral lands. That notwithstanding, during the preceding thirty-three years of the United States' dealing with indigenous North Americans, the treaty had proved to represent a most effective method of acquiring Native land. After *Fletcher v. Peck*, however, the Court emerged as the new medium for a foreign settler government to acquire indigenous peoples' lands

S. Neyooxet Greymorning (with Dr. Gregory Campbell)

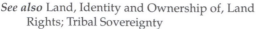

See also Land, Identity and Ownership of, Land
Rights; Tribal Sovereignty
References and Further Reading
Brightly, Frederick C., ed. 1904. *Fletcher v. Peck 10 US
(6 Cranch, 1810). Reports of Cases Argued and
Adjudged in the Supreme Court of the United
States, in February Term 1810,* 3rd ed. Reported
by William Cranch. New York: Banks Law
Publishing Co.
Haines, Charles. 1960. *The Role of the Supreme Court
in American Government and Politics 1789–1835.*
New York: Russell & Russell.
Hawke, David Freeman. 1988. *Everyday Life in Early
America.* New York: Harper & Row.

Forced Marches

As the U.S. government and its citizens took possession of indigenous lands and resources, forced marches were used to remove indigenous peoples and open their lands for European-American settlement. Though a practice originating from the earliest years of contact, forced marches reached their zenith in the nineteenth century when dozens of such "removals" occurred, affecting tens of thousands of indigenous people and the transfer of millions of acres of land to nonindigenous ownership.

In this context, forced marches are connected to broader U.S. policies, such as removal and relocation, that were used as a means to control and confine indigenous populations by concentrating them into small geographic areas. The death toll among those who were force marched to new locations was sometimes as high as 50 percent, but the most devastating consequences of forced marches were long term. Removal required the dispossession of indigenous peoples from their lands and the subsequent loss of the ways of life associated with their attachment to a particular land base. The repercussions of this tremendous sense of loss have reached into the twenty-first century as indigenous populations generally continue to suffer high mortality rates and a poor quality of life.

The best-known forced march is the 1838 Tsalagi (Cherokee) Trail of Tears in which seventeen thousand Tsalagi were removed from their southeastern homes to Indian Territory. After they were rounded up and placed in stockades, the population was removed in more than a dozen groups. Most traveled over land in small groups averaging 1,000 people, forming long refugee columns and suffering from starvation, disease, exposure, hardship, and

accidents. It is estimated that at least 4,000, and perhaps as many as 8,000 people died as a direct consequence of the forced removal and as many as half of the remaining population died within the first year after removal, largely due to disease. The extent of death and suffering as a consequence of the violent process of removal is not unusual, but is in fact characteristic of the forced marches experienced by indigenous peoples throughout American history.

The U.S. government carried out these brutal forced removals under the pretense of legality. After manipulating the Tsalagi population to obtain the signatures of a small, illegitimate faction, the United States ratified the Treaty of New Echota, which relinquished Tsalagi lands in the Southeast in exchange for lands in Indian Territory and $15 million. This bare semblance of legitimacy in dealings with indigenous peoples is all that remained after the passing of the Indian Removal Act of 1830 under President Andrew Jackson's administration. This Act authorized the president to exchange indigenous lands in the East for those in the West and to negotiate with tribes for their own removal. While the Act required indigenous agreement and support for removal, this aspect was ignored in practice. Furthermore, the U.S. government was indifferent to the fact that, in some cases, indigenous peoples already occupied lands in the West they were promising to others; this required taking land from some groups to make it available to others.

While Jackson has been associated most prominently with forced marches and acts of removal, he was not the first or last president to advocate indigenous removal. Early explorers such as Jacques Cartier, Martin Frobisher, and Henry Hudson practiced indigenous removal, as did early New England colonists who established "praying towns" and state reservations. Thomas Jefferson was a strong proponent of removal. He drafted a constitutional amendment, decades before Jackson, which would have allowed for the exchange of indigenous lands in the East for lands west of the Mississippi. In other contexts, he wrote that any Indians resisting American expansion should be met with the hatchet, concluding "if ever we are constrained to lift the hatchet against any tribe, we will never lay it down until that tribe is exterminated, or is driven beyond the Mississippi." This sentiment became manifest in forced removals across the continent. If invading settlers could not exploit the indigenous labor for their own purposes, they pressured them to leave areas so that European-Americans could get on with immigration and resource extraction. The complete subjugation through forced marches became a highly effective means of removal.

During the fall of 1862, Jefferson's sentiments were echoed by Minnesota Governor Alexander Ramsey, who stated, "The Sioux Indians of Minnesota must be exterminated or driven forever beyond the borders of the State." Unlike the Tsalagi, no segment of the Dakota population signed a treaty agreeing to its removal. Instead, the U.S. government considered the forced removal of Dakota people from their homeland to be a justifiable consequence of the U.S.–Dakota War of 1862. Rather than viewing warfare as a reasonable course of Dakota action in light of repeated U.S. violation of treaty obligations, the United States instead unilaterally abrogated Dakota–U.S. treaties and decided to take the remaining Dakota lands for European-American immigration.

The Dakota were removed from their Minnesota homeland in two successive waves. Women and children were force marched on a seven-day, 150-mile journey to Fort Snelling in St. Paul, where they spent the winter of 1862–1863. Forming a four-mile-long procession as they walked, an unknown number of the 1,700 women and children died along the way, many from the brutality of soldiers and citizenry who attacked them along the way as they were paraded through European-American towns. The following spring, the remaining thirteen hundred were sent down the Mississippi River on boats to St. Louis and then up the Missouri River to the Crow Creek Reservation in South Dakota. Three hundred and three Dakota men were tried and convicted of war crimes at the end of the war. While they awaited execution orders from Abraham Lincoln, they were shackled and placed in wagons that took them to a concentration camp at Mankato, Minnesota. After thirty-eight were hanged in the largest mass execution in U.S. history on December 26, 1862, the rest were sent down the Mississippi the following spring where they were imprisoned in Davenport, Iowa, for three years. After these forced removals were accomplished, Dakota lands were cleared for unimpeded immigration.

The Dine (Navajo) in the Southwest faced a similar forced march and removal in the 1864 Long Walk. As European-American immigration increased in the area and conflicts arose, Christopher Houston "Kit" Carson was sent to demonstrate that "wild Indians could be tamed." He implemented a brutal policy that included the destruction of crops and livestock, pillaging the land, and killing of the Dine. These scorched-earth tactics were meant to hurt not just the warriors of the nation, but also the noncombatants, the women and children, by forcing them into starvation and submission. Once the Dine were gathered at Fort Defiance, Arizona, they were force marched three hundred miles to Fort Sumner in the Bosque Redondo (in New Mexico Territory). The Dine named their concentration camp Hweeldi, the Place of Despair. Suffering starvation, disease, and harsh weather conditions with grossly inadequate clothing and shelter, at Hweeldi the Dine lost approximately thirty-five hundred out of their population of nine thousand. Unlike most indigenous peoples, however, the Dine were allowed to return to their homeland in 1868, where they continue to maintain the largest indigenous land base in the United States.

Forced marches were simply a means to an end. They allowed for large numbers of indigenous peoples to be transferred from one location to another, usually from their homeland to sites farther west, while their homelands were opened for nonindigenous settlement. Few indigenous peoples have ever recovered from the trauma caused by the disconnection from homeland and the accompanying destruction of their way of life. While the initial and significant loss of life caused from forced marches was enough to wreak havoc with any population, the devastation is compounded for indigenous peoples because of the simultaneous loss of land and way of life. Stories of suffering, particularly of the women and children, remain painful episodes in indigenous American history.

Waziyatawin Angela Wilson

See also Trail of Tears; Cherokee; Dakota; Navajo; Relocation; Jackson, Andrew.

References and Further Reading

Stannard, David E. 1992. *American Holocaust: The Conquest of the New World*. New York: Oxford University Press.

Wright, Ronald. 1992. *Stolen Continents: The Americas Through Indian Eyes Since 1492*. Boston: Houghton-Mifflin.

Fort Laramie Treaty (1868)

The Fort Laramie Treaty of 1868 was the second of two important midnineteenth-century treaty documents signed by Native nations of the American Great Plains and the United States government.

The terms of the treaty guaranteed ownership of *Paha Sapa* ("Black Hills") to the Lakota, the removal of military forts along the Bozeman Trail in the Powder River Country, and the establishment—on Lakota land—of the Great Sioux Reservation, a 26-million acre reserve of land that ran from the north line of the state of Nebraska to the forty-sixth parallel, bordered on the east by the Missouri River, and running westward to the hundred and fourth degree of longitude. Moreover, the treaty closed the Powder River Country to military and settlement incursions. The treaty, however, also prophetically designated this same country as "unceded Indian Territory" and therefore left the land in a temporary relation of ownership to the Lakota and outside the official "reservation." Additionally, the treaty articles specified the intention of the U.S. government to pursue the stated long-term goals of forced assimilation with agriculture, education ("They [the Lakota] therefore pledge themselves to compel their children, male and female, between the ages of six and sixteen years, to attend school"(Art. 7), and the division of land held in common. The treaty document is lengthy and relies heavily on dense legal language that often contradicts its own provisions. Red Cloud himself would later claim that the only provisions of the treaty that he was able to understand were the continued tenure of the Lakota in their own land and the expulsion of the United States military from the Powder River Country.

The Fort Laramie Treaty of 1868 was signed by representatives of the Oceti Sakowins, Seven Council Fires of the Lakota, the Sincangus (Brûlés), Oglalas, Minniconjou, Hunkpapas, Sihasapas (Blackfeet), Pabaskas (Cuthead), Itazipacolas (Two Kettle), and Oohenupas (Sans Arc) of the Lakota nation; by the Yanktonais of the Nakota nation; by the Mdewakantonwans and Wahpekutes of the Dakota (Santee) nation; by members of the Inuna-ina (Arapaho) nation; and by members of a U.S. treaty commission. The treaty document itself, as well as a year-long process of negotiating for signatures, was the result of a successful war waged against the United States by the Lakota, led by Makhpyia-luta (Red Cloud). Red Cloud's War (also known as the Bozeman War) was fought in the Wyoming and Montana Territories from 1866 to 1868 for control over the important hunting grounds of the Powder River Country in north central Wyoming.

Signatories of the treaty documents included Makhpyia-luta (Red Cloud), Tasunka Kokipapi

(Young Man Afraid of His Horses), Lieutenant General William T. Sherman, General William S. Harney, and General Alfred H. Terry. The Fort Laramie Treaty was ratified by the U.S. Congress on February 16, 1869.

For the Lakota and their Native allies, as well as for Euro-American immigrants and the U.S. government, the Fort Laramie Treaty was important to the history of the late nineteenth century, from the Battle of the Greasy Grass/Little Bighorn (1876) to the Massacre at Wounded Knee in 1890. Discovery of gold in the sacred *Paha Sapa* ("Black Hills") by George Custer's governmentally sanctioned expedition resulted in the Black Hills Gold Rush, which only increased the pressure on Lakota land already under attack by settlement, by the decimation of the great buffalo herds, by the demands of the Northern Pacific Railroad, and by unstable and changing governmental and military policy.

In September of 1875, President Ulysses S. Grant sent a special commission to Lakota territory to negotiate for the sale of "unceded Indian Territory" of the 1868 Fort Laramie Treaty and the *Paha Sapa* themselves; the Lakota refused to sell. In November of 1875, the Indian Bureau ordered all Lakota who were in the "unceded" hunting lands to come into the reservation and submit to agency control by January 31, 1875. The government launched a military campaign against the Lakota who were unwilling and unable to comply with the order; the campaign began in the winter of 1876 and lasted into the spring of 1877. The Battle of Greasy Grass/Little Bighorn—a military engagement in which an allied Lakota–northern Cheyenne force and the Seventh Cavalry of the U.S. Army—was one battle in the so-called Indian Wars of 1876–1877, fought by the Lakota to maintain the ownership of the land they believed the Fort Laramie Treaty of 1868 guaranteed them. The Massacre at Wounded Knee, December 29, 1890, in which 150 Minniconjou Lakota were killed while surrendering to the Seventh Cavalry, was the result of the same complex of factors involving struggle over land tenure in Lakota country and the United States' attempt to confine the Lakota to a shrinking and reconfigured reservation space.

As it was in the nineteenth century, the Fort Laramie Treaty of 1868 remained an important document in the struggle over native rights and land claims in the twentieth century. Two important events in the history of the Indian Movement during the 1960s and 1970s were predicated on the language

General William T. Sherman and Sioux leaders sign the Fort Laramie Treaty at Fort Laramie, Wyoming, in 1868. The treaty's signing ended Red Cloud's War and called for the closure of the Bozeman Trail and three U.S. Army forts. The war, led by Lakota Sioux Chief Red Cloud, started in 1868 in response to white advancement and the building of three government forts in the Powder River country and is best known for the Fetterman Fight of December 21, 1866. (National Archives and Records Administration)

and history surrounding the 1868 Fort Laramie Treaty: the occupation of Alcatraz in 1964 and again in 1969; and the occupation of Wounded Knee in 1973. On March, 8, 1964, a group of about forty Native people from various tribes took possession of the unoccupied island of Alcatraz off the coast of California and its abandoned prison complex under the provisions of the 1868 Fort Laramie Treaty, which guaranteed surplus or federally abandoned property to the Lakota. The first occupation of Alcatraz paved the way for another longer and more spectacular occupation of the island starting in November of 1969 and lasting until a forcible eviction in June of 1971. The dramatization of land claims, issues of tribal sovereignty, racism, poverty, and other important issues that characterized the two occupations of Alcatraz under the provisions of the Fort Laramie Treaty of 1868 also defined the American Indian

Movement's occupation in 1973 of the site of the Wounded Knee Massacre. The statement of demands made by the occupiers of Wounded Knee and passed to the Justice Department opened with an appeal to the Fort Laramie Treaty of 1868: "Communicate this to whomever [sic] is in charge. We are operating under the Provisions of the 1868 Sioux Treaty."

In the twenty-first century, the Fort Laramie Treaty of 1868 continues to be an important aspect of the long-standing Black Hills Land Claim wherein the Lakota nation continues to press the U.S. government for the return of the *Paha Sapa* that were guaranteed to them by the 1868 treaty. The Supreme Court of the United States itself ruled in 1980 that the sacred land was indeed unlawfully seized by the government and ruled that the monies that were never paid to the Lakota, along with interest accrued

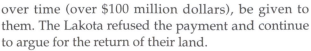

over time (over $100 million dollars), be given to them. The Lakota refused the payment and continue to argue for the return of their land.

Kathleen Kane

See also Alcatraz Proclamation: A Proclamation from the Indians of All Tribes; American Indian Movement; Battle of the Little Bighorn; Black Hills; Buffalo; Crazy Horse; Great Sioux Uprising; Occupation of Alcatraz Island; Red Cloud; Sacred Sites; Sitting Bull; Treaty Diplomacy, with Summary of Selected Treaties; Wounded Knee, South Dakota, Massacre at.

References and Further Reading

Allen, Chadwick. 2000. "Postcolonial Theory and the Discourse of Treaties." *American Quarterly* 52, no. 1: 59–89

Cook-Lynn, Elizabeth, et al., eds. 1988. *Black Hills Land Claim. Wicazo Sa Review IV* 1 (Spring, special issue): 1–59.

Deloria, Vine, Jr. 1990. *Behind the Trail of Broken Treaties: An Indian Declaration of Independence,* 3rd ed. Austin: University of Texas Press.

Deloria, Vine, Jr., and David E. Wilkins. 2000. *Tribes, Treaties and Constitutional Tribulations.* Austin: University of Texas Press.

Gonzalez, Mario. 1996. "The Black Hills: The Sacred Land of the Lakota and Tsistisistas." *Cultural Survival Quarterly* 19: 63–69.

Indian Affairs Laws and Treaties. Available at: http://digital.library.okstate.edu/kappler/Vol2/treaties/sio0998.htm. Accessed January 13, 2007.

Jones, Dorothy. 1982. *License for Empire: Colonialism by Treaty in Early America.* Chicago: University of Chicago Press.

Josephy, Alvin M., Jr. 1996. "Indian Policy and the Battle of the Little Bighorn." In *Legacy: New Perspectives on the Battle of the Little Bighorn.* Edited by Charles E. Rankin, 23–39. Helena: Montana Historical Society Press.

Kappler, Charles. 1996. *Indian Treaties: 1778–1883,* reprint ed. Mattituck, NY: Amereon.

Ortiz, Roxanne Dunbar. 1977. *The Great Sioux Nation: Sitting in Judgment on America: Based on and Containing Testimony heard at the "Sioux Treaty Hearing" held December, 1974, in Federal District Court, Lincoln, Nebraska.* New York: American Indian Treaty Council Information Center. [Distributed by Random House.]

Porter, Joseph C. 1996. "Crazy Horse, Lakota Leadership, and the Fort Laramie Treaty." In *Legacy: New Perspectives on the Battle of the Little Bighorn.* Edited by Charles E. Rankin, 41–62. Helena, MT: The Montana Historical Society.

Prucha, Francis Paul. 1997. *American Indian Treaties: The History of a Political Anomaly,* reprint ed. Berkeley: University of California Press.

Prucha, Francis Paul. 2000. *Documents of United States Indian Policy,* 3rd ed. Lincoln: University of Nebraska Press.

Smith, Paul Chaat, and Robert Allen Warrior. 1996. *Like a Hurricane: The Indian Movement from Alcatraz to Wounded Knee.* New York: New Press.

Hawai'i, Legal Status of Native Claims

In 1893, a cabal of American planters, supported by U.S. warships and a contingent of Marines, overthrew the Hawaiian monarchy by armed force. This "act of war," as even President Grover Cleveland admitted at the time, was invalid under international law. A century later, in 1993, the Kanaka Maoli (Native Hawaiians) secured an apology from the U.S. House of Representatives for this illegal act and are currently pressing a land claim that would return 1.8 million acres (of Hawai'i's 4.2-million acre land area) to the jurisdiction of a government to be elected at a Native Hawaiian constitutional convention.

Following the 1893 overthrow, the United States quickly recognized the "legitimacy" of what the insurgent planters called the Republic of Hawaii and in 1898 accepted a request by the resulting government that the islands be formally annexed as a "trust territory" of the United States. At no point in this process were the wishes of the Kanaka Maoli themselves taken into consideration. Instead, annexation occurred over the express opposition of Queen Lili'uokalani, the last of a long line of chiefs and constitutional monarchs ruling the Hawaiian kingdom (Budnick, 1992; Dougherty, 1992).

Over the next half century, as Hawai'i gained increasing importance as a strategic base for the U.S. military, as its land was increasingly converted for sugarcane production by a cluster of local corporations known as the Big Five (geared entirely to U.S. markets), and as the now rampant tourist industry began to take hold, the Kanaka Maoli were systematically dispossessed of what little property remained to them. By 1950, their destitution was endemic (Kent, 1993; Trask, 1999).

As a result of the dire poverty into which they were thrust, the Kanaka Maoli population underwent a steady decline throughout the first half of the twentieth century. Meanwhile, the number of whites moving to the islands from the continental United

States surged dramatically. Hence, when the holding of territories in perpetual trust was rendered illegal under the United Nations Charter, the United States was required to allow Hawai'i to determine for itself the nature of its political status. It circumvented this requirement simply by having the larger population of white settlers outvote the Kanaka Maoli on the matter. Consequently, although still not in accordance with international law, Hawai'i was made a U.S. state in 1959 (Churchill, 2003; Churchill and Venne, 2005).

Despite, or perhaps because of, this turn of events, a Hawaiian renaissance began in the 1970s. The native language, which had nearly died, began to flourish again; Hawaiians, all but homeless in their own land, began to recapture their heritage. Teams of seafarers built canoes capable of traveling to Tahiti to renew ties with indigenous people there. They sailed practicing ancient navigational skills that tied together the people of widely dispersed islands centuries ago.

At about the same time, Aloha Hawai'i, the first organization dedicated to asserting the legal and political rights of Native Hawaiians, was founded. Focusing first on the recovery of the sacred island of Kaho'olawe, used by the U.S. Navy as a bombing and artillery target range since World War II, the group had by the 1980s sparked a broad movement devoted to halting the increasingly widespread destruction of the islands' fragile environment through such military usage and ever more intensive commercial development (Churchill, 2003).

Over the next decade, the emphasis of such activism shifted steadily toward the recovery of a land base by the Kanaka Maoli themselves, and, with the decision to formally reestablish Kalahui Hawai'i (the Native Hawaiian nation) in 1987, the agenda was expanded to include the right to self-government as well. Both goals were pursued through a multipronged strategy combining demonstrations, litigation, and participation in the United Nations Working Group on Indigenous Populations (Churchill, 2003; Trask, 1999).

During the summer of 1993, pursuant to U.N. Resolution 1503 (XLVIII), an international tribunal convened in the islands to hear and receive evidence on U.S. violations of Native Hawaiian rights and the conditions suffered by the Kanaka Maoli as a result. Shortly thereafter, the House of Representatives issued its apology for abolishing the government of Queen Lili'uokalani 100 years earlier (Churchill and Venne, 2005).

The tribunal's findings strongly affirmed the rights of the Native Hawaiians to govern themselves within their own clearly defined territory. This was followed, in 1996, with a vote by some thirty thousand Kanaka Maoli—roughly 40 percent of the eligible electorate—who opted by a margin of three-to-one to resume a fully self-governing existence. An overwhelming majority also registered to participate in a referendum intended to resolve Kanaka Maoli land claims (Weinberg, 1996).

The land at issue includes all state and federal lands in the islands—about 1.6 million acres—but leaves private owners untouched. It has been proposed that another 200,000 acres presently occupied by U.S. military bases, a total acreage corresponding rather precisely to the quantity embodied in the so-called Hawaiian Home Lands the Kanaka Maoli were to have retained all along, might be leased to the Department of Defense at market value for some fixed period of time.

By the early years of the twenty-first century, no motion had been made in this direction, however, because the U.S. government asserts that only a government that it recognizes has the legal standing to resolve the claim to the so-called ceded lands. The Hawaiians as a group have no federal recognition of the type extended to many other Native peoples in the United States.

As of late 2005, a measure designed to accomplish such recognition remains stalled in the U.S. Congress. Only with the passage of the Akaka Bill, as the measure is known, would the Kanaka Maoli be in a position to engage in government-to-government negotiations with the United States and the state of Hawai'i regarding jurisdiction over and title to their lands (Meheula, 2005).

Such delays continue to exact an ugly toll. As long as the Kanaka Maoli continue to be "ruled by U.S. laws, not our own," as Native Hawaiian rights advocate Beadie Kanahele Dawson put it, they are all but certain to remain by far the islands' most "at risk people: seriously undereducated, overrepresented in prisons, overburdened with serious diseases and plagued with drug abuse and homelessness" (Dawson, 2005; McNarie, 2005).

Ward Churchill and Bruce E. Johansen

See also Genocide; Identity; Land, Identity and Ownership of, Land Rights; Language and Language Renewal; United Nations, Indians and.

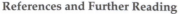

References and Further Reading

Budnick, Rich. 1992. *Stolen Kingdom: An American Conspiracy*. Honolulu, HI: Aloha Press.

Churchill, Ward. 2003. "Stolen Kingdom: The Right of Hawai'i to Decolonization." In *Perversions of Justice: Indigenous Peoples and Angloamerican Law*. Edited by Ward Churchill, 73–124. San Francisco: City Lights

Churchill, Ward, and Sharon H. Venne, eds. 2005. *Islands in Captivity: The International Tribunal on the Rights of Indigenous Hawaiians*. Boston: South End Press.

Dawson, Beadie Kanahele. 2005. "Native Hawaiian Struggle Is about Rebuilding a Nation." *Honolulu Advertiser* (January 16). Available at: http://the.honoluluadvertiser.com/article/2005/Jan/16/op/op07p.html/?print=on. Accessed on January 13, 2007.

Dougherty, Michael. 1992. *To Steal a Kingdom: Probing Hawaiian History*. Honolulu, HI: Island Style Press.

Kamakau, Samuel M. 1992. *The Ruling Chiefs of Hawaii*, rev. ed. Honolulu, HI: Kamehameha Schools Press.

Kent, Noel J. 1993. *Hawaii: Island Under the Influence*. Honolulu: University of Hawai'i Press.

McNarie, Alan D. 2005. "No Place of Refuge." *Hawaii Island Journal* (January): 1–15. Available at: http://hawaiiislandjournal.com/2005/01a05b.html.

Meheula, William. 2005. "Akaka Bill Opens Door to Talks with U.S." *Honolulu Advertiser* (January 16). Available at: http://the.Honolulu advertiser.com/article/2005/Jan/16/op/op07p.html/?print=o N.

Trask, Haunani-Kay. 1999. *From a Native Daughter: Colonialism and Sovereignty in Hawai'i*, 2nd ed. Honolulu: University of Hawai'i, Press.

Weinberg, Bill. 1996. "Land and Sovereignty in Hawai'i: A Native Nation Re-Emerges." *Native Americas* 13, no. 2 (Summer): 30–41.

Hudson's Bay Company

The Hudson's Bay Company exerted a powerful influence on the economic development of Canada since its formation as a commercial entity under an English royal charter dated May 2, 1670. The European desire and demand for fashionable animal pelts dates back to the Middle Ages, and the Company therefore originated in the fur trade. After the European intrusion into North America, competition sparked London merchants in the late seventeenth century to seek a charter for trading rights in the northern part of North America, in an area centered on Hudson and James Bays and extending south-ward and westward. King Charles II gave the charter to eighteen adventurers of London, who called themselves the "Governor and Company of Adventurers of England trading into Hudson's Bay." Under their charter, the Company was granted the:

> sole Trade and Commerce of all those Seas Streightes Bayes Rivers Lakes Creekes and Sounds in whatsoever Latitude they shall bee that lye within the entrance of the Streightes commonly called Hudsons Streightes together with all the Landes and Territoryes upon the Countryes Coastes and confines of the Seas Bayes Lakes Rivers Creekes and Soundes aforesaid that are not actually possessed by or granted to any of our Subjectes or possessed by the Subjectes of any other Christian Prince or State.

It further stated that the Company was to be the "true and absolute Lordes and Proprietors" of this vast territory, which was to be known as Rupert's Land after Prince Rupert. The only responsibility of the Company was to pay two elks and two black beavers in the event that the English crown ever set foot in this territory. This nominal amount in kind, which was never paid by the Company, illustrates the character of the bargain between the Crown and the Company for land and trading rights held by the latter.

The charter was based on a false assumption. One of the basic principles of English common law is that you cannot give what you do not own, and England did not own Rupert's Land. The First Nations have continued to use, occupy, and retain it as the true proprietors, even though France also claimed and occupied the territory until the Peace of Paris at the end of the Seven Years' War in 1763. Although the Hudson's Bay Company may have had trading rights in the area, these soon expired when, after the Company's royal charter was finally confirmed by the English Parliament in 1690 and renewed for seven years, the charter was not renewed in 1697. The legal fiction of the Hudson's Bay Company grew apace and did not deter the Company from claiming not only the exclusive trading rights to the area but also all of the surface and subsurface property rights.

In the 1950s, E. E. Rich wrote the Company's official history. Sir Winston Churchill, who believed in Britain's imperial mission (although it appears he had Iroquoian ancestry), as Grand Seigneur of the

Gwich'in Indians, an Alaskan indigenous people, are seen outside the Hudson Bay Company trading post at Fort Yukon in this late nineteenth-century illustration. Indigenous peoples gained wealth from trading with the company. However, problems, such as disease and social fragmentation, also emerged. (Corbis)

Company, wrote a Foreword to it in September 1957. In it, he said: "Many great merchant expeditions set out in the last four centuries from the shores of these Islands and materially the history of the lands to which they sailed. Of these, none was more prominent than the Hudson's Bay Company." Churchill continued, "Its interests have swelled from the early trading posts, where furs were the principal article of trade, to the vast commercial undertakings of the 20th century, when the Company is active in so many spheres of exploration and development in every Province of Canada. It is most fitting that the story of this epic of British enterprise, interwoven with the growth of the great country that Canada has become, should now be written" (Rich, 1960). Thus the Company's history has been written until recently largely by British imperial historians who have relied on the Company's own defense of the major challenges to its charter since 1670 rather than on an indigenous perspective, much less on a critical analysis of its relationships and histories with indigenous peoples.

The Company's relationship with indigenous peoples in what became Canada's North has always been both curious and ambivalent, stemming from a mutual interest in the gathering and the hunting of furs. The Company's partners in the fur trade—the First Nations, the Métis and the Inuit—collaborated reciprocally with the largely Scottish traders who ran the trade on the ground in Rupert's Land. The Company and aboriginal peoples benefited from the relationship in very different ways, creating wealth for one another. The fur trade even led to the creation of the Métis, who were the offspring of the miscegenation of aboriginal and nonaboriginal peoples. However, eventually there were problems. With the trade came the disease and epidemics and the social fragmentation of indigenous peoples that are still being felt in communities in Canada to this day. Along with pathogens, in response to increased competition from the Montreal merchants in the late eighteenth century, came the use of alcohol as a trading item, which led directly to alcoholism and the breakdown of many First Nation, Métis, and Inuit communities.

Aboriginal peoples who were not employed by the Company used their canoes and kayaks as well as their intimate knowledge of their lands and waters to resist its dominance. The alternatives to the company were twofold. First Nations and Métis people could refuse to trade with the Company and continue to trade within their own networks, or they could trade with the Northwest or other European companies instead of the Hudson's Bay Company. These options existed because of Canada's enormous geographical land mass as well as the fact that aboriginal people controlled the water routes into the interior of the country through the use of canoes. Even though the Company failed to win this economic war with the Montreal merchants, primarily the Northwest Company, British imperial legislation in 1821 joined the companies under the banner of the Hudson's Bay Company. Thereafter, and until 1870, the Company consolidated its trade in a ruthless manner under the manipulative, high-handed, and frequently racist tactics of Sir George Simpson, its governor, in its acquisition of new trading territories outside Rupert's Land into the Pacific Northwest and as far west as Hawaii.

Further challenges to the Company followed: The 1849 Sayer trial over free trade provided the Métis with a legal victory which allowed free trade in Rupert's Land and also effectively challenged the Company's charter. A select Parliamentary inquiry into the Company and its relationship with aboriginal peoples in the late 1850s challenged the Company's charter, which had been a legal fiction since 1697 and led eventually to the denial of the Company's license in 1859. Amid these challenges in the middle of the nineteenth century, two of the most prominent Métis leaders in London and Canada were almost singlehandedly fighting the Hudson's Bay Company's charter on the basis of aboriginal title and rights: William Kennedy (1814–1890) and his nephew, Alexander Kennedy Isbister (1822–1884). The Company gradually moved its trading posts northward and consolidated its efforts. The late nineteenth century saw the gradual decline of the Company's trading monopoly and its fortunes. Finally, the Company turned itself into an International Financial Society in 1863 and, on December 1, 1869, relinquished its trading rights and ostensibly its proprietary rights (which it did not possess) to Rupert's Land with its sale and deed of surrender to the new federal government of Canada.

Even after relinquishing its rights, the Hudson's Bay Company continued its ambivalent relationship with aboriginal peoples. Eventually its actions leading up to the sale of its trading rights of Rupert's Land provoked the Métis nation, led directly to the first of two armed resistance movements against the federal government in 1869–1870 and 1885, and perhaps were an unwitting cause of the Manitoba Treaty with the Métis under the 1870 Manitoba Act. In the years that followed, the Company, having retained its lands around its trading posts, operated as a commercial enterprise, still trading with aboriginal peoples, especially in the North.

Until recently, the Company survived commercially as a large department store with its headquarters in Toronto. Early in 2006, the American corporation, Target, took it over. Perhaps, fittingly, the Hudson's Bay Company, long the hunter, now became a "target" itself and was hunted down.

David T. McNab and Ute Lischke

See also Fur Trade; Trade.
References and Further Reading
McArthur, Patsy, ed. 2005. "HBC (Here Before the Company): The Saguingue Metis Community, Family History and Metis Trade and Trading." *Historic Saugeen and Its Metis People*, 11–16. Southampton: Sauguine Metis Council.

McNab, David T. 1978. "Herman Merivale and the British Empire, 1806–1874, with Special Reference to British North America, Southern Africa and India." Ph.D. dissertation, University of Lancaster.

McNab, David T. 2005. "Hiding in Plain View: Aboriginal Identities and a Fur Trade Company Family through Seven Generations." In *Hidden in Plain Sight, Contributions of Aboriginal Peoples to Canadian Identity and Culture*. Edited by David R. Newhouse, Cora J. Voyageur, and Dan Beavon, 295–308. Toronto, ON: University of Toronto Press.

McNab, David T. 2003. "Sovereignty, Treaties and Trade in the Bkejwanong Territory." *Journal of Aboriginal Economic Development* 3, no. 2: 52–66.

McNab, David T. 2001. "The Spirit of the Canadas: The Kennedys, a Fur Trade Company Family through Seven Generations." In *Aboriginal People and the Fur Trade, Proceedings of the Eighth North American Fur Trade Conference*. Edited by Louise Johnston, 114–121. Cornwall, ON: Akwesasne Notes Publishing.

McNab, David T., with Bruce W. Hodgins and S. Dale Standen. 2001 "Black with Canoes: Aboriginal Resistance and the Canoe: Diplomacy, Trade and Warfare in the Meeting

Grounds of Northeastern North America, 1600–1820." In *Technology, Disease and Colonial Conquests, Sixteenth to Eighteenth Centuries. Essays Reappraising the Guns and Germs Theories.* Edited by George Raudzens, 237–292. Amsterdam: Brill International.

Rich, E. E. 1960. *Hudson's Bay Company, 1670–1870.* 3 vols. Toronto, ON: McClelland & Stewart Limited.

Indian Act

Legislation concerning American Indians dates back to the first European and British settlers in North America. The one discernable commonality in all of the legislation is that it was focused on promoting the assimilation of Indians into mainstream colonial and later U.S. and Canadian society. These laws also had the effect of helping colonial officials secure political hegemony and destabilizing local Indian governing structures and philosophies. Several centuries after the initial legislation, the Indian Act of 1876 consolidated and amended all earlier statutes regarding the rights of indigenous peoples in Canada. Described as a coercive form of social control, the Indian Act was and, as some First Nations leaders would argue, remains Canada's best means of assimilating Indians into mainstream society.

When Native people first came into contact with Europeans and the British, political interaction was confined to treaty relationships and military alliances in times of war, a process that persisted until 1755 and the establishment of the British Indian Department in British North America. Indian affairs were administered by the Indian Department, a branch of the military, until 1830, when responsibility for Indians was detached from the military. The main goal of the civilian Department of Indian Affairs was to purchase and sell Indian lands in Upper Canada. In 1844, responsibility for the administration of Indian affairs was once again transferred, this time to the Province of Canada and away from the imperial authorities in England.

Beginning in the 1830s, a long line of legislation was implemented that directly affected how the colonial government in Canada dealt with Indians. By 1850, colonial officials attempted to consolidate the myriad Indian laws into two parallel acts (passed by Upper and Lower Canada respectively) designed to deal with the infiltration of settlers into Indian-held territories. These acts transferred control of and responsibility for leasing land and the collection of rents to the commissioner of Indian Lands. Canada's ostensible aim was to protect Indians and their lands from abuse until such time as they became "civilized." This was made clear in the next attempt to consolidate Indian legislation. The 1857 Gradual Civilization Act overtly promoted assimilation as the central goal of Indian policy, while also declaring that Indians of advanced education who were capable of managing their own affairs were eligible for enfranchisement. This legislation also established a separate legal status for Indian populations from equals in need of protection and civilization to that of wards in need of a guardian. Legislative activity increased with the passage of the Civilization and Enfranchisement Act of 1859, which consolidated all previous legislation regarding Indians. By 1860, authority for Indians and Indian lands was formally transferred to the colonial legislature. The Management of Indian Lands and Property Act of 1867 declared the Commissioner of Crown Lands to be the Chief Superintendent of Indian Affairs, while the 1869 Act for the Gradual Enfranchisement of Indians and the Better Management of Indian Affairs introduced the concept of local government to the reserves. By the 1870s, Canadian officials were involved in time-consuming, costly treaty negotiations in addition to fostering the conversion of British Columbia and Manitoba into provinces. Consistently revisiting and amending existing Indian legislation was deemed ineffective, and too many acts were considered cumbersome.

The Indian Act of 1876 consolidated all past Indian legislation into one law that created the legislative framework for an Indian policy that was generally applied uniformly throughout Canada. The Act granted considerable powers to the Superintendent General and to Indian agents located throughout Canada, while guaranteeing that Indians were subject to the Indian Affairs bureaucratic regime. In 1880, Indian Affairs attained departmental status, although it remained under the direction of the Minister of the Interior. An 1881 Indian Act amendment augmented the Indian agents' influence by making them justices of the peace, thereby enabling their prosecution and sentencing of Indians for violations of any Indian Act provisions.

The Indian Act provided for the administration of three key areas: (1) allocation of reserve lands, (2) defining "Indian" status, and (3) granting powers of enforcement to the Canadian government. The Act was (and remains) a comprehensive piece of legislation that regulated and controlled nearly every aspect of Indian life. Indian agents were in place to administer the Act directly in Indian communities. Provisions within it forced an end to traditional governing practices, which were replaced by municipal-style structures. The traditional and hereditary leadership selection processes were outlawed. Indian agents were empowered with extraordinary administrative and discretionary authority. From the beginning, the Indian Act was considered a temporary, stopgap measure that would outlive its usefulness following the absorption of Indians into Canadian society.

The Indian Act also structured an enfranchisement process, thereby permitting Indians to acquire full citizenship but only after relinquishing their ties to their community. In addition to giving up one's culture, enfranchisement required an individual to meet a number of standards that included obtaining higher education and being a person of strong moral character. In doing so, the Act distinguished between status and nonstatus Indians. Status Indians who were registered with the federal government according to the terms of the Act were eligible for minimal government services. Nonstatus Indians were not registered and were therefore not eligible for government programs. According to Section 12(1)b, an Indian woman who married a non-Indian man under the Act had her status taken away from her; her children would also lose their status. An 1880 amendment declared that an Indian person who obtained a university degree would automatically be enfranchised.

By the late nineteenth century, the Indian Act was constantly referred to in Department of Indian Affairs' dispatches to field agents when questions arose concerning issues of land ownership, land use, health regulations, tribal government elections, and justice issues. The Act was also open to amendment when a situation materialized that was not dealt with in the existing provisions. For instance, an 1881 amendment made it illegal for Indians to sell their agricultural produce. This provision was extended in 1941 to all Indians in Canada and to the sale of furs and wild animals. In 1884, the Act was again amended to outlaw the West Coast potlatch; a year later the Sun Dance on the prairies was also made illegal. A 1914 amendment banned Indians from wearing Native costumes in any dance, show, exhibition, stampede, or pageant without the

Department of Indian Affairs' official permission. A 1920 amendment made residential school attendance compulsory and set out penalties for parents who refused to part with their children; and a 1927 amendment made it illegal for Indians to raise money to hire a lawyer to pursue land claims against the government. This list represents but a handful of Indian Act amendments made from 1880 to 1951.

Despite the best efforts of Canadian officials, however, Native people held onto their native identity tenaciously. By the 1940s, Canadian officials were aware that their enfranchisement scheme had failed. The House of Commons special committee on reconstruction confirmed officials' fears while highlighting poor on-reserve living conditions. This resulted in the creation of the Special Joint Committee of the Senate and House of Commons (SJC) that sat from 1946 to 1948. The Indian Act was the catalyst for debate. The SJC held 128 sessions, heard 122 witnesses, including thirty-one Indian leaders, and published 411 written briefs (Belanger, forthcoming). The SJC called for the repeal or amendment of all the sections of the Indian Act to assist Indians in the gradual transition from wardship to citizenship, a strategy that would help Indians advance themselves. In 1951, the new Indian Act was unveiled and many of its more restrictive provisions were repealed, such as those concerning the potlatch and the Sun Dance. However, the new Act was a recycled version of the original, the main difference being that the 1951 Act increased the application of provincial laws to Indians.

Few changes to the Indian Act occurred during the next fifteen years. Then, in 1969, newly elected Prime Minister Pierre Trudeau (Liberal) proposed its repeal. Citing his just society mandate, he concluded in a White Paper that eliminating the Indian Act would abolish the existing chasm between Native and mainstream Canadians through the termination of Indian special status and federal responsibility for Indian affairs. However, opposition within the Native community was so strong that the White Paper was withdrawn in 1971. The next major change to the Indian Act occurred in 1985 with the passing of Bill C-31. This removed many of the discriminatory provisions of the Indian Act, especially those that discriminated against women. It also for the first time permitted the limited reinstatement of Indians who were denied or lost status and/or band membership in the past. Finally, it allowed bands to define their own membership rules. It is anticipated that the bill returned more than 22,000 men, women, and children to treaty status, giving them access to federal programs and services for off-reserve Indians. The next major attempt at change took place in April 2001, following Minister of Indian Affairs Robert Nault's announcement that he intended to alter the Indian Act by curtailing self-government in favor of mandated government structures. Given this proposed violation of their right to self-government, many Native people reacted negatively to Nault's plans, and in 2004 the bill died in Parliamentary process.

Yale D. Belanger

See also Assimilation; Canada, Indian Policies of; Citizenship; Royal Commission on Aboriginal Peoples.

References and Further Reading

Belanger, Yale D. Forthcoming. "Aboriginal Political Organizations in Canada, 1870–1951." In *Hidden in Plain Sight: Contributions of Aboriginal Peoples to Canadian Identity and Culture.* Vol. 2. Edited by David Newhouse, Cora Voyager, and Dan Beavon. Toronto, ON: University of Toronto Press.

Goikas, John. 1996. "The Indian Act: Evolution, Overview, and Options for the Amendment and Transition." In *For Seven Generations: An Information Legacy of the Royal Commission on Aboriginal Peoples.* Ottawa, ON: Canada Communications Group. [CD-ROM]

Leslie, John, and Ron Maguire. 1978. *The Historical Development of the Indian Act.* Ottawa, ON: Treaties and Historical Research Centre, Department of Indian Affairs and Northern Development.

Milloy, John Sheridan. 1979. "The Era of Civilization: British Policy for the Indians of Canada, 1830–1860." Ph.D. dissertation, Oxford University.

Milloy, John S. 1983. "The Early Indian Acts: Developmental Strategy and Constitutional Change." In *As Long as the Sun Shines and Water Flows: A Reader in Canadian Native Studies.* Edited by Antoine S. Lussier and Ian L. Getty, 56–64. Vancouver: University of British Columbia Press.

Tobias, John. 1983. "Protection, Civilization, Assimilation: An Outline History of Canada's Indian Policy." In *As Long as the Sun Shines and Water Flows: A Reader in Canadian Native Studies.* Edited by Antoine S. Lussier and Ian L. Getty, 39–55. Vancouver: University of British Columbia Press.

Indian Civil Rights Act (1968)

The Indian Civil Rights Act, enacted with the Omnibus Civil Rights Act of 1968, specifically delineated the civil rights of Indians as protected by the U.S. Constitution and as recognized by the federal government; in effect, it extended certain provisions of the Constitution to the Indian tribes. The crucial section of this Act, Title II, reads:

Sec. 201. For purposes of this title, the term (1) "Indian tribe" means any tribe, band, or other group of Indians subject to the jurisdiction of the United States and recognized as possessing powers of self-government; (2) "powers of self-government" means and includes all governmental powers possessed by an Indian tribe, executive, legislative, and judicial, and all offices, bodies, and tribunals by and through which they are executed, including courts of Indian offenses; and (3) "Indian court" means any Indian tribal court or court of Indian offense.

Sec. 202. No Indian tribe in exercising powers of self-government shall: (1) make or enforce any law prohibiting the free exercise of religion, or abridging the freedom of speech, or of the press, or the right of the people peaceably to assemble and to petition for a redress of grievances; (2) violate the right of the people to be secure in their persons, houses, papers, and effects against unreasonable search and seizures, nor issue warrants, but upon probable cause, supported by oath or affirmation, and particularly describing the place to be searched and the person or thing to be seized; (3) subject any person for the same offense to be twice put in jeopardy; (4) compel any person in any criminal case to be a witness against himself; (5) take any private property for a public use without just compensation; (6) deny to any person in a criminal proceeding the right to a speedy and public trial, to be informed of the nature and cause of the accusation, to be confronted with the witnesses against him, to have compulsory process for obtaining witnesses in his favor, and at his own expense to have the assistance of counsel for his defense; (7) require excessive bail, impose excessive fines, inflict cruel and unusual punishments, and in no event impose for conviction of any one offense any penalty or

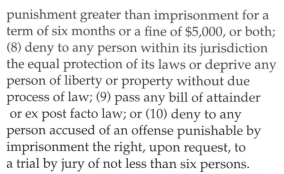

punishment greater than imprisonment for a term of six months or a fine of $5,000, or both; (8) deny to any person within its jurisdiction the equal protection of its laws or deprive any person of liberty or property without due process of law; (9) pass any bill of attainder or ex post facto law; or (10) deny to any person accused of an offense punishable by imprisonment the right, upon request, to a trial by jury of not less than six persons.

Sec. 203. The privilege of the writ of habeas corpus shall be available to any person, in a court of the United States, to test the legality of his detention by order of an Indian tribe.

President Lyndon B. Johnson signed the Civil Rights Act of 1968 in the East Room of the White House on April 11, 1968. Title II of the act confirmed the rights of Indians in the language of the U.S. Constitution and the Bill of Rights. A month earlier President Johnson delivered an address to Congress titled "The Forgotten American," in which he proposed a policy of "maximum choice for the American Indian: a policy expressed in programs of self-help, self-development, [and] self-determination."

Other portions of the law established a model code governing the courts of Indian offenses, asserted some state jurisdiction over criminal and civil actions involving Indians, amended an issue as to offenses within Indian country, allowed for the employment of legal counsel, called for the publication of materials relating to the constitutional rights of Indians, and set a policy regarding fair housing regulations for Indians. Further, the action ended Termination as a federal policy and expressly repealed the controversial Public Law 280 unless tribal councils specifically requested that states continued to oversee civil and criminal matters involving Indians. Senator Sam Ervin (Democrat, North Carolina) commented that the passage of this act "confer[red] upon the American Indians the fundamental constitutional rights which belong by right to all Americans."

C. S. Everett

See also National Congress of American Indians; Indian Self-Determination and Education Assistance Act.

References and Further Reading
Senator Sam Ervin. 1974. *Congressional Record*. 113: 35472.
United States Code Congressional and Administrative News. 1968. 90th Congress, 2d Session.

Indian Civilization Fund Act

The Indian Civilization Fund Act authorized the federal government to allocate money to instruct Native Americans in agriculture, reading, writing, and arithmetic. The Act went into effect on March 3, 1819, and it provided $10,000 per year to promote cultural assimilation among the nation's Indians.

Prior to the establishment of the Indian Civilization Fund, religious missionaries had long sought to teach Native Americans about Christianity and other elements of what they called "civilized" society. After the formation of the United States, and largely beginning with the Jefferson administration, the federal government took an active role in promoting the secular transformation of Natives. What became known as the Indian factory system began in 1795 to set standard rates and to control the behavior of traders and hunters. Indian agents, like Benjamin Hawkins, and other employees of the federal factory system, used their presence among the Indians to teach them to herd cattle, grow cotton, use written laws, adopt Western gender norms, and otherwise embrace elements of American "civilization." When Indian agents did not perform these functions, religious missionaries often did. A lack of steady funding for these efforts, however, frustrated many Americans who believed in the desirability of assimilating Native Americans.

In 1817, Thomas L. McKenney, the Superintendent of Indian Trade for the United States, began to lobby Congress to coordinate and fund a large-scale campaign to promote cultural change. He believed that such a program could be beneficial to both Indians and the United States. By expanding the federal factory system, McKenney believed that he could teach Indians to stop hunting and start practicing agriculture. He encouraged Indian agents to cooperate with religious missionaries, he provided agents with agricultural equipment and livestock to give to cooperating Indians, and he otherwise pursued policies that he believed would lead to acculturated Indians. These actions, McKenney hoped, would allow Indians to become citizens and at the same time bring Native lands under the control of the United States.

With the cooperation of Henry Southard, chairman of the House Committee on Indian Affairs, McKenney brought his plan for widespread schooling for Indians to Congress in 1818. After much internal haggling over who should be in charge of the education, whether profits from the factory system could fund the program, and, if not, how the program would be funded, Congress passed the Indian Civilization Fund Act. It provided a $10,000 annual allocation, far short of McKenney's $100,000 request. In addition, it authorized the president to use his discretion on how to spend the money. Rather than expand the factory system, President James Monroe chose to fund groups who were already engaged in educating Indians to do the work.

Most of the groups who received money from the Indian Civilization Fund were religious missionaries from Protestant sects, primarily Methodists and Baptists. With this new funding, they were able to expand their presence in Indian Country and to create new schools to teach Indians how to become part of American culture. Other allocations went directly to Indian nations, who could choose for themselves which schools to support.

Even with this additional funding, missionary schools did not become a prominent presence in Indian Country. Still, the money allowed the schools to expand and it made the education of Native Americans a central component of U.S. Indian policy. In 1824, the Indian Civilization Fund subsidized thirty-two schools and contributed to the ostensible education of more than 900 Indians. Funds allocated from various Indian treaties helped augment the program, and, by 1830, the Indian Civilization Fund helped support fifty-two schools with 1,512 enrolled students.

The Choctaw Academy was the most well-known institution that received money from the fund. Created in 1825, the academy also received federal funds as a result of several treaties and land sales by the Choctaws. The school was built in Scott County, Kentucky, outside of the Choctaw nation, and it was run by the Baptist General Convention. Students studied basic subjects like English and mathematics while also learning the mechanical arts. Most of the students were Choctaws, but students from other Indian nations attended as well. In 1835, the all-male academy had 188 students.

Andrew K. Frank

See also Assimilation; Baptist Church; Factory System.

References and Further Reading

Murphy, Justin D. 1991. "Wheelock Female Seminary 1842–1861: The Acculturation and Christianization of Young Choctaw Women." *Chronicles of Oklahoma* 69, no. 1: 48–61.

Prucha, Francis Paul. 1984. *The Great Father: The United States Government and the American Indian.* Lincoln: University of Nebraska Press.

Indian Claims Commission

The Indian Claims Commission (ICC) was a federal commission created in the 1940s to resolve the issue of awarding monetary compensation to Native Americans for the loss of their ancestral lands. More than six hundred claims were filed during its first five years. By the commission's expiration in 1978, over five hundred claims had been resolved, with over $800 million awarded to Native Americans.

The expanding United States had long acquired native lands through the treaty process. By 1868 Indian tribes had ceded to the United States over 2 billion acres of land through almost four hundred treaties, leaving Native Americans only 140 million acres. In 1855, some tribes began to file claims against the federal government for treaty violations in the newly established Court of Claims. The government restricted this practice in 1863, and, after 1881, a jurisdictional act of Congress was required before tribes could petition the Court of Claims. By World War I, only thirty-one claims had been filed, with fourteen positive verdicts for the tribes. In the 1920s, however, with a change in public sentiment toward American Indians, tribes had greater success using the Court of Claims to redress their grievances. By 1946, almost 200 native claims were on the dockets of the Court of Claims, a surge that prompted a new procedure to deal with the immense volume of cases.

The ICC was first proposed in 1910 by Commissioner of Indian Affairs Francis E. Leupp. The 1928 Meriam Report also suggested a special commission be created to examine existing claims without the passage of individual jurisdictional acts. After World War II, additional hearings on this topic continued, until finally H.R. 4497 passed through Congress on October 25, 1945, to create the ICC. Concurrent with the passage of the ICC Act, the federal government was in the process of altering its policy toward Native Americans. Termination—the attempt to "desegregate Indian communities, and to integrate Indians into the rest of society" (Fixco, 1986)—was gaining momentum. Historian Donald Fixco, in *Termination and Relocation*, further says that termination was also intended as "the ultimate destruction of had been filed, primarily concerning western lands. To develop a feasible system to accomplish their enormous charge, ICC commissioners decided to transform their organization into an official court. Since the majority of claims were land cases, they were heard in three stages: title, value-liability, and offsets. The long beginning of the ICC's early work troubled Congress, which desired a quick and speedy resolution of Indian claims. In addition to evidence that the petitioners supplied, outside expert witnesses, consisting of anthropologists, historians and land specialists, were required to present major portions of the testimony for these cases. These experts defined vital information concerning tribal boundaries, duration of tribal possession, and assessment of the land. This immense amount of data was presented at the ICC hearings. From the outset, the commission's work was full of unexpected complications. This was evident as the time involved in each step of the claims process lengthened. The challenge of presenting the historical, anthropological, and legal resources in the medium of a courtroom setting made progress sluggish in the early years of the ICC.

The legislation that enacted the ICC was based on the premise that the Indians would have "their day in court." The original conception of a court to hear these claims evolved into a commission format. Five broad categories of claims were permitted under the ICC Act:

> (1) claims in law or equity arising under the Constitution, laws, treaties of the United States, and Executive orders of the President; (2) all other claims in law or equity, including those sounding in tort . . . ; (3) claims which would result if the treaties, contracts, and agreements between the claimant and the United States were revised on the ground of fraud; (4) claims arising from the taking by the United States . . . of lands owned or occupied by the claimant without the payment for such lands of compensation . . . ; and (5) claims based upon fair and honorable dealings that are not recognized by any existing rule of law or equity (60 Stat. 1049).

The ICC sent out a notice to all eligible Native claimants, with an explanation of its function and procedure. The tribes could obtain any legal representative they desired, subject to the approval of the secretary of the interior. The attorney general and

Photographed after the signing of the Indian Claims Commission Act are President Truman, seated, and from left to right, Senator Joseph C. O'Mahoney of Wyoming; Reginald Curry of the Ute Tribe; Julius Murray of the Uintah Ute Tribe; and Oscar Chapman, acting Secretary of the Interior. The Indian Claims Commission operated for thirty-two years, adjudicating the long-standing land and accounting claims of Native Americans against the federal government. (Bettmann/Corbis)

tribal cultures and native life-styles." President Harry S. Truman ignored the issue that the federal government had a long history of unilateral appropriation of native lands. The ICC Act was passed to "absolve" the federal government from any obligation to honor treaties or to compensate Indians for these unilateral landgrabs in return for monetary compensation alone. The ICC Act did not mention the restoration of native lands to their original owners.

The ICC was officially created on August 13. The first cases came in gradually over the first few years, with only 200 claims filed by 1951. A remarkable increase in the quantity of cases occurred in that year, because Indian attorneys had previously refrained from filing until the earlier decisions had been determined. By the end of 1951 over 600 claims his associates represented the United States' side of the case. When a claim was finally decided, a final report was forwarded to Congress, and tribal petitioners were forever barred from "any further claim or demand against the United States arising out of the matter involved in the controversy" (Indian Claims Commission Act of 1946, Section 22). All awards were transferred to the Treasury, and the Bureau of the Budget was to include the allocation in the next appropriations bill. The Act specifically precluded land restoration. Final payment remained in the Treasury until Congress directed its dispersal. Additional compensation was awarded if the ICC found a "grossly inadequate" difference between the adjudicated price and fair market value. Other types of claims involved government accountability; for instance, the government might be held responsible if the ICC determined that tribal funds had been misspent.

After granting the ICC several five-year extensions, Congress finally shut it down in 1978. Two main problems confronted the commission during their last active decade. The first was confusion over the denotation of "unconscionable consideration" for claims filed, since no established formula existed to measure disparity between the payments made to tribes and land value. For example, if the ICC decided that less then 50 percent of the land value had been offered to the tribes by the government, then a disparity was deemed to have existed. A second problem was the lack of progress in compromise settlements, since only the claims attorneys could promote this avenue of settlement. New commissioners joined the ICC during the 1960s, for a total of five by 1968, and their addition expedited the resolving of claims; by 1971 over half the cases had been settled. By 1978 the ICC had only sixty-eight remaining dockets, which were remanded to the Court of Claims.

The ICC awarded over $800 million to Native groups. The claims took about two decades on average to reach their conclusion, The commission achieved other results as well. By hiring their own attorneys, Native people continued to guard their interests. The claims process also resulted in increased public awareness of Native land loss and the search for appropriate compensation. The ethnohistorical research gathered for these cases allowed for further study of Native American societies. The claims process and its difficulties united several Native groups as they strove toward a similar goal. Historians still differ on whether the ICC achieved

its goal of allowing Indian people to have "their day in court."

Susan Sánchez-Barnett

See also Meriam Report; Leupp, Francis Ellington; Land, Identity and Ownership of, Land Rights; Termination; Tribal Sovereignty.

References and Further Reading

Carrillo, Jo, ed. 1998. *Readings on American Indian Law: Recalling the Rhythm of Survival.* Philadelphia, PA: Temple University Press.

Fixico, Donald. 1986. *Termination and Relocation: Federal Indian Policy, 1945–1960.* Albuquerque: University of New Mexico Press.

Indian Claims Commission Act of 1946. Pub. L. No.726, ch. 959, § 12, 60 Stat. 1049, 1052.

Indian Claims Commission Records, RG 279. No date. Washington, DC: National Archives.

Kuykendall, Jerome K. 1979. *United States Indian Claims Commission: Final Report.* Washington, DC: Government Printing Office.

Rosenthal, Harvey D. "Indian Claims and the American Conscience." In *Irredeemable America: The Indians' Estate and Land Claims.* Edited by Imre Sutton. Albuquerque, NM: University of New Mexico Press.1985

Indian Gaming Regulatory Act

Prior to the 1988 enactment of the Indian Gaming Regulatory Act (IGRA), a few tribes ran small-scale commercial gambling operations on their reservations. Consisting of poker games and bingo, these businesses were conducted with federal approval but were not subject to state law. Gaming revenues at this time were modest, generating only about $212 million annually ("Indian Gaming," 2005, 858).

Because Native American tribes and nations have attributes of sovereignty, state law is inapplicable to tribal lands in some cases, absent express congressional intent to the contrary. For this reason, before IGRA, tribes were able to establish commercial gaming enterprises on tribal trust lands without regard for the law of the surrounding state. Yet conflicts arose between states and tribes as states tried to impose their laws on tribal gaming enterprises. An attempt by the state of California to enforce its laws on the Cabazon Reservation ended up as the Supreme Court case of *California v. Cabazon Band of Mission Indians,* 480 U.S. 202 (1987).

With Public Law (PL) 83-280, Congress had made state criminal laws applicable on tribal lands located in California. However, PL280 extended only state criminal laws to reservations—not civil and

Casino sign on the Morongo Indian Reservation, near Cabazon, California. (Bob Rowan; Progressive Image/Corbis)

regulatory laws. Thus, the primary issue in *Cabazon* became whether California's law limiting the conduct of bingo games to charitable organizations was criminal or regulatory in nature.

The state argued that, because the laws were enforced as misdemeanor criminal offenses, they should be considered criminal. However, the court found that, since California permitted gambling in some circumstances—a state lottery, parimutuel horse race betting, and charitable bingo and card games—gambling did not violate state public policy. Rather, the court found that California permitted gambling, although it was subject to regulation. As a result, the court concluded that the state's gaming laws were regulatory rather than criminal and therefore were not applicable to Indian reservations located in the state.

The general rule derived from *Cabazon* was that, if a state permitted any form of gambling, then tribes located in the state could conduct gaming operations. In contrast, tribes located in states that prohibited all forms of gambling were prohibited from operating gaming enterprises. By clearing up legal ambiguities, this ruling encouraged tribes across the country to open gaming enterprises. The expansion of tribal gaming in turn led to an increasing number of conflicts among states, citizen groups, and tribes. To ease the conflicts, Congress quickly acted to develop a comprehensive federal regulatory scheme for tribal gaming. In 1988, Congress passed the Indian Gaming Regulatory Act, which superseded the ruling in *Cabazon* by completely controlling the field of Indian gaming regulation.

Central to IGRA is the Act's division of gambling activities into three separate categories: Class I, Class II, and Class III. Each class is regulated differently. Class I gaming includes games played socially or as part of traditional activities for prizes of low monetary value. Tribes have exclusive jurisdiction over Class I games. Class II games are bingo, games similar to bingo, and some nonbanking card games, such as poker. Class III is a catchall category that incorporates all other games, such as slot machines and casino table games. IGRA limits Class II and III gaming to states in which such games are permitted. In addition, Class II and III games require the enactment of a tribal resolution, and Class III gaming requires the negotiation of a tribal–state gaming compact. (Additional regulations apply to tribal management and federal oversight of Class II and Class III gaming operations.)

Casinos and game designers are always at work developing new games to attract customers. Because Class II gaming can be conducted without a tribal–state agreement, determining whether a new game or machine fits into Class II or Class III is an important and sometimes contentious decision.

Tribes that wish to conduct full-scale casino gambling must negotiate a gaming compact with the state. A compact is a written agreement between the tribe and the state that sets out how the tribe will conduct its Class III gaming operations. IGRA sets out some suggestions for compact provisions, but the Act's parameters are quite broad and permit provisions regarding any "subjects that are directly related to the operation of gaming activities" (Indian Gaming Regulatory Act, fn 2 25 U.S.C. § 2710[d] [3][C][vii]). Existing compacts vary widely. Some common provisions relate to the waiver of the tribe's sovereign immunity related to gaming activities, state inspection of gaming facilities, licensing, enforcement of compact provisions, and casino security.

A key provision of IGRA is its waiver of state immunity from suit. States are generally immune from suit in federal court. However, to ensure that states will negotiate with tribes in good faith toward the adoption of a tribal–state gaming compact, Congress, under its Indian commerce clause authority, included in IGRA a provision giving tribes a cause of action in federal court against states that fail to negotiate a gaming compact in good faith. The U.S. Supreme Court invalidated this provision in a five-to-four decision in the 1996 case, *Seminole Tribe of Florida v. Florida*, holding that Congress does not have the authority to waive a state's sovereign immunity from suit. *Seminole Tribe*, which overturned earlier case law allowing Congress to waive a state's immunity from suit, has had repercussions stretching far beyond the field of Indian law. However, the immediate effect of the ruling was to preclude tribes from enforcing in federal court IGRA's requirement that a state negotiate a gaming compact in good faith. Although *Seminole* pulled some of the teeth out of IGRA, it left in place alternate remedies that have helped ensure the cooperation of states in the compact negotiation process.

IGRA represents a compromise between state and tribal interests. Similar to the ruling in *Cabazon*, the Act permits tribes to open gaming enterprises in states that allow some form of gambling. Yet the Act infringes on tribal sovereignty in several ways. First, it permits tribal gaming only in states where gambling is legal. In other words, the ability of a tribe to open a commercial gaming operation on tribal lands is dependent on state law. The Act also forces tribes to negotiate with states. In the course of these negotiations, states may demand that tribes allow state boards to license casino employees or permit state inspectors to inspect tribal facilities. In addition, although states cannot tax tribes directly, tribal–state gaming agreements often include a revenue-sharing provision that requires tribes to give a state a sizable percentage of tribal gaming revenues, often in exchange for the exclusive right to conduct casino gambling in the state. Tribes with gaming enterprises have been willing to accept these infringements on their sovereignty in exchange for the substantial economic benefits that gaming provides.

In the more than 200 years since the establishment of the first Indian reservations, gaming has been by far the most successful means of economic development. According to the National Indian Gaming Commission, the federal regulatory agency charged with oversight of Indian gaming, 2004 total revenue from the country's more than 300 tribal gaming enterprises was about $19.4 billion. Tribes have used gaming revenues to fund health clinics, schools and scholarship programs, tribal government, and infrastructure improvements. Some tribes also distribute gaming revenues as per-capita payments to tribal members. Today, casino gambling is one of the fastest growing sectors of the U.S. economy. However, the future of the industry and of tribal gaming in particular is uncertain. As a buffer against future uncertainty, some tribes have begun to use their gaming revenues to create more diverse tribal economies by investing in other enterprises.

Many tribes see gaming as the best option for tribal economic development and some have received a large financial benefit from their gaming operations. However, not all tribes are able to operate financially successful casinos. The tribes that have been the most successful usually have land close to a major highway or urban area. Tribes with land in remote rural areas far from major roads have had little success attracting nonmember customers to their casinos. In addition, market saturation can reduce revenues. Some tribes choose not to open casinos, for reasons of tradition, religion, or economics. Thus IGRA, while providing a boon to some, has caused a deep economic division and some political friction between successful gaming tribes and the many other tribes who are still struggling to develop viable economies.

Amy L. Propps

See also Economic Development; Gambling; Reservation Economic and Social Conditions; Tribal Sovereignty.

References and Further Reading

California v. Cabazon Band of Mission Indians, 480 U.S. 202 (1987).

Canby, William C., Jr. 1998. "Indian Gaming." In *American Indian Law in a Nutshell.* St. Paul, MN: West.

"Indian Gaming." 2005. In *Cohen's Handbook of Federal Indian Law.* Albuquerque, NM: American Indian Law Center.

Indian Gaming Regulatory Act. 1988. 25 U.S.C. §§ 2701–2721.

Mezey, Naomi. 1996. "The Distribution of Wealth, Sovereignty, and Culture Through Indian Gaming." *Stanford Law Review* 48 (February): 711–736.

Indian Mineral Leasing Act

Mining in Indian country is a matter of great significance both for the nation as a whole and for the tribes and Indian nations that contain mineral resources. Native nations constitute one of the largest owners of minerals in the country; only the federal government and the railroad companies have larger mineral holdings (Royster, 1994, 542–543). For many tribes, mining is the principal economic engine that brings revenues and employment to reservation communities (Royster, 1994, 544). Passed in 1938, the Indian Mineral Leasing Act (IMLA) has served as the principal piece of federal legislation that governs mineral leasing activities on Indian lands. The IMLA serves three primary purposes: (1) to obtain greater uniformity in the leasing of Indian lands for mining purposes, (2) to harmonize mineral leasing with the Indian Reorganization Act's policy of tribal self-determination by requiring tribal consent to mineral leasing on Indian lands, and (3) to foster greater tribal economic development by ensuring that Indians receive "the greatest

return from their property" (Senate Report, 1937, 2–3; House Report, 1938, 1–3)

Prior to the IMLA's enactment, mineral leasing on Indian lands was governed by several other federal statutes, including the Acts of 1891, 1909, 1919, 1924 and 1927 (Royster, 1994, 556). The multiple statutes governing Indian mineral leasing created a patchwork that varied with respect to types of Native lands subject to the statute, the kind of leasing permitted (oil and gas or non-oil and gas mineral leasing), whether tribal consent was required, and whether state taxation of the mineral leasing was permitted (Royster, 1994, 556). The IMLA introduced a much more uniform mineral leasing regime by imposing one set of rules governing nearly all mineral leasing on tribal lands.

The IMLA authorizes the leasing of unallotted lands and other tribal lands for mining purposes if a tribe and the Secretary of Interior both consent to the lease (25 U.S.C. § 396a). The terms of mineral leases entered into under the Act may extend up to ten years "and as long thereafter as minerals are produced in paying quantities" (25 U.S.C. § 396a). The statute provides for the public auctioning of oil and gas leases, with the right to set the terms of such auctions and the right to reject bids delegated to the Secretary of Interior, and requires that mineral lessees post surety bonds in amounts set by the Secretary of Interior (25 U.S.C. §§ 396b and 396c). Finally, the Act delegates authority to the Secretary to promulgate rules and regulations governing mineral leases (25 U.S.C. § 396d).

Congress's second major goal in enacting the IMLA was promotion of tribal self-government through a requirement that all mineral leases be tribally approved, coupled with a requirement that the Secretary of the Interior also approve mineral leases on Indian lands (Senate Report 1937, 2–3; House Report 1938, 1–3). Although the tribal consent requirement provides assurance that tribes have a critical role in the initial approval of mineral leases on their lands, the consent requirement does little to promote tribal self-government once mineral leasing is underway, since the Act does not include provisions that allow tribes to control mining exploration and development activities once commenced (Royster, 1994, 561). In 1982, Congress responded to the demand for greater tribal control of mineral development activities by enacting the Indian Mineral Development Act.

Congress's third purpose for enacting the IMLA was to ensure that tribes received the "greatest return" possible for mineral leasing conducted on their lands (United States, 1937, 2–3; United States House of Representatives, 1938, 1–3). The Supreme Court has held that the reference to the "greatest return" in the Act's legislative history is not intended to guarantee tribes the maximum profit available, but instead to provide tribes with a "profitable source of revenue" (*Cotton Petroleum v. New Mexico*, 1989, 179). The IMLA is designed to accomplish this objective through the surety bonds that the statute requires and through the system of bonuses, rents, and royalties that the IMLA's regulations establish.

Mineral leasing conducted in accordance with the IMLA has given rise to several controversies that strike at the core issues of federal Indian law, including the federal government's trust relationship with Indian tribes and tribal and state taxing authority in Indian country.

In *United States v. Navajo Nation*, the Supreme Court addressed whether the IMLA imposes a fiduciary duty on the federal government that, if breached, could mandate compensation for damages. The case involved a coal lease between Peabody Coal Company and the Navajo Nation. When the original lease was ripe for amendment, the Secretary of the Interior, after an ex parte meeting with a Peabody Coal representative, directed the Deputy Assistant Secretary for Indian Affairs to encourage the parties to renegotiate new royalty rates for the lease, rather than wait to accept an impending decision from the Deputy Assistant Secretary that was expected to affirm a substantial increase in the royalty rate to 20 percent of gross proceeds. In accordance with the new instruction, the parties resumed negotiations and agreed to a smaller adjustment, raising the original royalty rate to only 12 percent of gross proceeds.

The Navajo Nation sued the United States for $600 million in damages, claiming that the secretary's approval of the coal lease amendments constituted a breach of trust. The Supreme Court rejected the tribe's claim, holding that the IMLA does not impose a duty on the federal government that is enforceable in a claim for money damages. The court found that the IMLA creates a lesser role for the secretary, one that is limited to approving mineral leases and promulgating rules and regulations governing mineral leasing. The court concluded that the IMLA was distinguishable from other statutes that served as the basis for money damages following a breach of fiduciary duty, as in the case of *United States v. Mitchell* (*Mitchell II*).

In *Merrion v. Jicarilla Apache Indian Tribe*, the Jicarilla Apaches assessed an oil and gas severance tax on the production activities of oil and gas lessees that operated on the tribe's reservation, pursuant to mineral leases entered into under the IMLA. The Supreme Court affirmed the tribe's power to tax the lessees, holding that "the power to tax is an essential attribute of Indian sovereignty because it is a necessary instrument of self-government and territorial management" that enables tribal governments to raise revenues for essential services (*Merrion v. Jicarilla Apache Tribe*, 1982, 137).

In *Montana v. Blackfeet Tribe of Indians*, the state of Montana assessed several taxes that were applied against the Blackfeet tribe's oil and gas royalty payments under several oil and gas leases with non-Indian lessees. The state argued that the taxes were authorized because it claimed that the IMLA had incorporated a provision in an earlier mineral leasing statute, the Act of 1924, which had authorized state taxation of Indian mineral leases. The Supreme Court rejected Montana's interpretation of the IMLA, holding that the court will find that the general rule of tribal exemption from state taxation is lifted only when Congress has made its intent "unmistakably clear" (*Montana v. Blackfeet Tribe of Indians*, 1985, 765).

In *Cotton Petroleum v. New Mexico*, the Supreme Court upheld various state oil and gas production taxes assessed against Cotton Petroleum Corporation, a non-Indian party to oil and gas leases entered into with the Jicarilla Apache tribe in New Mexico. The court considered whether the tax was preempted by federal law through either an express or an implied prohibition of the tax, and the court looked to the history of tribal sovereignty, including the broad policies furthered by the IMLA, as a backdrop to its analysis. The court concluded that, although the legislative history of the IMLA referred to tribes receiving the "greatest return" from their property, this did not mean that Congress intended "to remove all barriers to profit maximization," with the effect of precluding all state taxation of non-Indian mineral lessees (*Cotton Petroleum v. New Mexico*, 1989, 180). The court also determined that tribes did not have a history of independence from the imposition of state taxes in the area of mineral leasing, since the Act of 1927 specifically authorized such taxes in the past. Furthermore, the court noted that the state had an interest in taxing Cotton Petroleum's on-reservation oil and gas production because it provided services to both the company and tribal members on and off the reservation. The court also held that states generally have the authority to tax the activities of non-Indians on the reservation unless Congress prohibited the tax.

The *Cotton Petroleum* court refrained from reexamining its prior rejection of a state tax imposed by Montana on a non-Indian mineral lessee on Crow tribal lands. In that case, *Montana v. Crow Tribe*, the state of Montana assessed extraordinarily high state taxes on coal mining activities that amounted to an effective rate of 32.9 percent. The Ninth Circuit Court held that the taxes were unlawful, and the Supreme Court summarily affirmed its holding. This case stands in stark contrast to *Cotton Petroleum*.

Wenona T. Singel

See also Economic Development; Indian
    Reorganization Act; Individual Indian Monies;
    Mining and Contemporary Environmental
    Problems; Reservation Economic and Social
    Conditions; Tribal Sovereignty; Trust,
    Doctrine of.

References and Further Reading

Cotton Petroleum Corp. v. New Mexico, 490 U.S. 163
    (1989).
Indian Mineral Leasing Act, 25 U.S.C. §§ 396a–396g
    (1988).
Merrion v. Jicarilla Apache Tribe, 455 U.S. 130, 137
    (1982).
Montana v. Blackfeet Tribe of Indians, 471 U.S. 759
    (1985).
Montana v. Crow Tribe, 484 U.S. 997 (1988).
Royster, Judith V. 1994. "Mineral Development in
    Indian Country: The Evolution of Tribal Control
    over Mineral Resources." *Tulsa Law Journal* 29:
    552–580.
United States House of Representatives. Report No.
    872, 75th Cong., 3d Sess. 1–3 (1938).
United States Senate. Report No. 985, 75th Cong., 1st
    Sess. 2–3 (1937).
United States v. Mitchell, 463 U.S. 206 (1983).
United States v. Navajo Nation, 537 U.S. 488 (2003).

Indian Removal Act

Provisions for Indian "removal"—the relocation of entire Native nations from areas about to be annexed by non-Indians—were first laid down in an 1817 treaty between the United States and the Cherokee Nation (7 Stat. 156). By 1830, the federal government had passed general removal legislation aimed at the Five Civilized Tribes (the Cherokees, Choctaws, Chickasaws, Creeks, and Seminoles) after they had adopted ways of life and political institutions resembling those of European-Americans. Many other Native American nations (such as the Osages and Poncas) also were removed to Indian Territory during the nineteenth century. By 1883, twenty-five Indian reservations occupied by a total of thirty-seven nations had been established in Indian Country.

The many trails of tears, mostly between the 1830s and 1860s, resulted in immense suffering among the estimated 50,000 to 100,000 Native people who were forced to move. Between one-third and one-fourth of those who were removed died either on the marches or shortly thereafter of exposure, disease, and starvation. Some Native nations, such as the Senecas, Seminoles, Navajos, and Poncas, resisted removal and won the right to remain (or return) home. Notable numbers of Native people, including many Cherokees, evaded removal, and they remain in their home territories to this day. Some, such as the Osages, found themselves forced to new lands that contained rich resources, such as oil.

Removals sometimes led to important legal conflicts that shaped U.S. law for centuries afterward. Such was the case with the Cherokees, on whose behalf Chief Justice John Marshall ruled in the early 1830s in *Cherokee Nation v. Georgia* and *Worcester v. Georgia.* The decision in the latter case did not keep President Andrew Jackson from illegally forcing the Cherokee from their lands, but it did define the relationship of Native Americans to the United States as one of "dependent domestic nations" that endures to this day. The removal of the Poncas led to the case of *Standing Bear v. Crook* (1879), which established Indians as human beings under U.S. law.

Mention "Andrew Jackson" to most Americans, and the phrase "Jacksonian Democracy" may spring to mind. To the descendents of Native Americans who survived the period, however, the first comparison may be to the Bataan Death March of World War II or to Joseph Stalin. There was very little that was democratic about Jackson's handling of relations with Native nations.

Andrew Jackson thought of Indian treaties as anachronisms. "An absurdity," he called them. "Not to be reconciled with the principles of our government" (Johansen, 2000, 88). As Jackson elaborated in a letter to President James Monroe (another advocate of Indian removal) in 1817, "The Indians are the subjects of the United States, inhabiting its territory and acknowledging its sovereignty. Then is it not absurd for the sovereign to negotiate by treaty with the subject? I have always thought, that Congress had as much right to regulate by acts of legislation, all Indian concerns as they had of territories, are citizens of the United States and entitled to all the rights thereof, the Indians are subjects and entitled to their protection and fostering care" (McNickle, 1949, 193).

Given the convoluted grammar, it is not easy to decipher what General Jackson is saying. Is he declaring the Indians to be citizens? Legally, that was not the case until a century later. Is he personally annulling the treaties, which had been signed by parties who regarded each other as diplomatic peers barely two generations earlier? Whatever the nature of his rhetoric, the ensuing decades made clear, especially for the Native peoples of the South, just what Jackson meant by "protection and fostering care."

The private rationale for removal was expressed by Henry Clay (like Jackson, a political product of the trans-Appalachian west). Clay's recitation, preserved in the *Memoirs* of John Quincy Adams, came at the end of a meeting of Adams' cabinet on December 22, 1825, during which the entire agenda was taken up by the conflict between the Creeks and Georgia. Clay was responding to a suggestion that the United States stop making treaties with the Indians and treat them as citizens. According to Adams, Clay said:

> It is impossible to civilize Indians. . . . There never was a full-blooded Indian who took to civilization. It was not in their nature. He said they are destined to extinction and, although he would never use or countenance inhumanity towards them, he did not think them, as a race, worth preserving. He considered them as essentially inferior to the Anglo-Saxon race, which were now taking their place on this continent. They were not an improvable breed, and their disappearance from the human family will be no great harm to the world (Drinnon, 1990, 179–180).

Clay's point of view was popular among Anglo-Americans in need of a rationale for relieving Native Americans of their lands. The fact that the civilized tribes had become, in some respects, as Europeanized as the immigrants seemed not to matter. Removal was less an ideological statement than a convenient method to transfer land from one group of people to another. During the 1820s, before their forceful removal from their homelands, the Chero-

kees developed prosperous villages, a system of government modeled on that of the United States, a written language, and a newspaper. The Cherokees owned 22,000 cattle, 2,000 spinning wheels, 700 looms, thirty-one grist mills, ten saw mills, eight cotton gins, and 1,300 slaves.

Passage of the Removal Act of 1830 climaxed a years-long struggle. The Creeks, for example, had become concerned about non-Indian usurpation of their lands as early as 1818, when the Muscogee (Creek) nation passed a law against the sale of any Native American land without council approval, under penalty of death for the transgressing party. The edict was enforced. In 1825, federal treaty commissioners bribed William McIntosh, leader of the Creek Lower Towns, to sign a land cession agreement, the Treaty of Indian Springs, with a few of his close associates. The National Council declared McIntosh to be a traitor and, on May 1, 1825, sent a delegation to torch his house. When McIntosh appeared at the door of his burning home, his body was riddled with bullets.

Removals of specific Native nations usually were negotiated by treaties (frequently under duress), in which the nations surrendered what remained to them of their aboriginal homelands in exchange for lands west of the Mississippi River. Although some small bands (and a few members of larger nations) had been moving westward since the War of 1812, the Removal Act forced the wholesale removal of entire Native nations, notably the Five Civilized Tribes, in the various phases of the trails of tears.

As the federal government prepared to remove entire nations of Native people west of the Mississippi River, little thought was given to the fact that Indians, European-Americans, and Afro-Americans had been intermarrying among Native peoples for more than a century. Many of the families who were forced to abandon their homes were nearly as European-American, genetically, as their nonreservation neighbors. John Ross, for example, the Cherokee best-known as an opponent of removal, was only one-eighth Cherokee. He lived in a plantation house and owned slaves.

These complications meant little to President Jackson, who had earned his national reputation as a general in the U.S. Army, whose primary business was subjugating Indians. When he ran for president, Jackson sought frontier votes by favoring removal. Once in office, Jackson considered the Removal Act of 1830 to be the fulfillment of a campaign promise.

Others felt less sanguine; even with extensive lobbying from the White House, the House of Representatives passed the Removal Act by only six votes (103 to 97). Representative William Ellsworth of Connecticut opposed Removal in a passionate speech delivered on the House floor, as he said, in part: "We must be just and faithful to our treaties. There is no occasion for collision. We shall not stand justified before the world in taking any step which shall lead to oppression. The eyes of the world, as well as of this nation, are upon us. I conjure this House not to stain the page of our history with national shame, cruelty, and perfidy" (Johansen, 1998, 275).

President Jackson's adamant support of Indian removal placed him on a direct constitutional collision course with Chief Justice John Marshall, who was evolving legal doctrines vis-à-vis Native American land rights on which he had been working before Jackson was elected. The Cherokee cases, which came before Marshall's U.S. Supreme Court between 1823 and 1832 would display, in broad and emphatic relief, how closely much of early nineteenth-century American life was connected to the land speculation machine that helped propel westward movement.

The removal of the "civilized tribes" from their homelands is one of the most notable chapters in the history of American land relations. Jackson's repudiation of John Marshall's rulings, which supported the Cherokees' rights to their homelands, constituted contempt of the Supreme Court (an impeachable offense under the Constitution). The subject of impeachment was not seriously raised, however. During the incendiary years before the Civil War, the removals became intertwined with the issue of state's rights vis-à-vis the federal government. Had Jackson followed Justice Marshall's rulings, the Civil War might have started in the 1830s.

The assertion of states' rights vis-à-vis Native American territorial sovereignty (against the background of removal legislation) provided the legal grist for an 1832 Supreme Court decision written by Chief Justice Marshall that has defined the relationship between Native Americans' sovereignty and state's rights for more than a century and a half.

Marshall's opinions outlining Native Americans' status in the U.S. legal system occurred as he defined the Supreme Court's place in U.S. politics. When Marshall became chief justice in 1801, the Supreme Court was little more than a clause in the Constitution. For the next thirty-five years, Marshall played a major role in defining the Court as an insti-

tution. According to author Jean Edward Smith, if George Washington founded the United States, John Marshall legally defined it.

Chief Justice Marshall had long-run political differences with President Jackson, and he agonized over the conflicts between states' rights and Native sovereignty. In 1831, in *Cherokee Nation v. Georgia*, Marshall held that the Cherokees had no standing in court to appeal the state of Georgia's seizure of their lands. This situation troubled Marshall so deeply that he said at one point that he thought of resigning from the Supreme Court because of it. A year later, in *Worcester v. Georgia*, Marshall held unconstitutional the imprisonment by Georgia of a missionary (Samuel Worcester) who had worked with the Cherokees. The specific issue was the refusal of Worcester, while a resident on Cherokee land, to swear loyalty to the state of Georgia in conformance with a state law.

The case began when three white missionaries living on Cherokee territory refused to swear an oath of allegiance to the state of Georgia. They were arrested, chained to a wagon, and forced to walk more than twenty miles to jail. Two Methodist preachers who objected to the cruelty that accompanied the arrests were also chained and taken to jail. The three missionaries were tried, convicted, and sentenced to four years of hard labor at the Georgia state penitentiary. Two of them later swore allegiance and were released; one (Worcester) did not. When the case reached the Supreme Court (as *Worcester v. Georgia*), Justice Marshall wrote that Native nations had a degree of sovereignty that denied Georgia the right to compel an oath of loyalty.

Historians disagree over whether President Jackson actually said, "John Marshall has made his decision, now let him enforce it." Whether Jackson expressed himself in those words may be a moot point; his implementation of removal flew in the face of the law as interpreted by Marshall in *Worcester v. Georgia*. Marshall wrote that the Cherokees had "always been considered as distinct, independent political communities, retaining their original natural rights . . . and the settled doctrine of the law of nations, that a weaker power does not surrender its independence—its right to self-government—by associating with a stronger, and taking its protection. . . . The Cherokee nation, then, is a distinct community, occupying its own territory, with boundaries accurately described, in which the laws of Georgia can have no force, and which the citizens of Georgia have no right to enter, but with the assent of the Cherokees, or in conformity with treaties, and with the acts of Congress" (Worcester, 1975).

Marshall reasoned in *Worcester v. Georgia* that the Constitution, by declaring treaties to be the supreme law of the land, had adopted and sanctified previous treaties with the Indian nations. The words "treaty" and "nation" are "words of our own language," wrote Marshall, "selected in our diplomatic and legislative proceedings, by ourselves, having each a definite and well-understood meaning. We have applied them to Indians, as we have applied them to the other nations of the earth; they are applied to all in the same sense" (Worcester, 1975). Marshall defined Indian nations neither as totally sovereign nor as colonies, but as "domestic dependent nations." The Congress, however, fearing that a confrontation over states' rights could provoke civil war, took no action against Jackson.

Although Ross continued to protest removal for several more years, the state of Georgia coerced Cherokees to sell lands for a fraction of their value. Marauding immigrants plundered Cherokee homes and possessions. They destroyed the *Cherokee Phoenix*'s printing press because it had opposed removal. The U.S. Army forced Cherokee families into internment camps to prepare for the arduous trek westward. As a result of unhealthy and crowded conditions in these hastily constructed stockades, many Cherokees died even before their Trail of Tears began. While failing in his efforts to stop removal, Ross did manage to gain additional federal funds for his people.

After almost six years of delays, the Trail of Tears was initiated in 1838. Before they were exiled from their homelands by force of arms, the Cherokees released a "memorial" expressing their feelings:

The title of the Cherokee people to their lands is the most ancient, pure, and absolute known to man; its date is beyond the reach of human record; its validity confirmed by possession and enjoyment antecedent to all pretense of claim by any portion of the human race.

The free consent of the Cherokee people is indispensable to a valid transfer of the Cherokee title. The Cherokee people have neither by themselves nor their representatives given such consent. It follows that the original title and ownership of lands still rests with the Cherokee Nation, unimpaired and absolute. The Cherokee people have existed as a distinct national community for a period extending into antiquity beyond the dates and records and memory of man. These attributes have never been relinquished by the Cherokee people, and cannot be dissolved by the expulsion of the Nation from its territory by the power of the United States Government (O'Brien, 1989, 57).

In preparation for the Cherokees' removal, John Ross was evicted from his mansion to a dirt-floored cabin. When John Howard Payne, author of the song "Home Sweet Home," came to visit him at the cabin, just across the Georgia state line in Tennessee, the Georgia State Guard crossed the state line and kidnapped both men. Realizing that the federal government did not intend to protect the Cherokees, Ross and others reluctantly signed the Treaty of New Echota in 1835 and prepared, with heavy hearts, to leave their homes.

During 1838 and 1839, the U.S. Army removed the Cherokees by force, except for a few hundred who escaped to the mountains.

The Cherokees' phrase for their long, brutal march (*nuna-daa-ut-sun'y*, "trail where they cried") gave the march its enduring name. At least one-fourth of the Cherokees who were removed died along the way. Ross's wife Quatie was among the victims of this forced emigration. James Mooney described how the Cherokees were forced from their homes: "Squads of troops were sent to search out with rifle and bayonet every small cabin hidden away in the coves or by the sides of mountain streams. . . . Families at dinner were startled by the sudden gleam of bayonets in the doorway and rose up to be driven with blows and oaths along the trail that led to the stockade. Men were seized in their fields or going along the road, women were taken from their wheels, and children from their play" (Van Every, 1966, 242). A U.S. Army private who witnessed the Cherokee removal wrote: "I saw the helpless Cherokee arrested and dragged from their homes, and driven by bayonet into the stockades. And in the chill of a drizzling rain on an October morning I saw them loaded like cattle or sheep into wagons and started toward the west. . . . Chief Ross led in prayer, and when the bugle sounded and wagons started rolling many of the children . . . waved their little hands goodbye to their mountain homes" (Worcester, 1975, 67).

Despite the cruelty of the marches they were forced to undertake, and the death and disease that dogged their every step, the surviving members of the peoples who were removed to Indian Territory quickly set about rebuilding their communities. Much as they had in the Southeast, the Creeks, Cherokees, and others built prosperous farms and towns, passed laws, and set about organizing societies once again. Within three generations, however, the land that in the 1830s had been set aside as Indian Territory was being sought by non-Indians. At the turn of the century, as a rush for "black gold" (oil) inundated Oklahoma, the Allotment Act (1887) broke up the Native estate much as Georgia's state laws had done a little more than a half century earlier. There would be no Trail of Tears this time, however: There was no empty land left to occupy.

Bruce E. Johansen

See also Cherokee Nation v. Georgia; Citizenship; Domestic Dependent Nation; Forced Marches; Genocide; Jackson, Andrew; Land, Identity and Ownership of, Land Rights; Ross, John; Trail of Tears; Tribal Sovereignty; *Worcester v. Georgia.*

References and Further Reading
Cave, Alfred A. Winter, 2003. "Abuse of Power: Andrew Jackson and the Indian Removal Act of 1830." *Historian* 65: 1130–1153.
Drinnon, Richard. 1990. *Facing West: Indian Hating and Empire Building.* New York: Schoken Books.
Jahoda, Gloria. 1975. *The Trail of Tears.* New York: Holt, Rinehart, and Winston.
Johansen, Bruce E. 1998. *The Encyclopedia of Native American Legal Tradition.* Westport, CT: Greenwood Press.
Johansen, Bruce E. 2000. *Shapers of the Great Debate on Native Americans: Land, Spirit, and Power.* Westport, CT: Greenwood Press.
McNickle, D'Arcy. 1949. *They Came Here First: The Epic of the American Indian.* Philadelphia, PA: J. B. Lippincott Co.
O'Brien, Sharon. 1989. *American Indian Tribal Governments.* Norman: University of Oklahoma Press.
Satz, Ronald. 1973. *American Indian Policy in the Jacksonian Era.* Lincoln: University of Nebraska Press.
Van Every, Dale. 1966. *Disinherited: The Lost Birthright of the American Indian.* New York: William Morrow & Co.
Wallace, Anthony F. C. 1993. *The Long, Bitter Trail: Andrew Jackson and the Indians.* New York: Hill and Wang.
Worcester, Donald, ed. 1975. *Forked Tongues and Broken Treaties.* Caldwell, ID: Caxton.
Worcester v. Georgia, 31 U.S. (6 Pet.) 515(1832).

Indian Reorganization Act

It has been more than eighty years since the passage of the Indian Reorganization Act (IRA) in 1934. During that time, there have been many opportunities to examine the conventional wisdom that it is a signal example of federal administrative reforms favorable to American Indians, reversing decades of land alienation and cultural abuses caused by the 1887 General Allotment Act. John Collier was Indian commissioner from 1933 to 1945 during President Franklin D. Roosevelt's Democratic administration, and the IRA was Collier's brainchild and the centerpiece of his reforms. Collier, a radical social worker who became an anthropologist, was both a prolific writer and a skilled propagandist. His books, *Indians of the Americas* (1947) and *From Every Zenith* (1962), have been widely read, and they put the best possible interpretation on the Indian New Deal. Until recently, conventional wisdom has followed Collier's interpretation. The question remains, however: Was the IRA truly an Indian agenda, and was it fairly and intelligently applied? In short, how should one evaluate the IRA legacy?

A twenty-year appraisal of the IRA took place in conjunction with the annual meeting of the American Anthropological Association in 1953. It included John Collier himself, along with several prominent Indians and anthropologists. When the fiftieth anniversary of the IRA occurred in 1984, scholars, Indian leaders, and political activists began another reevaluation. The Institute of the American West, for example, held a conference at Sun Valley entitled "Fifty Years Under the Indian Reorganization Act—Indian Self-Rule," in which many notables participated in a series of panels. Both appraisals during these reevaluations were uniformly positive.

In the past few decades, however, scholars have taken yet another look at the IRA and Collier's administrative reforms. Kenneth Philp's biographical study, *John Collier's Crusade for Indian Reform, 1920–1954,* came out in 1977, and Lawrence Kelly's *The Assault on Assimilation: John Collier and the Origins of Indian Policy Reform* appeared in 1983. Philp generally follows Collier's favorable view of the IRA. Kelly, on the other hand, emphasizes the failure of the IRA legislation to attain Collier's idealistic reform goals. He also faults the Collier administration for its failure to extend the Act's limited benefits to the majority of Indians. Two other scholars who have written major reevaluations are Graham Taylor and Lawrence Hauptman. They, too, are critical of the Indian New Deal as not being all that it was purported to be. We should also mention Deloria and Lytle, who present an insightful analysis of the IRA in *The Nations Within: The Past and Future of American Indian Sovereignty.*

In 1977 the American Indian Policy Review Commission reported its findings to Congress on the economic, social, and political conditions of the Indian tribes and nations. Its findings, as Graham Taylor observes, seem to indicate that the twin goals of the IRA (Indian economic development and the restoration of Indian self-determination through a council system of government) have been notable failures of existing Indian policy. As a result, as the Meriam Report found in 1928, American Indians continued to rank at the bottom of virtually every social indicator fifty years later.

New criticism of the IRA incorporates the views of traditional Indians, many of whom opposed the IRA and the Indian New Deal from its very beginnings. The traditional Indian movement has historically struggled to achieve three goals: (1) a viable land base for economic self-sufficiency and nationhood, (2) political self-determination through sovereignty under the treaties, and (3) cultural rights (language, religion, and heritage). John Collier's two aims under the Indian New Deal, on the other hand, were (1) to preserve the Indian people as a "race" and as distinct cultures, which Collier termed "grouphood," and (2) to preserve and develop resources, including land. The means to achieve these goals for Collier were "tribal" organization and economic incorporation under the IRA. For traditional Indians, however, the means to their goals is for the United States to return to the treaty relationship (treaty federalism) and to recognize the Indian peoples as sovereign with the right to self-determination.

The 1920s: Protest from the Pueblos

The first two decades of the twentieth century were particularly onerous for American Indians within the borders of the United States. Not only had the 1887 General Allotment Act resulted in reservation land loss and impoverishment, but the government's policy of Americanization and cultural assimilation ushered in a virulent period of ethnocide. One of the worst manifestations was the federal crackdown on Indian religious ceremonies. The proassimilationist Indian Rights Association led an attack on "indecent" ceremonies among the Indian Pueblos of the Southwest, and the Board of Indian Commissioners deplored the fact that tribal rituals were still being conducted on many Indian reservations. In its 1918 report, the Board described the Indian dances as evil and a reversion to paganism. On April 26, 1921, Indian Commissioner Charles H. Burke issued Circular 1665, which outlawed the Plains Sun Dance and other traditional religious ceremonies and made them punishable by fines or imprisonment. The Native American (peyote) Church also came under attack. This period of Indian policy also saw many other instances of religious abuse.

About the same time that the assault on Indian culture and religion was occurring, Secretary of the Interior Albert B. Fall led an attack on Indian rights through his sponsorship of the Bursum and Indian Omnibus bills in Congress. The former bill would have confirmed white encroachment on sixty thousand acres of Pueblo Indian land, while the Omnibus bill sought to individualize remaining tribal assets, including timber, coal, and other minerals, thereby ending federal trusteeship responsibility. Fall also attempted to create a national park out of part of the Mescalero Apache Reservation bordering on his Three Rivers ranch, which would have enhanced the value of his own property. When oil was discovered on the Navajo Reservation in 1922, he issued a ruling that opened all executive order reservations to exploration by oil companies under the 1920 General Leasing Act. These were the federal Indian policies that struck at Indian sovereignty, especially in New Mexico, and that led to the protest from the Pueblos and the entry of John Collier as an advocate for Indian rights.

Instead of destroying Native societies and cultures through forced assimilation, John Collier believed in a policy of cultural pluralism and Indian administration through indirect rather than direct U.S. rule. The controversy over the Pueblo land grants (part of a larger struggle against landlessness stemming from allotment) and religious dancing led to the formation of the American Indian Defense Association in May 1923. Facing criticism from Collier, the Pueblo Indians, New Mexico democrats, and the 2-million-member General Federation of Women's Clubs, Fall was forced to resign from the Harding administration. He was replaced in 1923 by Dr. Hubert Work, who was described as the last of the frontier commissioners. Secretary Work was under the influence of Christian missionaries and opposed Indian dancing, but he had to back off from former Commissioner Burke's order prohibiting the theocratic Taos and Zuni Pueblos from withdrawing selected Indian youth from Bureau of Indian Affairs schools for traditional religious training.

Despite Collier's advocacy work, the Bureau continued its policy of suppressing Indian religious ceremonies. The issue came to a head during the summer of 1925 at Taos when the Pueblos' officials disciplined two members of the Native American Church for invading traditional religious ceremonies. Acting unilaterally to "establish order," the Indian Bureau thereupon arrested virtually the entire governing body of Taos Pueblo. Collier's Defense Association provided bail and lawyers, and the All-Pueblo Council swung into action, denouncing the Bureau's effort to destroy Indian self-government. Collier took Pueblo representatives on a tour of Utah and California in the cause of Indian religious freedom and to raise money for its defense. Secretary Work denounced these activities, saying that "propagandists are touring part of the country with a company of dancing and singing Pueblos in full Indian regalia in order to awaken people to the 'crime' in New Mexico. There is no crime in New Mexico." Congressman Scott Leavitt of Montana sponsored a bill drafted by the Bureau that would give Indian superintendents the power to throw any reservation Indian in jail for six months and levy a $100 fine without trial. Because of the work by the Defense Committee the Leavitt bill did not get out of committee.

In 1928, on the eve of the Indian New Deal, a government commission issued a landmark report to Congress, "The Problem of Indian Administration." Collier declared that the Meriam Report, as it was popularly called, had "blasted apart the walls of the dungeon called the Indian affairs system" and constituted a major indictment of the Indian bureau. The report made it clear that allotment policy had not produced assimilation and was, in fact, an unmitigated disaster judging by any social or economic indicator. The Indian population had actually decreased since the passage of the 1887 General Allotment Act. There were more landless Indians than before; Indian trust lands had decreased in value; family income was as low as $48 per year on some reservations; the annual death rate had increased; and the Indian land base had shrunk from 137 million acres to a mere 47 million. Collier saw horrible material and spiritual decline as a result of the allotment policy.

As the Depression deepened, the Bureau began a retreat from instituting reform, and Congress was less inclined to vote for Indian appropriations. In March 1932, representatives of forty-nine Indian tribes petitioned the U.S. Senate, alleging that the Hoover administration had reneged on its promises for Indian reform as recommended in the Meriam Report. After his election in 1932, President Roosevelt received a document signed by more than 600 educators, social workers, and other concerned citizens, drawing attention to the extreme situation of the American Indians. The signers asserted that "your administration represents almost a last chance for the Indians."

The Indian New Deal (1933–1937)

Harold Ickes, who became FDR's new Secretary of the Interior, was a Chicago Progressive reformer and former director of the American Indian Defense Association. Ickes appointed Collier to become commissioner of Indian affairs on April 2, 1933. A cultural pluralist, Collier sought to reverse the policy of forced assimilation and its detrimental economic exploitation and land dispossession. He still believed in eventual assimilation, but at a slower and more equitable pace and without the loss of community solidarity and Indian values. He proposed that government follow a colonial policy known as indirect administration.

Upon taking office, Collier immediately instituted recovery measures legislated under the New Deal FDR administration. He successfully established a separate Civilian Conservation Corps (CCC, a jobs program for the unemployed) for Indians known as Emergency Conservation Work (ECW). The conservation of reservation lands and the training of Indians to utilize their own lands and resources distinguished it from the regular CCC. Before its demise in 1943, the ECW had employed 85,349 enrollees from seventy-one different reservations with a total of $72 million in appropriations. The ECW was perhaps the most successful of Collier's Indian New Deal reforms, and it was very popular at the grassroots level on the reservations.

Collier initiated many other reform measures as well, all of which became known as the Indian New Deal. The assimilationist-minded Board of Indian Commissioners was abolished in May 1933, and by the following August Collier persuaded Ickes to declare a temporary cessation of further Indian land allotments, of the sale of allotted lands, of the issuance of certificates of competency, and of similar measures. Of equal importance was the cancellation of debts owed by Indian tribes to the federal government. Because of the debt cancellation and the appropriation of more than $100 million in relief programs, American Indians were able to survive the worst years of the Great Depression and even enjoy a higher standard of living than they had a decade earlier. In some respects, the impact of the Depression in the wider society was already reversing the process of assimilation by driving Indians back to their reservation homelands for economic survival.

Other Indian New Deal reforms included the creation of an Indian Arts and Crafts Board, a reservation court system, and a directive ordering the Indian Service to observe "the fullest constitutional liberty in all matters affecting religion, conscience and culture." The ban against religious dances was lifted, and government repression of Indian languages in Bureau schools was ended. The major accomplishment of the Collier administration, however, was the passage of the Indian Reorganization Act.

Indian Reorganization Act

In a meeting held at the Cosmos Club in Washington, D.C., in January 1934, Collier laid out his ideas for a basic piece of legislation to correct the evils of forty-seven years of allotment policy. To this meeting he had invited representatives from organizations that formed the nucleus of Indian reform: the American Indian Defense Association, Indian Rights Association, National Association on Indian Affairs, American Civil Liberties Union, National Council on American Indians, and the General Federation of Women's Clubs. Later the same month, he tested the waters for his ideas in a circular to reservation superintendents, tribal council members, and individual Indians in a document entitled "Indian Self-Government." Despite the mostly negative replies, Collier nevertheless advanced plans to draft a bill for major Indian reorganization. The primary thrust of Collier's draft legislation was self-government, a policy that ran directly counter to the previous policy of assimilation. The completed Collier bill contained forty-eight pages and four major titles, each divided into a number of substantive sections. The final Indian Reorganization Act (IRA) as passed by Congress, on the other hand, omitted important parts of two of Collier's original titles and one title altogether, the one dealing with a proposed Court of Indian Offenses. Although the three remaining titles (self-government, education, and Indian lands) were all substantively reduced in content, they at least made it into the new law.

The bill was signed into law June 18, 1934, as the Wheeler-Howard, or Indian Reorganization, Act, but it bore little resemblance to Collier's original bill. Opposition to the Collier bill came from Indians who favored assimilation, western congresspersons (many of whom were reflecting special interests in their home states containing Indian reservations), missionaries, and Bureau personnel. The powerful Indian Rights Association still favored the melting pot concept, but hoped that the legislation with its provision for educational training would promote assimilation. Only the section of Title II in the original bill that dealt with education came through relatively unscathed. The act in its final form eliminated four key features of Collier's draft bill: (1) The tribes were denied the right to take over heirship lands; (2) the section setting up a reservation court system was eliminated; (3) social units smaller than the tribe, such as local or community level groups, were not empowered, although Alaska Native villages were later included when the IRA was amended in 1936; (4) the section on promoting Indian culture and traditions was deleted.

Self-government

Title I of the IRA gave Indian tribes the right to organize for the purposes of local self-government and economic enterprise. Collier's bill would have conferred limited self-government on reservation Indian groups or communities, treating them as municipalities, but the final version of the IRA limited this provision to tribal units only. The first step in the process was for a tribal committee to draft a constitution. Then an election would be held to ratify the constitution, with a majority vote of reservation members necessary for adoption. Approval by the Secretary of the Interior was also required. Congress modified this section of Collier's bill by cutting the annual appropriation for the organization of tribal governments from $500,000 to $250,000.

Deloria and Lytle, in *The Nations Within*, point out that the self-government provision of the IRA helped to define important powers of Native political entities. With the support of Collier, after the Act was passed, a ruling by the Solicitor of the Interior Department found that the powers conferred under the Act's self-government provision were inherent in the tribes' and nations' status as domestic dependent nations. These powers are a tribe's right to adopt its own form of self-government, to determine tribal membership, to regulate the disposition of tribal property, and to prescribe the rules of inheritance on real and personal property.

Tribal business corporations

An emphasis on economic development was an important feature of the IRA. Upon receiving a petition from at least one-third of the adult reservation Indians, the Secretary of the Interior could issue a charter of incorporation. When ratified by a majority of reservation members, a Native tribe or nation could then engage in business enterprises. The IRA also established a revolving loan fund of $10 million for economic development. This was twice the amount that Collier had suggested in his original bill.

Education and employment

The education provisions of Title II were not controversial, and Congress raised the appropriation from Collier's $50,000 to $250,000. Congress, on the other hand, limited the amount to loans rather than outright grants, and training was primarily for vocational education. An important clause in Title I waved civil service requirement for employment in the Indian service, thus establishing the principle of Indian preference in hiring. Omitted from Title II was Collier's draft section declaring that it would be the policy of Congress "to promote the study of Indian civilization, including Indian arts, crafts, skills and traditions." This entire section was struck. Congress, it would seem, was not interested in promoting the Indian heritage.

Indian lands

A key part of Title III was the section abolishing the 1887 Indian Allotment (Dawes) Act. Title III also declared it the policy of the United States to undertake a constructive program of Indian land use and economic development, with a pledge to consolidate Indian land holdings into suitable economic units. Two million dollars was set aside annually for land acquisition.

The new law also extended indefinitely the trust period of allotted lands as a protection against loss of Indian lands to non-Natives. Under the previous system, allotted lands were held in trust for twenty-five years, after which they were vested in the ownership of the Indian allottee. At the same time, however, they became subject to state taxes. As a result,

the Indian landowner almost always lost his land because of nonpayment of taxes or was forced to sell to a non-Indian.

The lands provisions of the Collier bill were so controversial in the congressional debate that its original twenty-one sections were reduced to eight, thus negating many of Collier's plans for significant land reform. The Collier bill had addressed the land alienation and heirship problems with language ensuring that previously allotted lands would be returned to tribal ownership. In the Collier draft, the Secretary of the Interior was empowered to compel the sale or transfer of trust allotments to tribal governments, and trust allotments not immediately returned would revert to tribal status upon the death of the landowner. Congress modified this section by making it voluntary rather than compulsory. In addition, the land title would now pass to the heirs and not to the tribe upon the death of the Indian landowner. This dealt a deadly blow to Collier's efforts to consolidate fragmented Indian parcels and return them to the tribal estate.

Under the IRA as passed by Congress, the Bureau of Indian Affairs became a real estate entity for thousands of Indian heirs possessing an interest in ever smaller pieces of inherited land from an original allotment. Today, the number of heirs to an original 160-acre allotment distributed under the 1887 Allotment Act in many cases exceeds one hundred. Tens of millions of dollars are lost every year to Indian tribes through the Bureau's practice of renting or leasing these uneconomical interests in allotted or heirship lands to non-Indian farmers and ranchers at low rates, who then combine the parcels into viable economic units. The heirship problem has continued to become more unmanageable with each passing generation. Because of allotment, which the IRA stopped but did not reverse, twenty-five reservations have greater non-Indian than Indian populations and thirty-eight have lost at least half of their original reservation land base to non-Indians.

Indian law and order

Title IV of the Collier bill that would have created a Court of Indian Affairs was eliminated entirely from the Indian Reorganization Act. It also would have removed IRA tribes from state jurisdiction in Indian cases, heirship cases, and appeals from tribal courts. Title IV also stipulated that law and order must be consonant with Indian customs and traditions. Although the then existing tribal court system needed significant improvement and stability, and the federal attempt to deal with Indian legal problems was woefully inadequate, Collier realized that it was politic to give up Title IV more or less as a sacrificial lamb to a not too friendly Congress.

Voting

Part of the congressional debate concerned the voting or ratification by the tribes and nations for self-government under the IRA provisions. An early version of the bill merely specified "three-fifths of the Indians on the reservation or territory covered by the charter." The House bill changed this to a simple majority vote. Finally, a supplementary act passed in 1935 resolved the question to "the vote of a majority of those voting."

Collier lost out to Senator Burton Wheeler, a sponsor of the legislation, with respect to the blood quantum legal definition of an American Indian under the IRA legislation. Collier wanted one-fourth "blood," but Wheeler insisted on one-half "blood."

Within a year after the passage of the IRA the Secretary of the Interior was to call for a referendum election on the reservations. Each tribe was to discuss the provisions of the act and then vote on whether to accept or reject it. Senator Wheeler favored a simple majority vote, but Collier managed to insert language that would make the IRA operative on a reservation *unless a majority of the tribal members voted to exclude themselves from the Act.* In other words, the adult Indians not voting could be counted as voting for the IRA. In this way, Collier's stratagem resulted in more tribes and nations coming under the IRA than would otherwise have been the case. No matter how small the number of eligible Indians voting in favor of the IRA, by counting the nonvotes as "yes," IRA acceptance was virtually assured. A case in point is the Santa Ysabel tribe in California that came under the Act because sixty-two eligible tribal members who did not vote were counted as being in favor of adoption. Another example is the vote manipulation that took place on the bitterly divided Hopi Reservation. A plurality of Hopi "progressives" voted for the referenda while a larger number of traditional Hopi "voted" by not voting. The Collier administration nonetheless ruled that the Hopi had voted to accept the IRA. As Kenneth Philp points out in his biography of Collier, at least seventeen Native polities that voted to reject the Act were considered as being in favor of it. Collier knew that on many of the reservations the more traditional, full-blood Indians would refuse to participate in the IRA elections, preferring instead to assert their tribal sovereignty under the treaties.

A related feature of the Act was the provision that allowed a tribe only one chance to either accept or reject the IRA. Any benefits of the new law would be lost forever if a tribe wanted to take a wait-and-see approach.

When administrative manipulation of the voting was exposed, Collier was forced to agree that Congress should amend the IRA. In June 1935, an amendment was passed that extended the deadline for referenda for another year. It also clarified the voting requirements by stipulating that a majority of those voting would determine whether a tribe accepted the IRA or not. At the same time, a distressing feature of the majority rule amendment was that it also contained a provision that 30 percent of the eligible adult Indian population had to participate in the referendum in order for a majority of no votes to reject the Act. If the number of voters did not amount to 30 percent, then even an overwhelming number of no votes could not result in the IRA being rejected. On the other hand, the same rule did not apply for a tribe voting to accept the IRA. Theoretically, even a 1 percent voter participation could effect acceptance of the IRA.

Extending and applying the IRA

Because a number of nations and tribes did not want to participate in certain provisions of the new law, and because of political pressure brought by special interest groups, a section of the IRA provided for exclusions and modifications.

Congress passed the Alaska Reorganization Act on June 1, 1936, which included Alaska Natives at the village level under the IRA provisions. The original IRA, on the other hand, had limited its provisions to tribes only. Ultimately, sixty-six Alaskan Native groups adopted constitutions and corporate charters under this law. The Oklahoma Indian Welfare Act was passed in the same month, which included the Indian tribes of that state.

According to the reorganization plan, after a tribe or nation voted to accept the IRA, it would draw up a constitution and bylaws, submit it to a referendum, have the Secretary of the Interior certify the results, and then start operating as a corporate tribal council. Of the 181 tribes accepting the Indian Reorganization Act between 1934 and 1945, only ninety-six adopted a tribal constitution, and only seventy-three tribes ever received corporate business charters. Seventy-seven tribes with a population of 86,365 members rejected the Act outright. Several of these were large reservation groups, such as the Klamath Indians of Oregon and the Crows of Montana. An especially bitter blow to Collier was the rejection of the IRA by the Navajo Nation. With 98 percent of the eligible Navajo voting, the tribe rejected the Act by 419 votes. The Navajo had not forgiven the Collier administration for its drastic livestock reduction program on the reservation, carried out ostensibly to protect the land against overgrazing, that had reduced many of the small herding families to destitution.

Councils vs. communities

Graham Taylor stood alone as the only contemporary critic to raise the question of Native political organization and the nature of Indian communities at the time the IRA went into effect. He believed that the Indian responses to the Act differed because each Indian group was at a different point on the assimilation–traditional continuum. There were great differences among the reservations in terms of intermarriage, English literacy, Anglo-American education, and acceptance of Christianity. These differences provoked factional strife on most reservations at the time. Many of the monolingual, full-blooded, traditional Indians were unfamiliar with parliamentary procedures, their aboriginal political systems having been a council of elders and chiefs acting on the unanimity principle. Consequently, many of the traditionals boycotted the IRA proceedings altogether. For most reservation Indians, the "tribal governments" established under the IRA constitutions were a totally new and unfamiliar form of political organization. At Hopi it was primarily the more acculturated villages on the First Mesa that strongly supported the IRA and drew up the tribal constitution, while the villages on the other mesas, being more traditional, either vacillated or withheld their support.

The misreading by Congress and Collier on the question of Indian social organization defies explanation because many of Collier's closest advisers were anthropologists. Yet Collier and his Applied Anthropology Unit, in pressuring Native peoples to accept the IRA, neglected the existing social organization of Indian communities, the nature of which varied tremendously from reservation to reservation. Many of the Six Nations Iroquois were still committed to a confederacy based on the clan system; the Choctaws, Cherokees, Chickasaws, and Creeks had a history of secular Indian republics; the Shoshones and Paiutes of Nevada, Utah, and Wyoming were organized only at the level of the extended family band; the Rio Grande Pueblo societies were settled, agricultural villages run as theocracies; and the full-bloods among the Plains Indians were organized into a complex of band councils under traditional chiefs. If the goals of the Indian reform were cultural preservation and economic self-sufficiency, then it would have made sense for reorganization to be tailored to each specific situation. Instead, the "tribal" governments established under the IRA constitutions were a totally new and unfamiliar level of sociopolitical organization for many Indian populations.

Evaluation

John Collier continually defended the IRA and the Indian New Deal programs during his tenure as commissioner of Indian affairs. He was forced to appear before Congress several times to justify the reforms, and there were two attempts by Congress to repeal the Act, although both were ultimately unsuccessful. The House Appropriations Committee underfunded IRA programs, and by 1944 the Senate Committee on Indian Affairs had also come to oppose the commissioner and his program of Indian reform. Among the most active Indian opponents of the IRA was the American Indian Federation, which joined forces with American pro-Nazi groups in labeling Collier a communist.

In hindsight one can conclude that the self-government provisions of the IRA, although important, had a problematic impact on Indian communities, but Collier's most lasting achievement was economic development. Much of the Indian New Deal involved bringing needed resources to economically depressed reservation communities. Collier's economic policies also helped Indians rebuild their badly depleted land base, if only modestly; Indian land holdings increased from 48 to 52 million acres, and almost 1 million acres of surplus land was returned to Native tribes and nations.

Following Collier's resignation in 1945, federal Indian policy became stridently regressive for the next two decades during the termination and relocation policy periods in which the limitations of Indian "self-government"—the relative powerlessness of the tribes under the IRA—became apparent. Federal policy did not improve until the federal War on Poverty in the early 1960s and the resurgence of American Indian activism.

Steve Talbot

See also Assimilation; Collier, John; Bureau of Indian
    Affairs: Establishing the Existence of an Indian
    Tribe; Identity; Indian Claims Commission;
    Land, Identity and Ownership of, Land Rights;
    Meriam Report; Reservation Economic and
    Social Conditions; Tribal Sovereignty.

References and Further Reading

Deloria, Vine, Jr., and Clifford M. Lytle. 1984. *The
    Nations Within: The Past and Future of American
    Indian Sovereignty.* New York: Pantheon.

Hauptman, Lawrence M. 1984 "The Indian
    Reorganization Act." *The Aggressions of
    Civilization: Federal Indian Policy Since the 1980s.*
    Edited by Sandra L. Cadwalader and Vine
    Deloria, Jr., 131–148. Philadelphia, PA: Temple
    University Press.

Jorgensen, Joseph G, and Richard O. Clemmer. 1980.
    "On Washburn's 'On the Trail of the Activist
    Anthropologist': A Rejoinder to a Reply." *The
    Journal of Ethnic Studies* 8, no. 2: 85–94.

Kelly, Lawrence C. 1983. *The Assault on Assimilation:
    John Collier and the Origins of Indian Policy
    Reform.* Albuquerque: University of New
    Mexico Press.

Philp, Kenneth R. 1977. *John Collier's Crusade for
    Indian Reform, 1920–1954.* Tucson: University of
    Arizona Press.

Taylor, Graham D. 1980. *The New Deal and American
    Indian Tribalism: The Administration of the Indian
    Reorganization Act, 1934–45.* Lincoln: University
    of Nebraska Press.

Indian Self-Determination and Education Assistance Act

Congress passed the Indian Self-Determination and Education Assistance Act (ISDEAA) in 1975 to implement its tribal self-determination policy. The Act began to loosen the tight grip of the Bureau of Indian Affairs (BIA) and several other federal agencies, such as the Indian Health Service (IHS), on the daily life of Indians and their tribal governments. Prior to passage of this law, the BIA and other federal agencies minutely regulated the delivery of educational, health, and a myriad of other services to the Indian people. The BIA, for example, operated a number of boarding schools, some for many years, with little meaningful input from tribal members or the tribal governments themselves. Some of these schools are still in existence.

Although this law deals primarily with the delivery of educational services, nearly all other federal support to Native Americans is also within the purview of the Act. Such services include agriculture, health care, law enforcement, and other programs in support of tribal government.

Essentially, the ISDEAA permits the tribes themselves or any group chartered by the tribe's governing body to assume the responsibility for delivering federal services to tribal members. Contracting organizations other than the tribe itself must meet certain requirements before they are eligible to enter into such agreements with the federal government. Elementary and high schools located on a reservation are among the most common organizations that have so-called 638 contracts (named after the number of the Indian Self-Determination and Education Assistance Act, Public Law 93–638). Where the BIA itself operates boarding or day schools for Indian students, it oversees every detail of their operation. Under the Act, the tribes and local tribally chartered schools contract with the BIA for it to take over school operations. The BIA or other agency allocates a fixed sum to the contractor, which must then furnish the services to the tribe.

This law also strengthens the Johnson-O'Malley (JOM) Act of 1934 by requiring all off-reservation schools that receive federal funding for the education of Indian children to involve Indian parents in decisions over how those funds shall be used. Local committees of Indian parents have considerable authority over how local schools may spend JOM monies.

The Act is not without its critics, however. Although tribes and allied organizations now deliver these services using their own employees, buildings, and equipment, the federal government retains significant oversight over the contracts. The government must approve each contract and must be provided with data regarding accounting practices, equipment, personnel, and other important details of the proposed contract. If the government is not satisfied with the agreement, it may reject it despite local community support. The contractor may, under the Administrative Procedures Act of 1946, appeal that rejection to the highest levels of the executive branch and ultimately to the federal courts. Such appeals, of course, are lengthy and expensive.

Some critics see the law as one step back toward the termination of federal responsibility for Indian services. They reason that the next step beyond turning over the running of federal programs to the tribes is eventually to end that assistance to the tribe entirely. Nonetheless, the current trend is to expand the number of federal programs to be operated by Indian tribes.

Later amendments to the law established a pilot project for ten tribes to take over the activities previously conducted for them by the BIA and IHS. In addition to those already mentioned, these endeavors include resource conservation, land use planning and zoning, among others. Many tribes have only limited 638 contracts with the government. These agreements must be negotiated one at a time. These tribes chosen for the pilot program administer all federal services themselves. Additionally, unlike the usual 638 contracts, the tribes chosen for this program have much more latitude in designing or altering their programs to meet the needs of their people and in reallocating the funds among the different programs. These 638 contracts are similar to block grants, in which recipients may use the funds in nearly any way they wish, subject only to some very limited restrictions.

Daniel R. Gibbs

See also Bureau of Indian Affairs: Establishing the Existence of an Indian Tribe; Education; Tribal Sovereignty.

Individual Indian Monies

The Individual Indian Monies (IIM) scandal has become the stuff of political and legal legend since the *Cobell v. Norton* class action was first filed in 1996. With half a million plaintiffs, the case concerning the abuse of royalty accounts for Native Americans kept by the federal government has become the largest class action ever filed against the U.S. government. Employing more than 100 lawyers on the payrolls of the Interior and Treasury departments, *Cobell v. Norton* (after Elouise Cobell, lead plaintiff, and Gale Norton, Secretary of the Interior) has become the largest single employer of federal legal talent in the history of the United States.

How much money is at stake? In 1997, the commonly accepted figure was between $2 and $3 billion. By late 2002, lead prosecutor Dennis Gingold placed the figure at "far north of $10 billion" (Kennedy, 2002). A report prepared for the Interior Department suggested that the federal government's total liability might reach $40 billion.

On December 21, 1999, Judge Royce C. Lamberth, who supervised the case from Washington, D.C. Federal District Court, issued his first (Phase One) opinion (the case is divided into two phases). The 126-page opinion stated that the government had massively violated its trust responsibilities to Native Americans. He called the IIM mess the "most egregious misconduct by the federal government." While *Cobell v. Norton* is certainly a high-stakes case, such a superlative overstated its historical scope. Perhaps it is the most egregious example of *financial* misconduct in a trust relationship by the U.S. government, which in its two-plus centuries has done worse to Native Americans than lose several billion dollars.

Judge Lamberth later ordered the government to file reports quarterly describing in detail its efforts to account for the monies. The judge also ordered the Interior and Treasury Departments to compile an audit of the Individual Indian Monies trust fund system reaching to its origins in 1887.

Judge Lamberth is a Republican appointee, a Texan with a taste for fancy boots and large cars, who seemed, on the surface, unlikely to take a serious interest in a Native American class action suit. However, he possessed a keen knowledge of bureaucratic politics and an ability to read and comprehend vast amounts of information. Like fishing rights judge George Hugo Boldt (also a Republican appointee), Lamberth also possesses a sharp sense of justice, regardless of vested interests. Like Boldt, he also has been hardworking and ruthlessly judicious.

The Education of an Indian Accountant

The IIM case produced evidence of what must have been the world's sloppiest banking record keeping. Even Elouise Cobell, who initiated the suit, has been amazed at the sorry state of the BIA's banking "system," if it can be called that. Cobell, a member of the Blackfeet tribe and a banker by profession, filed the suit in 1996. Cobell, of Browning, Montana, founded (and still has a hand in operating) the first Native American–owned bank in the United States. She also served as treasurer of the Blackfeet from 1970 through 1983.

Cobell's education in the BIA's ways of banking began with a detailed examination of the Blackfeet's trust accounts. After Cobell discovered a number of problematic transactions, she began asking questions. Her initial inquiries were rebuffed by the BIA. "They said, 'Oh! You don't know how to read the reports,'" Cobell recalled. "I think they were trying to embarrass me, but it did the opposite—it made me mad" (Awehali, 2003).

Cobell has spent much of her life in and near the reservation town of Browning, Montana. She was one of eight children in a house with no electricity or running water. The major form of entertainment was old-fashioned: oral history, sometimes describing Baker's Massacre, during which U.S. soldiers killed about two hundred Blackfeet, a majority of them women and children, following an ambush near the Marias River. She also sometimes heard stories from her parents and their neighbors about small government checks that bore no relationship to reality.

Cobell spends much of her time tutoring Blackfeet and other Native peoples in how to best start their own businesses. She also helps with chores on a ranch that she co-owns with her husband, Alvin. During a sojourn off the reservation in her twenties (she was nearly fifty in 2004), Elouise met Alvin, who is also Blackfeet, in Seattle. He was fishing off the Alaska coast, and she held a job as an accountant with a Seattle television station.

At the age of thirty, Cobell returned to Browning with Alvin, to resume a life on the family ranch. She also was offered a job as the reservation government's accountant. At the time, Browning had practically no Native-owned businesses; unemployment rose to more than 70 percent in the winter (which can last into May), when construction employment ceased. She found the Blackfeet accounting system "in total chaos" (Kennedy, 2003). Some trust accounts were being charged negative interest. Checks were being posted against accounts without her knowledge, even though she was supposed to be the only valid signatory. In 1987, Cobell moved on to start the first Native-owned bank in the United States, mainly to help finance local business ventures. In a few years, she could point to several businesses that she had helped to finance: the Glacier Restaurant, Browning Video, the Dollar Store (Kennedy, 2003).

Years before the class action suit was filed, Cobell asked questions within the system. As she began to delve into the trust issue on a national basis, in Washington, D.C., Cobell was introduced to Gingold, the lead prosecuting attorney for the case, who was quoted in the *Los Angeles Times* as saying of his first meeting with her: "From my experience, American Indians were not involved in banking. I was looking for a bunch of people with turbans" (Kennedy, 2003). Gingold admitted that he had a great deal to learn about how the government had separated Native Americans from their trust assets.

Cobell did not decide to file suit lightly, but only after several rebuffs by the government that displayed an unwillingness to take the trust accounts problem seriously. She realized that large legal actions were massively expensive. Her years of activism and her experience as the Blackfeet's accountant had suggested some sources of support, however. She contacted the Arthur Bremer Foundation of St. Paul, Minnesota, and won a $75,000 grant and a $600,000 loan. In 1997, a year after she filed the class action suit, Cobell also received, quite unexpectedly, a $300,000 genius grant from the John D. MacArthur Foundation, most of which went into the case. Shortly after that, J. Patrick Lannan of the Lannan Foundation read about Cobell's MacArthur grant, and traveled to Browning to meet with her. Lannan eventually donated $4 million to the cause. By mid-2002, the cost of the legal action had reached $8 million, still barely a drop in the proverbial bucket next to the hundreds of millions of dollars in tax money that the federal government has spent to defend itself.

Some in the government saw the problem coming before Cobell filed suit. During 1992, the House of Representatives Committee on Government Operations issued a report, "Misplaced Trust: The Bureau of Indian Affairs' Mismanagement of the Indian Trust Fund." During 1994, Congress passed the Indian Trust Fund Management Reform Act, with the stated aim of cleaning up the mess. As part of this law's implementation, Paul Homan, an expert at cleaning up failing private financial institutions, was hired. Homan, having taken stock of the situation, later quit in disgust, describing a banker's nightmare.

The BIA, for example, did not establish an accounts receivable system, so it never knew how much money it was handling at any given time. Partial records indicated that more than $50 million was never paid because the BIA had lost track of account holders. About 21,000 accounts were listed in the names of people who were dead. Large numbers of records had been stored in cardboard boxes, left to soak (and smear) in leaky warehouses. About $695 million had been paid—but to the wrong people or Native governmental entities. One property record valued chain saws at $99 million each. Some of the records were contaminated with asbestos, and others had been paved over by a parking lot. As he resigned, Homan said he had never seen anything like this in his thirty years as a banker.

Before he quit, Homan reported that no one knew just how many people were owed money. Of the 238,000 individual trusts that Homan's staff located, 118,000 were missing crucial papers, 50,000 had no addresses, and 16,000 accounts had no documents at all. Homan further reported that one could assume money had been skimmed extensively from the trust: "It's akin to leaving the vault door open," he said (Awehali, 2003).

In the meantime, before a dime has been paid to any of the half million Native people who are part of the class action, the Bush administration requested $554 million in its 2004 budget to "reform" the trust fund, an increase of $183.3 million over the $370.2 million budgeted in 2003. "Reform" in this case means, to a large degree, paying legal talent to resist the class action suit. In a January 2001 interview with Harlan McKosato on the national radio show, "Native America Calling," Cobell noted that "just by not settling the case, it's costing the government and taxpayers $160,000 an hour, $7 million a day, $2.5 billion a year" (Awehali, 2003).

"Pen and Ink Witchcraft"

With the government's mismanagement now so widely known, a sensible person might conclude that the time had come to find a way to reimburse the many Native people who have been cheated. If you are one of the 500,000 Native Americans who unwillingly did your banking with the BIA, when might you expect a corrective check in the mail? Don't hold your breath. If the Bush administration has its way, you could turn very blue before the guarantor of your trust makes you, as they say in financial litigation circles, "whole."

The spin doctors in the White House probably didn't realize that their designs resemble some treaty negotiations for its Alice-in-Wonderland quality (things are never what they seem). In 1791, the famed Ottawa speaker Egushawa, observing treaty negotiations, called such machinations "pen and ink witchcraft."

What Egushawa witnessed had nothing on the trust money mess. After eight years of legal song and dance by the federal government, the central fact of the case is this: The BIA and Treasury Department never built a record-keeping system capable of tracking the money owed to Native Americans based on income from its superintendency of their resources.

As time passed (the system, in its modern form, began with the advent of the Allotment Act in 1887), the lack of a functioning banking system made record keeping worse; the sloppiness of errant (or nonexistent) record keeping was compounded, for example, because of the divisions of estate required by generations of fractional Native inheritances. By the time Cobell and a few other banking-minded Native Americans began asking, seriously, what had become of their individual Indian monies, the Interior Department, by and large, did not have a clue.

In an average year, $500 million or more was deposited into the Individual Indian Trust from companies leasing Native American land for grazing, oil drilling, timber, coal, and other natural resources. According to law and financial theory, the money is collected by the Interior and sent to the Treasury, where it is supposed to be placed into individual trust accounts. Problems began with the roughly 50,000 accounts that lacked names or correct addresses. One such account contained $1 million (Awehali, 2003). Along the way, it also was learned that some companies simply neglected to pay as expected; they soon learned that, much of the time, no one seemed to be watching.

As early as 1999, the plaintiffs' legal team discovered that the Departments of the Interior and Treasury had "inadvertently" destroyed 162 boxes of vital trust records during the course of the trial, then waited months to notify the court of the "accident." "You tell me if that's fair," Cobell told Mike Wallace in a *60 Minutes* interview shortly after the discovery. "When they have to manage other people's money according to standards, why aren't they managing our money to standards? Is it because you manage brown people's money differently?" (Awehali, 2002).

Judge Lamberth was shocked when he discovered, in the course of the lawsuit, that the Interior and Treasury Departments had, as a matter of course, destroyed accounting documents and filed false reports with the court. In the course of the litigation, thirty-seven past and present government officials, including Bush's Secretary of the Interior Gale Norton and Clinton's Interior Secretary Bruce Babbitt, were held in contempt of court. On August 10, 1999, Lamberth ordered the Treasury Department to pay $600,000 in fines for misconduct.

As he delved into the trust account debacle, Lamberth found that some records were stored in rat-infested New Mexico warehouses. Others were dispersed haphazardly on several remote reservations. When the Interior Department kept computerized records at all, they were so inadequate and insecure that hackers could set up their own accounts (and presumably draw money from them).

During the first phase of the case, many experts testified that the Interior and Treasury lack the records to render any semblance of true accounting for the monies that the government was supposed to be managing. Instead, the plaintiffs suggested various methods of estimating what is owed. For example, the Geographic Information System (GIS) might use satellite-mapping technology to estimate the amount of oil produced by wells on Native lands and thereby derive an idea of royalties owed.

The "Midnight Rider"

In September 2003, Judge Lamberth ordered the Interior Department to conduct a thorough investigation into money that was supposed to be paid to Indians for oil, gas, timber, and grazing activities on their land, dating back to 1887. He said that the accounting must be completed by 2007.

Responding to Lamberth's first-phase opinion and this directive, Cobell was enthusiastic at the time. "This is a landmark victory," she said. "It is now clear that trust law and trust standards fully govern the management of the Individual Indian Trust and that Secretary Norton can no longer ignore the trust duties that she owes to 500,000 individual Indian trust beneficiaries" (Awehali, 2003).

The idea of a complete accounting, which sounded so simple, suddenly became very problematic in the land of pen-and-ink-witchcraft. The Interior and Treasury, with their allies on Capitol Hill and in the Bush White House, prepared a hastily inserted "midnight rider" to a federal spending bill that forbade spending that would have implemented Lamberth's directive. Funding, according to the rider, was to be frozen for a year or until an accounting methodology could be agreed on by the Interior, Treasury, and Congress.

In the meantime, the Interior Department was reported by several news organizations as complaining that the type of historical accounting required by Judge Lamberth's ruling would take ten years and cost $6 to $12 billion. Some feat of accounting that would be—the accounting equivalent, perhaps, of building the Panama Canal or putting many men on the moon, a rubber figure with an odor of obstructionist politics. (To illustrate just how rubbery the estimate is, let's crunch a few round numbers. At $100,000 each per year, very good pay for an accoun-

tant, $10 billion would hire a hundred thousand accountants. Even if they worked ten years each, $10 billion would still pay 10,000 number crunchers. Add a few zeroes here and there, and soon we're talking some very serious money. Bear in mind that the folks who came up with these quick estimates work at the same agencies that lost track of all that Native American money in the first place.)

With a federal budget deficit approaching $500 billion a year (including Iraq and Afghanistan war and reconstruction liabilities running at least $87 billion a year), the Bush Administration and the then Republican-controlled Congress seemed unwilling to seriously consider paying up a century-plus of Indian trust money bills that could cost as much as $40 billion—the bill that could come out of the second phase of the case, once the Interior and Treasury assessed the due bills, as ordered by Judge Lamberth. The midnight rider was sponsored in large part by a Republican-controlled executive branch and Congress that added 721,000 federal jobs to the federal payroll during George W. Bush's first term as president.

About fifty Republicans voted against the appropriations bill containing the rider, however, led by Representative Richard Pombo (Republican, California), chairman of the House Resources Committee, with Representative J. D. Hayworth (Republican, Arizona), cochair of the bipartisan House Native American Caucus. Pombo, who favors a legislative solution to the court case, called the rider a "poison pill that was added to the legislation in blatant violation of House rules and protocol" (Reynolds, 2003). The rider passed narrowly, 216–205, on October 30, 2003.

The Senate passed the spending bill (with the midnight rider) 87–2 on November 4, and sent it to Bush for his signature November 10. Cobell sharply criticized President Bush's administration, including Interior Secretary Norton, for sponsoring the rider. Said Cobell, "What this vote shows is the length that the Interior Secretary and the Bush administration will go to in their efforts to deny Indians the accounting for funds that belong to Indians—not the federal government. Now American Indians are being victimized once again by politicians in Washington" (Reynolds, 2003). Cobell said that she expected the courts to strike down the rider as an illegal interference with the judicial process, a violation of the Constitution's separation of powers.

"It's a clear act of bad faith to seek a stay based on an unconstitutional statute," said Gingold

(Appeals Court, 2003). The Senate's legal counsel and House members from both parties said the provision is probably unconstitutional because the administration cannot dictate to courts how to interpret the law.

Wither the Trust Fund Billions?

So wither the trust fund case? When all is said and done, will the plaintiffs in *Cobell v. Norton* ever get anything close to what they are owed? While optimism is always in season and justice sometimes does actually prevail, there is ample precedent in United States legal history vis-à-vis Native Americans to create doubts that right and reasonable outcomes follow the opinions of courts presided over by hardworking, honest judges, even after the government has copiously admitted its errors.

Some historical parallels present themselves: John Marshall, chief justice of the U.S. Supreme Court, found in favor of the Cherokees' sovereignty; President Andrew Jackson ignored him and his Court, leading to the Trail of Tears. Jackson's action was an impeachable offense—contempt of the Supreme Court and a violation of his oath of office. It was never prosecuted because Georgia made a states' rights case that could have started the Civil War thirty years before it actually began.

More recently, during the mid-1970s, the courts found in favor of a 250,000-acre land claim for the Oneidas. Thirty years later, they have yet to receive any land from this legal proceeding.

Might *Cobell vs. Norton* end up being another perpetual motion employment engine for lawyers, and another reminder that sometimes the legal system talks the talk as the executive branch fails to walk the walk of justice? Or might the contending parties, with judicial prodding, find a way to at least estimate what is owed the plaintiffs and take the necessary steps to pay them? The next few years may provide an answer, after the second phase of *Cobell v. Norton* is adjudicated and a final ruling is issued—but not by Judge Lamberth, who, in a virtually unprecedented decision, was ousted from the case by a U.S. Court of Appeals in 2006.

Senator Ben Nighthorse Campbell, who is Cheyenne, has insisted that all parties to the Cobell litigation must work together to resolve the case; he believes that, otherwise, it may not be resolved at all. "We have one year to reach settlement on this issue," he said during a hearing of the Senate Committee on Indian Affairs, as it considered his bill, S. 1770, to encourage individual beneficiary settlements in the lawsuit (Reynolds, 2003).

Native-owned companies could benefit from the requirement that the Interior Department compile an accounting for the 117-year record of Indian trust fund mismanagement. Earnings for such work may reach $50 million by some estimates. Tlingit and Haida Technology Industries has applied to do some of the court-ordered accounting work, according to Dan DuBray, an Interior Department spokesperson quoted in the Fairbanks *Daily News-Miner* and the Juneau *Empire,* both on November 5, 2003.

Blackfeet History at Ghost Ridge

"I've heard from friends that the government thinks I'm tired and that they'll wear me down, so that I'll just go away," said Cobell (Awehali, 2003). Near Cobell's hometown a marker describes the winter of 1884, when 500 Blackfeet died of starvation and exposure while awaiting supplies promised them by the federal government. The dead were buried in a mass grave that is now called Ghost Ridge. During the more difficult stages of the lawsuit, Cobell said she has visited Ghost Ridge, thinking of her ancestors who perished in the cold 120 years ago, while waiting for the government to fulfill its promises (Awehali, 2003).

The Blackfeet starved as U.S. Indian Agent John Young hoarded food that would have allowed them to survive. From Ghost Ridge, it is not difficult to draw parallels to the entire course of Indian–European-American relations, most notably to the case at hand. Once again, Native land and fiscal resources were taken, hoarded in faraway places, as the promises of the "trust" relationship between the United States and Native peoples were massively abused.

Bruce E. Johansen

See also Bureau of Indian Affairs: Establishing the Existence of an Indian Tribe; Trust, Doctrine of.

References and Further Reading

Associated Press. "Appeals Court Halts Indian Trust Accounting." 2003. *Billings Gazette.* November 14. Available at: http://www.billingsgazette.com/index.php?id=1&display=rednews/2003/11/14/build/nation/42-indiantrust.inc. Accessed January 14, 2007.

Awehali, Brian. 2003. "Fighting Long Odds: Government Continues to Shred, Evade, Obstruct, Lie, and Conspire in Indian Trust Case." *LiP Magazine*, December 15. Available at: http://www.lipmagazine.org. Accessed January 14, 2007.

Johansen, Bruce E. 1997. "The BIA as Banker: 'Trust' is Hard When Billions Disappear." *Native Americas* 14, no. 1 (Spring): 14–23.

Kennedy, J. Michael. 2002. "Truth and Consequences on the Reservation." *Los Angeles Times Sunday Magazine*, July 7 (Cover story). Available at: LATimes.com. Accessed January 14, 2007.

Reynolds, Jerry. 2003. "Bush Administration Likely Behind Cobell Appropriations Rider." *Indian Country Today,* November 1. Available at: http://www.indiancountry.com/?1067709828. Accessed January 14, 2007.

James Bay and Northern Quebec Agreement

The James Bay and Northern Quebec Agreement (JBNQA) was signed in 1975 and represents the first treaty in what has become Canada's modern treaty period. It also continues a long history of treaty making between the First Nations and the crown and, later, Canada. Treaties were regularly utilized by the crown from the 1870s until 1921, when the last of the numbered treaties, Treaty 11, was signed. A five-decade moratorium on treaty making followed. Canadian officials distanced themselves from engaging the First Nations in treaties largely because the land previously required to promote Canada's nation-building efforts had already been obtained from them. As federal officials found out in the early 1970s, however, territorial occupation did not necessarily signify fee simple title. This issue exploded when the James Bay Crees initiated an aggressive lobby effort demanding a formal treaty relationship that would protect their territorial integrity.

All of the lands that comprise the JBNQA area were at one time within the demarcated region known as Rupert's Land. Officially the domain of the Hudson's Bay Company, the land in question was ceded to Canada in 1868. In 1870, by imperial order in council, crown officials agreed to obtain formal title to the lands through treaties with the First Nations, a process that never occurred. Two boundary extensions—in 1898 and 1912—resulted in the transfer of territorial title to the province of Quebec, the latter of which promised formal recognition of the rights of the Indians inhabiting the lands. In return, the Indians were to release their rights to the province, and any agreements would then have to be approved by order in council, a commitment that was never honored. Nevertheless, Native people continued to utilize the vast region because the only non-Native presence consisted of a handful of Hudson's Bay Company employees, missionaries, and some members of the federal department responsible for Indian affairs.

Due to limited outside interest in the region, little thought was given to aboriginal rights in Quebec. The Native territorial presence notwithstanding, provincial officials in the mid-1960s began researching the region's hydroelectric potential. By 1971, the province of Quebec announced its intention to initiate development of the James Bay hydroelectric project. The project that government officials had in mind, however, would require blocking and, in certain cases, diverting rivers within the James Bay drainage basin. Subsequently, the province established the James Bay Development Corporation to develop all the territory's resources, which included hydroelectricity, forestry, mining, and tourism. Provincial officials failed to consult with the 10,000 Crees and 5,000 Inuits who occupied the area, people who discovered through media reports that their homeland was destined to be flooded.

The Crees quickly mobilized. Community leaders held information sessions and developed a political strategy they anticipated could end the onslaught of workers and heavy machinery moving into their territories. In 1972, the newly formed Quebec Association of Indians petitioned the Quebec Superior Court for an injunction to stop all construction in the region. The injunction was granted on the grounds that the province of Quebec had failed to settle all outstanding land claims as required by the 1898 and 1912 boundary extensions. This decision was overturned within days, once again opening the region to hydroelectric development. Many Native leaders, however, optimistically viewed the decision as affirming their claims and once again lobbied the provincial government for a land claim agreement.

By 1974, the Crees and Inuits of northern Quebec, the governments of Canada and Quebec, and the Quebec Hydro-Electric Commission concluded an agreement in principle, which led to the signing of the JBNQA in November 1975. Early in the negotiations, Cree Indians formed the Grand Council of

George Manuel (from left), president of the National Indian Brotherhood; Aurilien Gill, 3rd vice president of the Association of Indians, and Chief Max Louis, 2nd vice president of the Association of Indians speak in November 1974 at a news conference discussing the agreement between the James Bay Cree and the Quebec government. The agreement was finalized in 1975 and was the first treaty in the modern Canadian treaty period. (Bettmann/Corbis)

the Cree (of Quebec), with one chief and leaders from each of the eight Cree communities comprising the organization's board of directors. An executive group of four regional leaders was then selected, whereupon the Grand Council took over negotiations. Even though they represented the Cree people in negotiations, the Grand Council was not empowered to act without consulting the people at the community level. In sum, the Cree people remained the final decision makers.

The JBNQA total compensation package was worth $225 million, a sum to be paid over a period of twenty years to the Cree Regional Authority and to the (Inuit) Makivik Corporation, on behalf of the Inuit, by the Canadian and Quebec governments. This modern-day treaty settled all outstanding Native land claims in northern Quebec at that time. It also defined Native rights and established regional land use regimes for both Native and non-Native people in the region and among

local, regional, provincial, and federal governments. The Crees retained 3,100 square miles of territory while the Inuit retained 5,000 square miles of settlement land, in addition to exclusive harvesting rights over an additional 10,000 square miles of land. The JBNQA effectively extinguished Aboriginal title to 600,000 square miles of land (McCutcheon, 1991).

Under the JBNQA, the territory was divided into Category I, II, and III lands. Category I lands are for the exclusive use and benefit of Native people. Category II lands belong to the province, but Native governments share in the management of hunting, fishing and trapping, tourism development, and forestry. Native people have exclusive hunting, fishing, and trapping rights on these lands. Category III lands are a special type of Quebec public lands, whereby Native and non-Native people may hunt and fish subject to regulations adopted in accordance with the JBNQA. A provision was

The James Bay hydroelectric project flooded many Cree and Inuit lands. (Christopher J. Morris/Corbis)

included requiring the province to monitor the environmental impact and the social effects of development. Committees have also been established to advise governments about environmental issues, policies, and regulation. Each committee consists of federal, provincial, and Native representatives.

The JBNQA also recognized a form of Aboriginal self-government. Accordingly, Inuit communities were incorporated as municipalities under Quebec law, and municipal powers are delegated to them by Quebec legislation. Quebec also established the Cree Regional Authority to assist in creating services for Cree communities. Cree and Inuit school boards were also established as part of the agreement, with a special mandate and unique powers enabling them to adopt culturally appropriate educational programs. Canada and Quebec jointly fund the school boards, with Canada paying 25 percent of the Inuit budget and three-quarters of the Cree budget. A coordinating committee of federal and provincial representatives and Native delegates was established to administer, review, and regulate wildlife harvesting, while

ensuring that Native rights to hunting, as acknowledged in the agreement, are not abused.

Implementation of the agreement began almost immediately. However, the process was uneven and the results varied from community to community. Cree and Inuit leaders both identified problem areas and lobbied the federal and provincial governments to meet their obligations as outlined in the JBNQA. In 1982, all involved approved of a review of the JBNQA implementation process to deal with the concerns identified by the Crees and Inuits. Unfortunately for Cree and Inuit leaders, the implementation review focused specifically on the adequacy of program support up to 1981 and failed to resolve many fundamental problems plaguing program implementation or any of the anticipated problems. During this period, however, constitutional issues were the leading political issue in Canada, and Native people recognized that their treaty rights had constitutional protection. With the JBNQA now a constitutionally protected treaty, Crees and Inuits began aggressively lobbying both provincial and federal officials through the media for improved program implementation.

By 1986, the Canadian government approved the establishment of a mediated negotiation process between JBNQA beneficiaries and federal and provincial officials. The overarching goal was to address what had by now become problems endemic to the implementation process. Four years of protracted negotiations followed, leading to an agreement between the Canadian government and the Inuit in September 1990. The heart of the final agreement calls for the Inuits to receive a lump sum payment of $22.8 million in lieu of relieving the federal government of its financial obligations pursuant to the JBNQA. Pending final implementation of this agreement, all matters related to the Inuits and the JBNQA will be resolved. Despite the resolution of the Inuit negotiations, the Crees and the federal government have not come to terms. The Crees maintain that the operational matters associated with the implementation process must first be addressed before final-stage negotiations may proceed.

The cash and natural resources provided to the Crees by the JBNQA have proven inadequate to the people's needs. What appeared to be a large sum of money in 1975 turned out to be modest in relation to the costs of social and economic development and of self-government. Despite problems concerning the final agreement, however, the Crees are now well versed in the language of politics. They have also come to the realization that, notwithstanding their poor relations with the federal and provincial governments and project developers, they are capable of maintaining a political strategy to their benefit. Negotiations between true equals may be the only way to resolve a process now entering its second generation of negotiations.

Yale D. Belanger

See also Canada, Indian Policies of; Department of Indian Affairs and Northern Development.
References and Further Reading
Diamond, Billy. 1990. "Villages of the Damned: The James Bay Agreement Leaves a Trail of Broken Promises." *Arctic Circle*. November–December: 24–34.
Feit, Harvey. 1991. "Gifts of the Land: Hunting Territories, Guaranteed Incomes and the Construction of Social Relations in James Bay Cree Society." *Senri Ethnological Studies*, 30: 223–268.
McCutcheon, Sean. 1991. *Electric Rivers: The Story of the James Bay Project*. Montreal, QC: Black Rose Books.
Salisbury, Richard. 1986. *A Homeland for the Cree. Regional Development in James Bay, 1971–1981*. Montreal, QC, and Kingston, ON: McGill-Queen's University Press.
Vincent, Sylvie, and Garry Bowers, eds. 1988. *James Bay and Northern Quebec: Ten Years After*. Montreal: Recherches amerindiennes au Quebec.

Lancaster, Pennsylvania, Treaty Councils

In 1742, Pennsylvania officials met with Iroquois sachems in council at Lancaster to secure an Iroquois alliance against the threat of French encroachment. Canassatego, speaker (tadadaho) of the Haudenosaunee (Iroquois) Confederacy, spoke on behalf of the Six Nations to the Pennsylvania officials. He confirmed the League of Friendship that existed between the two parties and stated that "we are bound by the strictest leagues to watch for each other's preservation" (Colden, 1902, 2: 18–24)

Two years later, Canassatego would go beyond pledging friendship to the English colonists. At Lancaster, Pennsylvania, in 1744, the great Iroquois chief advised the assembled colonial governors on Iroquois concepts of unity:

> Our wise forefathers established Union and Amity between the Five Nations. This has made us formidable; this has given us great Weight and Authority with our neighboring Nations. We are a powerful Confederacy; and by your observing the same methods, our wise forefathers have taken, you will acquire such Strength and power. Therefore whatever befalls you, never fall out with one another (Van Doren and Boyd, 1938, 75).

Richard Peters described Canassatego at Lancaster as "a tall, well-made man," with "a very full chest and brawny limbs, a manly countenance, with a good-natired [sic] smile. He was about sixty years of age, very active, strong, and had a surprising liveliness in his speech" (Boyd, 1942, 244–245). Dressed in a scarlet camblet coat and a fine, gold-laced hat, Canassatego is described by historical observers

such as Peters as possessing an awesome presence that turned heads whenever he walked into a room.

Benjamin Franklin probably first learned of Canassatego's 1744 advice to the colonies as he set his words in type. Franklin's press regularly issued Indian treaties in small booklets, which enjoyed a lively sale throughout the colonies, from 1736 until the early 1760s, when his defense of Indians under assault by frontier settlers cost him his seat in the Pennsylvania Assembly. Franklin subsequently served the colonial government in England.

Canassatego's admonition would echo throughout the colonies for many years. For example, colonial representatives called upon them some thirty years later at a treaty council near Albany.

After some preliminaries, the sachems and treaty commissioners began their deliberations in earnest on August 24, 1775, at Cartwright's Tavern in Albany, New York. On the next day, the treaty commissioners (who had specific instructions from John Hancock and the Second Continental Congress) told the sachems that they were heeding the advice Iroquois forefathers had given to the colonial Americans at Lancaster, Pennsylvania, in 1744. At this point, the commissioners quoted Canassatego's words:

> Brethren, We the Six Nations heartily recommend Union and a good agreement between you our Brethren, never disagree but preserve a strict Friendship for one another and thereby you as well as we will become stronger. Our Wise Forefathers established Union and Amity between the Five Nations . . . we are a powerful Confederacy, and if you observe the same methods . . . you will acquire fresh strength and power (Proceedings, n.d.).

The Americans then said that their forefathers had rejoiced to hear Canassatego's words, which sank

> deep into their Hearts, the Advice was good, it was Kind. They said to one another, the Six Nations are a wise people, let us hearken to their Council and teach our children to follow it. Our old Men have done so. They have frequently taken a single Arrow and said, Children, see how easy it is broken, then they have tied twelve together with strong Cords— And our strongest Men could not break them— See said they—this is what the Six Nations

mean. Divided a single Man may destroy you—United, you are a match for the whole World (Proceedings, n.d.).

In this statement, the commissioners were not merely engaging in diplomatic protocol to flatter the Iroquois; they were actually summarizing a historical process of assimilating Iroquois ideas of unity that was expressed in subsequent meetings and in the papers of some of the Founding Fathers (Benjamin Franklin, James Wilson, and Thomas Jefferson, for example). Indeed, the Americans talked of creating a government of federated unity as an alternative to colonial conquest. The Americans continued and thanked the "great God that we are all united, that we have a strong Confederacy composed of twelve Provinces." The American delegates also pointed out that they have "lighted a Great Council Fire at Philadelphia and have sent Sixty five Counsellors to speak and act in the name of the whole" (Proceedings, n.d.).

Bruce E. Johansen

See also Canassatego; Franklin, Benjamin, Native American Influences.

References and Further Reading

Boyd, Julian Boyd. [1942] 1981. "Dr. Franklin: Friend of the Indian." In *Meet Dr. Franklin*. Edited by Roy N. Lokken, 244–245. Philadelphia, PA: The Franklin Institute.

Colden, Cadwallader. 1902. *History of the Five Nations*. 2 volumes. New York: New Amsterdam Book Company.

"Proceedings of the Commissioners . . . to . . . the Six Nations, August 25, 1775 at Albany, New York." No date. *Continental Congress Papers, 1774–1789*. Washington, DC: National Archives (M247, Roll 144, Item No., 134).

Van Doren, Carl, and Julian P. Boyd, eds. 1938. *Indian Treaties Printed by Benjamin Franklin 1736–1762*. Philadelphia: Historical Society of Pennsylvania.

Lone Wolf v. Hitchcock

In 1903, the United States Supreme Court issued a decision in the case of *Lone Wolf v. Hitchcock*, in which the Court allocated plenary authority over Indian affairs to Congress. This authority included the power not only to break Indian treaties at its discretion, but also to dispose of treaty-protected Indian land at will. Although widely discredited, the case

Lone Wolf, a Kiowa chief, led his people in resistance to the allotment of their reservation. (National Archives and Records Administration)

has never been overruled and represents a landmark case in American Indian law.

Lone Wolf v. Hitchcock was decided amid a background of separation, assimilation, and allotment. In an effort to confine Indian occupancy and use of land to specific territories, the earliest Indian treaties established the idea of reservations. However, the lure for gold, land, and other resources in Indian territory was a temptation too great for the settlers to resist. Consequently, many Indian tribes were removed westward to large blocks of land reserved for their use with the assurance that the new lands would remain Indian reservations forever. In fact, settlers soon encountered Indian Country as the nation expanded westward. Before long, homesteaders demanded more lands from the government, and the federal policy makers acquiesced by developing programs to diminish the Indians' reservation land base.

Specifically, in 1853 Commissioner of Indian Affairs George Manypenny instituted a general policy of attempting to negotiate allotment provisions in treaties, which converted communally held tribal lands into individually owned parcels. Any surplus lands remaining were then opened to settlement by non-Indians. Congress quickly adopted his policy and, by virtue of the General Allotment (Dawes) Act of 1887, Congress was able systematically to allot some 41 million acres of tribal lands. Former reservations soon became checkerboarded with non-Indian–owned land.

However, the Dawes Act did not apply to all Indian territory; rather, the allotment of certain areas, particularly those lands in the Oklahoma Territory, required a special act from Congress. In 1892, Congress sent three commissioners, known as the Jerome Commission, to negotiate with the Kiowas, a tribe whose reservation was located in the Oklahoma Territory, for the allotment and cession of their lands. According to the Treaty of Medicine Lodge, no further Kiowa land cessions would occur without the approval of a supermajority of the tribe. Specifically, Article XII of the treaty stated that any cession of tribal land required the signatures of "at least three-fourths of all the adult male Indians occupying the same."

Lone Wolf, the Kiowa chief, led his people in resistance to the allotment of their reservation. During negotiations, Lone Wolf reminded the commission that the Treaty of Medicine Lodge, which established their reservation, guaranteed their lands forever. In addition, Lone Wolf noted that the small farms that would result from allotment would not support tribal families. Realizing that the negotiations were going badly, the commission threatened the tribe, asserting that Congress has the power to take their land without payment or assent. Nevertheless, Lone Wolf and his tribe resisted any form of allotment.

Once negotiations faltered, the commissioners fraudulently induced some tribal members to sign various allotment documents under false pretenses. To obtain the supermajority required by the treaty for the cession of the Kiowa lands, the commissioners had members of other tribes sign the documents as well. By October 6, 1892, the government claimed that a majority of Kiowas had signed the agreement, which proposed to give every member of the tribe a 160-acre allotment and to pay $2 million for the surplus lands. The Commission then returned to

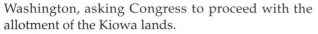

Washington, asking Congress to proceed with the allotment of the Kiowa lands.

However, Lone Wolf and several other Kiowas claimed that any assent to the agreements had been obtained by fraudulent misrepresentations of the terms by interpreters. In addition, they alleged that the agreement was invalid since, according to the tribal rolls, less than three-fourths of the adult male Indians signed the agreement. In October 1899, the tribes held a council and drafted a petition to Congress signed by a supermajority of eligible Kiowa members. The petition was a clear and simple statement of the tribes' repudiation of the agreement.

Despite the Kiowas' opposition and any congressional concerns about the fraudulent process used by the commission, in February 1900 Congress proceeded with the allotment. Subsequently, Lone Wolf filed a complaint in the equity division of the Supreme Court of the District of Columbia seeking to restrain the Department of Interior from carrying out the provisions of the Allotment Act, arguing that the Acts of Congress were unconstitutional, void, and a violation of solemn treaty provisions.

The Court refused to entertain any complaint concerning the statute or the federal policy of allotment in general. Instead, by recognizing the tribe's dependent relationship with the federal government, the Court upheld Congress's authority to allot the Kiowa reservation without any tribal assent:

> The contention in effect ignores the status of contracting Indians and the relation of dependency they bore and continue to bear towards the government of the United States. To uphold the claim would be to adjudge that the indirect operation of the treaty was to materially limit and qualify the controlling authority of Congress in respect to the care and protection of the Indians, and to deprive Congress, in a possible emergency, when the necessity might be urgent for a partition and disposal of the tribal lands, of all power to act, if the assent of the Indians could not be obtained (*Lone Wolf v. Hitchcock*, 1903, 564).

According to the Court, Congress, through its plenary power, has the authority to abrogate treaties unilaterally if that action is in furtherance of its obligation to care for and protect the Indians. Thus, the Court held that whether a supermajority of the tribe had signed the allotment documents was inconsequential. Rather, because Congress thought it necessary to allot the Kiowa reservation for the care and protection of the tribal members, it was entitled to do so without their assent.

In effect, the *Lone Wolf* decision granted Congress not only the plenary authority to abrogate treaties with the Indians unilaterally, but also an absolute, unchecked power to regulate in all aspects of Indian affairs. By relying on the Indians' special fiduciary relationship with the federal government, the Court established the presumption that any congressional actions taken toward Indian affairs are made in good faith: "We must presume that Congress acted in perfect good faith in the dealings with the Indians of which complaint is made, and that the legislative branch of the government exercised its best judgment in the premises" (*Lone Wolf v. Hitchcock*, 1903, 568). Furthermore, by characterizing such plenary actions as political questions, the Court announced that congressional legislation in the field of Indian law is "not subject to be controlled by the judicial department of the government" and is therefore unreviewable (*Lone Wolf v. Hitchcock*, 1903, 565). Thus, because any regulation of Indian affairs is presumed to have been taken in good faith and because such regulation is a political question, Congress has unfettered authority to act as it sees fit.

In recent years, *Lone Wolf v. Hitchcock* has been widely discredited, and the Supreme Court has attempted to mute its harsh ruling. Specifically, the Court now requires that any congressional intention to abrogate an Indian treaty or treaty right be clear and plain. In addition, the Court has declared that congressional activity in Indian affairs is no longer an unreviewable political question; rather, if such action cannot be characterized as that of a good faith trustee toward its beneficiary, the Court will subject the action as to the Takings Clause of the Fifth Amendment. Nonetheless, *Lone Wolf v. Hitchcock* remains a precedent in the field of American Indian law and provides authority for Congress, subject to few limitations, to deal with Indian tribes as it sees fit.

J. Landon K. Schmidt

See also General Allotment Act (Dawes Act); Plenary Power.

References and Further Reading

Clark, Blue. 1994. *Lone Wolf v. Hitchcock: Treaty Rights and Indian Law at the End of the Nineteenth Century*. Lincoln: University of Nebraska Press.

Estinn, Ann Laquer. 1984. "*Lone Wolf v. Hitchcock: The Long Shadow.*" In *The Aggressions of Civilizations: Federal Indian Policy Since the 1880's*. Edited by Sandra L. Cadwalader and Vine Deloria, Jr., 215–234. Philadelphia, PA: Temple University Press.

Getches, David H., Charles F. Wilkinson, and Robert A. Williams, Jr., eds. 1998. *Cases and Materials on Federal Indian Law*, 4th ed. St Paul, MN: West.

Gulig, Anthony G., and Sidney L. Harring. 2002. "'An Indian Cannot get a Morsel of Pork . . .' A Retrospective on Crow Dog, Lone Wolf, Blackbird, Tribal Sovereignty, Indian Land, and Writing Indian Legal History." *Tulsa Law Review* 38: 87–111.

Lone Wolf v. Hitchcock, 187 U.S. 553, 23 S.Ct. 216, 47 L.Ed. 299 (1903).

Treaty of Medicine Lodge. 1867. October 21. 15 Stat. 581.

Wildenthal, Bryan H. 2002. "Fighting the Lone Wolf Mentality: Twenty-First Century Reflections on the Paradoxical State of American Indian Law." *Tulsa Law Review* 38: 113–144.

Wilkins, David E. 1997. *American Indian Sovereignty and the U.S. Supreme Court: The Masking of Justice*. Austin: University of Texas Press.

Lyng v. Northwest Indian Cemetery Protective Association

This 1988 U.S. Supreme Court case concerned the protection of American Indian religious practices. The case exemplifies the difficulties that courts have in recognizing the holistic, connected nature of indigenous religious practices as opposed to mainstream religions and in applying constitutional religious principles to peoples not originally protected by such principles. The six justices who ruled in the majority stressed that the U.S. government was not prohibiting the free exercise of religion of members of three tribes by building a road near and allowing tree harvesting within a half mile of certain traditional ritual sites in the Chimney Rock section of Six Rivers National Forest.

Since the First Amendment applies only if the government prohibits the free exercise of religion, the constitutional claim of the American Indians failed. The majority felt that to rule otherwise would give the tribes effective ownership over public, government-controlled and -owned lands. The three dissenting justices noted that the Forest Service commissioned the Theodoratus Report, which examined Native religion. For Native peoples, land is living and the relationship to land and the natural world is an ongoing relationship of creation. These justices saw that the road and harvest would destroy the Indian religious practices and that the government should have a compelling interest before going ahead with the project.

In the 1970s, the U.S. Forest Service upgraded roads on federal lands in northern California. Part of the project included the Chimney Rock area of the Six Rivers National Forest. The Hoopa Valley Indian Reservation adjoins the national forest. The Chimney Rock area was used by the Indians for religious ceremonies and was considered especially sacred. The 1977 Forest Service draft environmental impact statement discussed the detailed project plans. The Forest Service commissioned a study of cultural resources of the area, the Theodoratus Report (1979). This study supported a 1979 recommendation not to proceed with the road project because of the irreparable and serious damage to the sacred areas so central to the Hoopa belief systems.

In 1982, the Forest Service decided not to follow the report. The road would be built in Chimney Rock as far away as possible from specific ritual sites. Routes that would have avoided Chimney Rock were rejected because they would involve the acquisition of private land. In addition, a management plan was approved that allowed substantial cutting down of trees in Chimney Rock with a half-mile distance between protected sites and the harvest. Thus, specific areas were preserved while the nature of the entirety was altered.

The majority opinion, by holding that the government had not prohibited the free exercise of any religion, negated the need to apply the test. The government, as landowner, was simply managing its land for the benefit of all. To allow the diminution of the government's property rights was substantial, and the Forest Service was not required to accommodate the Natives' religious needs either constitutionally or statutorily by the American Indian Religious Freedom Act, which created no cause of action or enforceable rights according to the Court. In any event, the government had accommodated the Indian religious practices by the half-mile zone and the placement of the road.

The dissenting justices attempted to understand the differences between European-derived religious practices and American Indian religious practices. The former is church-based, and the government is an entity apart from the church. For many American

Indians, spirituality pervades everything. For them, the attempts to build the road and harvest the trees while providing some core area protections essentially destroyed the practice of their religion and cultural beliefs. Such action clearly fails to accord with the First Amendment.

Michael W. Simpson

See also American Indian Religious Freedom Act.
References and Further Reading
Getches, David H., Charles F. Wilkinson, and Robert A. Williams, Jr. 1998. *Cases and Materials on Federal Indian Law,* 4th ed. St. Paul, MN: West.
Lyng v. Northwest Indian Cemetery protective Ass'n., 485 U.S. 439 (1988).
Pinter, Jeff. 2004. "Note: In Cases Involving Sites of Religious Significance. Plaintiffs Will Fall in the Gap of Judicial Deference That Exists Between the Religion Clauses of the First Amendment." *American Indian Law Review* 29: 289–318.
Reivman, Joshua D. 1989. "Comment: Judicial Scrutiny of Native American Free Exercise Rights: *Lyng* and the Decline of the *Yoder* Doctrine." *Boston College Environmental Affairs Law Review* 17: 169–199.

Maine Indian Claims Settlement Act

The 1980 Maine Indian Claims Settlement Act (MICSA) was the first major Native American land claim settlement of its kind in the twentieth century. It paved the way for similar federal settlements with eastern aboriginal nations such as the Pequots and Narragansetts. Following several court rulings in the 1970s, the Maine Wabanaki convinced the United States that they were entitled to compensation for illegal land acquisitions made by the states of Massachusetts and Maine. In exchange for giving up their claims to nearly two-thirds of the state of Maine, the Wabanakis, principally the Penobscots and Passamaquoddies, received a settlement of $81 million, federal recognition, the right to purchase at least 300,000 acres of land at fair market value, and limited immunity from state laws. Although MICSA was an impressive legal success, in the twenty-five years since its enactment, many Wabanakis feel the settlement poses some serious obstacles to their aboriginal sovereignty, economic growth, and environmental health.

The Maine settlement was flawed because it did not equally include all of the Maine Indians, namely the Maliseets and Micmacs. The Houlton band of Maliseets obtained federal recognition and $900,000 for land trust acquisition, but they remained subject to Maine's regulatory laws whereas the Passamaquoddies and Penobscots were exempt. The Aroostook band of Micmacs were not named at all in MICSA. Eleven years later, the Micmacs negotiated a separate settlement with the United States, gaining federal recognition and $900,000 to purchase lands. Because they neither signed nor were mentioned in MICSA, they argue that the Act does not apply to them, a situation that makes them unique among the Maine Wabanakis.

The central problem with MICSA, however, is that it explicitly equated the regulatory rights of sovereign Indian nations with those of state municipalities. The Wabanakis argue that Maine has refused to acknowledge their aboriginal claim to national sovereignty, which exists *in addition* to the municipality provisions of the settlement (Chavaree, 1998). The state, in turn, argues that the Indians are trying to claim a form of sovereignty that was explicitly extinguished by mutual agreement in 1980. As of 2005, the courts have steadily upheld the state's municipality arguments—such as denying the Wabanakis' request to build casinos under federal law—a situation that has embittered many of them.

The U.S. government was brought to the bargaining table with the Wabanakis because the Indians were able to prove in federal court in 1975 that the 12.5 million acres of Wabanaki land acquired by Maine and Massachusetts violated the terms of the 1790 Intercourse Act (see Brodheur, 1985). These Intercourse laws, modified several times in the early 1800s, stated that land purchases from Indian governments had to be attended by a U.S. commissioner and ratified by Congress. The Wabanaki sales usually met neither requirement. President Jimmy Carter appointed a task force to settle the Wabanaki claim out of court in late 1977. By March of 1980, a tentative agreement was reached, and at that stage it was endorsed by a vote of the participating Wabanakis. The governor and the legislature of Maine passed the Maine Implementing Act in April. The Maine agreement was then ratified by the U.S. legislature with some significant additions to federal law and then signed by President Carter in early October 1980.

MICSA involved state law, finances, and land. First of all, it revised the laws that are applicable to Natives and Native land in Maine, with the state basically withdrawing from legal supervision of the

President Jimmy Carter signs the 1980 Maine Indian Claims Settlement Act, using an eagle feather from the Penobscot Nation as Maine state officials look on. (Steve Cartwright/Wabanaki Alliance)

Indians (the Maine Implementing Act). Aware that disagreements were bound to occur under the new system, the Implementing Act established a nine-member advisory body called the Maine Indian Tribal–State Commission (MITSC). MITSC is equally composed by appointees from the state and the Wabanakis, with their chair chosen by the appointees. MITSC is charged to review the effectiveness of the Implementing Act, to make recommendations on land acquisition, to draft fishing rules, to conduct wildlife studies, and to review petitions by tribes for extensions to the reservations. As the commission admits in its report, *At Loggerheads*, MITSC has had some success negotiating fish and wildlife disputes, reviewing land trust issues, and educating people about Wabanaki lifeways, but it is grossly underfunded and lacks the authority to broker the sovereignty disputes that have arisen over the last twenty-five years.

MICSA's second achievement was financial, but it was largely directed toward the restoration of

Native land holdings. The Act established a $27 million trust to be shared equally between the Passamaquoddies and Penobscots, tax-free and with interest paid quarterly. It also set aside $54.4 million to buy 300,000 acres to add to Passamaquoddy, Penobscot, and Maliseet territory. These new land acquisitions would be held in trust for the Wabanakis by the United States and would be subject to oversight by the Secretary of the Interior. Although the Houlton Maliseets got $900,000 of this money for land trust acquisition, they did not get independent municipality status in their relationships with the state of Maine, nor did they get a trust fund.

The settlement was a great financial victory for the majority of the Wabanakis, but it also provided enormous benefits to the state of Maine. The federal government paid the $81 million settlement's cost. Maine paid nothing, and the state cleared title to all of its lands. The Implementing Act states that all Indian land claims were henceforth extinguished in

Maine. (The state argues that even Aroostook Micmac claims were extinguished by the Act, a claim the Micmacs currently dispute.) Maine was thus able to dismantle its Department of Indian Affairs, divesting itself entirely 150 years of supervision of some of the poorest Native populations in the country. The U.S. government would henceforth provide subsidies and care for the Wabanakis. (Again, until 1991, the Aroostook Micmacs were treated as if they did not exist.)

The greatest benefit of MICSA for the state, however, was that, even though Maine shed the *responsibility* for the management of Indian affairs in Maine, it retained extensive *regulatory authority* over the territory of the Passamaquoddies, Penobscots, and Maliseets.

The sections of the Maine Implementing Act that define this authority (30 M.R.S.A. 6204–6) appear to restrict the sovereign powers of the Indians to jurisdiction over "internal tribal matters." Except as otherwise provided in the Act, the Passamaquoddies and Penobscots have "the rights, privileges, powers and immunities of a *municipality*, including the power to enact ordinances, and collect taxes; be subject to all the duties, obligations, liabilities, and *limitations of a municipality*; and be subject to the laws of the State, except that 'internal tribal matters' are not subject to regulation by the State" (MITSC, 1997, 11).

According to the state's interpretation of this provision, the Native nations are thus at liberty to manage their own government and legal system for minor infractions. Like city governments, however, they are otherwise regulated by the state on almost any issue of consequence. Wabanaki leaders currently argue that an *exclusive* focus on the municipality provisions of the Maine Implementing Act disregards their simultaneous aboriginal rights as sovereign peoples that existed long before the arrival of European settlers. In May 2002, Wabanaki leaders were put in the embarrassing position of surrendering their documents on environmental pollution under the state's Freedom of Access Act, because the Maine Supreme court ruled that the Wabanaki nations were just like city governments in such situations.

An even more significant problem relating to the Maine Implementing Act, however, occurred at the federal level. The federal government was conscious that Maine's foremost concern during the 1980 settlement was to maintain authority over trade and government within the bounds of the state.

Thus, the federal act that *ratified* the Maine Implementing Act included provisions that reaffirmed the Wabanakis' former status as "state" Indians. Sections of the 1980 Maine Settlement Act (25 U.S.C. 1725 and 1735) state that federal laws and regulations that confer special status to Indians and that also preempt the jurisdiction of the state are *inapplicable* in Maine. Also, any federal law enacted after October 10, 1980, for the benefit of Indians that would affect or preempt the laws of the State of Maine "shall not apply within the State of Maine, unless [it] is specifically made applicable within the State" (MITSC, 1997, 13). As a result, the Wabanakis have been unable to take advantage of many of the recent federal court rulings allowing gambling casinos on Indian land.

The paradox of the federal 1980 Settlement Act is that the Wabanakis lost elements of their federal recognition. The U.S. government ratified the Maine Implementing Act *and* henceforth excluded the Wabanakis from some types of federal legislation expressly designed to have national effect. In the two decades since the 1980 settlement, federal legislation pertaining to casinos and pollution have made the Wabanakis painfully aware of the importance of maintaining regulatory authority over their own lands.

Granville Ganter

See also Trade and Intercourse Acts.
References and Further Reading
Brodeur, Paul. 1985. *Restitution: The Land Claims of the Mashpee, Passamaquoddy, and Penobscot Indians of New England.* Boston: Northeastern University Press.
Ganter, Granville. 2004. "Sovereign Municipalities? Twenty Years After the Maine Indian Claims Settlement Act of 1980." *Enduring Legacies: Native American Treaties and Contemporary Controversies.* Edited by Bruce Johansen, 25–43. Westport, CT: Praeger.
Chavaree, Mark, tribal counsel, Penobscot nation. 1998. "Tribal Sovereignty." *Wabanaki Legal New* (Winter). Available at: http://www.ptla.org/wabanaki/sovereign.htm. Accessed January 14, 2007.
MITSC (Maine Indian Tribal-State Commission). 1997 [rev. 2000]. *At Loggerheads—The State of Maine and the Wabanaki: Final Report of the Task Force on Tribal-State Relations.*
MITSC (Maine Indian Tribal-State Commission). 1995. "Maine Indian Land Claims Case." February 14. Available at: http://www.abbemuseum.org/d_scully_landclaims.pdf.

Meriam Report

The Meriam Report (1928), published as "The Problem of Indian Administration," was a government-funded report that underscored the failure of the U.S. policy of the forced assimilation of American Indians into American society. It was undertaken after a decade of growing concern about the direction of U.S. Indian policy. Events in the 1920s demonstrated the persistence of themes and concerns that had characterized white–Indian relations over the previous half century. Not only had the goals of the late nineteenth-century assimilation policy, including the division of tribal lands into individual holdings, not been achieved, but pressure from whites for more of the Indian land base continued. The study underlying the report was initiated in 1926 by Hubert Work, Secretary of the Interior, who named Lewis Meriam as the leader of a committee of ten that would examine the nation's Indian policy. Meriam's analysis broke with the pattern of earlier studies by analyzing statistical indicators of individual well-being, rather than asking for the opinions of those who had designed or administered existing national policies. By underscoring the vast disparities in the quality of life between Indians and society at large, the Meriam report indicted existing national policies and opened the door to new approaches that culminated in the creation of the Indian Reorganization Act in 1934.

Widespread dissatisfaction with the outcomes of Indian policy underscored the need for the study. The 1920s witnessed the continuing efforts to dispossess Native Americans of their resource base even as reform groups raised criticisms of existing policies. The most noted of the land grabs at that time was embodied in the Bursum Bill of 1922, designed to create a system for validating land titles on Pueblo holdings that would have given preference to the claims of individual white squatters over long-standing Pueblo tribal rights based on treaties. Reform groups coalesced in the successful effort to defeat this measure and remained vocal. John Collier created the American Indian Defense Association in 1923 as part of his opposition to the Bursum Bill. The Indian Rights Association was revitalized in the same period. In 1924 Congress extended citizenship to all Indians who had not yet acquired it (even though some Indians didn't want it). Some reformist Indian voices emerged in the Society of American Indians and the National Council of American Indians. Although not well financed, long lasting, or organically connected to the particular needs and perspectives of tribal organizations, these groups did offer coherent, compelling general criticisms of government policies.

The changing national mood from Anglo conformity toward cultural pluralism added to the willingness to reconsider forced assimilation. For example, missionaries' concern over the rising criticism of existing policies led to a sweeping study of socioeconomic aspects of Indian life as well as a defense of the efforts of the Bureau of Indian Affairs. The study, published as *Red Man in the United States*, was written by G.E.E. Lindquist for the Institute for Social and Religious Research in 1923.

Interior Secretary Hubert Work made two separate attempts to gain independent perspectives on living conditions among Indians. The first was embodied in the Advisory Council on Indian Affairs, also known as the Committee of 100, in 1923. Composed of people from outside the government, the group reflected growing national differences on policy rather than developing ideas of how to address these differences. Secretary Work tried again in 1927 when he contracted with the Institute of Government Research and appointed Lewis Meriam to head a committee to scrutinize Indian and national Indian policy.

The selection of Lewis Meriam to direct the study ensured that the work would be carried out in the spirit of pre–World War I progressivism, with its emphasis on efficient administrative actions as the key to successful reform. Meriam brought an array of research experiences to the study of Indian policy as well as a reputation as a disinterested social scientist who would not allow personal policy preferences to intrude on his objectivity. In addition to the nonpartisan Institute for Government Research (which later became the Brookings Institution), he had worked for the U.S. Census Office and the Children's Bureau. His previous work included job classification with the civil service and the creation of wage systems in government bureaucracies.

The people selected to work with Meriam reflected the range of issues as well as the operating assumptions that defined the work of the committee. Areas of expertise represented on the committee included economic conditions (Edward Everett Dale, University of Oklahoma), education (W. Carson Ryan, Jr., Swarthmore College), extant records (Fayette Mackenzie, Juniata College), family life and women (Mary Marks, Ohio State University), farming (William Spillman, Bureau of Agricultural Economics), health (Herbert Edwards, National Tuberculosis Association), Indian relocation to cities (Emma Duke, American Health Association), and legal issues (Ray Brown, University of Wisconsin). Yale-educated Henry Roe Cloud (Winnebago) served as general advisor and liaison for visits to Indian communities.

The reliance on social scientific expertise (rather than prior experience as an administrator of Indian policies) or on expertise on Indian issues underscored the desire of the committee to reach objective findings that would inform government policy. The work of the committee included extensive field visitation. The committee's staff visited all but fifteen areas under the jurisdiction of the Bureau of Indian Affairs, conducted over 500 home visits, and met with a wide range of groups on reservations, including many Indian-only sessions. Anthropologists were not included, in the belief that they were not value-neutral on issues of Indian life.

The summary of findings, presented as Chapter One, indicted the impact of past policies without assigning responsibility for the deplorable conditions. The report stated: "An overwhelming majority of the Indians are poor, even extremely poor, and they are not adjusted to the economic and social system of the dominant white civilization" (Meriam, 1928, 3). Policies intended to promote the individualization and assimilation of Indian people had failed. Debate about Indian economic or social "progress" from earlier eras was avoided because the report made comparisons with indicators of well-being in white society of the mid-1920s. This tactic undercut arguments used by some to claim that Indians were better off than they had ever been in the past. The committee's decision to examine the lives of Indians who had migrated to cities produced data demonstrating that social and economic difficulties were pervasive among Indians rather than confined to those who continued to reside on reservations. Statistics underscored the high incidence of disease, the alarming extent of infant mortality, the prevalence of extreme poverty, the absence of economic development, the disorganization of family life, and the failure of existing approaches to education. At each juncture, the report showed that the conditions were worse than most citizens could imagine and would be intolerable if experienced by white citizens.

The Meriam Report was premised on the desirability of assimilating American Indians into society at large. It called for the Indian Service to be con-

verted to an organization devoted to education for the social and economic advancement of Indian people in order to prepare them for fuller participation in general society or, absent that development, to be readied to live in parallel with white society. An underlying assumption of the report was that an improved Indian quality of life and a fuller participation in the national economy would reduce the degree of prejudice expressed toward Indians by white society. General recommendations included more respect for Indian people and the recognition that Indian rights extended beyond treaty provisions to embrace the full range of rights enjoyed by the general citizenry. Specific actions included the creation of a planning and development program that would make use of experts in areas such as agricultural economics, endemic diseases among Indians, marketing, and vocational guidance. These new workers would keep accurate records, maintain better relations with Indians, receive adequate salaries, be provided with better housing, and receive good retirement and health benefits. For the members of the Meriam Commission, the combination of professional expertise and social science methodology would yield an effective assimilation program.

Despite the Meriam Report's support for a more intelligent implementation of modified assimilation policies, symbolically the report marked the end of assimilation as a policy and stimulated the debate over the future direction of Indian policy. The report amplified growing criticisms of the Bureau of Indian Affairs from those who wanted more rapid assimilation and those who sought to restore traditional Indian culture to the extent possible. Proponents of radical assimilation saw the BIA as retarding assimilation by serving as a crutch that made Indians reluctant to "stand on their own" within American society. On the other side, a group of reformers led by John Collier sought to restore tribal sovereignty and traditional Native values to the extent possible and practicable. They believed that the BIA was destroying Indian ways. This debate was won by the Collier forces in the early years of Franklin Delano Roosevelt's administration with the passage of the Indian Reorganization Act in 1934. Although Lewis Meriam tried for a time to work with Collier on the promotion of IRA goals, he ultimately broke with the volatile reformer and moved into the ranks of conservative Republicans who favored assimilation.

David S. Trask

See also Collier, John; Indian Reorganization Act.

References and Further Reading

Critchlow, Donald T. 1981. "Lewis Meriam, Expertise, and Indian Reform." *The Historian* XLIII (May): 325–344.

Daily, David. 2004. *Battle for the BIA: G. E. E. Lindquist and the Missionary Crusade Against John Collier*. Tucson: University of Arizona Press.

Meriam, Lewis, et al. 1928. *The Problem of Indian Administration*. Baltimore, MD: Johns Hopkins University Press.

Parman, Donald. No date. "Lewis Meriam's Letters During the Survey of Indian Affairs, 1926–1927." Parts 1 and 2. *Arizona and the West* 24 No. 3 (1982), 253–280; 24 No. 4 (1982), 341–370.

Rusco, Elmer. 2000. *A Fateful Time: The Background and Legislative History of the Indian Reorganization Act*. Reno: University of Nevada Press.

Métis Nation Accord

In 1992, Canada, British Columbia, Alberta, Saskatchewan, Manitoba, Ontario, and the Métis nation of Canada, represented by the Métis National Council (MNC) and provincial Métis representative bodies, signed the Métis Nation Accord. The Accord set out provisions requiring all signatories to negotiate the implementation of aboriginal self-government. Unfortunately for the Métis, the Accord was directly tied to the success of the Charlottetown Accord (1992), which called for comprehensive changes of Canada's Constitution. These changes were designed in part to enable the First Nations political participation and representation in Canada, as well as formal recognition of the right to aboriginal self-government. It also represented a commitment on Canada's part to address the appropriate roles and responsibilities of governments as they relate to the Métis. The Charlottetown Accord was rejected in referendum by the Canadian people in 1992.

The Métis nation evolved during the eighteenth and nineteenth centuries from the miscegenation of French and Scottish fur traders with Cree, Ojibwa, Saulteaux, and Assiniboine women. The Métis developed as a unique people, distinct from Native people and Europeans. Today an estimated 200,000 Métis live in Canada, accounting for more than 20 percent of the aboriginal population living in Métis communities and urban centers. The Métis have long claimed national status and a unique culture, a distinct language, a unique economy, and enduring philosophies, but Canadian officials historically refused to accept this position. However, in 1982, the Canadian Constitution was amended to recognize the Métis as one of the country's groups of aboriginal peoples (along with Native Americans and the Inuit). By the end of the 1980s it appeared as though federal officials were willing to consider the social, political, and economic issues of the Métis.

The Métis Nation Accord represented a significant first step in relationship building between the federal government and the Métis nation. With the proposed constitutional changes in mind, the Métis National Council and its governing members initiated consultations with the Métis nation in September 1991. These discussions led to various MNC submissions to the federal constitutional processes through the spring of 1992. Central to the Métis strategy was forcing the federal government to assume its responsibility for the Métis's social and political betterment. The federal government responded by agreeing that the Charlottetown Accord would be amended to explicitly include the Métis. Resulting from this successful lobby, the Métis Nation Accord was established as a modern-day treaty between the federal government, all provinces west of Ontario, and the Métis nation.

The Métis Nation Accord was an impressive political accommodation that would have resolved many of Métis's legal questions and outstanding claims, including:

- Agreement on a definition of Métis.
- The establishment of tripartite self-government negotiations among the federal government, the Métis governments, and the respective provincial governments, as well as a commitment of financial resources for the negotiations.
- A commitment on the part of government to negotiate a land and resource base for Métis.
- A commitment on the part of government to undertake an enumeration of the Métis and establish a central registry.
- A commitment on the part of government to devolve programs and services to the Métis, provide transfer payments to the Métis government to support these programs and services, and to preserve existing funding and services already provided to the Métis.
- Provisions for the protection of the Alberta Métis settlements.

President of the Métis Nation of Ontario, Tony Belcourt (right), Steve Powley (center), and their lawyer Jean Teillet (left) celebrate their hunting rights victory in the Supreme Court of Canada in Ottawa, September 19, 2000. (Chris Wattie/Reuters/Corbis)

Following the failure of the Charlottetown Accord, none of the Accord signatories expressed a willingness to engage in multilateral discussions, leaving the Métis with few choices in their fight to see their aboriginal rights recognized. They may pursue recognition of these rights in the Canadian courts, or they can remain on the political periphery as provincial and federal officials engage in jurisdictional wrangling. Litigation proved successful, and in 2004, after more than a decade in the courts, the Métis were recognized by Supreme Court of Canada as possessing aboriginal rights. The case resulted from a Métis father and son, Steve and Roddy Powley, being charged in 1993 with hunting moose without a license and unlawful possession of moose meat, contrary to Ontario's *Game and Fish Act*. The Métis nation of Ontario determined to use this case to establish the existence of the Métis hunting rights. In 1998, a two-week trial resulted in the trial judge's determining that the Métis community at Sault Ste. Marie had an existing aboriginal right to hunt, a decision that was upheld by the Supreme Court of Canada.

The Métis Nation Accord was a progressive policy of accommodation that would have committed provincial and federal governments to negotiate: self-government agreements, lands and resources, the transfer of the portion of aboriginal programs and services available to Métis, as well as cost sharing agreements relating to Métis institutions, programs, and services. For now, the Métis will have to endure the complexities of Canadian Indian bureaucracy.

Yale D. Belanger

See also Nunavut Land Claims Agreement.
References and Further Reading

Indian and Northern Affairs Canada (INAC). "Proposed Métis Nation Accord." Available at: http://www.ainc-inac.gc.ca/ch/rcap/sg/sj5d_e.html. Accessed March 1, 2005.

Chartrand, Larry. 1992. "The Métis Settlement Accord: A Modern Treaty." Paper presented at the Indigenous Bar Association Annual Meeting. Montreal, ON.

Chartrand, Larry. 2000. "Agent of Reconciliation: The Supreme Court of Canada and Aboriginal Claims." In *The Judiciary as Third Branch of Government: Manifestations and Challenges to Legitimacy.* Edited by M. Mossman and Ghislain Otis. Montreal, ON: Canadian Institute for the Administration of Justice.

Hodgson Smith, Kathy, and Jason Madden. No date. "A Re-Engaged Métis Nation Multilateral Process: A New Journey Begins." *Otipemisiwak-Voice of the Métis Nation in Alberta:* Issue 1, Volume 1.

National Indian Gaming Commission

An independent federal agency created by the Indian Gaming Regulatory Act (IGRA) in 1988, the National Indian Gaming Commission (NIGC) regulates Indian gaming nationally. The commission consists of a chairman and two commissioners charged with assuring that Indian gaming is free from organized crime, primarily benefits American Indian communities, and offers fair games. The commission may conduct investigations, impose civil fines, close gaming facilities, review and approve gaming ordinances written by tribal councils, and do background checks and audits. The commission has headquarters in Washington, D.C., and regional offices in Portland, Sacramento, Phoenix, Tulsa, and St. Paul. The president chooses the chairman of the commission with the consent of Congress, and the Secretary of the Interior appoints the other two commissioners. Two members of federally recognized Indian communities must serve on the commission, and the NIGC must include members of both political parties. No commissioner can be affiliated with a gaming facility, and commissioners serve for three years. Fees assessed on revenue from Indian gaming operations fund the commission.

Congressman Morris Udall of Arizona began the Congressional effort to establish guidelines for the regulation of Indian gaming in 1983. By 1986, Udall had introduced H.R. 1920, which included provisions for the NIGC. The House passed Udall's bill, but it died in the Senate. The next year, Senator Daniel Inouye of Hawai'i, the new chairman of the Select Committee on Indian Affairs, introduced S. 555, which passed and became the IGRA. This legislation created the NIGC and defined its role in Indian gaming. The IGRA established three classes of Indian gaming. Class I games consisted of traditional social gambling for small prizes; Class II games included bingo, pull tabs, punch boards, tip jars, instant bingo, and nonbanked card games, and the law classified all other games Class III. The IGRA gave the NIGC a regulatory role in both Class II and III gaming and allowed tribal governments sole jurisdiction over Class I games.

Critics of the NIGC contend that it lacks the necessary power to regulate Indian gaming effectively and has failed to uncover any cases of major corruption in the industry. These criticisms have reached a popular audience through articles in popular publications such as *Time*. However, gaming communities insist that NIGC oversight is sufficient, noting the Minimum Internal Control Standards (MICS) for Indian gaming operations issued in 1999. These standards require Indian casinos to follow very specific guidelines in all facets of their operations. The NIGC even requires detailed plans for the spending of gaming profits, annual audits, and internal standard reports. Additionally, the National Indian Gaming Association (NIGA) maintains that Indian gaming is more highly regulated than other gaming operations because Class III operations are subject to regulations on the tribal, state, and federal levels.

The NIGC has used its authority on a number of occasions, shutting down gaming facilities for various reasons. In 2003, the NIGC shut down the Sac and Fox tribe's Meskwaki Casino in Iowa for six months until a formally recognized tribal council took control of casino profits, and in 2000 the commission closed the facility owned by the Kiowa tribe of Oklahoma for over five years for violations of the IGRA.

Gaming communities also have challenged the extent of NIGC authority through the courts. For example, in 1990, the Cabazon band of Mission Indians filed a suit against the NIGC protesting their designation of electronic facsimile games as Class III, and the courts upheld the commission's definitions in 1994. In 2001, the Colorado River Indian Tribes challenged the commission's right to audit their Blue Water Casino for MICS. In 2005, the district court in Washington, D.C., decided that the IGRA did not grant the NIGC this power. Despite this decision, the commission will continue to check for compliance with the MICS as part of their responsibility to both Indian gaming facilities and the public.

James Precht

See also Economic Development; Gambling.

References and Further Reading

Cramer, Renée Ann. 2005. *Cash, Color, and Colonialism: The Politics of Tribal Acknowledgement.* Norman: University of Oklahoma Press.

Light, Steven Andrew, and Kathryn R. L. Rand. 2005. *Indian Gaming and Tribal Sovereignty: The Casino Compromise.* Lawrence: University Press of Kansas.

Mason, W. Dale. 2000. *Indian Gaming: Tribal Sovereignty and American Politics.* Norman: University of Oklahoma Press.

National Indian Gaming Commission. Available at: http://www.nigc.gov. Accessed May 29, 2006.

Native American Graves Protection and Repatriation Act

For centuries, the skeletal remains of American Indians were removed from their burial sites, studied, catalogued, and relegated to the bins of museums and science labs. NAGPRA addresses the right of the dead to an undisturbed resting place among their own people. It also addresses the right of the living to ensure that their ancestors and their ancestral sacred items are interred with the respect they are due (Morris Udall, 1990).

Since 1906, the United States has taken management authority over the cultural and scientific resources under its jurisdiction. The 1906 Antiquities Act (16 U.S.C. §§431–433) and later the Archaeological Resources Protection Act (ARPA, 16 U.S.C. §§470aa-mm, 1979) established permitting authority for scientific data recovery on federal and Indian lands. The items removed from the ground, mostly

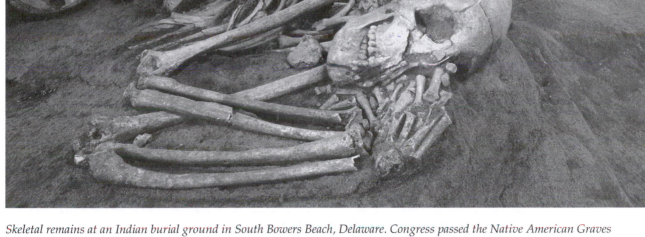

Skeletal remains at an Indian burial ground in South Bowers Beach, Delaware. Congress passed the Native American Graves Protection and Repatriation Act to achieve two main objectives: the protection of sacred objects like human remains from excavation and the return of such objects housed in federal museums to the appropriate Native American groups. (Kevin Fleming/Corbis)

Native American human remains and burial items, were to remain under government control and thus were stored largely in government and university repositories. Attempts by tribes to reclaim the remains of their ancestors and tribal property were unsuccessful (Echo-Hawk, 1986). When the Onondaga nation went to court in 1899 to retrieve the Wampum Belts held by the New York State Museum, they found that courts did not acknowledge the nation as having enforceable property rights (*Onondaga Nation v. Thacher*, 61 N.Y.S. 1027 [N.Y. App. Div. 1899]).

At the end of the twentieth century, largely due to pressure brought to bear by Indian activists, and despite opposition by various conservative scholars, the American public and the U.S. government began to recognize the culture of American Indians as meriting respect and protection on a formalized basis. Congress passed the American Indian Religious Freedom Act (AIRFA, 42 U.S.C. §1996, 1994) on August 11, 1978, and the president issued the Sacred Sites Executive Order (E.O. No. 13,007, 61 Fed. Reg. 26771, May 24, 1996), supporting the rights of Native Americans to practice traditional ceremonies. The National Historic Preservation Act (NHPA, 16 U.S.C. §§470a et. seq., 1992) was amended to recognize traditional cultural places meriting listing on the National Register of Historic Places and established Tribal Historic Preservation Officers who could replace state authority on tribal lands. Legislation specifically to address the cultural property rights of Native Americans is the Native American Graves Protection and Repatriation Act (NAGPRA, 25 U.S.C. §§3001–3013, 1990).

After compromises reached on the language and scope of the law by the archaeological, museum, and tribal communities, the NAGPRA legislation received unanimous support in Congress. NAGPRA is a law with four attributes. It comprises property law, Indian law, human rights law, and an administrative process.

NAGPRA as Property Law

NAGPRA enfranchises tribes and Native Americans in the common law of property and Fifth Amendment property rights. The law recognizes that, although human remains are not property and cannot be owned under the common law, descendents have the obligation and right to direct the disposition of their ancestors (Bowman, 1989). Funerary objects, sacred objects, and objects of cultural patri-

mony removed from tribes and Native American individuals without their permission, that are held in the control of federal agencies and museums that receive federal funds, must be returned to claimants under NAGPRA. If the museum has a lawful chain of ownership and transfer for the item, it may assert the right of possession. Under NAGPRA no taking shall occur.

Protected items in NAGPRA are the human remains of Native Americans and Native Hawaiians and cultural items. Cultural items include funerary objects (items placed with or intended for burials); sacred objects (ceremonial items needed by traditional Native American religious leaders for the practice of traditional religion by present-day adherents); and cultural patrimony (the inalienable items owned by the group that have ongoing historical, traditional, or cultural importance and were considered as such at the time the object was separated from the group).

The parties eligible to make a repatriation claim for NAGPRA-protected items held in the collections of federal agencies or museums are lineal descendents of named individuals with their associated funerary items. Also eligible are federally recognized tribes or Native Hawaiian organizations having a shared group identity with the cultural item when there is no claim of a lineal descendent for human remains, funerary objects, sacred objects, and objects of cultural patrimony. When newly exhumed burials and NAGPRA-protected items are located on federal or Indian land, the priority of claimants is as follows: lineal descendents; then tribal landowners on their tribal land regardless of cultural relationship; culturally affiliated federally recognized tribes and Native Hawaiian organizations on federal land; then federally recognized tribes or Native Hawaiian organizations that are the aboriginal occupants of the area regardless of cultural affiliation, unless another group with standing has a stronger claim of relationship.

NAGPRA as Indian Law

NAGPRA acknowledges the unique relationship between the federal government and tribes and Native Hawaiian organizations (25 U.S.C. §3010). As such, the law requires consultation with federally recognized tribes and with Native Hawaiian organizations on a government-to-government basis at each stage of the process. The NAGPRA process, further described in a following section, resolves years

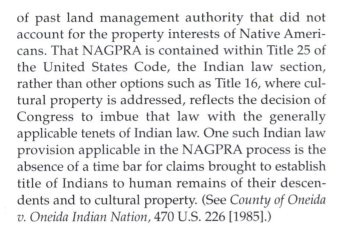

of past land management authority that did not account for the property interests of Native Americans. That NAGPRA is contained within Title 25 of the United States Code, the Indian law section, rather than other options such as Title 16, where cultural property is addressed, reflects the decision of Congress to imbue that law with the generally applicable tenets of Indian law. One such Indian law provision applicable in the NAGPRA process is the absence of a time bar for claims brought to establish title of Indians to human remains of their descendents and to cultural property. (See *County of Oneida v. Oneida Indian Nation*, 470 U.S. 226 [1985].)

NAGPRA as Human Rights Law

NAGPRA does not provide Native Americans with any greater rights than would otherwise be afforded to those seeking to make claims recognized under the common law and to seek relief from a "taking" under the Fifth Amendment of the Constitution. As such, NAGPRA may be seen as "equal protection" law. Enfranchising Native Americans with property rights due but not historically respected is the essence of human rights law.

NAGPRA as Administrative Process

The NAGPRA process establishes separate means to approach "repatriation" of Native American and Native Hawaiian human remains and cultural items separated from the land and held in museum and federal agency collections, from the immediate determination of "ownership" upon the discovery of human remains and cultural items excavated on federal or Indian lands after the date of the law, November 16, 1990.

Repatriation

Federal agencies and institutions that receive federal funds and have possession of or control over Native American cultural items must summarize their Native American and Native Hawaiian collections and enter into consultations to determine whether federally recognized tribes and Native Hawaiian organizations wish to make claims for the repatriation of items to which they are culturally affiliated. As to human remains and associated funerary objects, the consultation is intended to aid the museums and federal agencies in compiling an itemized inventory, containing decisions on cultural affilia-

tion, such that lineal descendents and culturally affiliated tribes can make claims for repatriation.

Inventories are sent to the National Park Service (NPS), National NAGPRA Program. Summaries are sent directly to all interested tribes as they trigger consultation. Notices of Inventory Completion are published in the *Federal Register*, as are decisions by the museum or federal agency as to the cultural affiliation of the human remains and associated funerary objects. Based on those decisions, lineal descendents and culturally affiliated tribes can claim the remains and/or items. When tribes or Native Hawaiian organizations come to repatriation agreements with museums or federal agencies as to cultural items in the summary, the museum or agency prepares a Notice of Intent to Repatriate that is sent to NPS for publication in the *Federal Register*. If there are no competing claims in response to either type of notice in thirty days, on the thirty-first day repatriation— that is transfer of control—can occur. As a practical matter, the claimant group and the museum or federal agency begin consultation on the manner of transfer once they have come to an initial agreement.

Those human remains and funerary objects for which no cultural affiliation determination can be reasonably made are listed in the inventory as culturally unidentifiable. To assist tribes, museums, and federal agencies in making further cultural affiliation determinations, NPS maintains a public access database of culturally unidentifiable Native American human remains and funerary objects in the inventories. Future regulations will direct the eventual disposition of culturally unidentifiable human remains. Until then, guidance may be obtained from the Review Committee.

NAGPRA does not require that science be undertaken to make a cultural affiliation determination, but it does not prohibit science undertaken in consultation with the interested parties. It does allow a museum or federal agency with NAGPRA-protected items in the collection to receive permission from the Secretary of the Interior to retain items until the end of a study that is of major benefit to the United States.

Disputes over repatriation factual issues may be referred to the Review Committee for an advisory opinion. This is not a predicate to court action but provides a means to have the facts examined by an expert neutral panel. Disputes can arise when tribes make competing claims and when the decision of the land manager or museum as to which tribe has the preponderance of evidence in its favor is questioned, or a dispute can arise between a tribe and a museum or federal agency if the claimant disagrees with a decision on cultural affiliation or repatriation. A tribe or Native Hawaiian organization making an initial claim must show (1) they have standing to make a claim, (2) the item is a NAGPRA-protected item, and (3) there is a relationship of shared group identify between the claimant and the item. A museum may then overcome the claim of a tribe if the museum can carry the burden to prove that they have the right of possession (that, under the common law of property, they hold title that began with permission of the initial owner to alienate the item).

Ownership

NAGPRA requires consultation with tribes and Native Hawaiian organizations prior to the removal of human remains or cultural objects from federal or tribal land, including Hawaiian Homes Commission land. When there is an agreement in place prior to the discovery of a NAGPRA-protected item, the event is called an "intentional excavation." The disposition of newly discovered items follows the agreement. When no agreement is in place, the event is called an "inadvertent discovery," and all work must cease for thirty days while consultation occurs to reach an agreement on disposition. Thus, advance planning is more effective than stopping a project to do remedial decision making. Native American human remains and associated funerary objects that are not claimed remain in federal control pending future regulations on disposition.

Illegal Trafficking in Native American Human Remains and Cultural Items

NAGPRA makes it a crime to traffic in Native American human remains and cultural items (18 U.S.C. §1170). It is illegal to sell, purchase, use for profit, or transport for sale or profit the human remains of a Native American, taken from any location, of any age, unless the actor has the right of possession. Under the common law this means that only the descendent with authority to put the remains into the marketplace may lawfully do so. The same is true of Native American cultural items. Violation of NAGPRA can be committed either by removing the item from federal or Indian lands, including the lands of a Native Hawaiian organization, or by trafficking in items from museum or federal agency collections that are subject to the repatriation provisions. For instance, a museum that holds back a NAGPRA-protected item from the NAGPRA process so that it may be offered for sale at an auction commits an act of trafficking. The first offense is a misdemeanor and the second offense is a felony. The new federal sentencing guidelines heighten the penalties but require a value calculation to determine the severity of the penalty.

Conclusion

NAGPRA has not caused all Native American and Native Hawaiian cultural items to be stripped from the collections of museums. Rather, the institutional knowledge about tribal culture has been enriched through the process of consultation. Post-NAGPRA collection protocols typically involve respectful treatment of the dead. Native Americans and tribes are regularly (although not always) regarded as necessary participants in consultation in the determination of rights to items in collections and as potential owners of human remains and cultural items that may be discovered on the landscape. It is also worth noting that many non-Native museums have profited handsomely from these laws, having received generous subsidies to conduct their inventories. In any case, the process is ongoing and the progress profound.

Sherry Hutt

See also Mound Cultures of North America; Native American Museums; Wampum.

References and Further Reading

Bowman, Margaret B. 1989. "The Reburial of Native American Skeletal Remains: Approaches to Resolution of a Conflict." *Harvard Environmental Law Review* 13, no. 167–208.

Echo-Hawk, Walter. 1986. "Museum Rights vs. Indian Rights: Guidelines for Assessing Competing Legal Interests in Native American Resources." *NYU Review of Legal and Social Change* 14, no. 437.

McKeown, C. Timothy, and Sherry Hutt. 2002–2003. "In the Smaller Scope of Conscience: The Native American Graves Protection and Repatriation Act Twelve Years After.UCLA Journal of Environmental Law," 21, no. 153.

Morris Udall, 136 Cong. Rec. E3484 (1990)

North West Company

Following Britain's conquest of Canada, French traders from Montreal were supplanted in the fur trade by independent Scotsmen. Many of these new

Scottish merchants allied themselves with the French already in the country but also competed against one another. Under the leadership of Simon McTavish and the brothers Benjamin and Joseph Frobisher, a few of the leading Montreal merchants united in 1779, forming a new power in the fur trade that in 1783 became officially known as the North West Company. This new company suffered much internal strife, yet it competed successfully with and was the chief rival of the Hudson's Bay Company from 1779 to 1821.

The company was headquartered on Vaudreuil Street in Montreal. Stockholders were the Montreal trading companies and the "wintering partners," the men who did the actual trading for furs with the Native Americans. The company also employed French-Canadian voyageurs familiar with the Indian trade. The Northwesters, as men of the company were called, tended to be more active and aggressive agents in expanding the Indian trade than their Hudson's Bay Company rivals. From their main supply depot at the Grand Portage, which linked Lake Superior and Montreal to the system of lakes and rivers and interior trading posts of the *pays d'en haut* (most of Ontario, the area west of the Mississippi and south of the Great Lakes and beyond to the Canadian prairies), Northwest Company men extended the Indian trade into new lands between the Hudson's Bay territories and Louisiana as well as westward. During the late 1700s the Grand Portage became a summer rendezvous site for Indian families, French voyageurs, Scottish clerks, *pays d'en haut* wintering partners, and Montreal and London agents.

The more intrepid character of the North West Company was embodied in one of the company's partners, Alexander Mackenzie, who began a series of explorations of the Northwest, which carried him to the Arctic (1789) and Pacific (1792–1793) Oceans. Another Northwester, geographer David Thompson, extended trade westward to the Missouri River and the Mandan Indians, and later to the Columbia River.

The bold enterprise of the North West Company stirred the older Hudson's Bay Company into action. Competition intensified between the two British companies as both suffered from a depressed fur market in Europe caused by the Napoleonic Wars and the overharvesting of animals. Rivalry escalated to bloodshed as the Hudson's Bay Company took bold steps to harass the North West Company. In 1811, a large tract of land in the Red River Valley was granted to Lord Selkirk (a major Hudson's Bay Company shareholder) for settlement. The colony's location would essentially cut off the North West Company from lands farther to the west and divide the territory to the east. In 1814, restrictions on the pemmican trade were enacted, which also alienated the Métis population who were the producers of pemmican, as well as occupants of the Red River area. The struggle reached a bloody pitch when war between the two companies peaked at the Battle of Seven Oaks (1816), resulting in Lord Selkirk's arresting several North West Company proprietors and seizing company property. With fears of a failing company and pressure from the British government to stop hostilities and ensure imperial stability, North West Company shareholders agreed to merge with their hated rival. In July of 1821, an agreement was signed with the Hudson's Bay Company, whereby it absorbed the North West Company.

The greater portion of labor for the trade came from the tribes who traded the pelts, hides, and pemmican to North West Company agents for manufactured goods. To strengthen trade connections, the North West Company (more than the Hudson's Bay Company with its stricter ideals of race and class) encouraged adopting Indian ceremonies and customs, the strongest connection being marriage *á la façon du pays* (after the custom of the country). The North West Company appreciated the advantage that marriages of its men to Indian women brought and allowed all ranks to marry. These unions strengthened trade relations and created reciprocal social and economic bonds for Indians that drew traders into tribal kinship circles. The result of such unions accelerated changes in many quarters of the Indian world including their economic, social, ceremonial, demographic, and political worlds as well as inter- and intratribal power. Perhaps the greatest evidence of change these unions created were mixed-blood offspring.

In its four decades of existence, the North West Company altered significantly the dimensions of the Indian trade, imperial claims to the West, and the lives of numerous western tribes.

S. Matthew DeSpain

See also Fur Trade, Hudson's Bay Company.
References and Further Reading
Carlos, Ann M. 1986. *The North American Fur Trade: A Study in the Life-Cycle of a Duopoly.* New York: Garland Publishing.
Davidson, Gordon C. 1967. *The North West Company.* New York: Russell & Russell.

Northwest Ordinance (1787)

Composed by the Confederation Congress (1787–1789) in the same year as the Constitution, the Northwest Ordinance is a multifaceted document. Ostensibly it is a design by the Congress for regional development of a territory it presumed it had acquired through its apparent success in negotiating the terms of independence in 1783. However, its character as a statement of republican ideals in a framework for the territorial governance (of non-Natives by choice and of Natives and slaves by force) renders it a catalogue of reference for a slate of issues relevant to contemporary cultural and political themes. Slavery, state's rights, religious freedom, habeus corpus, universal schooling, the financial ethics of politicians, and, not least, Indian relations are all addressed, if imperfectly and highly selectively, by the terms or context of the Northwest Ordinance. Truly, the audacity of the wide-ranging affairs brought together by the Congress under this document lies in its aim to provide development objectives for an extensive territory it had yet to bring under physical control and in its character as a precursor to the Bill of Rights. It was composed concurrently with the federal Constitution, which famously mentions Indians only as economically defined exceptions to the establishment of the new citizenry ("Indians not taxed" [*Article I, Section 2*, for example]) and elsewhere as simply trade concerns. As a result, many scholars of Indian affairs look to the Ordinance as an immediate predecessor to glean clues about the intentions of the Congress toward American Indians. In that context, the Ordinance is most recognized and referenced by its (cynical) statement of the apparent position of the Congress toward Indian Nations, articulated in the Third Article, which consists, significantly, of an exegesis primarily concerned with morality:

> Religion, morality, and knowledge, being necessary to good government and the happiness of mankind, schools and the means of education shall forever be encouraged. The utmost good faith shall always be observed towards the Indians; their lands and property shall never be taken from them without their consent; and, in their property, rights, and liberty, they shall never be invaded or disturbed, unless in just and lawful wars authorized by Congress; but laws founded in justice and humanity, shall from time to time be

made for preventing wrongs being done to them, and for preserving peace and friendship with them (Continental Congress, 1904–1937, 31: 340–341).

Among the earliest of formal statements of general intent toward Indian nations as a whole, the document, while not a treaty, is consistently utilized as a point of reference, with the "utmost good faith" and "without their consent" clauses suggesting the obligation of the federal government to act as the trustee of American Indian lands, an obligation that it would later codify and then proceed more or less to ignore. To limit the interpretation of the Ordinance to these assumptions would miss many critical aspects of the legislation and an understanding of its creators' strategic interests. Within the same year, preparations were made to make expedient use of the option reserved in the latter clause, "in just and lawful wars." The campaign against the tribes of the Northwest Territory began in earnest in 1788 with the assignment of Arthur St. Clair to the region as governor.

With the apparent inconsistencies between the document's stated intentions and the state of affairs in the region it aimed to administer, the Northwest Ordinance can be best understood through analysis of economic policy at the time of its writing and of the key figures shaping Indian policy. The Ordinance continued the Federalist-driven vision of a monopoly on Indian affairs, to the exclusion of the states, begun with the 1785 passage of the Indian Policy Act and continued with the 1786 Ordinance for the Regulation and Management of Indian Affairs; but this earlier legislation that attempted to bring Indian affairs under centralized oversight was not effective (Prucha, 1995, 47). Items such as the requirement for trading licenses to be issued only by Congress were all but ignored on the frontier.

Despite the ongoing state of war, many scholars believe that the Congress did intend to deal more peaceably with Indian nations than in the past, was aware of the standing of its actions in international law, and did hope to control and contain the settlement of the frontier, as opposed to allowing the wholesale overrunning of Indian lands (the "wrongs done to them" mentioned in the Ordinance) (Deloria and Wilkins, 1999, 17). However, assumptions must be seen as strategic: Congress had become convinced that it was far more efficient to treat Indians in a manner that recognized their autonomy and thereby maintained peace, but that exchanged the peace, as well as terms of trade, for their lands through purchase agreements made exclusively with the central government. The most significant obstacle to this strategy was, of course, the states themselves (through their anti-Federalist delegates), who generally wished to deal with Indians in a manner profitable for their own interests or that of their foremost citizens, until such conflicts arose that needed military backing. This was particularly the case in states such as Georgia, North Carolina, and New York, where representatives had already begun negotiating terms of trade with the Iroquois tribes without authorization from Congress.

The strategy to resolve this situation was a combined effort of military officials such as Secretary of War Henry Knox and, of course, George Washington, who knew only too well how expensive Indian wars were, and of the many economic thinkers among the Congress; the postrevolutionary government was deeply in debt and was, above all, concerned with securing financial stability. To that end, Congress—moving toward the centralization of power it articulated in the Constitutional Convention—saw that the control of Indian trade and of the wealth contained in title to Indian-controlled lands was essential to the new nation's financial future. Proposals to sell lands in the Ohio country were already before the Congress (Prucha, 1995, 45). This explains the immediacy with which the Congress secured the Northwest Territory militarily, as well as its treating with Indians, as General Knox had been persuasive in asserting, not as conquered peoples, but relatively liberally and on terms that would encourage them to deal only with the Congress (Horsman, 1967, 41).

Thus, with respect to Indian relations, the Ordinance is significant as a template for Indian relations and treaty making as it would be conducted into the 1800s. Indeed, the conflicts in the Northwest would be resolved at the Treaty of Greenville in 1795, in which, like the treaties of Fort Harmar (1789) and Canandaigua (1794) before it, "in consideration of the peace now established," the terms of agreement between apparently equal parties would become increasingly standardized, to more clearly define Indian rights and to negotiate the transfer of very specific tracts of land, treaty by treaty, from individual tribes, always with the proviso that if they "shall be disposed to sell" additional lands in the future they will deal only with agents of the United States.

This is the context for a much less referenced Ordinance passage, a statement of its objective to "lay out the parts of the district in which the Indian titles shall have been extinguished."

The Northwest Ordinance's evaluation by historians has been mixed. Many recognize it as the crowning achievement of the Confederation period, while others see it as a crowning act of hypocrisy. Apologists generally note its forethought for the future of the republic through its procedural provisions for the organization and incorporation of new states, and its pre–Bill of Rights narrative, with less attention to the source for such vision. It is important to note that recent scholarship has shown that an additional dimension of the document, with respect to American Indian history, is that its authors, like those of the Constitution, were familiar with existing forms of Indian governance that preserved individual liberties and that, in cases such as the Iroquois Confederacy, provided protocols for the incorporation of new member nations (Grinde and Johansen, 1991, 194). Their apparent ability to be influenced by Native thought and governance, and yet provide so calculatingly for their dispossession, gives critical evidence of the complex character of the founding generation. Further complicating this scenario is the clear conflict of interest of some members of Congress who were involved in regional planning legislation, yet who also held vested interest in the outcomes (for instance, Hauptman, 1995). The Ordinance would be ratified under the constitutional government in 1789; only its trade provisions would require further articulation in the Trade and Intercourse Acts.

Christopher Lindsay Turner

See also Assimilation; Canandaigua (Pickering) Treaty; Fur Trade; Haudenosaunee Confederacy, Political System; Trade and Intercourse Acts; Treaty Diplomacy, with Summary of Selected Treaties; Trust, Doctrine of.

References and Further Reading

Continental Congress. 1904–1937. *Journals of the Continental Congress, 1774–1789*. Washington, DC: U.S. Congress.

Deloria, Vine, Jr., and David E. Wilkins. 1999. *Tribes, Treaties, & Constitutional Tribulations*. Austin: University of Texas Press.

Hauptman, Laurence M. 1995. *Tribes & Tribulations: Misconceptions About American Indians and Their Histories*. Albuquerque: University of New Mexico Press.

Horsman, Reginald. 1967. *Expansion and American Indian Policy, 1783–1812*. Norman: University of Oklahoma Press.

Grinde, Donald A., Jr., and Bruce E. Johansen. 1991. *Exemplar of Liberty: Native America and the Evolution of Democracy.* Los Angeles: UCLA American Indian Studies Center.

Prucha, Francis Paul. 1995. *The Great Father: The United States Government and American Indians.* Lincoln: University of Nebraska Press.

Nunavut Land Claims Agreement

In 1993, the Inuit people of the central and eastern Arctic, the Canadian government, and the government of the North West Territories signed the largest aboriginal land claim in Canadian history. Following two decades of negotiations, the agreement covered 1.2 million square miles of territory and had the federal government recognize Inuit title to more than 220,000 square miles of land in the eastern Arctic. On 22,000 square miles of these lands, the Inuit were assigned mineral rights, and the agreement established land use regulations and control over the resources (Dahl, Hicks, and Jull, 2000, 58). The Nunavut Land Claims Agreement (NLCA) was brought into effect in June 1993, with the passing of the Nunavut Land Claims Agreement Act. The agreement contains forty-one articles that, in addition to providing land title to the Inuits of Nunavut, provide clear rules of ownership, rights, and obligations concerning Nunavut's land, water, and resources. In return for ceding certain territories, the Inuits also received $1.14 billion in compensation and an additional $13 million in the form of a Training Trust Fund to ensure that the Inuits have access to sufficient funding to assist in meeting their responsibilities under the claim (Légaré, 2003, 119). The NLCA also provided for the Inuits becoming full participants in a number of comanagement entities that are responsible for territorial resource management.

On April 1, 1999, Nunavut became the first territory to join the federation of Canada since Newfoundland in 1949. Representing the culmination of

Canadian Governor General Romeo LeBlanc (center) looks on as the flag of Nunavut is unveiled at the official ceremony to inaugurate Nunavut in Iqaluit, Nunavut, on April 1, 1999. (Tom Hanson/AFP/Getty Images)

nearly twenty-five years of negotiations between the federal government and the Inuits, Nunavut became Canada's third territory. The Inuit land claim was born of their long-standing territorial occupation. Yet despite Inuit territorial claims, by the 1940s, Canadian occupation of the north had become the norm. Threatened by U.S. troops stationed in the eastern Arctic and potential American sovereignty claims, Ottawa mobilized the Royal Canadian Mounted Police (RCMP), situating officers across the Canadian arctic in an effort to enhance Canadian sovereignty. This also accounted for the introduction of federal Indian policy and programming to the north. Promoting its long-standing civilization policy, the Canadian government facilitated program delivery by promoting the settlement of what federal officials at the time considered to be a nomadic people into small, easily accessible communities.

Reacting to the steady infiltration of non-Native people from the south and the imposition of Canadian programs, an organization called the Indian and Eskimo Association (IEA) was created in the mid-1960s to conduct research on the rights of indigenous peoples in Canada and to initiate a fight for territorial land claims. The goal was to augment Inuit social, economic, and political influence by wresting control over decision-making powers from the federal government. Following two IEA meetings in late 1970 and early 1971, the Inuits formed the Inuit Tapirisat Corporation (ITC). ITC delegates had many concerns, which were reflected in the significant organizational mandate. Founded to secure Inuit land title and establish resource management protocols with the Canadian government and other outside institutions, ITC began to lobby for the creation of Nunavut. Inuit leaders anticipated that Nunavut's formation would resolve their outstanding land claims in the region. In addition to fighting for aboriginal rights, ITC was to work with government officials to limit large-scale development, such as oil exploration, and to promote small scale and local development, such as northern tourism. It was also concerned with developing the proper devices to permit Inuit participation in policy formulation, the creation of programs and research for dealing with rights to territory and resources, all the while seeking protection and maintenance of traditional land use and harvesting practices.

The process that led to the establishment of Nunavut began in 1973. During this period the concept of aboriginal title was becoming a significant

Members of the Arctic Rangers raise the first Nunavut flag in Iqaluit, Nunavut, on April 1, 1999. (AP/Wide World Photos)

legal and political issue in Canada. That year the Supreme Court of Canada, in *Calder v. Attorney-General of British Columbia,* recognized pre-existing aboriginal rights, even those not exclusively outlined in the Royal Proclamation of 1763. This confirmed that a separate system of aboriginal rights did in fact exist, albeit a structure relegated to a lesser position in Western society. In this instance, aboriginal title arises from the long-term use and continuous occupancy of the land by aboriginal peoples prior to the arrival of European and British colonial powers to North America. The *Calder* decision was the first in Canada to use the terms "aboriginal rights" and "land claim." The message to Canadian officials who had previously ignored the concept of aboriginal title was clear: They needed to create a more flexible policy concerning the definition, classification, and recognition of aboriginal rights.

Such a policy would entail the extinguishment of aboriginal title held by Native groups who, until then, had never signed a treaty as indicated by the Royal Proclamation of 1763, which dictated that a public meeting be held and community agreement reached prior to Indian land being sold to the Crown. The Inuits were concerned with this strategy, having never signed a treaty with Canada. However, in 1974, the Canadian government implemented a new comprehensive land claims policy, which was described as a process in which the claimant group will receive defined rights, compensation, and other benefits in exchange for relinquishing rights relating to the title claimed over all or part of the land in question. The federal government then provided funding to, among others, the ITC to determine the land areas they wanted ownership rights over. ITC utilized the final report prepared as a working paper in the preparation of Nunavut land claim proposal. This was developed in part by a team of researchers, led by anthropologist Milton Freeman, who initiated an extensive land use and occupancy project that defined the boundaries of Inuit land use in Ketikmeot, Keewatin, and Baffin. These demarcations would eventually be adopted in 1979 as the Nunavut borders.

ITC worked diligently on their claim and, in 1976, submitted their grievance to the federal government. The ITC land claim proposed the creation of a new territory and representative government, an unprecedented request at the time. The Inuit goal was to resolve the land claim, which called for the Beaufort Sea and Yukon North Slope areas used by the Inuvialuit to be included in the Nunavut Territory, while simultaneously promoting Inuit political development. The proposal was later withdrawn due to its complexity and because the Inuits at the community level were upset that non-Inuit lawyers in Ottawa and Toronto drafted the proposal, eschewing an advocacy approach necessitating community-based guidance. The move toward a final land claim resulted in Inuit factionalism, which manifested itself when the Inuvialuit split from ITC to negotiate a separate land claim agreement. Nevertheless, that year the Federal Electoral Boundaries Commission recommended dividing the Northwest Territories into two federal electoral districts: Nunatsiaq and the Western Arctic.

The Inuits made clear that they intended to maintain their land base and that they would not consider any amount of compensation for sale of their territory. Further, the Inuits had no intention of remaining a part of the North West Territories (NWT). Rather, their territory was to remain under Inuit control. They would, however, accept in the new territory a "public government" as opposed to "aboriginal self-government." According to this model, all citizens could vote, run for office, and in general, participate in public affairs. All people, irrespective of aboriginal status, would fall under the government's jurisdiction. The NWT legislature expressed its dissatisfaction with the Inuit proposal, insisting that division of the NWT into two smaller territories was undesirable. The federal government considered these concerns. However, it was clear that both Inuit and Canadian officials favored the establishment of a separate Inuit territory, arguing that the Inuits would remain a minority in the NWT under the current structure and that the sheer size of the territory would make territorial program delivery increasingly difficult. The Inuits notified the federal government in 1980 that no final land claim agreement would be finalized that did not involve the creation of a separate and uniquely Inuit territory, to which the federal government conceded.

The North West Territories (NWT) Inuit Land Claims Commission (ILCC) was formed in 1977 to focus exclusively on land claims negotiations. That year, the ILCC submitted its claims proposal to Ottawa following an extended consultation process with northern Inuit communities. In September 1977, "Speaking for the First Citizens of the Canadian Artic" was presented, which was a necessarily less complex version of the ITC's previous proposal. The land claim component was well received; however, the negotiations came to an abrupt halt following the federal government's rejection of the Inuit request to resolve the issue of their future political development prior to moving on to land claims. This delay proved fatal for the ILCC, which disbanded in 1979, only to be replaced by the Nunavut Land Claims Project (NLCP). Inuit leaders agreed that year to participate in the NWT election, which was an historic first. A majority of Inuit members were elected to the NWT Legislative Assembly, and participating in the territorial political process warmed Inuit leaders to the prospect of pursuing their land claims on the basis of aboriginal rights. The NWT Legislative Assembly then established a Special Committee on Unity to determine how residents felt about the proposed territorial division. The final report indicated that residents favored the split, and, based on these findings, legislators voted in favor of division, sixteen to one.

In 1979, the federal electoral boundaries commission's recommendation to divide the NWT into two areas was executed, and the new eastern district (Nunatsiaq) roughly corresponded with the Inuits' proposed Nunavut territory. The ITC was following closely the evolution of the claims process, and, at their 1979 organizational meeting, drafted "Political Development in Nunavut," a proposal that incorporated the best aspects of all previous proposals. This document stated four objectives: (1) ownership rights over portions of land rich in nonrenewable resources; (2) decision-making power over the management of land and resources within the settlement area; (3) financial indemnity and royalties from resources developed in the area; and (4) a commitment from Ottawa to negotiate self-government once a land claim was signed. Once again, the ITC reaffirmed that land claims resolutions must also be accompanied by the division of the NWT to permit for the creation of Nunavut and Inuit governance. ITC established a fifteen-year policy attainment schedule. The following year, ITC delegates voted unanimously to pass a resolution, officially calling for the establishment of the Nunavut territory, and in March 1981 the NWT Legislative Assembly ordered a plebiscite to be called to settle the issue of division.

The federal government had previously been reluctant to consent to Inuit demands calling for the creation of a territory prior to resolving outstanding land claims. Officials did, however, accept the legitimacy of a plebiscite. John Munro, the Minister of Indian Affairs, announced that the Canadian government would abide by the plebiscite's results and the NWT Legislative Assembly's decisions, as based on the population's desires. Ottawa did set three preconditions to division. First, settlement of Inuit land claims must occur prior to the proposed division. Second, a boundary separating the east and west of the territories would have to be approved by the NWT residents. And, third, an accord would need to be reached defining the basic structural arrangements of the government of the Nunavut Territory.

Prior to the plebiscite, the Inuits received a vote of confidence concerning their land claims. In 1982, following the patriation of Canada's Constitution from Britain, included in the new Constitution Act, 1982 was Section 35(3). This clause protected land claims, "that now exist by way of land claims agreements or may be so acquired." This suggested that, upon the finalization of the land claims process, the accompanying agreement would become a constitutionally protected pact. Then, in April 1982, a plebiscite was held to determine support for the proposed division of the NWT into two independent territories. Despite low voter turnout, the majority of the NWT population (56 percent) favored the idea of division. In the eastern Arctic, where the Inuit population was highest, the percentage in favor of division hovered around 80 percent. Anticipating the establishment of an Inuit territory, a boundary settlement was pursued, albeit unsuccessfully.

The resolution of the NWT issue pleased Inuit delegates; they were now required to negotiate their territorial boundaries. A plebiscite held in April 1982, indicated that the majority of NWT population (56 percent) favored the idea of division into two new political territories. Anticipating the establishment of an Inuit territory, a boundary settlement was pursued in the late 1980s, albeit unsuccessfully negotiated. In April 1990, a former NWT commissioner was appointed to act as mediator in the boundary dispute, followed by one year of negotiations. In April 1991, the Inuit and Dene representatives recommended the proposed compromise border and, in a plebiscite held May 4, 1992, the majority (54 percent) of NWT residents approved the proposal.

Following the 1982 plebiscite, work began on a structured proposal intended to assist in the creation of a new government to be known as the Nunavut Territory. The Constitutional Alliance of the Northwest Territories (CA) was formed in 1982. Following dissemination of the plebiscite results, the CA created two forums intended to provide for debate and planning: the Nunavut Constitutional Forum (NCF) was established for the eastern arctic and the Western Constitutional Forum (WCF) for the western arctic. Anticipating significant revenues resulting from mineral extraction, the Tunngavik Federation of Nunavut (TFN) was established to succeed the ITC in 1982 and was now responsible to pursue land claims negotiations on behalf of the Inuits of Nunavut. Within one year of replacing the TFN, the NCI had drafted a comprehensive working proposal, entitled "Building Nunavut." A revised and expanded edition followed two years later.

The negotiations yielded early successes, and agreements were reached concerning the Inuits' role in wildlife management, on offshore rights, and on a resource management system that involved Inuit decision-making powers. Perhaps the most difficult component of the negotiations concerned the creation of a territorial boundary that everyone could agree on. There were overlapping areas in the central part of the territory where both the Inuits, who lived primarily in the eastern Arctic, and the Dene-Métis, who occupied the western Arctic, claimed traditional rights. In 1985, a tentative agreement was reached by the NCF and WCF that collapsed when the Dene-Métis refused to ratify it. Finally, John Parker, former NWT commissioner, was appointed to decide on a boundary in 1991. His proposed line was also disputed but later adopted in a territory-wide plebiscite. Even with a boundary in place, other questions remained. From the beginning, the Inuits were clear in their desire to see Nunavut and its government incorporated directly into the claims agreement. Federal officials were also clear in expressing their opinion that the land claims process was an inappropriate forum by which to create a public government that was meant to serve all people, including a non-Native minority. A compromise was reached that resulted in a caveat placed in the claim that would provide for the creation of the new territory without actually making division part of the claim.

A decade-long negotiations process took place, during which time myriad subagreements were reached and the creation of Nunavut became ever more a reality. Then, in 1985, the Coolican Task Force Report was released, leading to a revised federal land claims policy. The new policy recognized aboriginal decision-making powers for joint management boards, resource-sharing revenue, and inclusion of off shore areas. The Inuits were pleased, as were the various Inuit organizations involved in the negotiations. That same year, the final report of the Royal Commission on the Economic Union and Development Prospects for Canada was released, recommending that the creation of a new territory in the Eastern Arctic would make Canada's north "more governable." The commissioners also believed that a new territory would better accommodate different rates of political and constitutional development occurring. In the wake of a new land claims policy and the Royal Commission, the Inuit negotiators strengthened their resolve and refused to accept any federal offer that did not result in the creation of a separate Inuit territory. The federal government realized that this was a sticking point and made the decision to pursue the final land claim with the promise that a new Inuit territory would be established. This agreement was formalized in the Nunavut Political Accord, signed in April 1990 by the Canadian government, the NWT government,

and the Inuit negotiating body, the Tungavik Federation of Nunavut (TFN).

Although not directly involved in the Nunavut proposal, the Inuits from Inuvialuit who chose to break away from the Nunavut process in 1976 to settle their land claims did at times influence negotiations. Intense pressure from impending economic development initiatives led the Inuvialuit to settle the first comprehensive land claim settlement in the NWT with the government of Canada. Working together, Canada, the Dene, the Métis, and the Inuvialuit established the Iqaluit Agreement, which assigned the Inuvialuit surface ownership rights to 60,000 square miles of land as well as certain subsurface rights to another 8,000 square miles of land. The agreement afforded the Inuvialuit special harvesting rights, environmental protection, their participation in a number of comanagement regimes, federal support for economic development initiatives, and the establishment of a social development fund. Financial compensation in the amount of $45 million was paid to the Inuvialuit in annual installments until 1997. The final land claim notwithstanding, the Inuvialuit had to be consulted as the Nunavut process moved forward. This was followed by a proposal that the proposed boundary of Nunavut based on the Inuit land claim settlement area and the Dene/Métis and Inuvialuit claim settlement areas form the western territory. The Dene nation and Métis Association of the NWT did not reach an agreement with the TFN concerning the precise boundary of their respective claims areas; hence the Parker boundary.

Following years of negotiations, an agreement in principle was reached in 1990, and a single-line boundary between the claims settlement areas of the Dene/Métis and the Inuits was accepted in the 1992 plebiscite. The Government of the Northwest Territories (GNWT), the TFN, and the Canadian government adopted the boundary for division in the Nunavut Political Accord. In December 1991, negotiations were finalized and the final agreement committed Canada, the GNWT, and TFN to negotiate a political accord to deal with powers, principles of financing, and timing for the establishment of a distinct Nunavut government. The Inuit referendum was held November 3–5, 1992, with 69 percent voting in favor of the proposed land claims agreement. The agreement was also successfully passed through Parliament, received Royal Assent, and, on July 9, 1993, an order-in-council was prepared, realizing the agreement. Federal, territorial, and Inuit representatives signed the land claim agreement on May 25, 1993, which enabled the transfer of more than $1.1 billion to the Inuits.

The land claim was ratified and enacted by the Canadian Parliament in two pieces of legislation: the Nunavut Land Claims Agreement Act, ratifying the settlement, and the Nunavut Act, establishing Nunavut as a territory as well as enabling its government. In the six months following the Nunavut Act, the recently created Nunavut Implementation Commission worked with the federal government and various Inuit organizations to develop recommendations about the proposed locations of Nunavut's capital, the administrative structures of government, and the operating procedures for the Nunavut Legislative Assembly. Operating at an annual cost of $3 million, the commission ran until 1999. The Commission's final hundred-page report was divided into fourteen sections and made 104 recommendations concerning the political structures of the government of Nunavut.

The land claim settlement is the largest land claim in Canadian history. The 1993 agreement gives the Inuit territorial ownership to 220,000 square miles of land, mineral rights to about one-tenth of the area, and a financial settlement of $1 billion to be paid out over fourteen years. As part of the deal, the Inuits agreed to abandon their claims to all other northern lands. Under the Nunavut Act, the territory of Nunavut is designated as a 1.2-million-square-mile parcel of land that is separate from the NWT. Nunavut has the same territorial powers and responsibilities as the NWT; however, because the Inuits make up 85 percent of the population, Native interests dominate territorial governance (Légaré, 2003, 119).

Some of the more outstanding features of the agreement include:

- Title to approximately 220,000 square miles of land, of which about 22,000 square miles include mineral rights.
- Equal representation of Inuit within government on a new set of wildlife management, resource management, and environmental boards.
- The right to harvest wildlife on lands and waters throughout the Nunavut settlement area.
- Capital transfer payments of $1.148 billion, payable to the Inuits over fourteen years.
- A $13 million Training Trust Fund.

- A share of federal government royalties for Nunavut Inuits from oil, gas, and mineral development on Crown lands.
- Where Inuits own surface title to the land, the right to negotiate with industry for economic and social benefits with nonrenewable resource development.
- The right of first refusal on sport and commercial development of renewable resources in the Nunavut Settlement Area.
- The creation of three federally funded national parks.
- The inclusion of a political accord that provides for the establishment of the new Territory of Nunavut and through this a form of self-government for the Nunavut Inuit.

In 1995, Iqaluit was chosen over Rankin Inlet as Nunavut's capital city, and during the next four years, federal and territorial officials worked toward establishing Nunavut's government. Recognizing that the process would take some time, the federal government appointed Jack Anawak to serve as interim Commissioner of Nunavut responsible for establishing a functional government for Nunavut's official entry into Confederation. In 1998, amendments to the Nunavut Act were adopted by Parliament and received Royal Assent and, on February 15, Nunavut residents went to the polls to elect nineteen members to the new Legislative Assembly. On April 1, 1999, Nunavut and its new government were constituted, followed by the unveiling of the Nunavut flag and coat of arms. Once Nunavut's residents elect the Members of the Legislative Assembly (MLAs), the latter hold a secret ballot to elect a speaker of the assembly to oversee operations. The MLAs also elect by secret ballot the premier of Nunavut, as well as the executive (cabinet). Nunavut's government has ten departments, each headed by a minister. MLAs lacking ministerial portfolios form the opposition. Territorial elections are held every five years by popular vote, and one member of parliament (MP) and one senator represent Nunavut federally.

The federal government, according to a five-year formula financing agreement, funds Nunavut operations. The remainder of the budgeted operations is funded through taxation and the sale of goods and services. The inaugural allocation for the 1999–2000 governmental budget was $620 million, of which $580 million was allocated to cover the costs of programs and services.

The government of Nunavut conducts the majority of its business in Inuktitut, the language of the Inuit. Nunavut's other official languages are English and French. The government of Nunavut is decentralized, and the nearly 700 headquarters staffers are divided among Iqaluit, the capital of Nunavut, and ten other communities. Iqaluit is home to the ministerial, policy and planning, financial administration, and personnel-related functions of the government of Nunavut's other departments. Decentralizing was anticipated to provide Nunavut's three regions equal decision-making authority and to extend new jobs to as many areas as possible.

The more than $1.1 billion dollars in compensation money will pass from the federal government to the people of Nunavut over fourteen years, ending in 2007. This money is managed by the NTI (replacing the TFN), a highly centralized organization comprised of a General Assembly consisting of forty-eight delegates held annually, a ten-member Board of Directors that meets quarterly, and an Executive Committee that meets monthly. The General Assembly approves the annual budget, can increase or restrict spending, and can modify its programs and services, the latter of which must be approved by two-thirds of the delegates. The Board of Directors meets to review and evaluate the Executive Committee's decisions. Six of the ten board members come from Regional Inuit Associations, which gives significant weight to regional interests within the board. The Executive Committee is the most powerful cog in the machine. The Inuit beneficiaries elect the four-member committee that meets monthly to implement the decisions approved by the General assembly, while supervising the NTI's day-to-day operations (Légaré, 2003, 120–123).

The NLCA extends to various components of Nunavut's political economy, which includes its role in organizing territorial capital. The NLCA provides for representative hiring of Inuits within government, it outlines preferential procurement policies by the federal and territorial governments for Inuit firms, it specifies an Inuit Impact and Benefit Agreement be performed prior to implementing major development projects, and it affords greater Inuit control over natural resources and the right to harvest. Nunavut is a public government that provides the Inuit with political influence, because they constitute approximately 85 percent of the territorial population. The government of Nunavut incorporates Inuit values and beliefs into a public government model.

Yale D. Belanger

See also Canada, Indian policies of; Land; Royal Commission on Aboriginal Peoples; Tunkavik Federation, Nunavut.

References and Further Reading

Dahl, Jens, Jack Hicks, and Peter Jull, eds. 2000. *Nunavut: Inuit Regain Control of the Lands and Their Lives.* Copenhagen, Denmark: International Work Group for Indigenous Affairs.

Légaré, André. 1996. "The Process Leading to a Land Claims Agreement and Its Implementation: The Case of the Nunavut Land Claims Settlement." *Canadian Journal of Native Studies* 16, no. 1: 139–163.

Légaré, André. 1997. "The Government of Nunavut (1999): A Prospective Analysis." In *First Nations in Canada: Perspectives on Opportunity, Empowerment, and Self-determination.* Edited by J. Rick Ponting, 404–432. Toronto: McGraw-Hill Ryerson

Légaré, André. 2003. "The Nunavut Tunngavik Inc.: An Examination of Its Mode of Operation and Its Activities."In *Natural Resources and Aboriginal People in Canada: Readings, Cases, and Commentary.* Edited by Robert B. Anderson and Robert M. Bone, 117–137. Concord, ON: Captus Press.

McPherson, Robert. 2005. *New Owners in Their Own Land: Minerals and Inuit Land Claims,* 3rd ed. Calgary, AB: University of Calgary Press.

Oliphant v. Suquamish Indian Tribe

Oliphant v. Suquamish Indian Tribe was a landmark U.S. Supreme Court decision that eroded the legal standing of tribal governments' sovereignty. The far-reaching effects of the verdict's precedent are still being clarified today. Justice William Rehnquist authored the decision, a six-to-two split, arguing that tribal governments have no jurisdiction over non-Indians who commit crimes on their lands.

The two crimes instigating the litigation both occurred in the 7,276-acre Suquamish Port Madison Reservation across Puget Sound west of Seattle. The annual celebration of Chief Seattle Days on the reservation had become a popular event for non-Indians. The Suquamish petitioned state, county, and federal law enforcement officers for assistance in dealing with the thousands of visitors who attended. They were told to create their own enforcement using their own resources (Wilkins, 1997, 190).

On August 19, 1973, during the Chief Seattle Days celebration, Mark David Oliphant assaulted a member of the tribal police. He then resisted arrest and was summarily detained. Oliphant sought a writ of habeas corpus in the U.S. District Court for the Western District of Washington, maintaining that the authorities of the Suquamish Port Madison Reservation were not qualified authorities of the U.S. government and his civil rights had been violated. Oliphant lost the case. The case was appealed, as *Oliphant v. Schlie,* to the Ninth Circuit Court of Appeals, which also ruled against Oliphant. The lawyers for the tribe were quite surprised when, in 1978, the Supreme Court agreed to hear the case.

On August 12, 1974, the second petitioner in *Oliphant v. Suquamish Indian Tribe,* Daniel B. Belgarde, was charged with a high-speed highway chase that ended when he lost control of his vehicle and collided with a tribal police vehicle. He was detained, posted bail, and was allowed to leave. Nearly a week later, proceedings began against him for violating the tribal code and damaging tribal property. The tribal court proceedings were postponed pending a final decision of jurisdiction in *Oliphant v. Suquamish Indian Tribe.*

The Supreme Court ruled against the Suquamish. A majority of the judges used the legal justification that improper execution of habeas corpus was a violation of the Fourteenth Amendment. They stated that habeas corpus was improperly executed because the Suquamish tribal authorities lacked the specific written jurisdiction to detain non-Indians. Other rationales for lack of jurisdiction cited by Justice Rehnquist were that nineteenth-century congressional acts reflected a belief that tribes did not have "jurisdiction absent a congressional statute or treaty provision to that effect" (435 U.S. 191).

Rehnquist's reading of the Treaty of Point Elliot between the United States and Suquamish found no treaty language to guarantee the right to try non-Indians who commit crimes on treaty lands. Justice Rehnquist justified his decision for limited tribal sovereignty by citing a case in which the Choctaw nation requested from Congress the prerogative to punish non-Indians who entered their territory and committed crimes. Because the Choctaw treaty language concretely delineated this right, Rehnquist argued that by default most tribes were understood to lack this power (Wildenthal, 2003, 74–75).

Justice Thurgood Marshall, joined by Chief Justice Warren E. Burger, dissented from the majority opinion. Their rationale was that, without concrete treaty language specifically denying it, the right to keep the peace is "a *sine qua non* [essential quality] of the sovereignty that the Suquamish originally possessed" (435 U.S. 191, 213). This was the same rationale for the federal district court's ruling against Oliphant, which Justice Marshall cited in his written dissent.

Suquamish tribal lawyers were mystified by the legal logic of decision. One of these lawyers explained their opinion by quipping, "petitioner [Oliphant] takes the novel position that since his race differs from that of the government controlling the land on which he committed his offense, he is immune from prosecution by that government" (Wilkins, 1997, 194).

The ramifications of this decision reshaped the status of tribal governments' jurisdiction on reservations, as well as interpretations of Chief Justice John Marshall's famous reference to "domestic dependent nations" in *Cherokee Nation v. Georgia* (30 US 1 [1831]). The larger legal issue at contention in *Oliphant v. Suquamish Indian Tribe* was the precise legal parameters of a "domestic dependent nation" and the extent of its sovereignty. The Suquamish Port Madison Reservation had a population of only roughly 100 tribal members at the time of the decision. The small size of the reservation and the lack of many legal precedents in its history perhaps made this case an odd choice for the Supreme Court to review as indicative of the larger legal issue at stake. Several experts in law and tribal sovereignty agree that *Oliphant* was a poor case for asserting a tribal government's right to try criminals who commit crimes on their lands. The outcome of the case might have been different if it had involved a larger reservation with greater lands and population and a greater history of case law precedent, such as the Navajo Nation (Wildenthal, 2003, 77).

In 1973, the Suquamish tribal government established a Law and Order Code. The Code, which covered a spectrum of offenses from theft to rape, extended the Suquamish tribal government's criminal jurisdiction over Indians and non-Indians alike. The Suquamish Law and Order Code was held to be invalid for non-Indians because it provided similar but not identical protections to those guaranteed under the Constitution.

Yet, Rehnquist was adamant in his decision that he was arbitrating a case that protects encroachment on U.S. citizens' rights. The equal, if complex, U.S. citizenship of every American Indian appears absent from his legal logic.

Many advocates of tribal sovereignty were struck with disbelief by the decisions of *Oliphant v. Suquamish Indian Tribe* (1978) and *Duro v. Reina* (1990). Historically, the Supreme Court had shown a strong tendency to uphold the regulatory authority of tribal governments. The legal jurisdiction of such things as economic matters, land use, zoning, the environment, and family law had been consistently ruled as the domain of tribal governments (Wildenthal, 2003, 85).

The 1960s and the 1970s were times of great political activism as well as legal upheaval in Native–federal relations. Events such as the 1969 occupation of Alcatraz, and the 1973 occupation of Wounded Knee were coupled with unprecedented legal victories and rights secured from the executive, legislative, and judicial branches of U.S. government. These legal victories and new rights created resentment in certain circles of government. David Wilkins suggests that the *Oliphant* decision can be seen as a backlash among disaffected non-Indians against these legal victories secured in the previous decades (Wilkins, 1997, 186). This resentment is discernable in the comments by the vice chair of a congressional review commission on American Indian policy, a representative from the state of Washington, Lloyd Meeds. "'American Indian tribes are not a third set of governments in the American Federal system. They are not sovereign. The Congress of the United States has permitted them to be self-governing entities but not entities which would govern others. . . . [E]ven if *Oliphant* is upheld by the United States Supreme Court, the Congress must still decide whether Indian power over non-Indians is wise" (U.S. Congress, 1977, 587).

Two later decisions impacted by *Oliphant* also merit discussion. In *Duro v. Reina* (495 U.S. 676 [1990]), the U.S. Supreme Court considered whether tribal government jurisdiction was applicable to an American Indian who committed a crime on a reservation where the defendant was not a member. Justice Anthony M. Kennedy authored the decision, which found that tribal governments do not have the right to prosecute a nonmember Indian. Yet he upheld that tribal governments could eject whomever they chose from their lands. In *Means v. Chinle District Court* (1999) the well-known Indian activist Russell Means was prosecuted by the Navajo Nation for a crime he committed on their reservation. Means held that, under federal precedents *Oliphant* and *Duro,* he could not be prosecuted by a tribal government. Yet despite these precedents and

because the Navajo Nation's Supreme Court took a broad interpretation of the Navajo–United States Treaty of 1868, Means's case was rejected. Navajo Chief Justice Robert Yazzie ruled that the language of this treaty and Means's in-law relationship to the Navajo Nation allowed him to reject the precedent of *Oliphant* and *Duro* in this decision. Whether this represents groundwork for a potential reexamination of *Oliphant* at a later date remains to be seen.

Samuel Morgan

See also Occupation of Alcatraz Island; *Cherokee Nation v. Georgia;* Tribal Sovereignty.

References and Further Reading

Oliphant v. Suquamish Indian Tribe Et Al. 1978. 435 U.S. Reports 191–213.

Royster, Judith V. 2003. "Oliphant and Its Discontents: An Essay Introducing the Case for Reargument Before the American Indian Nations Supreme Court." *Kansas Journal of Law & Public Policy* 13: 59–68.

U.S. Congress. 1977. "*Final Report: American Indian Policy Review Commission.* Washington, DC: Government Printing Office. [Quoted in David E. Wilkins, *American Indian Sovereignty and the U.S. Supreme Court: The Masking of Justice* (Austin: University of Texas Press, 1997), 188–189.]

Wildenthal, Bryan H. 2003. *Native American Sovereignty on Trial.* Santa Barbara, CA.: ABC-CLIO.

Wilkins, David E. 1997. *American Indian Sovereignty and the U.S. Supreme Court: The Masking of Justice.* Austin: University of Texas Press.

Plenary Power

Its name derived from the Latin term *plenus,* meaning "full," plenary power is the full, complete, and unlimited power of Congress as granted under the Constitution. In practical terms, this power allows Congress to pass laws, levy taxes, wage wars, and hold in custody offenders of U.S. law. Although plenary power was intimated and exercised through earlier court cases, the Supreme Court first used the term in *Gibbons v. Ogden,* where the power of Congress to regulate interstate and foreign commerce was upheld (Wilkins and Lomawaima, 2001, 102). Many scholars view the exercise of such expansive federal power against the right of every citizen for equal protection under the law as the central tension of the U.S. government.

Legal scholar Nicholas Johnson argues that, while the "majoritarian perspective" typically views the "shifting boundary between rights and powers" as "unproblematic or even attractive" (i.e., as a sign of a reflective, organic democracy), the fluidity of this boundary is viewed differently from the minority perspective. He notes that critical race theorists have long critiqued this majoritarian perspective as a barrier to racial reform arguing, "the dilemma and danger for minorities is that plenary power tethered merely by majoritarian preferences and necessities leave minorities simply to gamble on the direction of future swings in the mood of the majority" (Johnson, 1996, 1556). Johnson's cogent critique of the implications of both fettered and unfettered plenary power for "minorities" seems particularly relevant to the impact of plenary power on American Indians.

While the exercise of plenary power in Indian affairs introduces the same rights–power paradox found in "minority affairs" discussed by Johnson (1996), there is an important difference: The pre- and extraconstitutional status of tribes places them outside the constitutionally defined "rights" discourse as it applies to states and enfranchised individuals (Wilkins, 1994, 355). As Wilkins notes, "the Bill of Rights . . . does not protect tribes or their members from congressional actions aimed at reducing tribal sovereignty, political rights, or aboriginal Indian lands" (1994, 354). Rather, the paradox for Indian tribes emerges through the tension between plenary power and sovereignty. American Indians exist in the precarious space between the congressional claim of an absolute and unlimited plenary power and treaty-defined rights to sovereignty that are greater than those of states but less than those of external nations. This tension is understood and theorized in American Indian law and policy as the concept of "irreconcilability" introduced by Ball (1987) in the seminal article, "Constitution, Court, Indian Tribes." He writes:

> [W]e claim that the Constitution, and the laws of the United States which shall be the supreme law of the land. But we also claim to recognize the sovereignty of Native American Nations, the original occupants of the land. These claims—one to jurisdictional monopoly, the other to jurisdictional multiplicity—are irreconcilable (Ball, 1987, 3).

Though they recognize the significance of this tension, Wilkins and Lomawaima (2001) maintain that this so-called irreconcilability remains only

when one presumes an unlimited and absolute definition of plenary power, begging the question: What is the actual extent of congressional power over Indian tribes?

Deloria and Lytle (1983) identify two sources of congressional power over Indian affairs: (1) Article I, Section 8, of the Constitution, which stipulates that Congress shall have the power to "regulate commerce with foreign nations . . . states . . . and *with* the Indian tribes," [emphasis added], and (2) the "guardianship theory," first suggested by Justice John Marshall in the landmark cases of *Johnson v. McIntosh* and *Cherokee Nation v. Georgia*, and subsequently conscripted into law by Justice Miller in *United States v. Kagama*. Deloria and Lytle contend, "taken together, these sources of power provide Congress with an almost omnipotent control over Indians" (1983, 40).

In contradistinction to this position, Wilkins and Lomawaima (2001) maintain that nothing in the Constitution provides for congressional power over tribes. They argue that the commerce clause empowers Congress only to regulate *in relation with* tribes, not over them. Also, instead of the "guardianship theory" cited by Deloria and Lytle, Wilkins and Lomawaima cite the treaty clause (Article 2, Section 2, cl. 2) as the most relevant source of congressional power. They maintain that, even though there is no explicit mention of tribes in the treaty clause, an implicit right operates since treaties "were the principal mechanism that linked tribes and the federal government," a right that also distinguishes tribes from states (Wilkins and Lomawaima, 2001, 103). In addition to differences regarding the appropriate sources and scope of congressional power, Wilkins (1994) notes that there is considerable disagreement among scholars over whether plenary power is a necessary power that protects tribes or a patently antidemocratic practice that represents an abuse of power.

To investigate the matter further, Wilkins reviewed 107 federal court cases involving plenary power between 1886 and 1914—the period in American history when plenary power was exercised in the "most virulent and unabashed form" (Wilkins 1994, 350). Through this comprehensive study, Wilkins found three major categories of interpretation and practice regarding plenary power: (1) absolute, (2) exclusive, and, (3) preemptive. *Exclusive plenary power* refers to the exclusive legislative power of Congress to engage in treaty making with tribes or to recognize particular rights that Indians have been deprived because of their extraconstitutional standing (Wilkins, 1994, 354, 355). *Absolute plenary power* refers to the exercise of power not limited by other textual constitutional provisions or other congressional objectives. *Preemptive power* is the congressional exercise of power that may preempt or supersede state law.

The era of plenary power examined by Wilkins commenced in 1886 with the Supreme Court's decision in *United States v. Kagama*. In this case, the defendant challenged the constitutionality of the Seven Major Crimes Act (23 Stat., 362, 385 [1885]), which authorized federal jurisdiction over "major crimes" (e.g., murder, rape, arson) in Indian Country. Despite the complete lack of constitutional authority, the Court ruled against Kagama, confirming federal jurisdiction over major crimes in Indian Country. The decision read:

> [T]hese Indians are within the geographical limits of the United States. The soil and people within these limits are under the political control of the Government of the United States, or of the States of the Union . . . What authority the State governments may have to enact criminal laws for the Indians will be presently considered. But the power to organize territorial governments, and make laws for their inhabitants, arises not so much from . . . [the Commerce clause but] . . . from the ownership of the country in which the Territories are, and the right of exclusive sovereignty which must exist in the National Government, and can be found nowhere else (*United States v. Kagama*, 1885).

Wilkins and Lomawaima (2001) delineate several errors inherent in this analysis. Most notably, they cite the irrational logic exemplified by the Court's use of extraconstitutional and/or extralegal constructs (i.e., Doctrine of Discovery, wardship, and dependency) while completely disregarding the extraconstitutional status of Indian tribes, who, as internal sovereigns, were neither governed nor protected by the constitution.

The inauspicious introduction of absolute plenary power is offset by the last case of the era—*Perrin v. United States*—which intimates an end to such unlimited and abuses of power. The case involved the sale of liquor on lands ceded to South Dakota by the Yankton Sioux by a treaty in 1894. Pursuant to this agreement, the chiefs forbid the sale of any liquor on ceded lands. After the cession, the U.S. government challenged the tribes' authority to enforce the terms of this agreement. In a change of tide, the Court upheld this initial provision, finding that plenary power should "not go beyond what is reasonably essential for [the protection of tribes], and that, to be effective, its exercise must not be purely arbitrary but founded on some reasonable basis." Deloria and Lytle explain the decision as follows:

> [The Court held that] the presence of Indians, with a peculiar status and a negotiated consideration for the cession of their lands, imposed a unique federal servitude on these lands so that, even though they were not wholly within the jurisdiction of South Dakota insofar as location, private title, and political independence from the federal government, they nevertheless were federal lands for the purposes described and would remain so until an affirmative congressional enactment released them from this servitude (1983, 73, 74).

Wilkins (1994) notes, however, that, while Perrin represents a victory of sorts, the Court still deferred to Congress to determine what counts as an "arbitrary" and/or "reasonable" basis for decision making.

Kagama and *Perrin* demarcate the beginning and end of an era when plenary power was interpreted in as many different ways as there were court cases. In the final analysis, the majority of scholars view both the preemptive and exclusive exercise of plenary power as authorized under the Constitution but criticize the absolute interpretations of plenary power as "fundamentally wrong" and in "violation of the treaty and trust relationship between the United States and Indian tribes" (Wilkins and Lomawaima, 2001, 115). Consequently, Wilkins and Lomawaima call for the U.S. government to honor the Constitution and treaty relationships and "resolve to use plenary power only in its exclusive and preemptive senses and explicitly . . . reject and renounce the unlimited/absolute definition as a violation of the democratic principles of enumerated powers, limited government, consent of the governed and the rule of law" (Wilkins and Lomawaima, 2001, 116).

Sandy Grande

See also *Lone Wolf v. Hitchcock; United States v. Kagama.*

References and Further Reading

Ball, Milner S. 1987. "Constitution, Court, Indian Tribes." *American Bar Foundation Research Journal* 1: 1–39.

Cherokee Nation v. Georgia 30 U.S. (5 Pet.) 1 (1831).

Deloria, Vine, Jr., and Clifford M. Lytle. 1983. *American Indians, American Justice.* Austin: University of Texas Press.

Gibbons v. Ogden 22 U.S. (9 Wheat.) 1 (1824).

Johnson v. McIntosh 21 U.S. (8 Wheat.) 543 (1823).

Perrin v. United States 232 U.S. 478)1914).

United States v. Kagama (118 U.S. 375 (1886).

Wilkins, David E. 1994. "The U.S. Supreme Court's Explication of 'Federal Plenary Power': An Analysis of Case Law Affecting Tribal Sovereignty, 1886–1814." *American Indian Quarterly* 18, no. 3: 349–368.

Wilkins, David E., and K. Tsianina Lomawaima. 2001. *Uneven Ground: American Indian Sovereignty and Federal Law.* Norman: University of Oklahoma Press.

Praying Villages of Massachusetts

Beginning in 1651, the Massachusetts Bay colony embarked on a mission to "civilize" and Christianize the Native peoples of New England. They attempted to accomplish this through the establishment of what came to be known as praying villages or praying towns. Many historians believe that these early settlements set the precedent for the reservation system, which came into prominence nearly 200 years later.

From the time it received its charter in 1629, one of the primary goals of the Massachusetts Bay Company was to spread Christianity and English culture. Indeed, the colony's original seal featured an Indian and the motto, "Come Over and Help Us." In the colony's formative years, however, there was little missionary activity. The Puritan settlers were more interested in simply subsisting and carving out a viable colony. Furthermore, they had first to consolidate their power and establish military dominance in the region, which was more or less accomplished after the Pequot War of 1637 and the submission of the Massachusett Indians in the mid-1640s.

In 1646, John Eliot began a rigorous campaign of proselytizing to the tribes of New England, including the Massachusett, Nipmuck, Pawtucket, and the Pennacook Confederacy. The success of this initial foray was limited, leading Eliot and the colony's leadership to believe that the Indians first had to be immersed in English culture before they could be converted. To accomplish this, they established protoreservations, or praying villages, where the Native people could be isolated and taught European customs. The first such village was Natick, which was soon followed by numerous others. By the outbreak of King Philip's War in 1675, there were fourteen such missions.

The Massachusetts Bay government set land aside for the praying villages and maintained control over them. Each reservation was laid out in an orderly manner, with English-style structures and streets spread across the village. The Native inhabitants also followed European subsistence patterns, tilling the surrounding fields and tending to livestock. In terms of government, the villages' adult male populations elected their own local leaders and drafted legislation. All laws and ordinances passed by the villagers, however, were subject to the approval of a superintendent who was appointed by the Massachusetts Bay General Court.

A staunch assimilationist, John Eliot insisted that the villages' inhabitants throw off their Indian culture. Native dress and religion, tribalism, polygamy, and powwows were strictly prohibited, while the European conception of private property was hammered home. A system of punishments and incentives was enacted: Those who transgressed or violated the villages' codes were fined; those who exhibited "good" behavior and made progress in adopting white ways were rewarded. This crash course in "civilization" was followed by a relentless effort to Christianize the Indians. Eliot worked with Indian converts to translate the Bible into Algonquian. He also wrote *The Indian Primer* and other texts outlining the cornerstones of Puritanical theology.

The success of the praying villages was limited. Most New England Indians shunned the missions and opted to keep their distance from the intruding non-Native world. The minority who did join the villages were from the most weakened tribes, such as the Massachusetts and Nipmucks. Their world had been decimated by disease and the English conquest of their lands. For these "praying Indians," the adoption of European culture seemed to be the only alternative. Nevertheless, despite the best efforts of Eliot and others, they remained caught between Puritan society and their former tribes, never fully accepted by either.

When King Philip's War broke out in 1675, many of the Indians in the praying villages sided with the

Wampanoag sachem, Metacom (King Philip), and his pan-Indian alliance. Others remained neutral or even fought alongside the colonists. Regardless of where they stood in the conflict, all New England Indians lost out once the war came to an end in 1676. Most of those who survived the bloody ordeal were pushed out of their traditional lands and summarily shipped off to isolated reservations or the West Indies. The colony's General Court eliminated all but three praying villages. The villages that remained were overrun and eventually absorbed by land-hungry whites in a few years. By the turn of the century, Eliot's initial experiment of assimilation and Christianization was just a fading memory.

Bradley Shreve

See also Assimilation; Metacom and King Philip's War.

References and Further Reading

Gookin, Daniel. [1674] 1970. *Historical Collections of the Indians in New England.* Spencer, MA: Towtaid Press.

Morrison, Kenneth M. 1974. " 'That Art of Coyning Christians:' John Eliot and the Praying Indians of Massachusetts." *Ethnohistory* 21, no. 1: 77–92.

Salisbury, Neal. 1974. "Red Puritans: The 'Praying Indians' of Massachusetts Bay and John Eliot." *The William and Mary Quarterly* 31, no. 1: 27–54.

Pyramid Lake Paiute Tribe v. Morton

The case of *Pyramid Lake Paiute Tribe v. Morton* brought to the courts' attention the fact that not all cases regarding Indian water policy necessarily involved water for agriculture. Early in the twentieth century, the Winters doctrine had set out the principle that Indian tribes had a reserved right to enough water to fulfill the purpose of their reservation, but that purpose had been almost exclusively defined by subsequent court decisions and Bureau of Indian Affairs policy as irrigated agriculture. Irrigation also was foremost in the minds of officials of the Bureau of Reclamation as they sought to develop the West's water resources for the benefit of non-Indian farmers.

In 1902, passage of the Reclamation Act, sponsored by Congressman Francis Newlands of Nevada, began the modern age of western water development. The first project funded by the new apparatus, devised by and named after Newlands

himself, was the first case in the new century in which Indians had to deal with a massive loss of water rights due to non-Indian water development (Wilkinson, 1992). The construction of the Newlands Reclamation Project in California's Central Valley, the first large-scale attempt by the federal government to subsidize irrigated agriculture in the West, involved diverting much of the area's water, including that of Pyramid Lake in Nevada, which is sacred to the Pyramid Lake Paiutes. Pyramid Lake, completely within the tribe's reservation boundaries and the source of their livelihood by fishing, became a shadow of its former self. The Newlands Project also entailed an immense construction on the Truckee River near Fallon, Nevada. The original proposal intended to divert the waters of the Carson River to feed the project, but, when those waters proved insufficient, reclamation officials turned their eyes toward the Truckee.

The construction of Derby Dam, about thirty-five miles upstream from Pyramid Lake, reduced the river's flow by half, which both lowered the level of the lake by about seventy feet and permitted the buildup of silt. This led to an insufficient flow to prevent the salination of the lake, a factor in the death of the Lahontan cutthroat trout, the primary source of livelihood for the area's Paiutes. Consideration of the lake and its associated wetlands as resources in their own right, apart from agriculture, was not something the courts or the Department of the Interior were prepared to accept. By the late 1960s, the Secretary of the Interior issued regulations regarding how much water could be diverted from Pyramid Lake, but by that time the fishery and wetlands were so seriously damaged that it would take a complete change in course to restore the tribe's asset.

In the case of *Pyramid Lake Paiute Tribe v. Morton,* a federal district court ruled that the allocation of water by the Interior Department violated the government's trust responsibility toward the Indians (Fixico, 1988). The court cited the trust responsibility of the federal government as requiring it to protect Pyramid Lake for the use of the tribe. The case pointed out the often contradictory nature of government policy in the area of water rights. While one federal agency within the Department of the Interior, the Bureau of Reclamation, was developing non-Indian water resources with no attention to Indian needs, the Bureau of Indian Affairs was ineffectively "advocating" for those Indian needs. In the end, it took the cooperation of environmentalist groups, reacting in response to the highly toxic materials leached out as a by-product of Newlands irrigation, to get the diversions from the Truckee River reduced. Unfortunately, this has had the unfortunate side effect of concentrating the leached toxins in the water that remained.

After fourteen years of negotiations, the California–Nevada Interstate Water Compact was signed in 1968 to allocate waters in Lake Tahoe and the Truckee, Carson, and Walker River basins. The agreement served the interests of local water user groups in Nevada and California but infringed, once again, on the water rights of the Pyramid Lake Paiutes. Eventually, the compact of 1968 was amended. The California and Nevada state legislatures approved the new version in 1971, but Congress refused to ratify it (Haller, 1989). It was not until 1990 that parties in the region were able to reach agreement on the Truckee-Carson-Pyramid Lake Water Rights Settlement, which ensured enough water flow into Pyramid Lake to resurrect the damaged wetlands, which are so integral to the Pyramid Lake Paiute identity and lifeways.

Steven L. Danver

See also Water Rights; *Winters v. United States.*
References and Further Reading

Fixico, Donald L. 1988. *The Invasion of Indian Country in the Twentieth Century: American Capitalism and Tribal Natural Resources.* Boulder: University Press of Colorado.

Haller, Timothy G. 1989. "The Legislative Battle Over the California–Nevada Interstate Water Compact: A Question of Might Versus Native American Right." *Nevada Historical Society Quarterly* 32 no. 3.

Wilkinson, Charles F. 1992. *Crossing the Next Meridian: Land, Water, and the Future of the West.* Washington, DC: Island Press.

Radiation Exposure Compensation Act

The Radiation Exposure Compensation Act (RECA), passed by Congress in 1990, provides payments to people who contracted certain cancers and other serious diseases as a result of their exposure to radiation released during aboveground nuclear weapons tests or as the result of their exposure to radiation during employment in underground uranium mines in Arizona, Colorado, New Mexico, Utah, or Wyoming between 1947 and 1971. Many of the Native Americans, mostly Navajos, applying for aid have had their requests denied because of difficulties with the strict rules for aid.

The dangers of radiation were not well understood by the public during the early years of the Cold War, although uranium was discovered to be radioactive in 1896. Uranium is a naturally occurring, silvery-white metallic element that is needed to create nuclear fission. Exposure to radiation from uranium can occur in various ways. The breakdown of uranium products creates radon progeny. These can attach to dust particles and, if workers inhale the dust, the particles lodge in their lungs, where they release intense doses of radiation.

People working with uranium need protective clothing to shield their bodies from radiation damage that causes cancer and kidney damage. Additionally, exposure to various agents in the mining community, such as silica and other dusts, can cause nonmalignant respiratory diseases such as pulmonary fibrosis, corpulmonale related to fibrosis, silicosis, and pneumoconiosis. Until the 1970s, miners typically wore only short-sleeved T-shirts, denim pants, and helmets. In that decade, mine managers started taking some precautions against radiation exposure.

RECA designated responsibility for establishing regulations for the submission and payment of claims to the Attorney General. In May 1992, the Department of Justice began accepting claims and making payments. Navajo workers formed about a fourth of the workforce in the uranium mines and mills of western Colorado and New Mexico, eastern Utah, and Arizona. However, they have not received a fourth of RECA benefits.

A substantial number of Navajos do not have a strong command of English, preventing them from understanding the RECA law and applying for benefits. Additionally, RECA regulations have been criticized for being unnecessarily stringent and unreasonably burdensome. Workers were required to provide proof that they were exposed to specified minimum levels of radiation, set at 200 Working Level Months. There is no scientific evidence that workers who were exposed to less than 200 months of radiation are safe from radiation-related ailments.

Uranium workers experience lung cancer at a rate that is twenty-eight times the normal rate. Despite this, the first version of RECA excluded lung cancer patients if they smoked more than one pack of cigarette products per year. Even Navajos who used tobacco for ceremonial purposes thus were banned from receiving compensation. The government also required documentation of marital status for wives of miners to get benefits but only accepted state-issued marriage certificates. Many Navajos do not have such documents, preventing widows of uranium miners from collecting benefits. Compounding the anger of the uranium workers and their relatives, the federal government did not sufficiently fund RECA. A "downwinder" (a person exposed to radiation during aboveground nuclear tests) was designated to receive $50,000, an on-site participant in testing was awarded $75,000, and a uranium miner received $100,000. However, the federal government issued IOUs and partial payments instead of full cash payments to those who qualified for aid.

To lobby the government for assistance, the Navajos have formed a number of organizations, including Diné Citizens Against Ruining Our Environment, the Eastern Navajo Agency Uranium Workers, the Northern Arizona Navajo Downwinders, the Utah Navajo Downwinders, and the Navajo Nation Dependents of Uranium Workers. Women and children who lived in uranium camps with their miner husbands and fathers were also exposed to radiation. Many of the wives have developed cancers and respiratory problems. The children also suffer from a high rate of birth defects. In response to Navajo complaints, the federal government amended RECA in 2000 to add new claimant categories, provide additional compensable illnesses, lower the radiation exposure threshold, and remove lifestyle restrictions.

Caryn E. Neumann

See also Mining and Contemporary Environmental Problems; Uranium Mining.
References and Further Reading
Eichstaedt, Peter H., and Murrae Haynes. 1994. *If You Poison Us: Uranium and Native Americans.* Santa Fe, NM: Red Crane Books.
Gallagher, Carole. 1994. *American Ground Zero: The Secret Nuclear War.* New York: Random House.
Udall, Stewart. 1998. *The Myths of August: A Personal Exploration of Our Tragic Cold War Affair with the Atom.* Piscataway, NJ: Rutgers University Press.
United States Department of Energy. "Final Report of the Radiation Exposure Compensation Act Committee, July 1996." Available at: http://www.eh.doe.gov/ohre/roadmap/uranium. Accessed January 18, 2006.

Royal Commission on Aboriginal Peoples

In the wake of the Oka crisis of 1990, Prime Minister Brian Mulroney (Progressive Conservative) established the Royal Commission on Aboriginal Peoples (RCAP) in August 1991. What began as a dispute over the expansion of a municipal golf course onto sacred lands between the town of Oka and the Kahnesatake Mohawk Reserve resulted in a seventy-nine-day, $500-million standoff between the Mohawks, the Quebec Provincial Police, and the Canadian Armed Forces. Concerned that similar events could erupt in other parts of Canada, the prime minister approached former Chief Justice of the Supreme Court Brian Dickson to prepare a report to determine whether a royal commission on aboriginal affairs should be established to investigate the issues. While praising aboriginal leaders for their forthright interface with federal officials in their efforts to solve the myriad problems plaguing aboriginal communities, Dickson's final report indicated that most aboriginal people were frustrated and disappointed with their treatment at the hands of provincial and federal authorities. Dickson recommended creating a royal commission to deal specifically with aboriginal issues as a central component of the national agenda. Although the commission began with high hopes, time has revealed that it has failed to live up to its potential.

Dickson further recommended that the established commission of inquiry investigate the evolution of the relationship among aboriginal peoples (Indian, Inuit, and Métis), the Canadian government, and Canadian society as a whole, to examine any and all issues that it deemed relevant to any, or all, aboriginal peoples in Canada. It was expected also to propose specific solutions, rooted in domestic and international experience, to resolve the existing problems confronting aboriginal peoples. Following the establishment of the RCAP, commissioners and federal officials determined that the realities of aboriginal life also needed to be understood by all Canadians prior to the formulation of effective solutions and that, until this education process took place, the renewal of the relationship among the "partners in Confederation" would be overly complicated. In their attempts to establish an effective mandate, the commissioners sought guidance from, and met with, members of the Assembly of First Nations (AFN), the Native Council of Canada (NCC), the Métis National Council (MNC), the Inuit Tapirisat of Canada (ITC), the National Association of Friendship Centres, and the Native Women's Association of Canada (NWAC).

The RCAP commissioners included as co-chairs the Honorable Rene Dussault, Justice of the Quebec Court of Appeal, and Georges Erasmus, former grand chief of the Assembly of First Nations. Filling out the commission were Paul Chartrand, Métis lawyer and academic; the Honorable Bertha Wilson, the first woman appointee to the Supreme Court of Canada; Mary Sillett, founding member and former president of Paukktuutit, the Inuit Women's Association; Viola Robinson, former president of the Native Council of Canada; and Peter Meekison, academic and former deputy minister of Federal and Intergovernmental Affairs for the government of Alberta.

The RCAP was concerned with demythologizing an array of preconceived notions about aboriginal people in order to build a new relationship that would aid in the development of aboriginal self-government. This would help aboriginal people to regain control of the direction of their everyday lives. Commissioners traveled throughout Canada during the public consultation phase of the process. Gaining access to people was important. Commissioners especially wanted the RCAP to be easily accessible to those people wishing to participate from remote areas of Canada. As a result, four aboriginal languages were used, and a special telephone line was also established to help secure these opinions. In all, the RCAP met 100 times, had 178 days of hearings, recorded 76,000 pages of transcripts, generated 356 research studies, and published four special reports and two commentaries on self-government. It cost close to $60 million. The final report was a six-volume set consisting of 3,536 pages dealing with myriad issues as diverse as justice, land claims, relocation of the Inuit, and health, to name a few (Belanger and Newhouse, 2004, 165).

The RCAP's recommendations were guided by five key principles commissioners were certain could enable the rebuilding of aboriginal life in Canada: (1) Aboriginal nations have to be reconstituted; (2) a process must be established for the assumption of governing powers by aboriginal nations; (3) there must be a fundamental reallocation of lands and resources; (4) aboriginal people need education and crucial skills for governance and economic self-reliance; and (5) economic development (or lack thereof) must be addressed if the existing rates of poverty and despondency of lives defined by unemployment and welfare are to change. The commissioners envisaged a new Canadian partnership based on mutual recognition, one in which aboriginal and nonaboriginal people would "acknowledge and relate to one another as equals, co-existing side by side and governing themselves according to their own laws and institutions."

As such, a sizable body of literature was devoted to the exigencies of aboriginal self-government that included twenty-five regional case studies, each focusing on a specific aboriginal nation. Some aboriginal academics and politicians saw the RCAP vision as a pooling of existing sovereignties requiring the formation of these varied groups into a unified entity in order to exercise their right to self-government. In all, those who made presentations to the RCAP considered self-government as one of the most important issues facing Native communities today. The RCAP insisted that Canadians take a proactive role by first sincerely acknowledging the injustices of the past. They also stressed the need to forge a profound and unambiguous commitment to establishing a new relationship for the future.

The RCAP was in the midst of its public consultation phase when, in 1993, the Jean Chrétien–led Liberal Party ousted the Progressive Conservative (PC) party from office. Even though PC leader Mulroney commissioned the RCAP, Chrétien and the Liberals chose to see the RCAP to its final report. Published in 1996, the RCAP forcefully argued that the right of aboriginal peoples to govern themselves is recognized in both international and domestic law. The principles of mutual recognition, mutual respect, sharing, and mutual responsibility helped define "a process that can provide the solutions to many of the difficulties afflicting relations among Aboriginal and non-Aboriginal people . . . When taken in sequence, the four principles form a complete whole, each playing an equal role in developing a balanced societal relationship. Relations that embody these principles are, in the broadest sense of the word, partnerships."

In January 1998, the federal government issued its comprehensive policy response to the RCAP. Entitled *Gathering Strength: Canada's Aboriginal Action Plan*, the strategy set out a policy framework for future government action based on four objectives. Stressing the renewal of the aboriginal–Canadian relationship, the government followed with an apology for the residential school debacle and the establishment of a $350-million "healing fund" to address those abuses. *Gathering Strength* also promoted the preservation and promotion of aboriginal languages; the increased public understanding of aboriginal traditions and issues; the inclusion of aboriginal partners in policy and program design, development, and delivery; government willingness to explore how existing systems might be improved; and addressing the needs of urban aboriginal people more effectively. Some of the major recommendations included:

- Legislation, including a new Royal Proclamation stating Canada's commitment to a new relationship and companion legislation setting out a treaty process and recognition of aboriginal nations and governments.
- Recognition of an aboriginal order of government, subject to the Charter of Rights and Freedoms, with authority over matters related to the good government and welfare of aboriginal peoples and their territories.
- Replacement of the federal Department of Indian Affairs with two departments, one to implement the new relationship with aboriginal nations and one to provide services for nonself-governing communities.
- Creation of an aboriginal parliament.
- Expansion of the aboriginal land and resource base.

Of the 470 recommendations contained in the RCAP's final report, recommendations that were the most profound and comprehensive ever made by a royal commission concerning the structure and functioning of Canadian society, none have as yet been endorsed by the Liberals or operationalized by the Canadian government. To date, aboriginal leaders and academics regularly refer to the RCAP findings as innovative and progressive. Historically, several royal commissions have been struck to investigate Indian affairs in addition to numerous parliamentary committees. Nevertheless, one decade after its release, the RCAP report is in danger of becoming yet another missed opportunity to improve the relationship between the federal government and one of its "partners in Confederation."

Yale D. Belanger

See also Language and Language Renewal.

References and Further Reading

Belanger, Yale, and David Newhouse. 2004. "Emerging from the Shadows: The Pursuit of Aboriginal Self-Government to Promote Aboriginal Well-Being." *Canadian Journal of Native Studies* 24, no. 1: 129–222.

Castellano, Marlene. 1999. "Renewing the Relationship: A Perspective on the Impact of the Royal Commission on Aboriginal Peoples." In *AboriginalSelf-Government in Canada: Current Trends and Issues*. Edited by J. H. Hylton, 92–111. Saskatoon, SK: Purich Publishing.

Ponting, J. Rick. 1997. "Getting a Handle on the Recommendations of the Royal Commission on Aboriginal Peoples." In *First Nations in Canada:Perspectives on Opportunity, Empowerment, and Self-Determination*. Edited by J. Rick Ponting, 445–472. Toronto: McGraw-Hill Ryerson.

Royal Commission on Aboriginal Peoples (RCAP). 1996. *For Seven Generations: An Information Legacy of the Royal Commission on Aboriginal Peoples*. 6 volumes. Ottawa, ON: Queen's Printer.

Standing Bear v. Crook

The *Standing Bear vs. Crook* court case began with the last request of a dying son and ended with a groundbreaking legal decision. For the first time, Native Americans were considered human beings under U.S. law.

In 1877, the U.S. government told Chief Standing Bear (Machunazha) and his Poncas that they must move from their Nebraska reservation to the Indian Territory (Oklahoma). The government sent several tribal leaders to examine their new land, promising the Ponca that they could return to Nebraska if they were dissatisfied. The chiefs rejected the land as being barren, full of rocks, and unsuitable for farming. However, they were told they had no choice; the tribe was moving.

Many Ponca died en route. By the end of 1878, only 430 of the 710 Poncas who had been sent to the Indian Territory were still alive; the rest had been lost to starvation and disease. One of the last to die was Standing Bear's sixteen-year-old son. He asked that his body be buried with those of his ancestors. Standing Bear promised, and, in January 1879, he headed north with a small burial party. They traveled by hidden trails and reached the Omaha Indian Reservation before soldiers caught up with them.

Standing Bear, a Ponca chieftain, filed suit against U.S. policy which ultimately resulted in the United States legally recognizing Native Americans as human beings. (Library of Congress)

General George Crook was ordered to arrest and return the Ponca. When he saw them, Crook was saddened by their pitiable condition and impressed with their stoicism. He contacted the *Omaha Daily Herald*'s assistant editor, Thomas Henry Tibbles, and enlisted his help. Crook believed his removal order was cruel but felt powerless to do anything about it himself. He encouraged Tibbles to use his newspaper to " . . . fight against those who are robbing these helpless people" (Brown, 1970, 340–341).

Tibbles was able to enlist the help of two prominent attorneys, A. J. Poppleton and J. L. Webster. Using the Fourteenth Amendment as the basis of their case, they persuaded Judge Elmer S. Dundy to grant an application for a writ of habeas corpus. Webster quoted from the amendment, which states that all *persons* born or naturalized in the United States are citizens of the United States and cannot be deprived of life, liberty, or property without due

process of law. Webster inferred that the Indians must then be citizens since they were born "on our soil." "If they are not citizens," he said, "what are they? Are they wild animals, deer to be chased by every hound?" (*Omaha Herald*, 1879, 8).

The second day of the trial climaxed with Standing Bear's testimony: "You see me standing here. Where do you think I come from? From the water, the woods or where? God made me and he put me on my land. But, I was ordered to stand up and leave my land. . . ? When I got down there it seemed as if I was in a big fire. One-hundred and fifty-eight of my people were burned up; now I stand before you. I came away to save my wife and children and friends. I never want to go back there again. I want to go back to my old reservation to live there and be buried in the land of my fathers" (*Omaha Herald*, 1879, 8).

The trial ended with Judge Dundy declaring Standing Bear "a person under the law" and thus entitled to basic human rights (*Omaha Republican*, 1879, 1). When the news reached the Ponca still in Oklahoma, Standing Bear's brother, Big Snake, decided to test the law and headed north with thirty of his followers. However, Dundy had written the law to apply only in the case of Standing Bear, so orders were sent to arrest Big Snake. He was bayoneted and killed while resisting arrest.

The first attempt by Indians to fulfill the high hopes created by Judge Dundy's decision had ended in the tragic death of an innocent man. Standing Bear, who had started the entire process by his simple desire to return his dead son to the land of his birth, now had a brother to bury as well. It had only been a few months since newspapers across the country had called for citizenship rights for peaceful Indians, but it was not until 1924, forty-five years later, that those citizenship rights, which had seemed so attainable in the spring of 1879, would finally be given to the First Americans.

Hugh J. Reilly

See also Jackson, Helen Hunt; LaFlesche, Susette Tibbles.
References and Further Reading
Berkhofer, Robert F. 1978. *The White Man's Indian.* New York: Alfred A. Knopf.
Brown, Dee. 1970. *Bury My Heart at Wounded Knee: An Indian History of the American West.* New York: Bantam.
Coward, John M. 1995. "Creating the Ideal Indian: The Case of the Poncas." *Journalism History* 21 (Autumn): 112–121.

Knight, Oliver. 1960. *Following the Indian Wars.* Norman: University of Oklahoma Press.

Martin, John L., and Nelson, Harold L. 1956. "The Historical Standard in Press Analysis." *Journalism Quarterly* 33: 456–466.

Omaha Bee. 1877–1879. June 20, 1877–May 21, 1879.

Omaha Herald. 1879. April 1–May 22.

Omaha Republican. 1877–1879. June 2, 1877–May 12, 1879.

Tibbles, Thomas Henry. 1957. *Buckskin and Blanket Days: Memoirs of a Friend of the Indians.* New York: Doubleday.

Tee-Hit-Ton v. United States

The United States purchased Alaska from Russia through the Treaty of 1867, but this treaty made no mention of the Natives or their land rights. The Tee-Hit-Ton band of the Tlingit Indians inhabited lands in Alaska that would later be established as the Tongass National Forest. In 1951, Congress sold timber from the Tongass National Forest to a private lumber company, and the Tee-Hit-Ton sued the United States for compensation under the Fifth Amendment of the U.S. Constitution. The Supreme Court decided against the Tee-Hit-Ton, affirming that, since Congress had never acknowledged their land rights, none existed.

The first Russian settlers of present-day Alaska arrived at Three Saints Bay in 1784. Tensions between these early settlers and Native peoples quickly arose over cultural differences, hunting and fishing rights, and land tenure. By the early nineteenth century, American traders were moving into Alaska to establish communities on lands occupied by indigenous groups such as the Eskimos, Aleuts, and Tlingits. Alaska is comprised of 365 million acres that contain a small percentage of inhabitable land but numerous natural resources. As these resources became known to non-Natives, white settlement increased, along with a growing call for statehood and the relentless usurpation of Native land. During the gold rush in 1898, for instance, non-Natives successfully filed claims for title to Native lands, causing severe Native displacement. Moreover, the diversion of streams and the disturbance of their natural environment caused Native people to lose access to and use of important natural resources. Slowly, Native rights developed into a legal issue.

In 1947, Congress passed a resolution instructing the Secretary of the Interior to contract for the sale of timber from land in and near the Tongass National Forest, "notwithstanding any claim of possessory rights" (61 Stat. 920). The resolution mandated that the receipts from the timber sale be placed in a special Treasury account until the Native land rights issues were settled. On August 20, 1951, the Secretary of Agriculture contracted to a private company all marketable timber from a section in the forest. The Tee-Hit-Tons filed suit claiming aboriginal title to the land and a proprietary interest in the timber harvested and sold.

The primary issue in the *Tee-Hit-Ton* case was whether aboriginal land ownership conferred protection under the Fifth Amendment. A Court of Claims ruled that, while the Tee-Hit Ton were an identifiable group of American Indians and possessed "original Indian title or Indian right of occupancy," their title had lost its legal standing since it was not explicitly mentioned in the Treaty of 1867. On these grounds, the Court of Claims dismissed the Tee-Hit-Ton case (128 Ct. Cl., at 92, 120F).

The Tee-Hit-Tons then appealed their case to the Supreme Court, which heard the appeal. Justice Reed delivered the final opinion denying the Tee-Hit-Ton claims. The Court made several important statements in this denial of Native land rights. The first was that Congress never recognized any permanent rights of Alaska Natives, a fact underscored by the 1947 timber sale. If Congress never affirmed the Tee-Hit-Tons' rights to occupy the forest section where the timber was cut, then it did not acknowledge Native title to this land. The Tee-Hit-Tons possessed aboriginal title only and did not qualify for compensation for the harvested timber. Congress's sale of the timber also implicitly denied Native possessory rights to timber on this land. An important second point was the Court's confirmation of the legal concept of the conqueror's sovereignty over, and ownership of, Native lands. Justice Reed wrote that "every American schoolboy knows that the savage tribes of this continent were deprived of their ancestral ranges by force and that, even when the Indians ceded millions of acres by treaty, it was not a sale but the conqueror's will that deprived them of their land" (348 U.S. 272 [1955] at 289–290). The Court supported this statement with previous land cases and quoted from *Johnson v. McIntosh* (8 Wheat. 543, p. 587) "that discovery gave an exclusive right to extinguish the Indian title of occupancy, either by purchase or by conquest." The Supreme Court determined that Indian occupancy can be extinguished by Congress unilaterally and without recompense.

The Supreme Court heard the *Tee-Hit-Ton* case in the 1950s, at the zenith of the termination policy. Since *Lone Wolf v. Hitchcock* (1903), the Court had supported congressional regulation of tribal domestic affairs but had allowed Native claims to be filed under the Fifth Amendment. The Court's decision was handed down prior to the admission of Alaska to statehood. When the Alaska Statehood Act passed on July 7, 1958, it formally repudiated any land rights held by Alaska Natives or those held in trust for them by the United States.

The *Tee-Hit-Ton* decision set a disturbing legal precedent for future cases that concerned property issues and Native sovereignty. The case implicitly permitted congressional confiscation of lands and resources, whether reservations were created by executive order or through treaty. Three years after the *Tee-Hit-Ton* decision, federal Indian law (414 U.S. 661, 670, 32–43, 583–645, 675–687, 1958) established some fundamental protections of Indian possessory and property rights with regard to aboriginal land title. These issues were significantly resolved according to the Alaska Native Claims Settlement Act of 1971, which provided that 44 million acres of land and $962 million be allocated for Alaska Natives, in exchange for the extinguishment of all indigenous claims. The land and monies were conveyed to Native peoples through regional and village corporations.

Susan Sánchez-Barnett

See also Land, Identity and Ownership of; Land Rights; *Lone Wolf v. Hitchcock*; Russians, in the Arctic/Northwest; Termination.

References and Further Reading

Newton, Nell Jessup. 1980. "At the Whim of the Sovereign: Aboriginal Title Reconsidered." *Hastings Law Journal* 31 (July): 1215–1285.

Wilkins, David E., and K. Tsianina Lomawaima. 2001. *Uneven Ground: American Indian Sovereignty and Federal Law.* Norman: University of Oklahoma Press.

Termination

The positive experiences of some American Indians during the post–World War II era living off the reservations, receiving a regular salary, and having control of personal finances led to a call by some of the more assimilated American Indian people, supported by much of the non-Indian population, to "free" the Native American from the reservation system. Accordingly, such a move would "free" the federal government from its trust responsibility to American Indian peoples.

Conservative members of Congress, unhappy with the reforms enacted during the Indian New Deal, worked to have them rescinded even before Roosevelt left office. The members wanted to redefine Indian policy and terminate federal relations with some tribes. Their sentiments reflected the national mood of intolerance toward cultural diversity, as well as a desire to trim the federal bureaucracy created by the Roosevelt administration. They saw withdrawing services to Native Americans as one way to cut federal spending.

Some in Congress determined that it was in the best interest of Native Americans to phase out tribal governments and any guardian responsibilities of the federal government. Thus Congress would remove its protection from Native lands and encourage business leaders to help Native Americans develop their own resources. These same congresspersons maintained that Indians would assimilate faster into the population if they owned their lands outright and were allowed to trade freely. This approach would also open the way for states to tax Indian lands so that Native Americans could help pay for public services (Trafzer, 2000, 389).

The Indian Claims Commission Act of 1946, which was part of the termination movement, turned out to be beneficial for the Native Americans. Under the provisions of this Act, Native Americans were allowed to file claims against the federal government for lands that had been illegally seized. Even though Native Americans could receive monetary compensation, no amount of money could make up for the upheaval and disruption to their way of life. Through the seizure of sacred lands and traditional hunting areas, the deeply held and sacred values of the tribes were disrupted and their usual means of support destroyed. However, compensation did provide Native Americans with funds that enabled them to get their economies moving, at least to some degree.

With conservatism growing strongly in the government and society, John Collier's successors, Commissioners of Indian Affairs William Brophy and John Nichols, were not able to withstand the pressure to roll back change. Conservative congresspersons and Dillon S. Myer, chosen by President Harry S. Truman in 1950 to head the Bureau of Indian Affairs, favored termination. They were able to push through their agenda.

During World War II, Myer had been the director of the War Relocation Authority, which had forcibly removed Japanese Americans from their homes into internment camps. Myer had also been responsible for managing the rural relocation of thousands of people. Throughout the war, Myer maintained the position that Japanese Americans and cultural groups should be assimilated into the dominant society, thereby reducing racial conflicts.

It is not surprising that, when Myer became commissioner, he would act to have Native Americans assimilated into U.S. society. Toward this end, he launched a major counterrevolution against John Collier's policies. Myer believed that a Native American culture was nonexistent and that it was wrong for the government to encourage Native languages, arts, literature, and governments. He had little interest in cultural preservation programs and little concern for cultural pluralism, and he ordered an end to these programs.

Myer played down the role of Indian Day Schools, especially those that were on or near the reservations. He perceived that these schools made too many accommodations to the culture and the customs of the Native American tribes. Myer wanted boarding schools to be enlarged so that more children could be taken from the reservations and their parents. He wanted students to be taught the regular class subjects so that their assimilation would be hastened.

After the election of Dwight D. Eisenhower as president in 1952, Myer realized he would have no place in the new administration. He then offered his services to Glenn Emmons, the new commissioner for Indian affairs. In this capacity he helped draft a document for Congress endorsing termination. Through Myer's work and influence, the Bureau of Indian Affairs had already advocated termination as the "new" national Indian policy by the time that Emmons took over the position of commissioner of Indian affairs in 1953. It is of interest that neither Myer nor Emmons considered it necessary or appropriate to seek Native American advice in formulating the new policy.

Termination was a policy designed by politicians to achieve the withdrawal of federal services and funds that had been promised in treaties, laws, and agreements. Assimilationists were in the ascendancy again, and Congress passed legislation to desegregate Indian communities from mainstream American culture (Fixico, 1991). The administrators implemented the policy quickly before Native Americans had time to respond to the new threat. It would appear that Emmons had his own agenda in supporting termination. He was a former banker from New Mexico, a state with a large Native American population. Many business interests in the state were eager to reopen reservation lands. Emmons and Senator Arthur V. Watkins of Utah, chair of the Senate Committee on Indian Affairs, championed termination as a way of abolishing the tax-exempt status of tribes. Conservative congresspersons chaired the committees on Indian affairs in both houses. They spent time and energy to move a resolution quickly through Congress. On August 1, 1953, Congress unanimously passed House Concurrent Resolution 108.

The thrust of the resolution was that Indians would be subject to the same laws and entitled to the same privileges and responsibilities as other Americans. The resolution abolished the status of Native peoples as wards and listed tribes in various states that were prepared to have federal services ended. Although House Concurrent Resolution 108 was not in itself law, it had the full support of Emmons and the Bureau of Indian Affairs, and it marked the beginning of an official congressional termination policy.

The Federally Impacted Areas Aid Act (20 U.S. C. 236), passed by Congress in 1951, was the second act—the first being the Johnson O'Malley Act of 1934—designed to aid Native American education in public schools. The Impacted Aid Act assisted school districts that had a reduced tax base because of federally owned land, that is, it provided monies to schools responsible for educating children from armed service bases so that the local schools would not have to sustain an unfair burden. It also provided monies for the education of Native Americans. With this increased funding, local schools now saw the Native American student as fiscally desirable.

In spite of the Johnson O'Malley Act of 1934 and the Impacted Aid Act, it was evident that the federal government would continue to play a primary role in the funding of Native education. The federal–Indian trust relationship, the statutes passed by Congress to maintain that relationship, and the federal funding required to execute the responsibilities in Native education ensured that the federal government would continue to be involved. For their part, the Native communities were concerned with the degree of control that the federal government exerted through the maintenance of its responsibilities (AIPRC, 1976, 167–170).

In the early days of the Impacted Aid Act and its amendments, the states officially were required to make a choice between the Johnson O'Malley or Impact Aid. The Johnson O'Malley Act of 1934 provided supplemental funds to support education programs for Indian students attending public school and for the culturally related and supplementary academic needs of Indian children attending public schools. The Impacted Aid Act was amended in 1958 to allow state school systems to collect both through the Impact Aid Act for the basic support of schools and through the Johnson O'Malley Act for the support of the special education needs of Indian students.

Debate in the federal government resulted in the passage of six termination bills in 1953. In the course of only two weeks, both houses of Congress passed Public Law 280. The president signed the law, but he noted that Congress had not included a provision asking for Native consent to the law. The law placed Indian lands in Minnesota, Wisconsin, California, Nebraska, and Oregon under criminal and civil jurisdiction of the states. The law also invited other states to assume jurisdiction over Indian lands (Trafzer, 2000, 390–392). As a result, states were to assume responsibility for the education of Native American children.

In 1954, Congress passed the Klamath Termination Act. As a result, in 1958 approximately 77 percent of the Klamaths voted to terminate and receive a one-time per-capita payment of $43,000. The 23 percent who voted to retain their Klamath status in 1973 voted to withdraw from the tribe and receive a payment of $173,000. Even though Klamaths had terminated their sovereign relationship with the federal government, they were still identified as Indians. The termination did not work out. The Klamath tribe found that it did not have the infrastructure to function successfully in the changed economic conditions. In 1975 the Klamaths readopted their tribal status, and in 1978 Congress recognized the Klamaths and restored their status (Trafzer, 2000, 393–395).

In 1961, the Menominee tribe of Wisconsin was selected by the federal government for release from its governmental ties under the Termination Act. This termination was a disaster for the tribe. As a result of misunderstanding the terms of the Act, members of the tribe failed to invest the money they received or plan for a future without regular subsidy from the government. The tribe quickly used its cash reserves and was left without resources to satisfy basic needs and continue education services. When the Menominee did not receive money regularly, as was the custom, poverty and then diseases ravaged the tribe. As conditions worsened, the tribe sold much of its prime lands along the rivers and surrounding areas and left itself without resources (Trafzer, 2000, 394).

In all, about seventy tribes were part of the termination era policies. The Menominees of Wisconsin had previously experienced quite a high level of economic development. Termination brought disaster to the economy and health of the tribe. They experienced the effects of tuberculosis as well as a rapidly increasing infant mortality. When the Menominees experienced threats to their power and self-determination, they formed the group Determination of Rights and Unity for Menominee Shareholders (DRUMS) to reverse the effects of termination. President Richard M. Nixon signed the Menominee Restoration Act December 22, 1973 (87 Stat730, 25 U.S.C. 903 et seq.), restoring most of the reservation to the tribe and recognized them as a tribe. Thus began the end of termination.

Another outcome of the Termination Act was the relocation of many other tribes to urban areas. This relocation also proved disastrous, as many Native Americans had great difficulty adjusting to their new surroundings. When they did not adjust to life in the city, they returned to their lands only to find that they were greatly reduced in size. Tribes had been forced to sell large tracts of land, as they needed money for survival. It did not take too long for the government and the tribes to recognize that the termination program, as it was passed and implemented, was a failure (Reyhner and Eder, 1994, 52).

Besides amounting to a failure, the policies of the termination era were in conflict with the existing body of federal Indian law. In 1948, Felix S. Cohen, in the *Handbook of Federal Indian Law,* had consolidated this body of law, which had set the groundwork for interactions between the federal government and the Native Americans. Beginning with the passage of House Concurrent Resolution 108, termination was specified as federal policy for Indian tribes. From that point until the early 1970s, the drive for termination was maintained by the decentralization policy of the federal government, a desire to open up Indian lands, a desire for Native Americans to be assimilated, and a wish to cut back on social programs. In order not to emphasize the discrepancies between new legislation and previous laws, the BIA simply revised Cohen's 1948 book, deleting or changing sections that were in contradiction with new legislation. The bureau included new opinions to support new policies. The final move was to issue a new edition of Cohen's book in 1972 without mention of any previous editions. This version was and continues to be a highly regarded legal reference (Kickingbird and Charleston, 1991, 16).

Jeanne Eder

See also Cohen, Felix; Indian Claims Commission; Indian Reorganization Act; Land, Identity and Ownership of, Land Rights; Relocation.

References and Further Reading

American Indian Policy Review Commission Final Report, submitted to Congress May 17, 1977.

Fixico, Donald. *Urban Indians.* New York: Chelsea House Publishers, 1991

Kickingbird, K., and G. Charleston. 1991. *Responsibilities and Roles of Governments and Native People in the Education of American Indians and Alaskan Natives* (Report No. RC 018 612). Washington, DC: Indian Nations at Risk Task Force.

Reyhner, J., and J. Eder. 1994. "A History of Indian Education." In *Teaching American Indian Students.* Edited by J. Reyhner, 33–58. Norman: University of Oklahoma Press.

Trafzer, C. 2000 *As Long as the Grass Shall Grow and Rivers Flow: A History of Native Americans.* Fort Worth, TX: Harcourt College Publishers.

Trade and Intercourse Acts

The first Trade and Intercourse Act of July 22, 1790, was enacted "to regulate trade and intercourse with the Indian tribes." Indian historian Francis Paul Prucha writes of this legislation:

Continuing the pattern set in the Ordinance of 1786 and earlier colonial legislation, the law first of all provided for the licensing of traders and established penalties for trading without a license. Then it struck directly at the frontier difficulties. To prevent the steady erosion of the Indian Country by individuals who privately acquired lands from the Indians, it declared the purchase of lands from the Indians invalid unless made by a public treaty with the United States. To put a stop to the outrages committed against the Indians by whites who aggressively invaded the Indian Country, the act made provisions for the punishment of murder and other crimes committed by whites against the Indians in the Indian Country.

One of the first laws of the new American nation to deal with Indian matters, the act reads:

Section 1. Be it enacted . . . That no person shall be permitted to carry on any trade or intercourse with the Indian tribes, without a license for that purpose under the hand and seal of the superintendent of the [War] department, or of such other person as the President of the United States shall appoint for that purpose; which superintendent, or other person so appointed, shall, on application, issue such license to any proper person, who shall enter into bond with one or more sureties, approved of by the superintendent, or person issuing such license, or by the President of the United States, in the penal sum of one thousand dollars, payable to the President of the United States for the time being, for the use of the United States, conditioned for the true and faithful observance of such rules, regulations and restriction, as now are, or hereafter shall be made for the government of trade and intercourse with the Indian tribes. The said superintendents, and persons by them licensed as aforesaid, shall be governed in all things touching the said trade and intercourse, by such rules and regulations as the President shall prescribe. And no other person shall be permitted to carry on any trade or intercourse with the Indians without such license as aforesaid. No license shall be granted for a longer term than two years. Provided nevertheless, That the President may make such order respecting the tribes surrounded in their settlements by the citizens of the United States, as to secure an intercourse without license, if he may deem it proper.

Sec. 2. And be it further enacted, That the superintendent, or person issuing such license, shall have full power and authority to recall all such license as he may have issued, if the person so licensed shall transgress any of the regulations or restrictions provided for the government of trade and intercourse with the Indian tribes, and shall put in suit such bonds as he may have taken, immediately on the breach of any condition in said bond: Provided always, That if it shall appear on trial, that the person from whom such license shall have been recalled, has not offended against any of the provisions of this act, or the regulations prescribed for the trade and intercourse with the Indian tribes, he shall be entitled to received a new license.

Sec. 3. And be it further enacted, That every person who shall attempt to trade with the Indian tribes, or be found in the Indian country with such merchandise in his possession as are usually vended to the Indians, without a license first had and obtained, as in this act prescribed, and being thereof convicted in any court proper to try the same, shall forfeit all the merchandise so offered for sale to the Indian tribes, or so found in the Indian country, which forfeiture shall be one half to the benefit of the person prosecuting, and the other half to the benefit of the United States.

Sec. 4. And be it enacted and declared, That no sale of lands made by any Indians, or any nation or tribe of Indians within the United States, shall be valid to any person or persons, or to any state, whether having the right of pre-emption to such lands or not, unless the same shall be made and duly executed at some public treaty, held under the authority of the United States.

Sec. 5. And be it further enacted, That if any citizen or inhabitant of the United States, or of either of the territorial districts of the United States, shall go into any town, settlement or territory belonging to any nation or tribe of Indians, and shall there commit any crime upon, or trespass against, the person or property of any peaceable and friendly Indian or Indians, which, if committed within the jurisdiction of any state, or within the jurisdiction of either of the said districts, against a citizen or white inhabitant thereof, would be punishable by the laws of such state or district, such offender or offenders shall be subject to the same punishment, and shall be proceeded against in the same manner as if the offence had been committed within the jurisdiction of the state or district to which he or they may belong, against a citizen or white inhabitant thereof.

Sec. 6. And be it further enacted, That for any of the crimes or offences aforesaid, the like proceedings shall be had for apprehending, imprisoning or bailing the offender, as the case may be, and for recognizing the witnesses for their appearance to testify in the case, and where the offender shall be committed, or the witnesses shall be in a district other than that in which the offence is to be tried, for the removal of the offender and the witnesses or either of them, as the case may be, to the district in which the trial is to be had, as by the act to establish the judicial courts of the United States, are directed for any crimes or offences against the United States.

Sec. 7. And be it further enacted, That this act shall be in force for the term of two years, and from thence to the end of the next session of Congress, and no longer.

The second Trade and Intercourse Act, enacted on March 1, 1793, was designed to improve on the Trade and Intercourse act decreed three years earlier. The law was established in reaction to a report from President George Washington, who told Congress that the original act was not working and needed to be strengthened. As historian Francis Paul Prucha explains:

The [1793] law was a considerably stronger and more inclusive piece of legislation than its predecessor of 1790. The seven sections of the earlier law were expanded to fifteen. Part of the increase came from the new sections authorizing the president to give goods and money to the tribes to "promote civilization . . . and to secure the continuance of their friendship," and from a long section that aimed to stop horse stealing, but the bulk of the augmentation came from the detailed provision enacted to stop criminal attacks of whites against the Indians and irregular acquisition of their lands. This act, too, was a temporary one, having the same limitations as the first trade and intercourse act.

Thomas Jefferson, in his annual message in 1801, called for a permanent renewal of the several trade and intercourse acts that had been enacted in the previous congresses. Historian Francis Paul Prucha writes, "Accordingly, on March 30, 1802, a new trade and intercourse act became law. It was for the most part merely a restatement of the laws of 1796 and 1799, but by now the period of trial was over. The act of 1802 was no longer a temporary measure; it was to remain in force, with occasional additions, as the basic law governing Indian relations until it was replaced by a new codification of Indian policy in 1834."

Enacted on June 30, 1834, the Trade and Intercourse Act of 1834 was the last of several such federal acts to "regulate trade and intercourse with the Indian tribes, and to preserve peace on the frontiers." Running for thirty sections, the most important portion of the Act, Section 1, reads:

> Be it enacted by the Senate and House of Representatives of the United States of America, in Congress assembled, That all that part of the United States west of the Mississippi, and not within the states of Missouri and Louisiana, or the territory of Arkansas, and, also, that part of the United States east of the Mississippi river, and not within any state[,] to which the Indian title has not been extinguished, for the purposes of this act, be taken and deemed to be the Indian country.

Note: The bracketed comma was added by the Supreme Court in the case of *Bates v. Clark* to clarify the legislation's meaning.

John L. WIlliams

See also Land, Identity and Ownership of, Land Rights; Trade.

Reference and Further Reading

Prucha, Francis Paul. 1970. *American Indian Policy in the Formative Years: The Indian Trade and Intercourse Acts, 1790–1834*. Bison Books, University of Nebraska Press.

Tribal Courts

Judicial systems are operated by Indian nations through laws and procedures enacted by the tribe. Like federal and state courts, tribal courts play a pivotal role in the functioning of the communities they serve and regularly adjudicate a wide variety of cases. Tribal courts, however, are not courts of general jurisdiction and maintain a limited authority to hear disputes. This is especially true for criminal cases, but often applies to civil and other disputes as well.

Although the passage of the Indian Reorganization Act of 1934 was an impetus for the creation of formal tribal courts, their development predates the Act. In *Ex Parte Crow Dog* (1883), a Lakota Sioux killed a fellow tribal member and was brought to justice by the tribe. There was no formal Lakota court system at this time and a traditional methodology was employed to bring about a resolution to the dispute. The federal government was displeased with the tribal resolution, so it prosecuted the defendant for murder and he was sentenced to death. The U.S. Supreme Court overturned the conviction because it found that the tribe, through a prior treaty, had a reserved the right to carry out its own justice.

Following *Ex Parte Crow Dog*, Congress moved quickly to pass the Major Crimes Act, which granted the federal government jurisdiction over Indians who commit certain felonies while in Indian Country. Passage of the Major Crimes Act undermined tribal sovereignty because it denied tribes the power to administer justice within their own borders. Around this same time, the Department of the Interior set up Courts of Indian Offenses, which are commonly referred to as CFR courts (Code of Federal Regulations). CFR courts were run by the Bureau of Indian Affairs superintendents and handled less serious criminal actions not covered by the Major Crimes Act. In addition to this, CFR courts were often used to advance the federal government's assimilationist goals and did not necessarily operate in a manner that was consistent with advancing tribal interests.

During 1934, Congress passed the Indian Reorganization Act, giving Native tribes and nations limited self-governing rights, among other things. With such rights, Indian nations often adopted constitutions and created systems of government that were similar to those of the United States. Accordingly, many tribes formed court systems to adjudicate disputes occurring within their respective nations. Funding for tribal courts comes from the federal government, private sources, and the Indian nations. Native tribes and nations that have not adopted court systems rely on federal courts, CFR courts, and sometimes state justice systems for their judicial needs. To date, more than 200 Indian nations and Alaska Native villages have established court systems.

Unlike state courts, reservation courts have limited authority over cases that arise within their nations. Although at one time it was presumed to be an inherent power, tribal courts presently have no general criminal jurisdiction over non-Indians and can impose only limited fines and prison terms of less than one year on Indians committing crimes in Indian country. Because of this, tribes often must rely on the federal government and on state governments in some instances to prosecute crimes occurring in Indian Country. A scarcity of resources and frequently a lack of interest by federal and state authorities to prosecute crimes in Indian Country are quite common. As a result, many offenses in Indian Country go unpunished.

Although the U.S. Constitution does not apply to tribal court actions, the Indian Civil Rights Act of 1968 guarantees many of the same protections found in the Bill of Rights. Therefore, defendants' rights in tribal courts are often similar to those found in the state and federal systems.

Tribal courts have a much more expansive authority to hear civil claims and routinely adjudicate such issues as domestic relations matters, tort cases, tribal tax issues, regulatory proceedings, and contractual disputes. In some instances, the tribal court has exclusive jurisdiction over a particular matter. One such area is divorce hearings. In divorce proceedings, the tribal court is often the only court that can adjudicate the matter if both parties are Indian and are domiciled in the respective Indian nation. In other cases, the state or federal courts and a given tribe may have concurrent jurisdiction, or the state or federal courts cannot hear a case unless the tribal remedies have been exhausted.

Even though tribal civil jurisdiction is noticeably broader than its criminal authority, it too has limitations. For example, tribal courts cannot hear probate cases involving assets held in trust by the United States. These types of hearings are conducted by administrative law judges in the Department of the Interior. Also, through acts of Congress and Supreme Court decisions, tribal civil jurisdiction has been severely diminished in other areas over the past few decades. This is particularly evident when one of the parties in a lawsuit is non-Indian.

The U.S. Constitution requires each state to enforce or give full faith and credit to the judgments of other states. With the exception of a few statutorily defined areas, full faith and credit does not apply to the tribes. As a result, tribes and states are not required to enforce each other's judgments. It is common, however, for states and tribes to regularly give full effect to each other's judgments. This is known as comity.

In some states, tribal criminal judicial authority has been significantly diminished, if not nullified, via Public Law 280. Public Law 280, which was enacted in 1953 by the federal government, gave six states exclusive jurisdiction over reservations within their boundaries. In these states, the Major Crimes Act is not applicable because the state has full authority to enforce their criminal laws. It should be noted that some tribes located in Public Law 280 states have retained some of their judicial authority and have managed to create tribal courts to enforce certain laws. Although Public Law 280 is applicable to civil jurisdiction as well, tribal courts can have concurrent jurisdiction in such matters if they choose to.

Tribal court systems range in both structure and size. For example, tribal courts may or may not operate independently of tribal councils. Some tribes have created a judicial branch that is separate from its other branches of government, while in other instances the tribal council retains authority over the judicial arm. There are also differences on how judicial positions are filled (appointment versus election) and what educational requirements are needed to become a tribal judge (law degree versus no formal legal education). Some tribes, like the Navajo, have an intricate judicial system, similar to that of a typical state judiciary, which addresses substantial numbers of cases per year. In contrast, other tribes have smaller systems that handle minimal numbers of cases in any given year.

Many Indian tribes have recently made traditional courts or peacemaker courts a vital part of their judicial systems. Through peacemaker courts, a tribe or Native nation attempts to settle disputes through traditional methods before it reaches the formal tribal courts. This approach resembles the growing trend among the Anglo system of adopting alternative dispute resolution as a viable alternative to the adversarial system.

Ryan Church

See also Indian Civil Rights Act (1968); Indian Reorganization Act.

References and Further Reading

Canby, William C. 1998. *American Indian Law in a Nutshell*, 3rd ed. St. Paul, MN: West.

Getches, David H. 2004. *Federal Indian Law: Cases and Materials*, 5th ed. St. Paul, MN: West.

Gould, Scott. 1996. *The Consent Paradigm: Tribal Sovereignty at the Millennium*. 96 Colum. L. Rev. 809.

Jones, B. J., Chief Judge, Sisseton-Wahpeton Sioux Tribal Court. 2000. *Role of Indian Tribal Courts in the Justice System*. http://www.ccan.ouhsc.edu/Tribal%20Courts.pdf.

Prucha, Francis Paul. 1994. *The Great Father: United States Government and the American Indians.* Lincoln: University of Nebraska Press.

Trust, Doctrine of

Since the nineteenth century, the U.S. government has considered itself to have a trust relationship with Native American nations within its borders. The trust relationship has been defined as a legal obligation of the United States to protect Native American lands and resources, as well as Indians' rights to self-government. In theory, this trust relationship is supposed to protect Indian interests; in practice, it has sometimes been a political and legal "cover" for the exploitation of land and resources, as well as of Indian people themselves. Trust has been exercised on a very pervasive, personal level under the related doctrine of wardship, by which the federal government, principally through the Bureau of Indian Affairs, has exercised nearly total control over Native Americans' personal lives.

The doctrine of a fiduciary or trust relationship toward Native Americans is said to have grown out of various court decisions. The best-known of these is *Cherokee Nation v. Georgia*, in which Chief Justice John Marshall held that Indian nations stood in U.S. law as wards to their federal guardian. In theory, trust responsibilities generally fall into three areas: (1) protection of Indian trust property; (2) protection of the Indian right of self-government; (3) provision of social, medical, and educational services necessary for survival of individual members.

Legal scholar Frank Pommersheim has written that "it was in this soil of expansion and exploitation that federal Indian law developed and took root. This was a soil without constitutional loam. . . . The theory of the trust responsibility with the U.S. government as owner and trustee of Indian land, natural resources, and [trust] provider of many services is in direct conflict with any meaningful theory of tribal sovereignty" (Johansen, 1998, 345). In other words, as the courts talk a measured sense of sovereignty for reservation residents, the government walks a potent form of colonialism through the trust doctrine.

Equally rootless in the loam of the Constitution and equally inconsistent with any meaningful theory of Native American sovereignty is the plenary power of Congress over Indian affairs. Plenary power, another assumption of control, largely evolved out of the Supreme Court's 1903 decision in *Lone Wolf v. Hitchcock*. For most of the rest of the twentieth century, U.S. courts held that Congress is the ultimate trustee and has virtually unlimited discretionary power in this relationship. The pervasive network of rules and regulations promulgated by Congress and administered by the Bureau of Indian Affairs and other agencies for the "protection" of Indians has often had the effect of diminishing the day-to-day operation of Native American sovereignty by subjecting nearly every move made by individual Native Americans to federal government approval.

The nature of this "protection" usually has been defined by the government vis-à-vis its own interests, with minimal Native consultation. During the late 1870s, for example, the General Allotment (or Dawes) Act was advanced as a means to "protect" (i.e., "civilize") American Indians. This form of protection cost Indians two-thirds of their collective land base over the next half century.

For many years, the BIA and the Treasury Department operated as Indians' bankers through Individual Indian Monies accounts. Following a class action suit in the 1990s, these accounts were found to be permeated with negligence and fraud that has and will cost individual Native Americans many billions of dollars. In 1995, an audit of funds being held in trust for Indians by the BIA could not account for perhaps $20 billion (the true figure remains elusive). The auditing firm, Arthur Andersen & Co., spent five years on its study and found trust accounts to be a total mess. Of the 2,000 accounts the BIA maintained at the time, 15 percent were missing paperwork, leaving little or no trace of the money in them. These 2,000 accounts represent only money held by Indian groups (such as BIA-recognized Native American governments), not the 300,000 individual accounts maintained by the BIA, of which a complete audit would be prohibitively expensive.

Occasionally, however, Native American governments have been able to use the trust relationship to their advantage. The Osages of Oklahoma, for example, faced in 1906 with allotment, accepted its provisions on condition that their nation retain collective control over copious oil and natural gas resources underlying their reservation, and they have retained control of these resources to this day.

Robert C. Coulter, executive director of the Indian Law Resource Center, and Steven B. Tullberg, a senior staff attorney at the Center, argue that trust status, as practiced by the U.S. government, has often been less than trustworthy:

> Advocates of the trust theory have forgotten or overlooked the fact that the federal government itself initiated the destructive policies of Indian removal, allotment, termination and other wholesale denials of Indian rights. Through these policies and a host of other federal acts, the federal government has confiscated massive areas of Indian lands for its own use and that of its non-Indian citizenry. One looks in vain through the historical record for actions by the Supreme Court to protect Indians from these confiscatory actions (Coulter and Tullberg, 1984, 188).

Legal scholar Felix S. Cohen reflected on the rather unusual status of Indian trusts in Anglo-American law:

> In the white man's business world, a "trust" is likely to be a property of great value; the trustee is required to protect the trust property and to turn over all the profits of the enterprise to the beneficiaries of the trust. The trustee has no control over the beneficiaries' person. In the Indian's world, the same principles should apply; there is no legal basis for the common view that the Indian bureau may deal with Indian trust property as if it were the owner thereof, or use such power over lands to control Indian lives and thoughts. Unfortunately, administrators often find it convenient to forget their duties, which are lumped under the legal term "trusteeship," and to concentrate on their powers, which go by the name of guardianship" (Cohen and Cohen, 1960, 333).

During recent years, some Native American nations have benefited from tardy enforcement of another aspect of the trust doctrine, the Trade and Intercourse Acts (1790, et seq. 1 Stat. 137 [1790 Act]; 25 U.S. C.A. Sec. 177 [1793 Act]). In 1789, in one of his first acts as president of the United States, George Washington asked Secretary of War Henry Knox to prepare a report on the status of Indian affairs. Knox prepared a lengthy report on Native Americans' rights and the mechanisms for dealing with them under the new United States Constitution. His conclusions closely resembled Spanish and English interpretations of the doctrine of discovery since the time of Francisco de Vitoria in the early sixteenth century. Knox found that the Indians had a right to their lands and that land could not be taken except by mutual consent (as in the signing of a treaty) or in a "just" war as defined by the European powers of the day. Knox determined that non-Indian squatters must be kept off Indian lands to keep the peace on the frontier.

Out of Knox's report came the first of several Trade and Intercourse Acts, passed by Congress between 1790 and 1834. The first Congress to convene under the Constitution passed the first such act in 1790 (25 U.S.C. para. 177). The act held that no sale of Indian lands was valid without the authority of the United States. This initial act was extended and amended several times (1793, 1796, 1802, 1817, 1822, and 1834). In addition to extending federal authority to land sales, many of the Trade and Intercourse Acts forbade European-American entry into Indian lands, regulated trade, and prohibited liquor sale on Indian land. The Trade and Intercourse Act of 1802 contained this clause providing for the prosecution of non-Indians who trespassed on Indian land:

> SEC. 2. And be it further enacted, that if any citizen, or other person resident in, the United States . . . shall cross over, or go within the said boundary line, to hunt, or in any wise destroy the game; or shall drive, or otherwise convey any stock of horses or cattle to range on any lands allotted or secured by treaty with the United States, to any Indian tribe, he shall forfeit a sum not exceeding one hundred dollars, or be imprisoned not exceeding six months.

Some of the Trade and Intercourse Acts made depredations by non-Indians against Indians a federal crime in protected areas and pledged monetary compensation to injured Indians if they did not seek revenge. The Acts also set uniform standards for the punishment of crimes by non-Indians against Indians (and vice versa) and enunciated a goal of "civilization and education" for U.S. Indian policy. Trade with Indians also came under federal regulation in the Trade and Intercourse Acts.

In a legal sense, the Trade and Non-Intercourse Acts were a double-edged sword for Indian sovereignty. On one hand, they were passed to protect Indians from land fraud; on the other, they were an extension of federal law over Indian Country. The later intercourse acts were drafted under the theory that "tribes should be considered foreign nations and that tribal lands protected by treaty, even though situated within the boundaries of a state, should be considered outside the limits of jurisdictions of states" (Act of June 30, 1834, 4 Stat. 729, 733).

Jurisdiction over trade and land sales concerning Indians had been an issue in the English colonies from the first settlements, but came into sharp focus at the Albany Congress of 1754, when Iroquois delegates led by Tiyanoga (Hendrick) advised Benjamin Franklin and other colonial delegates to develop a single system for trade, land dealings, and diplomacy. The individual colonies rejected the Albany Plan, but the idea that the federal government retains authority over the states for dealing with Indians was written into the Constitution and has been central to American Indian law in the United States for more than two centuries.

The Trade and Intercourse Act of 1817 (3 Stat. 383) attempted the first systematic regulation of criminal jurisdiction regarding both Indians and non-Indians in Indian Country. The Act held that anyone, Indian or not, who committed an offense in Indian Country would be subject to the same punishment as if the offense had occurred in the United States, except for offenses defined as domestic. This exception became an important influence on subsequent court decisions delimiting jurisdiction. This law became the source of opinions that defined the powers of Indian courts; generally, a non-Indian accused of a crime on Indian land has been held to be under the jurisdiction of the United States, while an Indian charged with an offense against another Indian is tried in a local (Native) court.

"Wardship," in American Indian law and policy, refers to a special version of the trust relationship in which the government assumes near total control of individual Native Americans' lives. This legal doctrine has been said to have been based on opinions by Chief Justice John Marshall (in *Worcester v. Georgia*) that Native Americans live in "dependent domestic nations" and are therefore wards of the federal government. The BIA was initially established to hold Indians' land and resources "in trust." Wardship status rationalized the establishment of Indian reservations and schools to assimilate Native Americans into mainstream U.S. culture.

In *Worcester v. Georgia*, Justice Marshall wrote that inhabitants of Native nations had assumed a relationship of "pupilage" (or wardship) in their relations with the United States. Using this doctrine, which has no Constitutional basis, the executive branch of the U.S. government, principally through the Bureau of Indian Affairs, has created a superstructure of policies and programs that have had a vast impact on individual Native Americans and their governments. Through the use of the plenary power of Congress, policies such as allotment divested much of the Indian estate between 1854 and 1934. The concept of wardship also lies behind the storage of thousands of Native skeletal remains and burial artifacts in many federal and state research institutions. The idea of Native sovereignty in modern times has been developed in large part in opposition to wardship doctrines. Indians reacted to a social control system that was so tight that in many cases (for example, if a will affected the status of allotted land) individual actions of Native American people were subject to approval by the Secretary of Interior.

A concept of wardship also has been used since the midnineteenth century to construct for American Indians a cradle-to-grave social control system that was described during the midtwentieth century by legal scholar Felix Cohen:

> Under the reign of these magic words ["wardship" and "trust"] nothing Indian was safe. The Indian's hair was cut, his dances forbidden, his oil lands, timber lands, and grazing lands were disposed of by Indian agents and Indian commissioners for whom the magic word "wardship" always made up for lack of statutory authority . . . (Johansen, 1997, 19).

While Chief Justice Marshall's opinions have been used as a legal rationale for government policies that have treated American Indians as "wards, "There is nothing," according to Robert C. Coulter, executive director of the Indian Law Resource Center, "in the rulings of the Marshall Court [which] even remotely suggested that the United States could unilaterally impose a guardian–ward relationship on Indians, that it held trust title to Indian lands, or that, as trustee, it could dispose of lands without Indian consent" (Coulter and Tullberg, 1984, 367–368).

Wardship, as historically practiced by the Bureau of Indian Affairs, differs markedly from the legal status of non-Indian wards. Under most conditions, wardship is viewed as a temporary condition, with established standards for cession. Civil guardianship and custody law must allow people who have been deprived of their civil rights means of regaining them in accordance with the due process clause (the Fourteenth Amendment) of the U.S. Constitution. As developed by the BIA, however, Indian wardship has no standard for cession and no ending date. An Indian is defined as a ward regardless of his or her accomplishments or other actions and as the object of a policy that may well have misinterpreted Justice Marshall's intent.

Bruce E. Johansen

See also *Cherokee Nation v. Georgia;* Individual Indian Monies; Plenary Power; Trade and Intercourse Acts; Wardship Doctrine; *Worecester v. Georgia.*

References and Further Reading
Barsh, Russel, and James Henderson. 1980. *The Road: Indian Tribes and Political Liberty.* Berkeley: University of California Press.
"BIA Missing Money." 1996. *Native Americas* 13, no. 1 (Spring): 4.
Canby, William C., Jr. 1981. *American Indian Law.* St. Paul, MN: West.
Cohen, Felix. 1960. *The Legal Conscience: The Selected Papers of Felix S. Cohen.* Edited by Lucy Kramer Cohen. New Haven, CT: Yale University Press.
Coulter, Robert C., and Steven B. Tullberg. 1984. "Indian Land Rights." In *The Aggressions of Civilization: Federal Indian Policy Since the 1880s.* Edited by Sandra L. Cadwalader and Vine Deloria, Jr. Philadelphia, PA: Temple University Press.
Hall, G. 1981. *The Federal–Indian Trust Relationship.* Washington, DC: Institute for the Development of Indian Law.
Johansen, Bruce E., and Donald A. Grinde, Jr. 1997. *Encyclopedia of Native American Biography.* New York: Henry Holt.
Johansen, Bruce E. 1998. *The Encyclopedia of Native American Legal Tradition.* Westport, CT: Greenwood Press.
O'Brien, Sharon. 1989. *American Indian Tribal Governments.* Norman: University of Oklahoma Press.
Pommersheim, Frank. 1995. *Braid of Feathers: American Indian Law and Contemporary Tribal Life.* Berkeley: University of California Press.

Tungavik Federation, Nunavut

On April 1, 1999, Nunavut became Canada's third territory and the first to join the Confederation since 1949. After a quarter century of Inuit–Canada negotiations, the Inuit received title and the mineral rights to a fixed parcel of land. Anticipating significant revenues resulting from mineral extraction, the Inuits created the Nunavut Tungavik Inc. (NTI) in April 1993, as a private corporation responsible for ensuring that the 212 sections contained in the forty articles of the Nunavut Land Claims Agreement (NLCA) are properly implemented (Légaré, 2003, 119). The NTI also represents the interests of the 24,000 Inuit beneficiaries of the NLCA (Légaré, 2003, 117).

The NTI succeeded the Tungavik Federation of Nunavut (TFN), which itself succeeded the Inuit Tapirisat of Canada (ITC) in 1982. That year, the TFN was incorporated to pursue land claims negotiations on behalf of the Inuits of Nunavut. In 1987, Canada, the Dene, the Métis, and the Inuvialuit established the Iqaluit Agreement, which proposed that the boundary of Nunavut be based on the Inuit land claim settlement area and that the Dene-Métis and Inuvialuit claim settlement areas form a western territory. However, the Dene nation and the Métis association of the NWT did not reach an agreement with the TFN concerning the precise boundary of their respective claims areas. As a result, the Iqaluit Agreement failed and the various federations were dissolved.

Despite this setback, negotiations over these issues continued, and in 1990 an agreement in principle was reached, and a single-line boundary between the claims settlement areas of the Dene-Métis and the Inuit was accepted in a May 1992 plebiscite. The government of the Northwest Territories, the TFN, and the Canadian government adopted the boundary for division in the Nunavut Political Accord. The final agreement committed Canada, the NWT, and the TFN to negotiate a political accord to deal with powers, principles of financing, and timing for the establishment of a distinct Nunavut government. Government and Inuit representatives signed the land claim agreement on May 25, 1993, which enabled the transfer of $1.1 billion to the Inuit.

The NTI is a highly centralized organization comprised of a General Assembly consisting of forty-eight delegates that meets annually, a ten-member Board of Directors that meets quarterly, and an Executive Committee that meets monthly. The General Assembly approves the annual budget, has the authority to increase or restrict spending, and can modify its programs and services, the latter of which must be approved by two-thirds of the delegates. The Board of Directors meets to review and evaluate the Executive Committee's decisions. Six of the ten board members come from regional Inuit associations, which gives significant weight to regional interests within the board. The four-member Executive Committee is the most powerful component. The committee, which is elected by the Inuit beneficiaries, meets monthly to implement the decisions approved by the General Assembly, while also supervising the NTI's day-to-day operations (Légaré, 2003, 120–123).

The NTI has a staff of fifty-five employees, 90 percent of whom are Inuits, and an annual budget exceeding $21 million (Légaré, 2003, 123). Working closely (if not always amicably) with the government of Nunavut, the NTI oversees the Nunavut Elders Benefit Plan, established as a reward for elders sharing their knowledge during the initial stages of the research that led to the creation of the Nunavut Territory, and the Nunavut Hunter Support Program, developed to promote traditional wildlife harvesting activities and to reinforce social cohesiveness. The NTI also supervises the operations of the Public Co-Management Boards responsible for the management of renewable and nonrenewable resources; the Nunavut Social Development Council, which conducts research on Inuit cultural and social issues and advises Nunavut officials regarding the social impact of their policies; and the regional Inuit associations, in addition to the Inuit Heritage Trust and the Nunavut Trust. The former exists to manage all archaeological sites and to establish by-laws related to archeological permits (and to deliver them); the latter is responsible for managing and investing the $1.1-billion land claims settlement.

Yale D. Belanger

See also Nunavut Land Claims Agreement.
References and Further Reading
Dahl, Jens, Jack Hicks, and Peter Jull, eds. 2000. *Nunavut: Inuit Regain Control of the Lands and Their Lives.* Copenhagen, Denmark: International Work Group for Indigenous Affairs.
Légaré, André. 1996. "The Process Leading to a Land Claims Agreement and Its Implementation: The Case of the Nunavut Land Claims Settlement." *Canadian Journal of Native Studies* 16, no. 1: 139–163.
Légaré, André. 1997. "The Government of Nunavut (1999): A Prospective Analysis." In *First Nations in Canada: Perspectives on Opportunity, Empowerment, and Self-Determination.* Edited by J. Rick Ponting, 404–432. Toronto: McGraw-Hill Ryerson.
Légaré, André. 2003. "The Nunavut Tungavik Inc.: An Examination of Its Mode of Operation and Its Activities." In *Natural Resources and Aboriginal People in Canada: Readings, Cases, and Commentary.* Edited by Robert B. Anderson and Robert M. Bone, 117–137. Concord, ON: Captus Press.
McPherson, Robert. 2005. *New Owners in Their Own Land: Minerals and Inuit Land Claims,* 3rd ed. Calgary, AB: University of Calgary Press.

United Nations, Indians and

The United Nations was formed in 1945, in San Francisco, when fifty nations came together to declare their commitment to the codification of international law for the purposes of promoting world peace and cooperation. Within the UN Charter's statements was the resolution to protect the equal rights and the self-determination of all peoples, as well as to bring an end to colonialism and to work with colonized peoples to develop self-determination. It was this clause that led American Indians to seek the redress of grievances through the United Nations.

The earliest attempt to petition an international body for recognition of Indian rights came in the 1920s when several members of the Iroquois Confederacy came together to appeal to the League of Nations, the predecessor of the United Nations, to recognize their right to sovereignty. After two years of exhaustive work, Deskaheah, the envoy's leader, realized he would not meet with success. International appeals were set aside until Vine Deloria, Jr. again raised the issue in *Behind the Trail of Broken Treaties: An Indian Declaration of Independence.* Published in 1974, Deloria's book introduced a new generation of American Indians to the concept of international justice and nationhood.

This new sense of nationalism took definitive shape in 1974 at the first International Treaty Council (ITC) held in South Dakota on the Standing Rock Reservation. The ITC, originally headed by Russell Means and Jimmie Durham, was a branch of the American Indian Movement (AIM). At the council, numerous elders from various Indian groups came together to discuss the principles and process of activism and determine a future route to pursue recognition of their rights from the U.S. government. It was agreed that, to attract broader international attention, they would need to frame their demands as that of one sovereign nation to another; therefore the group set about creating relationships with newly decolonized and independent countries. Such a legal context is well rooted in Native American history since treaties were often negotiated on similar terms. The ITC was granted the status of a nongovernmental organization in the UN and in 1977, in Geneva, appeared before the NGO Conference on Discrimination Against Indian Populations. There they testified about the land theft and discriminatory practices of the U.S. government.

In 1980, two delegations were sent to meet with the UN Commission on Human Rights and the Subcommission on Prevention of Discrimination and Protection of Minorities, as well as to speak at the Fourth Russell Tribunal on the wrongs committed by the federal government against American Indians. It was hoped by the International Treaty Council, who had organized these delegations, that the United Nations would hear and respond to their plea for self-determination. In 1981, at the NGO Conference on Indigenous Peoples and the Land, the Working Group on Indigenous Populations was formed as a subpart of the UN Economic and Social Council. Its purpose was to review and assess the living conditions and treaty rights of Native peoples.

By 1983, however, American Indian access to the appeals process of the UN was being constantly parried by the United States' invocation of a clause in the UN Charter that defines colonized territories as those that are geographically separated from their invaders by thirty miles of ocean and by another section of the clause that guarantees territorial integrity to all states. Nevertheless, the fight continues as people from nations around the world continue to take an interest in human rights issues for Native peoples in the United States and elsewhere.

The UN Working Group on the Rights of Indigenous Populations produced the Draft Declaration on the Rights of Indigenous Peoples in 1993, which became a framework for the desired relationship between nations. The Declaration called for the respect of basic human rights and cultural identity, as well as for the protection of indigenous land bases and natural resources, political rights, and, above all, Native self-determination. In addition, the United Nations has worked to incorporate the protection of Native rights into its program for environmental protection through the UN Conference on Environment and Development.

Vera Parham

See also Deskaheh.

Deloria, Vine, Jr. 1974. *Behind the Trail of Broken Treaties: An Indian Declaration of Independence.* New York: Dell.

Deloria, Vine, Jr. 1985. *American Indian Policy in the Twentieth Century.* Norman: University of Oklahoma Press.

Grounds, Richard A., George E. Tinker, and David E. Wilkins, eds. 2003. *Native Voices: American Indian Identity and Resistance.* Lawrence: University Press of Kansas.

Jaimes, Annette M., ed. 1992. *The State of Native America: Genocide, Colonization, and Resistance.* Boston: South End Press.

United States v. Dann

The U.S. Supreme Court decision in *United States v. Mary and Carrie Dann* is one event in a complex, ongoing land battle between the western Shoshone tribes and the federal government.

In the late 1600s, at the time of first contact between the western Shoshones and Europeans, the western Shoshones, a seasonally nomadic people, controlled over 60 million acres of land stretching from the Snake River in southern Idaho, through the Great Basin of Nevada, to Death Valley in California. The traditional lands of the western Shoshones are arid and rugged, consisting of many mountain ranges separated by deep, narrow valleys. Because most of the land is too dry and alkaline for farming, early European-American immigrants passed through the region and settled instead in the fertile valleys of California and Oregon.

The Shoshones were largely left alone to continue their traditional way of life until the 1840s. At that time, westward immigration, spurred in part by the discovery of gold in western Nevada's Comstock, caused a marked increase of European-American incursions into Shoshone territory. Construction of the first coast-to-coast railroad and telegraph networks caused further disruptions. Some Shoshone responded to these invasions by conducting "hostilities and depredations" on wagon trains, postal workers, and telegraph lines. The 1863 treaty between the United States and the western Shoshones, known as the Treaty of Ruby Valley, was designed to end these conflicts and ensure "the safety of all travellers passing peaceably" through western Shoshone territory in exchange for a $5,000 annuity. Upon signing the treaty, the Shoshone were given $5,000 worth of provisions and clothing; this was the only annuity the tribe ever received.

The Dann family, members of the Western Shoshone tribe, stand on their land near Elko, Nevada, in 1980. Mary and Carrie Dann have been in a legal battle with the U.S. goverment for the past thirty years over grazing rights. (Ted Streshinsky/Corbis)

Additional concessions contained in the treaty permit the establishment of U.S. military posts, as well as private mining, ranching and timber operations, within Shoshone territory. Even so, over the years, Shoshone territory remained sparsely populated. The small increase in European-American residents did not much disrupt the traditional lifestyle of the Shoshone, who, having turned from a subsistence lifestyle to cattle ranching, continued to occupy their traditional homeland, where they lived much as they always had. Today, although dense population centers have developed around Salt Lake City and Las Vegas, most of the Great Basin remains sparsely populated with an average population density of just one or two people per square mile.

Despite its small population, the commercial and military significance of the Great Basin has increased over time. The area is mineral rich; 64 percent of the gold extracted annually in the United States—almost 10 percent of the gold produced annually worldwide—is found there. In addition to its mineral wealth, the isolation and emptiness of the Great Basin are a source of military value. Due to the region's low population density, clear air, and general absence of private land ownership, the U.S. government has located a number of military bases and weapons ranges, as well as the proposed Yucca Mountain nuclear waste repository, in the Great Basin.

The ongoing legal conflict between the U.S. government and the western Shoshones in general and Shoshone ranchers Carrie and Mary Dann, in particular, began with a case brought before the Indian Claims Commission (ICC) in 1951.

The Indian Claims Commission was established by Congress to settle the outstanding claims of Indian tribes. The Commission's goal was to extinguish tribal claims by paying tribes for land that had been taken without compensation. Attorneys representing the Te-Moak tribe brought the ICC case on behalf of all western Shoshones. The ICC case was a source of conflict from its inception, largely because the Te-Moak tribe consists of just four of the more than fourteen bands that constitute the western Shoshone nation. Unrepresented bands argued that the Te-Moak attorneys did not have the authority to act on their behalf. Yet the ICC recognized the attorneys as representing the entire western Shoshone Tribe.

Although the attorneys (who under a contingent fee agreement were entitled to 10 percent of the tribe's recovery) told tribal members that the purpose of the ICC action was to reach an agreement for back annuity payments, some tribal elders feared that the action would result in a loss of tribal lands. Subsequent attempts by the Te-Moak to fire their attorneys and stay the proceedings were denied by the ICC. Attempts by other Shoshone individuals and bands to intervene in the action were also denied.

In 1966, the Te-Moak attorneys stipulated to July 1, 1872, as the valuation date for nearly 24 million acres of western Shoshone lands in the state of Nevada. By this stipulation, the attorneys and the government agreed that the western Shoshones had lost title to their aboriginal lands as of July 1, 1872, through gradual European-American encroachment and set the 1872 value of the land as appropriate compensation for its loss. The stipulation ignored the fact that in 1966 many western Shoshones were still in actual possession of their traditional land. In addition, the agreement contradicted the holding in *Johnson v. McIntosh* and the prohibition contained in the Non-Intercourse Acts against the transfer of tribally controlled land to non-Indians without prior government approval. The stipulation violated basic tenets of federal Indian law as well as the government's fiduciary duty to preserve and manage tribal resources.

In 1974, while the ICC case was still pending, the federal government brought a trespass action against the Dann sisters for grazing their livestock on federal land without a permit. This trespass action was the genesis of the U.S. Supreme Court case of *United States v. Dann*. The Danns, who had been grazing their cattle for thirty years on the land in question without a permit, responded that the western Shoshone tribe held aboriginal title to the land and, as tribal members, they were entitled to use the lands under tribal—not federal—law. The government argued that the issue of aboriginal title had already been decided by the ICC and so was not available to the Danns as a defense. The district court found in the government's favor.

The Danns appealed the case to the Ninth Circuit Court of Appeals, which reversed, holding that the ICC decision could not have decided the question of extinguishment of aboriginal title. The court reasoned that it was not within the ICC's jurisdiction to extinguish title to land and, further, the ICC had not yet issued a final decision in the case. The Ninth Circuit then sent the case back to the federal district court in Nevada on remand.

While the remanded case was pending in district court, the ICC issued a decision awarding $26 million to the western Shoshone tribe as compensation for loss of its aboriginal lands. According to the subsequent district court decision, the ICC award acted to extinguish the tribe's aboriginal title, thus barring the Danns' defense. The Danns again appealed to the Ninth Circuit, which once again reversed. The court held that since the tribe had not yet accepted payment of the award, the Danns could still raise the issue of extinguishment as a defense.

The government appealed this decision to the U.S. Supreme Court, which ruled against the Danns on the grounds that (1) Congress intended the decisions of the ICC to be final and (2) once the $26 million ICC award was appropriated into a Treasury account for the benefit of the tribe, payment had occurred. This 1985 decision arguably effected a judicial extinguishment of the western Shoshones' aboriginal title.

After the ICC award, many western Shoshone feared that distribution of the money would extinguish any remaining claim they might have to their traditional lands. For this reason, the tribe refused to accept a payout of the money in the Treasury account. By 2004, interest had increased the prospective award to more than $145 million, or roughly $30,000 per eligible tribal member. As the amount of money in the fund grew, so did pressure from many Shoshone for a distribution. By the time President George W. Bush signed the Western Shoshone Distribution Act on July 7, 2004, the tribe was deeply divided over the issue. While the Danns and other "traditionals" refuse to accept their individual shares, many others believe that the money is at least some compensation for the lands the Tribe has lost.

Despite the Supreme Court ruling, the Danns have continued to graze their livestock on rangelands managed by the Bureau of Land Management (BLM). In response, the BLM has assessed $3 million in grazing fees, penalties, and interest against the Danns. Since 1992, the agency has attempted to coerce the Danns' compliance with BLM regulations through threats, court action, and occasional roundups. In 2002, forty federal agents with guns, ATVs, and helicopters rounded up about 230 of the sisters' cattle. The animals were auctioned off for $60,000—much less than the cost of the roundup and auction—and many of the purchasers were Dann sympathizers who immediately returned the animals to the sisters.

In the years since the government's 1974 trespass action, the Danns' cause has been widely publicized and has received widespread international recognition and support. Having exhausted the remedies available to them in the U.S. courts, the Danns have taken their case to the tribunals of the Organization of American States and the United Nations, where they have received favorable decisions. Although these international decisions are not binding on the federal government, they put the United States in an embarrassing position by publicly censuring the government for its treatment of the western Shoshones. It remains to be seen what effect these decisions will have on U.S. Indian policy, the western Shoshones, and the Danns.

Amy Propps

See also Economic Development; Tribal Sovereignty; Uranium Mining.

References and Further Reading

Ragsdale, John W., Jr. 2004. "Individual Aboriginal Rights." *Michigan Journal of Race and Law* (Spring): 323.

United States Treaty with the Western Shoshoni Oct. 1, 1863. 18 Stat. 689.

United States v. Dann 470 U.S. 39 (1985).

United States v. Dann 572 F.2d 222 (9th Cir. 1978).

United States v. Mary and Carrie Dann Dec. 27, 2002. Case 11.140, Report No. 75/02. I/A Court H.R. Doc. 5, rev. 1 at 860.

United States v. Kagama

In *United States v. Kagama* [118 U.S. 375 (1886)], the U.S. Supreme Court enunciated a "superior position" of the federal government vis-à-vis Native nations (a doctrine that came to be known as plenary power) when it upheld the Major Crimes Act (1885). The court was upholding the federal trust responsibility against erosion by the states. The court said that "the people of the states . . . are often [the Indians'] deadliest enemies." This case was the first Supreme Court decision to directly address the legality of federal jurisdiction over both Indians and non-Indians in Indian Country.

A year after the Major Crimes Act was passed, attorneys for Kagama argued that it was unconstitutional. The Supreme Court ruled that the commerce clause of the Constitution did not authorize the Congress to regulate the internal affairs of Indian nations and their members. However, the court held that, since the states had no legal authority over Indians living on reservations, the role of sovereign must be played by the United States. Native American conceptions of sovereignty were omitted from this legal formulation.

The facts of the case concerned two Indians, Kagama and Mahawaha, who killed another Indian on the Hupa Reservation in California. They were arrested, tried, and convicted in federal court on grounds that the commerce clause of the Constitution gave the government jurisdiction on the Hupa reservation. The U.S. Supreme Court, following John Marshall's opinions in *Cherokee Nation v. Georgia* (1831) and *Worcester v. Georgia* (1832), held that Indian lands did not comprise foreign nations. "These Indian tribes are the wards of the nation," ruled the court. "They are communities dependent on the United States . . . From their very weaknesses and helplessness, so largely due to the course of dealing of the federal government with them and the treaties in which it has been promised, there arises the duty of protection, and with it the power." The court also held that "The Indians owe no allegiance to a state within which their reservation may be established, and the state gives them no protection."

Justice Samuel Miller, writing for the court majority, said that the government had always regarded Native nations as semisovereign entities, "not as states, not as nations, but as separate people, with power of regulating their internal relations and thus not brought into the laws of the Union or the States within whose limits they resided."

Kiowa attorney Kirke Kickingbird provided the following evaluation of Kagama's legal legacy:

The decision in Kagama and the line of cases which flowed from it led to an overly broad and often destructive exercise of federal power in Indian affairs. In these decisions, the courts have placed no legally enforceable standards or criteria on the trustee. Instead, they have designated Congressional power in Indian affairs as "plenary," or almost absolute (Kickingbird, 1983, 20).

Bruce E. Johansen

See also *Cherokee Nation v. Georgia; Lone Wolf v. Hitchcock;* Plenary Power; Tribal Sovereignty; *Worcester v. Georgia.*

References and Further Reading

Kickingbird, Kirke. 1983. *Indian Jurisdiction.* Washington, DC: Institute for the Development of Indian Law.

United States v. Kagama 118 U.S. 375 (1886).

John Marshall, Chief Justice of the Supreme Court, created the Wardship policy for Native Americans. (Library of Congress)

Wardship Doctrine

Wardship, in American Indian law and policy, is a legal doctrine, sometimes said to be based on opinions by U.S. Supreme Court Chief Justice John Marshall, that Native Americans live in "dependent domestic nations" and are therefore wards of the federal government. The Bureau of Indian Affairs was initially established to hold Indians' land and resources "in trust." Wardship status rationalized the establishment of Indian reservations and schools to assimilate Native Americans into mainstream U.S. culture. The concept of wardship also lay behind the storage of thousands of Native skeletal remains and burial artifacts in many federal and state research institutions. The idea of Native sovereignty in modern times has been developed in large part in opposition to wardship doctrines. Native Americans reacted to a social-control system that was so tight that in many cases (for example, if a will affected the status of allotted land) individual actions of Native American people were subject to approval by the Secretary of Interior.

The assertion of states' rights over Native territory in the southeastern United States provided the legal grist for an 1832 Supreme Court decision written by Chief Justice John Marshall. In *Worcester v. Georgia,* Justice Marshall wrote that inhabitants of Native nations had assumed a relationship of "pupilage" in their relations with the United States. Using this doctrine, which has no constitutional basis, the executive branch of the U.S. government, principally through the Bureau of Indian Affairs, has created a superstructure of policies and programs that has had a vast impact on individual Native Americans and their governments. Through the use of the plenary power of Congress, such policies as allotment divested much of the Indian estate between 1854 and 1934.

A concept of wardship also has been used since the midnineteenth century to construct for American Indians a cradle-to-grave social control system that was described during the midtwentieth century by the legal scholar Felix Cohen:

> Under the reign of these magic words ["wardship" and "trust"] nothing Indian was safe. The Indian's hair was cut, his dances forbidden, his oil lands, timber lands, and grazing lands were disposed of by Indian agents and Indian commissioners for whom the magic word "wardship" always made up for lack of statutory authority . . .

While Chief Justice Marshall's opinions have been used as a legal rationale for government policies that have treated American Indians as "wards," in the opinion of Robert C. Coulter, executive director of the Indian Law Resource Center, "There is nothing in the rulings of the Marshall Court [which] even remotely suggested that the United States could unilaterally impose a guardian-ward relationship on Indians, that it held trust title to Indian lands, or that, as trustee, it could dispose of lands without Indian consent."

Wardship as historically practiced by the Bureau of Indian Affairs differs markedly from the legal status of non-Native wards. Under most conditions, wardship is viewed as a temporary condition, with established standards for cession. Civil guardianship and custody law must allow people who have been deprived of their civil rights the means of regaining them in accordance with the due process clause of the U.S. Constitution. As developed by the BIA, however, Indian wardship has no standard for cession, and no ending date. An Indian is defined as a ward regardless of his or her accomplishments or other actions.

Bruce E. Johansen

See also Bureau of Indian Affairs: Establishing the Existence of an Indian Tribe; *Cherokee Nation v. Georgia;* Individual Indian Monies; Trust, Doctrine of; *Worcester v. Georgia.*

References and Further Reading

Barsh, Russel, and James Henderson. 1980. *The Road: Indian Tribes and Political Liberty.* Berkeley: University of California Press.

Cohen, Felix. 1960. *The Legal Conscience: The Selected Papers of Felix S. Cohen.* Edited by Lucy Kramer Cohen. New Haven, CT: Yale University Press.

Winters v. United States

The most generous basis for Indian water rights is the Winters (or reserved rights) doctrine, established in 1908 by the Supreme Court in *Winters v. United States.* It is also the most important point of contention among non-Indian water claimants. The roots of the case lie in a series of treaties signed by Montana Indian tribes, including the 1851 Treaty of Fort Laramie and four later treaties in 1855, 1874, 1888, and 1896, in which the tribes ceded much of their ancestral lands to the U.S. government. The last two treaties fixed the borders of the Fort Belknap Reservation, with its northern boundary, according to the 1888 treaty, as the "middle of the main channel of Milk River."

After the Indians began to settle on the new reservation, it became clear that government efforts to turn them into agriculturalists conflicted with their preference to raise livestock and maintain their cultural traditions. After 1888, non-Indian homesteaders began settling lands around the reservation and drawing off water for crop irrigation and stock watering. Reservation agents facilitated the opening of the reservation to non-Indian ownership and

leasing agreements so that, by 1920, non-Indians controlled over 58 percent of the reservation's irrigated lands. In 1905, a severe drought stuck the region, and upstream irrigation left little water for both the reservation and other downstream users. When off-reservation ranchers blocked the flow of the Milk River onto the reservation, Agent William R. Logan began to work for the restoration of Indian water rights—to aid not the Indians but rather the growing non-Native population on the reservation (Massie, 1987). The federal government sued on behalf of the Fort Belknap tribes to protect their rights to Milk River water.

The case was filed to adjudicate the water rights of the tribes of the Fort Belknap Reservation and local, non-Indian–owned farms that were located along the northern border of the Fort Belknap Reservation. Both Indians and non-Indians needed the Milk, because it was the only reliable source of water in the region. Further, the Bureau of Indian Affairs (BIA) had promised to develop irrigation for the reservation from the river while non-Indian settlers had been promised a federal reclamation project to irrigate their lands from the Milk. The Indians claimed that, when they ceded aboriginal lands surrounding the reservation, they retained for themselves the rest of the reservation land and enough water to make it useful.

In 1908, the Supreme Court acknowledged the existence of Indian water rights for the first time. In an eight-to-one decision, the Court held in *Winters v. United States* that, when Indian reservations were established, the tribes and the United States implicitly reserved sufficient water, along with the land, to fulfill the purposes of the reservations (Hundley, 1982). The case is significant not only because its decision restored water to the tribes, but even more so for the reasoning that led to the decision. Justice Joseph McKenna, speaking for the majority, reasoned:

The lands ceded, were, it is true, also arid; and some argument may be urged, and is urged, that with their cession there was the cession of the waters, without which they would be valueless, and "civilized communities could not be established thereon." And this, it is further contended, the Indians knew, and yet made no reservation of the waters. We realize that there is a conflict of implications, but that which makes for the retention of the waters is of greater force than that which makes for their cession. The Indians had command of the lands and the waters—command of all their beneficial use, whether kept for hunting, "and grazing roving herds of stock," or turned to agriculture and the arts of civilization. Did they give up all this? Did they reduce the area of their occupation and give up the waters which made it valuable or adequate? (*Winters v. United States*, 1908)

McKenna based his reasoning on the section of the 1888 agreement that said, "whereas the said Indians are desirous of disposing of so much [land] as they do not require, in order to obtain the means to enable them to become self-supporting, as a pastoral and agricultural people, and to educate their children in the paths of civilization." Even though no treaty or written agreement between the Fort Belknap tribes and the government specified water rights for the tribe, rights to enough water to make the land productive were implied to fulfill provisions of the treaty. The treaty stated that reservation lands were set aside so that tribal people could become self-supporting through an agricultural existence. The court then drew the inference that land without water is useless for the purposes of farming and ranching. Therefore, when the federal government set up the reservations, they also, the theory went, reserved enough water for the Indians to turn the terrain into productive farmland.

As a result of *Winters,* Indian water rights are defined and governed, at least in theory, by a body of federal law that recognizes Indian tribes' sovereignty over the water on their reservations. The Supreme Court held that tribal governments have jurisdiction over both tribal members and activities on the Indian reservations, and this ruling has affected the ways that Indians can use the water that flows through or adjacent to their reservations. However, by handing down a decision while not providing any way of reconciling it with the system of water allocation already in use throughout much of the West, the Court did more to provoke further conflicts over water between Indian and non-Indian populations than it did to settle them. *Winters* did nothing at all to determine either the scope of its application or the parameters for determining the amount of water Indian tribes could claim (Hundley, 1978). Almost from the time the decision was handed down and especially during the 1980s and 1990s, tribes have repeatedly been forced back to the courts in efforts to quantify their federal water

rights, even though such lawsuits have jeopardized the possible extent of those rights.

The main reason for the continued difficulty in securing water rights under *Winters* has been that the application of what came to be known as the Winters doctrine has constantly come up against prior appropriation, the prevailing method of allocating water claims in the western United States. When the doctrine of prior appropriation is taken to include Indian tribal use, the courts necessarily enter the picture to allocate the amounts that the tribe would have the rights to as determined by their use of the water source. Because so many Indian reservations were established before most other water uses began in the West, tribes often hold the oldest and thus most valuable water rights. Since many Indian groups have occupied their land since before non-Native settlement, they have strong, ancient priority claims to water for tribal uses. However, state water laws in the West often place a priority on the idea of beneficial use, which, more often than not, involves agriculture. Although many Southwestern tribes, such as the Pueblos, have a long agricultural tradition predating European contact, and others, such as the Jicarilla Apache, have a mixed subsistence tradition, the factors of modern reservation life do not always mean that the tribes will use water for agriculture. Since Indian tribes are theoretically not held to state laws regarding water use, conflicts have continually risen over which water rights allocation system is applicable to the adjudication of rivers that flow through both Indian and non-Indian lands. The Winters doctrine would seem to support the view that Indians have the right to sufficient water to irrigate reservation agricultural lands; yet the doctrine of prior appropriation supports the idea that, if the Indians did not historically irrigate their lands, non-Indian water claims would be substantiated. The courts then have to examine what water was reserved for use on the Indian reservations, how tribal water rights are quantified and used, and how these water rights are regulated and enforced. Because of the potential extent and great value of the water that could be claimed by Indian tribes under the Winters doctrine, especially in the American West, where water has become increasingly scarce, Indian water rights have constantly been under attack in the federal and state courts and in other political arenas as well.

As contradictory as the two dominant systems of allocation, Winters and prior appropriation, may appear, the situation in practice has been both less contradictory and more confusing than the various federal decisions would indicate. This is in part because the Justice Department's official position in favor of prior appropriation in the West conflicts with its legal obligation to uphold the reserved rights or Winters doctrine (McCool, 1987a). The Winters doctrine theoretically makes prior appropriation irrelevant. In practice, however, federal irrigation and reclamation programs have rarely been undertaken in the interests of Indian peoples, even when they were constructed adjacent to Indian lands. The Bureau of Reclamation (BOR), dedicated to the doctrine of prior appropriation and the promotion of non-Indian irrigated agriculture in the West, exercised great power and acted decisively in the interests of their constituents when allocating the waters made useful by their construction projects. Legal scholar Donald Worster was correct when he noted that "neither the courts nor Congress managed to settle the issue" and that "white appropriators had an uneasy but clear edge: they were already in possession" (Worster, 1985). *Winters* might have given the tribes a theoretically large claim to the waters of the West, but battles over gaining access to those waters continue to occupy the tribes, the federal and state courts, the Department of the Interior (as both the promoter of non-Indian development through the BOR and as the defender of Indian rights through the BIA), and Congress.

Steven L. Danver

See also Reservation Economic and Social
     Conditions; Tribal Sovereignty; Water Rights.
References and Further Reading
Hundley, Jr., Norris. 1978. "The Dark and Bloody
     Ground of Indian Water Rights: Confusion
     Elevated to Principle." *Western Historical
     Quarterly* 9.
Hundley, Jr., Norris. 1982. "The 'Winters' Decision
     and Indian Water Rights: A Mystery
     Reexamined." *Western Historical Quarterly* 13.
Massie, Michael. 1987. "The Cultural Roots of Indian
     Water Rights." *Annals of Wyoming* 59.
McCool, Daniel. 1987a. *Command of the Waters: Iron
     Triangles, Federal Water Development, and Indian
     Water.* Tucson: University of Arizona Press.
McCool, Daniel. 1987b. "Precedent for the Winters
     Doctrine: Seven Legal Principles." *Journal of the
     Southwest* 29.
U. S. Congress. 1888. *Agreement with Indians of the
     Fort Belknap Indian Reservation, Montana* 25 Stat.,
     113 (1888).
Winters v. United States 207 U.S. 564 (1908).

Worster, Donald. 1985. *Rivers of Empire: Water,
     Aridity, and the Growth of the American West.*
     New York: Oxford University Press.

Worcester v. Georgia

In *Worcester v. Georgia* presented before the Supreme Court in 1832, Chief Justice John Marshall determined that the Cherokee nation, as a distinct community, was empowered to exercise sovereign control over its internal affairs within the limits of its territory. According to the ruling, the U.S. federal government was duty bound to protect the Cherokee Indians from Georgia's violation of their treaty rights and from the interference of the state in their internal issues.

During the 1820s, the Cherokees held land in Georgia, North Carolina, Alabama, and Tennessee. In 1823, at the core of the Cherokees' crusade against removal from the Southeast, Cherokee leaders addressed President James Monroe to "remind him that the Cherokee are not foreigners but original inhabitants of America, and that they inhabit and stand on the soil of their own territory" (Vogel, 1972, 106). Recognition of Cherokee sovereignty and land rights by the federal government represented their strongest defense against removal.

By adopting their own constitution in 1827, the Cherokees rejected Georgia's jurisdiction. The state responded in December 1828, with an act by which it unilaterally extended its laws over the Cherokee people and nullified Cherokee legislation from June 1, 1830, onward. In answer to what they considered an infringement of their sovereignty, John Ross and three Cherokee representatives addressed a memorial to Congress on February 27, 1829, by which they declared, "the Cherokee are not prepared to submit to Georgia's persecuting edict. They would therefore . . . appeal to the United States government for justice and protection" (Ross, 1829).

To prevent non-Indians from aiding the Cherokee in their resistance against removal, Georgia passed an act in December 1830, whereby "all white persons residing in the Cherokee nation on the first day of March next [1831] without a license or permit from his Excellency, the governor, . . . and who shall not have taken the oath herein after required shall be guilty of a high misdemeanor, and upon conviction thereof, shall be punished by confinement in the penitentiary at hard labor, for a term not less than four years" (*History of the Presbyterian Church in the Cherokee Nation*, n.d., 84–85).

The missionaries who resided in the Cherokee nation were the primary targets of the Act. In 1825, Reverend Samuel Worcester started his service with the American Board of Commissioners for Foreign Missions to the Cherokees at the Brainerd mission in Tennessee. He was transferred to New Echota, the capital of the Cherokee nation, in November 1827. Despite the new legislation, Worcester did not leave the Cherokee nation and refused to take the oath of allegiance to the state of Georgia. As a consequence, on March 12, 1831, Reverends Worcester, Thompson, and Proctor were arrested and presented to Judge Augustin Clayton in the Court of Gwinnett County. Clayton released the missionaries because he believed they were under the protection of the United States as agents of the government. Samuel Worcester benefited more clearly than the others from this status as a postmaster in New Echota.

Upon the request of Governor George Gilmer of Georgia, Secretary of War John Eaton denied the missionaries the status of agents of the government (McLoughlin, 1984, 259–260). In a letter dated May 16, 1831, Gilmer informed Samuel Worcester of his dismissal as a postmaster. In July 1831, the Georgia Guard arrested eleven missionaries, and they were sentenced to hard labor on September 16, 1831. Unlike most of their colleagues who surrendered to the state's law by either moving out of Georgia or taking the oath of allegiance, Samuel Worcester and Elizur Butler stood firm in their original position until the case eventually reached the Supreme Court in January 1832.

Chief Justice John Marshall pointed out that the constitutional power to deal with the Indians resided with the federal government alone, thus affirming the United States' recognition of Native peoples' sovereignty. The treaties signed between the Cherokee nation and the U.S. government demonstrated the political autonomy of the Cherokee people. Consequently, Georgia had no authority to nullify Cherokee laws or to interfere in the regulation of the dealings between American citizens and the Cherokees within the Cherokee nation. As such, Georgia was not entitled to forbid or restrain by means of a license Samuel Worcester's and the other missionaries' presence in the Cherokee nation, since the Cherokees allowed the missionaries to reside in their territory.

On March 3, 1832, Chief Justice John Marshall concluded: "The Cherokee nation is a distinct com-

Samuel A. Worcester was a missionary to the Cherokee nation and refused to leave in spite of government regulations. (Library of Congress)

munity, occupying its own territory, with boundaries accurately described, in which the laws of Georgia have no force. . . . It is the opinion of this court that the judgment of the superior court of the county of Gwinnett, in the state of Georgia, condemning Samuel A. Worcester to hard labor, in the penitentiary of the state of Georgia, for four years, was pronounced by that court under color of a law which is void, as being repugnant to the constitution, treaties and laws of the United States, and ought, therefore, to be reversed and annulled" (Getches, 1998, 120–121).

Governor Lumpkin of Georgia did not enforce Marshall's judgment immediately. In his 1832 annual message, Lumpkin condemned the decision of the Supreme Court as "Federal usurpation . . . intending to prostrate the sovereignty of this State." In addition, the governor announced the continuation of his plan "to ensure a speedy settlement of the unoccupied lands in Cherokee Country" (Lumpkin, 1907, 104, 106). Samuel Worcester and Elizur Butler were finally released in January 1833, but Georgia continued with the implementation of removal. The Cherokees' forced removal from Georgia to the Indian

Territory in present-day Oklahoma was achieved from 1835 through 1838.

Although *Worcester v. Georgia* did not thwart Georgia's removal of the Cherokees, it has served as a cornerstone in the deliberations about Indian peoples' self-government from the 1830s to the present. Marshall's decision marked clearly the limits of the states' jurisdiction and the role of the federal government as a guardian of Indian sovereignty. The case is still cited to preserve Indian nations from unconstitutional intrusions of individual states in their internal affairs.

Anne-Marie Liberio

See also *Cherokee Nation v. Georgia;* Jackson, Andrew; Trail of Tears.

References and Further Reading

Getches, David H., Charles F. Wilkinson, and Robert A. Williams, Jr. 1998. *Cases and Materials on Federal Indian Law,* 4th ed. St. Paul, MN: West.

History of the Presbyterian Church in the Cherokee Nation. No date. Unpublished typescript. Arthur W. Evans Collection. Western History Collections, University of Oklahoma.

Lumpkin, Wilson. 1907. *The Removal of the Cherokee Indians from Georgia.* 2 volumes. New York: Dodd, Mead and Company.

McLoughlin, William G. 1984. *Cherokees and Missionaries 1789–1839.* New Haven, CT: Yale University Press.

Memorial of John Ross to the Honorable The Senate and House of Representatives of the United States of America in Congress Assembled (1829)", published in Niles Weekly Register, Baltimore, August 7, 1830, number 24, volume 2

Vogel, Virgil J., ed. 1972. *This Country Was Ours, A Documentary History of the American Indian.* New York : Harper & Row.

Index

Note: Page locators in **boldface** type indicate the location of a main encyclopedia entry.

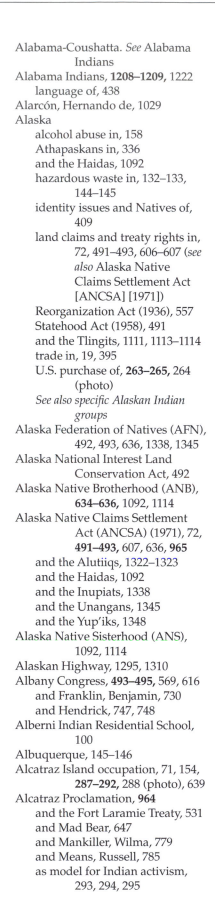

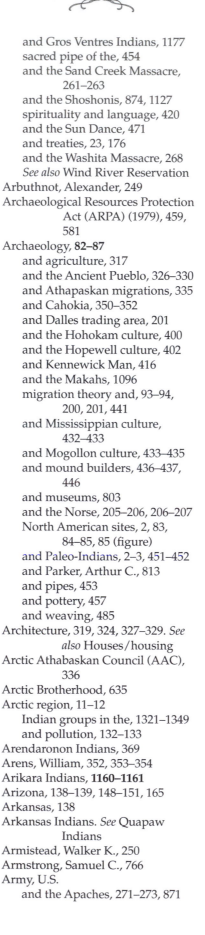

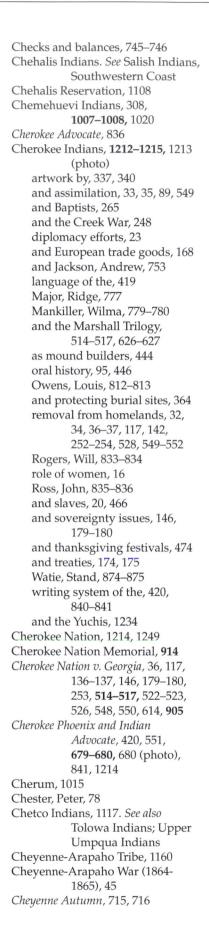

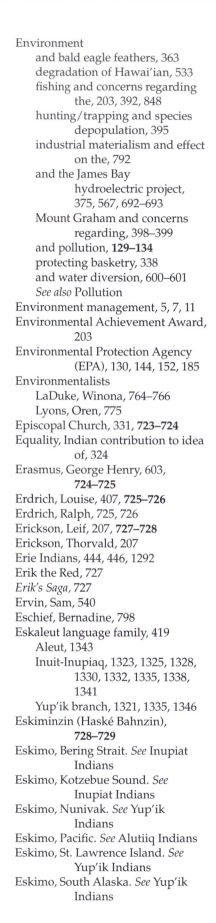

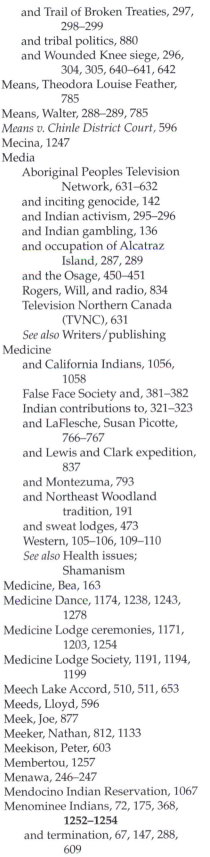

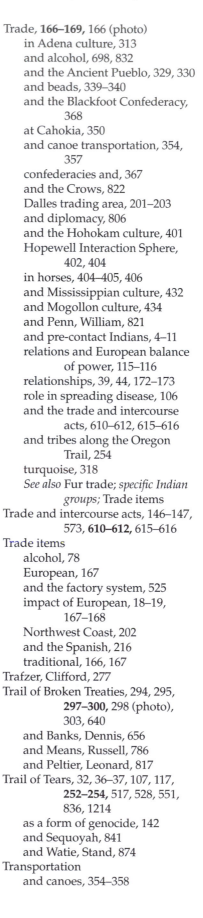

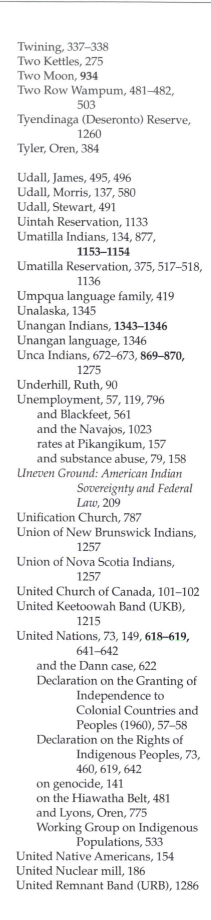

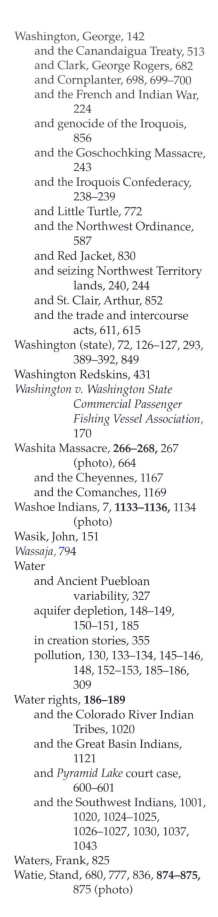

About the Editors

Bruce E. Johansen is Frederick W. Kayser Research Professor of Communication and Native American Studies at the University of Nebraska at Omaha. He is the author of dozens of books; his publishing efforts are concentrated in Native American studies and in environmental issues. His most recent publication is *The Praeger Handbook on Contemporary Issues in Native America* (Praeger, 2007).

Barry Pritzker is Director of Foundation and Corporate Relations at Skidmore College, where he occasionally teaches courses on contemporary Native America. He has authored books on Ansel Adams, Mathew Brady, and Edward Curtis, as well as *Native Americans: An Encyclopedia of History, Culture and Peoples* (ABC-CLIO, 1998). His most recent publication is *Native America Today* (ABC-CLIO, 1999).